W0050926

R. Mittermeir (ed.)

Shifting Paradigms in Software Engineering

Proceedings of the 7th Joint Conference
of the Austrian Computer Society (OCG) and
the John von Neumann Society
for Computing Sciences (NJSZT)
in Klagenfurt, Austria, 1992

Springer-Verlag Wien New York

Prof. Dipl.-Ing. Mag. Dr. Roland Mittermeir
Institut für Informatik
Universität für Bildungswissenschaften Klagenfurt, Klagenfurt, Austria

Printed on acid-free paper

With 77 Figures

ISBN-13: 978-3-211-82408-5   e-ISBN-13: 978-3-7091-9258-0
DOI: 10.1007/978-3-7091-9258-0

PREFACE

SPSE '92 - Shifting Paradigms in Software Engineering is held as part of the "Bildungswissenschaftliche Woche 92" at the University Klagenfurt, partially overlapping with the conference "Informatik in der Schule - Informatik für die Schule"[1]. SPSE '92 is the 7th joint conference of the OCG, the Austrian Computer Society, and NJSZT, the Hungarian John von Neumann Society for Computing Sciences. As such, it is a conference which has already substantial tradition. On the other hand, SPSE '92 is distinct from its predecessors, since - as a sign of maturity of computer science in the region - it limits its scope to a particular aspect of the computing sciences, to software engineering and notably to the shifting paradigms we currently witness in this discipline.

The shift of paradigms which currently takes place in software engineering has certainly many roots. Some of them can be found in object-orientation and the new opportunities and challenges offered by this approach for software construction. Building large software systems by combining interacting software objects might seem as frightening and revolutionary to a software engineer well trained in structured top-downism as the PC-revolution has been disturbing to the manager of a huge mainframe-based computing center. But the similarity might carry on: as PC's have not and will not replace mainframes, there will also be coexistence between classical and object-oriented approaches to software development.

The notion of coexistence is becoming ubiquitous though. The clear distinction into software systems on one hand, data base systems on the other hand, and artificial intelligence systems hopping on some shoulders can no longer be maintained. The boundaries become blurred and will eventually fade away. However, the textbook wisdom, especially as far as methodological aspects are concerned, is different in each of these three domains. Hence, the stability the discipline "Software Engineering" has acquired throughout the last 25 years is vanishing. Old teachings can no longer be fully backed, new ideas pop up - not all of them well tested, not all of them worth to be pursued, but several of them worth critical study and evaluation.

In the light of this situation of the discipline, where leading authorities in the field state that software engineering as needed in the 90s is both, beyond software and beyond engineering, the program committee has invited researchers and practitioners in the geographic domain of the two sponsoring societies and neighbouring countries to share with us what they consider as key factors with respect to application development, the underlying theory, and, last not least, the challenges for (continuing) education stemming from these shifting paradigms.

The response to this call for papers has been excellent. Hence, the program committee had an easy task to select out of the submissions those papers which warrant presentation and inclusion in the conference proceedings, those which have been accepted for presentation, but seemed to be yet too unrefined to warrant a full length publication, and finally, isolate those which just did not make it to this conference. I may state also with great pleasure, that in

---

[1] Mittermeir R.T., Kofler E., Steinberger H.: "Informatik in der Schule - Informatik für die Schule", Vol. 10 of "Bildungswissenschaftliche Fortbildungstagungen an der Universität Klagenfurt", Böhlau Verlag, Wien 1992.

spite of the regional focus of the conference which resulted from the partnership of the OCG and the NJSZT, we have been open to - and actively requested - papers from neighbouring countries. This openness was rewarded by submissions from the CSFR, Slovenia, Tunesia as well as speakers and (co-)authors from Canada, Russia and the US. So, we see this long established Austro-Hungarian partnership conference flourishing into a truly international venture.

The program consists of two keynote speeches, eight technical sessions, and one panel discussion. The latter should specifically address the chances and challenges facing (relatively) small countries in the light of concerted research efforts in the EEC, the US and Japan.

To conclude, I'd like to thank all authors for their effort and the members of the program committee as well as the referees for their kind support and cooperation. Special thanks go also to the two societies, notably their presidents and their secretariats, which deserve special mention.

Concerning the local organization, I have to say that this conference would not be, but for the dedication and support from Dr. Steinberger, Mag. Kofler, Mag. Janesch and Mr. Hüttel. My expression of gratitude goes to them as well as to all those who financially supported this conference.

Roland Mittermeir
Program Committee
Chairperson

CONTENTS

Shifting Paradigms in Software Engineering
Klagenfurt, 21. - 23. September 1992

PROGRAM COMMITTEE

CHAIR

R. Mittermeir, Universität für Bildungswissenschaften Klagenfurt

MEMBERS

B. Dömölki, IQSOFT Budapest
V. Haase, Technische Universität Graz
P. Hanák, Technical University Budapest
G. Haring, Universität Wien
G. Klimko, MTA Information Technology Foundation Budapest
E. Knuth, Hungarian Academy of Sciences Budapest
G. Pomberger, Johannes Kepler Universität Linz
D. Sima, Kandó Kálmán Müszaki Föiskola Budapest
P. Zinterhof, Universität Salzburg

ADDITIONAL REFEREES

P. Arató	G. Kovács	V. Risak
I. Bach	P. Krauth	L. Rónyai
K. Balogh	Z. László	E. Sántáné-Toth
M. Biró	A. Márkens	J. Samentinger
G. Csopaki	T. Marx	A. Stritzinger
J. Eder	T. Matlák	J. Szentes
I. Fekete	H.P. Mössenböck	T. Szép
U. Hoffmann	Pirkelbauer	P. Szeredi
P. Jedlovszky	P. Molnár	K. Tilly
P. Kacsuk	R. Plösch	T. Vámos
I. Kiss	J. Racz	Weinreich
K. Kondorosi	T. Remzsö	

ORGANIZING COMMITTEE

E. Kofler, Universität für Bildungswissenschaften Klagenfurt
H. Steinberger, Universität für Bildungswissenschaften Klagenfurt

This conference has been made possible by grants from the following organizations:

Bundesministerium für Wissenschaft und Forschung
Verein der Freunde des Instituts für Informatik
Digital Equipment Corporation
Siemens AG Österreich
BACHER Electronics

OPENING LECTURE

Chair: R. Mittermeir

Software Engineering:
Beyond Software and Beyond Engineering

L. Belady
Mitsubishi Electric Research Laboratories
Cambridge, Mass. USA

Two distinct types of software are emerging. One type includes traditional program "components" which are relatively easy to specify and to sell in large numbers. The other is the software "glue" to integrate islands of computer applications into enterprise-wide systems. Building the second type demands more than software engineering. Expertise in computer hardware and in the application domain are indispensible.

PROJECT MANAGEMENT

Chair: E. Knuth

Computer Integrated Work Management (CIW)

Univ.-Prof. Dr. Gerhard Chroust
Systemtechnik und Automation
Kepler Universität Linz
Altenbergerstr. 69
A-4040 Linz, Austria

Abstract

Software project management is often hampered by a lack of complete and up-to-date information on planned and actual activities, on their actual status, etc. At the same time **software engineering environments** have gained widespread acceptance and use within the last decade, providing **guidance** for the **development process** and integrating **access to tools**. They can provide most of the information needed for project management. An attainable vision of the future is the **integration** of classical project management with process guidance in order to arrive at **Computer Integrated Work Management (CIW)**.

Advantages are an effective communication between process guidance and project management and the ability to hide the added complexity from the user by adequate filtering on a need-to-know basis.

1 The Process Guidance/Project Management Gap

The need to control the development of systems (including software engineering projects) has long been understood. **Project Management** has a long standing tradition in engineering disciplines - building the pyramids was obviously an admirable achievement of project management. With respect to software projects it seems that we are not so successful [1]. Some of the reasons are eloquently discussed by F. Brooks in his famous paper 'No Silver Bullet" [2]. The reason for this state of affairs is partly due to the separation of Process Guidance and Project Management (see below).

1.1 Computer Aided Process Guidance

In order to bring a touch of industrialisation into software engineering we have seen the introduction of software engineering environments (also called Integrated Project Support Environments, etc. [7][10][11]) within the last decade.

The main purpose of these environments is threefold:

- providing an integrated, uniform access to a **tool set** [9][12],

- guiding the user through a pre-defined sequence of steps, defined in the **process model** [5][8].

- relieving the user from many administrative details like storing/retrieving results, finding standards and explanations, completing reports.

The availability of sufficient computing power fostered the idea to let the computer enforce observance of the intended (and pre-defined) process. The basic idea is rather simple, but nevertheless far-reaching. A **process model** defines like a template the way how development processes should be performed. This process model is in machine-readable form such that a **model interpreter** can present it step by step to the users (Fig. 1) via a so-called work bench. The model interpreter will help the users to follow the process (providing **process guidance**) and ensure observance of the intended process. At the same time the model interpreter takes care of the interface to the **tools**, relieving the developer of many boring and akward details. Additionally the model interpreter handles - in cooperation with an adequate repository - the retrieval and storage of the results. The result is a software engineering environments (Fig. 2) like ADPS [3].

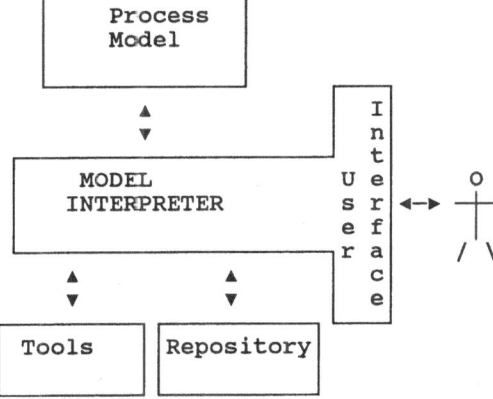

Figure 1: Process Model and Model Interpreter

1.2 Process Model

The process model plays a central role in guiding the user. It contains a detailed description of all activities to be performed in the course of the project. In its most basic form it consists of:

Result Classes: They describe all intermediate and final results of the development process.

Activity Classes: An activity class is the smallest unit of work identifiable at the chosen level of description. The activity class also defines the results to be used (the 'prerequisites') and the results to be produced (the 'deliverables'). Methods and/or tools are also identified.

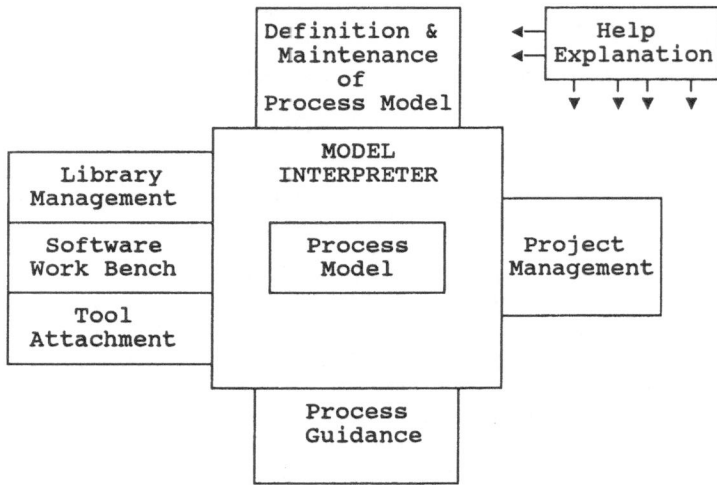

Figure 2: Components of the Software Engineering Environment

Result Class Structure: It describes the relationships between the various result classes (e.g. "object module *is compilation of* source module")

Activity Class Structure: It describes both the static relationships of activity classes (e.g. "coding *is part of* implementation phase") and their dynamic relationships (e.g. "coding *must occur after* design" [4]).

In most cases the process model is represented as a more or less strict network of activity classes and result classes, cf. Fig. 3 [3]). One has to keep in mind that the process model is a *template*. Each project will be an **instance** of the given process model, i.e. it will consist of activities, results, a result structure and an activity structure (cf. Fig. 6, left side), derived from the respective classes.

1.3 Classical Project Management

In the last few years we have seen a growth in project management tools [6] which provide all the functionality needed for successfully managing a project. Project management is mainly concerned with (cf. Fig. 6, right side):

Work Packages: These are the smallest units which are individually planned, they usually correspond to one or a small set of activities.

Resources: These comprise personell, money, software and hardware. In that respect we may also consider time as a resource, despite its slightly different nature.

Resource Constraints: Both the quantity, the timely availability and interdependencies between resources have to be taken into account.

Work Plan: The work plan tries to strike an acceptable compromise between the different requirements and constrains. It specifies a temporal ordering for the work packages based upon the logical dependecies (expressed in the Activity Structure) and the resource requirements.

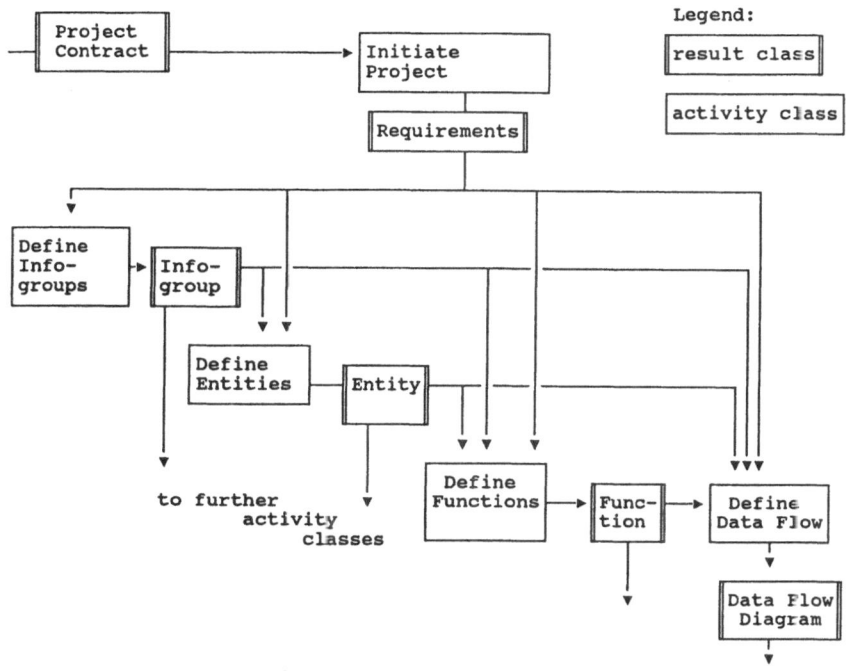

Figure 3: Section of the ADPS process model

2 Computer Integrated Work Management (CIW)

Project management, to do meaningful planning and control, needs accurate data about planned and actually performed activities and about the planned results and their status (Fig. 4). As long as the definition of the development process was largely intuitive or at best defined on paper [8], it was difficult to provide accurate data to project management (a developer is usually '90% finished', no matter how much more has to be invested in his module). And many of the necessary activities where forgotten when establishing a project plan. Only the integration of process guidance and classical project management is able to provide the needed synergetic effect, both providing to the process guidance the necessary information about additional, resource-based constraints on sequencing and to project management the information about the planned and actual activities and results. Obviously most of these considerations must be based on the actual instances of the respective classes in the process model .

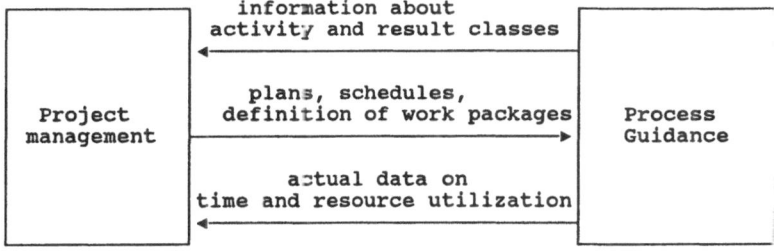

Figure 4: Cooperation of process guidance and project management

One can delineate the subareas of CIW as shown in Fig. 5. We may say that the areas of Configuration Management (including versioning), and Personell and Resource Management and Scheduling are well understood. The area of Activity Management just becoming state-of-the-art [5] [8].

What is new is the interface between the left and the right hand side of Fig. 5. This will be discussed in the sequel.

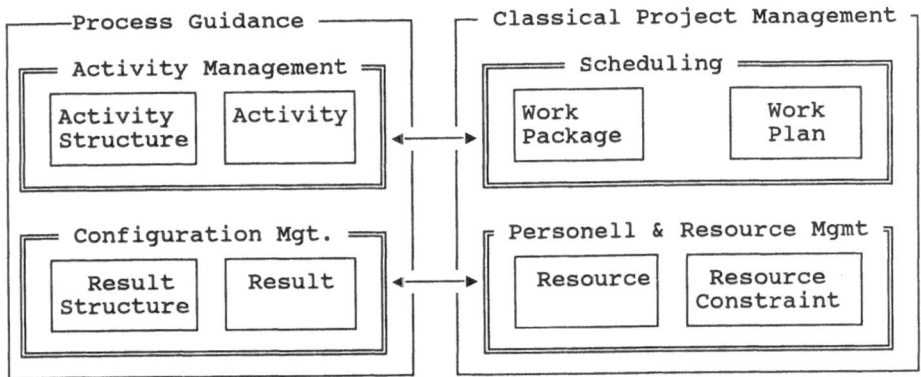

Figure 5: Areas of Computer Integrated Work Management

2.1 Components of CIW

CIW - as a synthesis of process guidance and resource management - will mainly involve the components shown in Fig. 6. In this figure the most important relationships between the individual components are shown, many others are implied. On the left hand side we recognize the domain of Configuration Management: results and their relationships. The relationships between the results imply the transformations of prerequisite results into deliverables (the activities). Additionally the ('dynamic') order in which the activities should be performed must be defined (the Activity Structure).

On the right hand side the components of classical project management (which is primarily resource management) are shown. Planning and control is based upon work packages (each usually containing several activities) of the process model. Work packages may also contain further activities which are not in the process model like vacation, education etc. Each of them needs certain resources (based upon the resource need of the contained activities). Resource constraints put restrictions on admissible work plans.

This point of view separates the influence of the *logical* structure of the process (expressed in the process model) from resource-oriented concerns (as reflected in the work plan).

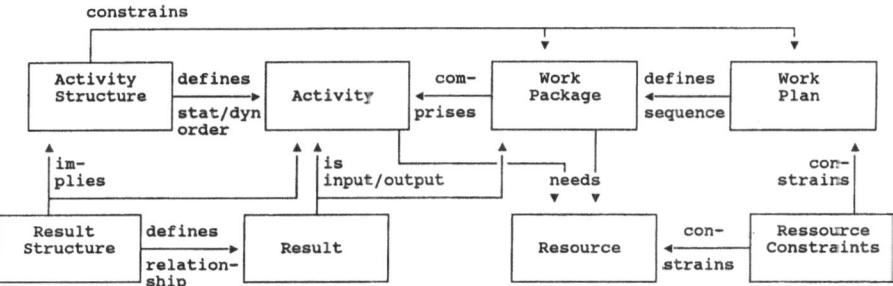

Figure 6: The basic components of Computer Integrated Work Management

2.2 Interfacing Process Guidance and Scheduling

Fig. 6 shows the necessary information exchange for integrating process guidance with project management. One can identify five key relationships:

Work Package comprises Activity: Usually several activities will be associated with one work package. Additionally not every activity needs planning. Typically a compilation, although usually an activity on its own, will not appear in the work plan. The actual granularity (and thus the number of activities collected in one work package) depends on numerous parameters like criticality of the project, experience of development team, size of project, enterprise culture etc. Despite the fact that two projects may use the same process model their work packages and the work plan may be drastically different.

Fig. 7 on its left hand side shows a rudimentary process model together with the produced results ('Spec0', 'Design0', ...). Several work packages (WrkP1 to WrkP5) have been defined. For the activity 'Code' two work packages have been defined, another work packages is concerned just with education.

Activity Structure constrains Work Package: The activity structure is mainly induced by the dependencies between the data produced and used. A work package may not contain an agglommeration of activities which violates the data dependencies.

Activity structure constrains Work Plan: Similarly the sequencing of the individual work packages must take into account the data dependencies between the respective work packages.

Work Package needs Resource: Based on the resource need of the activities contained in a work package, the resource demand of the work package can be derived.

Resource Constraint constrains Work Plan: Resource constraints (e.g. restricted availability of a specialist, of hardware, time constraints) impose further restrictions on the sequencing of otherwise independent work packages in the work plan.

10

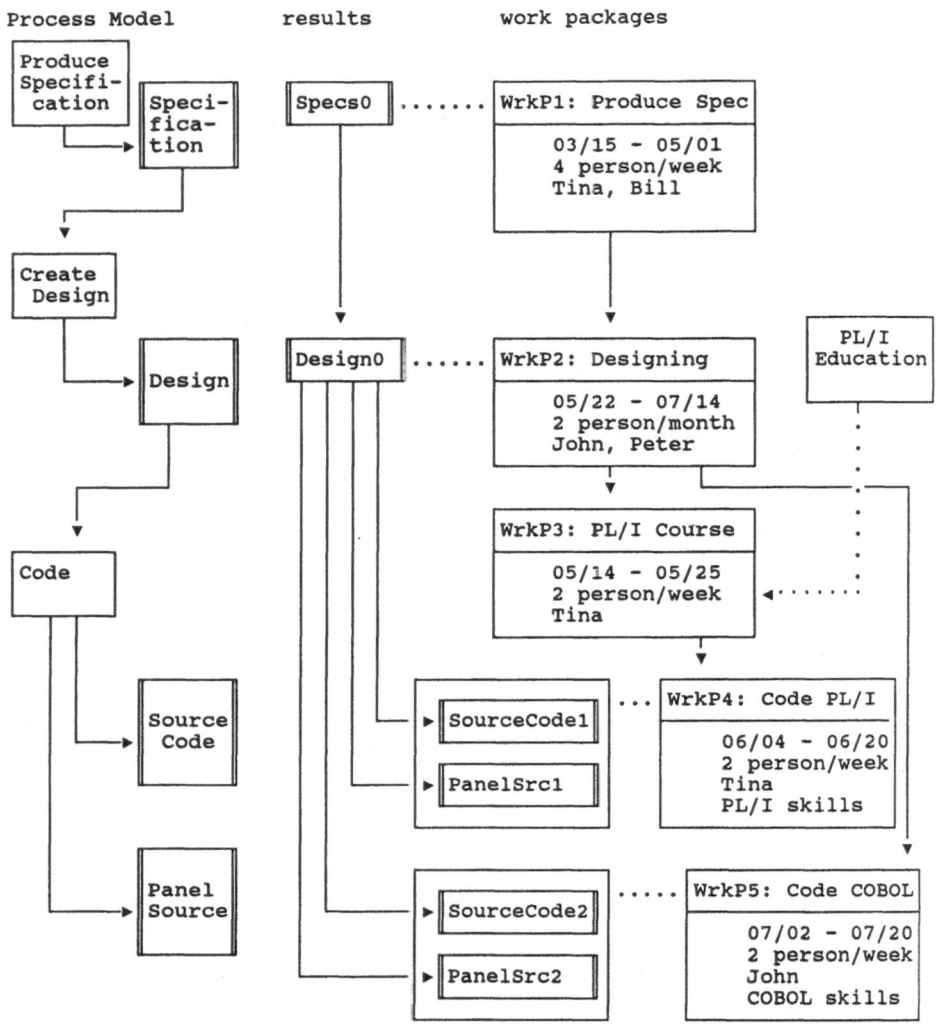

Figure 7: The relation of a process models to its instances and work packages

3   Personalizing the Work Management

Up to now the *whole* development process had been considered. The combination of process guidance and classical project management will obviously increase the complexity of the information to be administered and presented. In order not to overwhelm the individual user, it is necessary to *reduce* this complexity by providing individualized views. This can be achieved by providing a **resource-oriented view** of the process. For each individual resource - especially for a developer - one can isolate those activities which are his/her concern (Fig. 8). The project planner/leader still has access to the totality of information and can make the necessary adaptions. An individual user will generally only see those work packages which concern him (the 'need-to-know'). This can be achieved by a **To-do-List** (Fig. 10). In the example the To-do-List contains Tina's work packages from Fig. 7 plus a few others (these could even result from a different project assignment). The To-do-Lists are periodically updated by checking whether further work packages became ready, etc. (Fig. 9).

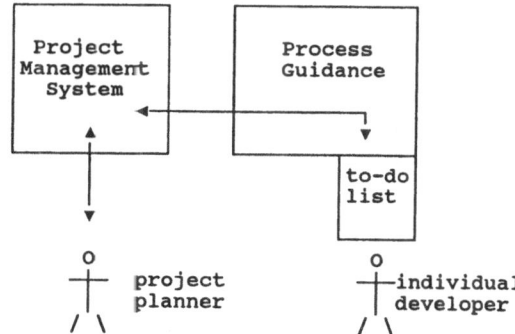

Figure 8: Attachment of Project Management

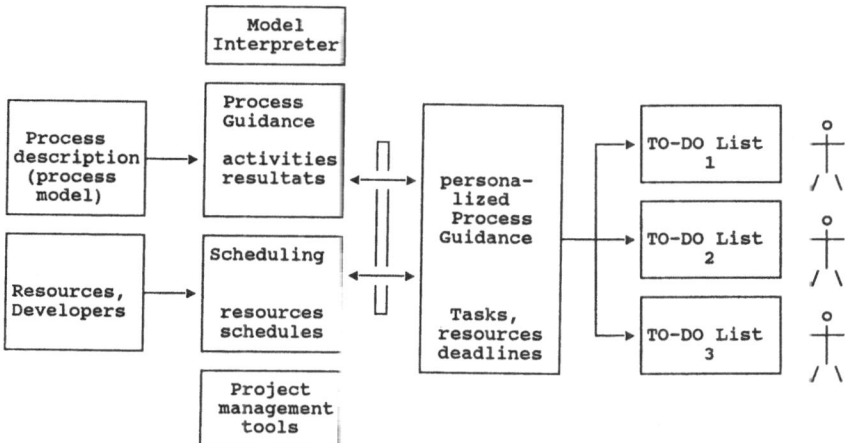

Figure 9: Personalized Task Management

Executable Tasks for: Tina			
Work Pack.	Plan from/to	Effort	Responsible
1: Produce Specif.	03/15-05/01	4 weeks	Tina, Bill
3: PL/I Course	05/14-04/25	2 weeks	Tina
* 4: Code PL/I	06/04-06/20	2 weeks	Tina
* -: Vacation	08/21-09/15	-	Tina
-: Project Meeting	06/10-06/10	1 day	Tina, John

* not ready

Figure 10: To-do-List

4 Summary

The proven usefulness of computer support for project management and the gradual acceptance of software engineering environments as the path to a more reliable, stable and productive system development make **Computer Integrated Work Management (CIW)** the next logical step. CIW carries with it the promise of integrating both project guidance and project management based on commonly available information. At the same time the complexity for the individual user can be reduced on a need-to-know basis.

References

[1] Brooks F.P.: The Mythical Man-Month.- Addison-Wesley 1975

[2] Brooks F.P.Jr.: No Silver Bullet - Essence and Accidents of Software Engineering.- Kugler H.J. (ed.): Information Processing 86, IFIP Congress 1986 pp.1069-1076

[3] Chroust G.: Application Development Project Support (ADPS) - An Environment for Industrial Application Development.- ACM Software Engineering Notes, vol. 14 (1989) no. 5, pp. 83-104

[4] Chroust G., Goldmann H., Gschwandtner O.: The Role of Work Management in Application Development.- IBM System Journal, vol. 29 (1990) no. 2, pp. 189-208

[5] Chroust G.: Modelle der Software-Entwicklung - Aufbau und Interpretation von Vorgehensmodellen.- Oldenbourg Verlag, 1992

[6] Elzer P.F. (ed.): Multidimensionales Software-Projektmanagement.- AIT Verlag Hallbergmoos 1991

[7] Huenke H. (ed.): Software Engineering Environments.- Proceedings, Lahnstein, BRD, 1980, North Holland 1981

[8] Humphrey W.S.: Managing the Software Process.- Addison-Wesley Mass 1989

[9] Martin J.: Information Engineering, Book I: Introduction.- Prentice Hall, Englewood Cliffs 1989

[10] Oesterle H.: Anleitung zu einer praxisorientierten Software-Entwicklungsumgebung, Band 1.- AIT Verlag München 1988.

[11] Oesterle H.: Computer Aided Software Engineering - Von Programmiersprachen zu Softwareentwicklungsumgebungen.- Kurbel K., Strunz H. (eds.): Handbuch der Wirtschaftsinformatik.- Pöschel Stuttgart 1990, pp. 345-361

[12] Stork B.: Toolintegration in Software-Entwicklungsumgebungen.- Angew. Informatik 1985, No. 2, pp. 49-57

Methods and Tools for Systems Engineering and Application Software Development

G. Klimkó, P. Krauth, B. Molnár

Information Technology Foundation of Hungarian Academy of Sciences
H-1525 Budapest 114. P.O.B. 49, Hungary,
Telephone: +36 1 169-9499, Fax: +36 1 155-3376
e-mail: h4445mol@ella.hu

Abstract. A general picture of the recent development in the field of systems engineering and application software development is presented. In the last years new aspects of systems development have been recognized. However, these are not technical ones, and they serve the users' interests rather than the developers'. Methodologies have been worked out for the new areas, and also supporting tools emerged. This process has an impact on the software providers, because the users expect them to be knowledgeable on the new areas, too. In short terms, the meaning of 'structured paradigm' has been widened, and we can talk a certain change of paradigms. The paper encounters some of the new areas and briefly describes a methodology of that area.

1. Introduction

The paradigm problem. When we are talking about 'paradigms', we might have to define what do we mean by this word. In the computing community people tend to use the word with a certain technical sense, like 'object-oriented paradigm', or 'knowledge-based paradigm'. This refers usually to the technical background, how the software engineer describes the system under investigation and how he builds the supporting software of the system. These questions mean problem for (and only for) the software engineer himself. Users of the system would perhaps be not too interested in such technical details.

Specifically, in the world of application software builders, the word 'structured paradigm' has a common use. This term usually refers to two separate meanings. Using a 'structured paradigm' indicates that during systems analysis and design a structured methodology is to be used, and in the implementation phase structured programming concepts will be followed. That way, the basic meaning of the word 'paradigm' was widened, because it pertains not only to the technical software design process, but to the phases of systems analysis and design, too.

The main structuring tools in the description of the application software building process are the *life cycle models* (waterfall [Layzell 1989], evolution [Booch 1991] etc.). Life cycle models for systems analysis and design were already formed in the 70s. Systems modelling techniques were invented (data flow diagrams, Petri nets, entity-relationship model, relational data analysis etc.), which tackle separate aspects of a system. These techniques serve two purposes. Firstly they give a systematic, conscious and usually semi-formal way of describing the given system. Secondly, they act as a communication tool with the user. The techniques were incorporated in a structured framework, that prescribes, how to use the techniques. The framework is based upon a life cycle model. Finally, methodologies were formed. Thus, a methodology is a combination of techniques and methods in a disciplined way. A methodology must have an underlying philosophy and life cycle model, Examples of such methodologies are JSP [Jackson 1992], Yourdon [Yourdon 1975], Merise [Matheron 1990], SSADM [NCC 1990], SDM [Turner 1990] etc. Different methodologies cover different extent of the life of systems building. For example the SDM (Systems Development Method) relates up to the implementation, however Merise does not cover implementation.

A standardization process have begun in the area of systems analysis, mainly in the governmental sector on a nation-wide scale. For example, in the UK there is SSADM, in France there is Merise, in the Netherlands SDM. In these countries, the standardization is in different stages (in the UK SSADM is just before becoming a British standard). As a consequence of the national governments forced standardization process, the *de facto standard* systems methodologies themselves has changed.

Having only national methodologies, however, is not enough. After 1992, on the new common European market there will be a demand for a commonly understandable systems analysis methodology. To achieve this, the Euromethod project was initiated. As a result of this project, in 1995 we shall have a *Generic Process Model* as life cycle model and a *Unified Terminology* [Euromethod 1991].

The life-cycle models focused again on the technical aspects of the development. They concern more about the systems analyst and the application developer rather than about the customers of that application. From the point of view of the customer there are other extremely important aspects in using information technology (IT). This aspect can be called as the business view of the usage of IT. Examples of the new areas (aspects) are IT strategy planning, IT project management, quality management, IT risk evaluation and security analysis, systems maintenance, software package evaluation and selection. The common attribute of these is that they serve more the interests of the user, rather than of the developer.

In summary, the way how the users of IT are thinking of the usage of IT has been changed. The applications software providers can not dictate anymore only with technical justifications. This phenomenon has a influence on the of the application software builder community. The meaning of 'structured paradigm' is widening now. In that sense we can speak about changing paradigms.

Slow industrial take-up. The surveys on the usage of methodologies or just the analysis techniques show a surprisingly low percentage of penetration [OECD 1991], [Rock-Evans 1989]. This is really astonishing if we think the governments (eg. UK, France) or big private companies (eg. Arthur Andersen, McDonnel-Douglas) how strongly favour the usage of systems development methodologies. There is a certain agreement on the fact, that the usage of methodologies result in better quality software, too. So the expectations for the new IT areas give a very sad predictions, if even such a well-known area like systems analysis is so badly handled.

The question is, how can we improve this situation ? The techniques and the methodologies must be obviously understandable and attractive. To demonstrate their power, we believe a good infrastructural background would be enough. A very good example of such a background is the support around SSADM. In the following paragraphs, a short description of this infrastructure is given.

SSADM is in the public domain, that is, the documentation of the method is publicly available. Other activities of systems analysis like estimating are covered in separate subject guides. Several textbooks on SSADM are available eg. [Ashworth 1989], [Eva 1992]. As SSADM is not committed to any company, there is no danger to stick to a specific vendor's method.

There is a central governmental organization, the Central Computer and Telecommunication Agency (CCTA) which is responsible for the maintenance of SSADM. The SSADM Users Group was formed to collect feedback on the method, and based upon this information the method is regularly updated.

SSADM is taught at the British universities. This approach assures that necessarily educated personnel is available. There are a large number of consulting firms that teach SSADM, too. The teaching materials are also evaluated by CCTA. This procedure assures the quality of the education.

There is an SSADM examination procedure controlled by the Information Systems Engineering Board of the British Computer Society. More than 2000 systems analysts has passed this examination up today, including non-UK experts, too. The existence of such an examination procedure makes it impossible to misuse the method. Because the usage of SSADM is forced at governmental sites, for applicants of IT jobs at these sites to have an SSADM certificate usually is a must.

The widespread usage of SSADM lead to the appearance of the SSADM computer support tools (currently there exist more than a dozen of this commercially available CASE tools). These tools are ranked by the CCTA on a 1 to 5 point scale. Every year there is review of the CASE tools at the regular meeting of the SSADM User's Group.

This infrastructure has been built up through almost a decade. It serves an excellent example how to support IT activities that could be followed on other areas. Therefore it is suggested, that the way how SSADM and its infrastructure was built, is to be used on the other areas, too. For this purposes the lessons learned on systems analysis can be applied in four stages. In the first stage techniques has to be developed and then into turn to be incorporated into structured frameworks. This forms a methodology. In the second stage a standardization approach would be reasonable on a nation-wide level. In the third stage a proper infrastructural background has to set up, that assures maintenance and feedback. In the fourth stage an European standardization process is to be initiated.

Design evaluation. Assessment of the goodness and validation of a particular design was always a crucial point in systems engineering. The problem is: how can we judge if a design decision were good, and how can we assure in advance that no 'bad' decision will be made. To answer such a question, first the real meaning of 'good' and 'bad' has to be defined in a objective way, that is, in quantifiable terms. This evaluation has to be incorporated into the systems analysis methodology. In order to be able to recognize bad points in the systems analysis documentation, the used methodology can use dichotomy. This means that an aspect of the system under investigation must be depicted from more than one viewpoint, and resulting documents (products) has to be cross-checked. The usage of graphical, formal or semi-formal description techniques are recommended in the documenting methods.

The detection of the bad decisions can be incorporated into the project management methodology. Software and design quality assurance is the way to handle this task. Organizing the quality assurance process is clearly different from the traditional technical activities of systems development. However, without quality assurance it is not possible to achieve good quality systems. In such parts of the world like chemistry or power plant control, quality assurance is an obvious must. The relevance of quality assurance in the IT industry, however, is not really recognized yet. Project management and quality assurance can be handled with help of methodologies the same manner, as we did earlier on the field of systems analysis.

In the paper we outline the current state-of-the-art on the areas of systems analysis, IT strategy planning, IT project management, IT risk analysis and management, looking at them from the user's perspective. These major areas all serve as a tool in order to achieve quality software products. For each area, an example of a corresponding methodology is given, and a supporting tool is mentioned. All the examples are excerpted from the UK practice. There are several reasons for choosing British examples. Most of the shortly described methodologies are in the public domain, so they are easily available. Very strong and well-sounded infrastructural support is available for IT services in the UK [CCTA 1990], [CCTA 1991a].

That is, there is a coordinating organization and therefore the ways of development and feedback are assured. According to the surveys, UK is the leader in the usage of analysis techniques (cca. 33%).

Among the IT leaders in Europe, the French practice could have been an other possible choice, but documents are mainly accessible only in the French language, which is not widely spoken in Hungary. In the UK, naturally all the documentation is in English, which is the *de facto* the working language of the computing society. In Germany, only at the military are standard methodologies, and it is very difficult even to have literature on them because of the nature of the applications.

Although in Hungary the different techniques and methods are taught, there is no widespread usage of methodologies and/or analysis techniques. There is no preferred or recommended systems analysis method even in the government sector. However, as Hungary likes to join the European Communities, it has to conform to the European expectations on the IT field, too. It has no sense to develop for Hungary own national methodologies for the separate IT fields. Rather, we have to choose from the elaborated ones. Taking into consideration the above mentioned facts, the British practice is a definite candidate for this purpose.

2. Systems analysis and design

In this section an overall view of the SSADM [NCC 1990] (Structured Systems Analysis and Design Method) will be presented, and supporting CASE tools will be mentioned. A short paragraph on the Euromethod standardization project closes the section.

Roots of SSADM. For UK governmental sites at IT development projects the use of SSADM is compulsory from the beginning of the 80s. The main reason of introducing such a recommendation was to get to such a situation, where different IT projects within the government can be compared against each other and thus be under control. SSADM was developed by LBMS (Learmonth and Burchett Management Systems, a private firm) then it was purchased by the British Government. The methodology is in the public domain, users need not have to pay for the usage of SSADM. The owner of the method is the CCTA.

SSADM framework. Being a structured methodology, SSADM breaks down the development process into modules. Modules are built from stages, stages are in turn defined by steps. At the end of any module the development can be cancelled by the user. This way the development process is more strictly controlled.

For all these building bricks it is clearly defined, what are its inputs and outputs, what are the preconditions to start, what techniques should be applied. The inputs and outputs are called products. Products are built up in a hierarchy structure. For all products, there is detailed description in the reference manual. The product descriptions include quality criteria and dependency descriptions, too. By these criteria the quality of the products can be checked and measured. Products are interdependent and are required to be updated at separate steps.

SSADM techniques. SSADM is a data- and user-driven methodology. There is a strong emphasis on the communication with the user. This is done mainly via graphical techniques rather than a verbal way. The base of most techniques is a Jackson-like notation. On the other side, a lot of investigation is done, what data is to be stored in the system and how will it change. SSADM applies the popular and well known-techniques of Data Flow Modelling, Entity-Relationship Modelling and Relational Data Analysis. The other, maybe not so well-known techniques include Event Modelling, Function Definition and Dialogue Design. Two special techniques, the Business System Option (BSO) and Technical System Option (TSO) make the user to be real control of the development. The selected BSO must define the scope of the IT system, the selected TSO must clearly define the hardware-software basis of the implementation of the selected BSO. The use of these two techniques help to lessen the usual debate on the delivered system.

Each technique is documented individually in the reference manual. Dependencies among the techniques are precisely described. For each step it is prescribed, which techniques should be used and what will be the result (product) of the techniques.

Computer support. Because SSADM uses lots of graphical techniques, and the results of the techniques are in often cross-checked, there was an obvious need for supporting CASE tools. However, only the technical need would have been enough to press CASE builders creating such tools. It was the widespread usage of SSADM that lead to the appearance of the SSADM computer support tools (currently there exist more than a dozen of this commercially available CASE tools). These tools are ranked by the CCTA on a 1 to 5 point scale. Every year there is review of the CASE tools at the regular meeting of the SSADM User's Group.

The price and quality of these CASE tools is disperse. Price categories start at 500 pound for single-user tools on an AT category machine (PC SELECT). In the midrange of the price categories, one of the leader products is SSADM Engineer from LBMS. The reason for pointing out this product is its very sound technical ground. This is a multi-user tool that supports most of the SSADM products. The designers chose the PC with DOS as the hardware/software basic platform, that can be usually easily provided. They also avoided the trap of developing their own database, network and user interface. For these purposes the tool uses off-the-shelf products, namely a commercially available relational database server for the data dictionary (with the SQL interface), the NETBIOS as network interface and Microsoft Windows as user interface. This foundation provides a technically superior solution, with excellent facilities. At the upper price bound (cca. 50.000 pound) you can find excellent product running on workstations only with superb supporting capabilities (SSADM-SF from Systematica).

European integration. There are nation-wide accepted systems analysis methodologies in other European countries. (in France Merise, in the Netherlands SDM, in Spain MEIN etc. [Euromethod 1991]) The European integration process obviously popped up the need for a common language. For this reason, the Commission of the European Communities initiated the so-called Euromethod project. This based upon six European and one American systems analysis and design methodologies. However, the wide-spread use of the national methodologies would make the introduction of a new super-method very difficult (if not even impossible). The purpose of Euromethod is therefore *...to help participants in IS planning and engineering activities choose the most cost effective approach to meeting their problems... It will be an umbrella methodology which harmonies the disparate methods currently use for Information Systems Engineering in Europe.'* [Euromethod 1991]. The scheduled finish of the Euromethod project is 1995.

3. IT strategy planning

IT strategic planning must not be confused with business planning, although the results of business planning can be utilized in the IT strategic planning process. In any organization that utilizes IT services, the costs and spendings must be justified for the management |CCTA 1991|. That supposes, that the organization does know its business aims and it is able to plan, where and how to use IT. Ideally, IT must serve the real business needs of the organizations. IT strategic planning concerns in the IT activities of an organization for a 3-5 year scope.

The aspect of making IT strategy planning is definitely not a technical one. The results of an IT strategy planning is more interesting for the business managers than to the IT people. One of the aims of IT strategy planning is, that business people have to understand and commit to the use of IT within their organizations.

There are structured methodologies in this area, too. Big consulting companies (eg. Logica) usually have an own IT strategy planning methodology, but these are not public. In the UK, on this area there is no recommended methodology for the governmental sector. However, the Information Systems Guides book A2 from CCTA does contain guidelines for IT strategy planning. The LBMS Strategic Planning Method (LSPM) , which will be shortly described here, is a commercially available and conform methodology to the IT Infrastructure Library [LBMS 1992]. LSPM education and reference manuals can be purchased and than internally used.

Roots of LSPM. The owner of the methodology is a consulting firm, their experience is summarized in LSPM. The economy related parts of LSPM are based upon the works of Porter and Parsons, the data analysis part bases on the entity-relationship model.

LSPM framework. In LSPM the strategic planning process is divided into steps, steps into tasks. There are role descriptions for the participants in the strategic analysis. Having studied the business environment, LSPM investigates the current use of IT first, then its future use. The investigations are done parallel from two viewpoint within LSPM. One is oriented toward a business description of the organization, the other is connected to traditional data analysis. At the end these two views are merged into a portfolio of IT project specifications. These projects are to be implemented in the organization in the next 3-5 years.

LSPM techniques. Simple identification and categorization techniques are used to describe the business/service areas, their importance and the used IT strategy. An organization can judge the necessity of IT on a specific area on this basis. The strategic analysis process involves a lot of interviews with upper management. To help this activity, certain techniques are presented for planning and making interviews.

The structure of the organization changes frequently, but the structure of data maintained at the organization does not vary so often. This is the reason, that simplified (not too detailed) data models are set up, that describes the ideal, the current and the transitional data structure for the organization. The well-known entity-relationship modelling techniques are used here, with a special attention not to run into the not necessary, deeper details. The transitional data models are connected to the project in portfolio.

Computer support. There is software support for LSPM. The tool supports the graphical data modeling techniques, and all the collected information is stored in one database. Various reports are available to present the results.

4. IT project management

Project management is classic bottleneck of IT projects. In the UK governmental sector the usage of the PRINCE (PRojects In Controlled Environment) methodology is compulsory on IT projects [CCTA 1991b]. PRINCE is definitely designed for (but not restricted to) IT projects. It interfaces to SSADM and CRAMM. SSADM itself does not contain project management guidelines (for example, as an alternate approach, the Merise systems analysis methodology does).

Roots of PRINCE. The ancestor of the method (called PROMPT) was developed by LEMS. The current form of PRINCE was worked out by the CCTA. CCTA is the owner of PRINCE, which is in the public domain.

PRINCE framework. PRINCE consists of five components. It defines the project organization, the necessary plans, gives controls, lays down the description rules of products and activities and has a configuration control component.

PRINCE has two underlying principles. In PRINCE it was recognized, that the three contributing but different views in IT development process, namely the business, the technical aspects and the user interests have to be separated. The different interests are represented by different persons in the separate project organizations. For each participant of an IT project, his/her role and responsibility is (and must be) precisely defined. The structure of the project is illustrated in Fig. 1. The usual practice of having just one powerful person (the project manager) is abandoned, a technique of controlling the project manager itself is included in the method.

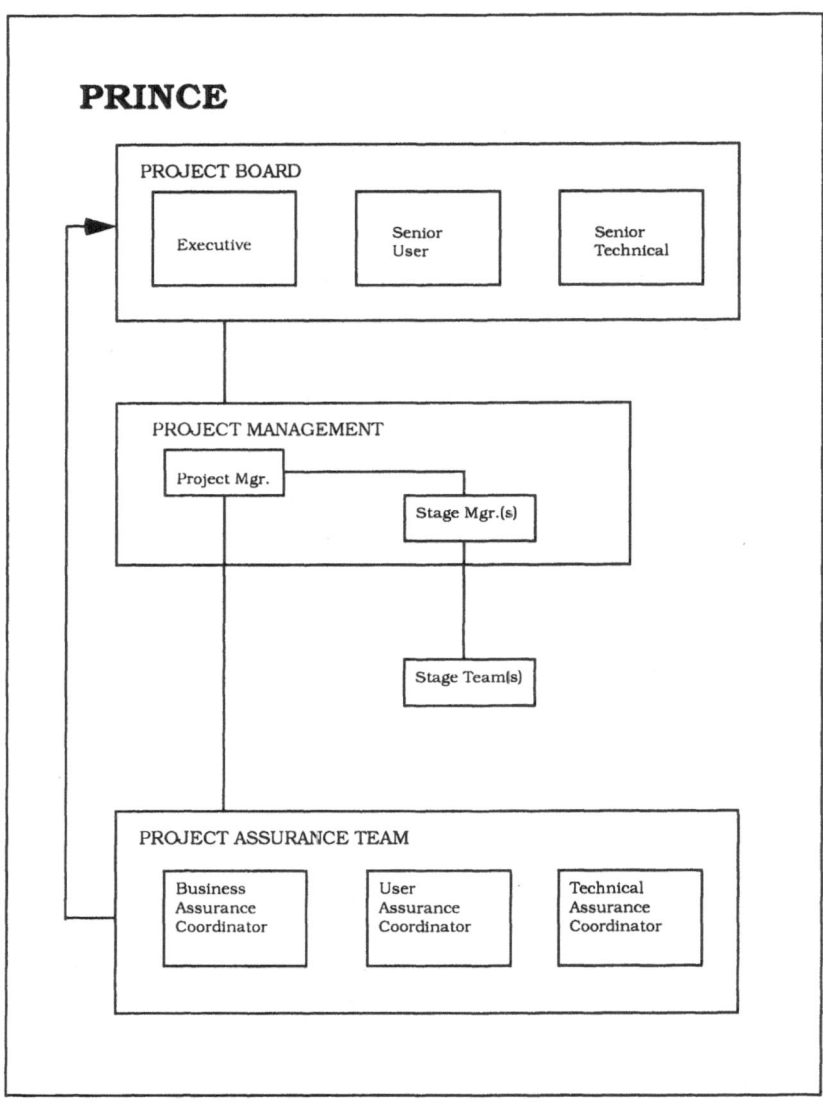

Fig. 1

On the other hand, PRINCE is product (and not activity) oriented. That is, before a development stage it has to be defined clearly, what are (and what are not) the deliverables of that development. A Product Breakdown Structure is to be created before any activity starts. The definition of the products must include quality criteria and must be agreed on between the user and developer. This approach helps to avoid the usual misunderstanding between the user and the developer, when the development is finished.

PRINCE techniques. For the organization component, PRINCE has a dictionary that describes precisely the roles in an IT project. This includes the responsibilities, the specific tasks and required knowledge and experience descriptions for each role, too.

In the techniques of the PRINCE planning component there is nothing IT specific. Types of plans include technical, resource and exception plans. Plans have to be produced on different levels (project, stage, detailed) for the technical process, for the usage of the resources, for the case of exception.

The controls component of PRINCE differentiate management and product controls. Management controls are built in at specific phases of the development, at the so-called control points. For each control point the objective, the attendees, their roles and an activity checklist is provided.

For product controls, the quality review and a technical exceptions handling technique is used. Procedures for both techniques are defined in a great detail. Technical exceptions are subdivided into project issue reports, off specification reports and requests for changes. Products are subdivided into technical, management and quality products. For each product there is a product description that contains the purpose, composition, format and quality criteria of that product.

Configuration management is built into the product controls. That is, there are elaborate configuration identification and status accounting schemas.

Computer support. Just currently are emerging the supporting tools for PRINCE. An example is Kernel-PMS/PRINCE from Transaction Point.

5. IT risk analysis

IT risk analysis has a growing importance. As more and more confidential data of vital importance are stored at the organizations, security aspects became essential. The increasing appearance of computer crimes stress the need to handle the risks and threats more formally. The main problem is, that no system could be made absolutely secure. What we can do is to recognize the possible threats and to decide if it is worth to have sufficient countermeasures or it is not.

In the UK CRAMM (CCTA's Risk Analysis and Management Method) is a preferred method for UK Government [CCTA 1991c]. It is widely used by Australian and New Zealand governments.

Roots of CRAMM. CRAMM was developed BIS Information Systems. CRAMM is owned now by CCTA.

CRAMM framework. CRAMM consists of three stages. Firstly, it identifies the assets, threats and vulnerabilities. Both the technical and the non-technical aspects of security are covered. Secondly, it recognizes the risks and offers countermeasures. Management can decide, if they see enough justification to implement specific countermeasures or not. At the end of each stage there is a management review meeting.

In Stage 1, the main task is to do a data, software and physical asset valuation. It is done by qualitative techniques on a scale 1 to 10. The techniques incorporate absolute figures in order to assure that the measurement is not subjective. Data and software assets are valued in different terms. Data gathering is done via interviews. In Stage 2, a threat and vulnerability assessment is to be done. Generic types of threats are defined as hardware and software malfunctions, accidental threats (eg. fire, disaster, staff shortage etc.) and deliberate threats (willful damage, infiltration etc.). The assessment is done by using questionnaires. These are available from the CRAMM supporting software. Having scaled the threat, vulnerability and asset values, measures of the risks to the system are calculated. In Stage 3, countermeasure selection is done. Based upon the identified risk values, specific countermeasures could be selected. These are presented together to the management with a prioritisation scheme and a 'what-if' scenario exploration. Management can then decide if they do want a specific countermeasure to be implemented.

CRAMM techniques. The most used technique is interviewing. For each threat there is a predefined questionnaire, and predefined roles for the interview.

Computer support. There is a software package called CRAMM itself, owned by CCTA. A lot of the technical details of CRAMM (like questionnaires, countermeasures etc.) are published via this software. That is, without the software the method can not be used.

6. Lessons learned

By the example of SSADM we have seen how a methodology can be a successful and accepted standard. If we want the IT community to accept the importance of the above described new areas, one can see the possibility to use the same approach as in the UK was done is the case of SSADM. So what do we need for the new areas ?

Solid foundation. The techniques of the methodology must be well understood and accepted. (Entity-Relationship Modelling and Relational Data Analysis are good examples in SSADM). The usage of such well-founded techniques encourages the users of the methodology. The structural framework and the products of the process must be also well defined.

Driving force. It is not easy to get people to use a methodology. There must be a true force behind it, but this force must be a competent one.

Strong infrastructure. Infrastructural background must support the maintenance and the education of the methodology. There must be an owner of the methodology which forces the evolution of the methodology. The feedback from the users of the methodology have to be taken into mind. The education of the methodology must centrally and periodically evaluated, in order to ensure the required quality of the education. If it is possible, software supporting tools must be developed for the methodology. These have to be also periodically evaluated.

7. Conclusions

Looking at IT from the user's point of view (that is, from the business view) has popped up new aspects. For these aspects, the technique of applying a structured methodology seems to be fruitful. This tendency is going on, the methods and methodologies are being defined (and refined). However, the industrial take-up of the different techniques and methodologies is still slow. In order to achieve better quality software products, policy makers must accelerate this process. The users of IT services must realize their need to force their suppliers to use such methodologies, and the suppliers must be supported with strong infrastructure of that methodologies.

There are other important aspects that surely will be involved in this process. These include package selection, systems maintenance and facility management. For these aspects methods and techniques are emerging, but they have not been stabilized yet.

CASE providers must have a close look at the new areas. These areas are candidates where to give support to the application software providers. For software systems houses it is vital to deal with these areas in order to keep their competitive position. As a consequence, the structured paradigm of systems building is widening and changing.

8. Bibliography and References

1. Asworth, C. Goodland, M. *SSADM: A Practical Approach,* McGraw-Hill Book Company, 1989
2. Booch, Grady, *Object-Oriented Design,* The Benjamin /Cummings Publishing Company, Inc. (1991)
3. Cameron, J.R., *JSP and JSD: The Jackson Approach to Software Development,* IEEE Comput. Soc., (1983)
4. CCTA, *IT Infrastructure Library,* HMSO 1990
5. CCTA, *The Information Systems Guides, Management and Planning Set,* John Wiley and Sons Ltd., (1991a)
6. CCTA, *PRINCE. Structured Project Management,* NCC Blackwell Ltd., (1991b).
7. CCTA, *CRAMM User's Guide Version 2.0, CRAMM Management Guide.* (1991c)
8. Euromethod Phase 1/3, *Introduction and Progress Report*
9. Eva, M., *SSADM Version 4: A User's Guide,* McGraw-Hill, (1992).
10. Hewett, J., Durham, T., *CASE: The Next Step,* Ovum Ltd., (1989)
11. Jackson, M.A., *System Development,* Englewood Cliffs, Prentice Hall, (1982).
12. LBMS, *LBMS Strategic Planning for Information Technology* 1992
13. Layzell, P., Loucopoulus, P., *Systems Analysis and Development,* (3rd edition), Chartwell-Bratt, (1989).
14. Matheron, J.P., *Comprendre Merise,* Outils Conceptuels et Organisationnels, Editions EYROLLES, (1990).
15. NCC (National Computing Centre), *SSADM Manual Version 4,* NCC Blackwell, (1990).
16. Noble, F.: *Seven Ways to Develop Office Systems: A Managerial Comparison of Office System Development Methodologies,* The Computer Journal, Vol. 34, No. 2. 1991 April
17. OECD: *Software Engineering: The Policy Challenge,* Computer Communications Policy, 1991.
18. Page-Jones, Meilir., *The Practical Guide to Structured Systems Design,* 2nd edition, Englewood Cliffs, N.J.: Prentice-Hall, (1988).
19. Rock-Evans, R., Engeline, B.: *Analysis Techniques for CASE: a Detailed Evaluation,* Ovum Ltd.(1989).
20. Turner, W. S., Langenhorst, R. P., Hice, G. F., Eilers, H. B., Uijttenbroek, A. A., *SDM system development methodology,* Elsevier Science Publishers B.V. (North-Holland)/Pandata, (1990).
21. Yourdon, E., Constantine, L.L., *Structured Design,* Yourdon Press, (1975).

Exploratory Software Development with Class Libraries

Johannes Sametinger, Alois Stritzinger

Christian Doppler Labor für Software Engineering
Institut für Wirtschaftsinformatik
Johannes Kepler Universität Linz
A-4040 Linz, Austria

Abstract. Software development based on the classical software life-cycle proves inadequate for many ambitious projects. Exploratory software development is an alternative way of building software systems by eliminating deficiencies of the conventional software life cycle. Instead of exactly defining the various phases of the life cycle, exploratory software development takes small development steps, whereby a single step results in an extension or an improvement of the existing system.

The object-oriented programming paradigm has resulted in increased reuse of existing software components. Therefore, class libraries will become very important in the near future. Exploratory software development is very well suited to this situation and thus provides a major step forward in economically developing software systems.

In this paper we depict deficiencies of the classical software life cycle, present the exploratory software development strategy, and especially illustrate exploratory software development in combination with the reuse of class libraries.

1 Classical Software Life Cycle

Software is usually developed according to the classical software life-cycle. Various models for this life cycle do exist, but basically they are very similar (see [Boehm79, Pomberger 86]). According to the software life cycle the software development process is divided in well-defined phases. In general, each phase has to be finished before the next one can be started (see Fig. 1). This enforces a linear process, which implies that executable programs are available very late. Therefore, any misunderstandings between customers and developers remain hidden for a long time. Besides, any technical problems (e.g., an inefficient file system) cannot be perceived before the test phase. Usually modifications becoming necessary are very costly because they are so late.

The classical software life cycle presupposes static requirements and does not deal with incomplete and inconsistent specifications. For given and static specifications, software developers have to deliver a tailor-made design and a corresponding implementation. The better the implemented program fulfills the given requirements, the better was the work of the

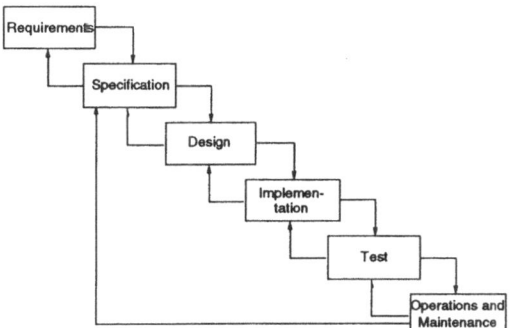

Fig. 1: Classical Software Life cycle

software developers. This approach is in contradiction to reality, because past experience has shown that programs need to be continuously modified and extended. This results in thousands of programmers being engaged with adapting existing software systems to new or changed requirements. Statistics even say that nowadays more time is spent on software maintenance than on software development (see e.g., [Gibson89]). This unsatisfactory situation is partly propagated by the classical software life cycle.

2 Exploratory Software Development

Recently the term *prototyping* has become a buzzword (see [Bischofberger91, Budde84]). The emphasis of prototyping is on the evaluation rather than on long-term use. Software prototypes very often implement the user interface of an application program in order to give potential users an early possibility to evaluate the usefulness and the proper design (of the user interface) of the product. This communication vehicle between developers and customers helps to avoid misunderstandings and usually improves the user interface considerably. However, software prototypes are not restricted to user interface aspects; they can be extended to the finished product step by step.

The term prototyping stems from industry, where prototypes are first models of a certain product. Such prototypes (e g., cars) are used to investigate certain aspects of a product before it goes into production. As software is simply copied rather than produced in quantity, the term software prototype is somewhat misleading. Besides, this approach can be used not only at the beginning of software development but throughout the whole life cycle. For that reason we prefer the term *exploratory software development*. To begin with, exploratory software development means the production of software to meet the known requirements. Testing the product leads to more requirements and results in modifications and tests to fulfill them. This process is repeated until the developed software system performs satisfactory (see [Sandberg87]). Exploratory software development is a strategy that is best suited when an inherent goal of the project is to identify elusive requirements (specification), to

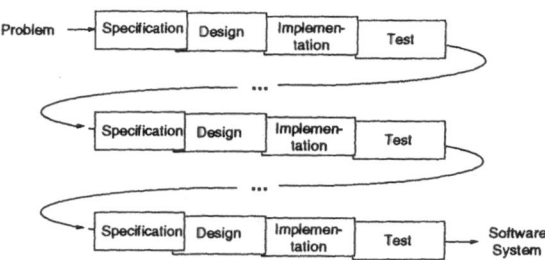

Fig. 2: Exploratory Software Development

establish a suitable system architecture (design), or to explore possible implementation techniques.

Exploratory software development involves repeatedly applying small steps. Each step results (ideally) in an improvement of the current program version until both the developer and the customer are satisfied with the result. Typically one step lasts several hours or even less (see Fig. 2).

When using exploratory software development, programmers have to work with utmost discipline. For example, extending the functionality of a system before its existing parts have reached a (preliminary) satisfactory condition is inexpedient. Additionally, programmers should be aware of writing all the code in a "quick and dirty" fashion, though sometimes it might be useful to temporarily use "quick and dirty" solutions.

The usefulness of exploratory software development emerges from the lack of alternatives in many situations. Both customers and developers not yet knowing exactly what they really want is a typical development situation. Programmers also might not know how to (best) solve certain (implementation) problems. In these cases it is appropriate to work with experimental versions of the software system. By experimenting both customers and developers can gain new insights into their problem domains and thus come closer to better solutions.

Another important justification for using exploratory software development is the increase in complexity of today's software systems. High complexity makes it impossible for human reasoning to deal with all the problems in a linear way, as the classical software life cycle proposes.

Software can best be developed in an exploratory way whenever one or more of the following conditions hold:

• The specification is very vague. Customers are unable to clearly specify their wishes and needs.

• Critical design decisions cannot be made based on theoretical considerations.

- Software developers do not have enough experience with the implementation of similar systems (and the system to be developed is sufficiently complex).

- Programmers do not have (enough) experience in using the programming language or library. (It is impossible to gain familiarity with a class library without experimenting.)

- The system to be developed is too complex and too ambitious to be built linearly.

In our opinion, about half of all projects satisfy one or more of the conditions mentioned above and thus are candidates for exploratory development. The main advantages of exploratory software development are:

- Experimental program versions are excellent vehicles for communication among developers and customers.

- The exploratory approach reduces risks because typically problems are perceived earlier than in the classical software life cycle.

- Stepwise developed programs are better structured and better suited for modifications and extensions because programmers are forced to permanently modify and extend the current version of the software system to be developed. This encourages and trains programmers to write better modifiable code.

- As modifying the system is part of the work being permanently done, it is easier to take new ideas into consideration. The statement: "The next time I would try a wholly different approach!" is more seldom among exploratory programmers.

- Programmers are strongly motivated by working on an executable program rather than writing specifications and design papers for a long time without having an executable program.

Unfortunately, there are also some disadvantages:

- Exploratory development in large teams is possible only when the software system can be clearly separated into various parts.

- It is difficult to estimate the duration and the costs of a certain project. New estimation methods have to be found for this purpose.

- Programmers have to be well trained and to work with discipline. This is extremely necessary in exploratory software development because otherwise the resulting programs are not easily modified ore extended.

- Documentation gets lost in the shuffle.

- Version control and backtracking need to be supported (by tools).

In commercial software projects these disadvantages may be too hard. In order to get estimates of the cost and the duration of a project, we suggest making a rudimentary specification and an initial design according to the classical software life cycle and applying the exploratory approach in the next steps only. This makes it possible to divide a project into small and easily surveyed parts that can be processed by small programming teams.

3   Reusable Class Libraries and Application Frameworks

Conventional libraries, toolboxes, drawing routines, etc. offer fixed functionality at a higher abstraction level than bare programming languages. In the design of the software system the designers have to consider the interfaces of the given components carefully and have to use the provided functions in an appropriate manner. Usually it is not a major problem to build a system upon such libraries when their functions and components are not strongly interrelated. This holds for simple user interface components, data containers, and mathematical and graphical operations.

When working with application frameworks, which define the core structure of the overall application, the designers cannot develop an architecture top-down. In this case the architecture is already predefined to a certain degree by the set of related framework classes which anticipate very early design decisions. The job of the designers is to append the application-specific functionality at appropriate places in the framework. The more powerful and extensive the framework is, the more design decisions are already anticipated in the provided classes.

Commercial applications usually do not use domain-specific interaction techniques or sophisticated algorithms. For such applications classical design methods become superfluous. Although complex software systems could never be designed by means of applying classical techniques and methods such as stepwise refinement or the Jackson System Development Method (see [Cameron89]) alone, application frameworks make these aids less useful. This does not imply that classical techniques will become obsolete as a consequence of frameworks, but their use will be restricted to certain domain-specific components.

Another drawback of classical design methods stems from the fact that applications made from frameworks are implemented in an object-oriented way. Object-oriented systems cannot be designed adequately by means of classical methods. A considerable number of software engineering scientists see the need for a new or modified design method to overcome the current dilemma. A rapidly increasing flood of articles and books about object-oriented design methods, e.g., [Booch86, Coad90, Rumbaugh91], mirrors the expectations of the unhappy software industry.

4   Exploratory Development Approach with Class Libraries

Powerful and well-structured class libraries are a crucial advantage for exploratory software development. The quality and extent of the library used are often more important than the power of the programming language or the development tools.

The exploratory approach has proven its excellence particularly in the development of highly interactive applications with graphical user interfaces. Below we will describe the various tasks that are typical in exploratory software development with class libraries. In general these tasks are seldom completed at once. Usually one does just a portion of a certain task; the next step is taken at the next iteration of the cycle. Furthermore, one should keep in mind that not everything can be done right the first time. But even when information is missing to make a sound design decision, one should not hesitate too much. Experimentation and exploration often lead to better solutions than intense analytical studies. The steps of the exploratory development approach are as follows (see also [Stritzinger92]):

Step 1:

Start with the design of the user interface in a prototyping-oriented way. Concentrate on the essentials first. Whenever some parts of the interface are unclear, try a rudimentary design.

Step 2:

Try to identify classes for the implementation of the user interface components. An extensive class library should offer a lot of support in this respect. Typical classes include: Window, Menu, View, TextView, ListView, and control elements like Button and Scrollbar. If you cannot find exactly what you are looking for, search for classes that already implement part of the desired functionality. Inheriting is most often cheaper than implementing.

Step 3:

Try to identify classes that describe important objects in your problem domain. These classes often correspond to object categories of the real world (employee, car, etc.). Although it is not as likely as with user interface classes, there is still a chance to find classes in the library from which you can inherit. If objects in your program have a close correspondence to real-world objects, slight changes in the real world will just cause slight changes in the program. All objects that describe application-specific data should be connected somehow. This complex object web is usually called the *model*. Relationships among model objects can either be established by application-specific compound objects (faculty, assemblyLine, etc.) or by general-purpose collection objects (queue, tree, etc.). The whole model should be accessible by a single (or a small number of) reference(s). If there are objects that share a lot of commonalties but differ in some respects, the commonalties should be described collectively (factored into a common superclass). In many cases abstract classes are rather useful. Abstract classes (e.g., GraphicShape) are classes that do not have instances; they just serve for factoring commonalties out of their subclasses. The more complex the problem is, the more imaginary classes have to be invented. Finding appropriate imaginary classes is a very difficult job that requires some experience. Fortunately, you can find such classes incrementally.

Step 4:

Identify relevant object states for all classes. Object attributes that carry state information are (usually) modeled as instance variables of the corresponding class. Redundancy among instance variables should be avoided.

Step 5:

Think about the messages (operations) your objects should respond to. Each instance variable has to be addressed; i.e., each variable must get a value and must be accessible somehow. The semantics of each message should be clearly describable. Messages should be as powerful as possible, but as flexible as necessary.

Step 6:

Implement a method for each message. Do not duplicate code from superclasses; send messages to invoke the overridden method instead. Extensive methods should be split into several, possibly private methods.

The above steps are often performed in a non-sequential way. For instance, it may happen that while implementing a method the need for an additional instance variable arises. Simultaneous development of various small life cycles is typical for the reuse of class libraries and is also called a *cluster model* (see [Meyer88], [Pree91]).

It is always advisable to define classes somewhat more generally than actually necessary. Modifying and extending existing code is typical in the exploratory approach. The more general classes are, the less widespread is the impact of changes and extensions.

5 Conclusion and Outlook

In summary, we claim that an exploratory, object-oriented development approach together with application frameworks is the most productive way to develop highly interactive applications with high quality standards. The problems in designing complex systems are rather a symptom of an insufficient strategy than a lack of methods. Innovative and sophisticated software systems can never be developed in a linear process of applying recipes. Similar to other high-tech products, knowledge, skills, experience and motivation play a crucial role in the successful realization of ideas.

In our opinion, one of the strongest drawbacks of object-oriented software development is the huge complexity of many widespread class libraries and application frameworks. This complexity, together with the manifold structuring options of object-oriented programming, make extremely high demands on programmers – even with an exploratory approach. Many programmers in the field are unable to take advantage of these powerful techniques. Therefore software engineering experts are called upon to develop tools that permit less experienced programmers to utilize the advantages of object-oriented programming with class libraries by helping to master the complexity and by supporting the comprehension process (see [Sametinger90] for an example).

A first step in the right direction is so-called interface builders. By means of interface builders construction of complex user interfaces can be done in a simple, interactive way by directly manipulating interface components. 4th generation systems form another possibility for a quick development of applications at a high level of abstraction. The drawback of 4th generation systems is often the connection between user interface and database, which usually have to be programmed with a rather conventional programming language. The developers are confronted with a huge gap in the abstraction level whenever the built-in functionality is not sufficient. Furthermore, only a minority of contemporary 4th generation systems are based on the object-oriented paradigm.

The goal of a thoroughly seamless development process at a very high abstraction level could be reached by a kind of tool (or tool set) which could be called *application builder* or

5th generation system. Such a system should support interactive, graphical construction of user interfaces and (external and internal) data models. In addition, a 5th generation system should offer the opportunity to combine predefined, reusable and user-defined building blocks in a comfortable, yet flexible and preferably visual way.

Unfortunately, such 5th generation systems are not available yet. But there is a good chance that mechanisms and tools will be developed which can fulfill the goal of a thoroughly seamless development process at a high abstraction level. Then object-oriented programming with extensive libraries will become a widespread technology available to almost everybody.

6 References

1. Bischofberger W., Kolb D., Pomberger G., Pree W., Schlemm H.: Prototyping-Oriented Software Development - Concepts and Tools, Structured Programming, Vol. 12, No. 1, New York, 1991

2. Boehm B., W.: Software Engineering, in Classics in Software Engineering, Yourdon N.E. Editor, pp. 325-361, Yourdon Press, 1979.

3. Booch G.: Object-Oriented Development, IEEE Transactions on Software Engineering, Vol. SE-12, No. 2, February 1986.

4. Budde R., et al (Editors): Approaches to Prototyping, Springer-Verlag, 1984.

5. Cameron J.: JSP & JSD: The Jackson Approach to Software Development, IEEE Computer Society Press, 1989.

6. Coad P., Yourdon E.; Object-Oriented Analysis, Yourdon Press Computing Series, Prentice Hall, 1990.

7. Gibson V.R., Senn J.A.: System Structure and Software Maintenance Performance, Communications of the ACM, Vol. 32, No. 3, pp. 347-358, 1989.

8. Meyer B.: Object-Oriented Software Construction, Prentice Hall, 1988.

9. Pomberger G.: Software Engineering and Modula-2, Prentice Hall, 1986.

10. Pree W.: Object-Oriented Software Development Based on Clusters: Concepts, Consequences and Examples, TOOLs Pacific (Technology of Object-Oriented Languages and Systems), pp. 111-117, 1991.

11. Rumbaugh J., et al: Object-Oriented Modeling and Design, Prentice Hall, 1991.

12. Sametinger J.: A Tool for the Maintenance of C++ Programs, Proceedings of the Conference on Software Maintenance, San Diego, CA, pp. 54-59, 1990.

13. Sandberg D.W.: Smalltalk and Exploratory Programming, ACM Sigplan Notices, Vol. 22, No. 10, 1987.

14. Stritzinger A.: Reusable Software Components and Application Frameworks—Concepts, Design Principles and Implications, to be published in VWGÖ, Vienna, 1992.

SOFTWARE PROCESS IMPROVEMENT BY MEASUREMENT
BOOTSTRAP/ESPRIT PROJECT 5441

Volkmar Haase   Richard Messnarz   Robert M. Cachia
Graz University of Technology   Graz University of Technology   Etnoteam SpA
Graz, Austria   Graz, Austria   Milan, Italy

Abstract. A new paradigm in software engineering claims that the quality of a product is highly impacted by the quality of the process which gives rise to it. To reduce the risk to product and project we therefore seek to quantify the quality of the development process. Software process measurement represents an evaluation of all the management activities, methods, and technologies that are employed to develop a software product. BOOTSTRAP developed a method to determine the profile of a Software Producing Unit (SPU) showing its strengths and weaknesses. This paper is intended to illustrate a methodology of software process measurement and will present some sample results.

1 Introduction

An SPU (Software Producing Unit) is a software producing company of small or medium size or a department in a large company in which projects are performed to develop software products. An SPU consists of projects that are software producing entities, and an organization and management built around these projects. A project is an entity within an SPU which has a well-defined goal and has to exploit the resources provided by the SPU to develop a certain software product according to a time schedule.

About 7 years ago the US DoD (Department of Defence) began to assess the development process of its contractors. Since then only contractors with a software process of high quality have been awarded further contracts. These SCEs (Software Capability Evaluations) have been performed by the SEI (Software Engineering Institute) [BOL91]. In addition teams of software development organizations wanting to develop software for the DoD have been taught by the SEI how to perform software process assessments. Software process assessments are based on a questionnaire which contains nearly the same questions as those used for SCEs. These assessments help to identify the key strengths and problems of an SPU, and to create action plans to improve the software process, so that the SPU has better chances of doing well at an SCE and getting a contract [BOL91, HUM91, HUM91a].

The SEI model differentiates between 5 different maturity levels of Software Producing Units [ESP91, HUM89, HUM91a, PAU91].

Level 1: Initial Process
Level 2: Repeatable Process
Level 3: Defined Process
Level 4: Managed Process
Level 5: Optimizing Process

A level between 2 and 5 is assigned to every question of the questionnaire. After the evaluation of the questionnaire it is possible to identify on which level of maturity the SPU is located.

BOOTSTRAP adopted and extended the SEI questionnaire and adapted it to the European software industry including non-defence. Further we developed an improved evaluation method to calculate the maturity level of an SPU [ESP91, HAS91].

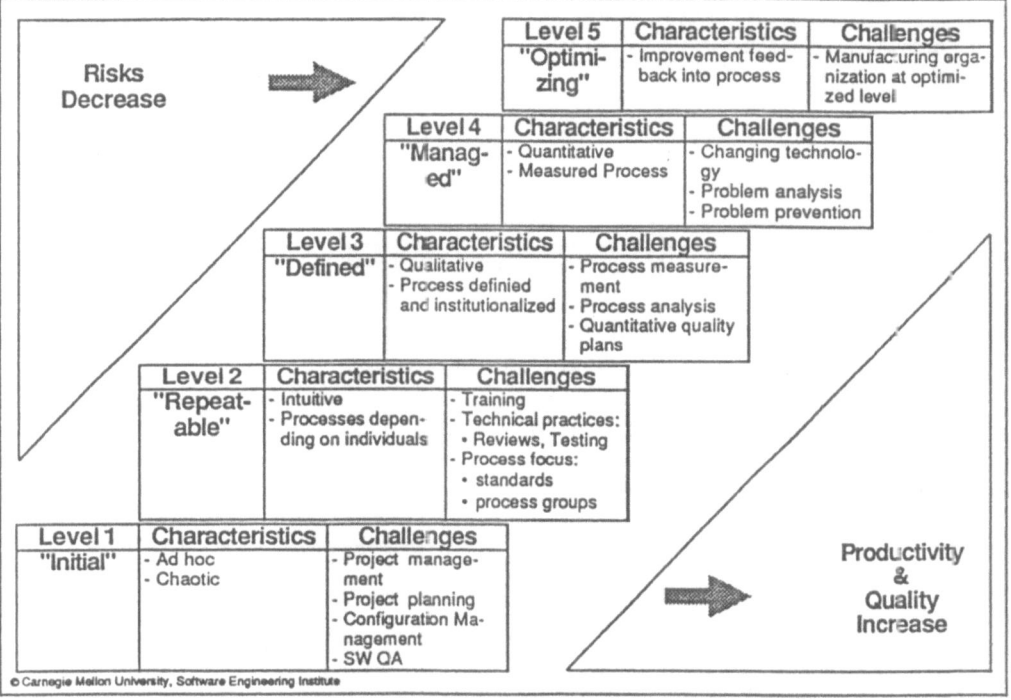

Fig. 1: Maturity levels according to the SEI

2 BOOTSTRAP's Approach

BOOTSTRAP attempts to identify all individual attributes of a software development organization or individual project and assigns all questions to process quality attributes as well as levels. It is not only possible to calculate the maturity level of an SPU or a project but also the attainment on a particular process quality attribute.

The SEI questionnaire initially only allowed a question to be answered by yes or no (black/white) [BOL91]. BOOTSTRAP, seeking to obtain more detailed and precise results, differentiates between 1 (0 percent / weak or absent), 2 (33 percent / basic or fair), 3 (66 percent / significant or strong), 4 (100 percent / extensive or complete). A maximum deviation of 0.5 on a discrete scale of 1 to 4 for the evaluation of a question corresponds to a deviation of approximately 17% on a percentage scale. This maximum deviation would be 50% in case of a yes/no scale. As in the real world, a process is seldom in a 0% or 100% state, a 4 point scale seems to be more precise and technically more sound.

BOOTSTRAP is not only based on the SEI model but also on the ISO standard 9000-3 [ISO87, ESP91] for quality assurance and quality management and on the ESA-PSS 005

standard [ESA91, ESP91] for the software life cycle. We also take into account some key aspects of the spiral model like risk management and prototyping. This, for example, has lead to a further process quality attribute entitled Risk Avoidance and Management.(see Fig. 2).
Initially we used weighted questions, because some questions seemed more important than others. After evaluating about 30 SPUs and 60 projects we found that evaluations based on weighted scores did not differ significantly from those based on non-weighted scores. For 86 percent of the evaluations the difference between weighted and non-weighted satisfaction percentage was equal or lower than 5 percent for each level. The maximum difference observed was 8 percent. There is a high correlation between weighted and non weighted satisfaction percentages. The correlation coefficient, which we derived from the comparison between weighted and non-weighted satisfaction percentages, is 0.98 for level 2, 0.9943 for level 3, and 0.9842 for level 4. Moreover it is quite difficult to select a weight set sensible for all situations. Thus the notion of question weights does not seem very useful.

Risk Avoidance and Management

Question Nr.	Assigned Level	Text
2219	3	Existence of requirements to identify, assess and document risks to project and product associated with modifying Software Life Cycle (SLC) or Non-SLC activities
2220	2	Existence of a requirement for identifying the parts of a specification more likely to show instability
2221	2	Existence of guidelines for taking into account, at high level design phases, the possible instability in parts of the specification
Answers:	absent / basic / significant / extensive	

Fig. 2: Sample questions of BOOTSTRAP's questionnaire

We have a 4 point scale for the evaluation of a question and if we assume that a question can be evaluated with a maximum deviation of $d = 0.5$, the following standard deviation can be derived:

$$Sigma = d * SQRT(Nq) \qquad (1)$$

Nq   ... Number of questions

Sigma   ... Standard deviation from the total score for Nq questions based on the assumption that scores might be given for a certain question with a deviation of 0.5.

From this standard deviation we can calculate a range for scores:

$$Score\_Low = (score[1]+score[2]+ ... +score[Nq]) - Sigma$$
$$Score\_High = (score[1]+score[2]+ ... +score[Nq]) + Sigma$$

If we calculate the maturity level of an SPU or a project based on the scores Score_Low and Score_High, the maximum difference between ML[Score_Low] and ML[Score_High] will be lower than 0.2 (Nq is over 100 for an SPU or a project).

ML[Score_Low] = Calculated maturity level based on Score_Low scores
ML[Score_High] = Calculated maturity level based on Score_High scores

Thus for the calculated maturity level of an SPU or a project we obtain a standard deviation of approximately 0.1, so that we have selected a scale going up in quarters, from 1.00, 1.25, .. up to 4.50, 4.75, 5.

BOOTSTRAP has separate questionnaires for the assessment of an SPU's quality system (Global Questionnaire) and the assessment of the projects within this SPU (Project Questionnaire) [ESP91]. In the Global Questionnaire we inquire into the recommendation of certain procedures, methods, standards or technologies, whereas in the Project Questionnaire we then ask about their adoption. This means that we check first if an SPU provides all necessary resources and secondly how effectively the projects are using these resources. Hence we can determine whether a project A uses some resources better than a project B and, if so, we can analyze this situation.

BOOTSTRAP emphasizes that organization is most important and that methodology is more important than technology [ESP91, HUM91, PAU91]. A project without organization is nearly certain to result in a disaster. And it does not help to buy a technology when the software engineers either cannot understand the method of the technology or do not accept the underlying methodology. Therefore the technology must be integrated in the existing environment. To be accepted the technology must adapt to the corporate culture, and management has to be sensitive to the need for training to enable the developers to use the methodology and technology effectively.

2.1 Individual Attributes of an SPU According to BOOTSTRAP

ORGANIZATION

Quality Assurance

Resource Management
  Staffing
  Training

METHODOLOGY

Process Related Functions

  Process Description
  Process Measurement
  Process Control

Life Cycle Independent Functions

  Risk Avoidance & Management
  Project Management
  Quality Management
  Configuration & Change Management

Life Cycle Functions

  Development Model
  Requirements
    User Requirements
    Software Requirements
  Architectural Design
  Detailed Design
  Testing
    Unit Testing
    Integration Testing
    Acceptance Testing & Transfer
  Operation & Maintenance

3 Considerations on Questionnaire Evaluations

A key question when performing assessments is how an SPU-wide, project-wide or attribute-specific maturity level can be calculated from the set of answers obtained during an assessment. Bootstrap has tried to develop an algorithm that produces more reliable results than the SEI one as it is able to take into account the following facts:

The Algorithm Fits the Complexity of Software Engineering. Our metric, which is based on the calculation of steps and a variable scale, is dynamic. This means that any change in the questionnaire automatically leads to a modified scale, which provides the basis for the calculation of the steps. Additionally we get different scales depending on the characteristics of the SPU type, so that our metric always automatically adapts to the current SPU profile. Nevertheless the results remain comparable because they are mapped onto a maturity level scale. We can even calculate the SEI maturity level. Thus we can compare our results with the SEI results, but this is not true the other way round.(see 3.1)

The Algorithm Minimizes the Dependence on Individual Assessors. The SEI algorithm uses key questions which have to be satisfied to fulfill a certain level [BOL91]. BOOTSTRAP does not use single questions but key clusters of questions (key attributes). Quality management, for example, is a key attribute consisting of 7 questions which have to be satisfied with a threshold percentage to fulfill a certain level. Thus we do not only count yes/no answers for important questions, but we look at clusters of about between 4 to 7 questions. That way the BOOTSTRAP algorithm seeks to minimize the dependence on "assessor behaviour" in judging individual questions. Avoiding such "singularities" resulting from strange SPU or project behaviour has been an explicit design objective of this algorithm. The same considerations led to our early choice of a 4 point reply set rather than yes/no. (see rule 3 in 3.3)

The Algorithm Awards Planned Innovation. The SEI algorithm is strictly sequential. Only if level i is satisfied by a minimum of about 80 percent and if nearly all key questions on level i are answered by yes, does the SEI algorithm take into account the scores on level i+1 [BOL91]. This does not award SPUs and projects which plan and stagger innovation over a period of time. Thus for the calculation of the steps we also take into account scores which the SPU or project gained on the next higher level. (see rule 2 in 3.3)

The Algorithm Is Based on Steps. If the evaluation is only based on percentages, you will get equal distances between the levels of the maturity scale, although there are different numbers of questions for each level. In the SEI questionnaire the number of questions decreases as the level increases.

$t[2] > t[3] > t[4] > t[5]$, with $t[i]$ ... total number of questions on level i, for $i = 2..5$

This is due to the fact that only few SPUs on levels 4 and 5 are known and well characterized so far. The experiences we gain from SPUs which are on level 4 will help us to define the full set of questions for checking characteristics of SPUs on levels 4 or 5. For levels 2 and 3 nearly 100% of the questions have already been identified.

From formula (1) we can conclude that the proportion between the standard deviation Sigma and the total score for Nq questions decreases if Nq increases. This means that with an increasing number of questions we obtain more reliable and precise results. To fulfill, for example, 75% on level 2 would mean to answer a lot more questions by yes than on level 4.

Even if we had the same number of questions for each level we would have to take into account that depending on the SPU type (e.g. commercial systems, embedded systems) different numbers of questions might be applicable for each level.

$$d[i] <= t[i], \text{ for } i = 2..5$$

t[i] ... total number of questions on level i
d[i] ... number of applicable questions on level i

BOOTSTRAP has developed an algorithm which uses steps instead of percentages and a scale with variable distances between the levels.
Only if d[1] = d[2] = d[3] = d[4] = d[5], is the calculation of steps equal to the calculation of percentages.

The Algorithm Has Enhanced Evaluation Capabilities. As BOOTSTRAP has two questionnaires, one for the SPU and one for projects, it is able to compare the SPU profile with the profile of the projects [ESP91]. Additionally we have designed an algorithm which cannot only calculate the maturity level of an SPU or a project but also of each individual attribute. (see rule 4 in 3.3)

3.1 Dynamic Scale

The distances d[i] between the levels (see Fig. 3) are defined by the number of applicable questions. There are different distances between the levels because we have different numbers t[i] of questions for each level and due to the size and structure of an SPU type different numbers of questions d[i] <= t[i] might be applicable. So the distances d[2], d[3], .., d[5] are not constant but variable. For an SPU A, for example, 40 questions might be applicable on level 3, whereas for an SPU B 44 questions might be applicable on the same level. Thus we obtain a scale depending on the particular characteristics of the SPU type.

I-----------I----------------I-----I----I
1   d2   2   d3   3 d4 4 d5 5

d[i] ... Number of applicable questions on
level i, for i = 2..5

Fig. 3: Scale According to the Maturity Levels

3.2 Motivation

We can compare the approach of the BOOTSTRAP level algorithm with a mountain, with a number of steps leading from the foot up to the peak. Each step represents one question in the questionnaire. Every SPU tries to master a number of steps to get as close as possible to the peak of the mountain. The foot of the mountain would be level 1 and the peak corresponds to level 5. We calculate the number of steps which the SPU has fulfilled in climbing up the mountain. (<--> Number of steps (questions) which the SPU has satisfied on the way from 1 to 5 on the scale above)

Thus we can identify on which level (or between which levels) the SPU is located. But this is only a first approximation of the appropriate maturity level and is a nominal value to be refined in subsequent steps (see 3.3).

3.3 Description of the Algorithm

A filled in BOOTSTRAP Questionnaire Q is a subset of NxLxS, with L=(2,3,4,5) representing the set of levels, S=(0,1,2,3,4) representing the set of possible scores and N representing the set of question numbers. Each evaluated question is an element of set Q. The maturity level ML is a function which maps Q, or a subset V of Q in case of an individual attribute, onto a value between 1 and 5 on the maturity level scale.

$$ML: V --> [1,5]$$

$$Q ... \text{subset of } N \times L \times S$$

$$V ... \text{subset of } Q$$

The algorithm works in two phases. First the number of steps is calculated regarding the restrictions which are described in the 4 rules listed below. Then the steps are put on the dynamic scale and the steps-value is transformed into a maturity level value.

$$ML(V) = G (F(V))$$

$$F: V --> [0,D], D = d[2]+d[3] + d[4] + d[5]$$

$$G: [0,D] --> [1,5]$$

F is a function of all scores given for questions which are elements of V and it calculates the number of the achieved steps:

$$F(V) = F(score[x1],score[x2],...,score[xn]), \text{ with}$$

$$|V|=n, \text{ and } x1,x2,.., xn ... \text{elements of } V$$

$$score[xj] ... \text{element of } S, \text{ given score for answer } j, \text{ for } j = 1..n$$

The following rules must be followed for the calculation of the number of steps:

1.
If all questions on level i are satisfied by a percentage[i] >= Defined Threshold, we define that level i is fully satisfied.

2.
If an SPU or project is between level i and i+1 after calculating the steps, the calculation has to be based only on the steps achieved on levels 2 to i+2.

3.
To reach the next higher level an SPU or project must satisfy all key attributes on the current level with a certain minimum.

4.
To calculate the maturity level of an SPU or project we need the restrictions of both 2. and 3. To calculate the maturity level of an individual process quality attribute we need the restriction in point 3, only if a defined key attribute is a subset of the process quality attribute.

Thus the BOOTSTRAP level algorithm allows the calculation of the maturity level of individual attributes, yielding synthetic indicators useful in identifying problem areas in the process. It is technically sound to have a global indicator (maturity level) and lower level synthetic indicators computed in the same way.

4 Sample BOOTSTRAP Results

We are reproducing histograms showing the maturity level of an SPU, of its projects, and of the individual attributes both for the SPU and its projects. (see Fig. 4 and 5)
Every Project Questionnaire contains nearly the same individual attributes as the Global Questionnaire. Using the BOOTSTRAP level algorithm we can calculate a characteristic profile for every project as we can calculate one for the SPU. We can then compare the profiles of different projects and the profile of a project with that of the SPU. This enables us to find weak points within an SPU quickly and easily.
The data analysis in Fig. 4 and 5 shows the structure of an SPU XX and one of its projects XX1 and is based on the calculation of appropriate levels for individual attributes according to the BOOTSTRAP level algorithm.

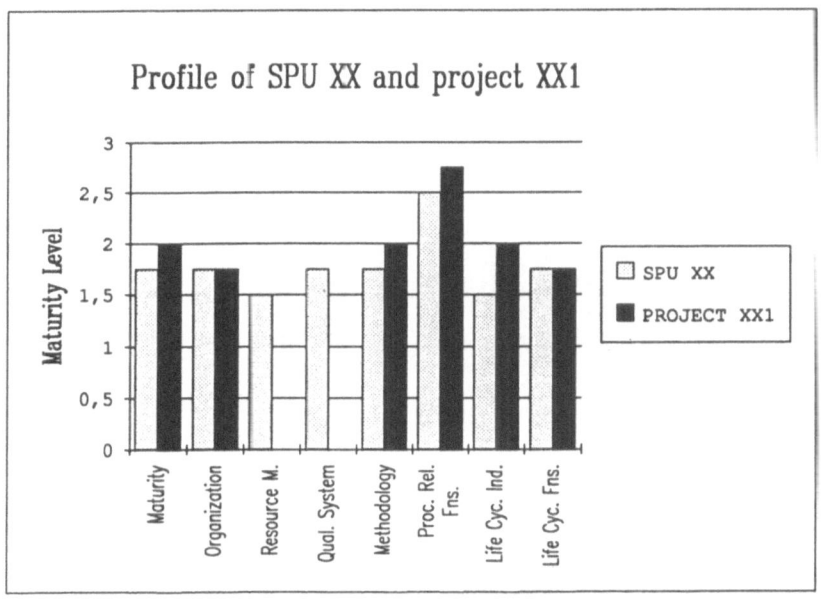

Fig. 4: Overview of the Maturity Levels of SPU XX and Project XX1

4.1 Comments on the Profiles of SPU XX and Project XX1 (see Fig. 4 and Fig. 5)

Resource management is low (1.5) and the quality system (1.75), which provides the basis for quality management, does not seem to work very well. The assessed SPU XX was found to be very weak in project management (1.25), although project management is basically performed at project level (2.00). This suggests that upper management does not recommend the use of project management methods, and nearly nothing has been done to select and refine methods and procedures. This caused the project managers to react by themselves and to develop their own individual methods. Such a situation, however, leads to the problem that all the projects use different methods, so that project management reviews are very difficult because no standard method is followed.

Further, the means for configuration and change management (2.00) are basically provided by the SPU and they are effectively used in project XX1 (2.75). The SPU XX does not recommend any method for analysis and design of the software system which has to be developed. Thus also project XX1 lacks an effective methodology for requirements specification and architectural design. Concerning detailed design project XX1 does not use all of the available resources and we have to check if this is caused by the project typology or if these resources could be used more effectively. The SPU recommends the use of a development model which is followed at project level. Quality management, testing, and maintenance are equally weak in the SPU XX as well as in project XX1.

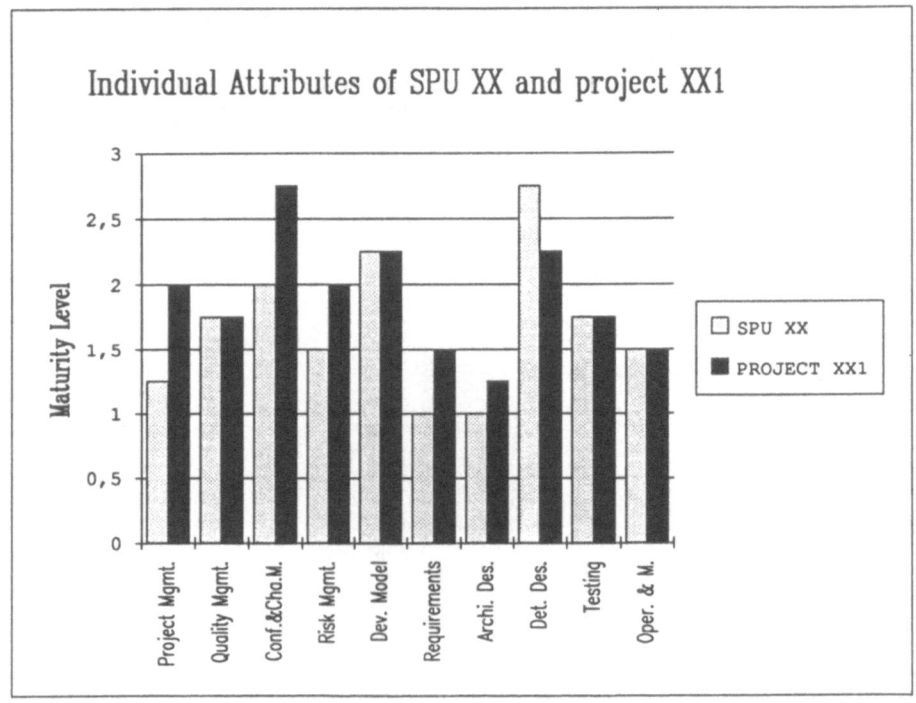

Fig. 5: Individual Attributes of Methodology of SPU XX and Project XX1

5 BOOTSTRAP's Future

BOOTSTRAP's long term task is to perform assessments all over Europe and determine a profile of the European software industry. We want to identify its key strengths and weaknesses. The profile of every assessed SPU can be compared with average values of appropriate subsets (e.g. similar size, same branch) of all European profiles. Thus we can determine the position of an SPU within the European market.

The SEI promotes the use of a SEPG (Software Engineering Process Group) [ESP91, HUM89, HUM91a, PAU91] which serves as the focal point of process improvement, performs assessments, and creates action plans to improve an existing environment. It also establishes standards and procedures [HAS91]. BOOTSTRAP's assessment activities can be seen as one possible instance of an international SEPG in the European context.

Acknowledgments

This work has been partly funded by the CEC commission under the ESPRIT project 5441, BOOTSTRAP. We would like to thank the commission and we are also grateful to the support of all the partners of the BOOTSTRAP consortium.

References

[BOL91] T.B. Bollinger , C. McGowan : A Critical Look at Software Capability Evaluations.IEEE Software, July 1991, pp. 25-41

[ESA91] ESA Board for Software Standardization and Control: ESA Software Engineering Standards, European Space Agency, Paris, France: 1991

[ESP91] ESPRIT Project 5441 BOOTSTRAP: Phase I Interim Report.Composite Deliverable 7, Commission for European Communities (CEC), July 1991

[HAS91] V.Haase, R. Messnarz: A Survey Study on Approaches in Technology Transfer, Software Management and Organization. Report 305, Institutes for Information Processing Graz, June 1991

[HUM91] Humphrey W.S., Bill Curtis : Comments on 'A Critical Look'. IEEE Software, July 1991, pp.42-46

[HUM89] Humphrey W.S.: Managing the Software Process, 494p., SEI Software Engineering Institute , New York , Amsterdam , Bonn , Madrid , Tokyo : Addison - Wesley Publishing Company 1989

[HUM91a]Humphrey W.S. , T.R. Snyder, R.R. Willis: Software Process Improvement at Hughes Aircraft. IEEE Software, July 1991, pp. 11-23

[ISO87] ISO 9000-3 : European Standard for Quality Management and Quality Assurance, European Committee for Standardization, Bruxelles: 1987

[PAU91] M.C. Paulk , B. Curtis , M.B. Chrissis : Capability Maturity Model for Software, Software Engineering Institute , Carnegie Mellon University, Pittsburgh, August 1991

ARTIFICIAL INTELLIGENCE -
MODELLING ASPECTS

Chair: V. Haase

A framework for reconciliation of the meta-structure of repositories and structured methodologies

Beyond Software Engineering

Bálint Molnár

Information Technology Foundation of Hungarian Academy of Sciences
H-1525 Budapest 114. P.O.B. 49, Hungary,
Telephone: +36 1 169-9499, Fax: +36 1 155-3376
e-mail: h4445mol@ella.hu

Abstract. In this paper, an attempt is presented in order to map the widely-accepted meta-structure of information resource dictionary systems (repositories) and the meta-structure of structured methodologies for systems analysis and design on the field of very large information systems. An effort is made to map these two architectures on each other using the object-oriented principles creating a theoretical framework, furthermore the applicability of object-oriented approach is investigated.
The aim of this research is twofold (1) to help understand the design process of very large information systems (VLIS) and (2) to create a base to analyze the problem solving activities.

1. Introduction

There are some standardized repository or Information Resource Dictionary System (e.g. ANSI IRDS [IRDS 1988, IRDS 1988b], ISO IRDS [IRDS 1990, IRDS 1990b], IBM AD/Cycle [IBM 1989], DEC ATIS, etc), some of them are defined by international standardization bodies, some of them are defined by huge organizations as a *de facto* standard. There are some similarities among them due to the early standardization efforts in their structures and in the applied concepts. The theoretical skeleton of these definitions provides a good opportunity to use their vocabulary of notions in practice even in the case when tools in a certain environment do not cling to one of the standards entirely.
The definition of repositories does not imply any particular methodologies but the conceptual structure can be used to arrange the entities and objects of a certain information systems design methodology in this framework.
There are some comprehensive meta-model of information system development methodologies [Hesse 1988] and there do exist meta-models for the single, concrete methodologies as well.
In this paper, the following theses might have to be proven:
- The structure of the repositories and meta-models of methodologies are orthogonal and this property can be exploited to reconcile these two viewpoints in a practically useful framework.
- The object-oriented approach is quiet useful but enforcing it on the meta-modelling of methodologies is not beneficial if it means to drop out the immanent dichotomy of the different system viewpoints in order to represent the universe of

discourse more smoothly and apparently with fewer conflicts.

The rapidly changing technology during long projects coerces that the employed tools for analysis, design and implementation have to be replaced with a more advanced one and even the methodology might have to be improved or enhanced either evolutionary or revolutionary way. However, if we have a sound base for representing and interpreting of the collected information in a meta-model, the right place for the pieces of information can be found more easily in a slightly or drastically changed environment so in spite of alteration in circumstances the project can be adapted to the new situation. Some project management methods can be considered as product-oriented (e.g. PRINCE [CCTA 1991]) so several entities of the meta-model as deliverables or products of a certain project have well-defined places in the meta-model and can be dealt with the project management in the same framework, this makes easier the adaptation process to changes caused by either the project or the methodology or the tool and environment.

The meta-modelling of the process of very large information systems may assist to build interfaces based on the theoretical framework to the various CASE tools utilizing the standard IRDS structure as a solid foundation. If we can identify the problem solving activities and associate them to generic task concept in this context [Chandrasekaran 1988] the software engineering or information engineering activities can be supported by artificial intelligence techniques and algorithms.

2. An overview about the Information Resource Dictionary Systems (IRDS)

There were some standardization efforts to define firstly an advanced data dictionary, later repository or recently Information Resource Dictionary System (IRDS). There is an ANSI standard [IRD 1988], there is an ISO standard [IRDS 1990] and there exists the IBM AD/Cycle Repository [IBM 1989]. But in fact, the tool vendors give lip service to the standards, most of them have a strategy to conform with one of them with added value. The users of the CASE (Computer Aided Software Engineering), I-CASE (Integrated CASE) or IPSE (Integrated Project Support Environment) [Gane 1990] face with a future with two or even three industry standards and a fair number of non-standard but technically advanced products which might apply object-oriented technology, object-oriented or entity-relationship database management systems, perhaps some expert database technology.

The premature endeavors to standardize the repositories have merit, the differences between the ANSI, ISO and IBM are matters of detail, not of basic notions.

We can conclude the flexibility and customizability can be considered as an important feature, the repository concept is proliferated in the industry among product vendors so it will become relatively easy to adjust a given project to the minor differences between two or even three realization of that concept.

2.1 The most important properties of repositories

In the following sections, the significant properties of the repositories are overviewed. The ANSI and ISO standard distinguishes four levels:
- IRD Schema Description - IRD Definition Schema Level
- IRD Schema - IRD Definition Level
- IRD (the Dictionary) - IRD Level
- "Real World" Instances - Application Level

These levels can be formed into a table in the following way [Sibley 1986] :

Level	Data Category	Name in the IRDS
0	Data	--
1	Meta-Data	IRDS Database
2	Meta-Meta-Data	IRDS Schema
3	Meta-Meta-Meta-Data	IRDS Meta-Schema

The level 1, the meta-data consist of entities, relationships and attributes, these form the dictionary database.

The level 2, meta-meta-data are meta-entities, meta-relationships and meta-attributes thus every type of component (entity, relationship, attribute) of the level 1 appears as a meta-entity, i.e., entity-type, relationship-type, attribute-type. The meta-relationships and meta-attributes can be used to describe the structure of the repository and can be employed to define rules, syntactic and semantic checkings to be imposed on the level 1 components. Hence, the permissible repository structure can be determined by meta-relationships. The meta-entity 'generic_procedure' or 'heuristic_rules' can realize the various constraint on the level 1 components (e.g. referential integrity constraint in a relational database system [Date 1981].

The level 3, meta-meta-meta-data termed as the meta-schema level is not yet implemented in commercial repositories, as far as we know. Nevertheless, in principle the level 3 components would be the types of the existing level 2 components.

The meta-meta-entities at the level 3 comprise the meta-entities, meta-relationships and meta-attributes at level 2. For information resource and life cycle management, some meta-meta-entities might be defined as attribute-validation-procedure, attribute-validation-data, life-cycle-stage-name, life-cycle-status-name [Goldfine 1985].

The ISO and ANSI approaches are very close to each other but the ISO is more SQL-oriented, i.e, the ISO strategy is to specify an IRDS that could be accessed through SQL. With the ANSI IRDS, the SQL is a potential implementation tool.

The AD/Cycle Repository manager distinguishes two domains - (1) specification, (2) run-time services.

The specification domain is further divided into three views:
- the conceptual view
- the storage view
- the logical view

The conceptual view operates with similar concepts as the IRDS four level model, supports the following modelling components [IBM 1989, Maciaszek 1991].
- *entity*
- *conventional relationship* with some limitations
- *is-attribute-of* relationships
- *is-part-of* relationships
- *is-a* relationships
- *is-constraint-on* and *is-heuristic-of*

3. A four level meta-model for information system development

In order to understand the development process of business application systems, several models are created to illuminate the various sides of the information modelling process [Hesse 1988, Brodie 1982, Essink 1986]. The modelling of a concrete information system is carried out by various methodologies, the most developed ones try to comprehensively perceive the diverse aspects of business areas [Cameron 1983, Eva 1992, Jackson 1982, Longworth 1986, Matheron 1990, Turner 1990, Yourdon 1975].

Meta-models are used to depict the information systems development process in a comprehensive and concise way and to structure the products and deliverables of a project and the related managing and controlling activities. A specific meta-model exists in the context of a project, an application domain and a methodology, furthermore it determines the basic concepts, vocabulary and terminology, relationships and organizing rules for the given situation.

3.1 A four-level meta-model

In this section, a brief overview will be given about a meta-model [Hesse 1988]. The original version of the meta-model uses the term 'level' so we do not want to deviate from it but we think of them as the various aspects or sides of the information system modelling.

The user level of the meta-model attempts to describe the universe of discourse, the application domain in terms of users. There is only one category and one relationship type in this model, namely, *user concept* and *refers to*.

The functional design level reflects the system analyst/designer viewpoint. The application of semi-formal description techniques (data flow diagrams, entity-relationship data modelling), the counterpoint of the active and passive elements of the application, i.e., the dichotomy of the data model and the function model [Brodie 1982] are the characteristic of this level.

The technical design level deals with the transformation of the functional design into the predefined technical system architecture, with the synthesis of the result of the analysis. This corresponds to the logical/physical design phase in the project life cycle. In this context, the terms 'building blocks' of the system can be used which consist of 'data types' and 'operations' or 'logical database transactions'. Object-orientation is suitable for that level, data are encapsulated in the building blocks and manipulated by operations which have exclusive access to the data. The interfaces to other building blocks are realized through those operations that can be accessed from outside. The Ada language [Pyle 1984] support such features but there are several other languages.

The implementation level takes care of programming, testing, integration and installation of the information system in a specific computer system environment.

3.2 A modified version of meta-model

The outlined meta-model is a good tool to arrange the components of the development process but it can be enhanced and adopted to an environment where for instance the newest version of SSADM is made use of [Eva 1992, NCC 1990] (Fig. 1).

One of the deficits of the meta-model is that it does not utilize the diverging viewpoints of the users and the business analysts. The user level is too simple although recently the computing-conscious users think in terms of dialogues, logical screens, menus and screens etc. This aspect should incorporate the functional requirements from the user side, the user roles and the related user activities. The differing perception of the system by the users and the analyst should be exploited through confronting the user and the functional aspects.

The functional level or aspect can be refined further. The classical models [Brodie 1982] fall into two categories dealing with the dynamic and static sides of an information system, i.e., the data model and the function/process model. The active components can be classified into process model, function model, event model, dialogue model according to the most modern analysis methods [Eva 1992, Matheron 1990, Turner 1990]. The function model means in this context the representation of the user requirements from the viewpoints of analysts so it is a variety of the functional requirements incorporated into the user level.

The technical design level should be adopted to the chosen technical environment whether 3 GL or 4 GL or object-oriented but because of the lack of space and complexity of the related questions we cannot go into detail. The meta-model at this level depends on the peculiarity of the concrete environment and in generality we cannot go beyond in [Hesse 1988] described structure.

4. The meta-model in the structure of IRDS

In this section, the relation of the user aspect and the functional design aspect to the structure of IRDS will be investigated, the connection of the technical and the implementation side is discussed briefly elsewhere [Goldfine 1985].

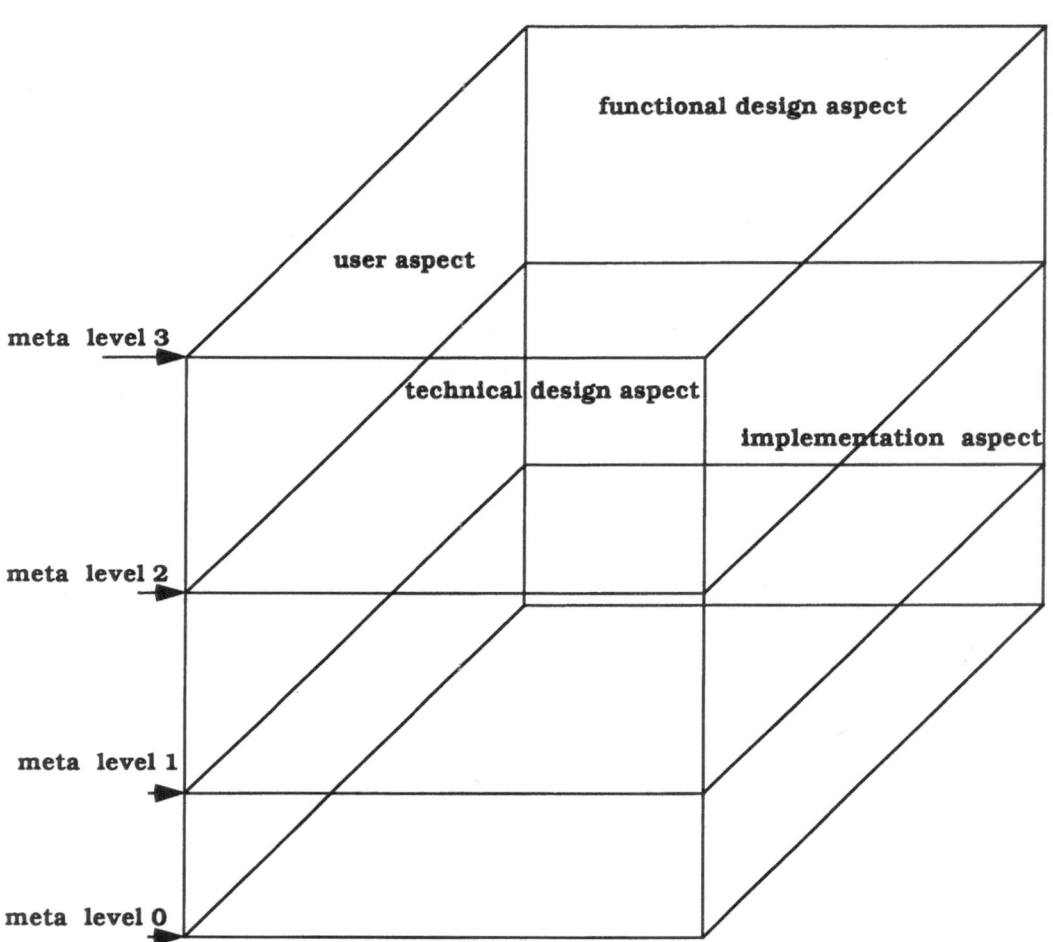

Figure 1.

4.1 The reconciliation of the orthogonal views

At the user level or aspect, the meta-meta-data is the *user concept*, the functional and user interface requirements appear at the meta-data level, the *is_a_part_of* relationships connect them to the outline or logical dialogue design, screen design, functional requirements for the system services, user roles and user activities. There exist relationship-types associating the previously mentioned entity-types to each other. For instance, a user-activity-instance *use* a logical-design-dialogue or a user-role-instance *execute* a user-activity., etc. The *use* relationship-type and the *user-activity-type* connected to each other through a meta-relationship. The functional requirements, the logical dialogues (screens, menus, etc.) and user roles can be connected similar way utilizing that the meta-relationships are able to describe more-than-binary relationships.

The functional design level or aspect of the meta-model provides the categories which comprise a sound base to build up a consistent and concise model of the concrete information or business application system. For this aim, an effective framework is needed in order to structure and exactly describe all relevant side of the application system and all significant pieces of information representing the properties and features of the system. This viewpoint showing the analysts' results is in a rival position to the user aspect.

The service requirements of the system should be collected into functions, the functions can be classified into a hierarchy of application functions, namely, main application functions, (normal) application functions and elementary application functions. The hierarchy can be defined by the recursive decomposed into relationship.

The same procedure can be followed in the case of the process and event model. The DFD (data flow diagram, [Eva 1992, Longworth 1986] technique offers a similar hierarchy for processes, for the different levels and other components (dataflow, external entity, etc.) of diagrams (Fig. 3).

The events can be structured into main events and sub_events in an analogue way using decomposed into relationship, but the events have relations to the effects and through the effects to the operations (logical database transactions). For example, an event-instance *cause* effect-instance on entity-type, an event-instance *trigger* a data-flow-instance in a DFD. The meta-entities are the *event-type*, the *entity-type*, *effect-type*, *operations-type*, *cause-relationship-type*, *trigger-relationship-type*, etc. The relationships are realized among them through meta-relationships (Fig. 2).

The effects on entities of events should be arranged into a Jackson-like structure diagrammatically in SSADM (ELH, entity life history). However, the Jackson structure is equivalent to a regular expression so the syntactic checking is well-defined and simply conceptualized so the generic procedure can be put into a meta-entity.

The semantic and syntactic checking , e.g. DeMarco level balancing [Longworth 1986], should be connected to certain components (meta-entities), that is, the information flows coming into or out of a higher level process (symbol) are equivalent to information flows appearing on an one-level-lower diagram crossing the boundaries and stepping in and out of this diagram which represents the higher level process in detail. These generic procedures can be placed into a meta-entity or meta-meta-entity and their effects can be imposed this way and then executed at the lower level.

The function and the processes should be correlated to each other, a function can *contain* several (elementary) processes. The principles of grouping the processes into functions may be based on the cohesion and coupling [Yourdon 1975], how much the processes close to each other in a certain metric. The classical properties are the data, control and common environment coupling, furthermore the coincidental, logical, temporal, procedural, communicational, sequential cohesion. These properties might be the attributes of the concrete relationships.

The structuring of the knowledge about the method in meta-entity or meta-meta-entity is important even in the case if there is not a computerized support in order that the right place may be seen where it belongs.

4.2 Object-orientation and the meta-model

Around the object-orientation, there is fairly great confusion, therefore our understanding should be clarified firstly.

Object-oriented languages and object-oriented database management systems offer the following features more or less.

50

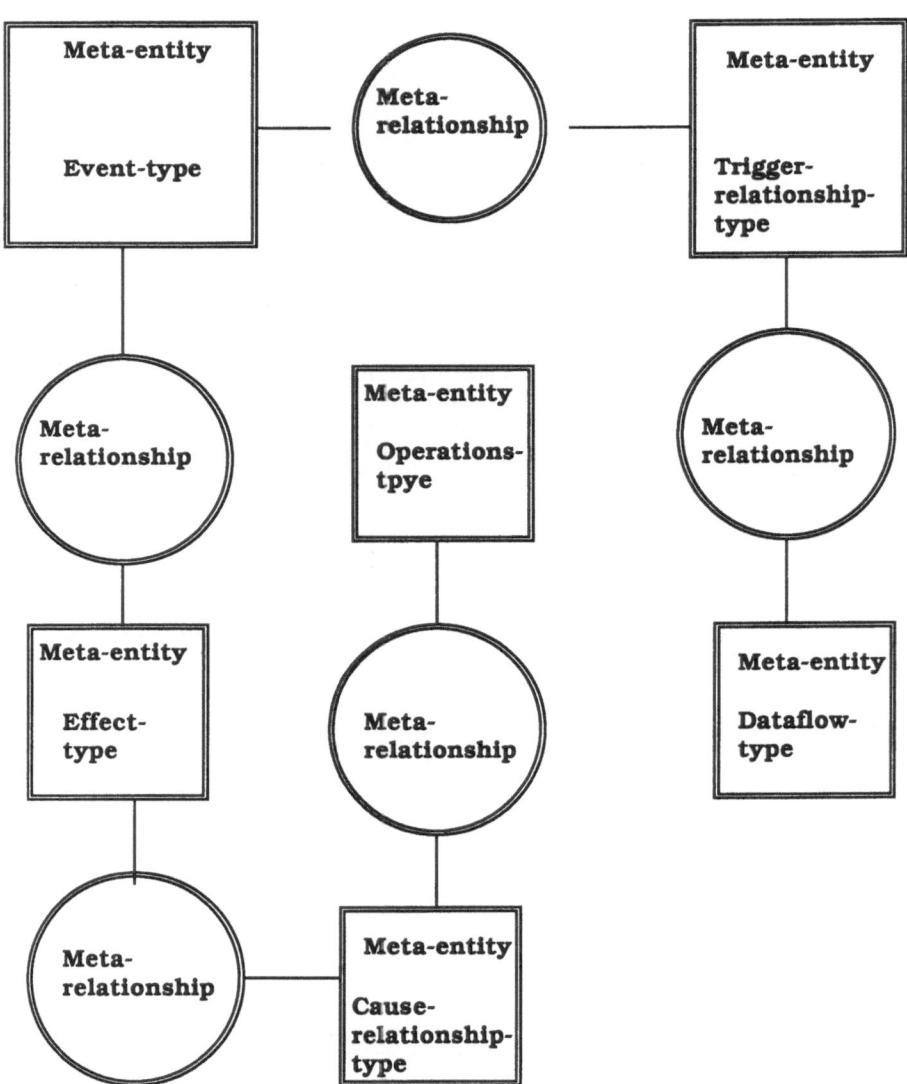

Figure 2.

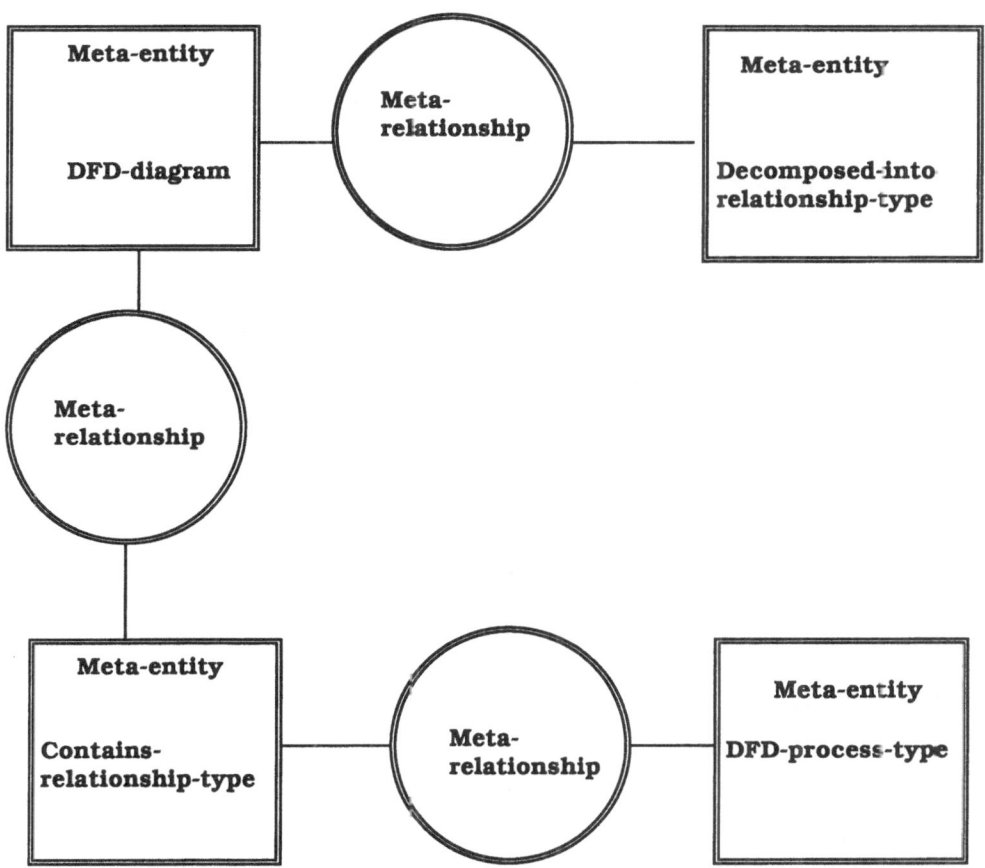

Figure 3.

Every entity (here "Any concrete or abstract thing of interest including association among things", [van Griethyuysen 82]) in the universe of discourse is an *object* and all objects are classified into classes that themselves are objects [Stefik 1986]. The class hierarchy has a single root, class *object*; all entities are instances of that class. Class *class* is the subclass of class *object* whose instances are entities which represent classes; class *object* and all its subclasses are thus instances of class *class*. Class *relation* is the subclass of class object whose instances are entities representing relations; example instances of that class are relations *subclass* and *instance*. Class *individual* is the subclass of class *object* whose instances are entities which neither represent classes nor relations.

More technically, object-orientation means:
- data encapsulation
- inheritance
- polymorphism.

A technical and theoretical feature is:
- abstraction which has two roles:
  - implementation role
  - modelling role, i.e, the correct description of the requirements

The knowledge about the universe of discourse can be structured along various ontological planes or meta-levels; relation *instance* achieves the transition between planes.

The components of meta-levels of IRDS and the elements of the different aspects of the application system meta-model can be considered as objects. The hierarchy among the meta-levels in IRDS can be regarded as a class hierarchy. A level or aspect of the application system meta-model consists of entities, meta-entities, meta-meta-entities can be identified with the hierarchy of *objects* or *classes*, the relationship-type-entities and meta-relationships may be with the *relations*.

4.3 Discussion

The above outlined identification or mapping of hierarchy of objects and entities is fairly superficial.

In the context of the IRDS, the hierarchy of notions about the universe of discourse is identified in the form of entity instances, entity types, entity classes (meta-entities). The behavior of the entities can be specified by propositions (or rules). The constraints and the rules may be placed in meta-entities (see 2.1) as generic procedures, i.e., in terms of IRDS, at least one level higher than the entities themselves.

The events in the context of the model of a certain information system can be considered as something happened in either the universe of discourse or the environment or in the information system. The events can cause the modification of entity instances, at the level of the environment or at the level of the universe of discourse can alter some meta-entities or meta-meta-entities.

In the object-oriented approach, events are modelled as messages that are passed on to other objects in order to respond. Object has states and records states [Booch 1986] so a part of the universe of discourse is altered by transitions from one state to another and reacts to events by changing the state of the object or certain objects and by this way the state of the given system.

The rules or propositions can be stored in the slots of objects which are only accessible from within methods attached to the class of objects in which the slots are defined.

The IRDS separation of entities representing data structures from rules specifying control does not match the object-oriented concept because objects specify a composite of data and activity.

In the IRDS meta-model, entities are not considered to possess attributes, instead attributes are regarded as entities in their own right. This is contrary to object-oriented approaches in which attributes are components of objects.

The IRDS view of relationships does not fit the object-oriented conceptualization of relationships between objects being either caused by events or specified in terms of a classification hierarchy. In the object-oriented approach, the most straightforward way of supporting a relationship between objects is to define a slot on one that holds the identifier of another, the IRDS relationship concept is close to the Entity-Relationships notion but the solution to implement it similar. The problem is that the standard object-oriented model cannot represent the constraint that the two objects must point at each other.

Hence, the object-oriented approach has several common features with the concepts of IRDS meta-model, but by no means all.

Booch's classification of objects by their behaviors is the following [Booch 1986]:

- actor objects; task-oriented objects may possess few data item and much complex algorithmic processing; perform actions which influence other objects in the system
- Server objects; data-oriented objects which undergo no operations other than simple updates to their attributes; the recipients of an actor activity and are related to the entity concept in the IRDS.
- Agent objects; mixture of the above outlined features

In order to resolve the differences in a theoretical framework, the entities at all level in the IRDS may be mapped onto server object type and the generic procedures onto actor object type. The behavior modelling remains within the meta-entities representing generic procedures and these are can be identified with the active objects, i.e. the actor object types By this way, the elements of the meta-model of information systems development can be symbolized by objects.

There is a temptation to define 'larger' objects in which the differences may vanish between the meta-levels of IRDS and the aspects or levels of meta-model. The argument is that such a simple object-oriented structure can be more easily handled, provides more opportunity for reuse of components, the transition between the functional and technical level might be smoother, etc.

We do not agree with such an approach because the confronting views give chances to exploit the deviations in order to understand more profoundly the system. The object-oriented approach helps to structure the available knowledge in a comfortable way in the above mentioned style and if a tool is accessible which more or less object-oriented the outlined orthogonal views can be implemented.

If the collected information is represented in objects or frames, some reasoning mechanism might be used. For instance, the processes can be grouped into functions, the inconsistencies between the user aspect and functional aspect can be disclosed, etc. Some conflict resolution algorithm can be used to make the model consistent and to eliminate the deviations, namely the assumption based truth maintenance, the blackboard architecture and the reasoning with objects can be combined together [Bachimont 1991, Barbuceanu 1990, Molnár 1991].

Even if there is not available a tool the outlined structure aids to locate the places where a certain piece of knowledge about the methods and techniques should be used.

5. Summary and conclusions

The outlined framework is only a brief introduction how the meta-model of information system development process and the structure of IRDS can be used and these two orthogonal views how can be fitted together. In this framework, there is an intention to collide the diverse viewpoints and explicitly exploit it in order to build up a consistent model.

Such a framework gives a good guidance how the components, products, deliverables or documents relates to each other and therefore makes it easier to map a concrete project into a concrete tool or environment (e.g. CASE). This mapping process may need a more detailed meta-model of the concrete methodology but this framework can be refined further.

It seems worth investigating the object-oriented approach in this context too as the object-oriented models focus on the definition and inheritance of behavioral capabilities, in the form of operations or methods embedded within the objects, and also support simpler capabilities for structuring complex objects to view object-oriented models as having both structural and behavioral *encapsulation* facilities.

This framework facilitated creating the product descriptions for a large project with a new CASE tool and finding sub-optimal solutions for defining relationships and entities in the data dictionary of the CASE tool so it proved its usefulness.

If there were available a development dictionary which has services for customization and representing the knowledge attached to the methodology this framework and the collected and structured knowledge straightforwardly can be used.

Several systems and approaches are proposed and experimented [Demetrovics 1982, Molnár 1991, Konsynski 1984, Rouge 1990] whose architecture appearing in the practice would provide a good opportunity for incorporating the outlined framework of application system development.

6. Acknowledgements

The author thank the referees for their important and valuable comments and remarks which the author was not able totally incorporate in the text because of the short of space.

7. Bibliography and References

1. Bachimont, Bruno., 'DOTMS: A Dynamic Object-Based Truth Maintenance System to Mange Consistency in a Blackboard', in *Proc. 11th International Conference, Expert Systems and Their Applications, General Conference, Second Generation Expert System*, Avignon, France, EC2, pp 109-122 (1991).
2. Barbuceanu, M. , Trausan-Matu, S., Molnar, B. Concurrent Refinement: A Model and Shell for Hierarchic Problem Solving, *Proc. 10th International Workshop, Expert Systems and Their Applications, General Conference*, Avignon, France, EC2, 873-891 (1990).
3. Booch, G., 'Object Oriented Development' , *IEEE Transactions on Software Engineering*, Vol. 12 No. 2, pp 211-221, (1986).
4. Brodie, M. L., Silva, E., 'Active and passive component modelling: ACM/PCM' in Olle, T. W., Sol, H. G., Verrijn-Stuart, A. A. (eds.), *Information system design methodologies: A comparative view*, Elsevier Science Publishers B. V. (North-Holland), (1982).
5. Cameron, J.R., *JSP and JSD: The Jackson Approach to Software Development*, IEEE Computer. Soc., (1983).
6. CCTA (Central Computer and Telecommunication Agency), *PRINCE, Structured Project Management*, NCC Blackwell Ltd., (1991).
7. Chandrasekaran, B., 'Design: An Information Processing-Level Analysis', Technical Report, The Ohio State University, Department of Computer and Information Science, Laboratory for Artificial Intelligence Research, (January 1988).
8. Gane, C., *Computer Aided Software Engineering, the methodologies, the products and the future*, Prentice-Hall, (1990).
9. Date, C.J., *An Introduction to Database Systems*, Addison-Wesley, (1981).
10. Demetrovics, J., Knuth, E., Rado, P., 'Specification Metasystems', *Computer*, pp 20-35, (April 1982).
11. Essink, L. J. B., 'A modelling approach to information system development', in Olle, T. W., Sol, H. G., Verrijn-Stuart, A. A. (eds.), *Information system design methodologies: Improving the practice*, Elsevier Science Publishers B. V. (North-Holland), (1986).
12. Eva, M., *SSADM Version 4: A user's guide*, McGraw-Hill, (1992).
13. Goldfine, A., 'The Information Resource Dictionary System', in Chen, P.P. (ed.), *Entity-Relationship Approach, The Use of ER Concept in Knowledge Representation*, IEEE Computer Society Press/North-Holland, pp 114-122, (1985).
14. Hesse, W., Bosman, J. W., ten Damme, A. B. J., 'A four-level metamodel for application system development', in Bullinger, H.-J., et al. (eds.), *EURINFO '88, Information Technology for Organizational Systems*, Elsevier Science Publishers B. V. (North-Holland), pp 575-581, (1988).
15. Hewett, J., Durham, T., *CASE: The next step*, Ovum Ltd., (1989).
16. IBM, *Systems Application Architecture. AD/Cycle Concepts*, GC26-4531-0, (1989).
17. *IRDS: Information Resource Dictionary System*, American National Standard for Information Systems, X3.138-1988, (1988).
18. *IRDS: Information Resource Dictionary System Services Interface*, draft proposed American National Standard for Information Systems, (1988b).
19. ISO 10 0027: *Information Resource Dictionary System - Framework*, (1990).
20. ISO 10 0728: *Information Resource Dictionary System - Services Interface*, draft International Standard, (1991).
21. Jackson, M.A., *System Development*, Englewood Cliffs, Prentice Hall, (1982).
22. Konsynski, B.R., 'Databases for Information Systems Design' in *New Directions for Database Systems*, Ariav, Gad., Clifford, James. (eds.), Ablex Publishing Corp., pp 124-145, (1984).
23. Longworth, G., Nichols, D. *SSADM Manual Vol. 1-2*, NCC Blackwell, (1986).
24. Maciaszek, L. A., 'AD/Cycle Repository Manager from Object-Oriented Perspective', *ACM SIGSOFT Software Engineering Notes*, Vol. 16, No. 1, pp 50-53, (Jan 1991).

25. Matheron, J.P., *Comprendre Merise, Outils Conceptuels et Organisationnels*, Editions EYROLLES, (1990).
26. Molnár, B., Frigó, J., 'Application of AI in Software and Information Engineering, *Engineering Applications of Artificial Intelligence*, Vol. 4, No. 6., pp 439-443, (1991).
27. NCC (National Computing Centre), *SSADM Manual Version Four*, NCC Blackwell, (1990).
28. Pyle, I.C., *The Ada programming language*, Second Edition, Prentice-Hall, (1985)
29. Rouge, A., 'Techniques et Outils Intelligence Artificielle Comme Support Methodologique du Developpement & de la Maintenance des Bases de Donnees'. *Proc. 10th International Workshop , Expert Systems and Their Applications, General Conference*, Avignon, France, EC2, pp 807-821, (1990).
30. Sibley, E. H., 'An Expert Database System Architecture Based on an Active and Extensible Dictionary System', in Kerschberg, L. (ed.), *Expert Database Systems*, The Benjamin/Cummings Publishing Company, Inc., pp 401-422, (1986).
31. Stefik, M., Bobrow, D., 'Object-oriented programming: themes and variations', *The AI magazine*, No. 6, pp 40-62, (1986).
32. Turner, W. S., Langenhorst, R. P., Hice, G. F., Eilers, H. B., Uijttenbroek, A. A., *SDM system development methodology*, Elsevier Science Publishers B.V. (North-Holland)/Pandata, (1990).
33. van Griethyuysen (ed), *'Concepts and terminology for the conceptual schema and the information base, computers and information processing'*, ISO/TC97/SC5/WG3 International Organization for Standardization, Geneva, Switzerland, (1982).
34. Winkler, J., 'The entity-relationship approach and the information resource dictionary standard', in Batini, C., (ed.), *Entity-Relationship Approach*, Elsevier Science Publisher B. V. (North-Holland), pp 3-19, (1989).
35. Yourdon, E., Constantine, L.L., *Structured Design*, Yourdon Press, (1975).

The Use of Deep Knowledge from the Perspectives of
Cooperative Problem Solving, Systems Modeling, and Cognitive Psychology

Miklós Biró and István Maros*

Computer and Automation Institute
Hungarian Academy of Sciences
Budapest, Kende u. 13-17. H-1111, Hungary

Abstract. One of the points of the paper is that the exploitation of deep knowledge may well contribute to the appreciation of technology supporting small groups. The term deep knowledge is used in this paper for knowledge that is not only derived from rules acquired from experts, but is complemented with the application of usually numerical algorithms which incorporate a deep body of mathematical knowledge. A natural requirement in this context is the involvement of end-users in the mathematical modeling process. The selective usefulness of relational and functional modeling is analysed from this point of view. A graph theoretic algorithm is proposed for the support of relation building by end-users. The idea of spreadstructure is highlighted. Modeling is analysed from the perspective of cognitive psycholgy. Finally, a prototype modeling support system is presented which is built on the Microsoft Windows environment.

1. Introduction

The primary objective of this paper is the synthesis of ideas and techniques that could promote the use of group decision support technology for cooperative problem solving by even small groups. The issues are examined and the ideas are synthesized from a broad range of perspectives.

The concept of deep knowledge can be approached from different points of view. In artificial intelligence deep knowledge is usually considered as knowledge which can be accessed by going deeply down into the search tree. In the more specific field of expert systems, "the term

---

* Research supported by OTKA grants no. 2571, 2575 and 2587.

second- generation expert system is used to denote systems which employ both experiential, shallow knowledge and theoretical, deep knowledge" [18]. These approaches are not contradictory at all, even if there may be disagreement about definitions. The importance of the concept is nevertheless unquestionable.

The term deep knowledge is used in this paper for knowledge that is not logically derived from rules acquired from experts, but is generated by usually numerical algorithms based on underlying mathematics. The input of these algorithms is usually a mathematical model. In this paper we focus on linear programming models.

A central theme of the paper is that the most appropriate model representations and tools are different in each of the phases of the cooperative problem solving process. The difference is caused by both the nature of the task to be performed, and the professional background of the principal human actor of each phase.

An issue with an effect opposing to the consideration of the above one, is that the transition between the phases and their corresponding representations should be as smooth as possible for technical and psychological reasons.

Ideas contributing to the alleviation of the above conflict are discussed from the perspectives of the problem solving process, systems modeling, and psychology. The sections of the paper are organized around these perspectives. New ideas are discussed in the context of a prototype modeling support system which supports hierarchical concept generation and the building of relations from the concepts. These relations represent matrix entries in a linear programming model.

2. Inhibiting factors and their neutralization

Two extreme factors which inhibit the use of group decision support technology for cooperative problem solving are:

(1) The technology intervening between the participants in the cooperative problem solving process.

(2) The usual requirement for the knowledge and domain specific interpretation of a number of mathematical terms and approaches.

Let us discuss these factors in more detail.

2.1. Factor (1)

Nunamaker, Applegate and Konsysnski [25] give account of extensive experiences with advanced group decision support software (PLEXSYS) and hardware facilities. They report that small groups were frustrated despite of the high level of technology whose intervention between participants may be more inhibiting than stimulating. Their conclusion is that the inhibiting effects are only counterbalanced by information processing benefits if the group size is large enough. These experiences are drawn from unstructured problems, where ideas can only be generated by the participants themselves.

We propose that the unstructured, brainstorming style generation of ideas be coupled with a natural generation of deep knowledge producing models. Deep knowledge may be successfully exploited by even small groups since the generation of optimal alternative solutions through model experiments assumes the use of a computerized system anyway. Thus, the inhibiting effects of the intervening technology are counterbalanced by the computing power necessary in this case.

2.2. Factor (2)

The primary concern here is the complexity of formulating and manipulating a sophisticated model which presumes the use of the technology (see factor (1) above) in the first place.

Even though the complexity of deep knowledge generation is not relevant to cooperative problem solving only, model formulation issues are more acute in this context because of the need to support users with a large variety of possible backgrounds. In this paper we focus on techniques which cause the least mental strain on the end-user while switching between unstructured idea generation and deep knowledge generation environments.

Our approach is based on the opinion that if "the final user is also the model builder, the modeler understands and trusts the model, and is likely to implement the solution" [27]. Model building and model management techniques meant for modeling-experts are only considered in this paper from the point of view of their potential applicability by non-expert users. Not neglecting however the dangers of end-user modeling [13], we consider these tools as most useful in the model rectification phase performed by a modeling-expert after the completion of the brainstorming and initial relational model building phases performed by the end-users. These phases are discussed in the following section.

3. Perspective of the problem solving process

Since our focus is deep knowledge generation in a cooperative problem solving environment, we isolate the following phases of the cooperative problem solving process:

(1) Idea and concept generation through brainstorming. These include decision criteria as well as potential alternatives suggested by the decision makers.
(2) Initial relational model building by the end-users.
(3) Model rectification by a modeling-expert, solution of the model, and interpretation of the results (sensitivity, postoptimality analyses).
(4) Inclusion of the generated solution among the decision alternatives with any comments and assumptions related to the underlying model.
(5) Evaluation of the alternatives (sensitivity analysis, ranking).

Of course, these steps may be performed repeatedly according to the classical modeling cycle and can be complemented by problem partitioning techniques as analysed in [32].

Phase (1) is usually supported by group decision support systems. Model building systems also support phase (1), they do not allow however for a self-contained structuring of the concepts independently from the model under construction. This problem is discussed in more detail in the following section.

Phase (2) for deep knowledge generation is one of the central issues of this paper. It is not supported by either existing group decision support systems or model building systems. The target users of model building systems are usually supposed to be modeling-experts, not end-users. Spreadsheets and even relational data base management systems prove however the viability of the phase suggested above. Its necessity, as a means of building end-users trust in the model, has already been discussed in the previous sections. We will return to this issue from other perspectives.

Phase (3) encompasses the usual phases of modeling in existing model building systems. Since the details are extensively discussed in the literature, they are omitted in this paper.

Phase (4) is also pertinent to the central theme of the paper. In our approach, the solution generated by a mathematical model is only considered as an alternative to creative solutions suggested by the decision makers. In addition, the same model may yield several alternative solutions when model experiments are performed with varied parameters. Comments and opinions may be attached to these solutions by either the modeling expert or the decision makers.

Usual model representations and techniques appropriate in phase (5) include spreadsheets, and multi-attribute utility decomposition (MAUD). The methods enhancing the choice from the set of suggested or generated alternatives (AHP [29], ELECTRE, PROMETHEE [28], [8]) are not detailed in this paper.

The system described in [3] is based on MAUD and supports the hierarchical development and evaluation of decision criteria. Its advantage is that it can be readily coupled with the modeling support system described in this paper, since their concept structures can be identical. This is an example of the support of smooth transition between the brainstorming and modeling phases. The smooth transition between these and the final evaluation phases will be supported by the later defined spreadstructures.

4. Perspective of systems modeling

It has been discussed in the introduction that different model representations are more or less appropriate in different phases of the cooperative problem solving process. In our opinion the building of a concept hierarchy is appropriate in the brainstorming phase, relation matrices in the initial model building phase, semantic nets or relation matrices in the model rectification phase, and spreadsheets or later defined spreadstructures in the interpretation and evaluation phases. These representations are discussed below and their selective application is suggested according to the above opinion.

4.1. Hierarchies and semantic nets

The following are the fundamental reasons for the hierarchical structure of complex systems as discussed by Herbert A. Simon [30] [31]:

(1) Hierarchical systems are most apt for evolution among systems with given size and complexity, since the components of a hierarchy are themselves hierarchies which are stable structures.
(2) The information transfer requirement between the components of a hierarchical systems is less than in other systems.

(3) The local complexity of a hierarchical system is highly independent on its size.

Let us examine some essentially different applications of hierarchies for problem solving.

• Conceptual hierarchy.

In the brainstorming phase, a hierarchy is useful as a mental guidance for the consideration of all relevant concepts of the problem. For the above reasons, an appealing hierarchy building tool is particularly important in a system which is meant to motivate the user who enters the concepts himself.

The "modular structure" in the framework of structured modeling introduced by Geoffrion [14] [15] and the AHP by Saaty [29] are designed to accommodate hierarchical conceptual structures.

Psychological reasons for using a hierarchy and motivating the users to enter their own concepts are discussed later.

• Functional hierarchy and semantic net.

Gerlach and Kuo [16] apply a semantic network representation of model components, which is a hierarchy at the same time. This is a functional hierarchy which is meant to be built by an expert. This semantic network is similar to the functional hierarchies used by Müller-Merbach [24], the networks (element graph, genus graph) defined by Geoffrion [14] [15], the frame-based representation by Binbasioglu and Jarke [1], the graph based representation by Liang [19], and the LPN network introduced by Egli [11] and further developed by Hürlimann [17]. Its advantage is the fortunate combination of the classification and functional relationships in a single graph. The element and genus graphs of Geoffrion are, however, not restricted to hierarchies, but can be directed acyclic graphs. The inclusion of this latter feature into the combined semantic network would unfortunately make it much less manageable.

• Block decomposition hierarchy.

A third type of hierarchy relevant to our study is block decomposition appearing in the LPFORM system developed by Ma, Murphy, Stohr [20]. LPFORM provides a consistent graphical interface for building the matrix of a linear programming problem starting from blocks with interconnections. The detailed content of the blocks can be specified interactively or even retrieved from a database using a relational query language. The interconnections are specified using the activity modeling approach of [10], which is relatively natural for novice users as well. However, "the target user for LPFORM is primarily someone knowledgeable about LP". A semantic net (not a tree) representation is also provided in LPFORM for representing the relationships of models in the model base. Even though the semantic net defined in [16] is restricted to trees for usability reasons, it serves partially the same purpose.

4.2. Relational modeling

A serious drawback of the use of semantic nets in the model building phase of the cooperative problem solving process is that partial structures and definitions are to be fixed early, making subsequent changes more difficult. Vepsalainen [33] suggests a relational modeling approach based on diagonal semantic and activity matrices. This technique makes it easy to experiment with structures without committing to a specific decomposition.

The superiority of relational modeling to semantic networks in the model building phase can also be traced to reasons similar to those of the superiority of the relational data model to the network data model in data base management. "It provides a means of describing data with its natural structure only - that is, without superimposing any additional structure for machine representation purposes." [9] The underlying reason of the success of spreadsheets is also related to this fact.

After the above arguments for relational modeling, it must be remarked that nevertheless, network models have an undeniable expressive power. The controversy could be dissolved with techniques that would allow a smooth transition between the two representations. The spreadstructure idea described later in this paper is a contribution in this direction.

5. Perspective of psychology

There is a paradigm in the science of cognitive psychology which is built on the concept of cognitive patterns [22]. Cognitive patterns are models of the complex knowledge structures appearing and evolving in the human brain. It is an experimental fact that even the perception of our everyday environment is restricted to those phenomena for which we already have cognitive patterns. A model of the storage area of these cognitive patterns is called Long Term Memory (LTM). The buffer between LTM and the real world is called Short Term Memory (STM). It is a stable experimental fact as well, that the capacity of STM is 7 plus or minus 2 units of information. Nevertheless, a unit of information may mean a highly complex cognitive pattern transferred from LTM. New and improved patterns migrate to the LTM from the STM, but the details of this process are very little known.

Cognitive patterns can be categorized into everyday patterns and professional patterns which are connected. This connection is however much looser for an apprentice and it becomes mature at the master level [22].

How are the above concepts related to the issues of this paper?

Experts participating in a cooperative problem solving process may have different professional backgrounds which implies that their professional cognitive patterns are different. A tool supporting cooperative problem solving must provide support for each individual expert and for the group as a whole. Thus, the model representations offerred by the system must be appealing to all of the participants, which implies that they must be as close as possible to everyday cognitive patterns. Tabular representations in both ralational matrices and spreadsheets satisfy this requirement since tables are incorporated among our cognitive patterns at the elementary school level. This is another fundamental reason of their general success.

A point of view opposing but in fact complementary to the above one, is that an individual expert will find the system appealing if he can find model representations close to his professional patterns. It is an experimental fact as well, that there may be an essential decrease in problem solving efficiency if the representation of the problem is not familiar, even if it is completely isomorphic to a familiar one [22]. By consequent, it is important to offer model representations most appropriate for each of the experts in the different phases of the cooperative problem solving process.

The following are further psychological factors which contribute to the popularity of the system:

(1) The user must not be a passive observer or plain server of the system.

This means among others that the concept hierarchy must be built by the users themselves since the model will only be familiar to them in this case. This gives a feeling of active participation at the same time. We discussed earlier that users should stay involved with the building of even a deep knowledge generating model, so that they do not lose contact. An expert can give technical advice and help however.

(2) The user must not be expected to perform complex operations or interpretations.

This issue is related to the inhibiting effects of excessive learning requirements imposed on the user. Gerlach and Kuo [16] highlight the importance of user interface design in this respect. In their approach however, it is an expert who predefines the model. In the modeling support system described below, user involvement is stressed in the model definition phase as well, not leaving the user interface design out of sight either. This will naturally reduce learning problems even if an expert performs rectifications on the model as discussed earlier.

(3) The advantages provided by the system must overweigh the burden imposed by the intervening technology.

The issue of the facility for deep knowledge generation for this purpose is a central theme of this paper. Most of the discussed ideas are focused on relieving the contradiction of this requirement with the previous one.

(4) The psychological fact that humans cannot take much more than seven concepts simultaneously into consideration has already been mentioned.

The use of hierarchies helps in this respect, since the number of direct descendents of an entry can be restricted to be no more than the magic number.

(5) Floyd, Turner, and Roscoe Davis [12] highlight the importance of "computer based gaming" as a means of unfreezing the users.

The "point and shoot" style generation of new relations between entities in the modeling support system below has resemblance with the style of computer games. This will increase the willingness of the participants to experiment with the system.

6. Modeling approach and new ideas to be implemented

The prototype MOdeling Support SYstem MOSSY takes advantage of the Microsoft Windows environment running on IBM/PC compatible computers. MOSSY supports the initial generation and hierarchical structuring of ideas in the form of objects that can be manipulated on the screen using a mouse. In addition to the hierarchical structuring of the objects, relations can be established between any pair of them. The entity-relationship model generated in this way is explicitly visualized and made accessible in a window. MOSSY incorporates a user interface management system (UIMS) which allows the coupling of any information to the objects in the most suitable form.

6.1. The prototype system

In the example presented in the appendix, relations represent matrix entries in a linear programming model. MOSSY is developed to the point of generating an MPS format input file and solving the model.

The target user of MOSSY is not necessarily knowledgeable about LP. However, keeping the requirements for widespread use and deep knowledge handling in focus, MOSSY allows any user to first build a hierarchy of his own concepts, then relate these concepts by simply clicking with the mouse on their window representations. This is a rather simple, even relaxing process, during which even data or any information characterizing the relations can be entered. The block structure of the resulting complete relation matrix is instantly seen on a proportionally sizeable map of the relation window whose visible area may actually contain relatively few of the entities.

Even though it cannot be expected from end-users that they build a correct mathematical model, there are essential psychological benefits in motivating them to go as far as possible. These benefits have already been discussed. An LP expert can be called upon to rectify the model after the end-user has partially defined it. The model building systems mentioned earlier can provide the necessary support for the expert.

The presence of a modeling expert is also necessary for enforcing compliance with the verification and validation requirements of the model life-cycle as cautioned by Gass [13] and mentioned earlier. The approach proposed above guarantees however both the preservation of user interest and the compliance with professional standards.

An ultimate solution to the above problem would be the elaboration of a model building expert system which could partially relieve the requirement for direct expert involvement [6].

The matrix representation of the entities and their relationships in MOSSY bears the same advantages over functional network representation as those mentioned in the section on relational modeling. A further advantage of building a matrix as suggested in MOSSY is that only the relevant relations have to be dealt with preserving in this way the advantages of sparse matrix definition techniques (e.g. MPS format). This approach is on the other hand at a far higher level. The entities are immediately visible and accessible in matrix form and can even be transferred into a spreadsheet.

Direct simultaneous contact with spreadsheets (e.g. Microsoft Excel) is supported by MOSSY through the clipboard of Windows. There is a possibility for dynamic data exchange as well.

6.2. Support for building a relation matrix from differently structured or unstructured concepts.

When a network representation is used, the activity model is considered to be the definition of flows with various inputs and outputs. When a relational representation is used, relations are established between selected entities. Let us assume that relations are established by the user as suggested in MOSSY, and not by an expert. A problem occurs when the entities on both sides of the relation selected by the user have to be assigned to either rows or columns of the matrix. When an entity is selected for the first time in any relation, it is assigned to a row if it is the first operand of the relation and to a column if it is the second. It cannot be expected however, that the user will always select entities already assigned to rows as first operands and entities assigned to columns as second operands. The question is whether the selected operands of a new relation can be assigned to a row and a column in consistency with previous assignments of the entities in other relations.

MOSSY is designed to provide support for this assignment by applying algorithmic techniques. The problem can be formulated in graph theoretical terms, and turns out to be a special case of the Precoloring Extension problem introduced and extensively studied in [4], [5]. The problem in graph theoretical terms is deciding whether a given two-coloring of a bipartite graph can be extended when a new edge and a new node are introduced. Precoloring Extension can be efficiently solved in this special case, since the problem is simply deciding whether the new graph is still bipartite.

6.3. Spreadstructure

Some fundamental reasons of the success of spreadsheets have already been mentioned. In fact, spreadsheets were among the first software tools which have led to the widespread use of DSS within organizations [25]. In MOSSY we are planning to learn from the success of spreadsheets, and include immediate expression evaluation capabilities naturally attached to the conceptual hierarchy built by the user [26]. This facility is an important step toward widespread use, since one of the drawbacks of spreadsheets is that they do not visually support the manipulation of complex structures other than tables and matrices. This is, however, meaningful only if the conceptual hierarchy built for managing the complex structure reflects functional relationships at the same time.

A general system supporting immediate expression evaluation based on an arbitrarily structured construct could be called SPREADSTRUCTURE instead of spreadsheet. Such an object-oriented spreadstructure could even prompt for unspecified values or expressions, and take advantage of artificial intelligence techniques. A spreadstructure would provide an appropriate transitional representation between the brainstorming and evaluation phases of the problem solving process. The implementation of dynamic link between a functional spreadstructure and a corresponding relational spreadsheet would provide smooth transition to the model building phase as well. (A commercial realization close to the spreadstructure idea is Borland ObjectVision for Windows which was announced after the publication of an earlier report [7] already containing the idea.)

7. Conclusion

Deep knowledge generation has been shown to be a necessary facility of group decision support technology for cooperative problem solving intended for widespread use by small groups. On the other hand, widespread use presumes that the system satisfies a number of requirements which have been examined from the points of view of the problem solving process, systems modeling, and psychology.

A facility for building a concept hierarchy is shown to be useful in the brainstorming phase of the cooperative problem solving process.

In order to keep the interest of the users alive, it has been suggested that they get involved in the initial building of the model. Once the model is solved, its solution is considered as an alternative to creative solutions suggested by the decion makers and to other solutions obtained through model experiments.

Relational modeling has been found to be more suitable for end-user model building than the semantic net approach, similarly to the superiority of relational data base management to network data base management.

Smooth transition between the different representations should be supported since the cognitive patterns of the end-users and modeling experts may be different, and different representations may be more or less appropriate in the various phases of the cooperative problem solving process.

Support based on a combinatorial algorithm is provided for the establishment of relations by the end-user.

The idea of a general system supporting immediate expression evaluation, in the spreadsheet tradition, on an arbitrarily structured construct has been raised under the name SPREADSTRUCTURE.

Acknowledgment

We express our thanks to Prof. Tibor Vámos for his helpful criticism of a previous version of this paper.

References

[1] M. Binbasioglu and M. Jarke, Domain Specific DSS Tools for Knowledge-Based Model Building, Decision Support Systems, 2(1986)213-223.

[2] M. Biró, P. Turchányi and M. Vermes, CONDOR-GDSS CONsensus Development and Operations Research tools Group Decision Support System, MTA SzTAKI Report, Budapest, Hungary, 23/1989.

[3] M. Biró, P. Csáki and M. Vermes, WINGDSS Group Decision Support System under MS-Windows, Proceedings of the Second Conference on Artificial Intelligence, John von Neumann Society for Computer Sciences, (ed. by I.Fekete and P.Koch), Budapest, Hungary, (1991) pp.263-274.

[4] M. Biró, M. Hujter, On a graph coloring problem with applications in scheduling theory, in: H. Sachs, Ed., Proceedings of the International Conference "Discrete Mathematics" (Eisenach), Technische Hochschule Ilmenau, Germany, (1990).

[5] M. Biró, M. Hujter and Z. Tuza, Precoloring Extension I: Interval Graphs, Discrete Mathematics 100(1992)(to appear).

[6] M. Biró, J. Mayer, T. Rapcsák and M. Vermes, Building Mathematical Programming Expert Systems, Proceedings of the Second Conference on Artificial Intelligence, John von Neumann Society for Computer Sciences, (ed. by I.Fekete and P.Koch), Budapest, Hungary, (1991) pp.155-162.

[7] M. Bíró, I. Maros, Deep knowledge for group decision support, MTA SzTAKI Report, Budapest, Hungary, 42/1991.

[8] J.P. Brans, Ph. Vincke and B. Marechal, How to select and how to rank projects: The PROMETHEE-method, European Journal of Operational Research, 24(1986)228-238.

[9] E.F. Codd, A Relational Model of Data for Large Shared Data Banks, Communacations of the ACM, 13, no.6(1970)377-387.

[10] G.B. Dantzig, Linear Programming and Extensions (Princeton University Press, Princeton, New Jersey, 1963).

[11] G. Egli, Ein Multiperiodenmodell der linearen Optimierung für die schweizerische Ernährungsplannung in Krisenzeiten, Dissertation, University of Fribourg, Switzerland, (1980).

[12] S.A. Floyd, C.F. Turner and K. Roscoe Davis, Model-Based Decision Support Systems: An Effective Implementation Framework, Computers Opns. Res., 16, no.5(1989)481-491.

[13] S.I. Gass, Model World: Danger, Beware the User as Modeler, Interfaces, 20, no.3(1990)60-64.

[14] A.M. Geoffrion, An Introduction to Structured Modeling, Management Science, 33, no.5(1987)547-588.

[15] A.M. Geoffrion, The Formal Aspects of Structured Modeling, Operations Research, 37, no.1(1989)30-51.

[16] J. Gerlach and F. Kuo, An Approach to Dialog Management for Presentation and Manipulation of Composite Models in Decision Support Systems, Decision Support Systems, 6(1990)227-242.

[17] T. Hürlimann, LPL: A Structured Language for Modeling Linear Programs (Verlag Peter Lang, Bern, 1987).

[18] M. Klein and L.B. Methlie, Expert Systems A Decision Support Approach (Addison-Wesley, Wokingham, England, 1990).

[19] T. Liang, Development of a Knowledge-Based Model Management System, Operations Research, 36, no.6(1988)849-863.

[20] P. Ma, F.H. Murphy and E.A. Stohr, Representing Knowledge about Linear Programming Formulation, Annals of Operations Research, 21(1989)149-172.

[21] I. Maros, MILP linear programming optimizer for personal computers under DOS, Preprints in Optimization, Institute of Applied Mathematics, Braunschweig University of Technology, (1990).

[22] L. Mérö, Ways of Thinking. The Limits of Rational Thought and Artificial Intelligence (World Scientific Publ., London, 1991).

[23] F.H. Murphy and E.A. Stohr, An Intelligent System for Formulating Linear Programs, Decision Support Systems, 2(1986)39-47.

[24] H. Müller-Merbach, Model Design Based on the Systems Approach, J. Opl. Res Soc., 34, no.8(1983)739-751.

[25] J.F. Nunamaker, L.M. Applegate and B.R. Konsynski, Computer-Aided Deliberation: Model Management and Group Decision Support, Operations Research, 35, no.6(1988)826-848.

[26] W.E. Pracht, An Object Oriented Approach for Business Problem Modeling, in: M.G.Singh, K.S.Hindi and D.Salassa, Eds., Managerial Decision Support Systems (Elsevier Science Publishers B.V., North-Holland, 1988).

[27] A. Roy, L. Lasdon and D. Plane, End-user optimization with spreadsheet models, European Journal of Operational Research, 39(1989)131-137.

[28] B. Roy and Ph. Vincke, Multicriteria analysis: Survey and new tendencies, European Journal of Operational Research, 8(1981)207-218.

[29] T.L. Saaty, The Analytic Hierarchy Process (McGraw Hill, 1980).

[30] H.A. Simon, The Sciences of the Artificial (M.I.T. Press, Cambridge, Massachusetts, 1969).

[31] H.A. Simon, The New Science of Management Decision (Prentice Hall, Englewood Cliffs, New Jersey, 1977).

[32] R.G. Smith and R. Davis, Frameworks for Cooperation in Distributed Problem Solving, IEEE Transactions on Systems, Man, and Cybernetics, 11, no.1(1981)61-70.

[33] A.P.J. Vepsalainen, A Relational View of Activities for Systems Analysis and Design, Decision Support Systems, 4(1988)209-224.

LESSONS OF A FIRST-YEAR USE OF THE AUTOMATED REASONING TOOL

J. Váncza and A. Márkus

Computer and Automation Institute
Hungarian Academy of Sciences
H-1518 Budapest P.O.B. 63
e-mail: hl40van@ella.hu

Abstract. The paper discusses problems we have encountered while using the advanced knowledge representation and reasoning system ART for developing an automated process planning system. First, key concepts and distinct *modus operandi* of ART are presented through showing how they match the requirements of the process planning task. Then we discuss the lessons that previous experience and skill in application of conventional programming methods is the main factor that makes programming in an integrated knowledge based environment more cumbersome than expected. Finally, a knowledge compilation strategy is outlined that would enable us to deliver results to more traditional and simple computing environments.

1 Introduction

Artificial intelligence applications progress along two paths: while one path leads through the selection or development of tools to be given to the domain experts, choosing the other way means that AI is used mostly for analyzing the domain and the perspectives of the solution processes. Having chosen this way, what the end user meets is rather a result of AI methods than actual AI tools and techniques themselves.

Working in a project in computer-aided generation of manufacturing process plans (CAPP), it has turned out soon that the complexity of our tasks and the fragmented nature of relevant domain knowledge are very much against the application of straightforward algorithmic methods and call for the application of AI tools. Moreover, aiming at an efficient use of the limited human and computing resources through the separation of research, development and application environments, we have adopted the second approach of AI applications. The aim of this paper is to present the lessons of our first-year use of the Automated Reasoning Tool of Inference Corp. (henceforth ART), as applied for building this process planning system.

ART is one of the most advanced integrated knowledge representation and reasoning systems that was conceived in the mid eighties as a complete tool-kit for building large-scale knowledge based applications. It supports object-oriented and rule based programming, hypothetical and temporal reasoning, and access to conventional languages. Major components of this integrated system are: (1) a language for knowledge representation and rule based programming, together with its inference engine, and (2) an environment for supporting program development. For a detailed description we refer to the tutorials and manuals (ART Reference Manual 1988, Clayton 1987).

The paper first discusses the problems encountered while developing this process planning system: there will be shown what kinds of engineering knowledge have been represented by what features of ART, what issues have turned out simple, and what are the hard ones. The second half of the paper tries to form generalizations of the lessons we have got and advocates for a new style of program development.

2 Process planning and ART - how they fit to each other

2.1 Our approach to the process planning problem

The primary objective of manufacturing process planning is to specify and arrange the order of manufacturing operations and to select resources (machine tools, tools, fixtures) that are needed for transforming the blank part to its final form. Moreover, process plans have to be executable in the sense that the selected machine tools be capable to produce the part and be available when actually needed. Economic considerations of improving cost effectiveness and productivity are also of primary importance.

In process planning, so-called manufacturing features of workpieces (slots, pockets, holes, faces etc.) are the key concepts that permit the localized representation and manipulation of planning knowledge. A manufacturing feature is a maximal technological entity for which all applicable processing methods have been collected. (N.B., maximal here means that, with respect to processing methods, no more complex entities can be constructed without facing the need of considering other features.) The set of the applicable manufacturing processes provides an implicit definition of the feature and, at the same time, it establishes links to the representation of related concepts (such as machines, tools, sequencing and equivalence constraints between processes). In spite of the fact that our planning method is being built on the concept of features, i.e. on a concept with much local flavor, planning inevitably must incorporate the concept of global economical optimum as well.

Our process planning method works as follows: a global and robust optimization process runs in the middle of several, highly domain-specific, local reasoning and optimization steps that are handled by dedicated tools. These steps have been defined so that combinatorial complexity of global optimization could be focused into a single, well formalized step, even if this step grows unusually large. For driving the global optimization process, genetic algorithms have been applied (see Váncza and Márkus 1991).

Within the above framework, domain specific knowledge is represented and manipulated by ART; it is ART who builds up the search space for the genetics-driven optimization. Through representing domain knowledge in ART we could get rid of several simplifying assumptions that became unwarranted *de facto* standards of present days' process planning systems.

2.2 A correspondence schema

ART has provided appropriate tools and reasoning techniques for capturing and modeling basic concepts as well as thinking particular to process planning. Below there are given pairs of closely related concepts of process planning versus ART (mappings in square brackets have not yet been verified by implementation):

objects (as features, processes, machines)	--- schemata
taxonomies	--- inheritance networks of schemata
geometric, tolerance relations	--- customized relations
part model	--- network of schema instances
rules for selecting, reference features, processes, setups, machines, ordering constraints, etc.	--- forward chaining rules

70

rules analyzing the part model	--- backward chaining rules
local scope of rules	--- patterns
external procedures, global optimization	--- rule and LISP processing intermingled
satisfying constraints on reference features	--- hypothetical reasoning
maintaining alternative part interpretations	--- [hypothetical reasoning with worlds]
causal reasoning on the part model	--- [hypothetical and temporal reasoning]

2.3 Definition of conceptual models

The world of process planning consists of complex objects like the workpiece to be produced, manufacturing features that build up the workpiece, machine tools, fixtures, cutting tools and other equipments that may have a contribution to the production process. Moreover, we consider also the manufacturing processes as objects of this world. Typically, these objects (especially features and processes) have a large, heterogeneous set of characteristics, that, however, do not provide clear-cut conceptual boundaries. Hence, techniques for constructing open-ended flexible conceptual models are sought for.

ART supports linking the facts which are related to a particular object. Such objects are called schemata; once a schema is defined ART can reason about it in terms of its related facts. A schema may be defined by inheritance relationships to other schema(ta). Both kinds of standard inheritance relations, i.e. **is-a** and **instance-of**, are supported.

Using schemata and **is-a** relations, we have structured and defined many concepts of our domain. First of all, conceptual taxonomies for the types of features and subfeatures of prismatic parts, machining processes, machine tools as well as cutting tools have been created. As an example of the hierarchical taxonomy of features, see. Fig. 1.

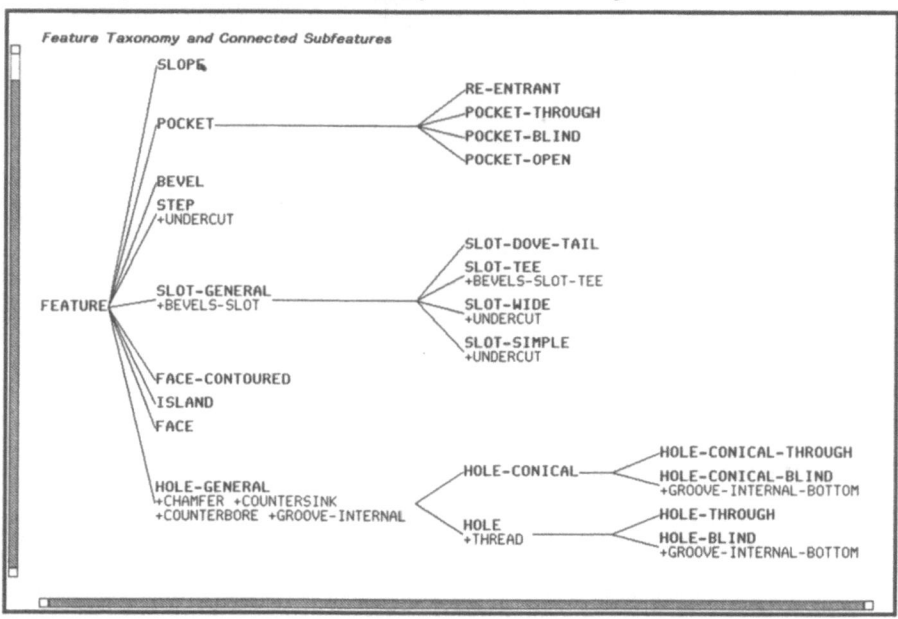

Fig. 1 The hierarchical taxonomy of features and subfeatures

With using the above concepts, actual planning tasks (i.e. descriptions of a particular part, available machines and applicable processes) are specified as instances of the general objects. As an example, see the description of a particular hole in Fig. 2.

```
                        Schema TH5

(DEFSCHEMA TH5
            "threaded hole in H7"
    (BELONGS-TO-PART PART#2-SLIDE)
    (CHILD-OF H7)
    (IS-A COMPOUND-FEATURE)
    (INSTANCE-OF HOLE-BLIND)
    (INSTANCE-OF HOLE)
    (INSTANCE-OF HOLE-GENERAL)
    (INSTANCE-OF FEATURE)
    (LOCATION (X F5 -12.5))
    (LOCATION (Z F4 18))
    (ORIENTATION (+Y))
    (DIAMETER 4)
    (DEPTH 35)
    (BOTTOM-TYPE FLAT)
    (HAS-SUBFEATURES TH5-THR1)
    (FEATURE-NAME HOLE-BLIND)
    (FEATURE-HU-NAME ZSAKFURAT)
    (SURFACE-FINISH)
    (MATERIAL-QUALITY)
    (LOCATION-TOL)
    (APPROACH-DIRECTIONS)
    (INITIAL-STATE RAW)
    (PLAN-TYPES)
    (STATE)
    (NETWORKS)
    (BASE-TYPE 0-POINT)
    (INDEX 17)
    (BASE (Z F4 SMOOTH))
    (BASE (X F5 SMOOTH))
    (BASE (Y F3 SMOOTH))
    (FIRST-STATE)
    (LAST-STATE)
    (THROUGH-TYPE BLIND)
    (DIAMETER-TOL)
    (CIRCULARITY)
    (STRAIGHTNESS)
    (COLLINEARITY)
    (PARALLELISM)
    (ORTHOGONALITY)
    (ANGULARITY)
    (DEPTH-TOL)
    (SIDE-SURFACE-FINISH)
    (BOTTOM-SURFACE-FINISH)
    )
```

Fig. 2 Schema of a particular instance of a feature

2.4 Definition of relations and semantic networks

Instances of features correspond to subproblems of the planning problem among which several relations and dependencies may exist. Geometric relations between features can be interactions (when two feature volumes physically meet each other through nesting or intersection), or non-contact type relations (when no physical interaction occurs but other geometric relations - parallelism, coaxiality or perpendicularity - exist between features). Since tolerance and other requirements have to be dealt with in the planning problem, a rich vocabulary of relations is needed for constructing a useful model of the part.

As a matter of fact, an ART schema is a semantic net that organizes knowledge by defining objects in terms of their mutual relations. The user has the means to define his custom relations, characterized by the arity, inheritance procedures, direction, transitivity, and input/output format (see Fig. 3). If needed, relations may also call new relations into existence.

```
                    Schema HAS-SUBFEATURES

(DEFSCHEMA HAS-SUBFEATURES
        "secondary - primary feature relations"
  (INSTANCE-OF RELATION)
  (INSTANCE-OF SLOT)
  (INSTANCE-OF SCHEMA)
  (SLOT-HOW-MANY MULTIPLE-VALUES)
  (SLOT-HOW DEFINITE)
  (SLOT-WHAT NOTHING)
  (SLOT-MULTIPLE PROMPT)
  (SLOT-INPUT-OUTPUT (A ?SLOT OF ?SCHEMA IS ?VALUE))
  (SLOT-INPUT)
  (SLOT-OUTPUT)
  (INVERSE SUBFEATURE-OF)
  (ELEMENT-OF RELATIONS)
  (ELEMENT-OF SLOTS)
  (ELEMENT-OF SCHEMATA)
  (TRANSITIVITY (REPEAT (STEP HAS-SUBFEATURES $) 1 INF))
  (TRANSITIVITY-GENERATE-FUNCTION DEFAULT-STATIC-218)
  )
```

Fig. 3 The definition of a relation

A part is modeled by a semantic network of instances of features that build up the part. Moreover, features themselves may be compound objects consisting of primary features and subfeatures, like a hole and a chamfer on its mouth. The consistence of the part model is checked up automatically while the model is constructed, i.e. when the declarations of the features are compiled: relations of particular objects that are in conflict with the standard and/or customized declarations about the characteristics of the relations are detected by a built-in mechanism of ART.

2.5 Pattern matching and forward reasoning

A typical process planning problem contains a huge body of facts form which solutions must be constructed. Departing from an analysis of the required properties of the part and the capabilities of available resources, the CAPP system has to suggest alternatives of machining processes, machines, tools, orientations and reference surfaces. In order to avoid negative interactions between manufacturing processes, precedence constraints should be set on the ordering of the actions. (E.g., whenever a cross hole intersects a deep hole, the deep hole must be drilled prior the cross hole in order to avoid the leaking of the coolant and the subsequent breaking of the drill).

The above activities can be supported by forward reasoning made by rules that detect either the existence or absence of certain facts and act whenever a specific situation is found. The left-hand side of a rule is a conjunction of positive and/or negated conditions expressed in terms of existentially quantified predicates, which themselves may contain negations (so a condition may say that in the database "there exists no slot with a surface finish that is not rough"). Pattern matching in ART performs much more than a simple test of Boolean conditions on a set of variables when matched with a given set of database elements: it makes a search to determine all combinations of variable bindings that simultaneously satisfy the conditions.

We have many groups of rules for accomplishing distinct planning subtasks. Most of these rules have a rather limited, local scope; they look for a specific feature plus some closely related, neighboring features. This fragmented, fine-grained representation of the domain knowledge has several benefits: (1) it fits to the cognitive structures of process engineers (for a detailed discussion, see (Váncza and Márkus 1992)), (2) the rule base can be upgraded relatively easily, and (3) it allows for an efficient execution of the program.

```
                  Rule BASE-TYPE-SELECT-2-POINTS-3

(DEFRULE BASE-TYPE-SELECT-2-POINTS-3
        "cylindrical features appropriate for 2-point bases"
  (DECLARE (SALIENCE *BASE-SELECTION-SALIENCE*))
  (INSTANCE-OF ?FEATURE FEATURE)
  (NOT (BASE-TYPE ?FEATURE ?))
  (INSTANCE-OF ?FEATURE HOLE)
  (DIAMETER ?FEATURE ?D)
  (LENGTH ?FEATURE ?L)
  (INSTANCE-OF ?PART PART)
  (WEIGHT ?PART ?W)
  (TEST (OR (AND (>= ?W 0.5) (>= ?D 20) (>= ?L 10))
            (AND (< ?W 0.5) (>= ?D 10))))
  =>
  (ASSERT (BASE-TYPE ?FEATURE 2-POINTS))
  )
```

Fig. 4 A forward chaining rule

2.6 Interrogating object descriptions by backward chaining

For keeping descriptions compact and concise, we do not require that all details (actually slots) of features making up a part be fully specified at the very beginning. However, there is often a need to derive missing information from available data. E.g., if the location tolerance of a particular subfeature is not given explicitly, then it should be derived from the tolerance of its primary feature, or, if even this data is missing, then from the tolerance of a feature-pattern, or, as the last resort, from the value of the general tolerance assigned to the whole part.

ART has a backward chaining mechanism for creating such facts that may be required by partially matched rules. Once a pattern on the left hand side of a forward rule cannot be matched due to lack of some data, such missing data can be regarded as a goal, and backward chaining rules can be activated to supply these facts, either by transforming information stored in another form or by interrogating the user. Accordingly, part models can be kept as small as possible.

We have applied backward reasoning for analyzing the description of the part, i.e. for filling in details that had not been given in the original description but are needed at the present stage of problem solving (see Fig. 5).

```
                      Rule SEARCH-CIRCULARITY

(DEFRULE SEARCH-CIRCULARITY
        "looks for the circularity of a rotational (sub)feature"
  (DECLARE (SALIENCE *SEARCH-SALIENCE*))
  (GOAL (CIRCULARITY ?X ?))
  (NOT (CIRCULARITY ?X ?))
  (OR (AND (INSTANCE-OF ?X HOLE-GENERAL)
           (BELONGS-TO-PART ?X ?PART))
      (AND (INSTANCE-OF ?X SUBFEATURE)
           (SUBFEATURE-OF ?X ?Y)
           (INSTANCE-OF ?Y HOLE-GENERAL)
           (BELONGS-TO-PART ?Y ?PART)))
  (GENERAL-TOL ?PART ?TOL)      ;default is the general tolerance
  =>
  (ASSERT (CIRCULARITY ?X ?TOL))
  )
```

Fig. 5 A backward chaining rule

However, when using backward rules, there is a danger of futile deduction: as a matter of fact, the superfluous generation of goals can be stopped by specific means of ART that discriminate explicit facts from those that could be implied from facts already in the database. (By the way, there is another use of backward chaining when intermediate results produced by forward reasoning are checked by backward rules.)

2.7 Hypothetical and temporal reasoning

There are situations when planning must be pursued in several parallel directions by maintaining alternative hypotheses until some of them become infeasible. This situation originates from the fact that the structure of process planning problems, as produced along features of the part, rarely suggest a unique decomposition of the problem: due to feature interactions there might emerge several competitive interpretations of the same part, each one as valid as the other, but with different major consequences in terms of cost factors of the plans.

As we have pointed out (Váncza and Márkus 1992), for the purposes of process planning a domain theory is needed that allows causal reasoning about changes caused by manufacturing processes themselves. (E.g., if the planner sees that a hole H within slot S is to be made before milling slot S, it should be able to infer that, if made in this sequence, hole H is deeper than it is in the case when H is made after slot S. Similarly, when planning a milling process for the slot the planner should know, actually infer, whether a specific tool trajectory will cause a clash between the tool and other regions of the part.) By eluding an explicit and exhaustive representation of preconditions and effects of manufacturing processes, causal reasoning gives a handy opportunity not to hide laws of the domain. From the assumptions that (1) nothing changes unless it is caused by some factor, and that (2) cause always precedes effect, it follows that nothing changes until it actually has to change. Given a causal domain theory, manufacturing processes would trigger only initial changes on the part model and the causal rules of the world would govern all subsequent changes.

ART has a so-called viewpoint mechanism that is appropriate for exploring hypothetical alternatives and/or modeling situations that change with time. Information whose validity depends on specific hypothetical assumptions can be stored in viewpoints, too. A tree of viewpoints can be developed whose nodes represent distinct assumptions. A viewpoint can be discarded if its facts or their logical consequences are unacceptable or contradictory to each other: the so-called poisoning of such viewpoint deletes all descendant viewpoints. As another extreme, viewpoints that are not contradictory to each other may be merged into a single one.

The concept in ART dedicated to handling temporal information is the so-called extent of facts: assigned to a fact extents delimit the set of situations in which that fact is true. Viewpoints that keep track hypothetical dependencies of facts on the one hand, and extents that constrain the temporal validity of facts can be combined to form multiple-level viewpoints. As a matter of fact, this platform provides efficient means for non-monotonic reasoning, so we hope that the viewpoint mechanism of ART will support the construction of a full-fledged causal domain theory for process planning.

We have made experiments with the viewpoint mechanism of ART in order to find good combinations of reference surfaces for all applicable machining processes of the plan. The above problem has quite a few solutions to be found in a huge search space (Váncza and Márkus 1991). First results suggest that the viewpoint mechanism is indeed appropriate for this purpose, provided that one (1) can define strong enough constraints for poisoning unfeasible hypotheses, and (2) has sophisticated strategies for controlling the order in which hypotheses are generated, merged and discarded.

2.8 Integration of external processes

Rule based reasoning is suggested for tasks for which neither a single, nor an optimal solution is sought (Cooper et al. 1988). In rough terms, rules should define only a set of constraints which the final solution must conform. However, this style of problem solving is certainly inappropriate for handling the global optimization objectives of process planning.

There are stages of the planning process when engineering analysis is to be performed (e.g., when chains of dimensioning and tolerances are to be checked up or transformed). For dealing with such cases, pieces of procedural code are handy for formulating numeric algorithms. Fortunately, ART is smoothly embedded into the underlying LISP environment since it supports calling LISP programs on both sides of the rules. External programs on the left-hand side help to express further constrains for pattern matching that are beyond the capabilities of the pattern language. On the right-hand side any LISP programs can be evaluated, e.g. for making computations that supply further data to be stored in working memory. (As a matter of fact, passing variable bindings from rules to external procedures is not always the very best way to pass data, especially when large amounts of facts are concerned. Thus we have written transformation rules that build bridges between ART and external optimization programs; they work by generating ART data structures from LISP structures and back.)

3 How to learn the art of using ART

3.1 The ART way of pattern matching

The efficient use of a rule based system largely depends on whether its built-in pattern matching mechanism can do the bulk of the work by itself. This general statement, far from being a novelty (Brownston et al. 1985), is particularly relevant when programming in ART: compared with other tools for building knowledge based systems (Mettrey 1991, Mettrey 1992) ART has an outstanding capability for matching conditions of rules to the actual contents of the database.

By the way, if one starts ART with some logic programming background, it is better to forget the Prolog meaning of pattern matching at all: considering the *facts* of ART, patterns are lists, matching supports the use of single- and multiple field variables and wild-cards, augmented with the use of built-in and external predicates for constraining the values of variables. Considering *schemata* of ART, all this gets even more difficult and the parallel with Prolog pattern matching nearly disappears.

3.2 The procedural semantics of the ART rules

Although the well known but rather superficial doctrine of rule based programming says that rules should be used to capture the declarative knowledge of the application domain piece by piece, our experience suggests that in all but the simplest cases an additional, procedural meaning is attached both to the rules as seen one by one and to the whole set of rules of an application. Users usually consider that (1) both the conditions on the left hand side and the actions on the right are visited in their textual order, and (2) rules will fire before, together with, or after some other rules. While the first kind of expectations causes not much trouble with ART, the rules' ordering in time is a far more intricate issue.

First of all, not the rules are the atomic entities that should be related to each other: since the same rule may be used at different stages of the problem solving process again and again, objects to be sequenced in time are not the rules themselves but the activations of the rules. As a matter of fact, this difference is especially important in cases when problem solving consists of goal-driven stages mixed with forward chaining ones: having ended a long sleeping period, a forward chaining rule may start a new phase of activities as soon as some goal driven rule provides the facts that have been missing up to this point.

While writing a set of related rules, let they either be forward or backward chaining ones, one has to be attentive of the relative timing of their activations. The exact order of the activations is, however, hard to predict since it is influenced by several factors. Although some handles are offered to the user just for expressing control aspects (e.g. assigning a constant priority to the rules by the so-called salience values of rules), there are further, sometimes rather intricate factors that are not documented as control features of the system (maybe worst of all these factors is the order in which the rules are (re)declared and (re)compiled).

3.3 Hidden factors of control

The most important factor within the gray area of control is, as a matter of fact, just the conflict resolution strategy of the inference engine: nowhere in the manuals is it specified which one of the pending rule activations will fire, so the user may not know more than a statement that the activated rule must be of the highest salience present on the agenda at that moment.

In comparison with logic programming, the situation with hidden control factors of ART is quite interesting: Why may a Prolog user have a full control of the execution of his/her program, in spite of the fact that the underlying logic mechanism has no concept of sequencing conditions and rules? Why can the execution of ART not be defined by a meta inference engine, just as Prolog can simply defined by a meta interpreter?

Although we do not know answers from the authors of ART, our suspicion is that one should share preference among factors such as disciplined use of the rule based programming paradigm, or efficiency issues, or a business-like interest in hiding valuable implementation details. Another, more highbrow reason may be that leaving these control issues open (or at least, undocumented) enforces a kind of discipline on the user who has to adhere to a style that is thought as best for rule based knowledge representation. If rules are indeed separate pieces of knowledge, then their run-time relation belongs to the authority of the inference engine and not of the user. Accordingly, when the user has some specific course of actions in mind, it is better for him/her not to use rules for executing these actions but to call for traditional algorithmic tools. Since ART supports both starting its engine from another program and calling up non-ART programs from both sides of ART rules, this standpoint is hard to be questioned. On the other hand, one can not access, even in read-only mode, ART working memory through any other means than using rules. So the above argumentation can hardly be accepted as an ultimate answer: a duplication of the data (in one representation for ART, in another for the procedures whenever they need it) can be defended neither on the theoretical nor on the practical level. Accordingly, the gray area of control should be considered as a matter of efficiency and of the implementors' development and business strategy. As for efficiency, aspects of human and machine efficiency are nicely coordinated in ART and we claim that this coordination is a key factor of the success of ART. Accordingly, even if the integration of these two faces of efficiency have lead to a considerable loosening of the user's control over the system, the result may be worth the price.

As for hiding design details, this is again a matter of style: down to a level, near to uniform in depth across the whole system, users may see anything by using services of a friendly set of tools. However, anything below this level is strictly hidden so that users can not drive ART crazy or inefficient.

In addition, procedural (or, better to say, control) aspects of problem solving with ART can not be described even in terms of rule activations: activations are made in an autonomous way by the inference engine who chooses them from an agenda. Accordingly, if the user wants to have a feeling how ART works on solving his/her problem, he/she has to conceive the changes of the agenda.

3.4 Conventional programming constructs versus rule interactions

In traditional programming languages well-proven control cliches provide the means for (1) coercing the sequences of computing steps (conditionals, cycles), (2) avoiding interaction between parts of the code that should remain unrelated and (3) writing similar code only once (procedures). All this together makes the problem-solving process more tractable and comprehensible to humans, and, at the same time, more efficient in machine terms.

However, in case of rule based programming the role of control cliches and interaction among the pieces of code is just reversed: we can't help but try to implement the above cliches by rule interactions. (An interaction between two activations happens when the order in which the rules fire results in a difference of the result of these actions. Activations interact either directly, if an activation asserts or retracts an element of the database that is a precondition of another matching, or indirectly, through modifying the sequence of the instantiated rules waiting on the agenda.) Actually, for this purpose there are no other means in our hands; e.g. if we want that certain rules fire in a predetermined sequence then we have to distribute this information of ordering among the rules concerned.

In other words, programming in ART largely disables the use of our conventions for expressing the control of programs. No wonder, questions emerge whether we really need these programming cliches and/or what can rule based programming offer instead of them.

3.5 Pattern matching and control

To begin with a simple example, let's consider iteration: it is needed whenever the extreme of some similar elements is looked for (e.g. one needs to find the deepest of the holes on a face of the part). Supposing that no results of a previous investigation have been stored, object(s) with the extreme value can be found only by visiting and comparing all candidates. Accordingly, if the inference engine does not provide a wired-in solution, then there is no other choice than the search cycle implemented manually.

Furthermore, what to do if there are more than one objects with the same extreme value; e.g. there can be found two holes of the same, maximal depth? Should the rule referring to these objects fire immediately after each other as many times as many instantiation it actually has? Indeed, such a regime could be regarded as the most natural extension of selecting from among activations; but what to do if the firing with the first of the equivalent extremes results in actions that destroy conditions of the next rule activations? Anyway, even this most simple thought experiment could suggest that extending the power of the rule syntax and providing more fixed constructs, e.g. for iteration, may easily lead to messy situations; accordingly, the use of hand-made cycles may be more safe, as far as the outcomes of using such constructs are easier to browse and debug.

Summing up, the powerful pattern matching causes no troubles as long as the user can imagine all the situations he/she can ever meet while running the program. Beyond this point, ART presupposes a working knowledge of classical data structures and computing algorithms, as well as skill in the use of traditional languages, especially LISP. No wonder that a widely used introduction to rule based programming (Brownston et al. 1985) regards mastering of basic computer-science concepts covered in (Wirth 1976) as a prerequisite of mastering rule based systems.

What can we do on a higher level of abstraction of representing declarative knowledge, i.e. when dealing with schemata, with multiple levels of viewpoints etc.? After this first year, we can't say more than it is better to shadow prior knowledge, to begin with a *tabula rasa*, as far as concepts and techniques of traditional programming are concerned. The double view may cause serious conflicts and is a source of perplexity.

3.6 Will rule based systems deliver new control structures?

Up to now, there is no widely accepted choice of control structures suited to complex rule based systems. A technical reason might be that each rule based system has its own version of pattern matching and a strategy, or even more ones, for choosing the next rule firing from the agenda. A control concept that is good for one system may be inefficient, unclear if used with another version of pattern matching and firing strategy.

In our opinion the basic contradiction lies deeper, between the global and hierarchical nature of the conventional control structures versus the fact that, as for rule based systems, control should be implemented in a distributed manner, in a medium that has no conceptual mechanism other than that of rules.

Although the way out from this situation may lead towards handling the agenda in novel ways, our immediate aim is to have a better understanding of control in rule based systems and to develop a transparent style of programming through working only with specific rule interactions. The application of rule interactions for implementing typical control structures should be elaborated case by case, within each environment.

4 Directions of further work: knowledge compilation or ART as a delivery system

Running on a Symbolics 3620 with Genera 7.2., ART is now being used as a tool for generating an automated process planning system. At a later stage of the project, for everyday practical use our results are to be delivered to more traditional and simple computing environment.

We deem the task of rewriting the prototype process planning system into a form that is executable on a simpler computing platform unfeasible. This skepticism is grounded by the following facts: (1) a good deal of expertise is captured by the patterns of rules that heavily exploit the powerful pattern matcher of ART, (2) control of the whole program is distributed among interacting rules, (3) most rules are senseless outside the context of some other rules, and, finally, (4) the genetic algorithm performing plan optimization requires large enough dynamic memory and high speed of computation. Due to the first three reasons (those that might be common to most ART applications), the re-implementation of even a less competent version of the prototype system would be extremely difficult.

Instead of rewriting the prototype system by hand-coding, now we are looking for automatic methods for picking up and putting together those fragments of domain knowledge that may bear relevance to the solution of a particular class of the planning problem. Fortunately enough, the problem domain encourages the use of a method known as knowledge compilation (Goel 1991). In our cast of the method, given the model of a manufacturing system together with the local manufacturing practice and the set of its products, the question is how the system's production can be improved by taking advantage of the similarity of the parts and technologies. A well-established approach leads through working out so-called group technologies: similar parts are collected into groups, each of which will have its so-called group technology. In case when a new part arrives, its process plan will be generated through the part's classification into one of the groups and by adapting the corresponding technology.

The main difficulty with generating group technologies is caused by the incomplete and conflicting nature of available domain knowledge, the intermingled relations bound both to the production environment and engineering practice, and to the particular solutions of earlier tasks. This problem can be approached as formation of concepts and theories by means of symbolic learning: departing from empirical facts and a domain theory, one should create a representation of the pieces of knowledge that is adequate with the domain and, at the same time, can be used efficiently.

Accordingly, our aim is a learning system that is able to create group technologies for the families of parts, based on individual part and technology descriptions, and the linked representations of parts, process plans, tools, machines, and manufacturing processes. While inductive, similarity based learning methods should be used to find shared features and technologies, analytic methods should refine the plans to the right level of specificity and abstraction. Final results are to be delivered for other, more conventional computing platforms where they should be able to work independently both from the original, general-purpose process planning and the learning components.

Acknowledgement

The authors wish to thank M. Horváth for many helpful discussions on process planning issues. This research was supported by the National Research Found of Hungary (OTKA), grant No. 412.

References

1. ART Reference Manual, Inference Corp. 1988.
2. L. Brownston, R. Farrel, E. Kant and N. Martin, Programming Expert Systems in OPS5, Addison-Wesley, 1985.
3. B. D. Clayton, ART Programming Tutorial, Vol. 1-4, Inference Corp. 1987.
4. T. A. Cooper and N. Wogrin, Rule-based Programming with OPS5, Morgan Kaufmann, 1988.
5. A. K. Goel, Knowledge Compilation, *IEEE Expert*, April 1991, 71-73.
6. W. Mettrey, A Comparative Evaluation of Expert System Tools, *Computer*, Vol. 4 No. 2, 19-31, 1991.
7. W. Mettrey, Expert Systems and Tools: Myths and Realities, *IEEE Expert*, February 1992, 4-12.
8. J. Váncza and A. Márkus, Genetic Algorithms in Process Planning, *Computers in Industry*, Vol. 17., 181-194, 1991.
9. J. Váncza and A. Márkus, Features and the Principle of Locality in Process Planning, to appear in *Int. Journal of Computer Integrated Manufacturing*, 1992.
10. N. Wirth, Algorithms + Data Structures = Programs, Prentice-Hall, 1976.

ARTIFICIAL INTELLIGENCE -
TOOL BUILDING ASPECTS

Chair: P. Zinterhof

Architectural Considerations
for
Extending a Relational DBMS with Deductive Capabilities[1]

Michael Dobrovnik, Roland T. Mittermeir

Institut für Informatik
Universität Klagenfurt
Universitätsstraße 65-67
A-9020 Klagenfurt, Austria
e-mail: {michi,mittermeir}@ifi.uni-klu.ac.at

Abstract

This paper describes the development rationale and the architecture of a prototypical expert-database system. Knowledge processing capabilities of SQL were enhanced by extending the language by recursive views. This work is based on an evolutionary approach; smooth integration with the base language was an important development aim.

After a discussion of the main design alternatives, the architecture of a prototype is presented. Finally the progress of the project is described and possibilities for further extension are indicated.

1 Recursive Views

1.1 Motivation

A host of modern applications demand knowledge processing capabilities in combination with the support of large scale volume data processing capabilities and multi-user support for concurrent access and flexible combination of persistent information as provided by todays data base systems. But classical expert system shells lack important features needed in conjunction with bulk transaction processing, support for persistence, and integrity preservation over long spans of time. Hence, systems supporting multi-paradigm applications become increasingly important.

---

[1]The work on this project was partly supported by the Austrian Fonds zur Förderung der wissenschaftlichen Forschung under Contract P6772P.

At the time this project started, various options to achieve the above aim have already been proposed in the literature (see e.g. [Gall81, Gall84, Brod86, Kers86, Wied 86]). They can be classified into three broad categories:

- extensions of logical programming languages or expert system shells by appropriate permanent storage management (back-end storage management);
- development of database systems with "logical" query languages;
- extensions of database systems by "reasoning facilities".

In the project on which we are reporting here, the latter approach had been adopted. However, we wanted to follow this approach in such a way that we could fully build SQL's high acceptance in the marketplace. To achieve this aim, a solid formal definition of certain SQL features became necessary before searching for an adequate linguistic and architectural design of such an extension. While the formal aspects have been reported already, this paper presents the architectural considerations which guided this project.

The choice for this approach has been founded on the consideration that relational database systems enjoy high penetration into a host of application areas. One reason for this success surely is the widespread use of standard database languages such as SQL [SQL86,Date87]. SQL can be characterized as an end user oriented, mainly declarative language which plays a central role in the database field, even in spite of its well known deficiencies [Date87].

One of the most important restrictions of SQL is its lack of computational completeness [Aho79]. So, an important class of systems such as knowledge based systems or decision support systems, but also technical systems demanding special search characteristics [Boud92], are not well supported. A particular reason for this deficiency is that recursive problems cannot be adequately attacked by means of standard SQL. But recursion plays an important role in deductive systems. Two of the most prominent textbook examples for this class of problems are path problems and bill of material calculations. Hence, the main idea of the XPL*SQL-project was to extend the capabilities of SQL in such a way that the extended language provides good support for a broad range of recursive problems.

The linguistic mechanism we needed for obtaining our aim was the well known view mechanism. It allows to create virtual relations by declaring a rule that describes how to compute them. The view construction mechanism has been extended to support **recursive views**.

1.2 General Transitive Closure

The transitive closure T of a relation R is defined as [Eder90a]:

$$LFP(T = union(R, COMP(R,T)))$$

COMP means composition and is an equijoin where the join-attributes are eliminated by projection. The least-fixpoint operator LFP evaluates T to the smallest set, for which the equation is valid.

To demonstrate this concept, let us consider a binary relation *flight(from,to)*, which associates cities that can be reached with one single flight. This relation clearly is transitive, so it makes sense to compute the transitive closure *connection* of *flight*, which contains all flight connections between two cities, formally:

$$LFP(connection = union \ (connection, \ flight \bowtie_{flight.to=connection.from} connection))$$

It has to be pointed out, though, that the concept of transitive closure of a relation may not contain any attributes pertaining to the specific association just established. E.g. in the example, it is not possible to total the distance or the duration of connections. Certainly, this is a main disadvantage of pure transitive closure and makes it unsuitable for a large class of applications. Therefore, the concept was generalized [Eder90a,Eder90b] in the following way:

$$LFP(GT = union(R,COMPEX(R,GT)))$$

There, R is a base relation as before, GT is the generalized transitive closure. The main difference between transitive closure and general transitive closure lies in *COMPEX*. *COMPEX* stands for composition-expression and is a selection on the carthesian product of R and GT, combined with a projection which may also contain arithmetic expressions. The introduction of this composition-expression allows the definition of attribute values as computable functions, whereas the generalization from the equijoin to a selection on the carthesian product allows to formulate non-trivial conditions for linking tuples. An example for general transitive closure will be given in a subsequent section.

1.3 Integration of Generalized Transitive Closure into SQL

General transitive closure is a special form of a linear recursive deduction rule. When one considers SQL, there is a mechanism which allows for the definition of derived relations, which are better known as **views**. A view is a virtual relation whose extension is computed according to a declarative specification, the view definition, which can be seen as a deduction rule. Whereas one could argue that from such a perspective, SQL is a language with deductive components, there is one main shortcoming of views in standard SQL. The language explicitly forbids to reference the view to be defined in the definition part itself, i.e. recursion is not permitted.

Considering the fact, that views can be interpreted as nonrecursive deduction rules, and that views are a well understood feature of SQL which is broadly used in practice, it seems to be promising to extend the view concept and to explicitly allow the definition of **recursive views**. This evolutionary approach not only integrates very well with the basic language, it has as main advantage, that it does not require any change in the application pattern. Neither a user querying a view, nor any special tool (application generator, report writer, ...) using those views, need to take special consideration as to whether a view is defined recursively or in the usual way.

However, there are some minor deficiencies one has to bear in mind using recursive views. In general, recursive views may not be updated, queries on them can take longer to complete than on conventional views, and the results of a query may be infinite. While the first and second points are inherently connected with recursive views, the possibility for infinite results requires special treatment (see [Eder90a]).

Nevertheless, besides increasing the expressive power of the language, this specific approach meets some important criteria for extending a language [Mitt88]. The principle of recursive views is easy and safe to use and it incorporates a minimal number of new constructs. The new feature is orthogonal to existing language elements, it can be formally described, and it can be optimized to some extent.

1.4 Syntax of Recursive Views

The syntactical extensions of the definition of SQL are mainly captured in one single place, namely the *recursive-view-definition-statement* which is presented (in a slightly simplified form) in Figure 1. Other aspects of the language, notably the select statement, remained unchanged.

A simple example of the application of the new construct can be found in the appendix. Now we briefly give an informal description of some of the nonterminals mentioned in Figure 1. For a more thorough treatment, we refer to [Eder90a, Eder90b, and Dobr91].

The *attributed-column-list* extends the standard *column-list* of SQL. With *INC* and *DEC* respectively, the specification of monotonous characteristics of certain attributes is allowed. This information is crucial in optimization and assuring the finiteness of certain queries. The *set-type* specifies, whether a certain view should be treated as a set-relation, having only distinct tuples and where duplicates have to be eliminated, or as a multiset-relation, where duplicate tuples must be taken into account.

It should be noted that recursive views can be used as targets of queries like any other table or conventional view (with some minimal restrictions, see [Eder90a]). As small as the syntactical extensions to standard SQL for the definition of recursive views may be, the possibility to use recursive views in virtually all contexts where ordinary views are permitted implies that fundamental changes in the SQL-interpreter must be made.

```
statement ::= ... |
             create-view-statement |
             create-recursive-view-statement |
             ...

create-view-statement ::=
             CREATE VIEW viewname [ (column-list) ]
             AS SELECT [ set-type ] select-list
             FROM table-reference-list
             [ where-clause ]
             [ group-by-clause ] [ having-clause ];

create-recursive-view-statement ::=
             CREATE VIEW viewname (attributed-column-list)
             AS [ set-type ] FIXPOINT
             OF table-name [ (column-list) ]
             BY SELECT select-list
             FROM table-reference, view-reference
             where-clause;

attributed-column-list ::=
             column-name [ INC | DEC ] [, attributed-column-list ]

set-type ::=
             ALL | DISTINCT
```

Fig. 1: Syntax Extension

2 Considering Architectural Alternatives

The main design variants we investigated have been to build an entirely new system completely from scratch, to integrate the new functionality into an existing system, and to construct an add-on or a frontend to an operational system. We will weigh these alternatives against each other in the sequel.

In deciding on the architectural alternative to be pursued for the proposed extensions, we considered technical as well as economic aspects. The reasons for considering technical arguments need no further explanation. The economic aspects have been considered in spite of us being located at a university institute. Since our research is mainly sponsored by governement money, we considered it important that its results would be at least in principle exploitable by some local software producer or software house without placing undue risks on the developer of customer of such a system.

2.1 Build from Scratch

The design and implementation of a new DBMS, which supports the concept of recursive views would not only be challenging, but would also offer a wealth of advantages:

*   No restrictions from existing systems would have to be taken into account.
*   The whole system could be constructed with special considerations to the deductive component and its implications.
*   The recursive views would be deeply integrated into the DBMS (Fig. 2).
*   The highest degree of optimization and, hence, highest performance, would be possible.
*   One single interface for tools and application programs could be defined and the tools provided could support the complete language.

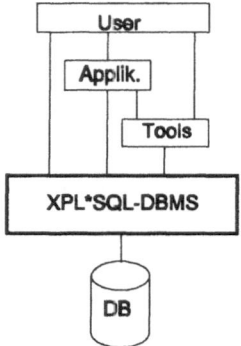

Fig. 2: Build Totally New System

The main drawbacks of this approach are the extremely high costs and the long development time that would be needed to build a DBMS totally from scratch. A great deal of the effort would be used for the design and implementation of functional aspects, which would have been only of subordinate interest in the given context. These aspects have been particularly important in our design considerations. Not only, that we didn't feel in a position to acquire the ressources for a full fledged development of an operational knowledge-base management system which would show all properties of a modern database system. We have even been sceptical about our own greediness, which might arise from good ideas in several directions off the mainstream line of thought, endangering the project to result in a never ending venture.

Besides these aspects, several aspects which might stem from the particular economic context (small country with moderate DP-industry only) in which our university is placed were considered. There is no large scale international vendor of data base systems around. Hence, the acceptance of a system based on a full integration of the database and knowledge-base aspects of the system with managers responsible for the applications to be supported by this system would have to be projected as being very low. The risk, that the developer of such a huge system might not survive would probably be too high for a responsible DP-manager.

Further, the evolutionary idea behind the construct and the language extension would be reduced to the appearance of such a system to the user (investment in training and education), since changing the vendor of one's DBMS would rather have the flair of a revolution than that of a smooth change in most of the cases.

2.2 Extending an Existing System

The internal extension of an existing system, which is well established in the market, has a much higher degree of potential for success. In contrast with the development of a totally new system, this approach poses major restrictions on design decisions, because of the high amount of investments in the basic SQL-DBMS, which must be protected. Yet it is possible to construct and present a uniform interface for users, application programs and tools. The integration of recursive views into the system and the supporting tools could be quite strong (Figure 3).

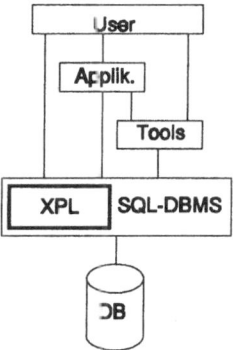

Fig. 3: Embedded Development

The extension based development would allow for moderate costs. It would also have a much higher acceptance in the market, because it would not look like a major change in the computing environment. The impact of such a system could be compared to that of a new release of a DBMS, just incorporating some (very nice) new features. However, one has to see very clearly, that such an argument would be deceiving, since the coupling between the extensions and the base-DBMS would have to be so tight, that with most modifications (new versions) of the base DBMS, a new version of the XPL-extension would also have to be supplied. This, however, would also require not only the adequate economic resources but also very intimate contact between the developer of the DBMS and the developer of the expert system extensions.

The main disadvantage of this kind of extension is that the developper of the extension must have full access to all internals (source and documentation) of an existing DBMS, and that one would have to constantly adapt the extension to the new releases of the database system itself, which usually would mean that if the developer of the extensions is not also the developer of the base system itself, he would be heavily dependend on him.

2.3 Add-on to some Existing System

This alternative form of enhancement of a DBMS is implemented in the same way as every other application program (Figure 4). Therefore, (virtually) no knowledge of the underlying DBMS internals is required.

This variant has a lot of disadvantages, if seen from a solely technical point of view. The uniform interface to other application programs and the possibility to make use of the language extension in the tools supplied with the DBMS must be given up. Further, the user has to make right from the beginning a choice, whether working with XPL or with pure SQL is needed. An awkward consequence of this choice would be that in cases, where recursive views and base views have to be used concurrently, the results of the recursive views would need to be materialized and explicitly transfered into the "ordinary" database management system, or the add-on has to be powerfull enough to process also data contained in the conventional data base of stored facts. This later option would require however full SQL capabilities and, hence, would lead us to the fourth option.

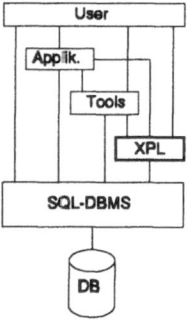

Fig. 4: Add-On to Existing System

2.4 Frontend to an Existing System

The merits of this option become directly visible, when considering the shortcommings of the adds-on alternative. Here, we do not consider the extension to be just an add-on where the clients (user, application programs and tools) have to switch between the base system and the enhancement. We rather assume it to be a real front end, allowing the clients to access the system in a completely transparent way (Figure 5).

The advantage of this solution would be - like with the previous case - that it could be implemented and maintained with comparatively moderate effort. Further, the interfaces to both, the data base management system it utilizes underneath, as well as to applications and tools would be clear cut. Therefore, no severe dependence between the developer of the DBMS and the developer of the XPL-extension would come up. Hence, even in the economic and institutional environment in which this development had to be undertaken (and for which it had been targeted), this approach seemed feasible.

Of course, there is also a price to be paid for such an architectural decision: Any SQL statement needs to be first analyzed by the XPL system and in case it is an "ordinary" SQL statement, the same analysis has to be repeated within the DBMS itself. Given the predominant structure of SQL-statements, this overhead would be marginal though. Hence, performance surely will be suboptimal due to the partly duplicated execution of operations and due to the coarse tuning of the frontend with respect to internals of the base system. Additionally, main components of the SQL-DBMS must be reimplemented (in a simplified form) in the frontend itself.

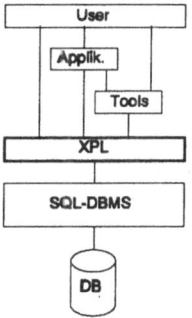

Fig. 5: Frontend to existing System

Despite the shallow integration of the frontend, it will not be completely independent from the SQL-DBMS and it will also not be portable per se, since the (highly implementation specific) catalog of the underlying system must be accessed.

From a broader perspective, however, this model doesn't look so bad as stated above, especially if one considers the possibility to market it as a special "preprocessor". This poses absolutely no hidden risk for potential customers. They can continue to use their existing DBMS, existing applications are totally unaware of the extended functionality whereas new applications can make instant use of the frontend. Since the development costs for the frontend itself can be held at a relatively low level, it would also be affordable.

This model also allows for real third-party development of the system in contrast with the internal extension of an existing system. Besides the fact that the specifications of a DBMS's external interfaces are publicly available, they also tend to be relatively stable, as compared to internal interfaces. Further, the evolutionary risk is reduced by the fact that new releases of systems are usually upwards compatible. Hence, even if the developer of the frontend cannot keep pace with the developer of the main system, the detrimental effects on the applications will be limited.

3 Architecture of the Prototype Actually Implemented

In this section, we sketch the architecture and the components of the implemented prototype, which is a frontend to an existing system (Figure 6). This decision is based on several reasons. First, we had no access to all internal information of an existing DBMS which would be necessary to extend it. Second, we had no intention to put much effort into components which are not in the center of our interest. Further, we didn't feel in the position to develop YADE (yet another database environment) and to become another DBMS vendor.

The aim of the prototype was to provide an extended SQL-based command interface, which allows one to define and query recursive views in addition to the functionality of standard SQL, and which can be used for further study.

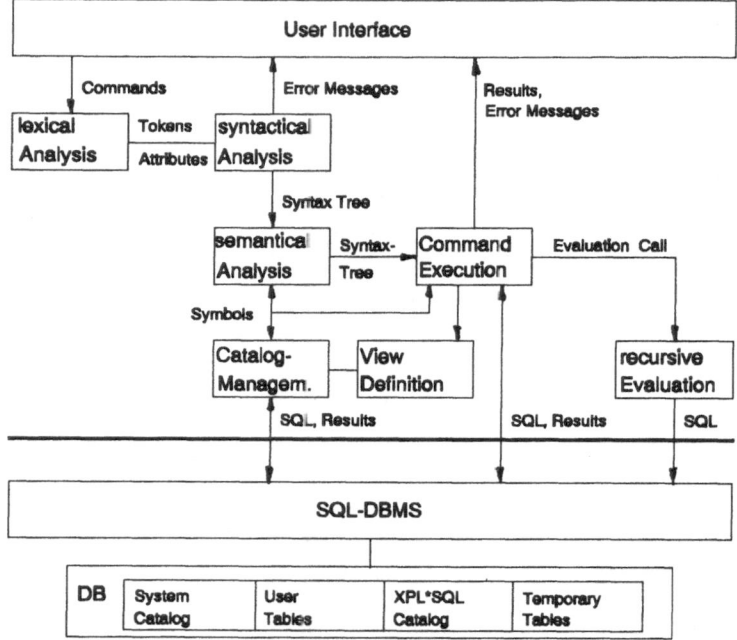

Fig. 6: Architectural Overview

The user interface component consists of a very simple line editor, which can be used to enter the extended data definition and data manipulation commands, and a rather rudimentary formatting capability for query results. Error messages are also displayed through these components. The user interface is solely character based.

All SQL commands coming from the user interface are fed into a lexical analyzer which transforms the commands from the textual form into an attributed stream of tokens.

This stream of attributes and tokens is the input for the parser. This component analyzes the stream for its syntactical correctness and constructs a syntax tree representing the structure of the command.

The semantic analysis component processes the syntax tree and extends it with new attributes. Here, not only name resolution of database objects (tables and attributes) by means of queries performed by a catalog component is carried out, but also the semantic correctness of the command is checked (at least to a certain degree).

The command executor decomposes the (possibly complex) command into smaller units, which can be executed in isolation from other units. Each unit is classified, whether it references a recursive view or just makes use of standard tables and views. If recursive views are referenced, termination and efficiency become key issues. To allow for the broadest set of safe applications [Eder90a], we check what expressions can be propagated into the computation. What is to be propagated is determined in a special part of the command executor. The thus rearranged statements are then ready for recursive evaluation. The results of this evaluation are stored in temporary tables, which are maintained by the base DBMS.

Knowing the temporary tables just computed, the command executor reconstructs an SQL-statement from the syntax tree. This SQL-command may not only be just a part of the initial SQL-command, it may also differ from it. This difference is due to the fact, that the names of the recursive views have to be substituted by the names of the temporary tables which contain the evaluation results of the recursive views referenced. The modified statement will be evaluated directly by the SQL-DBMS. Results and error messages are sent to the user interface component.

Note, that up to this point in the analysis process, all SQL-statements need to be analyzed, regardless of whether they do define or reference recursive views or not. The user does not need to switch between two different systems, and the extension is totally transparent to him.

The catalog management component updates the symbol table, based on the information contained in the system catalog of the underlying SQL-DBMS as well as in a special catalog which is used solely for the storage and retrieval of the definitions of recursive views and their corresponding attributes.

The view definition component computes the attribute dependency graph [Eder90a], which is used to classify the attributes of the view. This classification information together with the view definition is stored in the special catalog tables.

The recursive evaluator implements the algorithms to compute the results of recursive views [Eder90a, Eder90b]. It uses information from the special extendend catalog (XPL*SQL-catalog) and those constraints of the query at hand which can be propagated. The schema information concerning the relevant temporary tables is passed as a parameter to the recursive evaluator.

4 State of the Project

Currently, the implementation of a first version of the prototype is finished. It builds on the ALLBASE DBMS, running under HF-UX. It allows to interactively define recursive views and to query a database including tables, regular views and recursive views. Its actual design and implementation took about six person month.

As extensions, we forsee that the prototype could be extended to offer a programming interface allowing application programs to use the enhanced abilities of the system. A lot more of semantic checks could be added and performed in the frontend itself. This would allow for the detection of a large number of errors early in the interpretation process; errors could thus be caught before a lot of time is consumed by the evaluation of recursive views. This computation could be enhanced further by incorporating the propagation of additional kinds of restrictions into the evaluation process.

Further work will include adapting the frontend to other DBMSs and to integrate further extensions, namely extreme-value selections and aggregates. There are also plans to make use of the enhanced functionality in the context of a software engineering environment, which demands the ability to define and to use recursive views.

5 Assessment

The choosen architectural variant was adequate and allowed us to concentrate mostly on the new and specific aspects of the system without forcing us to deal with lots of internals of existing DBMS or tons of (unavailable) documentation. It was possible to demonstrate major aspects of the concepts reported in [Eder90a, Eder90b] and to substancially increase the expressive power of a relational DBMS with a rather limited effort.

We conclude that this architectural variant may be well suited when development takes place under the assumption of a third party producer with limited resources. It poses few risks, because it guarantees the highest possible independence from the vendor of the basic DBMS, and promises rather short development time with moderate cost.

Appendix:

Example of General Transitive Closure

Consider a relation *direct* with the following schema

$$direct(from, to, km, mins, hops)$$

where each of its tuples represent a direct flight which starts in city *from* and is destined to city *to*. The distance and duration of the flights are recorded in columns *km* and *mins*. The attribute *hops* contains the number of intermediate landings, which is zero in all tuples of relation *direct*, since we are considering direct flights only.

The following definition of a recursive view computes all possible flight connections between all pairs of cities, summing up distance, durations and number of hops:

```
CREATE VIEW connection (from, to, km INC, mins INC, hops INC)
AS FIXPOINT OF direct
BY SELECT d.from, c.to, d.km + c.km, d.mins + c.mins, c.hops + 1
FROM direct d, connection c
WHERE d.to = c.from;
```

This view can be used as a query target like every other table or conventional view (with some minimal restrictions, see [Eder90a]). A more complex example of an application of recursive views in the context of CPM-charts can be found in [Dobr91].

References

[Aho79]   A. Aho, J. Ullmann: "Universality of Data Retrieval Languages", ACM Symp. on Principles of Programming Languages, 1979, pp. 110-120

[Boud92]   N. Boudriga, A. Mili, R. Mittermeir: "Semantic Based Software Retrieval to Support Rapid Prototyping", Structured Programming, Vol. 13, No. 3, 1992

[Brod 86]   Brodie M.L., Mylopoulos J.: "On Knowledge Base Management Systems', Springer Verlag, 1986

[Date87]   C.J. Date: "A Guide to the SQL Standard", Addison-Wesley, Reading, 1987

[Dobr91]   M. Dobrovnik: "IXPL*SQL. Erweiterung der Abfragesprache SQL um rekursive Views", Diplomarbeit, Institut für Informatik, Universität Klagenfurt, Klagenfurt, 1991

[Eder90a]   J. Eder: "Extending SQL with General Transitive Closure and Extreme Value Selections", IEEE Transactions on Knowledge ans Data Engineering, Vol. 2, No. 4, Dec. 1990, pp. 381-390

[Eder90b]   J. Eder: "General Transitive Closure of Relations containing Duplicates", Information Systems, Vol. 15, No.3, 1990, pp. 335-347

[Gall81]   Gallaire H., Minker J., Nicolas J.-M.(eds): "Advances in Database Theory", Plenum Press, 1982

[Gall84]   Gallaire H., Minker J., Nicolas J.-M.: "Logic and Databases: A Deductive Approach", ACM Computing Surveys, Vol. 16/2, June 1984, pp. 153 - 185.

[Kers86]   Kerschberg L. (ed).: "Expert Database Systems", Benjamin/Cummings, 1986

[Mitt88]   R.T. Mittermeir, J. Eder: "XPL*SQL. Research on new AI-Languages", Proc. 6th European Oracle User's group conference, Paris, April 1988

[SQL86]   Database Language SQL, Document ANSI X3.135-1986

[Wied 86]   Wiederhold G.: "Knowledge and Database Management", IEEE Software. Vol. 1/1, Jan. 1984, pp. 63 - 73

FuzzyExpert: A Case Study in PC-Based Expert System Development

Jan Žižka

Computer Center, Brno Technical University

Údolní 19, 602 00 Brno, Czechoslovakia

Abstract. Like many other complex software products, expert systems are leaving their original hardware platforms – mainframes and minis. In particular, the fuzzy set theory-based expert system *FuzzyExpert* was developed for the personal computer (PC) environment using various integrated paradigms. However, as the experience described in this paper indicates, the process of downsizing encounters many problematic issues. For the hardware base, *FuzzyExpert*'s developers chose the *IBM/PC* compatible, but this environment presents memory-related constraints. To circumvent these problems, *FuzzyExpert*'s developers employed a virtual memory mechanism. Software issues primarily concern performance, derived from the absence of multitasking in *MS-DOS*. As a solution to this problem, the system uses a preempting technique. This paper further presents principles of *FuzzyExpert*'s user interface, which is based on object-oriented programming.

1. Introduction

Artificial intelligence and, especially, the area of expert systems (ES) has progressed in a relatively short time from an academic discipline to a commercially viable technology. Expert systems offer the opportunity to organize human expertise and experience into a form that the computer can manipulate. However, much of human knowledge is incomplete, imprecise, approximate, or subjective. Consequently, conventional method-based computer modeling of many non-numeric problems does not provide satisfactory results. With improvements in problem solving tools, expert systems now represent an alternative programming model, yet the technology is complex and not easily mastered. Successful adoption of an expert system as a practical, useful tool depends on several important features, which constitute today's widely recognized expert system paradigms (Payne and McArthur 90; Giarratano and Riley 89):

- suitable knowledge representation;
- user confidence in the system's conclusion;
- high speed of execution;
- appropriate user interface.

To satisfy such needs, expert system developers must possess adequate hardware and software tools. The following sections describe one experience with developing a PC-based expert system, *FuzzyExpert*, which processes vague knowledge. *FuzzyExpert*'s development team strove to create an expert system efficiently running on standard *IBM/PC* compatibles under *MS-DOS*, equipped with a friendly user interface, and providing as simple knowledge and fact representation as possible. The system has been, above all, intended for users who need to experiment with fuzzy knowledge bases before they implement particular applications, such as fuzzy process control, decision-making systems, diagnostic systems, empirical research processing, etc. Aside from these application areas, *FuzzyExpert* can be used for knowledge base tuning (e.g. reducing sets of rules to a necessary minimum), for testing correctness and completeness of knowledge bases, or simply as a training tool. The developers started with a fuzzy set theory-based prototype originally developed on a mainframe. With the complete change of hardware and software environments, the team had to sort out many problems.

2. *FuzzyExpert*'s Fundamentals

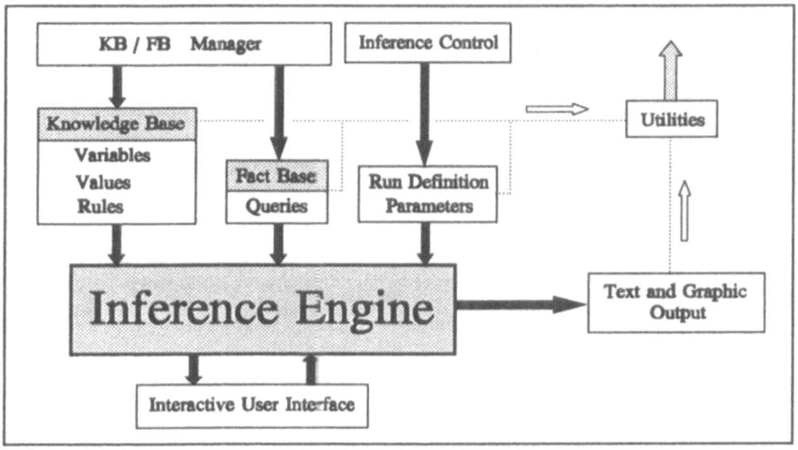

Fig. 1. *FuzzyExpert*'s **general architecture**

FuzzyExpert is a rule-based expert system supporting approximate reasoning based on fuzzy set theory (Zimmerman 85). Fig. 1 shows the basic components of the system. Besides the core (i.e. the inference engine, knowledge base [**KB**], and fact base [**FB**]), several additional constituents are integrated within the expert system. *Knowledge Base/Fact Base Manager* assists knowledge engineers and users in creating rules and queries. Moreover, it checks data integrity inside individual KBs and FBs as well as between a KB and its related FBs. *Inference Control* enables the inference engine to run with various parameters. *Interactive User Interface* supports communication between the user and the system during computation. *Utilities* provides, for example, file management, report generation, and data format conversion. The following sections describe these components in more detail.

2.1. Knowledge and Fact Base

The system's inference engine processes two input data sets:

– *rules*, which are stored in a knowledge base;
– *queries*, which represent a base of facts.

Setting up KBs is the task of knowledge engineers who must transform experts' knowledge into computer-acceptable data. These data represent a certain reality, described with various linguistic attributes (variables).

FuzzyExpert enables its users to define attribute values as fuzzy sets. [A fuzzy set is defined, in turn, using a membership function that assigns a value $\mu(x)$ to each coordinate x within a universe U ($0 \leq \mu(x) \leq 1$).] As shown in Fig. 2, nine predefined shapes of the membership function serve to represent particular attribute values, allowing the system to model both crisp and vague **linguistic values**. In practice, these shapes prove to be sufficient. To define any value, the user must select one of the shapes that is suitable for a given case, then specify the fuzzy set's location on its universe with 1 to 4 breakpoints. When the user wants to express the value "I do not know" or "it does not matter" for one or more values, the rightmost shape in Fig. 2 accommodates this need; no breakpoints are necessary because the value is defined on the whole universe and it has no influence on the result.

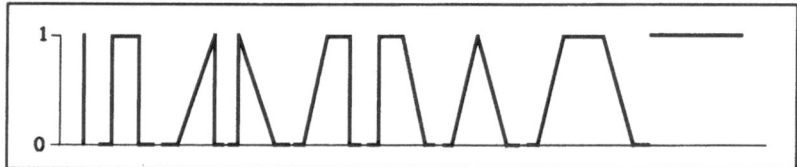

Fig. 2. Predefined shape of the membership function

Any effective combination of attribute values can make up a rule, which takes the form of an *IF–THEN–ELSE* clause. Attribute values in rules are usually assigned by a knowledge engineer as a result of the process called "knowledge acquisition". To create a new fuzzy KB, the knowledge engineer must complete several steps in the specified order:

    1) defining all linguistic attributes that describe the problem modeled;
    2) detailing the output attribute;
    3) assigning linguistic values to each attribute;
    4) making up rules as combinations of linguistic values.

A **rule** can be formally introduced in the following way:

Let $x_j \in U_j$ ($j=1,2,...,n$) denote an independent attribute taking its linguistic (fuzzy) values A_{ij} from a universe U_j. Let $y \in U_B$ stand for a dependent attribute defined on a universe U_B; furthermore, let B_i mean a fuzzy value defined on the universe U_B. Then, the following clause:

$$R_i \equiv if\ x_1 = A_{i1}\ and\ x_2 = A_{i2}\ and\ ...\ and\ x_n = A_{in}\ then\ y = B_i\ else\ ...$$

represents the i-th rule ($i=1,2,...,m$) in the formal description of a problem.

All attributes can be defined on different universes with different units of measure, which makes *FuzzyExpert* work with cylindrical extensions of the attribute values to the Cartesian product of the universes. Consequently, the system can easily look for an answer in the multidimensional space.

A **query** (hypothesis) can be expressed in a similar way:

$$Q \equiv x_1 = A_1\ and\ x_2 = A_2\ and\ ...\ and\ x_n = A_n$$

Here A_j (j=1,2,...,n) stands for a fuzzy set defined on its corresponding universe U_j. Queries are created by the user, who assigns values A_i to the set of attributes. The user can define values or, when convenient, take advantage of the values defined by the knowledge engineer in the KB.

2.2. Inference Process

Generally, attribute values in a query can differ to a greater or lesser degree from their counterparts in rules: $A_j \neq A_{ij}$. The inference engine's targets are to find which rules match a given query and what is the degree of match. For the expert system designer to decide which inference method would provide the best results is not an easy and straightforward task, especially when the system is intended for approximate reasoning with non-crisp values. However, *generalized modus ponens* (GMP) seems to be the contemporary paradigm for fuzzy set-based ESs.

The GMP's principle can be briefly explained as follows. Let $\mathcal{A}$ stand for an antecedent, let $\mathcal{B}$ stand for a consequent (i.e. the answer), and let $\mathcal{A} \Rightarrow \mathcal{B}$ denote the implication. Unlike traditional two- or multi-valued logic, GMP makes possible the conclusion $\mathcal{B}'$ when an antecedent $\mathcal{A}' \neq \mathcal{A}$ (provided that $\mathcal{A} \Rightarrow \mathcal{B}$ is valid). The inference engine computes the consequent $\mathcal{B}'$ as the composition of $\mathcal{A}'$ and $\mathcal{R}$:

$$\mathcal{B}' = \mathcal{A}' \circ \mathcal{R} = Q \circ \mathcal{R},$$

where $\mathcal{R}$ is a fuzzy relation made up by an aggregation of rules and $\circ$ means the operator of composition. Rules in a KB are aggregated by way of interpreting the *else* operator between each pair of rules with the operator of disjunction (the *disjunctive model*):

$$\mathcal{R} = R_1 \cup R_2 \cup ... \cup R_m,$$

where $\mathcal{R} \subset U_R = U_1 \times U_2 \times ... \times U_n \times U_B$ (Cartesian product). A query $Q \equiv \mathcal{A}'$ is a fuzzy relation, too, on the universe $U_A = U_1 \times U_2 \times ... \times U_n$.

As its output, the inference engine provides values of the membership function of $\mathcal{B}'$. To obtain these values, the system interprets the operators *and* and *then* as *min* (minimum) and the operator $\cup$ as *max* (maximum). Then, it computes individual matches between the query Q and each rule R_i. Any match contributes to the result, so the answer $\mathcal{B}'$ consists of superimposed values of all relevant B_i, which are cutoff at the height corresponding to the degree of the match.

The general form of a rule can also be rewritten in this way:

$$R_i \equiv A_{i1} \cap A_{i2} \cap ... \cap A_{in} \cap B_i,$$

where the operator $\cap$ means *min*. This form has one interesting implication: because the *min* operation is commutative (i.e. $A \cap B = B \cap A$), the order of B_i and any A_{ij} can be changed. Consequently, the user is allowed to look for an attribute value A_{ij} provided he/she knows (or supposes) the value B_i.

If the user requires a single value instead of the resulting fuzzy set, two possible ways have been suggested (Graham and Jones 88):

– *Defuzzyfication* of $\mathcal{B}'$ into a single scalar. *FuzzyExpert* computes the gravity center. (The other possibility would be to compute the point of maximum.);
– *Linguistic approximation* of $\mathcal{B}'$ using a verbal description. Because of its ambiguity, this method is left to the user.

Remark: Generalized modus ponens and the disjunctive model are not, of course, the only candidates for the inference mechanism. It is possible to use other tautologies, such as modus tollens, syllogism, or contraposition; however, GMP is widely preferred. On the other hand, experimenting with the *conjunctive* model (rules are aggregated using the operator ∩) seems to be quite meaningful (Kopřiva 88). Unlike its disjunctive counterpart, the conjunctive model provides more determinate answers, which usually do not cover such a wide interval on the output universe. If a knowledge base, interpreted with the conjunctive model, contains at least one rule that disagrees with a query, the inference engine would not provide an answer. This approach can be called "pessimistic" in contrast to the "optimistic" disjunctive model, which gives a positive answer whenever it finds at least one rule matching a query. The structure of *FuzzyExpert*'s inference engine allows an exchange of both models.

3. Implementing *FuzzyExpert* in a PC Environment

The PC environment often seemingly lacks speed, a suitable platform for software development, and sufficient screen size and resolution. Most PCs depend on *Intel 80x86* technology, which restricts operating systems and applications working in the real mode to a 1MB address space (although, in practice, only 640KB are accessible). PC operating systems, such as *MS-DOS*, provide relatively simple capabilities and do not directly support true multitasking or more advanced techniques like virtual memory.

To complete the PC implementation in a short period of time, developers choose Borland's *Turbo Pascal* programming language (version 6.0) for two main reasons: 1) the mainframe prototype was written in Pascal and 2) *Turbo Pascal* is a commonly used programming language, providing a rich set of tools.

3.1. Memory Issues

During the inference process, *FuzzyExpert* looks for a match between a query and a set of rules. Because the search for a match occurs sequentially – the inference mechanism consecutively compares the query against each rule – the system should keep as much data in the computer's main memory as possible. This strategy, however, often meets with serious space problems because a knowledge base can contain hundreds or thousands of rules; each rule, in turn, can hold many values.

The last mainframe prototype version of *FuzzyExpert* ran on the *EC-1045* computer, a Soviet *IBM/370* clone with 4MB of RAM. The *EC-1045*'s operating system allows a program to access up to 16M of virtual memory transparently. For that reason, the prototype previously could handle huge amounts of data without any special programming considerations. Given an *IBM/PC* compatible environment, by contrast, the expert system must process data in the comparatively small heap. Unfortunately, memory restrictions do not stop here. Due to the *Intel 80x86* chip's architecture, an individual data item cannot exceed the address space of one segment (i.e. 64KB). This particular stumbling block arises when a program defines a large array of variables using long data structures such as records.

The simplest solution to the drawback of memory constraints might entail limiting the number of attributes and rules that a user can specify. However, attributes and rules maintain an inversely proportional relationship: the lower the number of attributes, the higher the number of rules and vice versa. The expert system designer cannot easily set the upper bounds of these two parameters because any reasonable combination is allowable; from the perspective of memory utilization, therefore, expert systems demand dynamic control.

A radical technique was employed to solve the problem – a virtual memory mechanism. Specifically, it uses *Object Professional*, TurboPower Software's development tool for object-oriented *Turbo Pascal* programming, which provides a nearly effortless means to circumvent *MS-DOS*'s inherent memory constraints through its virtual large arrays. In fact, this mechanism dynamically uses RAM, expanded memory, extended memory, or disk-based paging, allowing individual data items to exceed 64K bytes in size. The dimensions and data type of a large array may be specified at run time rather than during compilation. Objects for managing a large array are arranged according to the hierarchy shown in Fig. 3.

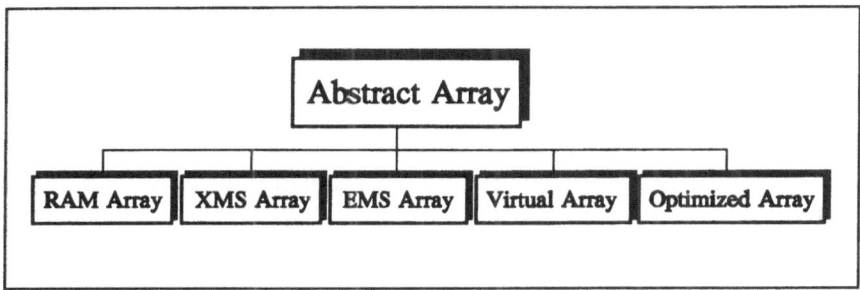

Fig. 3. Hierarchy of large array objects

AbstractArray defines the common methods (e.g. storing or retrieving an array element) used by all of the array types. *RAMArray*, *XMSArray*, *EMSArray*, and *VirtualArray* implement the storage mechanism for heap, *XMS*, *EMS*, and disk-based arrays, respectively. *OpArray* (Optimized Array) can store an array using any of the four types; the choice depends on the computer resources available at run time and on a user-defined priority. Any of the large array types can be stored on disk as a file and later reloaded by any other array type.

This flexibility exacts inevitable costs in overhead, leading to slower access of data types exceeding 64KB. Overhead results mainly from the fact that for each access to a dynamically allocated array element, the routines must calculate a page (segment) and an offset within the page to locate the data.

The *OpArray* method minimizes overhead and slowdown, namely in cases with a low number of attributes and rules, because it automatically uses free space in *RAM* or *XMS/EMS* (if available). This approach brings the mainframe's advantageous virtual memory techniques nearer to the PC world and thus enables downsizing of programs and systems originally developed in a quite different environment.

3.2. Performance Issues

Performance of an expert system (specifically, the inference engine's response time) is a very important criterion. Two fundamental factors affecting system performance are efficient hardware and effective software implementation.

When the system's inference engine was carefully profiled, it revealed disappointing response times in many cases, so the program developers looked for its bottlenecks. Because processing of real numbers engrosses the main CPU load, critical strictures appeared among functions that frequently work with reals. Specifically, the function that compares two real number arrays (often used by *FuzzyExpert*'s inference engine to find a degree of match between a query and a rule) presented the most serious problem. In spite of using various artificial intelligence methods to speed up extensive searches (e.g. alpha-beta pruning) the program developers could not overcome the ultimate flaw: *Turbo Pascal*, like almost all programming languages, surprisingly does not provide any high-level means to compare arrays of the same type directly. The only possibility involves comparing pairs of individual elements in a loop, which is a time-consuming process even with a math coprocessor. Replacing the Pascal code with assembler instructions resulted in a suitable solution for the following reasons: 1) *Turbo Pascal* 6.0 readily supports the use of inline assembler code through its built-in assembler and 2) the inline assembler code can directly refer to the Pascal code (e.g. labels and data items). Of course, such a solution reduces the ability to move the source code to another hardware platform. However, if a sequence of assembler instructions forms a closed unit, such as a function or a procedure, the program developer does not sacrifice too much portability (replacing a unit of code so the program can run on a computer from a different family is always easier than trying to isolate machine-specific code dispersed throughout the program). The result of replacing the *Turbo Pascal* loop with a sequence of assembler instructions was astounding, for the speed of the comparison function improved roughly 10 times. Interestingly, the mainframe predecessor of *FuzzyExpert* suffered from the same problem, and the solution was similar – an assembler routine.

Another substantial speed improvement was achieved through passing large data items (e.g. arrays and records) as variable rather than value parameters. With a variable parameter, the caller passes only a pointer to the parameter without copying the data itself into an auxiliary area in main memory, as value parameters typically do.

Perhaps the most burdensome obstacle to better utilization of a PC concerns *MS-DOS*'s lack of support for true **multitasking**. This deficiency is particularly detrimental in situations when the user views results displayed on the screen while the program idly waits. Instead, the inference engine could process another query in the background, thus reducing the inescapable time interval needed to obtain the next result. As the user examines the screen, the inference process simultaneously runs in the background. Whenever the display process needs the CPU, it preempts the background computation; after finishing its action, the display process returns control to the inference process. This procedure decreases CPU dead time and provides faster total system response. (The display process gives a user supplemental information, such as explanation of the result, the gravity center coordinate, individual components of the result, etc.) Implementation of the interrupt handling was not very difficult, but one serious problem emerged. *Turbo Pascal*'s input/output routines and memory management routines, which invoke *MS-DOS* non-reentrant system calls, cannot be used in an interrupt service routine (ISR). The principal solution to this problem (i.e. essentially rendering input/output operations possible in an ISR) is shown in Fig. 4. The ISR first clears the interrupt, restores the previous interrupt vector, disables subsequent interruptions, and then passes control to the Interrupt server. The server routine, which is a part of *FuzzyExpert's* Interactive User Interface, communicates with the user, displays what is asked for, and then returns control back to the ISR and, in turn, to the Inference process.

4. User Interface

FuzzyExpert's interface gives users the ability to effectively maintain various data files required by its inference engine, a characteristic fostered by the consistency inherent to object-oriented programming (OOP). Unfortunately, problems abounded on the path to this interface, related both to specific requirements of the system and to inherent drawbacks of OOP.

Almost every aspect of *FuzzyExpert*'s front end depends on OOP. Specifically, each user interface-related object (e.g. pick list, entry screen, or dialog box) originates with a window object, which consists of data and methods to handle features common to all objects, at the root of the object hierarchy. For example, a window can include a title header. It can support scroll bars for vertical or horizontal adjustments. If the user wants a hot spot that, when clicked, closes a window, the object complies. A window moves, too. The most powerful method of a window, however, processes keystrokes entered by the user when the window is active. Essentially a large **CASE** statement in a control loop, the Process method fields a key press that it anticipates, then returns to the top of the loop to await the next

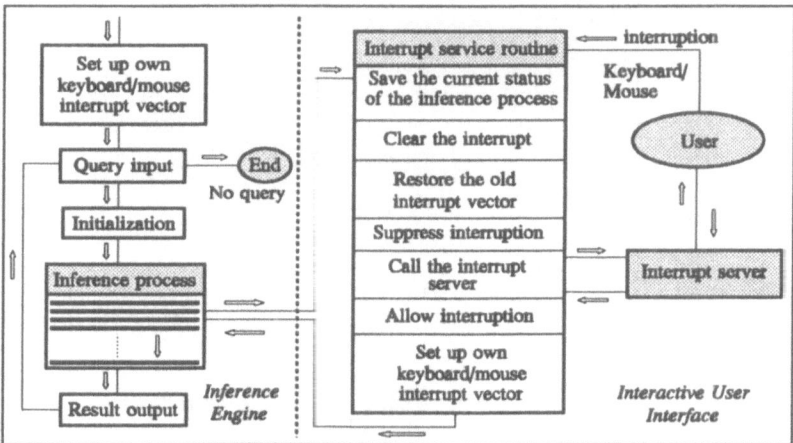

**Fig. 4. Principle mechanism for preemption
of the background computation**

keystroke. Some key presses cause the Process method to exit, allowing the user to provide unique handling. Obviously, any user interface object might have a need for these capabilities. Through object-oriented programming, a descendant object can very easily utilize a window feature simply by calling the appropriate method.

Development of *FuzzyExpert*'s user interface encountered one significant problem. Although the system runs in text mode, which entails less arduous programming than graphics mode, the full complement of 256 ASCII characters does not contain some odd symbols required to paint a fuzzy set shape on the screen. Consequently, *FuzzyExpert* programs the computer's EGA or VGA video display card to create 11 of these unusual characters.

4.1. *FuzzyExpert*'s Knowledge Base/Fact Base Manager

FuzzyExpert's user interface provides a highly structured means to create the input data files necessary to run the inference engine. Through the **Variables** option on the main menu, the user can build a linguistic attributes file. *FuzzyExpert* displays a dialog box containing an entry screen for 14 linguistic attribute records (actually, a 14-record view of a whole file). By clicking on a pushbutton, the user can define the values associated with the currently highlighted linguistic attribute. In response, *FuzzyExpert* draws a dialog box containing an entry screen for 14 linguistic attribute value records (again, a 14-record view of a whole file). The user can only edit a value's name in this dialog box (its value type and breakpoint coordinate fields are read-only), but by clicking on a pushbutton, the user can determine the fuzzy set shape (i.e. type) and breakpoint coordinates of the currently highlighted linguistic attribute value. *FuzzyExpert*, in turn, presents another dialog box that includes a pick list of predefined fuzzy set shapes and the appropriate number of entry fields for the selected shape's breakpoint coordinates. In Fig. 5, for example, a triangular-shaped fuzzy set is currently chosen in the pick list, and as a result, only three entry fields appear. Thus, with a few keystrokes, the user can construct the linguistic attributes and values files essential for the inference engine.

To create a file of rules or a file of queries for an inference engine run, *FuzzyExpert* offers two separate options on its main menu: **Rules** and **Queries**. However, with some minor exceptions, identical processing occurs for these input data file types. *FuzzyExpert* displays a read-only window that lists existing rules or queries. By clicking on a pushbutton, the user

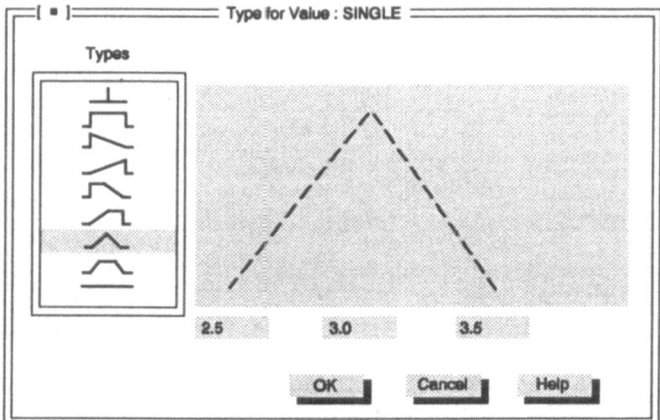

Fig. 5. Attribute value type dialog box with predefined fuzzy set shapes

can update the currently highlighted rule or query. Because a rules or a queries file must relate to a specific linguistic attributes file, *FuzzyExpert* draws a dialog box containing a scrolling entry screen with exactly one field for each linguistic attribute; the user must enter a previously defined value in every field. Thus, the user can generate two more elements – the rules file and the queries file – necessary for a run of *FuzzyExpert*'s inference engine.

Another important role of the Knowledge/Fact Base Manager is preventing the inference engine from crashing due to problems concerning data integrity. Rules and queries files derive from a linguistic attributes file; each rule or query must include one value for every defined attribute. Assuming the user creates a rules file then deletes a record from the linguistic attributes file, an incongruity exists that would force the inference engine to abort. To remedy this problem, *FuzzyExpert* tracks all modifications to a linguistic attributes file and its associated values file. When the user finishes editing these files, *FuzzyExpert* automatically reflects changes in the related rules and queries files.

4.2. *FuzzyExpert*'s Run Definition Facility

Integrating these distinct files and delineating parameters for execution of the inference engine, *FuzzyExpert* offers the simple mechanism of a run definition file. Through the main menu's **Inference** option, the user can design up to 100 different run definition files for a single linguistic attributes file. *FuzzyExpert* presents a rich dialog box containing, among other items, entry fields for a description of this particular run definition file, the specific rules file and queries file that the inference engine should read, as well as many parameters. Parameters in the file enable a number of special functions, for example:

- omitting some attributes from the run (so called non-live variables);
- selecting a constant or a variable scale of the output attribute universe;
- restricting the percentage of activated rules (when a query does not result in an answer after processing the requested percentage of rules, the inference engine ignores the rest of the rules to prevent long, unnecessary computations for ill-formulated queries);
- displaying only those components of an answer that have cutoff values greater than a user-demanded threshold;

- computing primary consistencies of KBs (the left side of each rule is treated consecutively as a query, and the inference engine looks for a match between the rule and the rest of the KB; this function assists users and knowledge engineers in searching for knowledge gaps in KBs);
- stretching original attribute values in a query when the inference engine cannot obtain an answer (fuzzy set breakpoints on the universe axis are stretched to the left and to the right so each value becomes "wider", which increases the possibility of getting a conclusion). This feature can help users to find out what additional knowledge is necessary to improve the system's inference results. Fig. 6 illustrates the effect of stretching.

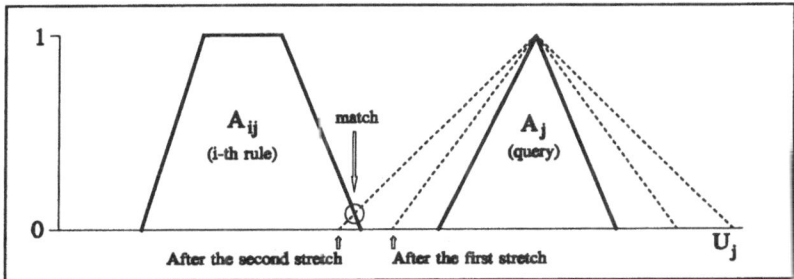

Fig. 6. The value A_j matches the value A_ij after the second stretch

After the user establishes a run definition file, he/she can start the inference process merely by selecting the run definition file.

4.3. Output Interface

FuzzyExpert displays its output in conformity with the input data: answers to the user's queries appear on the screen in graphics mode as compound fuzzy set shapes. The user can ask for supplemental information, including the gravity center, outlines of individual fuzzy set components, and an explanation window. *FuzzyExpert* saves each answer on disk so it can be easily redrawn later. Moreover, a detailed description of the inference process's conclusions is stored in a text file. *FuzzyExpert*'s supporting utilities enable printing of these graphic and text files as well as exporting of graphic screens to several common file formats (e.g. PCX, TIFF). Fig. 7 illustrates a graphic output screen of the inference engine.

5. Conclusion and Recommendations

This paper presents problem areas that developers of PC-based expert systems can encounter, stemming from hardware specificities and from software complexities. Effective memory management remains mere wishful thinking: a user's process must control utilization by itself. In spite of these imperfections, PCs now dominate the computing world, so expert systems must shift to this platform. On the software side, *FuzzyExpert* was implemented in Borland's *Turbo Pascal*, although profiling revealed several serious bottlenecks that only inline assembler instructions could bypass. This solution, while improving *FuzzyExpert*'s performance, decreased its portability. *Turbo Pascal*'s object-oriented extension supports such important and, at the same time, difficult tasks as developing *FuzzyExpert*'s user-friendly interface. To briefly summarize *FuzzyExpert*'s implementation experience, today's hardware and software provide a powerful base for complex software system development; however,

104

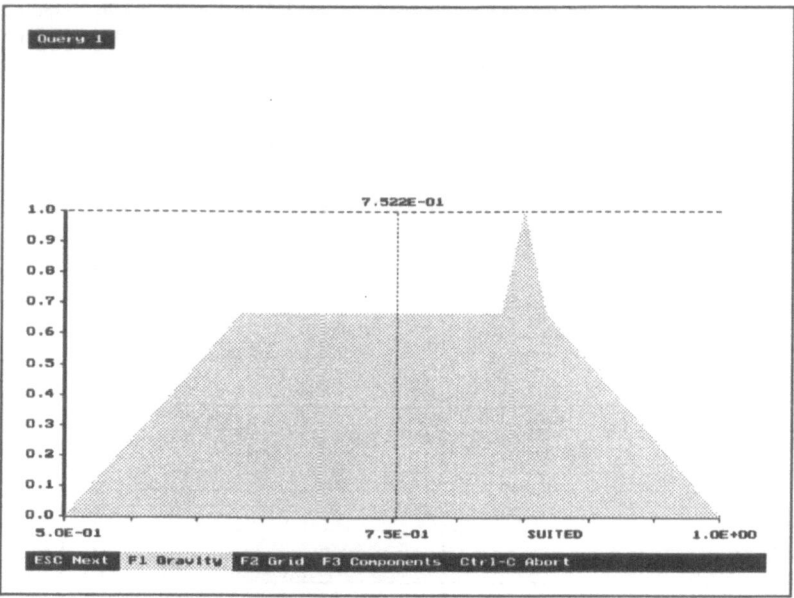

Fig. 7. An example of the inference engine graphic output

many issues still await their perfect solutions. A brief study showed that *UNIX*-based systems would provide a far more convenient environment for developing and running expert systems. The *UNIX* operating system naturally includes a virtual memory mechanism as well as multitasking. Despite the implementation difficulties, the result – *FuzzyExpert* for PCs – is a useful tool with many possible applications.

6. References

1. Giarratano, J. and Riley, G. *Expert Systems: Principles and Programming.* PWS-KENT Publishing Company. U.S.A., 1989.

2. Graham, I. and Jones, P.L. *Expert Systems: Knowledge, Uncertainty and Decision.* Chapman and Hall, London, 1988.

3. Kopřiva, J. *Fuzzy Deductive System, Its Implementation and Application.* Proceedings of "Modern programming 1988", pp. 119-130, Červený Kláštor, Czechoslovakia, May 29 – July 3, 1988. In Czech.

4. Payne, E.C. and McArthur, R.C. *Developing Expert Systems.* John Wiley & Sons, Inc., U.S.A., 1990.

5. Zimmerman, H.-J. *Fuzzy Set Theory and Its Applications.* Kluwer-Nijhoff Publishing, U.S.A., 1985.

A CLAUSE INDEXING METHOD

Kálmán Balogh

"IQSOFT" SzKI
INTELLIGENT SOFTWARE CO. LTD.
H-1251 Budapest,P.O.Box 73.Hungary
(H-1011 Budapest, Iskola u. 10.)
E-mail: BALOGH@IQSOFT.HU
H1395bal@ella.UUCP
Phone: (36-1)201 67 64
Telefax: (36-1) 201 71 25

Abstract

An indexing method for clauses of predicate logic is discussed. The method is based on the decision tree corresponding to the argument expressions of procedure heads. The method is efficiently applicable for procedures containing a lot of clauses, to direct both or- and and-parallelism. It is indicated, how to apply the method to a knowledge base of frames or objects. This indexing method suits well to common inheritance operations, and increases their efficiency.

Keywords: predicate logic, Prolog, knowledge base, data base, indexing, decision tree, frame, object, inheritance.

1 Introduction

Traditional execution method of Prolog evaluates a call of a predicate through linear search for alternative clauses in the corresponding procedure when backtracking. This search is inefficient, if the procedure contains a lot of clauses. Introduction of any indexing methods would increase efficiency. In fact, DEC-10 Prolog [1] and some other implementations of Prolog apply indexing of clause heads according to the main functors of their first arguments for a long time.

Indexing can be explored not only when searching for matching alternatives, that is evaluating "or" branches of the execution tree. Evaluation of conjunctive subgoals in a parallel, mutually dependent way can be supported by indexing their definitions (the corresponding procedures) in accordance with each other.

Indexing of procedures should not be treated independently of the evaluation mechanism. When determining the indexing method described here my aim was

- to prepare evaluation of procedures statically as far as possible;

- to store procedures in an irredundant way, where it does not conflict with functional requirements (e.g. order prescription for alternatives, generality of argument expressions) or with the former aim.

According to the different kinds of functional and evaluation requirements, a variety of index structures and searching algorithms is determined.

The paper is divided into two main parts. In section 2 the indexing method based on decision trees is introduced, while in section 3 it is shown, how the method can be explored when structuring a knowledge base.

2 The indexing method

This indexing indexing method is generalized from that of MProlog [2] for static clauses.

The method is introduced in three steps. In the first step a variable free world is supposed, which is extended in the further steps with handling variables in calls, then in heads of procedures, too. These steps result in three main variants of the indexing method, as described in section 2.1, 2.2 and 2.3.

Refined versions of the above variants can be derived, if other requirements, being orthogonal to the former one (dealing with indexing from the point of view of variables) are considered, too. Two further dimensions of such requirements are investigated here. The first one is, at what extent the original order of clauses constituting a procedure should be preserved. The other dimension is, whether during parameter passing the input/output role of some arguments of the defined predicate is restricted or not. Treatment of these additional requirements is discussed within the three-step description of the main variant.

Further refinement possibilities, being common for the previous variants are mentioned in section 2.4 .

2.1 The variable free case

The main purpose is to prepare matching of a given procedure to its possible calls as far as possible. This aim is reached, if clauses of the procedure are stored in a decision tree corresponding to the expressions occuring in the heads of clauses of that procedure.

First a special case of simple constant arguments is described, then handling of compound arguments is discussed.

2.1.1 Treatment of heads containing simple arguments

Let us see an example of a unary procedure:

$p(a)$:- $Body_a$.
$p(b)$:- $Body_{b1}$.
$p(c)$:- $Body_c$.
$p(b)$:- $Body_{b2}$.

The decision tree corresponding to this procedure is

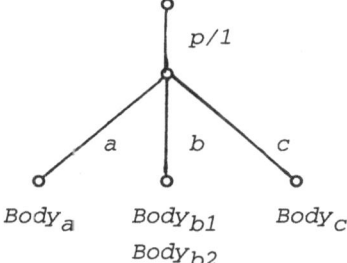

Let us call the list of clauses referred by the same leaf of the tree to be a *partition*.

The example shows, that the second aim of the introduction of indexing - irredundancy of both data structures and processing - is also reached, as common components of different clause heads are extracted. In this example it is trivial, but this property will hold for the more complicated versions of the method, too.

Another important property of the decision tree (which also will hold for further variants) is, that branches of the decision tree originated at the same node are exclusive alternatives. Original order of the clauses of the procedure is preserved (if it is preserved within partitions), when searching for matching alternatives to a call.

As the order preserving property of the method is independent of the order of the branches of a node, it is possible to use any kind of indexing methods (e.g. logarithmic search within lexicographically ordered symbols, B-tree handling,hashing) to improve efficiency of search within a great number of alternative branches.

If the defined predicate has arity more then one, then (in case of simple arguments) one can attach a layer of the tree to each argument position. Order of the layers shows the order of the decisions according to the arguments. This order is arbitrary; either it may be the original order of arguments, or it can be prescribed by the user through a so-called match-order declaration [2].

2.1.2 Treatment of heads containing compound arguments

If the arguments of the predicate definition may contain variable free expressions, then indexing the definition according to the designator of the head argument expressions can be made in a way analogous trivially to the former case. The *designator* of an expression is the term *Name/Arity*, where *Name* is the name and *Arity* is the arity of the main functor of the expression. The designator of a simple constant C can be regarded to be $C/0$.

Indexing according to the designators can be extended to the deeper level of argument expressions. The decision tree can be built according to the processing of the argument expressions, e.g. in a depth first left to right order.

The branches introduced so far are said to be of type *des-branch* (branches for given distinct designators).

2.2 Handling variables in the call

When calls with (unbound) variables are allowed, a further type of branch should be introduced. The new branch is called *var-branch*, which lists all clauses attached to the node.

In case of the example of 2.1.1, the tree corresponding to the procedure for *p/1*, when calls with variable arguments are allowed is

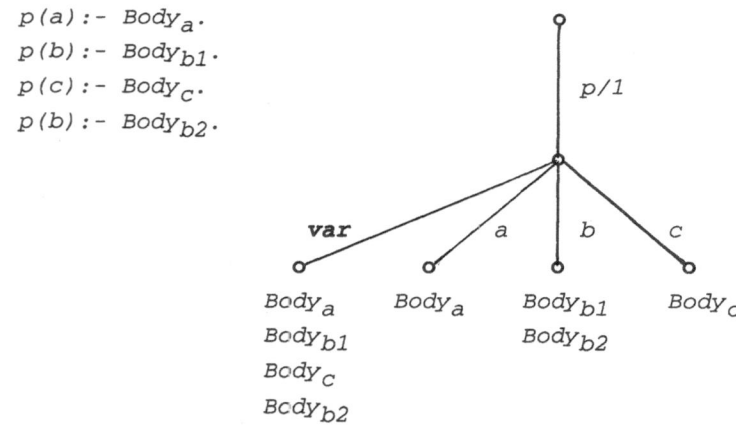

$p(a):- Body_a.$
$p(b):- Body_{b1}.$
$p(c):- Body_c.$
$p(b):- Body_{b2}.$

Explicit representation of the var-branch in the tree

- causes redundancy in storage (multiple references to the same clauses)

- preserves original order of matching clauses.

Indexing is equally efficient in each variation of i/o role (during parameter passing) of the arguments. This property will hold also in further versions of the method, but speed of execution of the indexing is slower, where we choose an irredundant representation.

In the next refinement of the method var-branches are eliminated from the representation, so each clause is referred to only once from the tree. The price of it is, that the algorithm should enumerate all the branches corresponding to a call with a variable, and the method preserves original order of the clauses only within partitions.

A var-branch is not needed for an argument position, if the user states in a so-called mode declaration, that the arguments should be concrete in the procedure calls for that argument position. This possibility is given e.g. in MProlog [2] for main designators of arguments.

2.3 Handling variables in the heads of the procedure

Clauses of a procedure, heads of which contain variables in the position in question, can be successfully matched with an arbitrary call of the predicate.

The method does not take account of multiple occurences of the same variable in a head; the tree contains only context free information.

In order to handle the above mentioned clauses, a new type of branches,called *else-branch* is introduced. Such a clause should be inserted into all alternative branches of the else-branch, too. For this price original order of matching clauses is preserved.

Let us extend the example of 2.1.1, to see the effect on the representation. The new procedure for $p/1$ is

$p(a):- Body_a.$

$p(b):- Body_{b1}.$

$p(X):- Body_{x1}.$

$p(c):- Body_c.$

$p(b):- Body_{b2}.$

$p(X):- Body_{x2}.$

The tree corresponding to the above procedure in the general case is

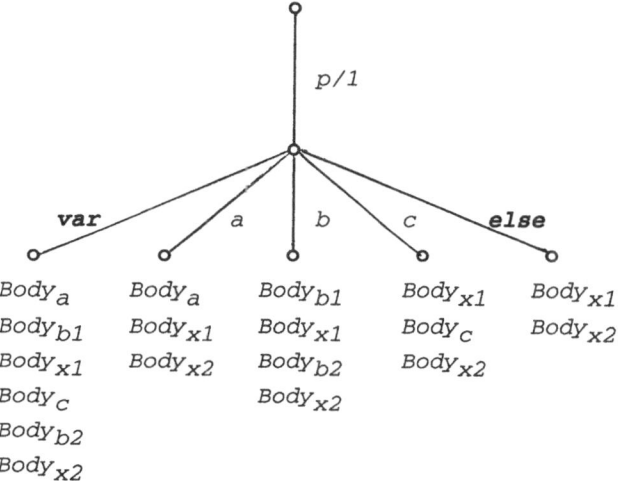

If the clauses, heads of which contain variables in the position in question are deleted from the var- and des-branches of the representation, then each new clause is referred once by the tree. In this case the algorithm should enumerate the clauses on the else-branch, having enumerated those referred by the matching des-branch(es). Original order of the matching concrete and general clauses is preserved only separately, within the two groups, but each of the concrete alternatives will precede any of the general ones.

Else-branch is needless, if the user states in a declaration, or it is verified by preprocessing the definition, that the corresponding arguments should be concrete in the heads of the procedure.

2.4 Common refinement possibilities

Let us suppose, that execution of the procedures is preceded by preprocessing of the bodies of the clauses in addition to that of their heads. This allows us to bind each call to those subtrees within their definition, which can be determined by the statically existing argument expressions. The binding can be refined during the execution, thus focussing on the smallest possible subtree.

Binding information is valuable for dynamic memory management. On one hand it helps increasing the effect of garbage collection. On the other hand it makes possible increasing efficiency of secondary storage management through a dedicated paging system built on a hardware virtual memory.

According to our purpose whether to apply the method for static or dynamic procedures, different refinements of the method are suitable to implement.

On the other hand, specification of the built-in dynamic procedure handling predicates should be synchronized with the method. Refering to clauses via an external (source level) sequence number allows only a low level, algorithmic interface for the user. This facility can be overridden by giving (also) more Prolog-like nondeterministic and backtrackable procedures, based on general searching possibilities, which can be efficiently implemented by the indexing method.

3 Application of the indexing method for frames

Each way of indexing helps in efficient implementation of structured knowledge bases, e.g. that of frames or objects. In the following it is shown in a frame terminology, that the above method of indexing helps both structuring of knowledge and inheritance in an extremely efficient way, compared to other indexing methods.

3.1 Representation of frames

Let us assume for simplicity, that frames have the following form

frame Frame_id with parameter P.

    slot S_name$_1$: S_value$_1$.

    . . . .

    slot S_name$_m$: S_value$_m$.

endframe.

Here *Frame_id* and *P* are arbitrary terms [3].

This form will be sufficient to show, how the previous indexing method can be applied.

A frame of the above form can be represented in Prolog as a set of clauses corresponding to the predicates frame/2 and slot/4

    frame(Frame_id,P).

    slot (Frame_id,P,S_name$_1$,S_value$_1$).

    . . . .

    slot (Frame_id,P,S_name$_m$,S_value$_m$).

In general, if frames have further kinds of components, a frame system can be represented in Prolog through partitioning the procedures according to the frame identifiers

predicate designator / partition corresponding to a frame	frame/2	slot/4	. . .
Frame_id$_1$			
Frame_id$_2$			
. . .			
Frame_id$_n$			

3.2 Description of frame structure and inheritance through inheritance rules

Inheritance can be described directly by clauses [4] of form

Frame_id$_1$ inherits Component from Frame_id$_2$
   if Body.

Indirect description of inheritance by using binary relations between frame identifiers has the following form

Frame_id$_1$ is related to Frame_id$_2$ by Rel.

Frame_id inherits Component through Rel
   if Body.

3.3 Reflecting frame structure through the construction of the frame identifiers

An example is shown, how to avoid redundant storage of overlapping frames by properly constructed frame identifiers.

If we have two overlapping frames, named f_1 and f_2, we do not want to store their common components twice. This is the case, if, for instance, one wants to store production rules of form

$$\textit{if}\ \ f_1\ \textit{is\_in\_working\_memory}\ \ \underline{and}$$

$$f_2\ \textit{is\_in\_working\_memory}$$

$$\underline{then}\ \textit{Conclusion}$$

knowing, that role of the two components of the condition part of the rules is symmetric.

In order to access these rules both from f_1 and from f_2, but store them irredundantly, an auxiliary frame named $f_1 \cap f_2$ is introduced, and the rules are placed into this frame. More generally, we make the representation disjoint by introducing the auxiliary frames named $f_1 \backslash f_2, f_1 \cap f_2$ and $f_2 \backslash f_1$

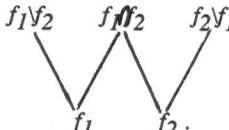

Inheritance can be expressed stating the following rules

$$F\ \underline{inherits}\ All\ \underline{from}\ (F\backslash\_).$$

$$F_1\ \underline{inherits}\ All\ \underline{from}\ F_2$$

$$\underline{if}\ F_1\ \textit{is\_conjunctive\_component\_of}\ F_2.$$

(The last predicate can be defined in Prolog easily.)

3.4 Reducing inheritance back to subsumption

Special frame structures can be described using properly constructed frame identifiers through the subsumability of these identifiers. We say, that *term T1 subsumes term T2*, if *T1* and *T2* are unifiable without binding any variables in *T1*. E. g. the term *parallelogram(square(X))* subsumes the term *parallelogram(X)*.

By the subsumability of frame identifiers the most frequent common situations can be expressed, among others hierarchic structures.

Execution of inheritance operations in general needs inference, that is evaluating inheritance rules. Deriving inheritance back to subsumption checking puts execution to unification level, so it allows a far more efficient execution. Implementation of subsumption checking is even more efficient, if it is specialized according to the indexing method described in section 2 .

3.5 Inheritance strategies

Tools are needed for the user for conflict resolution among multiple sources of inheritance. Possible reasons of nondeterminism of inheritance are enumerated first, then ways for solutions are sketched.

The pure method of inheritance through subsumption has a serious drawback: the user cannot control, which component of the frame is to be inherited from where (if the frame has more than one parent according to the frame identifiers, or there are exceptional connections among frames, which are given by inheritance rules). This problem arises also, when the inheritance rules are conflicting.

It is also worthy to give possibilities to indicate types of inheritance (whether the inheritance should be e.g. deterministic, classic or default).

Means are needed to describe the strategy, which determines, whether to search for the source of inheritance within the ancestors of a parent (to search first in depth), or within the brothers of the parent (to search first in breadth), and in the latter case determines the source of inheritance within the parents.

The above problems can be solved efficiently by assigning suitable built_in predicates to specific strategies, argument of which is the reference to the frame component. A more general solution would be to give for the user a binary predicate, to allow encapsulating also the description of strategy beside the frame reference into an argument of this predicate.

It is worth assigning strategies not only to references (dynamically), but rather to slots of a frame definition by declaration. It is nice and clearly arranged, if this declaration is part of the creation of the frame.

4 Conclusion

Ways of indexing of procedures and kinds of evaluation mechanisms should be related suitably, when building and processing knowledge bases. Consequences of this observation corresponding to a rather abstract level of notions are described above. If one concretises stepwise the notions in question, further fruits of the method can gather.

Some of the benefits of the decision tree based indexing method are indicated here. Further investigation should be taken to elaborate and implement these possibilities and find other correlations between indexing and evaluation mechanisms, e.g. depending on whether

- the evaluation mechanism is based on structure sharing or copying

- the programming language is Prolog or LDL [5], [6]

- the method is applied to a static or a dynamic definition (supplied with a variety of basic operations).

The indexing method based on decision trees can be generalized to be based on decision graphs [7].

References

[1] *Warren, D., Pereira, F. and Pereira, L. M.: User's Guide to DECsystem-10 Prolog*, Occassional Paper 15, Dept. of Artificial Intelligence, University of Edinburgh, 1979.

[2] *MProlog Language Reference Manual. MProlog* is a registered trademark of IQSOFT SzKI, Intelligent Software Co. Ltd., H-1251 Budapest, P.O.Box 73., Hungary

[3] *C. Zaniolo: Object-oriented programming in Prolog*, IEEE, Proc. Symposium on Logic Programming, 1984, Atlantic City, pp. 265-270.

[4] *A. Domán: Object-Prolog:Dynamic object oriented representation of knowledge*, Proc. SCS Multi Conf. on AI & Simulation, 1988., San Diego.

[5] *S. Naqvi - S. Tsur: A Logical Language for Data and Knowledge Bases*, Computer Science Press, New York, 1989.

[6] *G. Gardarin - P. Valduriez: ESQL: An Extended SQL with object and deductive capabilities*, Rapports de Recherche No 1185, INRIA, Le Chesnay, France, 1990.

[7] *S. Kliger - E. Shapiro: From Decision Trees to Decision Graphs*, Prceedings of ICLP, 1990.

KEYNOTE LECTURE

Chair: G. Pomberger

Software Engineering for Real-Time Systems

H.Kopetz

Technical University of Vienna
Austria

Abstract. A hard real-time system has to produce the correct results at the intended points in time. In such a system a failure in the time domain can be as critical as a failure in the value domain. In this paper it is claimed that an engineering approach to the design of the application software for a hard real-time system is only possible if the run-time architecture is based on the time triggered paradigm.

1. Introduction

At present, real-time system development resembles sometimes a "black art". Modules of conventionally designed software are integrated by "real-time specialists" who tune the system parameters (e.g., task priorities, buffer sizes, etc.,) during an extensive trial and error testing period, consuming more than 50% of a projects resources. Why the system performs its functions at the end is sometimes a miracle, even to the "real-time specialists".

Temporal properties are system properties. They depend on the behavior of all levels of an architecture, e.g., the hardware, the operating system, and the application software. A systematic design of real-time software is only possible if the underlying hardware and operating system guarantee a predictable temporal behavior. In this paper we examine the architectural prerequisites for an engineering approach to the development of real-time systems, as proposed in [1].

This paper is organized as follows. After a classification of real-time systems we present a set of key design problems that have to be solved in any rational real-time software development process. We then examine proposed solutions and conclude that only time-triggered architectures support an engineering approach to hard real-time system design.

2. What is a real-time system ?

In many models of natural phenomena (e.g., Newtonian mechanics), time is considered as an independent variable which determines the sequence of states of the considered system. The basic constants of physics are defined in relation to a standard of time, the physical second. If we intend to control the behavior of a natural system, we have to act on the system at precise moments in time.

We define a *real-time system* as a system that changes its state as a function of (real) time. Our interest focuses on real-time systems that contain embedded computer systems. It is sensible to decompose such a real-time system into a set of *clusters*, e.g., the *controlled object*, the *computer system* and a *human operator* (Fig.1). We call the controlled object and the operator the *environment* of the computer system. The computer system must react to stimuli from the controlled object (or the operator) within time intervals dictated by its environment. Such a computer system is called a *real-time computer system*.

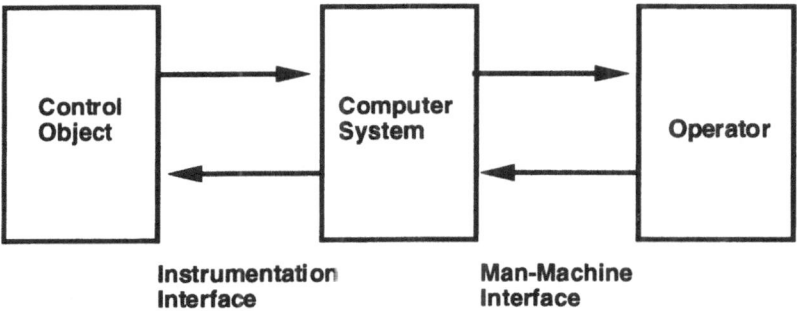

Fig.1: A real-time computer system

Since the real-time computer system is only a part of the total real time system, there must be interfaces between the real-time computer system and its environment. We call the interface between the real-time computer and the controlled object the *instrumentation* interface, consisting of sensors and actuators, and the interface between the real-time computer system and the operator the *man-machine* or operator interface.

Nowadays, most real-time computer systems are distributed. They consist of a set of nodes interconnected by a real-time communication system. Access to this real-time communication system must be controlled by a *real-time protocol*, i.e. a protocol that has a known small maximum execution time.

Based on the above definition of a real-time computer system it follows that the duration between a stimulus from the environment and the response to the environment must be time constrained. We call the sequence of all communication and processing steps between such a stimulus and response a *real-time (RT) transaction*. A RT-transaction must deliver the correct result at the intended point in time. Otherwise, the real-time computer system has failed.

Any real-time computer system has a finite processing capacity. If we intend to guarantee by design that the given temporal requirements of all critical real-time transactions can be satisfied then we have to postulate a set of assumptions about the behavior of the environment. The *load hypothesis* and the *fault hypothesis* are two of these important assumptions.

Load Hypothesis. The load hypothesis defines the *peak load* that is assumed to be generated by the environment. It can be expressed by specifying the minimum time interval between--or the maximum rate of--each real-time transaction. Peak load implies that all specified transactions will occur with their maximum specified rate. In many applications the utility of the real-time system is highest in a *rare event situation* that leads to a peak load scenario. Consider the case of a nuclear power station monitoring and shutdown system. It is probable that in case of the rare event of an reactor incident--e.g., the rupture of a pipe--many alarms will be activated simultaneously and will thus generate a correlated load. Statistical arguments about the low probability for the occurrence of peak load, based on the argument that the tail of a load distribution of independent events is very small are not valid in such a situation. If a real-time system is not designed to handle the peak load it can happen that the system will fail when it is needed most urgently.

Fault Hypothesis. The fault-hypothesis defines the types and frequency of faults that a fault-tolerant system must be capable of handling. If the identified fault scenario develops, the system must still provide the specified level of service. If the environment generates more faults than specified in the fault-hypothesis, then even a fault tolerant system may fail. The worst scenario that a fault-tolerant real-time system must be capable of handling exists if the peak-load and the maximum number of faults occur at the same time.

Even a perfect fault-tolerant real-time system will fail if the load-hypothesis or the fault hypothesis are unrealistic, i.e., they do not properly capture the behavior of the environment. The concept of *assumption coverage* defines the probability that the fault and load hypothesis--and all other assumptions made about the behavior of the environment--are in agreement with reality.

3 Classification of RT-Systems

We call a real-time system as *soft*, if the consequences of a timing failure are in the same order of magnitude as the utility of the operational system. Consider, e.g., a letter sorting machine. If a letter is placed in the wrong bin because of a timing failure, the consequences are not very serious--the letter will have to be sorted again.

If the consequences of a timing or value failure can be catastrophic, i.e., the cost of such a failure can be orders of magnitude higher that the normal utility of the system, then we call the system a *hard real-time system*. A railway signalling system is a good example of a hard real time system.

For some hard real-time systems one or more safe states can be identified that can be accessed in case of a system failure. Consider the example of the railway signalling system. In case a failure is detected it is possible to stop all trains and set all signals to red to avoid a catastrophe. If such a safe state can be identified, than we call the system a *fail-safe system*. Note, that fail-safeness is a characteristic of the control object, not the computer system. In fail safe applications the computer system must have a high error detection coverage, i.e., the probability that an error is detected, provided it has occurred, must be close to one.

There are, however, applications where such a safe state cannot be identified, e.g., a flight control system aboard an airplane. In such an application the computer system must provide a minimal level of service even in the case of failure in order to avoid a catastrophe. This is reason why these applications are called *fail operational*.

In the rest of this paper we will focus on hard real-time systems.

4. Key Design Problems

In this section we discuss some of the key problems in the design of fault-tolerant distributed hard real-time computer systems.

4.1 Flow Control

Flow control is concerned with the synchronization of the speed of the sender of information with the speed of the receiver, such that the receiver can follow the sender.

Since the controlled object in many real-time systems is not in the *sphere of control* of the computer system, there is no possibility to limit the occurrence of events in the controlled object in case the computer system cannot follow. Therefore provisions must be made that correlated event showers can be buffered at the interface between the controlled object and the computer system. Several engineering solutions are applied to restrict the flow of events at this interface. These include hardware implemented low pass filters, intermediate buffering of events in hardware and/or software, etc.. However it is still one of the difficult design problems to devise a flow control schema for a real time system that

* protects the computer system from overload situations caused by a faulty sensor or a correlated event showers and at the same time

* makes sure that no important events are suppressed by the flow control mechanism.

4.2 Scheduling

In general, the problem of deciding whether a set of real-time tasks whose execution is constrained by some dependency relation (e.g., mutual exclusion), is schedulable, belongs to the class of NP-complete problems[4]. Finding a *feasible schedule*, provided it exists, is another difficult problem. The known analytical solutions to the dynamic scheduling problem [7] assume stringent constraints on the interaction properties of task sets that are difficult to meet in distributed real-time systems. In practice most dynamic real-time systems resort to *static priority scheduling*. During the commissioning of the system the static priorities are tuned to handle the observed load patterns. No analytical guarantees about the peak load performance can be given.

4.3 Testing for Timeliness

In many real-time system project more than 50% of the resources are spent on testing. It is very difficult to design a constructive test suite to systematically test the temporal behavior of a complex real-time system if no temporal encapsulation is enforced by the system architecture.

4.4 Error Detection

In a real-time computer system we have to detect value errors and timing errors before an erroneous output is delivered to the control object. Error detection has to be performed at the receiver and at the sender of information. The provision of an error detection schema that will detect all errors specified in the fault hypothesis with a small latency is another difficult design problem.

4.5 Replica Determinisms

In many real-time applications the time needed to perform checkpointing and backward recovery after a fault has occurred is not available. Therefore fault-tolerance in distributed real-time systems has to be based on active redundancy. Active redundancy requires *replica determinism*, i.e., the active replicas must take the same decisions at about the same time in order to maintain *state synchronism*. If replica determinism is maintained, fault-tolerance can be implemented by duplex fail-silent selfchecking nodes (or by Triple Modular Redundancy with voting if the fail-silent assumption is not supported).

5. The solution space

Depending on the triggering mechanisms for the start of the communication and processing activities in each node of a computer system, two distinctly different approaches to the design of real-time computer applications can be distinguished. In the *event triggered* (ET) approach all communication and processing activities are initiated whenever a significant change of state, i.e., an event, is recognized. In the *time triggered (TT)* approach all communication and processing activities are initiated periodically at predetermined points in time. In the following sections we will analyze the problem solving potential these two competing design philosophies.

5.1 Event triggered systems

In a purely event triggered (ET) system all system activities are initiated by the occurrence of significant events in the control object or the computer system. In many implementations of ET-systems the signalling of significant events is realized by the well known interrupt mechanism, which brings the occurrence of a significant event to the attention of the CPU.

Flow Control. Within an ET-system, *explicit flow control* mechanisms with buffering have to be implemented between a sending and a receiving entity. The time span which an event message has to wait in a buffer before it can be processed reduces the temporal accuracy of the observation and must thus be limited. The provision of the proper buffer size is a delicate problem in the design of ET-systems.

Scheduling. Operating systems for ET-systems are demand driven and require a dynamic scheduling strategy. Since it is difficult to systematically tackle the complex scheduling problem in the available restricted time span, in practice most ET-systems resort to a simple static priority scheduling. During the commissioning of the system the static priorities are tuned to handle the observed load patterns. No analytical guarantees about the peak load performance can be given.

Testing for Timeliness. The confidence in the timeliness of an ET-system can only be established by extensive system tests on simulated loads. Testing on real loads is not sufficient, because the *rare events*, which the system has to handle (e.g., the occurrence of a serious fault in the controlled object), will not occur frequently enough in an operational environment to gain confidence in the peak load performance of the system. The predictable behavior of the system in rare-event situations is of paramount utility in many real-time applications

Since no detailed plans for the intended temporal behavior of the tasks of an ET-system exist, it is not possible to perform "constructive" performance testing at the task level. In a system where all scheduling decisions concerning the task execution and the access to the communication system are dynamic, no *temporal encapsulation of the tasks* exists, i.e., a variation in the timing of any task can have consequences on the timing of many other tasks in different nodes. The critical issue during the evaluation of an ET-system is thus reduced to the question, whether the simulated load patterns used in the system test are representative of the load patterns that will develop in the real application context. This question is very difficult to answer with confidence.

Replica Determinims. State synchronism is difficult to achieve in asynchronous ET-systems based on a dynamic preemptive scheduling strategy.

Consider the case a fault-tolerant distributed system. Two identical fail-silent nodes operate in parallel in order to tolerate a crash failure of one of the nodes. Since the two processors are driven by different quartz crystals, their processing speeds will not be identical. In case a significant external event requires an immediate task preemption, the two processors will most probably be interrupted at different points of their execution sequence. It may even happen that the faster processor has already finished its current task, while the slower one has to execute a few more instructions. Since in this case only the slower task will have to perform a context switch, the state synchronism between the two processors is lost.

Error detection. In an ET architecture the point in time, when a message will be sent, is only known to the sender. Therefore a message loss can only be detected by a bidirectional communication protocol, e.g., of the PAR type. Error detection at the receiver requires an additional mechanism, e.g., a watchdog timer.

5.2 Time triggered systems

In a time-triggered (TT) architecture all system activities are initiated by the progression of time. There is only one interrupt in the system, the periodic clock interrupt, which partitions the continuum of time into a sequence of equidistant granules. The state variables of the control object are observed (polled) at recurring predetermined points in time.

Flow Control. The flow control in a TT-system is *implicit*. During system design appropriate observation, message, and task activation rates are determined for the different state variables of the RT-object, based on their specified dynamics. It has to be assured at design that all receiver processes can handle these rates. If the state variables change faster than specified, then some short lived intermediate states will not be reflected in the observations and will be lost. Yet, even in a peak load situation, the number of messages per unit time, i.e., the message rate, remains constant.

This implicit flow control will only function properly if the instrumentation of a TT-system supports the *state view*. If necessary, a local microcontroller has to store the events that occurred in the last polling cycle and transform them into their state equivalent. Consider the example of a push button, which is a typical *event sensor*. The local logic in this sensor must assure that the state "push button pressed" is true for an interval that is longer than the granularity of the observation grid.

Scheduling. Operating systems for TT-systems are based on a set of static predetermined schedules, one for each operational mode of the system. These schedules gurantee the deadlines of all time-critical tasks, observe all necessary task dependencies and provide an implicit synchronization of the tasks at run time. At run time a simple table lookup is performed by the operating system to determine which task has to be executed at particular points in real time, the grid points of the *action grid* [5]. The difference between two adjacent grid points of the action grid determines the *basic cycle time* of the real-time executive. The basic cycle time is a lower bound for the responsiveness of a TT-system.

In TT-systems all input/output activities are preplanned and realized by polling the appropriate sensors and actuators at the specified times. Access to the LAN is also predetermined, e.g., by a synchronous time division multiple access protocol.

In the MARS system [1], which is a TT-architecture, the gridpoints of the observation grid, the action grid and the access to the LAN are all synchronized with the global time. Since the temporal uncertainty of the communication protocols is smaller than the basic cycle time, the whole system can be viewed as a distributed state machine [8].

Testing for Timeliness. In a TT-system, the results of the performance test of every system task can be compared with the established detailed plans. Since the time-base is discrete and determined by the granularity of the action grid, every input case can be reproduced in the domains of time and value. The temporal encapsulation of the nodes, achieved by the TDMA communication protocol, supports constructive testing.

Replica Determinism. In a TT-system all task switches, mode switches, and communication activities are synchronized globally by the action grid. Nondeterministic decisions can be avoided and replica determinism can be maintained without additional interreplica communication.

The basic cycle time of a TT-system introduces a discrete time base of specified granularity. Since a TT-system operates quasi-synchronously, TMR structures as well as selfchecking duplex nodes can be supported for the implementation of active redundancy without any difficulty.

Error Detection. In a TT-system the error detection is performed by the receiver of the information based on the global knowledge about the expected arrival time of each message. Fault-tolerance can be achieved by massive redundancy, i.e., sending a message k+1 times if k transient failures are to be tolerated.

The periodic transmission of message rounds makes it possible to implement efficient membership protocols in a TT architecture. Such a membership protocol informs sender and receiver about the proper operation of all nodes.

6. Consequences for the software engineer

Many real-time system designs are based on the principle of resource inadequacy[3]. It is assumed that the provision of sufficient resources to handle every possible situation is economically not viable and that an event triggered dynamic resource allocation strategy based on resource sharing and probabilistic arguments about the expected load and fault scenarios is acceptable. We call such systems *best effort systems*. These systems do not require a rigorous specification of the load and fault hypothesis. The design proceeds according to the principle "best effort taken" and the sufficiency of the design is established during the extensive test and integration phase.

At present, the majority of real-time systems is designed according to this best effort paradigm. It is expected that this will change radically in the future. The widespread use of computers in safety critical applications, e.g., in the field of automotive electronics, will raise the public awareness and concern about computer related accidents and force the designer to provide convincing arguments that the design will function properly under all stated conditions. On the other side, the decreasing cost of microelectronic components diminishes the economic necessity for resource sharing.

These developments offer excellent new possibilities for the software engineering community. If a software engineer can start from the specified fault and load hypothesis and can deliver a design that makes it possible to reason about the adequacy of the design without reference to probabilistic arguments, even in the case of the peak load and fault scenario, then we speak of a system with a *guaranteed response*. Guaranteed response systems are based on the principle of resource adequacy, i.e., there are enough computing resources available to handle the specified peak load and the fault scenario. The probability of failure of a perfect system with guaranteed response is reduced to the probability that the assumptions will hold in practice, i.e., the assumption coverage [6].

Considering the present state of understanding and the discussion in the previous sections, guaranteed response systems can only be designed in time triggered (TT) architectures. A consequent development of a software engineering methodology for the design of TT systems will thus have a marked impact on the computer industry.

References

1. Kopetz, H., Zainlinger, R., Fohler, G., Kantz, H., Puschner, P, and Schutz, W.The design of real-time systems: From specification to implementation and verification, Software Engineering Journal, May, 1991, p. 72 - 82

2. Kopetz, H., Kim, K., Temporal Uncertainties in Interactions among Real-Time Objects, Proc. of the 9th IEEE Symp. on Reliable Distributed Systems, Huntsville, Al, Oct. 1990

3. Lawson, H.W., Cy-Clone: An Approach to the Engineering of Resource Adequate Cyclic Real-Time Systems, Journal of Real-Time System, Vol.4, 1992, pp.55-83

4. Mok, A.K., Fundamental design problems of distributed systems for the hard real-time environment, Ph.D. dissertation, M.I.T., 1983

5. Specification and Design for Dependability, Esprit Project Nr. 3092 (PDCS: Predictably Dependable Computing Systems), 1st Year Report, LAAS, Toulouse, 1990

6. Powell, D., Fault Assumptions and Assumption Coverage, PDCS report RB4 (2nd year deliverable 1991) and Report LAAS, Toulouse Nr. 90.074, Dec. 1990

7. Sha, L., Rajkumar, R., Lehoczky, J.P., Priority Inheritence Protocols: An Approach to Real-Time Synchronization, IEEE Transactions on Computers, Vol. 39, No. 9, Sept. 1990, pp. 1175-1185

8. F.B. Schneider, Implementing Fault-Tolerant Services Using the State Machine Approach: A Tutorial, ACM Computing Surveys, Vol 22, Nr. 4, December 1990, pp. 299-320

FEATURES OF PROGRAMMING LANGUAGES

Chair: G. Pomberger

A Comparison of Modula-3 and Oberon-2

Laszlo Böszörmenyi

Institut für Informatik
Universität Klagenfurt
Universitätsstr. 65-67
A-9022 Klagenfurt / Austria

Keywords

Object-oriented programming languages, Modula-3, Oberon-2, Evaluation of software, Comparison of programming languages.

Abstract

Two modern programming languages - *Modula-3* and *Oberon-2* - are compared in respect to the way how they handle module interfaces, type equivalence, subtyping, concurrency and exception-handling. An assessment of the two languages is given discussing the value and cost of every feature.

Introduction

Two new programming languages are compared: Modula-3 [Nelson91] and Oberon-2 [Mössenböck91a, Wirth88]. Both languages are successors of Modula-2 [Wirth82]. Thus, they are quite similar, which makes it easier to compare them, but more difficult to evaluate the differences.

The comparison relys on the following principles: Features which can be implemented without compiler support (e.g., in a module or in a class) should not be incorporated into a language. Even those features should be omitted, which are expensive in the compiler, and could be implemented easily and with an almost full functionality without compiler support. On the other hand, features, which cause high costs in many user programs, should be incorporated into the language, even if it is expensive in the compiler. Features that enhance the safety of large programs should also be incorporated for (almost) any price.

The following comparison tries to concentrate on the *essential* features, which have a major influence on the global *structure* of programs, such as modules, classes, procedures, and processes. Moreover, the type systems of the two languages are compared. The presented features are investigated first of all from the point of their *cost/performance* ratio. *Safety* properties and *understandability* are also considered. An exhaustive comparison of the two languages is beyond the scope of this paper.

Both Modula-3 and Oberon-2 support strong type checking. They both support the notion of a module as the unit of compilation and static encapsulation. Both language support object-oriented programming by providing tools for subclassing with single inheritance. Both languages rely on garbage collection. The most essential differences are in their type systems, i.e., in the way they define type equivalence, abstract data types and inheritance.

Modula-3 is more powerful: it offers some features, which have no counterpart in Oberon-2. The following chapters will compare those features which are available in both languages and will make some cost/performance statements for those features which are only available in Modula-3.

1. Information hiding and module interfaces

Information hiding is one of the most important concepts of modern programming languages. Many object-oriented languages use the notion of a class both for specifying abstract data types and for information hiding [Meyer89]. In these languages the class is the basic unit for software construction, often it is the compilation unit as well.

Modula-3 and Oberon-2 share the notion of a module for information hiding and separate compilation. Modules are static units grouping together closely related data and code. They constitute a syntactical wall against other modules hiding their private data from illegal access. A module may explicitly export names which can then be imported by other modules (clients). The declarations of the exported names make up the interface of a module.

The module was already a central concept of Modula-2, where the interface of a module is given in a so-called definition module and the actual implementation in a corresponding implementation module. The designers of Oberon-2 and Modula-3 have agreed that the solution used in Modula-2 is insufficient. Consequently, the concept has been changed in both languages, and the differences between the two approaches are very instructive.

In Oberon-2 we have no explicit definition module. We write a module and simply mark those identifiers which should be exported, by an export mark (normally a "*"; the mark "-" can be used for read-only export). This solution is not only simple, but even selective. It makes it very easy to make only a part of a structure visible. In the following example

```
MODULE M;
    . . .
TYPE
  Rec* = RECORD
            f1*: INTEGER; f2-: REAL; f3: LONGREAL
         END
    . . .
END M.
```

the field *f1* is accesible in any other module that imports *M*, *f2* is accessible for reading and *f3* is unknown outside *M*.
The interface of a module can be extracted with the help of special tools (this extract may miss - depending on the tool - the original comments), resulting in a pseudo definition module.

In Modula-3, the concept of the explicit interface unit has not been omitted, quite the opposite, it has become more powerful than in Modula-2. In contrast to Modula-2, an interface can be implemented by more than one implementation modules, and an implementation module may export more than one interfaces. The first feature can be used to break a large implementation into several modules. The second feature can be used to distinguish between parts of an interface, e.g., to export one interface for everybody, and a second one only for trusted clients. For hidden and partially hidden types the notion of opaque types is introduced (Modula-2 has the same notion, but with poor semantics). An opaque type is a name that denotes an unknown subtype (see below and [Nelson91]) of some reference type. Different scopes can reveal different information about an opaque type, i.e., there may be several partial revelations and one complete revelation of an opaque type. The complete revelation must be branded (see below); this makes the type unique.

These differences are very typical for the different views (or "paradigms", to say it nicely) behind the two languages. If we look at the implementation cost, it is obvious that Oberon-2's solution is much cheaper for the compiler, because it does not have to check, whether the declarations given in an interface are equivalent with those in the corresponding implementation. In Modula-3, even the linker must be involved, because it has to check whether the impelmentation of an interface is complete and unambiguous. Even at the user's side, on first sight, it seems to be cheaper to just mark some names rather than to write out an explicit interface specification. Oberon-2's solution has a programmer in mind, who explores his data structures and algorithms, and eventually marks those names he believes to be useful for the outer world. This idea works fine in the case of smaller systems. However, in the case of large systems, it is the interfaces which play the central role in the design process, the actual implementations are almost secondary. Therefore, the additional burden, put by the necessity of defining explicit interfaces is an advantage rather than a disadvantage. Modula-3 suggests (almost forces) the programmer to design his/her interfaces separately from the actual implementation. Oberon-2 does not forbid that either, but it is not the implicit suggestion. Programming languages are not just tools for ideally trained programmers; they teach through their implicit suggestions as well.

As a consequence, we may say that the way to sepcify module interfaces in Oberon-2 is efficient and convenient. However, Modula-3 suggests a better style of programming, which - in the case of large systems - may be worth the additional effort, made by the compiler and the user.

2. Types

The most interesting part of the comparison of Modula-3 and Oberon-2 is their type systems.

2.1. Type equivalence

Modula-3 uses *structural equivalence*, Oberon-2 uses *name equivalence* (similar to Modula-2).

Name equivalence in Oberon-2 means that two types are the same, if they are denoted by the same identifier, or if they are declared explicitly to be the same (in the form of T1 = T2). Oberon-2 defines the notion of *equal* types as well in the sense that two types are equal if they are the same, or if they are open array types with equal element types, or procedure types with the same formal parameter list. The latter notion is obviously a kind of structural equivalence, so we can say, Oberon-2 uses mainly name equivalence, and makes an exception for open array and procedure types. (Open arrays were stepchildren already in Modula-2, and they still have an exceptional status in Oberon-2.)

Let us take the following example:

```
TYPE
    T1 = ARRAY 10 OF INTEGER;
    T2 = ARRAY 10 OF INTEGER;
    T3 = T2; T4 = T3;
    O1 = ARRAY OF INTEGER;
    O2 = ARRAY OF INTEGER;
```

In Oberon-2, T1 and T2 are distinct, T2 and T3 are the same (T4 and T2 are hoped to be the same, actually it does not follow necessarily from the definition), and O1 and O2 are equal. It is not so easy to understand, why O1 and O2 are "more equal" than T1 and T2.

Structural equivalence in Modula-3 means that two types are the same if their definition becomes the same when expanded; i.e., if all constant expressions are replaced by their values and all type names are replaced by their definitions. (In the case of recursive types, expansion is defined as the infinite limit of the partial expansions, which is probably not an easily understandable concept.)

To give some examples [Nelson91]:

```
TYPE
  R1 = RECORD a: INTEGER END;
  R2 = RECORD b: INTEGER END;
  List1 = REF RECORD x: INTEGER; link: List1 END;
  List2 = REF RECORD x: INTEGER;
        link: REF RECORD x: INTEGER; link: List2 END;
    END;
```

Types R1 and R2 are different (the type constructor is the same, but the arguments of the type constructor - the name of the record fields - are different). List1 and List2 are the same, because they both lead to the same infinite expansion (and therefore, they both can be reduced to the same canonical form: List1).

The main problem with structural equivalence is that equivalence of the structure of two types may be accidental. For example, if we write

```
TYPE
  Apples  = REF RECORD count: INTEGER END;
  Oranges = REF RECORD count: INTEGER END;
  Fruits  = REF RECORD count: INTEGER END;

PROCEDURE Q(fruit: Fruits) = . . .
PROCEDURE P(apple: Apples) = . . .
```

structural equivalence allows us to call Q with arguments of type Fruits, Apples and Oranges (which is probably desirable), but it also allows us to call P with an argument of type Oranges (which is probably undesirable). The latter problem can be solved in Modula-3 by using branded types. A branded type is unique, regardless of its structural identity with other types. The brand may be a user-defined string, or an implicit unique brand, assigned by the system.

So, we can say that Modula-3 uses structural equivalence which has to be restricted in certain cases and Oberon-2 uses name equivalence which has to be extended in some other cases.

The important question is: which type system is better? In [Nelson91] we find the honest statement that it is lastly a matter of taste. Maybe that's the true answer, but a bit more exact evaluation might be more helpful. Implementing name equivalence in the compiler is obviously much cheaper than implementing structural equivalence (it is trivial to compare two names, but it is non-trivial to compare structures that may be even recursive). However, there are cases, where user programs have to pay a high price if structural equivalence is not available. Many operations are only related to the structure of some data, and in those cases name equivalence is a severe restriction. Another benefit of structural equivalence is that it makes it easier for two programs to exchange data structures (via a file or a network) that are structurally equivalent but not necessarily declared with the same type identifier. The Modula-3 environment allows the programmer to store a data structure of type T1, together with its type information. When the data structure is read into some variable which has the type name T2, it is automatically checked whether the two types are equivalent. The Oberon-2 environment also allows a programmer to store a data structure together with its type name. However, other programs can read this data only into variables with the same type name.

From a didactical point of view, structural equivalence seems to be more natural. On the other hand, structural equivalence combined with opaque and branded types might be more difficult to understand than name equivalence with its few exceptions. As a consequence, we may say that for an undergraduate course, Oberon-2's type equivalence notion can be preferred. However, if we want to consider persistent or remote objects (either in education or in practice), then Modula-3's concept of type equivalence seems to be a good value for its price.

2.2 Classes and inheritence

For object-oriented programming, probably the most important question is: how does a language express classes (abstract data types) and class hierarchies (inheritance)?

Oberon-2 provides *extensible record types* and *type-bound procedures* to express classes with methods. It is interesting to mention that Oberon - the direct predecessor of Oberon-2 - had no type-bound procedures, actually the only language feature for expressing classes was the notion of extensible records. It should be mentioned as well that this very fundamental concept was already sufficient to implement a substantial object-oriented operating system [Wirth89a, Reiser91].

Modula-3 provides the *object* type to express classes with methods. An object is always a reference (if not NIL) to a data record paired with a method suite. If o is an object, f a data field, and m a method of the object, then $o.f$ is a reference to the field f, and $o.m(...)$ is a call on the method m. Object types cannot be dereferenced, i.e., the entire data record cannot be referenced, only the individual fields.

Modula-3 defines a general subtyping rule, which can be applied to several kinds of types. The subtyping relation is denoted by "<:", and the general rule says: If T <: U, then every value of type T is also a value of type U. This rule can be applied to objects, procedures, arrays, references, subranges and packed types.

The declaration and usage of classes in Modula-3 and Oberon-2 is compared in Table 1. (Note that in Modula-3, objects are always references, in Oberon-2, they may be both pointers and records.)

	Oberon-2	Modula-3
	TYPE	TYPE
1	SuperR = RECORD f1: INTEGER END;	- - -
2	SubR = RECORD(SuperR) f2: REAL END;	- - -
3	Super = POINTER TO SuperR;	Super = OBJECT f1: INTEGER END;
4	Sub = POINTER TO SubR;	Sub = Super OBJECT f2: REAL END;
	VAR	VAR
5	superR: SuperR; subR: SubR;	- - -
6	super: Super; sub: Sub;	super: Super; sub: Sub;
	... ...	
7	super:= sub;	super:= sub;
8	sub:= super(Super);	sub:= super;
9	superR:= subR;	- - -
10	subR:= superR(Sub);	- - -
11	IF super IS Sub THEN ...	IF ISTYPE(super, Sub) THEN ...
12	super(Sub).f2:= 1.1;	NARROW(super, Sub).f2:= 1.1;

Table 1.

In Oberon-2, SubR is an *extention* of SuperR (SuperR is the *base* type of SubR) and therefore *inherits* the field f1. SubR adds a new field f2. Pointers take over the extention relation of records, so Sub is also an extention of Super. Extended types can be regarded as subtypes of their base types (which correspond to supertypes in this case).

In Modula-3, Sub is a *subtype* of Super (Super is a *supertype* of Sub). Sub inherits the field f1 and adds the field f2.

A subtype object can be assigned to a supertype variable (lines 7 and 9). In the record assignment (available only in Oberon-2) only the field f1 is assigned (corresponds to a projection of the variable's value onto the subspace spanned by the base type [Wirth89b]). A supertype object can only be assigned to a subtype variable if its run-time type (its dynamic type) is this subtype. This requires a run-time type check which has to be written as an explicit *type guard* in Oberon-2 and is done implicitly in Modula-3 (lines 8 and 10). If this type check fails, a run-time error occurs. Line 11 shows a *type test*. It checks whether the dynamic type of super is Sub. Line 12 shows, how to use fields which are not part of the static type but which belong to the dynamic type - via a type guard in Oberon-2, and via the narrow statement in Modula-3.

Both languages allow to associate operations with objects, i.e., to specify methods (in Oberon-2 they are called type-bound procedures, in Modula-3 they are called methods). The methods associated with a supertype are inherited by the subtype and can be overridden there. Both languages allow to call an overridden method of a supertype (to make a super call). In Modula-3, method names can be even redeclared in a subtype, in which case the original names are masked by the new ones. The old names can, however, be accessed by using *narrow* (which should be better called *broaden* in this case). Redeclaring a method can be used among others to change a method's parameters in the subtype (the parameters of the overriding and the overridden methods must be of course the same). The possibility to both redeclare and override a method is powerful but maybe confusing.

Let us now try to compare the two approaches.

The concept of extended records in Oberon-2 is simple and together with the appropriate rules for assignments, it can be used to express a class hierarchy. The interesting point is that in Oberon-2 subclassing is expressed in terms of "conventional" concepts, i.e., Oberon-2 introduces object-oriented programming in terms of non-object-oriented concepts. However, the lack of an explicit subtyping rule is confusing - to my opinion. The concept of type extension alone is not sufficient to express subclassing. This must be explicitly expressed with the help of the rules of assignments. These are even different for pointer and record variables, because the latter normally do not change their dynamic types, except when they are passed via a *var* parameter - which might be not so easy to understand for undergraduate students.

Modula-3 has a general subtyping rule, and the object type-hierarchy is a natural application of this rule on object types. Therefore, in Modula-3, the assignment rules of objects *follow* from the subtyping rule, while in Oberon-2, subtyping is partly *defined by* the assignment rules. Thus, this issue is better defined in Modula-3. In Modula-3, records, referenced by an object type, do not fall under the subtyping relation, therefore, the rules defining the cases when a variable changes its dynamic type are simpler. The price for the this is that objects are always references. Apart from this difference, the two approaches have about the same power and their implementations should cost about the same.

2.3. Procedures

Both languages support the notion of a procedure. Procedures in Oberon-2 are very similar to procedures in Modula-2 (apart from type-bound procedures). In Modula-3, there are quite a few additional properties of procedures. Besides value and variable parameters, read-only parameters are available as well. Functions may return values of any type but an open array. (Oberon-2 restricts function return types to basic types and pointers.) Formal parameters may have default values which are taken if the corresponding actual parameter is missing. Binding of parameters may be by position or by keyword.

These features can all be implemented efficiently. Read-only parameters can be used to pass larger types efficiently (via a reference). Default parameters can be used to simulate procedures with a variable number of parameters. Restricted function return types are a matter of discussion. In principle, basic types and pointers are sufficient, since a complex type can always be substituted by a pointer. However, this restriction is not only inconvenient for the programmer but also expensive because working with data on the heap is usually more expensive than working with data on the stack.

3. Exceptions

Modula-3 provides exception handling, Oberon-2 does not. In Modula-3, exceptions can be declared (with an optional parameter), they can be raised and can be caught by exception handlers. Raising an exception exits active scopes repeatedly until a scope is found for which an exception handler is declared. If there is no such scope, the computation terminates in some system-dependent way (e.g. by calling the debugger).

An exception can be caught by the TRY statement:

```
TRY
Body
EXCEPT
id1 (v1) => Handler1
| . . .
| idn (vn) => Handlem
ELSE Handler0
END
```

id1 to idn stand for exception names, v1 to vn for parameters of the exceptions.

Exceptions are in dispute, especially because they can be easily misused for masking some errors [Meyer89]. With that point of view, the *else* clause is especially dangerous, because it catches and handles all non-expected errors. This could be extremely bad if an implementation module hides an ill-designed exception handler which simply "swallows" some errors without notifying its clients. Another difficulty with exceptions is that they are often used in a bad style. For example, in the module *Scan* in the SRC library [Harbison92], which exports procedures for reading data in an expected format, e.g. integers, reals etc., the exception *BadFormat* is raised, if the input does not conform to the expected format. This usage of exceptions regards a mistyped user input as an exceptional case - which should be considered rather normal.

Another form of exception handling is used for finalization. In this case, the TRY statement has the form:

```
TRY S1 FINALLY S2 END
```

This statement excutes S1 and after that S2 even if an exception was raised in S1. After executing S2 the exception is propagated to the enclosing scopes to be caught by an exception handler there. This kind of try statement construct can be used for finalization (e.g. closing files) in the case of errors. It can enhance the safety of programs considerably.

The question is again, is it worthwile to burden the compiler with exception handling? An ill-designed exception handling system could confuse everything by ignoring errors that shouldn't be ignored or by handling them at the wrong place. On the other hand, the lack of exception handling can easily lead to systems which react to exceptional cases in an extremely rigid way. Compiler support for exception handling is worth its price, if a fast reaction on errors is required, or if the loss of data (e.g. loss of files that could not be closed by a crashed program) is critical.

4. Concurrency

Oberon-2 does not provide any special support for concurrency, Modula-3 provides the data type *mutex* and the *lock* statement to support concurrency. Moreover, a standard library module is available that provides threads.

It is interesting to look at the way how concurrency is supported in the Modula family of languages. The original Modula language [Wirth77] still had the concept of concurrent processes, of mutual exclusion and a slightly modified version of Hoare's monitor concept. These concepts were replaced in Modula-2 by the more fundamental concept of coroutines. In Modula-2, a coroutine is a procedure that can be started as a quasi-parallel process with explicit points of control transfer. Thus, Modula-2 threw some concepts out of the language and expressed them in terms of others (coroutines are expressed in terms of procedures). Beside the theoretical beauty, the solution of Modula-2 gives entire freedom in writing schedulers, without forcing any given concept (e.g. that of the monitor) on the user. The price for this freedom is the loss of language support for expressing parallel concepts, which is quite a high price.

Regarding this history it is not too surprising that in Oberon-2 all support for concurrency has been moved from the language to a module providing coroutines. This is especially understandable if we consider the Oberon operating system, which uses a very special approach to support multi-tasking without multi-processing [Wirth89a].

Now, let us compare the costs. The Oberon implementation has obviously no costs at all. In Modula-3, the actual costs in the compiler are quite low, since the language supports only the mutex type and the lock statement. Mutex is an opaque subtype of *root* - the root of all objects. As a consequence, we can declare additional object types which are subtypes of mutex. This way to define objects for which mutual exclusion is necessary, is not only a convenient but also an efficient way.

The semantics of the lock statement is defined as follows. If S is a statment, we may write:

```
VAR m: MUTEX
...
LOCK m DO S END.
```

The lock statement is equivalent to:

```
Thread.Acquire(m);
TRY S FINALLY Thread.Release(m) END
```

Thread.Acquire(m) and Thread.Release(m) are procedures exported by the Thread interface [Nelson91] and do what their names suggest; Aquire locks m (waits if the lock is already held) and Release unlocks it. The essential part of the story is the way how Release is used. The *finally* part of the try statement is executed even if S fails. Thus, even erronous programs can use the locking feature safely. This kind of safety can hardly be achieved without language support.

Let us consider another example:

```
LOOP
...
LOCK m DO
...
IF b THEN EXIT END
(*EXIT raises the exit-exception and jumps to the statement after the END of LOOP*)
...
END (*LOCK*)
...
END (*LOOP*)
```

A loop statement (LOOP S END) executes S repeatedly until the exit-exception is raised. As a consequence, in the above example, the exit-exception forces the call of Thread.Release, and m will be unlocked. This is another example of how to get safer and simpler user programs for a moderate price in the compiler.

Coming back to the comparative question, we may state that the lack of any support for concurrency in Oberon-2 is only acceptable if we really do not need concurrency. The solution of Modula-3 is efficient and moderate and, therefore, is worth its price. However, Modula-3 supports concurrency adapting an implicit model of communication - via a common store. It is an open question at the moment, which language could provide a better support for a distributed memory model.

5. Additional features of Modula-3

5.1. Modified features from Modula-2

Some features that are unsatisfactory in Modula-2, are omitted in Oberon-2 and redefined in a clean way in Modula-3.

The type *cardinal*. Cardinals were introduced in Modula-2 with poor semantics (e.g., they are assignment-compatible but not expression-compatible with integers). In Modula-3, cardinal is defined as a subrange of integer (which is a clean notion).

Subranges. Modula-2 subranges are not quite clean either (they follow a special type equivalence rule). In the elegant solution of Modula-3, the subtyping rule is applied to them.

Enumerations. Identifiers of a Modula-2 enumeration list may cause name clashes if the enumeration type is imported. In Modula-3, the identifiers of an enumeration list must be qualified by the name of the enumeration type.

5.2. New features in Modula-3

The following list contains a number of Modula-3 features, which are neither available either in Modula-2 nor in Oberon-2.

Initialization of variables. Variables can be initialized at their declaration. This feature is especially useful in the case of arrays and records.

Generics. In a generic interface or module, some of the imported interface names are treated as formal parameters, to be bound to actual interfaces when the generic module is instantiated.

Isolation of unsafe code. In unsafe modules low-level programming features are available, as explicit storage disposal or unchecked type transfer.

6. Implementation

It is a difficult question, to which extent actual implementations should be considered, when comparing languages. Implementability surely has to be considered, but probably not actual implementations. However, it must be stated that at the time being, there is a specific difference between the implementations of Oberon-2 and Modula-3.

Oberon-2 has an extremely fast compiler, integrated into a convenient programming environment. Modula-3 has a slow compiler with some modest support, embedded in a not very friendly environment.

This difference could be regarded as a temporary prove that the design of Oberon-2 is superior. It is noteworthy to mention that the design process of the Oberon-2 language started with the absolute minimum considered [Wirth88], and later, on the basis of experiences, some further features (e.g. type-bound procedures) were added. The opposite approach - first provide more features than necessary, and select the necessary ones later - has no chance to succeed. If a feature is introduced into a language, one can be sure that some people will use it and find it indispensable.

If a better Modula-3 implementation will be available soon, which allows for an efficient use of the more powerful features of this language, we may hope that users will be able to choose between the two languages on the basis of their needs and not on the basis of the availability of appropriate implementations.

Conclusion

There is a continuously growing need for evaluating programming languages (and other software designs as well). However, there are no exact methods to do that, programmers prefer to speak about their "favorite" languages, which is a sign for the "subject-oriented" approach, used in selecting programming languages. In this paper, an attempt was made to compare and evaluate two programming langugaes in a fairly objective manner, with moderate efforts. Two modern languages, Modula-3 and Oberon-2, were compared. Both languages were found to be clean and consistent. Oberon-2 generally takes the simpler way, Modula-3 is more powerful and more expensive. As a consequence, Oberon-2 fits better for small programs and undergraduate courses, Modula-3 fits better for large programs (possibly in a distributed environment) and for teaching more advanced features.

Acknowledgements

My thanks go to H. Mössenböck, J. Templ, H. Eberle, G. Nelson, M. Jordan, B. Kalsow and R. Mittermeir for many inspiring discussions.

References

[Harbison92]   S. P. Harbison: *Modula-3*; Prentice-Hall, Englewood Cliffs, NJ, 1992

[Nelson91]   Greg Nelson et al.: *Systems Programming with Modula-3;* Prentice Hall, Englewood Cliffs, NJ. 1991

[Meyer89]   From Structured Programming to Object-Oriented Design: *The Road to Eifel;* Structured Programming Vol.10, No.1 1989

[Mössenböck91a] H. Mössenböck, N. Wirth: *The Programming Language Oberon-2;* Structured Programming Vol.12, No.4 1991

[Mössenböck91b] H. Mössenböck: *Object-Oriented Programming in Oberon-2*; 2nd International Modula-2 Conference; Loughborough, September, 1991

[Reiser91]   M. Reiser: *The Oberon System;* User Manual and Programmer's Guide Addison-Wesley, 1991

[Wirth77]   N. Wirth: *Modula - A language for Modular Multiprogramming;* Software Practice and Experience, Vol.7, No.1, 1977

[Wirth82]   N. Wirth: *Programming in Modula-2;* Springer Verlag, 1982

[Wirth88]   N. Wirth: *The Programming Language Oberon*; Software Practice and Experience, Vol.18, No.7, 1988

[Wirth89a]   N. Wirth J. Gutknecht: *The Oberon System;* Software Practice and Experience, Vol.19, No.9, 1989

[Wirth89b]   N. Wirth: *Modula-2 and Object-Oriented Programming;* Proc. of the First International Modula-2 Conference; Bled, Yugoslavia, 1989.

Appendix

As a matter of interest, two simplified versions of a generic binary tree are given, implemented in Oberon-2 and in Modula-3. The tree is generic; it does not make any assumption about the type of the search keys. The Oberon-2 version was designed by H.P. Mössenböck, the Modula-3 version by the author.

The Oberon-2 version consists of a single module, the exported identifiers are marked (by * or -):

```
MODULE BinTree;  (* HM 11.6.91 *)

  TYPE
    Node* = POINTER TO NodeDesc;
    NodeDesc* = RECORD
      left, right: Node
    END;

    Tree* = RECORD root: Node END;

  PROCEDURE (x: Node) less* (y: Node): BOOLEAN;  (*abstract method*)
  END less;
  PROCEDURE (x: Node) equal* (y: Node): BOOLEAN;  (*abstract method*)
  END equal;

  PROCEDURE (VAR t: Tree) Insert* (n: Node);
    VAR p, father: Node;
  BEGIN p := t.root; father := NIL;
    WHILE p # NIL DO
      IF p.equal(n) THEN RETURN END;
      father := p;
      IF n.less(p) THEN p := p.left ELSE p := p.right END
    END;
    n.left := NIL; n.right := NIL;
    IF father = NIL THEN t.root := n
    ELSIF n.less(father) THEN father.left := n
    ELSE father.right := n
    END
  END Insert;

  PROCEDURE (VAR t: Tree) Init*;
  BEGIN t.root := NIL
  END Init;

END BinTree.
```

The Modula-3 version consists of an interface and an implementation. The types *PublicNode* and *PublicTree* are entirely revealed in the interface. The methods in *PublicNode* are deferred [Meyer]: they must be overriden by the user, otherwise an exception is raised. *Tree* and *Node* are revealed in the impelementation module.

```
INTERFACE BinTree;  (*LB 30.01.92*)

  TYPE
    Node  <: PublicNode;
    Tree  <: PublicTree;

    PublicNode = OBJECT
        METHODS
          less (y: Node): BOOLEAN; (*abstract method*)
          equal (y: Node): BOOLEAN; (*abstract method*)
        END;

    PublicTree =  OBJECT
        METHODS
          init ();
          insert (n: Node);
        END;

END BinTree.
```

```
MODULE BinTree;  (*LB 30.01.92*)

  TYPE
    REVEAL Node = PublicNode BRANDED OBJECT
          left, right: Node;
        END;

    REVEAL Tree = PublicTree BRANDED OBJECT
          root: Node;
          OVERRIDES
            init:= InitTree;
            search:= Search;
            insert:= Insert;
        END;

  PROCEDURE Insert(t: Tree; n: Node) =
  VAR father: Node := NIL; p: Node := t.root;
  BEGIN
    WHILE p # NIL DO
      IF p.equal(n) THEN RETURN END;
      father:= p;
      IF n.less(p) THEN p:= p.left ELSE p:= p.right END;
    END; (*WHILE*)
    n.left:= NIL; n.right:= NIL;
    IF father = NIL THEN t.root:= n
    ELSIF n.less(father) THEN father.left:= n
    ELSE father.right:= n
    END
  END Insert;

  PROCEDURE InitTree(t: Tree) =
  BEGIN
    t.root:= NIL
  END InitTree;
BEGIN
END BinTree.
```

Discrete event simulation in object oriented languages

Gy. Gyepesi, T. Szép, F. Jamrik, G. Janek, E. Knuth

Computer and Automation Institute
Hungarian Academy of Sciences
H-1519 POB. 63, Budapest

Abstract. Those who remember SIMULA 67, the grandmother of object oriented languages, know that it contained powerful and elegant mechanisms for the control of quasi-parallel processes and a high level technique for discrete event management based on the concept of an abstract time axis. Surprisingly, none of the modern object oriented languages implemented these particularly useful concepts. This paper presents an approach how two of the leading object oriented languages C++ and (a dialect of) Smalltalk have been extended to incorporate such mechanisms.

1. Introduction

As it is known, the language SIMULA [9] (formerly called SIMULA 67) played a pioneering role in the advent of object oriented technologies. Though it lacked some of the important modern concepts like polimorphism and encapsulation, however, it contained a particularly effective concept the discrete time oriented quasi-parallel behaviour, never again implemented by other object oriented languages.

The fundamental notion in SIMULA is the abstract time axis which transparently and dynamically controls the scheduling of all process objects of the system (amongst them the user program as a whole too). To implement this behaviour, SIMULA used a special version of basic quasi-parallel control primitives. Of course, the higher level behaviour and the language formalisms associated can also be built over any other known parallel or parallel engines (like the ones given in papers [Ghezzi 85, Muhlbeim 88, PARLE 87, Ruppelt 89, Thomas 87]).

The following paragraphs summarize the concepts used by the SIMULA language.

1.1. Quasi-parallel sequencing

This concept offers a low-level control mechanism enabling us to suspend the execution sequence of statements at certain points in class bodies in such a way that a) the whole environment is preserved and; b) the control can at any time be resumed again. At a given moment any number of suspended execution sequences (in object instances) can coexist. Suspended objects can later be resumed by sending them a "resume" message from any other object (that is they are awakened explicitly, in contrast to the way explained in 1.2).

Statements implementing this behaviour in SIMULA are denoted as *detach, resume(object)*, and *call(object)*. They are accessible for the users, though normally they are not used explicitly. The main purpose of these procedures is providing a basis for the discrete time oriented behaviour of processes as described in the next point.

1.2. The time axis

Historically, the simulation of discrete event based parallel processes was the basic paradigm SIMULA addressed (and solved, in fact, in a far more elegant way than its competitors like GPSS [3], and SIMSCRIPT [Johnson 72]). It invented a more general concept, nowadays called "object orientation" by chance.

The main concept of SIMULA for discrete time oriented behaviour is the class *process*. Instances of this class (i.e. process objects) can be scheduled dynamically in a simulated time axis (called the *sequencing set*). The real fun starts when the main program (by convention, a process object too) suspends itself. At this point the time axis gains control and governs all further behaviour. Processes schedule continuations of themselves (or of other processes) for given time points dynamically at the time axis. These continues until no further events are scheduled.

More exactly, the behaviour based on the time axis is implemented by the following main commands:

hold(interval)
> The process issuing this command is suspended. When the time interval specified is elapsed (in simulated time), the process is resumed automatically.

passivate
> The process issuing this command is suspended, but not scheduled for reactivation. (Passive processes can only be activated by other processes in an explicit way.)

activate process *at/delay* time
> By this command processes can schedule (or reschedule) the activation time of other processes. The clause "at" refers to (simulated) absolute time points, while "delay" refers to relative ones.

cancel process
> Cancel the scheduling of a given process (if exists).

There are several other useful commands available, but not detailed here.

1.3. An example

The above concepts can well be illustrated by the following beautiful example (published by the University of Oslo many years ago, nevertheless it does nothing with simulation indeed). It is perhaps the most elegant prime number generator available in the literature. The whole program looks like as follows:

```
1:      begin
2:      process class prime(p); integer p;
3:      begin print(p);
4:        while true do begin
5:          if nextev.evtime-time>2
6:          then activate new prim(time+2) delay 2;
7:          hold(2*p);
8:      end end;
9:      activate new prime(3) at 3;
10:     hold(limit);
11:     end;
```

The algorithm prints (for simplicity, only the odd) prime numbers until the number "limit", and works as follows. Line 9 creates the first prime (prime 3) and schedules its activation at simulated time 3. Line 10 suspends the main program (until the limit is reached in simulated time) and passes control to the time axis. Since there is only one event scheduled at this moment (prime 3 at time 3), the time advances to 3 and prime 3 gains control (gets resumed, activated).

Prime 3 prints the number 3 according to line 3. An "infinite" loop begins then. First it is checked if the next scheduled event is farther than two units. (In fact, this is the essence of the algorithm. If not, the number time+2 is not a prime, as it will be obvious later.) Now the only further event is the main program scheduled at "limit" which we suppose is far enough. Therefore a new prime namely prime 5 is generated and scheduled at 3+2. Prime 3 is suspended then for a period of 2*3, that is it will continue - its own filtering work - at time 9.

After time 3, the next event prime 5 gains control at time 5. Since the next event (prime 3 at time 9) is farther than 2 units, it will generate a new prime, the prime 7, and the process continues. All the generated new prime processes advance filtering then in parallel.

The essence of the algorithm is a careful and elegant balance of control. Though the parallel processes proliferate, however, only those events are scheduled which are really needed for the temporal decision whether the next odd number is prime or not. This results in a particular efficiency in addition to beauty of the program.

2. The "Yarn" model

Below we introduce a model which can generally be used as a basis to implement quasi parallel behaviour in a variety of modern languages. We will use common terminologies of object oriented languages (like class, method, message, descendant, object, receiver, etc.) without explaining them.

Yarn

This phrase will refer to parallel branches in our model. Yarns are created by a special message which duplicates the creating branch (its local environment). Methods needed to implement the quasi parallel behaviour will be defined in a generic class named Yarn. The user code of a particular quasi parallel process is to be given by the method named *body* in a descendant class of Yarn. This way, any number of coexisting user processes can be created.

stitch

On creating a new branch the old one still keeps the control. The control can actually be passed by the special method "stitch(branch)".

back

A branch always remember the one activated it. The control can be given back by the method "back". (The method "stitch" can also be used for the same purpose.) On terminating a branch, the "back" method is automatically invoked.

Parallel branches can also communicate by the control passing methods. For this purpose parametric versions of them named *istitch* and *iback* are provided too. The parameter used can be of any object (except a Yarn one).

For more details of the exact behaviour and for additional methods introduced we refer to the technical definition of Yarn [Szep 92].

3. Extending the Actor system

3.1. The Actor language

The Actor language and environment [Franz 90] (trade mark of The WhiteWater Group, Evanston, Illinois, USA) is a true SMALLTALK [10] dialect. It differs only in certain notations and implementation techniques both for efficiency reasons. In fact, presently, Actor is the only professional SMALLTALK-type development environment for MS WINDOWS [5]. For this reason, we chose Actor as the basis for our extensions.

Like SMALLTALK, Actor is based on the message sending paradigm. Actor's general notation is the following:

    message(receiver, arguments)

3.2. Implementation of Yarn in Actor

A single class named Yarn implements all the required behaviour. The Actor version of Yarn is based on a stack-saving technique. For efficiency reasons, only the part the stack which is used in the parallel work is duplicated. (Special tools are available to set or adjust its level.) The basic stack-saving methods are implemented on a binary level, and are not available for the users. On loading the Yarn extension of Actor, all the necessary binary adjustments are done automatically.

3.3. Methods implemented

The following methods are provided to realize the functionality defined in the Yarn model:

Def back(YarnClass)
Def iback(YarnClass,arg)
    Return control to the calling branch.

Private body(Yarn,arg)
    Dummy at the generic level. Must not be called explicitly.

Def close(YarnClass)
    Terminate and delete all branches except the main one.

Def close(Yarn)
    Terminate a particular branch.

Def fibre(YarnClass)
    Returns the currently active branch.

Def from(Yarn)
    Returns the branch which activated the current one by "stitch" or "istitch" (but not by "back" or "iback").

Def stitch(Yarn)
Def istitch(Yarn,arg)
    Transfer control to the body of the receiver branch.

Def main(YarnClass)
    Returns the main branch. This contains the original Actor environment and can not be terminated.

Def new(YarnClass)
    Create a new parallel branch.

Def state(Yarn)
    Return the current state of a branch. Possible values are: #active, #inactive, #terminated.

3.4. Example

All collection objects in Actor posses a *do* method having a block argument. On sending a "do" to any collection, the argument is executed for each of its elements. (This technique is elegant and particularly useful when members of the collection are not addressable directly like in cases of sets and trees.)

Unfortunately, the "do" can be sent to a single collection only. In many cases, it would be useful to traverse structures in parallel (like comparing or copying them). Using the Yarn technique, parallel versions of "do" methods can easily be defined however. An example is provided with Yarn which looks like:

parDo(Yarn,anArray,aBlock)

Parallel *do*. The array argument can be any array of collection objects. For instance, we can send the method in the following way:

parDo(Yarn, tuple(aTree1, aTree2), aBlock);

Now, if our purpose is to find the number of differences between the trees given, the argument block can be defined as:

```
aBlock :=
{ using(pair)
  if pair[0] <> pair[1]
  then differences := differences + 1
  endIf
}
```

(We note that this version of parDo terminates if any of the collections traversed are exhausted. For different behaviour, the user can define a private parDo in any other way.)

4. Simulation technique in Actor

Based on the methods of Yarn a discrete event oriented layer is also built. The corresponding simulation methods are given in three classes:

4.1. The Process class

This class is defined as a descendant of Yarn. Therefore, its time-controlled behaviour should be described in its "body" method. Special methods available are the following:

Def activateAt(Process,time)
Def activateAtPrior(Process,time)
Def activateDelay(Process,interval)
Def activateDelayPrior(Process,interval)

Schedule the activation/reactivation time of the receiver process at the given time or after the given interval. Prior schedules it as the first event at the given time point.

Def activate(Process)
Def activateBefore(Process,aProcess)
Def activateAfter(Process,aProcess)

Schedule with respect to another process on its activation time. The direct form "activate" means: after "current".

Def passivate(Process)

Stop the execution of the process (self) without terminating. Transfer control to the hidden time-control mechanism. (Passivated processes can then be activated by other ones.)

Def hold(Process,interval)
> Suspends self for the specified period. (Schedules self at the time point current time + interval; and passivates self then).

Def wait(Process,EventQueue)
> A useful utility which passivates the process and also adds it to an ordered collection (a queue - a typical one in simulation applications).

Def time(ProcessClass)
> Returns the current value of the simulated time (as real).

Def current(ProcessClass)
> Returns the process object currently possessing the control.

Def activity(Process)
> This is the name of the method to be used to describe the body of the user process. Dummy at the generic level.

Def status(Process)
> Returns the status of the process. Possible values are: #scheduled, #passive, #terminated.

Def cancel(Process)
> Removes the scheduling notice of the receiver process.

Def evtime(Process)
> Returns the time point (as real) at which the receiver is scheduled.

4.2. MainProcess

As a descendant of Process with a different body method, it serves to store the main simulation program. The only additional method provided is:

Def simulation(MainProcess)
> Start the simulation.

4.3. The time axis

The time axis is simulated by the class named *SequencingSet* which is defined as a descendant of the Actor class OrderedCollection. It has no public methods. Once the "simulation" method is sent to the MainProcess, the SequencingSet governs all the control needed for the model.

4.4. Example

The following example is a simplified outline for a traffic simulation where cars arrive at a traffic light and wait in a queue until it is green. (For more exact description of the example we refer to [4].)

```
inherit(MainProcess,#TrafficSimulation,#(#queue,#lamp));
Def activity(self)
{ queue:=new(EventQueue,1);
  activate(lamp:=new(TrafficLamp));
  activate(new(CarGenerator));
  hold(self,limit);
}


inherit(Process,#CarGenerator,#(#no))
Def activity(self)
{ no:=0;
  loop while true begin
    no:=no+1;
    activate(new(Car),no);
    hold(self,random);
  endloop;
}


inherit(Process,#Car,#(no))
Def activity(self,n)
{ no:=n;
  hold(self,random);
  if size(queue)>0 or not(green(lamp))
  then
    wait(self,queue);
    continue(self)
  endif;
}


inherit(Process,#TrafficLamp,#(#green))
Def activity(self)
{ loop while true
  begin
    hold(self,random);
    green:=not(green);
    if green
    then
      activate(first(queue));
    endif;
  end;
}
```

5. Implementation in C++

The C++ implementation of both Yarn and Simulation is fundamentally the same as above, here, however, these are adapted to the different nature and style of the whole environment. Main differences are as follows:

a) The C++ version of Yarn is implemented by the stack-changing technique. It means that for each parallel branch a new stack is allocated from the Windows global heap. This leads to a different stack initialization technique (required to be tailored by the user, - not detailed here).

b) Since the C++ development environment is not interactive (in the way as Smalltalk), a couple of methods are not needed, however, a special technique is necessary to handle program termination.

Some of the most important methods implemented are the following:

static LPvoid back();
static LPvoid iback(LPvoid par);
Transfers control back to the one called the current.

virtual LPvoid body(LPvoid par) = 0;
Abstract method for the user body. All descendants must define it concretely.

static void exit(int status);
Equivalent to the standard "exit", but attempts to return to the main branch.

static LPvoid stitch(Yarn& dest);
static LPvoid istitch(Yarn& dest,LPvoid par);
Quasi parallel version of transferring the control. Returns when the control is returned from the called branch.

Further available methods are similar to those given for the Actor version. The simulation layer is also elaborated for the C++ case, this, however, is not detailed here.

6. Conclusions

A new technique with corresponding tools has been presented for MS Windows application programming consisting of two self-contained layers, one for pure quasi parallel programming, the other for a simulated time-controlled behaviour of processes built of discrete events. Quasi parallel programming is a reasonable alternative of the real parallel one for problems containing parallel components in nature. The simulation layer provides the forgotten special power of the SIMULA language in modelling the interaction of discrete processes.

The tools experimentally developed are now available for MS Windows 3.0 with Actor version 3.0 or 3.1, with Borland C++ 2.0 or 3.0 (moreover for Turbo Pascal for Windows too, - not detailed in the paper).

References

1. Franz, M. Object-Oriented Programming Featuring Actor. Scott, Foresman IBM Computer Books, USA, 1990.

2. Ghezzi, C. Concurrency in Programming Languages: A Survey. Parallel Computing 2(3), pp229-241, 1985.

3. GPSS, General Purpose Simulation System V, User Manual, IBM Corporation, 1991.

4. Johnson, G.D. SIMSCRIPT II.5. User's Manual, Release 6, C.A.C.I. 1972.

5. Microsoft Windows, version 3.0. Microsoft Corporation, 1991.

6. Muhlbeim, H. et al. MUPPET: A programming environment for message-based multiprocessors. Parallel Computing 8, pp201-221, 1988.

7. PARLE. Proc. Parallel Architectures and Languages Europe. Eidhoven, The Netherlands, Lecture Notes in Comp. Sci. Springer, 1987.

8. Ruppelt, Th., Wirtz, G. Automatic transformation of high-level object oriented specification into parallel programs. Parallel Computing 10, pp15-28, 1989.

9. SIMULA Standard. Simula Standards Group, Oslo, Norway. 1989..

10. Smalltalk-80. Byte Magazine, August, 1981.

11. Szep, T. Technical reference for Yarn (in Hungarian). Hungarian Academy of Sciences, Budapest, 1992.

12. Thomas, I. Object oriented programming on transputers. Proc. BCS Workshop on Parallel and Distributed Object Oriented Programming, 1987.

OBJECT-ORIENTED SOFTWARE DEVELOPMENT

Chair: P. Hanak

150

An Approach to the Classification of Object-Based Parallel Programming Paradigms

Georg Pigel
Institut für Statistik und Informatik
Abteilung für angewandte Informatik
Universität Wien
Lenaug. 2/8
1080 Wien, Austria

Abstract

This paper tries to present a classification scheme for object-based concurrent paradigms. Based on the discussion how concurrency is introduced into a system a classification scheme will be presented and applied on examples. Then the classification will be refined and corresponding features of our example systems discussed. In the end a summary will be presented and an outlook on further research will be given.
Keywords: Object-based, concurrency, classification.

1 Introduction

Creating software systems is a task proposing high demands on the developer's intellectual skills and creativity. Programming was thought to be an art for a long time, and it took until the mid-seventies to develop widely accepted software engineering techniques. But these techniques were not able to cope with the ever increasing demands on today's software. Especially high maintenance costs, missing concepts for reusability, and enormous difficulties in creating portable software together with the rise of new user interaction techniques (GUIs) and an increasing demand for distributed and parallel programming lead to the wish for new software development paradigms. So the new software development paradigm of "object-orientedness"* was born. The arguments for the use of object-oriented programming concepts stated by different authors are manyfold:

- Object-orientedness catches the whole world, consisting of data and functional aspects. It was claimed that functional decomposition (e. g. structured analysis [Gane 79]) only can catch the half of the real world, that consists of functional aspects. Data modelling (e. g. entity-relationship diagrams [Bach 73]) can describe the "data half" of the real world very well, but lacks of descriptive power of the functional aspects. Doing data modelling and functional decomposition in parallel leads to inconsistencies between the different documents produced as results, due

---

*As the definitions of object-oriented, class-based, and object-based are given some sections below, I will use object-oriented where I mean object-based, as it is the more known word, whereas the term "object-based" could spread confusion about its meaning.

to the different views of the world, thus opening a gap which sometimes becomes nearly unbridgeable and containing severe impacts on software quality [Coad 90].

- In [Cox 87] it is stated that bulk is bad. Long programs are harder to write, to debug, to maintain and to understand and reuse. With object-oriented techniques one can produce shorter programs, that are therefore easier to debug, maintain and reuse.

- Similarly it is claimed in [Cox 87] that "surface area" is bad. With "surface area" it is meant, what the programmer needs to know about a piece of code if he wants to use it. The concepts of information hiding, abstraction and the message passing mechanism contained in object-oriented systems make it not necessary to know anything about the implementation of an object, i. e. objects have well defined, clean interfaces. The programmer only needs to know a small "surface area" when using existing code.

Creating systems containing parallelism is even more complex than creating sequential systems. First of all not only shorter or longer pieces of sequential code (dependent on the grain of parallelism exploited in the system) have to be correct, but also the additional complexity of entities communicating in a practically unpredictable sequence has to be taken into account. There is a couple of reasons, why concepts related to object-oriented systems could help coping with this additional complexity:

- Thinking in terms of objects helps the developer to understand the problem space better, and therefore makes it easier to exploit the parallelism inherent to a certain application.

- Objects lend themselves to define the grain of parallelism to be exploited in the system. Of course it often is usefull to exploit parallelism inside an object to improve performance, but this does not add to the overall complexity, if this concurrency is strictly hidden from the outside, with objects seen as selfcontaining entities.

- As communication patterns were found to be the most important feature to classify parallel algorithms [Levi 87] [Nels 87] [Babb 87], the fact, that communication via message passing is an essential part of the object-oriented paradigm, and has not to be added in a more, but often less natural way makes this paradigm even more suited.

Parallel programming is most often motivated as being the most natural way of improving performance of a problem solution. But performance is one of the not-so-good points of current state of the art object-oriented environments.[†]

2 Examples for Object-Based Parallel Programming Paradigms

In the last years numerous programming languages and paradigms for object-oriented concurrent programming were introduced. The need to find out common trends or differences between those ideas, but also to gain a sound basis for comparing the different ideas, leads to the neccessity of a classification of the introduced models.

Due to lack of space, we will restrict ourselves to five widely known models for object-oriented concurrent programming. We will introduce them shortly and then we will use these models in the remaining part of this paper to demonstrate how to apply our scheme of classification.

[†]Interpretation instead of compiling, automatic garbage collection and late binding are the most power consuming features found in most object-oriented systems.

2.1 Actors

As there is a wide range of actor-based languages [Lieb 87] [Atta 87] [DiSa 91] [Loya 91] we have chosen to discuss the implementation independent basic concepts behind Actors as described in [Agha 89] [Agha 86].

Actors are computational agents, distributed in time and space. Each actor has a *mail address* and a *behaviour*. An actor can influence the actions of another actor by sending it (or itself) a message. To send a message, the mail address of the receipent must be known to the sender. In the actor model buffering of messages is provided, leading to asynchronous communication. Actors can be created dynamically. The state of an actor is defined by its *behaviour*. An actor is able to compute a *replacement behaviour*. Actors never change their behaviour (this is similar to the "singles assignment rule" known from dataflow languages), but create new actors with these newly computed replacement behaviours.

2.2 Smalltalk-80

As Smalltalk-80 is probably the most known object-oriented laguage, we will reference to [Gold 83] for a detailed language description and only explain how Smalltalk-80 handles parallelism. Without going into any details, it can be said, that concurrency is obtained in Smalltalk-80 by sending a *fork* message to a block context. In the following example, taken from [Yoko 87], after sending a *fork* message part (i) and part (ii) are executed concurrently .

```
/t1/
.....
[...(i)...]fork.
....(ii)....
.....
```

In the example $t1$ is a common variable. Mutual exclusion must be done explicitly by the methods which want to use the object using semphores. Semaphores are provided by a class *Semaphore*. This leads to a distributed form of control of synchronization which is hard to develop and debug, and a bit contrary to seeing objects as self contained entities. Messages have the semantic of function calls, i. e. the sender sends a message and is blocked until it receives a return value. Smalltalk-80 has been critisized because its extension to concurrency reminds more on conventional languages as *Parallel Fortran*, not fitting well into the object-oriented world. For details see [Gold 83].

2.3 ConcurrentSmalltalk

ConcurrentSmalltalk [Yoko 87] was developed on the basis of Smalltalk-80, but although one of the primary goals of its implementation was to keep binary code compatability to Smalltalk-80, there are certain differences. ConcurrentSmalltalk has objects as grain of parallelism. There are two kinds of message-passing mechanisms: *Synchronous method calls* which are compatible to Smalltalk-80 message passing. *Asynchronous method calls*, which have no equivalent in Smalltalk-80, allow the sender to continue working without waiting for the receiver to reply. Asynchronous method calls return a *CBox* to the sender. The return value of the object which received an asynchronous method call is buffered in the CBox until the caller retrieves the value. If the calling object tries to retrieve a return value not delivered yet, it is blocked. Therefore CBoxes also can be seen as a synchronization mechanism. For compatibility reasons to Smalltalk-80 shared variables are supported. As the mechanism of shared variables is contrary to the basic idea that an object is a selfcontained entity their use should be avoided. In ConcurrentSmalltalk there is no concurrency inside an object.

2.4 DistributedConcurrentSmalltalk

DistributedConcurrentSmalltalk is the extension of DistributedSmalltalk to a distributed interpersonal environment [Naka 89]. In DistributedConcurrentSmalltalk there can be multiple threads inside an object, differently to ConcurrentSmalltalk. These threads have to synchronize internally inside the objects by using guarded commands.

2.5 HOOD Nets

HOOD nets, as described in [Giov 90], are no programming language but a design paradigm. "HOOD (Hierarchical Object Oriented Design) is the standard ESA (European Space Agency) method for the architectural design phase of the Software Life Cycle" [Giov 90]. Details on HOOD can be found in [HOOD 89a] [HOOD 89b]. HOOD nets are based on the Petri net formalism, exactly said on high-level Petri nets [Genr 91] [Jens 91]. HOOD nets are normally used for developing systems implemented with ADA. Nevertheless they are programming language independent. HOOD objects consist of a public interface and an internal implementation (as is normal in object oriented concepts). A HOOD design document is a tree. A complex object can be splitted into several child objects of less complexity. Objects are re-entrantable, that means that synchronization mechanisms for conflicting methods inside an object must be provided. The control flow of the system is modelled by a OPeration Control Structure (OPCS). An OPCS net can be seen as a sequence of net blocks. Net blocks can be invoked iteratively, alternatively or in parallel.

3 Basic Features of Object-Based Concurrent Systems

Having introduced our example paradigms, it is time to define the basic terms, following the definitions in [Wegn 90] as far as possible. The definitions 1,2,3 and 4 are directly adapted from [Wegn 90].

Definition 1 (Object-Based Systems) *Object-based systems are systems whose basic entities are build on the concepts of consisting of data plus methods communicating via a message passing mechanism.*

Definition 2 (Class-Based Systems) *Class-based systems are object-based systems where each object belongs to a class.*

Definition 3 (Object-Oriented Systems) *Object-oriented systems are class-based systems where hierarchies of classes are build by inheritance relations.*

Let's apply these definitions on our examples. HOOD nets have objects as basic entities but no classes. Therefore they are object-based. Actors have objects, classes (because an equivalence relationship between actors with the same behaviour can be defined), but no inheritance relationship between classes. Consequently the Actors paradigm is class-based. Smalltalk-80, ConcurrentSmalltalk and DistributedConcurrentSmalltalk have objects, classes, and inheritence. Therefore they are truly object-oriented systems by the definition in [Wegn 90].

In the remainder of the paper we will not distinguish between object-based, class-based and object-oriented models, but lead our discussion in the widest possible range, i. e. object-based systems, for the following arguments:

- Classes are a very powerfull means for structuring the system statically, but per se have no impact on concurreny in a system, which is a dynamic feature.

- Inheritance has an impact on the run time behaviour of a system, but does not change the pattern of communication between objects. Besides that, we do not want to go into details of the semantics of inheritance and therefore will not take it into considerations in this discussion.

- As stated before, performance considerations are often the driving force behind the creation of concurrent systems. But object-oriented paradigms are normally inherently coupled with very dynamic allocation and freeing of system resources, most often done in a way transparent to the user. Hardware specific details are hidden from the user very strictly. But as parallel programming for reasons of performance often forces to make use of special features of the hardware, we do not want to exclude such systems from the discussion here and therefore take the most general approach.

To avoid possibly arising confusion in the following discussion, we want to cite another definition from Wegner [Wegn 90]:

Definition 4 (Active Objects) *Active objects are objects, which may already be active, when receiving a message, so that incoming messages must synchronize with ongoing activities of the object.*

We do not consider this definition to be usefull, because in any system containing any kind of concurrency, it always may happen, that a message is sent to an object, which is currently working. The only way to prevent this, would be to provide a systemwide global clock, which would supply points at the time axis, at which messages could be sent. But we can not imagine, why this should be usefull. Therefore, we always have active objects in a concurrent object-based system in the sense of Wegners's definition.

Having spoken so much about parallelism and objects-based models of concurrency, it is time for the basic question: How is concurrency introduced into an object-based system? One possibility consists of more than one object knowing what to do without receiving a message first. Then there is more than one flow of control in parallel in the system right from the beginning, although all method calls may follow strictly the function call semantics as is the case in the Remote Procedure Call (RPC) model. The combination of several starting objects in combination with RPC leads to a static number of concurrent tasks in a system. This can simplify the administration of resources in the system and therefore the prediction of system performance. How can objects know what they have to do without receiving a message first? It might be, that their "job" is kind of "hard coded" into them, e. g. such objects always have to control a system resource, or the objects are producing periodic signals. Otherwise the object could be an interface to the environment of the system, for example a window retrieving input from the user. It is quite natural, that there is more than one such object, just think of a database system, to which more than one terminal is connected. Naturally the terminals are internally modelled by objects.

The second possibility is, that there exists some means of splitting the control flow similiar to the UNIX *fork()* system call. That means introducing some kind of asynchronism into the system. As the only means of communication between objects (and all entities in an object-based system are objects) is message passing there must be an asynchronous message passing mechanism.

These two possibilities can be considered as being the generic constructs to introduce concurrency into an object-based system. These constructs may either be found alone or both in combination in a system, but one of these generic constructs has to be included in a concurrent object-based system, otherwise the system neccessarily is strictly sequential. Let's define:

Definition 5 (Vivid Objects) *Vivid objects are objects which can send messages without receiving a message first.*

An example for a system consisting of vivid objects would be a distributed process controlling system where each sensor sends its values either periodically or if some limit value is reached, e. g. a certain temperature has been exceeded. ADA tasks are vivid objects for instance.

Definition 6 (Passive Objects) *Passive objects can send messages to other objects or to themselves only in response to a message received first.*

To continue the example above, if the sensors were being polled by some master station periodically, they would be passive objects. The master station would be vivid of course. In general, objects as known from popular object-based languages as C++, Objective C , or Simula) are passive objects. Of course, even in such systems, there must be one initial object, which ist the starting point of program execution and therefore must be vivid.

Definition 7 (Vivid System) *A vivid system is an object-based system where more than one object is vivid (i. e. can send messages, which are not sent in response to a message received first) at a time.*

The definition of a **passive system** is analogous.

Now it is time to pay attention to the second generic construct, the asynchronous message passing. To clarify our point of view, we first of all propose the following definitions:

Definition 8 (Synchronous Message Passing) *Synchronous message passing means that the sender is blocked until it receives a return value, i.e. message passing has function call semantics.*

This mechanism is very convenient to the developer and reduces synchronization problems significantly. Nevertheless it can lead to unsatisfying solutions: Imagine a vector object, having several point objects as attributes. If another vector has to be added, with synchronous message passing, one coordinate of the vector has to be added sequentially after the other. The more natural solution, adding coordinates in parallel would be impossible, if only this mechanism is supplied.

Definition 9 (Asynchronous Message Passing) *The sender may continue to work without retrieving a return value. The receiver can process the message independently of the sender.*

Now the vector object could send *add*-messages without waiting for a return value before sending the next, thus splitting up the flow of control and exploiting additional parallelism.

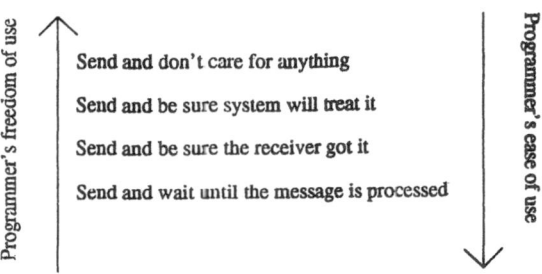

Figure1: Four communication paradigms

These last two definitions must be handled carefully. First of all consider that, according to this definition, the communication mechanism used in OCCAM would be asynchronous ! Only a full rendezvous as for example provided by the RPC mechanism of ADA would be considered synchronous. Let's clarify our view by dividing communication mechanisms into four classes:

a) The sender sends and does not care at all what happens to the message. This may look very awkward at a first glance, but can be very efficient in certain situations. This point of view is treated exhaustively in [Salt 84].

b) The sender gives his message to the underlying communication mechanism and can be sure, that this underlying mechanism has really received this message for further treatment. It is now in the responsibility of the communication system to buffer the message if necessary and deliver it at the right address reliably. This mechanism is very convenient for the programmer but adds additional complexity to the system and makes it harder to predict the performance of the system on one hand. It also adds the full burden of supplying a buffering mechanism and some kind of flow control to the system. There also exists the danger of deadlocks and system breakdowns due to a runout of internal resources.

c) The sender is blocked until the receiver is ready to retrieve the message. This does not mean that the object which has got the message will process it successfully. Therefore special considerations concerning error handling in a system based on this message passing mechanism have to be kept in mid. A similar mechanism of message passing (where message passing of course has different semantics) is used in OCCAM.

d) The sender is blocked until it receives a return value signalling the successful processing of the message. This means sending a message has function semantics. This last model is known as "rendezvous" in the literature and was first implemented in the RPC mechanism of ADA. This is very convenient for the programmer, as he can use message passing the same way as he is used from function calls in sequential programming. But we are convinced, that most often the restrictions imposed on the flow of control and the lack of being able to distribute a computation over several entities limits the applicability of this mechanism if system performance is the primary goal.

The reader should be aware that only the last model does not allow a split of control flow and therefore will be called synchronous according to our definition.

	passive objects	vivid objects
synchronous message passing	class 1	class 2
asynchronous message passing	class 3	class 4

Table1: Basic classification

4 Classification

Object-based concurrent systems now can be classified by applying the definitions of vivid systems and synchronous and asynchronous message passing given above. This leads to four possible classes (see table 1).

We try to give a short charcterization of the most basic features of these four classes: Class one is a purely sequential system as implemented in C++ for example and therefore not of interest to us. Class two systems contain a static amount of parallelism, which cannot be extended at run time. In systems of class three a number of object working in parallel is dynamically changing during run time, but all messages being sent in such a system have a common root, as change of flow of control with ongoing time can be described by a tree. The systems in class four combine the features of class two and class three systems and allow least prediction of their runtime behaviour.

Let's apply this classification on our examples now:

Smalltalk-80 Smalltalk-80 does not allow objects to send messages without an impetus from the outside. Therefore it has passive objects. But it has a kind of asynchronous message call, even only in a very restricted form: The class *block* has a method called *fork* which is asynchronous in our definition and allows split of control flow. So Smalltalk-80 turns out to be a class three concurrent object-oriented system.

ConcurrentSmalltalk ConcurrentSmalltalk also falls into class three. Nevertheless its asynchronous method call fit better into the object-oriented context: Concurrency is not limited as being a method of a special class, but possible in connection with every object. Secondly, although for reasons of compatability the questionable concept of Smalltalk-80 is still supported, it is adwised to see objects in ConcurrentSmalltalk as self-contained entities, which is better conforming to the concept of objects.

DistributedConcurrentSmalltalk As DistributedConcurrentSmalltalk is an extension to ConcurrentSmalltalk, it also provides the asynchronous message passing mechanism described above. But as DistributedConcurrentSmalltalk is an interpersonal system, it is a vivid system, as there may be more than one user in the system at a time. Therefore DistributedConcurrentSmalltalk is a class four system.

Actors As stated in [Agha 86] "all computation in an actor system is the result of processing communications". Therefore it is a passive system[‡] Communication is buffered in an actor system, as explained before under communication mechanism b). This means that message passing is asynchronous according to our definition. Consequently actors is a class three system.

[‡]There are models of actor systems seen as vivid systems (e. g. [Kafu 91]), but we will keep to the basic description of actors, where the possibility of more than one "initial actor" is not stated explicitely.

HOOD nets Due to their tree structure with a root node as starting point, HOOD nets are a passive system. Child nodes, which are subnets modelling an object, can be called in parallel. Consequently there exists some kind of asynchronous message passing. Due to this feature HOOD nets are a class three system by our classification.

So far there is still missing the discussion of an important feature of concurrent object-based systems: Can an object handle more than one message in parallel? Can there be more than one method in process inside an object? Although the implementation of concurrency inside an object should be invisible from the outside, as such parallelism can influence the system performance considerably, it has to be seen as a crucial feature, which must be taken into consideration. To exploit this charcteristic for our classification, we give these definitions:

Definition 10 (Multi-Threaded Object) *An object is multi-threaded if there can be more than one method of an object in process at a time.*

Definition 11 (Multi-Threaded System) *A system is a multi-threaded system if it contains at least one multi-threaded object.*

Single-Threaded Systems are defined analogously.

Multi-threaded objects can be a very natural source of parallelism: Let's think of an object, which behaves like an undivideable logical entity to the outside. As an example, there can be an object "employee" in a payroll program with a number of attributs like working hours, salary, number of children and first name of her husband, all of which themselves are objects. It consequently would be a severe violation against object-oriented concepts to change any of these attributes from the outside, but there must be methods of the "employee"-object which will consequently also result in messages addressed to the attribute objects. Now everyone can imagine methods, which are sent to the employee, but only concern one of the attributes. Can there be anything more natural than allowing such methods, only concerning different attributes, to be processed in parallel inside the object? Only allowing single-threaded objects could prevent improving system performance, given the existence of such compound objects in a system.

Nevertheless it is clear that a multi-threaded system must provide some synchronization concept to ensure mutual exclusion between methods which concern the same attributes as semaphores [Dijk 65], guarded commands [Hans 78], monitors [Tane 87] or even some special communication mechanism as in CSP [Hoar 78]. We do not want to discuss the question, which of these mechanisms is most suited for the object-based paradigm, but we do have the feeling, that semaphores are not fitting well into object-based concepts, because they lead to a distribution of control in a non-modular way, contrary to concepts of abstraction and information-hiding.

By taking into account that a system may be multi-threaded or not, we have eight possible classes (see table 2). Nevertheless it should be clear that a multi-threaded class one (i. e. a sequential) system has no sensible interpretation.

Let's classify our examples once again:

Smalltalk-80 In Smalltalk-80 an object cannot protect itself against violation of the consistency of its internal attributes because of receipt of multiple messages at a time. The objects sending messages have to ensure mutual exclusion by using global semaphores. Nevertheless such semaphores also could be used for mutual exclusion of methods inside an object. As a consequence Smalltalk-80 is multi-threaded, though the implementation must be seen as a violation of basic concepts of objects.

	passive objects		vivid objects	
	single threaded	multi threaded	single threaded	multi threaded
synchronous message passing	class 1 S	class 1 M	class 2 S	class 2 M
asynchronous message passing	class 3 S	class 3 M	class 4 S	class 4 M

Table2: Extended classification

ConcurrentSmalltalk For reasons of compatibility to Smalltalk-80 there are so called non-atomic objects in ConcurrentSmalltalk, which are multi-threaded with the problems described above. There are also atomic objects, which only allow one method being executed at a time. Consequently, according to our definition ConcurrentSmalltalk must be considered multi-threaded, although only due to its compatability to Smalltalk-80.

DistributedConcurrentSmalltalk DistributedConcurrentSmalltalk has single activity objects and multiple activity objects, which are called multi-threaded according to our definition. DistributedConcurrentSmalltalk supports an exclusive and a conditional synchronization mechanism. Exclusive synchronization is done by an object by defining exclusive relations between two methods. This relation leads to serialization between several activities inside an object. Conditional synchronization is done by each method having a guard, similiar to ADA. By including all these concepts DistributedConcurrentSmalltalk must be called a multi-threaded system, with an implementation perfectly fitting into the object-based paradigm.

HOOD nets As objects in HOOD nets are re-entrantable they are multi-threaded. HOOD nets have their own definition of active and passive objects. Passive objects, as defined in HOOD nets, have no control over the execution of methods on their data. Therefore they only can be used if all methods are executable in parallel on them without leading to inconsistencies. This means, that they must be "functional objects" with no state associated. Otherwise, if the object must contain a state, an active object has to be used, which can delay the execution of methods, this way enforcing mutual exclusion. The mechanism used for internal synchronization is not specified.

Actors Actors only fetch another message from their message queue if they have finished processing the previous communication, which does not mean that the task has been processed. The message could have been forwarded to another actor, which can still be processing it. Therefore an actor based system follows a strictly single-threaded concurrent object-based paradigm.

Table 3 sums up the application of our classification scheme for a set of object-based concurrent pragraming paradigms, presented at the ECOOP-OOPSLA workshop on object-based concurrent programming during the last years.

5 Summary

After motivating the use of object-based techniques in the development of systems containing concurrency five related, but rather different object-based example systems were introduced. Then the basic definitions of *object-based*, *class-based*, and *object-oriented* systems were given. The ways of introducing concurrency into object-based systems were

Name of the System	Classification	
ABCL/1	class 3	S
Actors	class 3	M
ConcurrentSmalltalk	class 3	M
CORAL	class 3	M
DistributedConcurrentSmalltalk	class 4	M
HERAKLIT	class 2	M
HOOD nets	class 3	M
Matroshka	class 3	M
Orient84/K	class 3	S
POOL	class 2	S
Smalltalk-80	class 3	M

Table3: Application of the extended classification

discussed, and a classification scheme, based on the discussion, was introduced and applied on example systems. Lastly the question of concurrency inside objects was raised and added to the classification scheme as being discovered a basic feature of object-based concurrent systems. Our examples were classified again and their mechanisms to control concurrency inside objects (if any) were examined. At the end a table containing the application of our proposal for classification on a larger set of systems, which were not discussed here due to lack of space, was given.

6 Further Research

First of all the performance as being one of the most important reasons for developing concurrent systems of the different classes has to be examined. Are systems falling into one class are performing significantly better than the others? Is the additional complexity needed by multi-threaded systems paid back in an adequate gain of performance? Another point of interest are error handling mechanisms applied in those classes of our classification containing asynchronous message passing. Of course, one also has to ask, if the classification presented above is valid for all possible systems, can it be extended, refined? And, to come to an end, the basic question, if there is one class superior to all others, has to be investigated.

To answer these questions must be the goal of further work.

References

[Agha 86]   G. Agha. *Actors: A Model of Concurrent Computation in Distributed Systems.* MIT Press, 1986.

[Agha 89]   G. Agha. "Foundational Issues in Concurrent Programming". *SIGPLAN NOTICES*, Vol. 24, No. 4, pp. 66 – 65, April 1989.

[Atta 87]   G. Attardi. "Concurrent Strategy Execution in Omega". In: *Object-Oriented Concurrent Programming*, MIT Press, 1987.

[Babb 87]   R. G. Babb and D. C. DiNucci. "Design and Implementation of Parallel Programs with Large-Grain Dataflow". In: L. H. Jamieson, D. B. Gannon, and R. J. Douglass, Eds., *The Characteristics of Parallel Algorithms*, pp. 335 – 349, MIT Press, 1987.

[Bach 73]   C. W. Bachmann. "The Programmer as Navigator". *ACM*, Vol. 16, No. 11, 1973.

[Coad 90]   P. Coad and E. Yourdon. *Object-Oriented Analysis*. Prentice Hall, 1990.

[Cox 87]   B. J. Cox. *Object Oriented Programming*. Addison-Wesley, April 1987.

[Dijk 65]   E. W. Dijkstra. "Co-operating Sequential Processes". In: F. Gennys, Ed., *Programming Languages*, London Academic Press, 1965.

[DiSa 91]   M. DiSanto and G. Iannello. "Implementing Actor-Based Primitives on Distributed Memory". *OOPS Messenger*, Vol. 2, No. 2, pp. 45 – 49, April 1991.

[Gane 79]   C. Gane and T. Sarson. *Structured Systems Analysis: Tools and Techniques*. Prentice-Hall, 1979.

[Genr 91]   H. J. Genrich. "Predicate-Transition Nets". In: K. Jensen and G. Rozenberg. Eds., *High-level Petri Nets*, Chap. Section A, pp. 3 – 43, Springer-Verlag, 1991.

[Giov 90]   R. D. Giovanni. "Petri Nets and Software Engineering: HOOD Nets". In *11th International Conference on Application and Theory of Petri Nets*, pp. 123 – 138. June 1990.

[Gold 83]   A. Goldberg and D. Robson. *Smalltalk-80: The Language and its Implementation*. Addison-Wesley, 1983.

[Hans 78]   P. B. Hansen. "Distributed Processes, A Concurrent Programming Concept". *CACM*, Vol. 11. No. 21, pp. 934 – 941, 1978.

[Hoar 78]   C. A. R. Hoare. "Communicating Sequential Processes". *CACM*, August 1978.

[HOOD 89a] *HOOD Reference Manual*. HOOD Working Group, European Space Agency. wme/89-173/jb. issue 3.0 Ed., September 1989.

[HOOD 89b] *HOOD User Manual*. HOOD Working Group, European Space Agency, wme/89-353/jb, issue 3.0 Ed., December 1989.

[Jens 91]   K. Jensen. "Coloured Petri Nets: A High Level Language for System Design". In: K. Jensen and G. Rozenberg, Eds., *High-level Petri Nets*, Chap. Section A, pp. 44 – 117, Springer-Verlag, 1991.

[Kafu 91]   D. Kafura, D. Washabaugh, and J. Nelson. "Progress in the Garbage Collection of Active Objects". *OOPS Messenger*, Vol. 2, No. 2, pp. 59 – 63, April 1991.

[Levi 87]   S. P. Levitan. "Measuring Communications Structures in Parallel Architectures and Algorithms". In: L. H. Jamieson, D. B. Gannon, and R. J. Douglass, Eds., *The Characteristics of Parallel Algorithms*, pp. 101 – 138, MIT Press, 1987.

[Lieb 87]   H. Lieberman. "Concurrent Object-Oriented Programming in Act 1". In: *Object-Oriented Concurrent Programming*, MIT Press, 1987.

[Loya 91]   J. P. Loyall, S. M. Kaplan, and S. K. Goering. "Specification and Implementation of Actors with Graph Rewriting". *OOPS Messenger*, Vol. 2, No. 2, pp. 73 – 77, April 1991.

[Naka 89]   T. Nakajima, Y. Yokote, M. Tokoro, S. Ochiai, and T. Nagamatsu. "Distributed Concurrent Smalltalk, A Language and System for the Interpersonal Environment". *SIGPLAN NOTICES*, Vol. 24, No. 4, pp. 66 – 65, April 1989.

[Nels 87]   P. A. Nelson and L. Snyder. "Programming Paradigms for Nonshared Memory Parallel Computers". In: L. H. Jamieson, D. B. Gannon, and R. J. Douglass, Eds., *The Characteristics of Parallel Algorithms*, pp. 3 – 20, MIT Press, 1987.

[Salt 84]   Saltzer. "End to End Arguments in System Design". *ACM Transactions on Comp. Systems*, Vol. 2, No. 4, pp. 277 – 288, November 1984.

[Tane 87]   A. S. Tanenbaum. *Operating Systems: Design and Implementation*. Prentice Hall, 1987.

[Wegn 90]   P. Wegner. "Concepts and Paradigms of Object-Oriented Programming". *OOPS Messenger*, Vol. 1, No. 1, pp. 7 –87, August 1990.

[Yoko 87]   Y. Yokote and M. Tokoro. "Concurrent Programming in Concurrent Smalltalk". In: *Object-Oriented Concurrent Programming*, MIT Press, 1987.

Finite State Machines and Object Orientation

R. Lewandowski
M. Mulazzani
Alcatel Austria–ELIN Research Centre
Ruthnergasse 1–7
A–1210 Vienna, Austria

Abstract

Finite State Machines (FSM) are an established approach for modeling the behavior in reactive systems. At the same time object oriented techniques are spreading on the market. This report investigates Finite State Machines and their similarities to and extensions with object oriented concepts.

First, basic similarities of the traditional Finite State Machines with respect to object orientation are explored, covering encapsulation, typing, system structuring and instantiation. Then, some object oriented extensions of FSMs (inheritance, virtual transitions, ...) are shown with the example of OSDL (currently under standardization by CCITT, an OO extension of SDL from CCITT). Finally, state charts from Harel are investigated. They provide extensions to FSMs which are not object oriented. But there exists an interesting mapping of their extensions to classes, inheritance and composition, providing a new view on FSMs, states and transitions.

1. Introduction

For several years now Finite State Machines (FSMs) and Extended Finite State Machines (EFSMs) are used in the area of real time systems as a standard technique. They provide the means to effectively describe system behavior and they are well suited to model the change of behavior in systems. One big application area are telecommunication systems. CCITT (International Telegraph and Telephone Consultative Committee) recommends the use of SDL [CCIT89], [Saca89] (based on the FSM concept) for the software development of telecommunication services.

On the other hand, object oriented technology has strongly emerged on the market. The concepts of encapsulation, information hiding, abstract data types and inheritance provide new means for system development. Availability of object oriented languages and programming environments, as well as the emergence of object oriented methods allow for the adoption of the object oriented technology into an industrial context.

So coming from the application area of telecommunication systems, the question arises, how object oriented concepts will fit or will be integrated into the development process. It is the goal of this report to discuss the concept of finite state machines and their links, similarities and extensions with object oriented concepts.

Section 2 starts with the basics about FSMs. It gives a short introduction to FSMs and their representation forms, which is then evolved into a discussion on structuring aspects with FSMs, showing a first set of similarities to object orientation. A different approach is presented in section 3. OSDL is an object oriented extension of SDL under standardization from CCITT, the section discusses how object oriented principles are integrated into the FSM approach. As the third main approach, the state charts from Harel [Hare87] are presented in section 4. They are a powerful, not object–oriented extension of FSMs. But it turns out that there exists an interesting object oriented analogy of the extensions which is presented in section 5. Finally, the summary collects the results and gives an outlook for further topics and open questions.

2. Finite State Machine (FSM)

FSM Definitions

Sequential Machines (Finite State Machines): A FSM is a machine with memory containing the state. Operations are determined by input events and the current state.

Mathematically a FSM is a 5–tuple, (I, S, O, NSF, OF), where

- I is a finite set of input symbols.
- S is a set of mutually exclusive states (static waiting).
- O is a finite set of output symbols.
- NSF is a mapping of I and S onto S called the next state function (this mapping is often called transition).
- OF is a mapping of I and S onto O called the output function.

FSMs are characterized by discrete–valued inputs, outputs and internal elements [Hatl87], [Hopc79].

With such a FSM it is possible to express behavioral aspects of a system. The states are used to define conditions in which the system reacts to specific events. Reaction here means the transition to another specific condition. Only very simple systems can be sufficiently described by the usage of FSMs. This is because the number of different conditions in which a system can be, is usually too large. The number of states in a software system equals the number of all possible combinations of values of all data. This phenomena is called "the explosion of states".

An example for the application of an FSM is a traffic light. There exist four different states: green, yellow, red and red–yellow . Only one input signal named *change* is defined for this FSM. Depending on the current state and the input signal the next state is determined. If the actual state is green, the input signal *change* will cause a transition to yellow a.s.o..

Extended FSM: In EFSMs not all conditions of a system are modelled with states. States are only used to model the essential conditions. States are abstractions representing *groups* of conditions of a system. For these states also transitions can be defined as for normal FSMs, but in an extended form.

In an EFSM the output signal and the next state is determined not only from the previous state and the input symbol (here called signal) but also from other data. Data of an EFSM can be classified into four categories:

- the state variable which holds the actual state

- the local variables which hold additional information to the state
- the temporary variables which are used temporally during state transition e.g. a counter variable which needs no remembrance
- the input signal variables and the output signal variables.

In EFSMs the behavior is defined with states as abstractions of conditions. Transitions depend on actual state, input signal and values of additional data.

Representation of FSMs

Different representations are used in order to define FSMs. Common notations for FSMs are *state transition diagram, state transition matrix* and *SDL diagrams.*

State Transition Diagrams: State transition diagrams are directed graphs. The different states are represented as nodes. The transitions (caused by incoming signals) are represented with directed edges between the states. The incoming and outgoing signals are shown as annotation of the edges. The state transition diagram shows the sequence of signals and conditions within a system (see Figure 1 where A, B, C are states, r, s, t are incoming signals and u, v, w, x, y, z are outgoing signals).

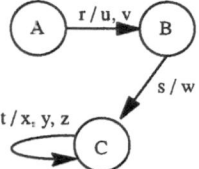

Figure 1: Example of a state transition diagram with incoming and outgoing signals

State Transition Matrix: In a state transition matrix the states are represented by rows. The incoming signals are shown as columns. Whenever an incoming signal is accepted in a state the according transition and output signals are written into the specified field of the matrix. This matrix tends to have a lot of empty fields due to the number of not allowed signals in a state. Figure 2 gives an example.

	onhook	offhook	ring
onhook state		offhook state/ dial_tone_on	ringing state/ ring_line
offhook state	onhook state/ dial_tone_off		
conversation state	onhook_state/ disconnect_line		
ringing state	onhook state/ disconnect_line	conversation state/ connect_line	

Figure 2: Example of a state transition matrix

Software Description Language (SDL): While the previous notations are only able to define FSMs, the *software description language* [Saca89] is able to define EFSMs. SDL has a graphical and a textual representation. Graphical SDL is a kind of *flow chart* extended by special symbols like *state symbol, incoming signal* and *outgoing signal.* This allows to express both, the FSM aspect and the control flow of transitions.

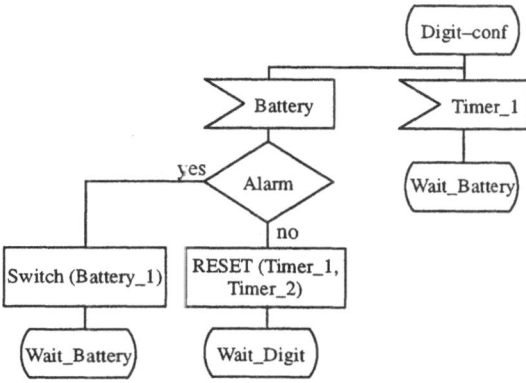

Figure 3: SDL example

An example of this notation is shown in Figure 3. Two transitions are defined for the state *Digit-conf*. Receiving the signal *Timer_1* will change the state to *Wait_Battery*. In case of receiving signal *Battery* the condition of *Alarm* will be tested. If the condition is true the procedure *Switch(Battery_1)* is called. The transition ends by changing the state to *Wait_Battery*. If the condition *Alarm* is false the procedure *RESET(Timer_1, Timer_2)* is called and the state is changed to *Wait_Digit*.

SDL offers additional constructs which allow to model typical situations. A special symbol can be used for "all other signals", i.e. defining a transition for the unexpected signals in a state. It is possible to store signals for later use. A transition can be associated to an incoming signal which is valid in any state, and many other possibilities.

Structuring of FSMs

A large and complex FSM is hard to understand, even for the designer himself. A state transition graph showing all states and transitions of a FSM possibly does not even fit on a single page.

But it is possible to show views of the FSM thus helping a reader to understand it. Different groups of signals are shown on different state transition diagrams. Figure 4 gives an example which shows two separate views of a FSM for two different logical parts of behavior. The addition of both diagrams results in a more complex diagram which would be more difficult to read and understand.

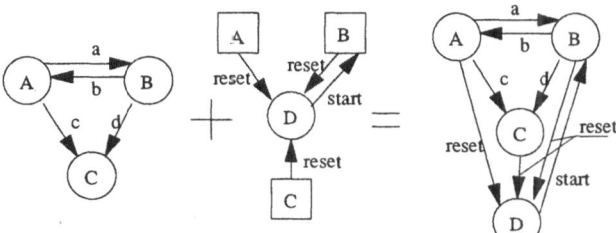

Figure 4: Managing complexity with different views

To indicate copies of states in the different diagrams they are shown by a rectangle instead of a circle.

Structuring of Systems with several FSMs

Systems and especially large systems have to be structured in order to master their complexity. FSMs, when combined with the process model (a FSM instance is a thread of control) are well suited to express the behavior of a system. The system is divided in several parts (processes) each of them being modelled with a FSM. So the system is seen as being built out of several FSMs, each of them having data (current state) and input signals.

166

With such a view of cooperating FSMs, several issues become important which are discussed hereafter: How to express interaction between FSMs ? How are FSMs used (instances of FSMs) ?

Message Sequence Charts (Scenarios): Message sequence charts show the interaction between different FSMs, they show the signal flow and its timing. Each such scenario shows one example of an interaction, i.e. one specific situation of interaction. In the notation the FSMs are drawn as vertical bars, the vertical dimension represents the passing of time. The signals are shown as directed lines between the FSMs. In this notation it is easy to express the duration of signal exchange, sequence of signals and concurrency.

Figure 5 shows an example of a message sequence chart. One specific flow of signals is shown for four FSMs. The directed arrows do *not* show the transitions but the *flow* of signals from one FSM to another.

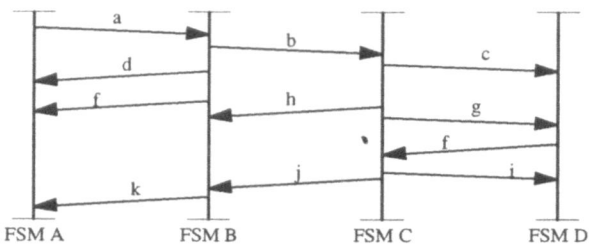

Figure 5: Example of a scenario

Instances of FSMs: Each FSM has to store the actual state and its local variables. An additional concept is the instantiation mechanism for FSMs (e.g. process instance in CHILL [CCIT86]). Figure 6 shows the relation between several instances of a FSM and the FSM itself. The FSM shows the common behavior of all instances. The FSM is used as a *type*. The instances of the FSM hold their *own* local variables and the *actual state*. In languages without special language constructs for FSM the storage allocation for each instance has to be implemented explicitly (or has to be generated automatically).

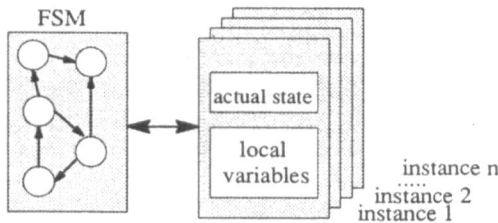

Figure 6: FSM and Instances

Similarities to Object Orientation

Although the discussion up to now focused on properties and usage of FSMs, some similarities of FSMs with object oriented concepts can already be seen:

The notion of FSMs having data (including state) and input signals is quite analogous to objects, FSMs encapsulate data and allow a client only to operate on these data by means of signals.

The system being seen as consisting of interacting FSMs is another similarity to OO. Communication between several FSMs is done by means of sending and receiving signals. It is worth noting, that the scenarios used for FSMs are quite equivalent to the object interaction diagrams as recently introduced into the Booch method [Booc91b].

Another similarity exists between FSMs and OO. A FSM can be seen as type. Instances of a FSM exist, each having its own data. This allows to create several copies of the FSM in a system. Each of these instances has the same properties as defined for the FSM. FSMs map to classes, and the instantiation of FSMs directly corresponds to object oriented approaches.

Finally, the question of granularity and complexity (combination and splitting of FSM) is valid also in object oriented systems and vice versa.

However, it should be noted here, that it is not our argumentation that FSM and object orientation is the same (there are certainly differences). We just want to point out that there are certain similarities.

The following sections now explore in more detail the links of FSMs with the object oriented approach, covering object oriented extensions of FSMs as well as object oriented views of FSMs.

3. Concepts of OSDL

OSDL is an extension of SDL with concepts of object oriented techniques [Moll87]. It was intended to keep the changes within the semantics of SDL as small as possible. SDL supports encapsulation by means of the process concept. A process encapsulates data and the associated operations.

OSDL distinguishes between types and instances. Process instances are derived from process types. Inheritance is used to support specialization of process types.

Single inheritance of a process type (FSM) allows to add new transitions with new input signals to the inherited ones. A state transition matrix is well suited to visualize this. Figure 7 shows a state transition matrix of an SDL specification. This process type has two states: *Even* and *Odd*. The following input signals are used in transitions: *Probe, Result, Endgame and Bump*. Figure 8 now shows *Special Game*, a specialization of *Game*. *Special Game* inherits from *Game* which could be seen in the new state transition matrix: several transitions (with new input signals) and states are added (here *Evil* and *WereEvil* are added signals and *Chance* is an additional State). Defined transitions from the super–type cannot be redefined (overwritten) within the definition of the sub–type.

	Probe	Result	Endgame	Bump
Even				
Odd				

Figure 7: State transition matrix of *Game*

	Probe	Result	Endgame	Bump	Evil	WereEvil
Even	These transitions are inherited from *Game*					
Odd						
Chance						

Figure 8: State transition matrix of *Special Game*

Another object oriented concept introduced for process types in OSDL is the *virtual procedure*. Virtual procedures of a super–type can be defined concretely in sub–types (derived process). This allows to define a transition in an abstract process type only partly and leave some parts open (virtual procedures) to be defined within specializations of the process type. Figure 9 shows for the already mentioned example *Game* the process definition of *General Game*. Two procedures *ProbeWhenEven* and *ProbeWhenOdd* are defined virtually (grey boxes). Figure 10 shows the definition of process *Game*. The process *Game* inherits all transitions defined by *General Game*. The virtual procedures *PropeWhenEven* and *ProbeWhenOdd* are defined in detail with the SDL notation.

168

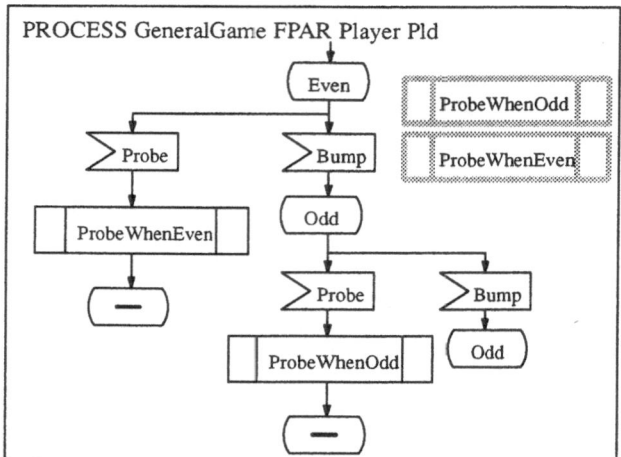

Figure 9: Virtual procedures

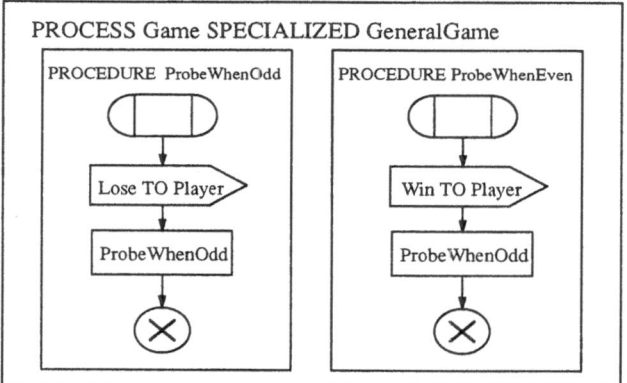

Figure 10: Definition of virtual procedures

While *virtual procedures* are used to leave specific parts of transitions undefined, *virtual transitions* allow to define the complete transition in detail in the derived process. For a *virtual transition* only the *state* and the *input signal* are defined. The super–type allows to define a default transition which can be overwritten within derived types. This concept stresses a subtype either to use the default transition or to redefine a transition to a more specialized one. Figure 11 shows two process types inheriting from a super–type. The super–type defines that there has to exist a transition for *State A* and signal *S*. The super–type also defines a default transition. The derived process drawn on the left hand side defines the *virtual input* (= virtual transition) to a concrete transition. The other derived process defines the virtual input to a *save* (storing of the signal for later usage).

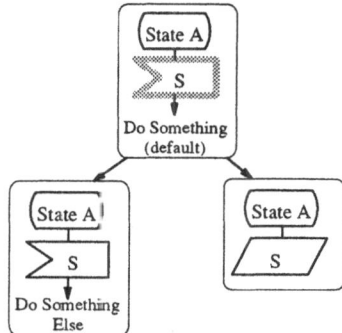

Figure 11: *Virtual Input* specialized to an *Input* or *Save*

The following table 1 gives an overview how the concepts introduced by OSDL can be mapped to object oriented concepts.

Systems modelled with Finite State Machines	Systems modelled with Objects
Finite State Machine	Class
State	Data (members)
Process	Instance
Input signal	Operation
Transition	Operation implementation
Output signal	Called operations in operation implementation
Virtual procedure	Virtual operation
Virtual transition	Virtual operation

Table 1: Finite State Machine and Object Oriented Concepts

4. State Charts, Non Object Oriented Extension of FSM

While *OSDL* allows for abstraction of transitions, *State Charts* [Hare87] provides a different idea of abstraction of states. State charts are a visual formalism for describing states and transitions in a modular fashion, enabling clustering, orthogonality (i.e. concurrency) and refinement.

State charts have a similar semantic like state transition diagrams but with some extensions. Simple state transition diagrams are expressed with the same notation as used for state transition diagrams. The small difference is that states are drawn with rounded boxes instead of circles.

Refinement of States: One of the extensions to state transition diagrams is the refinement of states. A superstate can be refined into substates with the semantics of XOR. The superstate can only be exactly one of its substates at a time. As usual for FSMs, transitions are attached to these substates. Transitions can also be attached to superstates with the following semantic: A transition defined for a superstate means that this transition is defined for all of its substates.

An example is shown in Figure 12 where picture I. shows a superstate *D* which is refined into substate *A* and *C*. If the system is in the superstate *D* it is either in state *A* or *C* (XOR semantics). Signal *b* is valid for both of the substates *A* and *C*. Therefore the transition is attached to the superstate D. Signals *a* and *c* can be received in state *B* and cause transitions to *A* respective *C*. Picture II. gives an equivalent FSM without superstates.

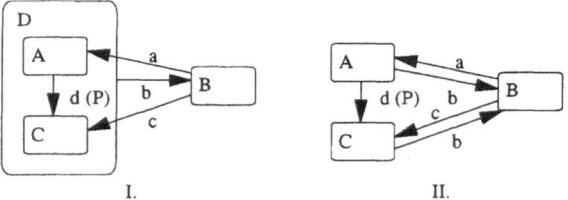

Figure 12: Abstraction in State Charts

Figure 13/I. shows the previous state chart at a higher level of abstraction (no inner details). Picture II. then shows the inner details of state D, the substates and their transitions. At the same time it shows another extension, the annotation of signals by conditions e.g. $d(P)$ were d is the input signal and P is a condition. The transition is only made if the condition is true.

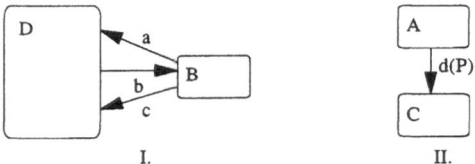

Figure 13: Abstraction in State Charts

The superstate/substate concept offers two ways of usage: refinement (as it was introduced in this section, i.e. top–down approach) or clustering and abstraction (bottom–up approach). What to choose depends on the situation.

Orthogonality (Concurrency) of States: State charts also allow AND decomposition, capturing the property that, being in a state, the system must be in *all* of its AND components. The orthogonal product of the components is called the *AND state*. For the orthogonality it is required that the transitions of one state machine are independent of the actual state of the other state machine and vice versa.

Figure 14 shows an example of an AND state. The dashed line in picture I. between state A and D shows the AND composition of A and D. Y is called the orthogonal product of A and D and is itself a state. In picture I. the arrow with the black spot on its shaft defines the initial state. A and D are not completely orthogonal, in A there exists a transition from C to B which is annotated by b *(in G)* indicating that the transition takes only place if the current *substate* of D is G. Picture II. shows an AND–free equivalent to picture I.

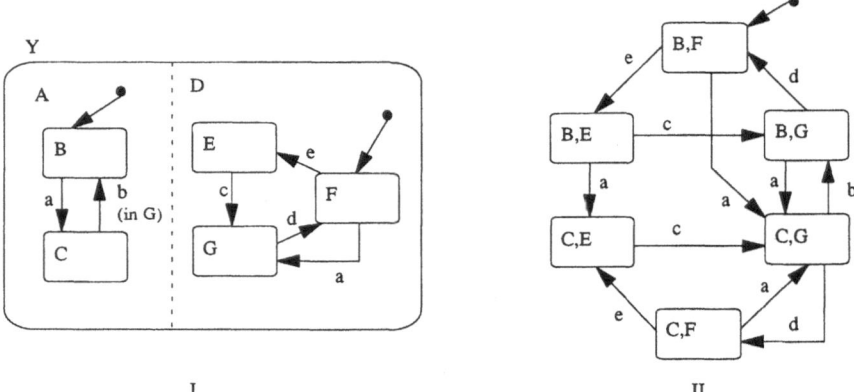

Figure 14: Orthogonality in State Charts

There are several further extensions in State Charts, including *history, condition and selection entrances, delays and timeouts*. However, they are beyond the scope of this paper, for details see [Hare87].

State refinement (XOR) and state orthogonality (AND) are quite abstract means. They provide new concepts for structuring FSMs and are intended to increase the power of FSMs for behavior modelling. The next section investigates the similarities of these extensions with object orientation.

5. Object Oriented Analogy to State Charts

The object oriented view of the state chart extensions follows the basic idea to map states to classes [Hüne91], [Vans91]. Input signals accepted in the states are mapped to the operations of the class. Figure 15 shows an example of a FSM and the corresponding classes. The names of the classes are taken from the states, the signals from the FSM are mapped to operations. The transitions (the arrows from one state to another) are indicated as comments (they would correspond to the implementation of the operation).

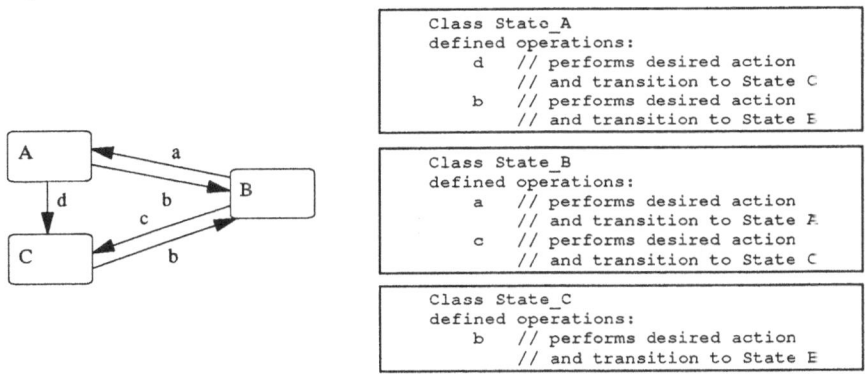

Figure 15: FSM mapped to Classes

With this object oriented view, the analogy of state refinement (superstate, XOR) is easy to express. State charts use the superstate to show common properties of states. In the object oriented paradigm it is possible to show common properties of classes with inheritance. If we look at class *State_A* and class *State_C* we will find an operation *b* which is defined similar for both classes. In the object oriented paradigm this could be modelled with inheritance. A new class *State_D* is introduced with operation *b*. Both classes *State_A* and *State_B* inherit from class *State_D*. Classes *State_A* and *State_D* which are derived from *State_D*, have to define only the remaining operations.

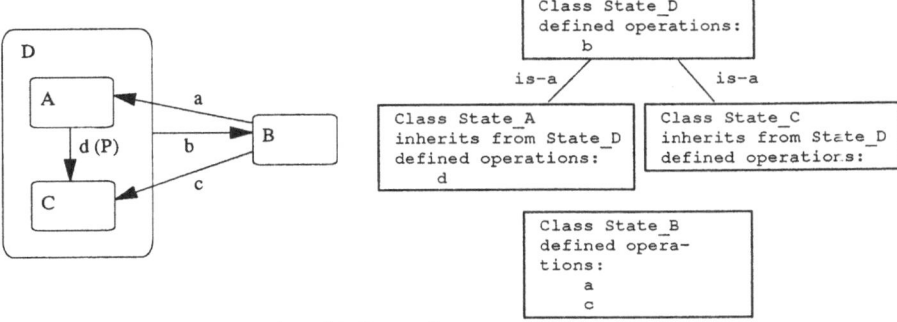

Figure 16: Abstract States mapped to Classes

Figure 16 shows Harels notation on the left hand side and the object oriented equivalent on the other side. The object oriented analogy of superstates is the inheritance between classes.

In contrast to that, the AND decomposition in state charts captures the property that, being in an AND state, the system must be in *all* of its AND components. The AND state can be seen as a composition of all its states. In the object oriented paradigm there exists a composition hierarchy (whole–part), each class can be seen as the composition of other classes. These classes are often modelled as data (members) of the *composite* class.

Figure 17 shows an AND state Y defined by Harels formalism. This AND state has two components, state A and state D. The AND state consists always of both components A and D. There is no point in time where state Y is either only in state A or state D. This semantics is similar to the semantics of whole–part relation in the object oriented paradigm shown on the right hand side. Composite class *state_Y* is built out of class *state_A* and class *state_D*, composition–relation is modelled with data members of a class *state_Y*.

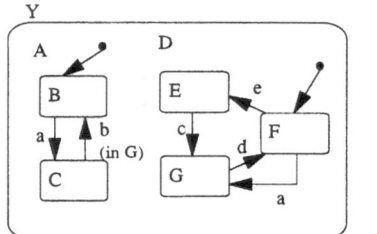 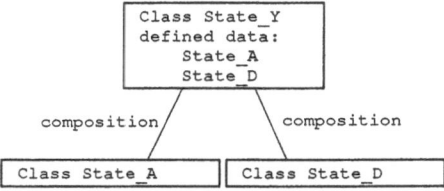

Figure 17: AND States mapped to Classes

The object oriented analogy to Harels AND states is the whole–part relation.

It is also interesting to see, that for the combination of AND and XOR states for state charts maps to the combination of inheritance and whole–part: Class *State_A* (in Harels state chart an XOR of B and C) and *State_D* (XOR of E,F, and G) from figure 19 can be refined in the object oriented view by inheritance (is–a relation) analogous to Figure 16.

Harel extended the FSM and gave a complete new view of states and FSMs. The similarities between Harels states and the object oriented paradigm allows now to map ideas from one model to the other. This allows to find new aspects in state charts by looking at the object oriented paradigm and vice versa. How do virtual operations map to states? What does multiple inheritance or access control for members of classes mean for states. There are a lot of unanswered questions which are under further investigation.

The following table 2 summarizes the mapping of Harels formalism to object oriented concepts.

Systems modelled with State Charts	Systems modelled with Objects
State	Class
XOR state	Base–class (inheritance)
AND state	Composite class (data members)
Signal	Operation
Transition	Operation implementation

Table 2: Harels Formalism and Object Oriented Concepts

6. Summary

The question "How will Finite State Machines integrate object oriented principles?" does not have a single answer. This report addresses three approaches: the link of traditional FSMs with object orientation; specific object oriented extensions to FSMs in OSDL; and an object oriented view of the state structuring in Harel's state charts.

Traditional FSMs and EFSMs show several characteristics, which are similar to object oriented concepts. The property of FSMs to allow access to its data only by means of signals corresponds to encapsulation. With FSMs, systems are modeled as sets of interacting and cooperating FSMs, which fits to object orientation. Finally, FSMs are types (behavior templates) which are instantiated at run–time. However, this should not be over–interpreted, these are just similarities in characteristics. It is not our argumentation that FSMs are object–oriented.

One actual enhancement of FSMs with object oriented constructs is being done for CCITT with the definition of OSDL (extension of SDL from CCITT). This mainly includes inheritance, but also virtual procedures, virtual transitions and other aspects. OSDL shows how object oriented constructs can be used within the formalism of FSMs.

Harel's state charts extend the FSM approach with state structuring, including state refinement (XOR state) and orthogonality of states (AND state). While these extensions are not directly connected to object orientation, it turns out that from an object oriented point of view, these extensions nicely map to inheritance and composition structure. This interpretation of state charts raises interesting questions concerning the mapping of ideas from the FSM model to the object oriented model and vice versa.

These three approaches only show some aspects of the issues involved when considering the link between FSMs and object orientation. Areas for further investigations include:
–   Conflicting and contradicting issues between FSMs and OO
–   OO extensions of FSMs (e.g. OSDL) and their link to OO languages
–   link of FSMs with object oriented analysis and design methods [Booc91a], [Coad91], [Rumb91] as well as the extensions of real time methods (based on FSMs) with object oriented concepts.

7. References

[Booc91a]   G. Booch, "*Object Oriented Design with Applications*", Benjamin/Cummings Publishing Company, 1991.

[Booc91b]   G. Booch, M. Goldberg, "*Object Oriented Design*", Rational Course Handout, 30. Oct. 1991.

[CCIT86]   ——, "*The CCITT High Level Language CHILL User's Manual*", International Telegraph and Telephone Consultative Committee (CCITT). Geneva, 1986.

[CCIT89]   ——, "*CCITT Blue Book, Recommendations Z.100: Functional Specification and Description Language (SDL)*", International Telegraph and Telephone Consultative Committee (CCITT), Geneva, 1989.

[Coad91]   P. Coad, E. Yourdon, "*Object Oriented Analysis*", Yourdon Press Computing Series, 1991.

[Hatl87]   D.H. Hatley, I.A. Pirbhai, "*Strategies for Real–Time System Specification*", Dorset House Publishing, 1987.

[Hare87]   D. Harel, "*Statecharts: A visual formalism for complex systems*", Science of Computer Programming, Vol. 8, pp. 231–247.

[Hopc79]   J.E. Hopcroft, J.D. Ullman, "*Introduction to Automata Theory, Languages and Computation*", Addison–Welsey Publishing Company, 1979.

[Hüne91]   I. Hüneke, "*Finite State Machines. a model of behavior for C++*", The C++ Report, Vol. 3/1, Jan. 1991

[Meye88]   B. Meyer, "*Object Oriented Software Construction*", Prentice Hall, 1988.

[Moll87]   B. Moller–Pedersen, D. Belsnes, "*Rationale and Tutorial on OSDL: An Object–Oriented Extension of SDL*", Computer Networks and ISDN Systems, Vol. 13/2, pp. 97–117, 1987.

[Rumb91]   J. Rumbaugh, M. Blaha, W. Premerlani, F. Eddy, W. Lorensen, "*Object–Oriented Modeling and Design*", Prentice Hall, 1991.

[Saca89]   R. Sacaro, J.R.W. Smith, *Telecommunications System Engineering using SDL*", Elsevier Science Publishers B.V., 1989.

[Stro88]   B. Stroustrup, "*What is Object–Oriented Programming?*", IEEE Software, Vol. 5/3, pp. 10–20, May 1988.

[Vans91]   J. Vanslembrouck, "*Relating Extended Finite State Machines with Object–Orientation*", Software Engineering Report nr. 914009, Alcatel Bell Telephone, Jan 1991.

Enhancing Reusability and Simplifying the OO Development with the Use of Events and Object Environment

Krista Rizman, Ivan Rozman

University of Maribor, Faculty of Technical Sciences
P. O. Box 224, 62000 Maribor, Slovenia, Europe
E-mail:rizman@uni-mb.ac.mail.yu

Abstract. Object-oriented(OO) software development enhances reusability. But reuse and object composition are not straightforward. Only compatible components, which conform to the same client-server protocol, can be composed. In this paper we propose an event-driven approach to OO software development which enhances reusability by increasing the openness of objects and provides a simple composition principle. It bases on concepts of events and object environment. Object environment serves as a mediator among independent objects. It consists of agents that monitor and respond to object notifications of events that occur through the life-cycle of each object. Events enhance object openness and so reusability and allow uncoupled programming style. Uncoupled programming style together with a simple composition principle provided by the use of the object environment allow easy production of powerful building blocks and simple construction of the complex software from powerful building blocks.

1 Introduction

The last ten years, there is an explosion of complexity in construction of software development. First, there is the complexity of behavior of real world system, part of which has to be modeled and verified in the early stages of development, i. e. in the requirement specification step.

The complexity of results of analysis and also of design is the second form of complexity. Mountains of documents and diagrams contained by traditional specifications are very hard to be exactly verified by end users. But only end users can exactly verify specifications, because only they exactly know what for a system they want and how it must work. Operational specifications called prototypes reduce the complexity of specifications and increase understandability of them. Executable specifications make the verification process to the end user easier. Problems caused by complexity of system structure and behavior can be avoided with iterative - spiral or fountain development life-cycle [1]. We found prototyping to be the best technique for performing the iterative development [2]. The prototype grows with each iteration, and refined each time, eventually becomes the end product.

2 Object technology

Prototyping approach is particularly appropriate when object technology is used which enhances reusability.

Libraries that have been around for a long time, are more difficult for using than libraries of classes. At using procedures an assumption must be made about the context in which they are to be invoked. For instance when using a GKS procedure for drawing a circle we must know in which viewport the circle will be and viewport has to be opened before drawing so as the workstation and GKS.

Since objects "are" self-contained behavioral units, it is easier to create units (objects) that can be taken out of the context and reused in another context. Generalization of features is possible via inheritance. We have written above "are", because *objects communicating by methods are interconnected too much, in our opinion. In order to make objects self-contained, it is required that interaction abilities of an object are described independently of formalisms to ensure these interactions. In other words, compositions have to be separated from components to increase reusability of components and to enhance understandability of applications.*

During the development of an object-oriented system, developers are faced with problems appearing at reuse of components, that are *interconnected to much* and *with the lack of a simple composition principle.*

There is a move in object-oriented software development methodologies from the data-driven object-oriented design to the responsibility-driven design [3, 4] and interaction-oriented development [5] with the goal to increase encapsulation. But, both new approaches to software design, the responsibility-driven and interaction-oriented, base on the description of object responsibilities and thus client-server relationships although the client-server protocol *limits the reuse* of object-oriented software. Only components which are compatible - which obey the same client-server protocol may be composed and may collaborate and perform some system functionality.

Software reusability is of great importance for the efficient development of large systems. Object-oriented approach to software development enhances software reusability because it provides a simple mechanisms for incremental modifications and compositions of software. These mechanisms are inheritance, dynamic binding, and message passing [5]. The composition of reusable components is made difficult by incompatibility of two or more existing components which perform the required functionalities but they do not satisfy the same client-server protocol.

As an example, consider the designing of an information system about people, where the required statistical data about people are graphically presented by dial or histogram. Consider that we have classes People, Dial and Histogram from other applications in a class library. They can be reused for this system. They are written in Smalltalk in Listing 1.

These three classes do not satisfy the same client-server protocol and cannot be reused without modifications for our application. Instead of the message show: aValue, the paint: aValue message should be sent to objects of class Dial and draw: aValue to objects of class Histogram. These are interface incompatibilities. Then message getValue is unnecessary. This is an incompatibility, where an object does not perform required actions in response to a received message. It is called causal incompatibility. In strongly typed languages (such as C++, Eiffel) also type incompatibilities can occur.

The design of reusable classes is also made difficult because in message passing systems a process cannot disseminate new results without knowing precisely where to send them. Objects have to know about its surrounding objects.

This and all forms of incompatibilities can be avoided by introduction of an object environment and by designing objects that instead of invoking the behavior of other objects with sending messages to them, inform the environment about interesting changes of values of its state variables [6]. Changes of object state variables are called events. Environment monitors and responds to notifications of events by initiating actions.

The introduction of an object environment for description of compositions of objects allows the separation of components from compositions which has already been mentioned as a request for increasing object reusability and understandability of applications.

```
class            People
superclass       Set
instance variables   views
instance methods
init ...
setValue: aValue
  views do:[:view|view show:aValue]
attachView: aView
 ...views  add:...
detachView: aView
 ...
older: years
    |anumber|
    anumber := 0.
    self do:[aPerson|
      (aPerson age > years)
      ifTrue:[anumber := anumber + 1]]
    self setValue:anumber.
younger: years
    ...
    self setValue:anumber.
old: years
    ...
    self setValue:anumber.
```

```
class            Person
superclass       Object
instance variables surname age...
instance method    ...
age
  ^age        ...
```

```
class              Dial
superclass         Object
instance variables  boundingBox subject
instance methods ...
boundingBox: aValue    ...boundingBox := aValue.
paint                  ... subject getValue.
setSubject:anObject   ...subject:=anObject.
```

```
class              Histogram
superclass         Object
instance variables  boundingBox
instance methods
boundingBox: aValue
  boundingBox := aValue.
draw : aValue  ...
```

Listing 1: Classes People, Person, Dial and Histogram

3 An Object Environment

Besides classes representing all real world entities involved in an application, an object environment is a constituent part of each object-oriented application.

Each object can inform the object environment about a number of named events that occur in an object through its life-time. Each event has a name and each may have no, one or more attributes. When an event occurs in an object, the object sends a message to the environment of the form:

E event-name [: event-attribute { keyword: attribute}]

where [] means option and {} means iteration (0,1 or more times) of parts of an event message.

After getting information about the occurrence of an event in an object, the environment activates appropriate actions performed by one or more objects of the application.

Environment is the set of application event agents which bind together objects of an application. Event agents are event-action rules. One or more rules, called a subsystem manager, define the run-time interactions and enforce the required behavioral relationships or constraints between two or among more objects forming a subsystem. A subsystem consists of a set of objects dedicated to a special goal (functionality) according to a set of local event-action rules performed by a subsystem manager.

A number of run-time interactions between objects correspond to enforce relationships or constraints between objects. Such interactions can be simple defined by interobject rules (i.e. event-action rules named event agents) and they need not necessarily be explicitly described by means of procedural transactions. Besides agents which monitor and respond to events, the environment contains also transactions. Transactions instantiate the system, initiate objects of the system, prompt the user to initiate events, or remind the user that some action is to be performed. All other required application processes are expressed by behavior relationships among objects defined in an object environment by subsystem managers.

The suggested event-driven design provides a way of declarative description of application functionality by means of event-action rules defined in an object environment.

Listing 2 shows the realization of our application - information system about people by the use of an environment E.

Because an object can belong to more subsystems, more subsystem managers can require object to perform the different or the same actions (defined by methods of a class of the object).

```
class              Dial          class              Histogram
superclass         Object        superclass         Object
instance variables boundingBox   instance variables boundingBox
instance methods                 instance methods
boundingBox: aValue              boundingBox: aValue
  boundingBox := aValue.           boundingBox := aValue.
draw : aValue                    paint: aValue
```

Listing 2: Information system about people designed by means of an object environment

178

```
class              Person
superclass         Object
instance variables surname age...
instance method    ...
age
  ^age       ...
```

```
class              People
superclass         Set
instance variables
instance methods
init ...
setValue: aValue
  E valueChanged:aValue.
 ...
older: years
    |anumber|
    anumber := 0.
    self do:[aPerson|
      (aPerson age > years)
      ifTrue:[anumber := anumber + 1]]
    self setValue:anumber.
younger: years
    ...
    self setValue:anumber.
old: years
    ...
    self setValue:anumber.
```

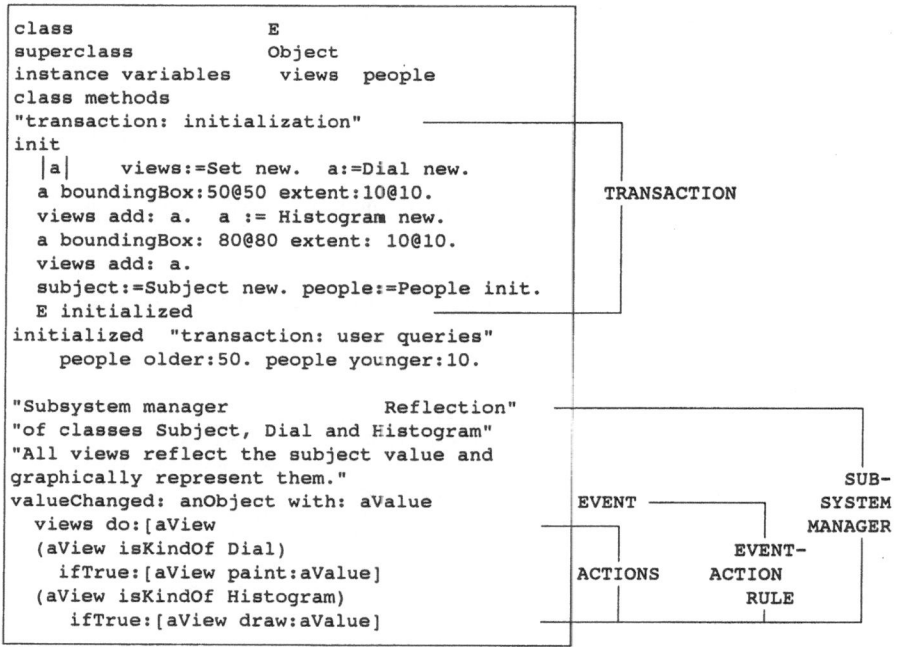

```
class               E
superclass          Object
instance variables   views  people
class methods
"transaction: initialization"
init
  |a|     views:=Set new. a:=Dial new.
  a boundingBox:50@50 extent:10@10.
  views add: a.  a := Histogram new.
  a boundingBox: 80@80 extent: 10@10.
  views add: a.
  subject:=Subject new. people:=People init.
  E initialized
initialized  "transaction: user queries"
    people older:50. people younger:10.

"Subsystem manager              Reflection"
"of classes Subject, Dial and Histogram"
"All views reflect the subject value and
graphically represent them."
valueChanged: anObject with: aValue
  views do:[aView
  (aView isKindOf Dial)
    ifTrue:[aView paint:aValue]
  (aView isKindOf Histogram)
    ifTrue:[aView draw:aValue]
```

Listing 2 (continued)

4 Benefits of Introduction of Events and Object Environment

The introduction of events and object environment as an event management system solves many problems in the object-oriented software development.

- Simple composition principle.

Incompatible objects can be composed without any modifications, because the object environment plays the role of adapters between otherwise incompatible objects. It receives messages about events that occur in an object (client of the client-server communication protocol) and translates them to calls that the other object (server) can understand.

- Increasing the reusability.

The use of an object environment enhances the class reusability by delaying the client-server binding. The environment permits the description of behavior specific to a particular application after the application components have been fully specified. This can be done without modifying the implementation of any component.

- Uncoupled programming style, which facilities establishing a

powerful libraries of easy reusable classes.
The fact that the client objects in the suggested events-environment model need not know anything about the servers and vice-versa, is central to the programming style. The sender notifies the environment about an event and sends event attributes. An environment then calls required actions and sends them all necessary received event attributes. Such communication enhances reusability and promotes uncoupled programming style. This facilitates establishing a large collection of independent reusable classes for software communities [7].

- Easy understandable and reusable programs.

It cannot happen that pieces of code failed to be object-oriented and at the same time difficult to be reused, because objects are not responsible for performing the ordered sequences of actions required to provide all application functionalities. This task is done by the object environment where the control flow of program is implemented.

5 How the Contents of an Object Environment can be Reused

Object environment defines all relationships among objects of an application. But same relationships can appear among many different objects in different applications. The question is how to reuse definitions of relationships. Complex structure and behavior of many applications from different domains can be the same. The same relationship as it is between People and Histogram in upper application exists for example between ball and obstacles in a Brickles game, where each movement of ball should be followed with position changes of obstacles. Obstacles in one way reflect the position of ball.

The common complex structure and behavior should be defined very abstractly to facilitate reuse. The complex structure and behavior of both applications consists of views (histogram and ball obstacles respectively) which always reflect the value of a subject (required statistical data about people and ball position respectively). Abstract description of this common complex structure and behavior is given in Figure 1 by means of E-R diagram and in Listing 3 with a class SubjectView which manages more subjects, each of which is presented with more views.

180

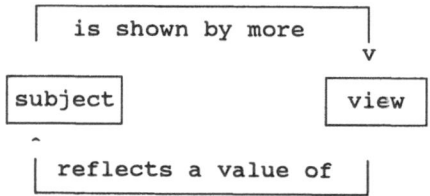

Figure 1: E-R diagram modeling relationships between parts and whole.

```
class SubjectView                    class Net
superclass  Object                   superclass   Object
instance variables dic               instance variables
instance methods  ...                instance methods
init                                 init
  dic:=Net new.dic init.               connections:=Dictionary new
attachView:aView to:aSubject         connect:aNode with:aNode
  dic connect:aSubject with:aView      ...
allViewsOf: aSubject                 connectedWith:aNode
^dic connectedWith:aSubject             ^...
"After initiation of subject,
 views have to be initiated."
initedS:aSubject
  self allViews:aSubject
   do:[:aView|E initW:aView]
    E do:aSubject
" All views allways reflect
subject value."
changedS:aSubject on:aValue
 self allViews:aSubject
  do:[:aView|
   E update:View for:aValue
endS
   self allViews:aSubject do:[
   aView| E end:aView .
```

Listing 3: Class SubjectView

6 The Event-Driven Object-Oriented Development

The use of events and object environment for the late binding of objects of an
application enhances reusability by increasing the openness of objects. This nice property
of suggested   object design is not very efficient for software development without an
appropriate development methodology. Following steps are suggested in the suggested
event-driven object-oriented software development:

▪ Identify objects (and classes) in the application domain.

▪ Identify relationships between objects. Represent entities and relationships in E-R
diagram.

▪ Identify and define structure and abstract behavior of each object. Develop or find and
extent specification (class) for each object if necessary. Some objects are designed to be

active. Active objects inform the object environment about changes of its states by event messages.

▪ Identify and define complex relationships. Classes which define parts of the E-R diagram of application are founded and reused or new classes have to be described.

▪ Put all classes together by means of an object environment and by abstract classes in strongly typed languages. First define transactions and then describe each relationship between two or among more objects by an event-action rule of the object environment. Event-action rules can define the required relationships also by reuse of existing classes modeling required relationships.

7 Conclusions

The use of events as a support for describing the system behavior is an old one. Events are used together with the triggering mechanism in many extensions of the data-flow analysis method for description of the system behavior.

The lack of efficiency is a major problem of many systems using some form of triggering concept. We have avoided this problem by the exact description of the order of actions executed at each event. In this way, there is no necessary search among objects of a system interested in particular event. Events are handled immediately after they occur.

The use of an object environment and events allows the extension of the traditional client-server communication paradigm. Events and object environment provide a simple mechanism for modeling system complexity and behavior. They increase object openness and reusability and provide a simple mechanism for describing the behavior compositions, constraints and dependencies among objects of an application.

Events generated by objects of a class are a part of a class and should be appropriately specified. Most events should be placed by the class designer, because they are a part of a class description. Environments containing subsystem managers are designed by the application developer.

Problems concerning the generation of events are not simple ones. There are many questions about generation of events: Which are active objects or which objects should be designed as active? What events should be generated? What event arguments are necessary? These questions have a great effect on the reusability and suitability of the event-driven design for the development of large library of reusable classes for software communities.

The suggested development methodology and design enable assembling applications rather than programming, what we still do today. We think, that the construction of complex software systems from powerful building blocks can greatly increase productivity.

At the moment, we can not give any experimental results about the efficiency of the suggested design for real applications in terms of software productivity and quality.

The suggested event-driven design enhances reusability. And considering the fact that when the effort required to produce a new code is larger than the effort of reusing the existed code the reusability is in proportion to productivity, we can conclude that the suggested approach improves productivity.

Software complexity theory suggests that a program with a larger variable span and live variable, decision count and readability will be more sensitive for future modifications. Thus, the software quality of a program with a large decision count, readability, variable span and live variable is considered to be poor. With observing of Listings 1 and 2 and the design of our information system about people done by means of an object environment which reuses SubjectView class for modeling complex behavior and structure between people and views can be concluded that variable span and number of live variables is decreased.

References

1. B. Henderson-Sellers, J. M. Edwards, "The object oriented system life-cycle", Communication on the ACM, vol 33, no. 9, Sept. 1990.

2. K. Rizman, I. Rozman, A computer aided prototyping methodology, ACM SIGSOFT SOFTWARE ENGENERING NOTES, Vol 14., No. 6, 68-72 (1989).

3. R.Wirfs-Broock, Object-Oriented Design: A Responsibility-Driven Approach", OOPSLA'89 Proceedings, 71-75 (1989).

4. R. Wirfs-Brock, B. Wilkerson, L. Wiener, "Designing Object Oriented Software", Prentice Hall, 1990.

5. R. Helm, I.M. Holland, D.Gangopadhyay, "Contracts: Specifying Behavioral Compositions in Object-Oriented Systems", ECOOP/OPSLA'90 Proceedings, October, 1990, pp. 169-180.

6. B. Meyer, Reusability: The Case for Object-Oriented Design, IEEE Software, March 1987, 50-64 (1987).

7. S. Gibs, D. Tsichritzis, E. Casias, O. Niersatz, X. Bintando: Class Management for Software Communities, Communications of the ACM, vol. 33, no. 9, September 1990, 90-103 (1990).

8. G.Booch, Object-Oriented Design, The Benjamin Cummings Publishing Company Inc., (1991).

9. P. Coad, E. Yourdon: Object-Oriented Analysis, Yourdon Press, Prentice Hall, 1990.

10. A. Goldberg, D.Robson, Smalltalk-80: The Language and its Implementation, Addison-Wesley, 1983.

11. W. LaLonde , J. Pugh: Designing is Hard: Object-Oriented Software Is Different!, Journal on Object Oriented Programming, March/April 1989, 46-55 (1989).

12. D. Teanzer, M. Ganti, S. Padar, "Object-oriented Software Reuse: The Yoyo Problem", Journal on Object Oriented Programming, Sept./Oct. 1989, 30-35 (1989).

THE CHALLENGE OF COPING WITH COMPLEXITY

Chair: B. Dömölki

Usability is a Good Investment

Dipl.O.W.Sc.Inst. Tamas Marx
IQSOFT SzKI Intelligent Software Co.Ltd.

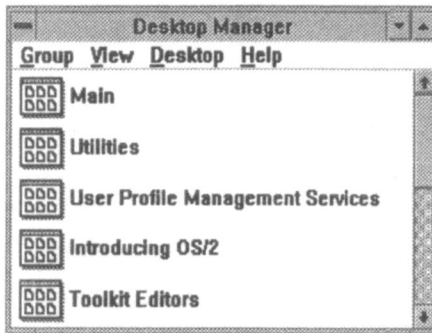

Figure 1

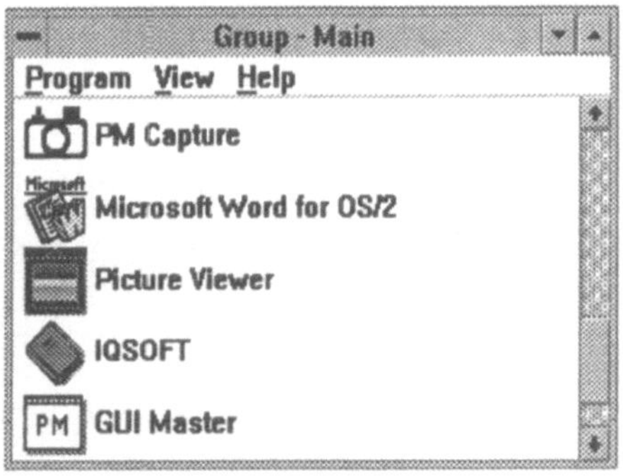

Figure 2

Abstract: Visual identification is certainly quicker than reading. However the above three examples show us that the use of grafical user interface is not as simple as puting little pictures everywhere. They are useful in Figure 2 but they are useless in Figure 1.

Figure 3

Technology has changed. New interfaces gave programmers possibilities they have never dreamt of. How and when to exploit these possibilities are the question!

- User interfaces are the decisive factors of the success on the market of a new software or your application in your company.

- There are terminals in front of more and more people, this should be the quickest growing branch of data processing. It is not.

- Usability testing is the part of the computer industry where we have do deal with the human factors.
  Software engineers alone can not handle this problem.

- How to mesure usability and how to estimate the profitability on any investment in usability are the question we will have to answer.

The speach will try to address the above problems with real examples on the screen and numbers from real projects will try to show you how to make your applications more usable and how to estimate its profits.

A Metaphor-Based Design Approach of a Graphical User Interface for Database Systems

G. Haring and M. Tscheligi

Department of Applied Computer Science
Institute of Statistics and Computer Science
University of Vienna
Lenaugasse 2/8
A-1080 Wien
Email: A4424DAF@AWIUNI11.BITNET

Abstract. The appropriate design of user interfaces has a fundamental influence on the acceptance of software systems. Today´s technology supports the realization of attractive user interfaces, which represent the functionality of the application to the user, based on the mental model. The paper describes the prototype design of a direct manipulative, graphical user interface for the core functionality of database systems. A new two-phase interleaving prototype development cycle is proposed for the design process. The general design philosophy and some basic interacting user interface objects, based on the real life look metaphor, are described in detail. Finally the embedding software architecture is outlined.

1 Introduction

Beside the processing of text the management of data is the main centre of interest of today´s office activities. The support of data management activities is presented to the human by data base systems. These systems offer a wide and complex range of functionalities including schema design, querying, browsing and manipulation for different classes of users (database designer, application developer, end user). A lot of database knowledge is necessary to use the data base system with the aimed success.

The amount of theoretical database knowledge should be minimized by an intuitive and easy understandable user interface. The importance of the user interface nowadays is widely accepted by the computer community. Due to this importance the solution of the user interface problem has to be considered as a leading activity in every software development process . Therefore steps of user interface development must be integrated in software engineering methodologies to achieve a sophisticated form of human computer communication.

* this work was supported by the Austrian National Bank under grant 3692

Graphical user interfaces are becoming mandatory for every interactive software system. This modern type of user interfaces takes advantage of the visual channel of humans. The states of the application are transferred to the user by graphical presentations and the user is able to manipulate these presentations to transmit the intentions to the computer system. The manipulation of the graphical objects results in an altered internal state. Direct manipulation [7] is an important term often mentioned in this context. Graphical interaction techniques and direct manipulation have to be used to hide the complexity of data base systems to the user. Too frequently the user interface is oriented to the underlying data model. In this paper we describe the result of going in the opposite direction: hiding basic and theoretical data base concepts to the user. The design of the user interface is primarily influenced by the users mental imagination of data management tasks and is based on a collection of real life looking interacting objects.

Prototyping is accepted as the leading approach for the development of user interfaces due to the early evaluation possibility. Unfortunately existing implementation environments for graphical user interfaces are not the ideal platform for an efficient and rapid evolutionary prototyping process. This statement is extremely valid when alternative user interface techniques have to be tested, without any alignment to existing user interface standards. Therefore a two step prototyping process was introduced during the development of our user interface prototype.

The aim of this paper is to show the general concepts of an alternative user interface for common database functionalities, where look and feel is based on the usage of user oriented metaphors. Before the specific appearance and behavior of the user interface is demonstrated we outline the above mentioned prototyping process together with a clarifying discussion of nomenclature necessary to describe activities of the user interface development process. Afterwards some remarks are made concerning the specific software environment and software architecture where the development of the user interface prototype took place. In the last section some conclusions are drawn from this design project.

2 A Prototyping Oriented Development Approach

So far a well defined characterization of necessary activities for the construction of a graphical user interface is missing. To define a structured methodology for this task we use terms already established in the software engineering community to circumscribe the process of development: the analysis of existing designer models and mental models of potential users results in a user interface requirements definition, the user interface design activity yields in a user interface specification (in our case a written specification is almost completely replaced by a first prototype), the user interface implementation design results in a general software architecture for this type of user interface and the user interface implementation activity leads to the second prototype.

This activities are shown in Fig. 1 in a top down form unless some of the activities can be overlapping and iteratively repeated. In particular this is necessary during the design, where several versions of prototypes have to be produced before a sophisticated level was reached. Regarding this overlapping the user interface implementation design started before the first prototyping process was finished. The general user interface philosophy created during the design activity is suffice for the conceptual work on the architecture.

2.1 Designer Models and User Models

The designer model is the mental imagination of the basic data base functionality on the side of the user interface designer transferred to users by existing data base systems. With already existing and running software and the accompanying documentation a specific mental model from the functionality of underlying data management tasks is built on the user's side. The evaluation of some existing data base systems aimed at the identification of existing designer models and to get a feeling of implemented data base system functionality. In the evaluation mainly PC-based products were used including Apple's Hypercard approach to get an input also from non traditional data base oriented solutions.

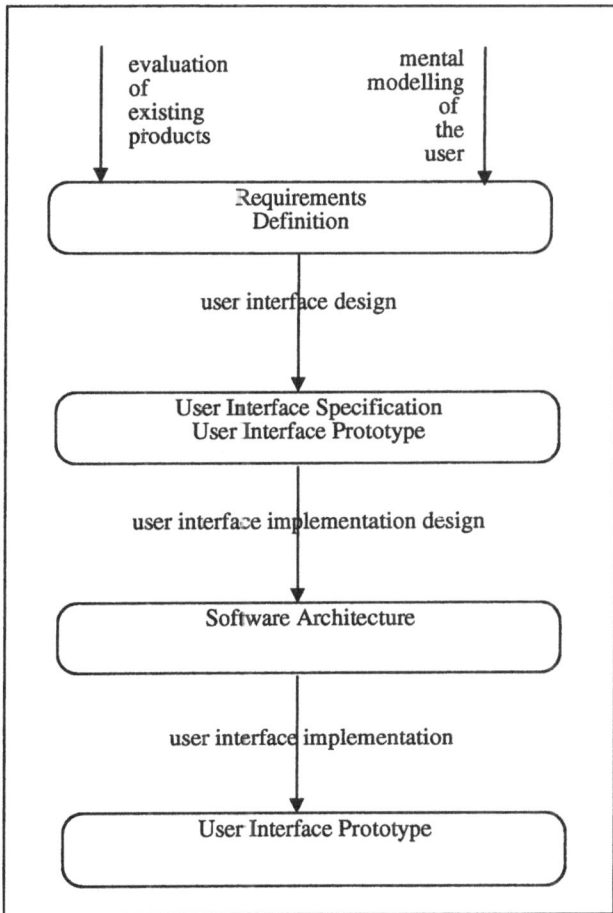

Figure 1

For the second activity leading to the requirements definition we tried to identify the ideas of potential data base system users without any reference to existing software solutions of data base management functionality. The users had to show the different ideas by sketching it on paper. In Table 1 the results of evaluation is shown for the principle data base concepts "database" and "file".

group	database	file (table)
1	filing cabinet	folder
2	wall cabinet	folder
3	archive	cardfile
4	wall cabinet	table book
5	collection of books	book
6	cabinet with books	folder
7	cabinets	folder, books

Table 1

This survey shows a clear preference for objects already used within non computer supported data management in everyday office life. The results of this evaluation encouraged our attempt to maximize the integration of a real life oriented metaphor.

2.2 User Interface Design - The First Prototype

As the first step within this activity the general principles of the intended user interface were specified. The whole user interface is totally composed of objects, each with a specific semantic regarding data base tasks or general object manipulation tasks. A set of general manipulation primitives [6, 10] were defined to reach a consistent and object independent manipulation style. In the following individual graphical objects are invented for specific data base functionalities to get a starting point for the following prototyping cycle.

There was already mentioned that available user interface implementation platforms are not the ideal environment for really rapid prototyping. User interface implementation within a window environment requires a lot of programming to yield a working piece of software. User interface toolkits at a higher level of abstraction are oriented towards a predefined and specific user interface style with minimal freedom for the goal of alternative user interface testing.

Therefore we decided to use another type of product for the user interface design activity to experiment with different design alternatives not restricted by common user interface implementation conditions. In particular MacroMind Director [5] was used which is a tool for the assembly of multimedia presentations. In this case multimedia presentations denote the production of high quality animated color graphics for different purposes. With this orientation to animation the intended user interface can be demonstrated not only statically but also dynamically. Several steps of evaluation and redesign were necessary to yield a sophisticated prototype which could be used as basis for further development and transformation to the target implementation environment.

2.3 User Interface Implementation Design

As every software system user interface code demands for a careful design of the internal software structure. The term implementation design was chosen to create a distinction to the external (user oriented) activity of user interface look and feel design.

Within this activity a general object oriented software architecture was introduced to realize this type of user interfaces with reusable components. The activity of user interface implementation design started before the previous activity was finished with the general interaction possibilities defined at the beginning of the design activity as general guideline for the software structure.

2.4 User Interface Implementation - The Second Prototype

Based on the software architecture defined in the above mentioned activity the user interface objects specified within the first prototyping cycle were transformed to the target environment successively. Though we denote this activity with the term implementation it is a matter of fact that in this activity also prototyping took place. This is due in part to different software and hardware platforms. The first prototyping process was done with a Macintosh and a one button mouse and the second prototype was produced on a SUN workstation with a three button mouse. In addition the permanent attempt to improve the user interface is another reason.

The prototype was oriented to the NeWS windowing environment [3] and implemented in the Postscript extension of NeWS for the device dependent part together with some amount of C++-Code for a device independent part. Due to availability of a working prototype many problems of communicating the ideas of the user interface designer to the implementation group was weakened.

3   The General User Interface Philosophy

The whole user interface is composed out of different objects. The available objects conceptually put the user into an office environment. All database functionality is embedded in manipulation relationships between these available objects. With this approach menus common in usual systems are obsolete. The mouse cursor acts as special object with which the semantic of the interaction relationships between different objects are triggered for the most part. Some manipulations of the objects are directly carried out by the mouse. In a metaphorical sense the mouse cursor acts as the lengthening of the user hand and touches the objects in question. This corresponds to the general directness   demand of direct manipulative systems [4]. The keyboard is only used for data entry (characters, numbers).

Three possible operations with the mouse are mapped to higher level manipulation primitives. The general idea of defining manipulation primitives results in a clear and consistent manipulation philosophy which is intuitively understandable and rememberable for the user of the system. If the primitive is applicable the general semantic of the manipulation primitive is the same regardless of the object type involved.

The mouse operations used for this purpose are a single click (pressing and releasing a mouse button without any movement in between), a double click (pressing and releasing a mouse button without any movement twice in a very short period) and dragging (pressing the button, dragging the mouse to another position on the screen and releasing the button).

The mapping of mouse buttons to higher level manipulation primitives is defined in Table 2. With the *activation* of an object the user defines special interest on the object mainly to prepare the object for further operations or select associated object attributes as current adjustments. The activation is accompanied with object specific feedback to show the user possible usage possibilities. With the *open/close* primitive the user usually toggles between an external and an internal presentation for objects which are used as data containers. The *positioning* manipulation primitive allows the user to alter   the current object position. If there exists a special interaction relationship between the manipulated object and another touched object the specific functionality is initiated if both objects are overlapping. Objects can be rotated by a *rotate* primitive and resized by a *resize* primitive as known from some window managers.

interaction primitive	mouse operation
activate	single click with left mouse button within object region
open/close	single click with right mouse button within object region
position	dragging with the left mouse button within object region
rotate	dragging of a object corner with the left mouse button
resize	dragging of an edge or corner with the right mouse button

Table 2

The problem of getting objects for the first time is solved by the usage of a special catalogue object. The catalogue contains all the objects available in the system and the user gets them by simply opening and dragging the objects out.   The catalog is self reproducing to enable more than one instance of a special object. In addition to the general manipulation primitives some other interaction relationships are collectively in existence: copying with a copying machine, printing with a printer object, coloring of objects with a color bucket and a subsequent selection from a color palette which represents available color possibilities, deleting objects with a trash can and scrolling with an fully independent scrollbar with an alternative look and feel.

4 The Look and Feel of User Interface Objects

In the following subsections objects from the prototyped data base user interface are described according to the object oriented organization of the user interface. These objects and their relationships together result in the user interface for this type of functionalities. If other objects are referenced in the object specific description these are written in italic form.

4.1 Cardfile

For this object a rectangular colored cardfile representation is used also showing cards within the cardfile (Fig. 2). The amount of visible cards shows the current utilization of the cardfile. On the front side a label object can be placed. With this label the user is able to enter the name of the card file. With the open/close manipulation primitive the cardfile can be opened and then cards are presented in a stack form. Cards only exist behind a special object mask.

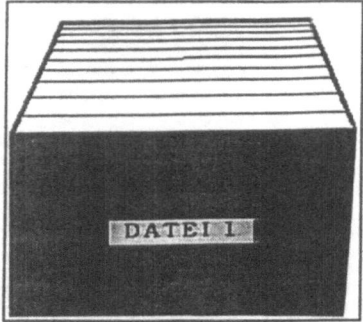

Figure 2

The presentation of the stack is visually strengthened by a background color in which the stack is contained. This background color can also be used to close the cardfile. By positioning the cardfile (in an opened or closed state) to another cardfile the contents of the cardfile can be transferred to the target object. At the end of each stack an empty card is available to input new data. For changing the visible card the interaction relationship with the *scrollbar* can be used.

4.2 Label

By activating the label a cursor appears at the beginning of the label. Now the user is allowed to input or edit a name. The label adapts to the length of text. One or more labels can be positioned to a cardfile or another object. The label also interacts with the scrollbar to see hidden (e. g. the label was reduced in size before) contents of the label.

4.3 Masks

Masks are a special form of card dedicated to the definition of views on existing cardfiles. Without a mask nothing can be seen from the data contained on a specific card. The mask is also an object which comes in an open and closed presentation. The closed form can be seen in Fig. 3. Available masks (open or closed) can be attached (in conceptual terms the mask is inserted before the data cards) by activating or by positioning. At any time only one mask can be active.

The open mask is presented in an A4 paper sheet form and can contain fields. This fields are the placeholders for the data. On every place in the card additional text can be inserted without fields. The fields can be selected from an object called attribute list, from the list of computed fields and/or from the list of joined fields. The contents of the fields can be protected from editing by placing a grid over some part of the mask.

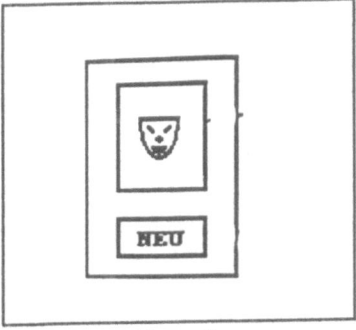

Figure 3

4.4 Fields

Fields are represented by a rectangular white bar. Fields can be obtained from the attribute list, the list of computed fields or the list of joined fields. By activating the field the cursor is positioned at the beginning of the field and the user is able to enter something. The field is aimed to different forms of data (text, images, sound) and automatically alters the size if necessary by the contents. If a field does not show all the data at once the srollbar is usable again.

4.5 Query Card

The catalog contains also a special form of card for the execution and definition of queries (query card tool, Fig. 4). By activating a special query card the query associated with the manipulated query card is applied. Several queries can be active at the same time. A subsequent query is applied to the state of the cardfile after the already activated query.

At the same time the query card is integrated into the appropriate place at a special presentation called the top view (Fig. 5). The top view shows the partition of the card file caused by applied queries. An activated query card partitions the card space according to the query condition.

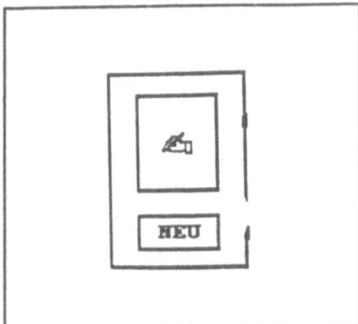

Figure 4

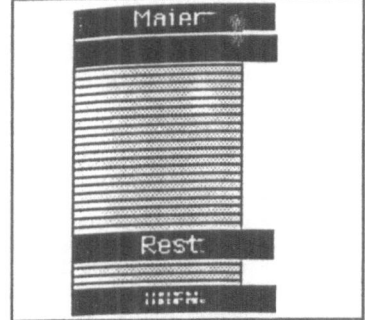

Figure 5

The query card is shown between the cards which fulfill the query condition and the cards where this is not the case. In the top view existing query cards can be activated and removed directly. An empty query card is always shown at the back of the top view, which is replaced automatically by a new one if it is used. To deactivate any queries the correponding cards can be placed behind the empty card for further usage.

The query card can be opened. In the opened presentation one or more conditions can be attached to fields selected from the attribute list. With a special object billiard ball a sorting direction can be specified.

4.6 Scrollbar

The scrollbar can be attached to any object with scrollable contents in order to see other parts of the content. The scrollbar is shown in Fig. 6. Visually the scrollbar comes with two triangles within the scrollbar frame. The triangles serve as slider which can be moved. By activating one of the triangles the scrolling is executed by one line, the activation out of the triangles but within the scrollbar borders causes a page oriented movement.

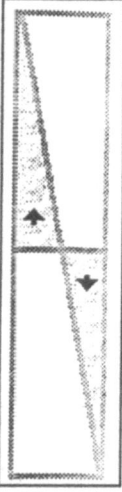

Figure 6

As special feature of this type of scrollbar is the possibility of scrolling in alternative directions. The same scrollbar can be used to scroll horizontal, vertical or diagonal. This is simply adjusted by rotating the scrollbar object with the rotating primitive. So scrolling towards the third dimension necessary within the used cardfile representation can be done.

4.7 Browsebox

The browsebox is an object to give the user another possibility to view the data inside a cardfil. By opening the browsebox a table is presented with all available data within a specific cardfile. The first line shows the names of the fields which values are shown on the subsequent lines in traditional form. Usually the available space is restricted and therefore the scrollbar can be used again. By activating the desired portion of the table some data can be edited or added. As soon as the data is altered within the table it is also taken over to the card representation.

4.8 Tab

This object is intended for marking special data cards, mask cards or query cards (Fig.7). It is for example useful if the user wants to find a particular card out of the lot of card usually found in a cardfile. The tab can be designated by the object label, as any other object. To attach a tab to a card the tab has to be positioned on top of the target card. The association holds as long as the tab is not removed from the surface of this object. By activating the tab the associated card is activated.

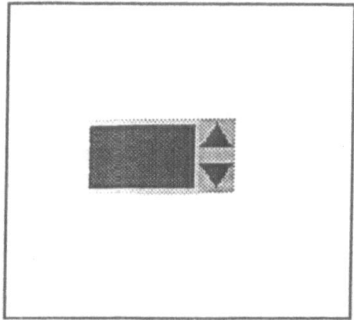

Figure 7

4.9 Attribute List

In the opened presentation the attribute list contains all available fields of a cardfile (Fig. 8). This object is always presented on top of all other objects and gets a transparent appearance. New fields can be added and existing fields can be edited. By opening the attribute list (the closed is shown Fig. 9) the fields are shown from all existing cardfiles with the current color of the cardfile. If the cardfile is positioned over a cardfile only the fields of the touched cardfile are visible. The activation of special field entry causes the field to appear on a mask object.

Figure 8

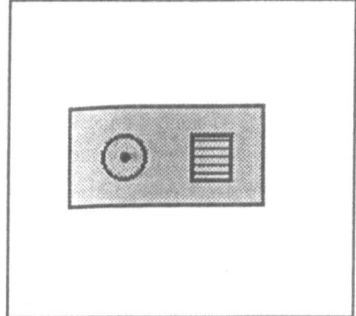

Figure 9

4.10 List of Computed Fields

All computed objects of a cardfile are represented with this type of list. Again this list always lays on top of other objects and the visual presentation is transparent. Computed fields are defined by an arithmetic expression using fields of the attribute list. The opened presentation allows editing of existing and creation of new computed fields. By simply opening the list of computed fields the fields from all cardfiles are presented. After the positioning over a specific cardfile only a specific set of computed fields is presented. The activation of a special field entry results in an integration into a mask card.

4.11 Billiard Ball

The billiard ball object acts as a possibility to define fields used for sorting the cardfile. The user has to activate the billiard ball for that field which should be used for the sorting. If within a sorting definition another sorting is requested a further billiard ball has to be used. This ball is used with the subsequent number to indicate the next sorting level. The defined sorting order also can be stored with a query card.

4.12 Data Base Manager

Joining data base parts is very complex task very hard to understand especially for the naive user. In particular this sort of task in this form is not existent in reality without a computer supported solution. Nevertheless an object had to be defined with some connection to real life appearance supporting the formation of the mental model based on analogy.

A database manager consists out of different regions: a head, a body and some hands (Fig. 10). The hat of the data base manager shows the operators forming the condition under the card files are joined. The connection is established by positioning one hand of the data base manager to the first cardfile and the second hand of the data base manager to the second cardfile. Automatically the data base manager gets a new hand which also can be used to integrate another cardfile. The specific fields are selected by the finger of the corresponding hand using the attribute list.

Figure 10

The activation of the head stands for the start of the execution of the defined functionality. As special progress feedback the eyes of the data base manager are rolled. The result of the join is represented within the body as a different object virtual cardfile.

4.13 Virtual Cardfile

The virtual cardfile is represented within the body of the data base manager and represents the result of a join. By activating the head of the data base manager the user is able to learn more about the join conditions used. Automatically the connections are shown with the hands of the data base manager. In a special list object called list of joined fields the involved fields and operators are visualized. The structure of the virtual cardfile can be changed by using other fields or another operator. By opening the virtual cardfile virtual cards are represented.

4.14 Virtual Cards

On one card the stacks of all involved cardfiles are visualized which cards satisfy the join conditions. To indicate the source cardfile the same underlying color is used. The activation within a virtual card leads to the possibility of editing the contents. An empty card is available at the end of each stack. By srolling to the card of one stack the corresponding card of the other stack is also visualized. As with the regular form of a cardfile objects like the browsebox, query card, mask card or billiard balls are also applicable.

4.15 List of Joined Fields

Like the other lists in this user interface approach this object shows the fields involved in the join on a separate list. This list is also applicable for mask cards by the activation of a special field. The list of joined fields cannot be edited.

4.16 Freezer

The freezer object is used to transform a virtual cardfile to a "normal" cardfile. The fields are combined and presented on one card. Joined fields exist only once. By default the fields are layouted in a column format but the user can redefine it or create other masks.

4.17 Grid

As already mentioned the grid object is used to restrict the access to some objects. If an object is protected by a grid only a well defined group of persons is able to manipulate the object. In the current version the grid is only used for protecting fields.

5   Software Architecture

In this section some remarks are made concerning the software architecture of the second prototype. A detailed description of the implementation can be found in [8, 9]. The architecture is based on the principles of application frameworks or user interface frameworks [2]. Application frameworks offer some amount of user interface code in form of reusable and extendable standard objects. Application frameworks utilize the techniques of object oriented programming for the implementation of graphical user interfaces.

Usual frameworks only support primitive mouse events. All higher level manipulation primitives have to be implemented for every new problem situation. Therefore direct manipulative user interfaces as introduced in this paper are not supported in a sufficient way.

So the support of interaction primitives defined above was the first important goal for our specific software architecture. The user interface programmer has the possibility to control the interaction primitives (enable, restrict or forbid) and select suitable forms of notification after an manipulation.

The second goal was to combine the higher level of abstraction with a sophisticated form of portability and reusability for different windowing platforms. Therefore the whole framework was splitted up into two functional parts.

The first application framework implements dialog control functionality [1] without any consideration to the presentation peculiarity regarding the concrete presentation of objects. The presentation part is the second application framework which is aimed at the presentation of the different graphical objects and the preparation of user interaction within a concrete windowing environment and without the consideration of their effects to and the triggers within the dialog control part.

The dialogue control part contains the whole user oriented semantic of the user interface. Only in this part objects are created and destroyed. As already mentioned the dialogue control was implemented in C++. The presentation part was mainly realized in Display Postscript with a C interface to the control part. Display Postscript is an extended version of Postscript used in the NeWS windowing environment for the application programmer interface.

6 Conclusions

This paper presents results from ongoing research regarding alternative methods of human computer communication. The user interface style introduced here is characterized by an exceptional object orientation from the user side of the system. The explicit usage of metaphors is another goal for the system. Several functions of database functionalities are considered and transformed into the selected interaction philosophy but by no means our system covers all available functionality of today´s data base systems. Due to the object based style missing objects can be easily integrated into the overall interaction style.

Existing user interface objects have to be refined in particular regarding the formulation of queries or other types definition tasks using a more visual oriented definition language. Additional objects are also necessary for the organization of the office due to the huge amount of existing objects. Further releases of the design not reported here include some objects for this task.

The two phase prototyping cycle used for the development of the user interface was very helpful to achieve an early discussion base for the evaluation of ideas concerning the design and the transformation of user interface concepts to more implementation oriented development activities. Future work regarding the development methodology is necessary for a better support of the requirements definition support and a better orientation of existing prototyping tools to the needs of alternative user interface designs to weaken the need of using different development environments.

References

1   L. Bass L., J. Coutaz J.: Developing Software for the User Interface. Reading, Mass.: Addison-Wesley 1991

2   M. Dodani, C. Hughes, M. Moshell M.: Seperation of Powers. Byte, March 1991

3   J. Gosling, D. S. H. Rosenthal, M. J. Arden: The NeWS Book. An Introduction to the Network/extensible Window System,.SUN Technical Reference Library. New York: Springer 1989

4   E. L. Hutchins, J. D. Hollan, D. A. Norman: Direct Manipulation Interfaces. In: D. A. Norman, S. W Draper (eds.): User Centered System Design: New Perspectives in Human Computer Interaction. Hillsdale: Lawrence Erlbaum 1986, pp. 87-124

5   MacroMind Inc., 410 Townsed St., Suite 408, San Francisco, CA 94107.

6   F. Penz, M. Manhartsberger, M. Tscheligi: The World of Objects - A Visual Object Based Interaction Language. In: Proceedings of the 10th Interdisciplinary Workshop on Informatics and Psychology, Schärding, Austria, May 21-23 (1991)

7   B. Shneiderman: Direct Manipulation: A Step Beyond Programming Languages. IEEE Computer 16, 8, 57-69 (1983)

8   B. Strassl B., F. Penz: CommonInteract - ein objektorientiertes System zur Entwicklung direkt manipulativer Benutzerschnittstellen. In: Proceedings UNIX Forum IV, Vienna, Austria, Oktober 1991 (in german)

9   B. Strassl B., F. Penz: CommonInteract - an Object Oriented Architecture for Portable Direct Manipulative User Interfaces, appears in Journal of Object Oriented Computing

10 M. Tscheligi, F. Penz, M. Manhartsberger: N/JOY-The World of Objects. In: IEEE Workshop on Visual Languages, Kobe, Japan, October 8-11 (1991)

Links in Hypermedia Systems

Frank Kappe, Hermann Maurer

Institute for Foundations of Information Processing
and Computer Supported New Media (IICM),
Graz University of Technology, Graz, Austria

Ivan Tomek

Jodrey School of Computer Science, Acadia University,
Wolfville, Nova Scotia, Canada

Abstract

In hypermedia systems, pieces of information (so-called nodes) are tied together by so-called links. This paradigm is often considered the as the single most important feature cf hypertext/hypermedia systems. However, in actual implementations of such systems there are a number of questions (open or partially resolved), design issues, and tradeoffs related to features and attributes of links.

In this talk, we discuss these questions as well as possible answers, including:

- Should links be single-ended or multi-ended?
- Should links be unidirectional or bidirectional?
- What types of entities should links be attached to?
- What kind of media should links be attached to?
- What should be the granularity of link attachment points?
- What information should be displayed before activating a link?
- Should links be typed?
- Should links have attributes?
- Should links be used for specification of node attributes?
- Should links be cold, warm or hot?
- How should links be displayed?
- How should links be created?
- How should consistency of links be maintained?

In addition, some notes concerning the actual implementation of links in a general-purpose, large-scale, multi-user hypermedia system will be made.

A NEW APPROACH TO DEFINING SOFTWARE DESIGN COMPLEXITY

László Varga

Department of General Computer Science

L. Eötvös University,

H-1117. Budapest, Bogdánfy u. 10/b.

Abstract: A general method is given for defining architectural design complexity measures. Desired properties of a measure are described by functional equations. Two cases of descriptions are considered. Complexity measures are given as the solutions of functional equations. Other complexity measures can be regarded as special cases of the solutions. A new measure is also presented.

Introduction

Software design is the most critical part of the software development process. In this period of software life cycle the structure of the pending software system is defined and the system is fully specified. The quality of a software design plays an important role in reducing software cost. This is because, researchers have attempted to find quality measures for characterizing software design. Among the quality measures probably the most important is the complexity measure.

In spite of the importance of software complexity it is insufficiently known and defined. It is necessary to distinquish between computational and psychological complexity of software.

Computational complexity is a qualitative characterization of algorithmic solution of a problem. It is measured by the amount of resources used by the solution.

Psychological complexity is a qualitative characterization of the misunderstandebility of a software. It can be measured as the difficulty of performing programming tasks as coding, testing and modifying software. Objective of this paper is psychological complexity.

The most often cited software complexity measures [Halstead 1977, McCabe 1976, Prather 1984] treat a program as a symple body of code. More recently, complexity investigations have attempted to characterize complexity of the relationships among the modules of a system [Card 1988, McCabe 1989].

In the paper [McCabe 1989] the cyclomatic complexity is applied to architectural hierarchical design of a system.

Common feature of almost all measures mentioned above is that measures are based on intuitions. For example, idea of cyclomatic complexity measure is that the difficulty in understanding a program can be approximated by the maximum number of linearly independent paths through a program.

In the paper [Daróczy 1988] the authors proposed a new approach to defining complexity measures. New feature of this approach is the following: Intuition is used for describing the desired properties of a measure and functional equations are used for describing properties.

The objective of this article is to extend the functional equational method into architectural hierarchical design of a programming system.

Architectural design

During the design phase of program life cycle, the system which satisfies the requirements, must be decomposed into seperate components. In this paper, the components are modules.

There have been many design methodologies developed in different applications. Among them the top-down functional decomposition has been widely used. At this method the programming system as a hierarchy of parts can be described by structure chart. An example of a structure chart is shown in Figure 1.

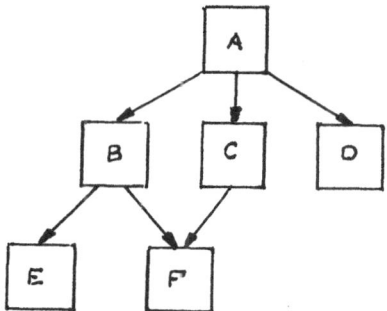

Figure 1. Sample structure chart.

Generaly, a sturcture chart defines how modules work together, but it does not define how each module works.

Software design is described by a suitable language. Design description languages generally use the control structures of high level programming languages with natural language description of operations. Variants of high-level programming languages such as ADA could be used as design description languages. For example, a high-level description of the well known spelling checher could be:

```
procedure SPELLCHECK is
begin
        produce list of words in document in short order
        loop
                get word from word list
                if word not in dictionary then
                        handle unknown word
                end if
                exit when all word processed
        end loop
        create new dictionary
end SPELLCHEK
```

Compound operations such as

"produce list of words in document in short order"

"handle unknown word" etc.

can be realized by procedure call.

Module specification generally gives precondations to procedure calls. For example the operation

"handle unknown word"

has the precondation

"not all word processed and the given word is not in dictionary".

According to this comments the stucture design of a programming system is defined as follows:

Definition 1. A structure chart $SC = (N, E, m, T)$ is a directed graph with a finite, nonempty set of nodes N, a finite, nonempty set of edges E, a master node $m \in N$, and a finite, nonempty set of terminal nodes $T \subset N$.

- Each node $n \in N$ lies on some path from m to $t \in T$.
- $m \in M$ is a unique node which has no predecessor.
- Terminal nodes ($\forall t \in T$) are characterized by the property that they have no successor.
- Each path in SC has no cirle.
- Nodes are used for representing modules.
- An edge is an ordered pair of nodes $n_1 \to n_2$ and it means, that module n_1 calles module n_2 or module n_2 is called by module n_1.

Definition 2. The module is a "case" structure plus its module function.

$$\text{case } (\alpha_1 : \text{ call } m_1; \ \alpha_2 : \text{ call } m_2; \ \ldots \ \alpha_n : \text{call } m_n); \ S$$

where $\alpha_i (i = 1, 2, \ldots, n)$ is logical expression, $m_i (i = 1, 2, \ldots, n)$ is module name and S is the module function. Terminal modules in SC have no case structure.

Definition of design complexity measures

A recursive definition could be given for design complexity measures using the hierarchical structure of SC.

Let the module

$$m = \text{case } (\alpha_1 : \text{call } m_1; \ldots; \alpha_n : \text{call } m_n); S$$

be given with the complexity measures

$$a(\alpha_1); \ a(\alpha_2); \ \ldots; \ a(\alpha_n); \ b(S);$$

$$c(\text{call } m_1); \ c(\text{call } m_2); \ \ldots; \ c(\text{call } m_n).$$

The design complexity measure of module m is

$$dc(m) = f(a(\alpha_1), c(\text{call } m_1); \ldots; \ a(\alpha_n), c(\text{call } m_n); \ b(s))$$

where f is a function to be determined.

The question is what kind of function f characterize the design complexity of a program sufficiently? To find an appropriate measure its properties should be formulated.

Let

$$f(x_1, y_1; \ldots; x_n, y_n; z)$$

be the function in demand. Obvious to investigate the result of changes in its argument.

<u>First appromation</u>

The function

$$f(x_1 + x_1', y_1 + y_1'; \ldots; x_n + x_n', y_n + y_n'; z + z')$$

is characterized by the property:

$$f(x_1 + x_1', y_1 + y_1'; \ldots; x_n + x_n', y_n + y_n'; z + z') \geq$$

$$f(x_1, y_1; \ldots; x_n, y_n; z) + f(x_1', y_1'; \ldots; x_n', y_n'; z')$$

Our requirement is not very profound. It means that the complexity of a system is greater than or equal to the complexity of its original complexity plus the complexity of increments. A solutions for f could be get using the equality relation.

Theorem 1.

Let us now suppose that

$$f(x_1 + x_1'; y_1 + y_1'; \ldots; z + z') = f(x_1, y_1; \ldots; z) + f(x_1', y_1'; \ldots; z'),$$

then

$$f(x_1, y_1; \ldots; x_n, y_n; z) = \sum_{i=1}^{n}(d_i x_i + e_i y_i) + gz$$

with convenient constants $d_i, e_i, i = 1, 2, \ldots, n; g$.

The formula could be proved by using the solution of the well known Cauchy equation.

How can we get a better approximation? It is obvious to suppose that the difficulty of understanding the relationships among modules depends on the complexity of decisions. In this case we get the following:

Second approximation

$$f(x_1 + x_1', y_1 + y_1'; \ldots; x_n + x_n', y_n + y_n'; z + z' =$$

$$f(x_1, y_1; \ldots; x_n y_n; z) + f(x_1', y_1'; \ldots; x_n', y_n', z') +$$

$$f(x_1, y_1'; \ldots; x_n, y_n'; 0) + f(x_1', y_1; \ldots; x_n', y_n; 0)$$

Theorem 2.

$$f(x_1, y_1; \ldots; x_n, y_n; z) = \sum_{i=1}^{n} h_i x_i + gz$$

with convenient constants $h_i, i = 1, 2, \ldots, n; g$.

Proof of the theorem also could be derived from the solution of Chauchy equation.

If we suppose, that

$$c(\text{call } m) = i(m) + dc(m),$$

where $i(m)$ is the complexity of modula interface, then both approximations provide a recursive definition for the design complexity measure.

Really, the second approximation yields an extension of the measure given by [Prather 1984] to arhitechtural design of a system.

An example

The question is what kind of weights could be choosen in our formulae? Let all be equal to unit.

Let us see the structure chart in Figure 1., with its associated functions:

$$A = \underline{\text{case}}(\alpha_{AB} : \text{call } B; \ \alpha_{AC} : \text{call } C; \ \alpha_{AD} : \text{call } D); \ S_A;$$
$$B = \underline{\text{case}}(\alpha_{BE} : \text{call } E; \ \alpha_{BF} : \text{call } F); \ S_B;$$
$$C = \underline{\text{if}} \ \alpha_{CF} \ \underline{\text{then}} \ \text{call } F; \ S_C;$$
$$D = S_D; \ E = S_E; \ F = S_F.$$

Using the short forms:

$$a(\alpha_{XY}) = a_{XY}; \ i(X) = i_X; \ b(S_X) = b_X,$$

second approximation gives the following design complexity measures:

$$dc(D) = b_D; \ dc(E) = b_E; \ dc(F) = b_F;$$
$$dc(C) = a_{CF}(i_F + b_F) + b_C$$
$$dc(B) = a_{BE}(i_E + b_E) + a_{BF}(i_F + b_F) + b_B$$
$$dc(A) = a_{AB}c_{BE}(i_E + b_E) +$$
$$(a_{AB}a_{BF} + a_{AC}a_{CF})(i_F + b_F) +$$
$$a_{AB}(i_B + b_B) + a_{AC}(i_C + b_C) +$$
$$a_{AD}(i_L + b_D) + b_A$$

Let $a_{XY} = 1$ and $i_X = 0$ for all X, Y in the system. If the structure chart is a tree then the formula is reduced to McCabe design complexity measure.

REFERENCES

1. Card, N.D. and Agresti, W.W., Measuring software design complexity. The J. of Syst. and Softw. 8.(1988) 185-197
2. Daróczy, Z. and Varga, L., A new approach to defining software complexity measures. Acta Cybernetica 8(1988) 287-291
3. Halstead, M.H., Elements of software science. Elsevier, New York, (1977)
4. McCabe, T.J., A complexity measure. IEEE Trans. Software Eng. 2.(1976) 308-320
5. McCabe, T.J. and Butter, C.W., Design complexity measurement and testing. Communications of the ACM, 32(1989) 1415-1425
6. Prather, R.E., An axiomatic theory of software complexity measure, The Comp. J. 4(1984) 340-347

METHODOLOGY AND EXPERIENCE

Chair: G. Klimko

SOFTWARE DEVELOPMENT ON THE BASIS
OF FRAME-CHANNEL MODEL

H. Maurer, N. Scherbakov
IIG, Technical University
Graz, Austria.

Abstract. In this article, a new paradigm in software engineering is discussed. In accordance with this paradigm a software system can be seen as a number of so-called frames connected by a number of channels.

Hence, we call this model the frame-channel model. Frames can encapsulate concrete actions such as execution of procedures, interpretation of database queries, infer procedures, and so on. The concept of channels allows to combine a number of frames into single software system in an elegant fashion.

The model can also be used in coauthoring numerous, large, software-related documents throughout the software life cycle.

1. INTRODUCTION

In order to successfully develop large software systems more or less formal models must be used. Such formal models are particularly important in the context of computer aided design of software systems [3]. In this case, the users i.e. the software developers, prepare and assess concrete decisions about a certain software project by means of computer systems [1]. In this paper we introduce a novel computer-based model for the described purpose.

Basically our idea is to describe an object-oriented software design approach in which we deal with the problem of addressability in a new way. Usually, messages in an object-oriented system are either sent to explicitly named objects (creating the well-known problems of naming conflicts, etc.) or else they are sent to all objects and only those with specific properties will act on them. The latter approach leads to serious problems in systematic program debugging and specification. We are choosing as alternative a hypermedia-kind of network consisting of links (which we call channels) allowing to pass messages from an object to a selected number of others.

We hope that such a "hypermedia" structure of a large software system leads to new possibilities in software development, verification and specification including reusability of source codes and software documents. The main motivation for reusing existing source codes and software documents in general is to improve qualities and productivities within a well-coordinated organization and increase usabilities of resources.

2. FRAME-CHANNEL MODEL

The frame-channel model is a paradigm which allows to formally define the structure of a large software product and, thus, manage the process of its development [5].

Within this model, the internal structure of a software system is perceived as a frame structure which includes:
- a number of so-called frames;
- and a number of channels ,which are functional relationships ("links") between frames.

A certain frame can be defined in the form of either a basic procedure or a frame structure. Note the recursive definition which allows to apply the same model on different levels of abstraction.

In analogy, channels can be seen as an unified approach to the interface between functional parts of a software product.

A frame includes a number of *switchers* which are special logical conditions, and a body which is either a basic procedure or a frame structure.

The main action which can be applied to a frame is to activate it. When a certain frame is activated, body is evaluated i.e. analysed or interpreted. If the body is a basic procedure, then this procedure is executed. If the body is another frame structure, then the activation is recursively applied to this structure.

One channel can connect an arbitrary number of frames. More precisely, each frame can be connected to a number of so-called input channels, and to a number of output channels. In analogy, some frames can be defined as sources of a certain channel, and some - as results.

For instance,

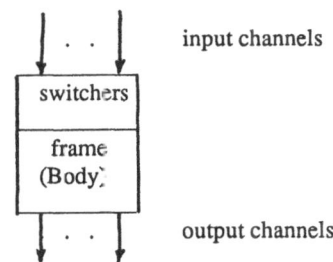

and from the "channel´s" point of view:

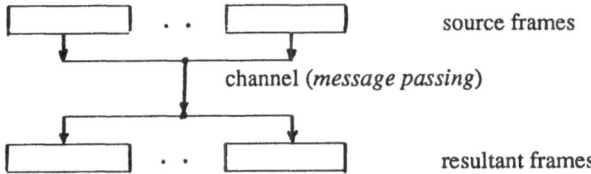

A channel can be also activated. A certain channel is activated as a result of the activation of one of its source frames.

At this point, we can describe the frame activation process in more detail.

Once a certain channel is activated, it contains a number of so-called messages which are available to resultant frames. The term "message" is to be understood as a number of words. For instance, (READ FILE), (25 16) (1) and so on. Such messages are called mails during our discussion. Thus, an activated channel includes 0, 1 or more mails which are available to resultant frames. Resultant frames have a fixed order within a certain channel. Hence, we may use terms "first", "last" and "next" resultant frame. In order to activate a concrete resultant frame, we scan through the sequential list of resultant frames, and check the value of the corresponding switchers i.e. their logical conditions. If a "current" switcher has the logical value "TRUE", then a frame which includes this switcher is activated. Once a certain frame is activated, the input channel immediately ceases to be activated. Thus, only one resultant frame can be activated.

3. SOFTWARE OBJECTS

In accordance with the frame-channel paradigm, a software system can be seen as a kind of software object. A certain software object implements a concrete algorithm by judging a certain collection of input messages and by generating output messages. In turn, this judging of input messages can be seen as a multi-steps process of activation of "internal" frames and channels which define different reactions (or responses) to certain messages (i.e. algorithms). The term "internal frames and channels" is perceived here as purpose-oriented structure of a particular software object. The judging procedure results in the activation of exactly one output channel which corresponds to the result of the algorithm.

For instance,

In addition to these two active data structure types - frames and channels, the internal representation (or topology) of software objects may also include mail boxes.

Each mail-box has unique name, and contains either a number of concrete messages (mails) or the special code NULL-value. In the latter case the mail box is empty.

Note that a mail box is a passive data structure. That is, messages within a certain mail box can be used or modified at any time by means of the unique name of this mail box, but the mail box cannot modify other messages, activate frames and channels.

Messages within a concrete channel or a concrete mail box have a fixed order. Thus, we can refer to a "first" message, to a "second" message and so on. When a certain action refers to a message by means of a channel name or a mail box name, the "first" message is refered to. If the same action puts a new message into a certain channel or a mail box, the new message becomes the "last" one. Thus, mail boxes act as queues.

4. MESSAGE PROCESSING AND SWITCHERS

In most respects, the activation procedure of a certain frame can be seen as a number of actions which deal with messages. To address a certain message, the message operations use a *reference* to the message.

The form of a reference is:

$$<message> = \left\{ \begin{array}{l} \underline{USER} \\ <name>\ \underline{CHANNEL} \\ <name>\ \underline{BOX} \\ "<message>" \end{array} \right\}$$

Thus, a certain reference can address or point to:
- a message on the user´s screen ("USER" option);
- a first message within a certain channel ("CHANNEL" option)
- a first message within a certain mail-box ("BOX" option);
- a concrete message which is defined in the form: "message"

Generally, a switcher is a special *logical function* which takes two messages as parameters, and produces the logical value "TRUE" or "FALSE". In order to distinguish between parameters of a switcher, we call the first message an input message, and the second - a pattern.

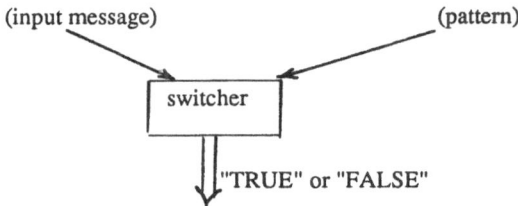

Let us also introduce some operations which deal with messages.
The operation

$$GET(<reference>)$$

gets the message from the user's screen, from a certain channel or from a certain mail-box. Note that the message taken from either a channel or a mail-box is deleted either from that channel or mail-box. The accepted message is available for further processing using the GET operation under discussion. If the operation is applied to an "empty" mail box or to an "empty" channel, then the result of the comparison

$$GET(...) = NULL\_VALUE \quad yields\ "TRUE".$$

Thus, the mail box can be seen as a special type of external variable which is assigned either a patricular value or a special code "value is unknown". Such a variable can be used in order to define rather sophisticated algorithms of logical inference.

The operation

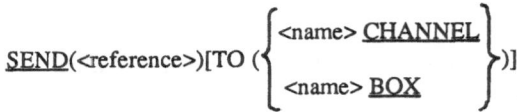

$$\underline{SEND}(<reference>)[TO\ (\begin{Bmatrix} <name>\ \underline{CHANNEL} \\ <name>\ \underline{BOX} \end{Bmatrix})]$$

sends the message
- to the user's screen (default option)
- into a certain channel ("CHANNEL" option);
- into a certain mail-box ("BOX" option).

There is the concept of frame type and of an instance of a certain type. Thus, users can build new types on the base of previously defined ones and then apply instances of certain types in concrete software projects. This corresponds to the concept of <u>modularity</u> and <u>reusability</u>.

In our context, the possibility to parametrize (and hence <u>generalize</u>) the structure of a concrete software object is of particular importance.

To accomplish this, an arbitrary number of so-called <u>unresolved references</u> can be used.

More precisely, the definition of a frame type includes the number of parameters, i.e. the number of unresolved references to abstract messages. An unresolved reference is coded in the form: & <name_of_parameter>

Thus, a concrete instance of a software object can defined as an instance of one previously defined frame type or as a certain combination of such instances by means of assigning concrete sources of messages (channels or mail boxes) or particular messages to unresolved references.

The term "combination" implies a number of connections between input and/or output channels of different instances.

It should be especially noted that the discussed methods allow to build new frame types in analogy to building concrete instances of software objects. In other words, the designers are allowed to build <u>new frame types</u> on the basis of a current set of existing types.

5. THREE LEVELS OF ABSTRACTION

We now come to the essence of this method, i.e. its actual application.

Three levels of detail exist during the definition of a certain software object.

On the first level, the prototype developer (can be the author or a specially appointed person) deals with a number of basic functions, and with the rules of frame type definition. These rules are fairly trivial ones and include special statements to define a switcher, and a special statement to define a body as sequential set of basic functions. It should be noted that all frame types defined on this level contain exactly one input channel i.e. unresolved reference &INPUT, and exactly one output channel i.e. unresolved reference &OUTPUT.

For instance, the frame type F2:

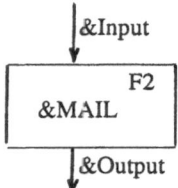

Can be defined by:

```
DECLARE FRAME F2
    SWITCHER: EQ(&INPUT, &MAIL)
    BODY: SEND(GET(&INPUT)) TO (X)
          GET(&MAIL)
          SEND(X) TO (&MAIL)
          SEND(&INPUT,&OUTPUT)
END FRAME F2;
```

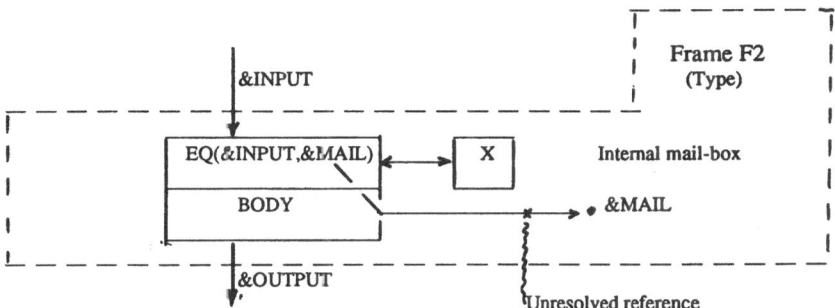

Of course, within the body of a certain frame some additional functions can be used. These additional functions are perceived as a possibility to invoke external procedures or a whole software system during the interpretation of this frame. The results of the execution of such external procedures can be handled by this frame for further processing by means of the concept of messages. Thus, we can say that the concept of frames allows us to encapsulate external procedures or operations within a certain frame arbitrarily.

On the second level, the prototype developers deal only with previously defined types of frames i.e. with the current library of types. They can apply simple rules in order to build new frame types on the basis of the current library of types. The building rules are fully defined by the described concept of internal presentation of software objects. That is, the developer can connect frame types using the channel metaphor, and can assign concrete references to unresolved ones.

For instance,

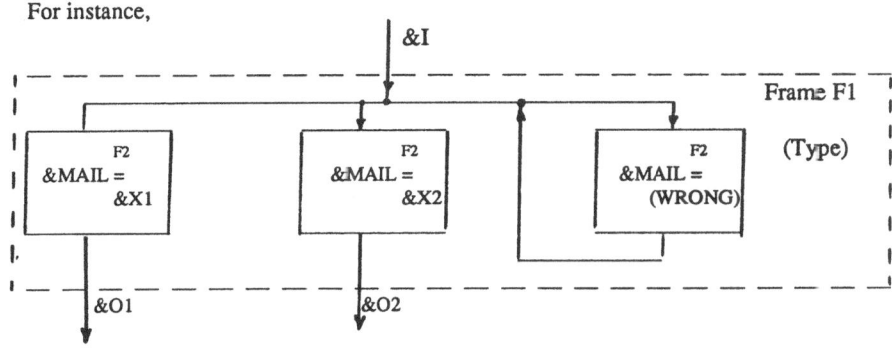

Now this structure can be seen as a new type of frame having two unresolved references: &X1 and &X2.

On the third level, the user has got a number of frame types which can be interpreted as completed software objects. The subset of such software objects is a user's own software design philosophy. This philosophy can be easily applied by means of setting a prescribed collection of parameters i.e. unresolved references.

It is very important to realize that the number of currently available frame types (the current library of frame type) can be dynamically changed at any time as a result of experience gained.

In other words, when the user starts to apply the software design system, the system can be seen as a prototype of the real system that is needed. This prototype can be successfully applied because it contains a collection of typical software objects, but what is more important, the prototyped number of software objects can be dynamically extended by means of the previously described possibilities to define new frame types.

6. CONCLUSION

There are some properties of our model which are of potential benefit from the point of view of the management of software projects[1,2]:
- the model includes a clear and convenient graphic notation;
- the model can be easily metaphorised for a concrete application[4];
- the model allows the formal verification of a project or of its part[3];
- the model can be applied on the different levels of software specification and implementation;
- the model supports rapid *prototyping*, including the possibility to apply a previous version of the software system within the latest version[2].

The model is mainly oriented towards the specification of so-called database systems, it pays a lot of attention to compatibility between different data models, between different data sub-languages and/or conventional programming languages.

The model was successfully applied in the number of rather big software projects. For instance, a working prototype of database system applied to control manufacturing activity of one of the biggest factories of St.Petersburg (around 15000 employees), was developed and installed during 3 months. Then, the system was applied as developing prototype for the period of 5 years. Now the system includes about 100 working versions. The most attractive feature of this approach is that the end-users were actually involved in the process of system development. They feel themselves as authors of this system and the painful transformation of end-users' needs to software was considerably simplified.

The same approach was applied during the development of a hyper-media system at Technical University of Graz. This approach permitted the usage of different types of end-user interfaces and dynamical assessment of their comparative efficiency from the user's point of view.

REFERENCES:

1. P. Bruce, S. M. Pederson: The software development project, Wiley-Interscience, NY, USA (1982), pp. 210
2. C. Choppy, S. Kaplan: Mixing abstract and concrete modules: Specification, Development and Prototyping In :12th International Conference on Software Engineering, IEEE Computer Society Press, Los Alamitos, CA, USA (1990), pp. 173-185
3. P. Freeman: Strategic directions in Software Engineering: Past, Present and Future, in: Ritter G.X. (Ed.), International processing 89. Proceedings of the IFIP 11th World Computer Congress, pp. 205-210, North-Holland publishing Company 1989.
4. R.H. Thayer: Software Engineering project management: A Top-Down View, in E. Nahouraii et. al. (Eds.): Software Engineering Management, pp. 230-235, IEEE Computer Society Press, Washington, DC, USA (1988).
5. H. Maurer, N. Scherbakov: The HM-Data Model; IIG Report Graz (1992).

Design Environment and Technologies Applied within the AXE 10 Software Design Process

Sead Kotlo

Ericsson Technika Kft., Hungary
1108 Budapest, Venyige u. 3

Abstract. Software design process for the digital switching system AXE 10, the main Ericsson's product in the field of digital switching as regards the public telecommunication, is divided in a number of subprocesses/phases. Further on, each of them includes a number of activities logically related to each other.

In order to make possible and successful cooperation of a number of dislocated design centres being involved in huge or medium size development projects going on within the company, to provide for all of them the same design conditions, to ensure the quality required by international standards as well as to increase the productivity, a special design environment, methods and tools have been developed by Ericsson supporting different phases within the AXE 10 software design process.

On the example of the Software Design Centre built up at Ericsson Technika Kft. in Budapest/Hungary, enabling actually performance of a remote software development, the following aspects regarding design of AXE 10 software products will be discussed :

- connectivity environment which makes possible a software development using resources on geographically distant locations;
- well defined development methodology, supported both by standards and design and implementation tools, providing conditions for several groups of mutually unknown people with different backgrounds and experiences to work and act as a team;
- comprehensive testing methods/tools which permit the extensive verification of the software remotely from, or even without, the hardware to be controlled by it.

Integration of Object-Oriented Software Development and Prototyping: Approaches and Consequences

Wolfgang Pree

Department of Computer Science, Washington University
One Brookings Drive, St. Louis, Missouri 63130, U.S.A.
wolfgang@amadeus.wustl.edu

C. Doppler Laboratory for Software Engineering
Johannes Kepler University of Linz, Austria

Abstract. Although object-oriented application frameworks like MacApp [13], AppKit [8] and ET++ [12] substantially ease the building of graphic, direct-manipulation user interfaces, the level of abstraction is considered to be too low to support prototyping such interfaces in a comfortable way. Thus we implemented a user interface prototyping tool based on an object-oriented application framework.

The most important part of a software prototype is its dynamic behavior. On the basis of the tool mentioned above we discuss several ways in which means of adding dynamic behavior to a user interface prototype can be smoothly combined in one tool, in particular combining conventional and object-oriented software. Finally, we categorize user interface prototyping tools available today according to the concepts they offer for dynamic behavior specification.

Keywords: graphic direct-manipulation user interfaces, prototyping, object-oriented programming, application frameworks, multi-paradigm systems, C++

INTRODUCTION

We presuppose that the reader is familiar with object-oriented concepts (independent of a specific language): encapsulation, data abstraction, inheritance, polymorphism and dynamic binding, as well as with principles of graphic user interface application frameworks like MacApp, AppKit and ET++.

Such user interface frameworks offer several advantages: User interface look–and–feel standards are "wired" into the framework components. Furthermore, experience has proven that writing a complex application based on an application framework can result in a reduction in source code size of 80% and more compared to software written with the support of conventionally implemented libraries.

Apart from this enormous code reduction, application frameworks have other important benefits: the abstraction level is raised, and a standardization is achieved in terms of both the user interface and the code structure. However, the abstraction level of an application framework is considered to be too low to support prototyping in a comfortable way. Implementing applications with a framework absolutely requires specialized programming ability (especially in object-oriented programming). Furthermore, the programmer must become familiar with the particular application framework—a time investment that cannot be neglected.

This fact is contrary to the philosophy of prototyping. Therefore we implemented DICE[1] [9, 10] (Dynamic Interface Creation Environment) for/with the application framework ET++ in order to extend this tool in the direction of prototyping. The subsequent section describes several ways to specify dynamic behavior as offered by DICE. What sets DICE apart from other available prototyping tools is that it elegantly combines commonly used concepts to add dynamic behavior to a prototype. Furthermore, due to its object-oriented implementation DICE's specification component is extensible in a straightforward fashion.

We implemented DICE with the application framework ET++ for the following reasons: Compared to other available application frameworks, ET++ was the cleanest object-oriented implementation, based on a small set of

---

[1] This project was supported by Siemens AG Munich

basic mechanisms. ET++ provides a homogenous object-oriented class library that integrates user interface building blocks, basic data structures, and high level application components. ET++ was implemented in C++ and runs under UNIX and either SunWindows, NeWS, or the X11 window system. The design and implementation of ET++ is described in detail in [4, 11, 12].

ADDING FUNCTIONALITY TO A DICE PROTOTYPE

Prototyping is a paradigm that is well established in research and practice for enhancing the Software Life Cycle and improving software quality. There are various publications discussing definitions of prototyping in depth (e.g., [2, 3, 9]). User Interface Prototyping in particular is important for the development of applications that have graphic direct-manipulation user interfaces by providing better requirement definitions. Prototyping this kind of user interfaces with proper tools can significantly reduce the implementation effort (especially if the prototype can be enhanced to the final product).

It is not enough to just describe screen layouts, since the most important aspect of a user interface prototype is its dynamic behavior. In order to support evolutionary prototyping it should be possible to portray the dynamic behavior of a system and at the same time to enhance the prototype to an accomplished application. For this purpose most tools available today provide interfaces to procedural languages or some kind of an integrated procedural language.

DICE supports the graphic specification of the (static) user interface layout similar to other available tools: User interface elements offered in a palette (e.g., action button, labeled radio/toggle button, editable text field, non-editable text field, menu, text subwindow—a subwindow containing a full-fledged text-editor, list subwindow—a subwindow containing a list of selectable text items) are placed into windows simply by dragging them from a palette to the appropriate window. Attributes of interface elements (like the text displayed inside an action button) are defined in dialog boxes. For example, Figure 1 shows the attribute specification of an action button labeled "Stop".

In order to enhance a prototype's functionality DICE offers three possibilities:

- Without programming: Interface elements communicate with one another by sending *predefined messages*.
- With conventional or object-oriented programming: A protocol was developed that allows the prototype to be connected with other *UNIX processes* using one of UNIX's Interprocess Communication mechanisms.
- With object-oriented programming: *Subclasses of ET++ classes* can be generated. Application-specific behavior is added in subclasses of the generated classes.

DICE either operates in a specification mode or a test mode. DICE lets the user transform the specification of a prototype (its static and dynamic behavior) into an operational one within a neglectable amount of time (a fraction of a second on a SUN Sparc Station 1+).

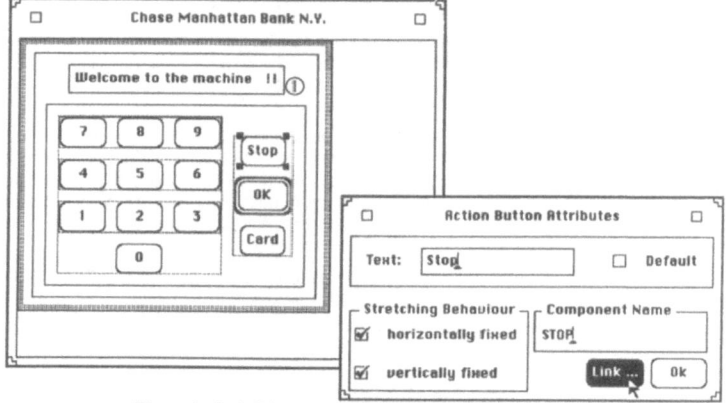

Figure 1: Cash Dispenser prototype (in specification mode)

Predefined Messages

Each user interface element has certain messages assigned that it "understands": For instance, the messages "Open" and "Close" are assigned to a window. All other interface elements understand at least "Enable" and "Disable". In addition, text subwindows, non-editable text fields and editable text fields change their text if they receive a "SetText(...)" message. A list subwindow switches its list if it receives a "SetList(...)" message. Labeled radio and toggle buttons alter their state depending on the parameter value of a "SetState(...)" message.

DICE realizes *state transitions* (in finite automata terminology) in the following way: From each element that can be activated (buttons and menu items), any number of messages to other elements can be specified by means of DICE's Message Editor (see below). If the prototype is tested (i.e., the prototype specification is transformed into an operational prototype) and an interface element is activated in the test mode, the messages specified for that element are sent to their receivers. They effect the corresponding change(s) (=state transition(s)) in the user interface. Thus rudimentary dynamics are realized without programming effort.

Let us take a simple cash dispenser prototype (see Figure 1) as an example. We want the display (① in Figure 1) to show the text "Oops—Stop Button Pressed" when the button labeled "Stop" is pressed. To specify this functionality, one presses the "Link..." button in the attribute sheet (= the dialog box where attributes of the selected user interface element can be edited) of the "Stop" button (see Figure 1). (We assume that the component name of the display field is "Display" and that the button labeled "Stop" has the component name "STOP".) By means of DICE's Message Editor (see Figure 2), the desired dynamic behavior can then be defined for the "Stop" button (i.e., that the message "SetText(...)" is to be sent to the non-editable text field "Display" when the "STOP" button is pressed—the button with the component name "STOP" as its sender (see ① in Figure 2)). After the button "Set Up Link" of the Message Editor (see Figure 2) is pressed the appropriate text string has to be provided as parameter of the message "SetText(...)" by means of a text editor.

The left list ("Target Objects") in the Message Editor displays component names of already existing user interface elements. After a component name is selected in the left list, all messages that are understood by the selected user interface element are displayed in the list "Possible Messages". The right list of already defined messages shows message names together with the component names of their receivers (in our example the message "Disable", which is to be sent to the button with the component name "OkButton", is already defined, the button with the component name "STOP" being the sender). After the "Set Up Link" button is pressed as demonstrated in Figure 2 and the appropriate text string is specified, the message "SetText(...)" (to be sent to the component named "Display") will be added to the list of already defined messages.

Connection of a Prototype with Other UNIX Processes

Algorithmic components of a DICE prototype can be implemented in any formalism and communicate with the user interface prototype specified with DICE by means of a simple protocol that is described below. The integration requires *no code generation* for the user interface part and thus no compile/link/go cycles. An arbitrary number of components implemented in different formalisms can be connected with a user interface prototype that is specified and tested within DICE.

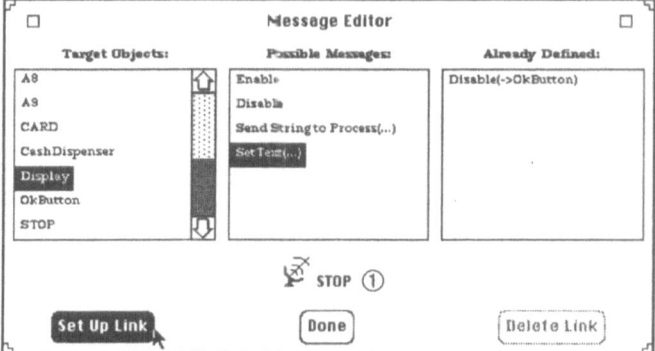

Figure 2: DICE's Message Editor

Communication Concept: Since DICE is implemented on UNIX systems, the UNIX Interprocess Communication mechanisms (e.g., sockets, shared memory) are used for interprocess communication of independent processes (see Figure 3). The interface specified with DICE and the process(es) interacting with the interface form a UIMS (User Interface Management System) with mixed control [1, 5]. This means that an application's "work" is accomplished by various loosely coupled parts of a software system. In case of DICE a DICE user interface prototype forms all visible parts of the user interface and maybe some basic functionality specified by means of predefined messages. Other functionality may be spread over several system parts that are coupled with the user interface by a simple protocol as described below.

Figure 3: Connection between a user interface prototype and an arbitrary process

Communication Protocol

We illustrate this protocol as far as it is necessary to understand DICE's interprocess communication concept.

User Interface Prototype -> Connected Process: If a user interface element of a prototype is activated in DICE's test mode (activatable user interface elements are all kinds of buttons, text items in a list subwindow, and menu items), an element identifier and its value are sent to the connected process(es) in the following format: identifier=value The identifier is usually the component name of the activated element. If a menu item is selected, the identifier is the component name of the user interface element the menu is part of (e.g., a list subwindow) concatenated with a dot (".") and the text of the selected menu item. If a text item in a list subwindow is selected, the identifier consists of the component name of the list subwindow concatenated with a dot (".") and the text of of the selected text item.

Activated action buttons, menu items, and text items in list subwindows always send TRUE as their value. Labeled radio and toggle buttons send either TRUE or FALSE as value (depending on their state).

Connected Process -> User Interface Prototype: A connected process can ask for the value of an interface element by sending identifier ? to the user interface prototype. If a user interface element exists that matches identifier, it "answers" as if it had been activated using the format described above. Values of user interface elements can be changed from the connected process by sending identifier=value to it. This allows some special changes in the user interface, too: windows, for example, can be opened or closed using the value OPEN or CLOSE. A list subwindow accepts EMPTY as value (to empty the list). A text string sent to a list subwindow as value means that this text is to be appended as a list item in the correspondent list subwindow.

The communication protocol is the precondition that a user interface developed with DICE can be connected with any conventional or object-oriented software system. E.g., the functionality of the cash dispenser specified in Figure 1 was implemented in C. (It could also be implemented in Cobol or Fortran or what else is available.) Necessary modifications or enhancements of the functionality are implemented in a C program. Immediately after compiling and starting this program, the modified functionality can be tested together with the user interface prototype (in test mode) without restarting DICE, even without switching from the test mode to the specification mode and back to the test mode.

The development of software systems that are to be connected with the interface prototype can be supported by available methods and tools. Pomberger [9], for instance, describes a tool that allows prototyping-oriented incremental software development. Due to DICE's Communication Protocol it was easy to combine this tool with DICE.

On the other hand, it is, of course, possible to connect a user interface prototype specified and tested in DICE with object-oriented systems developed by means of any domain-specific class libraries that might be available.

Generating Application Framework Subclasses

DICE simulates the static and dynamic behavior of a specified prototype when that prototype is tested. Thus no code generation and no compile/link/go cycles are necessary for testing. In order to enhance the prototype by means of the application framework ET++, DICE allows the creation of subclasses of ET++ classes. The compilation of the generated classes results in an application which works exactly like the specified prototype.

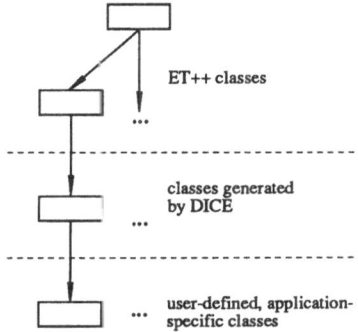

Figure 4: Code generation concept

The generated classes need not (and should not) be changed when further functionality is added in the sense of evolutionary prototyping. Additional functionality can be implemented in subclasses of the generated classes by overriding or extending the corresponding dynamically bound methods (see Figure 4).

Let us look at the cash dispenser interface (Figure 1) again: When the "Ok" button in the window titled "Chase Manhattan Bank N.Y." is pressed, the correctness of the displayed amount should be checked. This functionality could not be provided by DICE's prototyping facilities. Therefore we would like to add special code in order to implement this behavior.

DICE uses the component names of user interface elements in the generated code. Component names can be defined for each user interface element in the corresponding attribute sheet (see, for example, Figure 1: the component name of the button labeled "Stop" is "STOP"). We assume that the button labeled "Ok" has the component name "OkButton" and that the window titled "Chase Manhattan Bank N.Y." has the component name "CashDispenser".

So DICE generates a class CashDispenser. DICE reuses behavior implemented in the ET++ class Document by generating CashDispenser as subclass of it. Document, for example, manages a window in which the appropriate contents is displayed. Furthermore, the ET++ class Document has a dynamically bound method Control which is called each time a user interface element is activated inside a window associated with a Document object. Thus the method Control is used in the generated code to implement the behavior of user interface elements specified by means of predefined messages. Since no behavior was specified by means of predefined messages for the button with the component name "OkButton" the code generated by DICE is the following:

```
class CashDispenser: public Document {
    ...
    void Control(int id) {
        ...
        case OkButton:
            break;  // no action
        ...
    }
};
```

In order to check the correctness of the amount, we implement a class ExtCashDispenser (stands for "Extended Cash Dispenser"). The presented code fragment is simplified in order to stress the essential idea of adding functionality in subclasses of generated classes.

```
class ExtCashDispenser: public CashDispenser {
    ...
    void Control(int id) {
        ...
```

```
case OkButton:
        int  disp=Display->Val();
        if  (AmountOk(disp))
                ...
        break;
...
CashDispenser::Control(id);
```
        }
    };

To sum up, this kind of code generation separates changes of the user interface from hand-coded functionality as far as possible. For instance, if the user interface layout is changed, code (i.e., ET++ subclasses) must be generated again. The user-defined classes that have been derived from the originally generated classes are not concerned. Changes of these classes only become necessary if interface elements are removed (which would result in extrenous code) or switched between windows of the prototype.

CATEGORIZATION OF USER INTERFACE PROTOTYPING TOOLS

Prototypes built with DICE (i.e., prototypes that are executable within DICE in the test mode as well as ET++ applications generated from the prototype specification) are *finite* automata consisting of a finite number of states (the static layout of user interfaces) and state transitions (the dynamic behavior). We call this basic structure of a prototype its *application model*.

Applications built with state-of-the-art application frameworks are typically *infinite* automata: states and state transitions are described in classes from which an arbitrary (and theoretically unlimited) number of instances can be created. So the number of states and state transitions is not limited. For instance, a text editor application may have an arbitrary number of documents (= windows) in which text can be edited. Though the windows of one such text editor can be specified with DICE (e.g., by means of the text subwindow), the prototype as well as the eventually generated application have only the specified windows—the text editor application is not instantiable.

Thus the underlying application model of DICE prototypes and the application model of typical applications that are built on top of state-of-the-art application frameworks differ considerably. Since DICE's application model is a subset of the application model of a modern user interface framework, it is easy to generate subclasses of such a framework (ET++ in case of DICE), so that the transformation of the generated classes into an executable program results in an application which works exactly like the prototype specified with DICE. In order to project DICE's application model to an application framework, the generated classes have to eliminate many mechanisms provided by the framework classes: in ET++, for example, the complete document management done in class Application becomes superfluous.

Abstraction Level of Dynamic Behavior Specification

In general, the abstraction level of the specification of dynamic behavior determines whether the application model of the specified prototype can correspond to the application model of typical framework applications. User interface prototyping tools known today that allow the specification of dynamic behavior on an abstraction level higher than that of a programming language rely on the concept that applications with graphic, direct-manipulation user interfaces are finite automata—an application model that does not match that of modern application frameworks. The main reason for this fact is that the application model represented by finite automata can be specified with graphic editors in an easy and intuitive way.

The more sophisticated application models of modern application frameworks would require other graphic-oriented specification techniques. Such *visual programming* editors have not reached the maturity to allow use in this context [7]. NeXT Interface Builder [8] supports the building of applications that adhere to the application model of a modern application framework (AppKit) at the cost of specifying dynamic behavior on the programming language level (At first glance, the possibility offered by NeXT Interface Builder seems to be identical with predefined messages in DICE, but there is one crucial difference: In NeXT Interface Builder message connections between objects (called *sender* and *target* in this context) are method calls of the target object issued by an activated sender object. The messages that objects "understand" must be implemented in classes.)

Supported Application Area

Another important issue of user interface prototyping has to be taken into consideration, too: Many commercial data processing applications heavily rely on database management systems. Evolutionary prototyping of applications belonging to this category could benefit a lot if the user interface prototyping tool or the generated executable prototypes could be integrated with a (relational or object-oriented) database management system. Tools that allow user interface prototyping and the development of a database management system are often called fourth generation systems [6]. Though the term fourth generation system has not been standardized yet, we give a possible definition of such a system: fourth generation systems are built around a database management system and enable the developer to specifiy/implement not only the user interface layout but also data models, reports and consistency rules on a high abstraction level. They typically provide standard search and sort facilities and procedural languages for implementing dynamic behavior.

If a user interface prototyping tool is used within a fourth generation system the kind of code generation (based on a conventionally implemented toolkit or an application framework) is almost irrelevant because the user interface of commercial data processing applications (often called *information systems*) can be completely specified with available user interface prototyping tools in most cases: text fields, buttons, lists and text editors are sufficient for this application category. The system developer usually does not need (user interface) application framework classes in order to enhance a prototype. Moreover, the finite application model of almost all user interface prototyping tools available today meets the requirements of information systems: it is, for example, not desirable to instantiate an arbitrary number of input masks that are used to enter data into a database.

SUMMARIZING REMARKS

Depending on the level of abstraction of the specification of dynamic behavior we can divide high-level user interface prototyping tools into two categories: tools which support prototyping of information systems and tools that help to reduce the implementation effort if an application framework is used. All tools which are based on the finite automata application model are especially suited for prototyping information systems and thus belong to the first category. Their application model is only a subset of the infinite automata application model of user interface application frameworks. Thus the development of software systems with the infinite application model of user interface application frameworks is not supported.

An example of a tool that belongs to the second category is NeXT Interface Builder. Research (especially in visual programming) is necessary in order to allow the specification of dynamic behavior on an abstraction level higher than that of a programming language and to retain the application model of a state-of-the-art user interface application framework.

REFERENCES

1. Betts B., et al.: Goals and Objectives for User Interface Software; in: Computer Graphics, Vol. 21, No. 2, April 1987.

2. Budde R. et al.: Approaches to Prototyping; in Proceedings of the Working Conference on Prototyping, Namur, October '83, Springer 1984.

3. Floyd, C.: A Systematic Look at Prototyping; in: Approaches to Prototyping, Springer, 1984.

4. Gamma E., Weinand A., Marty R.: Integration of a Programming Environment into ET++: A Case Study; Proceedings of the 1989 ECOOP, July 1989.

5. Hayes P.J., Szekely P.A., Lerner R.A.: Design Alternatives for User Interface Management Systems Based on Experience with COUSIN; in: Human Factors in Computing Systems: CHI'85 Conference Proceedings, Boston, Mass., April 1985.

6. Holloway S.: Background to Forth Generation; in Fourth Generation Languages and Application Generators, The Technical Press, 1986.

7. Myers B.: User-Interface Tools: Introduction and Survey; IEEE Software, 6(1), January 1989.

8. NeXT, Inc.: 1.0 Technical Documentation: Concepts; NeXT, Inc., Redwood City, CA, 1990.

9. Pomberger G., Bischofberger W., Kolb D., Pree W., Schlemm H.: Prototyping-Oriented Software Development, Concepts and Tools; in Structured Programming Vol.12, No.1, Springer 1991.

10. Pree W.: Object-Oriented Versus Conventional Construction of User Interface Prototyping Tools; PhD thesis, Johannes Kepler University of Linz, 1991.

11. Weinand A., Gamma E., Marty R.: ET++ - An Object-Oriented Application Framework in C++; OOPSLA'88, Special Issue of SIGPLAN Notices, Vol. 23, No. 11, 1988.

12. Weinand A., Gamma E., Marty R.: Design and Implementation of ET++, a Seamless Object-Oriented Application Framework; in Structured Programming Vol.10, No.2, Springer 1989.

13. Wilson D.A., Rosenstein L.S., Shafer D.: Programming with MacApp; Addison-Wesley, 1990.

Trademarks:

MacApp is a trademark of Apple Computer Inc.

App Kit is a trademark of NeXT Inc.

SunWindows and NeWS are trademarks of Sun Microsystems.

UNIX and C++ are trademarks of AT&T.

Object-Oriented Analysis and Design — A Case Study

Wolfgang Eder[1]   Gerti Kappel[2]   Jan Overbeck[1]   Michael Schrefl[3]

[1] Inst. f. Informationssysteme Technische Universität Wien
[2] Inst. f. Statistik u.Informatik Universität Wien
[3] Inst. f. Wirtschaftsinformatik Universität Linz

Abstract

Several methods for object-oriented system development have been published by the scientific community. Recently, industrial software developers are also attracted by the object-oriented paradigm and consider switching from structured techniques to an object-oriented approach to system development. A question commonly asked by industry is, how both approaches compare on industrial applications. To investigate on this issue, a case study has been undertaken.

A configuration management system, which had originally been developed following the structured analysis and design approach, was modelled using an object-oriented modeling technique[1]. The main lessons learned are the following:

1. The effort put into the analysis was considered higher in contrast to our experience in non object-oriented projects. During design and implementation, however, the analysis effort proved useful as there was a smooth transition from analysis to design and from design to implementation.

2. The object classes of the design could be easily mapped into object classes of the implementation using the MacApp application framework. The application framework proved highly reusable and easily customizable for implementing the case study.

3. The object-oriented model proved stable against major changes in the system's requirements. It is believed that the object-oriented approach is suitable for applications with evolving reqirements.

4. Some "objects" of the object-oriented solution were already present in the original (non object-oriented) solution in terms of a set of procedures manipulating the same data structure. As object-orientation was not known to the original project team, some of the semantics of these "objects" had to be handcoded while others were not present at all. Thus the benefits of object-oriented development could be fully exploited in the object-oriented solution.

The presentation gives an overview of the case study introducing the object-oriented analysis model, the object-oriented design model, and selected parts of the object-oriented implementation. The above mentioned experiences will be discussed on behalf of these models.

---

[1] J.Rumbaugh, etal. *Object-Oriented Modeling and Design*. Prentice Hall, Englewood Cliffs, NJ, 1990.

SOFTWARE ENGINEERING EDUCATION

Chair: D. Sima

Small Is Beautiful, Isn't It?

Contradictions in Software Engineering Education

Péter Hanák, Zoltán László

Hanak@inf.bme.hu, h4245las@ella.hu

Faculty of Electrical Engineering and Informatics,
Technical University Budapest
H–1521 Budapest, Hungary

Abstract

Staff and students have recently faced the latest reforms in informatics education at the Section of Technical Informatics, TU Budapest. In this paper, partly *post factum,* we pose ourselves such questions as

- which topics of informatics, and in particular of software engineering, ought to be taught,
- how these topics should and could be taught,
- who and how will present these topics,
- how to convince students of their importance and usefulness (i.e. how to motivate students),
- what jobs will be open for software engineers in Hungary or in other countries,
- what are the skills a university student should acquire,
- what is the optimal ratio of theory and practice, etc.

We do not promise the answers to these and many similar questions. However, we do try to reveal contradictions in software engineering education in a small country, partly by comparing our problems to those discussed in the literature, and partly by presenting our experiences and approaches at TU Budapest — in the hope that it will trigger vivid discussions at the conference on Shifting Paradigms in Software Engineering in Klagenfurt.

1 Introduction

Informatics (as it is called in Continental Europe) or computer/computing science (as the American/British traditionally call it) is related to mathematics, engineering and management. Depending on the School where it is taught one of its aspects is emphasized. Nonetheless, in the curriculum a proper balance is desirable. In Section 6 the newest curriculum of *technical informatics* at TU Budapest, centred around software engineering (SE), is presented, and the sequence of courses that determine its SE content is discussed, with an eye kept on this balance.

Engineering is defined in [10] as 'creating cost-effective solutions to practical problems by applying scientific knowledge to building things in the service of mankind'. SE is claimed in the same paper to be more 'a statement of aspiration' than a 'description of accomplishment' because of the 'lack of widespread routine application of scientific knowledge to a wide range of practical design tasks'.

It's not at all easy to determine the necessary content of a degree programme in informatics and in particular in SE. Beside personal ambitions, local expertise and available infrastructure the *immaturity of the subject* causes most difficulties: the 40-year history of computing education is the history of *permanent shifting*, triggered by technological changes, from technical peculiarities to higher-level concepts and solutions.

By now, programming-in-the-small is more or less well understood, and the educational community has the necessary skill in teaching the widely accepted, sound principles of algorithmic and data abstraction. On the other hand, programming-in-the-large is far from being established: it is a field of discussions and beliefs. After all, small is beautiful, isn't it?

While we still strive for theories, methodologies and tools necessary to create huge but correct and secure software systems one wonders if the well-known educational difficulties are only due to this lack of knowledge, or if they are of intrinsic character. That is, we have to face the problem of teaching complex things while being restricted in resources, time and prerequisite knowledge. Although this situation is not unusual in the engineering education we again have to 'reinvent the wheel' in the SE field — as it occurred e.g. with structured programming.

Then, we should ask ourselves whether the idealized practice of system design can be abstracted and taught at all, or only some well-sounding principles and slogans can be collected and presented in the classroom. The authors, graduated in electrical engineering and gained practice in the design of medium-size hardware/software systems, have the impression that systematically only small-scale design of digital systems is and can be taught. It would be interesting to study other, more mature and less dramatically changing fields of engineering (e.g. civil or mechanical engineering) in order to reveal the similarities and the differences, and to see whether there are any general methods applicable also to SE.

Education is usually told to be *the art of concealment,* but it could well be called *the art of selection,* i.e. of choosing things worth to know. Very frequently, we teach nonessential and unimportant topics just because they are well known and easy to teach.

The dilemma was also admitted during a workshop at Brown University in 1990 [3] many invited speakers questioned even the widely accepted contents of introductory programming courses describing them as nonrelevant. Further, 'it was a humbling experience to see that after twenty-five years of teaching computing in major universities, we still don't know how to do it' [4].

In the first paragraph we used the term 'technical informatics'. In Hungary, it has been used since 1991 meaning informatics education at universities and colleges of *technology,* in contrast to 'theoretical informatics' being or to be taught at universities of natural sciences, 'econometrics' at universities of economy, and 'library informatics' at universities of liberal arts, etc. In the courses of technical informatics 'much more attention is given to the hardware aspects of information systems than anywhere else' [8], and to its engineering character.

2   Contradictions and other problems

Here is a list of the most striking contradictions that deeply affect engineering education in general, and SE education in particular. We suppose they are understandable without further explanation.

- Things easy to teach and grade vs. things essential to know;
- things motivated by fashion ('attractive knowledge') vs. things worth to know ('painful knowledge');
- theoretical background vs. practical skills;
- concrete and specific vs. abstract and universal knowledge;
- student's self-motivation vs. teacher's pressure;
- real things (languages, tools, etc.) with practical value vs. educational versions with didactic value;
- exact facts and algorithms vs. philosophy and descriptive methodologies;
- stand-alone knowledge vs. system-wide or embedded knowledge;
- bottom-up approach in education vs. top-down approach in application.

Below is another list of important problems related to informatics and SE education; more problems and detailed explanations can be found, for example, in [3] and [11].

- Small classroom problems does not strive for methodologies and development tools; what's more, methodologies and tools cause additional problems;
- larger classroom problems are usually too specific and need detailed background knowledge of some other field;
- larger problems, to be solved as projects, imply management problems and increased trainer's effort;
- most phases of a development project (writing project plans, specifications, detailed designs, documentation, test plans, manuals, etc.) are much more boring than simply coding and debugging programs;
- there are plenty of bad patterns to follow while good patterns are rare in practice;
- most students lack the experience of unsuccessful projects, therefore they don't feel the need for formals methods and systematic approaches;
- engineering students, accustomed to facts and algorithms, are reluctant to descriptive methodologies and philosophy;
- students rarely study programs written by others (be good or poor ones);
- the effort needed to read, check and comment student projects is tremendous;
- because the profession of SE lacks self-confidence, we do not dare to demand thorough and precisely documented designs from the students — in this respect, we should learn from mechanical design and architecture;
- an interesting phenomenon is the following: as soon as we fully understand a problem of programming methodology (structured language constructs, abstract data types, etc.), we usually consider it as an unworthy topic for a university-level course on computing (that's why the content of introductory programming courses changes so frequently);
- development tools and environments are rapidly becoming obsolete (often triggered by the business interests of huge, multinational corporations), requiring additional training efforts from staff members. (E.g. between 1987 and 1991 the following Turbo Pascal versions were used with first-year students in informatics at TU Budapest: 3.0, 4.0, 5.0, 5.5 and 6.0, i.e. a new version each year! Add to them various versions of assemblers, editors, "C" compilers, CASE-tools under MS-DOS, plus other machines, other operating systems, other languages...)

Obviously, most of these problems can only be overcome if we carefully select the topics to be taught. Experience (e.g. [3]) shows that it is far from being simple.

3   Paradigm shifting

The word 'paradigm' is relatively new to informatics, and made as fast a carrier as the terms 'modular', 'structured', 'software engineering', 'object oriented', etc. did earlier. (Eventually, fashion can be traced on titles of professional books that often appear with the same traditional content but under attractive titles.) One feels temptation to define what 'paradigm' might mean but a definition would hardly contribute to its better understanding (like with the other terms mentioned above). We need time to get familiar with this new term and its possible meanings.

Paradigms are changing because so far no paradigm has solved the problem of the mass-production of software — and because *only new promises bring money.*

If we forget this last remark for a while, and try to reveal other driving forces of paradigm shifting, the title of this conference also assumes, then we have to admit that, above all, it is *the technological development* that made these changes possible and inevitable. Indeed, the development of technology has made those tools available and those methodologies implementable *that had already been known earlier.*

Table 1 below enumerates some concepts, the approximate dates when they first appeared, and when they became or will presumably become generally accepted, implemented and productive. (Of course, dates are rough estimates.)

Table 1: Some concepts

Concept	Appearance	Acceptance
Structured Programming (SP)	1965	1985
Structured Analysis (SA)	1970	1990
Object-Oriented Programming (OOP)	1967	1990
Functional Programming (FP)	1950	1990
Logic Programming (LP)	1960	1988
Artificial Intelligence (AI)	1960	1990
Program Proving (PP)	1960	????
Formal Specification (FS)	1960	1995
Software Metrics (SM)	1965	????
Software Reuse (SR)	1980	1995

We should admit that general acceptance is by no means influenced by scientific value or theoretical superiority: implementation and technology are that really count. For example, take the case BASIC we know too well: computing scientists, methodologists and didacticians fought bitterly over two decades against BASIC whose popularity had even been fortified by first generation PC's — with almost no result. Then, faster than it arrived, it has been blown away by the IBM PC/AT boom of recent years. Those who like similar debates should draw the moral of the story themselves.

[12] describes another convincing example: although the term *algebra* had been known and *paper-mills* had been used in Europe since around 1200,

> 'it was not until the 16th century that algebra was really accepted as a formal method. In that century, there was the struggle between the Abacists and the Algorithmists, between the concrete calculation by means of *calculi*, little stones or coins, and the abstract calculation on paper and by more and more formal rules. The Algorithmists won, because *suddenly paper could be produced at a much lower price* — which shows once more how much we depend on technology, even in such mental aspects.'

In the following section we try to argue for a necessary change in SE education.

4 Approaches in Software Engineering Education

Software engineering, like many technical terms, has various interpretations. It's no surprise that there are different approaches to SE education.

In the narrow sense, it means a single course or a few related courses (for undergraduates) trying to cover the whole process of software development, usually based on the waterfall-model, including principles, methodologies, tools and techniques, see e.g. [11].

In a broader sense, however, we may extend the concept of SE to include other courses related to software development: courses on introduction to programming, algorithms and data structures, program design and programming technology, object-oriented programming, mathematical logic and logic programming, functional programming, formal specification and program proving, compiler construction, operating systems, database technology, software quality assurance, etc.

Since program development is a constructive discipline it is hard to imagine a series of pure lectures without related project activities. [11] classifies various models of SE courses and project styles many of them we have also applied. Later, while surveying past and present of informatics education at TU Budapest, we shall summarize our experiences with these models.

Like other disciplines, SE has also been passing through various phases of self-development: empirical, descriptive and formalized.

It is well known that the theory of software development is lagging behind practice; nonetheless, it is more than regrettable that at most universities of sciences and of technology SE courses are only taught as empirical and descriptive subjects.

Formal description and specification

Formalization is going into two directions: graphical and algebraic. In some cases graphical formalization is based on strict mathematical models, and can be manipulated mathematically (e.g. Petri-nets). In most cases, however, this correspondence is missing.

Recent graphical formalization methods, supported by CASE-tools, are mainly used in architectural design, and does not help much in transforming the design into an executable program. The gap is large, and research results do not promise fast solution. Repository-based object-oriented techniques are now claimed to diminish this gap [9]. Graphical formalization methods are gaining popularity since (1) computer graphics is fashionable; (2) they are attractive at first sight and claimed to be 'easy-to-use' (which is rarely true), (3) have a long tradition (e.g. blueprints, flow-charts), (4) have some software support (e.g. Teamwork, SSADM Engineer), and therefore (5) software firms are interested in their dissemination.

On the other hand, algebraic methods, based on sound mathematical theory, pencil and paper — or a text editor, proved their usefulness in the formal specification of small pieces of programs (its supporters like to remark that even huge programs are small depending on the level of abstraction). The authors would also like to believe in the superiority of these techniques that promise — at least in the *far* future — the possibility of automatized transformation from specification to executable code. As for the present, these methods are distinguished by their unambiguity, precision and rigour; virtues that we eagerly need in SE education. Unfortunately, current formal specification methods are limited; their acceptance by students is at least controversial, by colleagues is even worse.

One leading expert, who advocates algebraic methods, writes [5]:

> 'No professional architect, bridge builder or car designer would work with specifications of the same shoddy nature that one finds in software engineering. ... One hears

that software projects are larger and more complex than other classical engineering projects, but that is even more — and not less — reason to be more professional.

...while texts on discrete mathematics for computer science students have a chapter on logic, the material is rarely used in the rest of the text. Hence, the student and the instructor come away with the feeling that the mathematical tools are of academic interest only. They have seen some of the techniques, but lack skill in their use and question their applicability. ...The retort "We know what we want to do, and it's too big a task to formalize" is heard far too often. ...Have you ever heard a physicist say that their problems are too big and complex to be handled by mathematical techniques?

...I am not advocating the formal proof of correctness of all programs. ...In developing a calculational skill, one learns that formalization can lead to crisper and more precise descriptions. One learns that the form of the formalization can itself lend insight into developing a solution. One acquires the urge to clarify and simplify, to seek the right notation in which to express a problem. One acquires a frame of mind that encourages precision and rigor.'

In the ideal case, the rigour of the algebraic formalization and the transparency of the graphical approach should be combined.

Variety or diversity

Unfortunately, there is little consensus about how a standard undergraduate informatics curriculum should be improved. [7] enumerates four contradicting opinions:

1. recent informatics education should be replaced with a traditional program based on standard engineering and the usual topics in mathematics;
2. informatics should be a new form of mathematics that deals with the verification of symbol manipulators;
3. (bookstore shelves give the impression that) informatics is primarily a matter of learning BASIC — or Pascal, if you like;
4. programming, as an engineering discipline, should be based on a minimal number of concepts: recursion, prefix notation and the list structure.

Then, continuing, [7] completely denies the formal specification approach:

'...fundamentalist views ...leave little or no room for incremental system building. In addition, the proof techniques apply to the elementary constructs of a programming language and use a tedious notation that has the flavor of an assembly code. This approach seems to encourage the view that each program must be proven correct as if it were the only one of its kind in the world.'

Reasonings, like this one, show that most of us hear only what we want to hear. Those, who remember the bitter fight between followers and opponents of structured programming, would recognize the only unrefutable argument in a somewhat modified form [5]: 'Calculational techniques deserve to be given a fair chance, especially since nothing else has appeared on the horizon to solve the ills of the profession.'

In summary, not much help can be found in the literature when someone tries to determine the fundamental content of SE education. Usually [3], there is an introductory course on computing (based on Pascal or similar language), another one on algorithms and data structures, and then an undergraduate course on SE based on one out of four popular textbooks [11]. Other courses, if any, rely too heavily on local people, their research interest and faith. As [6] writes, career success in United States universities 'depends very much on ... obtaining outside funding through grants, publishing in journals and teaching — in precisely that order'. He and others blame this practice for ignoring engineering and didactic issues in informatics education: 'Many of those who are most interested in educational issues are at institutions that do not afford faculty much time for scholarly activities. Unfortunately, the reverse is often true as well: too many faculty at research-oriented institutions are not as concerned as they should be with issues in undergraduate education' [1].

5   Local history and experiences

The degree programme in *informatics* at TU Budapest, like at many other universities of technology, grew out of Electrical Engineering rather late, in 1986, as a new curriculum offered for a number of students by teams composed of lecturers of existing departments. The electrical engineering topics still dominated this curriculum, only ca 1/3 of the courses were specific to informatics.

Based on former experiences and in answer to the changing demands of a changing society, a significantly modified (hopefully improved) degree programme in *technical informatics* has replaced the previous one since 1991 (see Section 6 and [8]). It is distinguished by a ca 2:1 ratio in favour of subjects related to informatics. The tendencies are also reflected in the new name of the Faculty: since May 1992 it is called *Faculty of Electrical Engineering and Informatics*.

So far, the history of programming and software engineering education at TU Budapest can be divided into three phases. Below, we try to characterize the SE content of these phases, and draw some lessons if possible. Of course, this summary necessarily contains simplifications — and it reflects how the authors see the happenings now. (The notation Sx below means Semester x in which the course is taught.)

5.1   Phase I. Electrical engineering (ca 1970–1986)

Computer hardware and programming education started around 1970 at TU Budapest.

Lectures: Introduction to Programming: assembly + ALGOL or FORTRAN, later assembly + Pascal (S1), Digital design, incl. microprocessors (S3–S4), Computer systems, incl. programming issues (S5), Peripherals & interface design (S6–S7), Computer networks (S8).

Labs: Digital measurements (S4–S5).

Projects: Peripheral interface design for microprocessors; individual student projects and thesis works (more and more shifted from hardware to software development).

This somewhat 'overmature' pioneering phase extended over almost two decades. Software development was only marginally treated in the courses while more and more student projects and thesis works dealt with program development, in response to external needs and student motivation. The inflexible curriculum structure, strengthened by the selfish interests of most engineering departments, hindered the inclusion of new subjects for a long time.

Projects were carried out by usually one, sometimes two students under the guidance of a staff member — cooperation in larger teams was not required. The size of the projects was rather small: typically a peripheral interface board and a device driver, or some stand-alone program had to be developed. Measurement labs covered SSI and MSI, later LSI circuits, incl. microprocessors, with some assembly-level programming. The ultimate goal of the education was to produce electrical engineers who were *able to develop* new equipment, devices and systems.

As design methodology, the well-known Karnough-tables, state-transition diagrams and tables, etc. were introduced for small hardware systems. For medium and large systems, because no systematic methods were known, standard MSI and LSI elements, principles and thumb rules, combined with block-diagram techniques, were taught. In case of software nothing better than flow-charts, NS-diagrams and pseudo-languages were used, based on principles of T-D and partly B-U methodology.

5.2 Phase II. Informatics (1986–1991)

Last graduates of this programme will finish their studies in 1995.

Lectures: Programming and problem solving: assembly + Pascal (S1–S2), Principles of program design (S3–S4), Systems programming (S5–S6), Program design (S7), Informatics systems (S7).

Labs: Computing in assembly, Pascal and C (S1–S2–S3).

Projects: Programming projects in small teams (2–4), individual development projects, causally participation in faculty teams, thesis works.

Developers of Curriculum 1986 preferred a small number of comprehensive courses. As a consequence, the course Principles of program design comprised two, more or less independent parts: Theory of algorithms and Formal languages; the course Systems programming consisted of three parts: Operating systems, Computer networks and Databases.

The content of the course Program design, sometimes also called Software engineering — the authors' main field of interest — has slightly changed over the years. It has covered the phases of software life cycle, but not necessarily in the same order and detail: requirements analysis has only been mentioned; Jackson, Jackson–Warnier and DeMarco notations have been introduced as formal techniques of program design, finite automata modelling and SSADM methodology have also been discussed. Testing, reliability, software metrics, quality assurance, maintenance have been covered to some extent. The course has been concluded with a summary of formal specification methods and an introduction to program proving, based on predicate calculus and the guarded command notation.

The content of a related course, Informatics systems, was only vaguely described in Curriculum 1986, and since then it has changed a lot. Based on invited lecturers from external firms, topics of artificial intelligence, expert systems, relational knowledge bases, man-machine communication, and later Prolog and logic programming have been presented. However, as it has never turned into a well-structured course, this title has been left out from Curriculum 1991.

It should not be left unmentioned that the intensive involvement of external lecturers resulted in a number of problems: it proved (once again) that no single course can be given by many people (more than two), and that education must not be based on non-staff members deeply involved in business or management.

The five-year existence of informatics education at TU Budapest has also yielded other useful experiences; let's see a short account.

Programming projects. First-year informatics students had intensive laboratory exercises in semesters 1, 2 and 3 on IBM PCs. In the first half of each semester they acquired some skills in a programming language and environment (assembly, Pascal and C, respectively), and then in the second half they were given larger tasks — toy projects (simulate a programable calculator, design and implement a graphical editor, simulate a three-cabin elevator, etc.) — to be solved in teams of three or four, supervised by staff members. The students were asked to refine requirements, divide the task into subtasks and assign them to team members, design the whole program and split it into modules, design, implement and integrate these modules, and finally complete the user and developer documentations.

Almost everybody worked with enthusiasm and spent uncountably many hours with the project (lecturers of other courses were less enthusiastic...). In some teams, instinctive team leaders emerged capable to coordinate activities of other team members. In most students' life, it was the first time they had to cooperate in teams. Nonetheless, as it turned out later when they took the course on Program design, they had not known much about systematic specification and design methods; therefore they suggested to shift the Program Design course into the early semesters.

Teams consisted of 2 to 4 members; we have never tried to start big (say, 20-member) projects with students as we feared of preparation and management problems. (As a counter-example see [11] describing a successful, real-life campus-project). It should also be mentioned that some supervisors (lab coaches) preferred to give the students one-person tasks. (Small is beautiful, isn't it?) It would be interesting to ask those students if they felt later that they had missed something; or to study their attitude towards programming projects, and look for possible differences.

Lectures. Course titles often did not correspond to their content. Two-semester courses frequently consisted of completely distinct topics. The content of some courses was poorly defined, and in a number of cases there were also 'implementation problems'. Textbooks were almost completely missing. Further, the number of electrical engineering courses was still too high while important topics (e.g. logic, functional programming, compiler construction) were missing from Curriculum 1986.

Labs and projects. The curriculum imposed a high amount of lab and project activities: programming exercises in semesters 1 to 3, individual projects in semesters 4 to 7, pre-thesis and thesis projects in semesters 8 to 10. These activities required very intensive participation, both of students and of staff. In the beginning, insufficient hardware resources caused problems, later the lack of manpower — a new phenomenon at TU Budapest – caused most difficulties. Therefore, we have involved senior students as supervisors. They have the advantage that they know the programming environments much better than we do but they need supervision and guidance themselves — an additional burden on staff.

Within the course on Program design, we applied various project models. At first, student teams were asked to systematically redesign a project they carried out earlier. As it turned out, nobody applied the methods presented in the classes but used the old *ad-hoc* ones. They complained because of the number of pages they had to write. Nevertheless, many colleagues liked the idea since documentations that otherwise would not be completed were finished. One year later no project accompanied the course — we regretted it afterwards. In the next year all student teams were given the same design-without-implementation task (Tangram). In the beginning, most teams worked with enthusiasm but only a few produced a systematic, well-considered design; probably, its main reason was that they had not confronted with implementation problems that would forced them to reconsider and improve the original design.

5.3 Phase III. Technical informatics (1991–)

Many of the above experiences and other considerations were taken into account in the (often controversial) design process of the new curriculum (see Section 6). Very importantly, university authorities have been challenged to react to social and political changes in the country, namely

- the weakening of COCOM-restrictions and the appearance of multinational computer companies in Hungary have slowly been resulting in a better infrastructure;
- the anticipated collapse of Hungarian industry, including electronics and computer manufacturers, and at the same time a vivid interest in information and computing

services result more students at sections of informatics and less in other branches of engineering;

- in answer to these changes and utilizing new opportunities, more universities and colleges of technology, including newly established, private ones, offer degree courses in informatics.

For example, for the year 1992/93 the Faculty of Electrical Engineering and Informatics could enrol only 382 (1991/92: 460) freshmen in electrical engineering while the acceptance level at the entrance examinations has been lowered to 80 scores (1991/92: 101!) out of 120. At least for a while, technical informatics has not been losing its attractiveness: for 1992/93 the faculty has enroled 146 (1991/92: 75) freshmen in informatics while the acceptance level was set at 100 scores (1991/92: 111).

University authorities and staff should overcome many other problems if TU Budapest wants to remain attractive and keep its leading role in informatics education in Hungary, e.g.

- Since universities in Western-Europe and the United States, further private firms, home and abroad, offer more attractive and in many cases easier professional careers and first of all much higher wages many younger colleagues have left TU Budapest.
- For the same reason, it is not easy to recruit new staff members with proper educational background or experience. (On the other hand, there is a surplus of 'real' electrical, mechanical, etc. engineers.)
- Departments devoted to one or another field of informatics are still missing at TU Budapest. Partly due to this fact, no significant working groups and personalities have emerged. While the establishment of one or even more informatics departments can no longer be delayed without long-lasting consequences, the conditions, both personnel and financial, are much worse than it was a decade ago.
- While many of our graduates go abroad to work, higher education is still free of charge in Hungary — this is, however, another story.

Fortunately, conference papers on informatics education, like e.g. [3], mitigate, to some extent, this rather dim picture: at least we know we are not completely alone! For example, [2] complains as in Germany 'there are more vacancies for faculty staff than good candidates, because industry offers so many interesting job opportunities.' And what [6] says we also know too well: 'From the beginning, computing scientists have had to convince colleagues from other, more mature disciplines that computing is a discipline.'

6   Revised curriculum

The Curriculum 1991 of the degree programme in technical informatics at TU Budapest reflects a two-level structure: an undergraduate level (3 years) and a graduate level (2 years), with no formal boundary between these two levels. The undergraduate programme is divided into three main blocks. One of them consists of courses related to mathematics, information and coding theory. Another one contains subjects specific to electrical engineering. The third block is devoted to informatics: courses related to programming, computing science and software engineering. The content of the graduate level varies since it consists of modular and elective courses. They give the students the opportunity to acquire special knowledge according their interests and abilities.

In the first six semesters, the exercises in the computing laboratory help the students gain the necessary skills in programming and computer applications. The project laboratories in semester 8 and 9 give them the opportunity to work in bigger teams; traditionally, they join a research or development group of the faculty.

Below, an excerpt from the schedule of courses is reproduced. (See [8] for a fuller account. In case of possible deviations the current report is valid since it reflects newer developments.) Only the undergraduate courses closely related to SE are shown in Table 2. For comparison: the total number of hours is 24 a week, ca 20% less than in Curriculum 1986.

Table 2: Undergraduate courses related to SE
(e – examination, p – practical exercise, s – signature, i.e. no grade)

Course name	Hours/week with requirement						
	total	in semester					
		1	2	3	4	5	6
Programming	4	2e	2p				
Programming Technology	4			4e			
Theory of Algorithms	4			4e			
Formal Languages	4				4e		
Mathematical Logic	4				4e		
Programming Paradigms	4					4e	
Operating Systems	4					4e	
Databases	4						4e
Computing Laboratory	12	2s	2s	2p	2p	2p	2p

Graduate courses are much more flexible than in earlier curricula. Only the framework is set up, the content depends on future needs and possibilities. Their structure is depicted in Table 3. Course descriptions may be obtained from the authors.

Table 3: Framework for graduate courses

Course name	Hours/week with requirement			
	total	in semester		
		7	8	9 10
Module 1	12	4e	4e	4e
	4	4e		
	6	2p	2p	2p
Module 2	12	4e	4e	4e
	4	4e		
	6	2p	2p	2p
Elective courses	12	4e	4e	4e
Project laboratory	12		6p	6p
Thesis work	24			24

Further, the development of Curriculum 1991 aimed at

- decreasing the cost of education (by reducing the extent of labs and projects);
- decreasing the number of weekly hours in classes;
- increasing the flexibility of studies and meeting individual needs of students (modules, electives);
- adding courses to the core curriculum that strengthen its computing science and software engineering character (Math logic, Paradigms, Programming technology);
- creating space for formal specification and design techniques, functional and logic programming, etc.

Many important topics like compiler construction, artificial intelligence and expert systems, network and information systems management, neural networks, robotics, etc. will be covered by modular and elective courses.

7 Conclusion

It is not enough that we, computing professionals at academia, are convinced about the necessity of informatics education: it is our duty, too, that government and university authorities, professionals in business and industry, colleagues in other engineering disciplines accept *informatics as a discipline*. In the long run, 'information industry' could fill the space caused by the collapse of other branches (electronics, metallurgy, mining, etc.) in Hungary. However, to promote its proper development, *positive discrimination is necessary* at TU Budapest. Conferences, like this, contribute to make a clear picture: where we are, what we do, where we go. Even more if nobody knows *the* answer.

Acknowledgements

The authors express their thanks to their colleagues at TU Budapest who, like them, took part in the elaboration of the computing science and SE courses for the section of technical informatics. Nonetheless, their views, manifested in this article, are not necessarily shared by the others.

References

[1] Bruce, K.B.: *Creating a new model curriculum: a rationale for* Computing Curricula 1990. In [3], pp. 23–35.

[2] Brauer, W.: *Informatics education at West German universities.* In [3], pp. 125–131.

[3] *Education & Computing.* Issue on 'Informatics Curricula for the 1990s'. Vol. 7, Nos. 1–2, ISSN 017–9287, Elsevier.

[4] Gries, D. – Levrat, E. – Wegner, P.: *Foreword. Informatics Curricula for the 1990s.* In [3], pp. 3–8.

[5] Gries, D.: *Improving the curriculum through the teaching of calculation and discrimination.* In [3], pp. 61–72.

[6] Gibbs, N.E.: *Software engineering and computer science: the impending split?* In [3], pp. 111–117.

[7] Habermann, A.N.: *Introductory education in computer science.* In [3], pp. 73–86.

[8] Györfi, L. – Hanák, P. – Selényi, E.: *The Degree Programme in Technical Informatics at the Technical University Budapest.* Budapest, 1992.

[9] Reé, B.: *Feasibility of Repository-Based CASE Environments.* Master thesis. TU Budapest, 1992.

[10] Shaw, M.: *Prospects for an Engineering Discipline of Software.* IEEE Software 7, 6 (November 1990), pp. 15–24.

[11] Shaw, M. – Tomayko, J.E.: *Models for Undergraduate Project Courses in Software Engineering.* CMU–CS–91–17. September, 1991.

[12] Zemanek, H.: *Formalization. History, Present, and Future.* Programming Methodology, 4th Informatik Symposium, Germany, Wildbad, Sept. 25–27, 1974, in Lecture Notes in Computer Science, Vol. 23, pp. 477–501.

Teaching Programming
Via Specification, Execution and Modification of Reusable Components:
An Integrated Approach

Ahmed Ferchichi
Université de Tunis III
Institut Supérieur de Gestion de Tunis
Département Informatique
41 Rue de la Liberté 2000 le Bardo

Abstract. In computer science curriculum, it is a challenge to define and teach a first programming course including software engineering concepts and integrating programming paradigms. The aim of this paper is to present a teaching approach to address this problem. Experimented in the university of Tunis III, the approach is caracterised by the use of software library units representing actually Prolog and Ada programs respectively as specifications and implementations. Specifically, at the level of its goal, the approach is oriented by external and internal software qualities; at the level of its strategy, the approach is based on program execution and program modification; and at the level of its conceptual formalisation, the approach uses a relational view.

Keywords. Teaching Programming, Software Engineering, Software Reuse, Software Modification.

1. Introduction

The debate of how to teach a first year programming course is as old as programming itself and, in all likelihood, will remain in the center stage of computer science education. In recent years, several important languages specifically designed for software engineering [1] have emerged, most notably Ada. These languages may be used at both the software design and the implementation stages of the development process [8].

Good Programming involves the systematic mastery of complexity. It is not an easy subject to teach. The principal tenet is that abstraction and specification are necessary for any effective approach to programming ([5],[6]).

In this paper, we present a teaching approach related to a first programming course including software engineering concepts and integrating programming paradigms.

We consider that the first contact of students with programming is of prime importance and ought to be controlled carefully [3]. Based on the use of a software library components where some units are considered as specifications and others as implementations, our teaching approach uses successively external then internal program use. So, it introduces external program qualities by external program execution and internal qualities by internal program modification, hence tools and concepts achieving this goal as defined recently in software engineering [8] are progressively introduced.

The next section presents the programming course concerned by the approach. Section 3 deals with the presentation of our teaching approach based on two kinds of activities: program execution and program modification. In section 4, we present an illustrative example. In section 5, we present some remarks showing the interest of the selected approach. And section 6 outlines future work and perspectives.

2 Course Description and Organisation

2.1 Course Objectives

We are concerned by a first programming course caracterized by the following premises:
        - The integration of functional, logic, and object oriented programming paradigms as programming tools.
        - The introduction of a simplified software life cycle for program development as programming model [7].
        - The study of software product and process qualities as programming goal.

2.2 Software Libraries and Case Studies

2.2.1 Software Libraries

All the teaching activity is based on the use of the following software libraries:
        - Environment library,
        - Programming language library,
        - Data structure library,
        - Domain oriented library.

These libraries represent the teaching library and are respectively related to:
        - The used programming environment as the operating system, the editor, and the compiler.
        - The programming langage represented by the primitive data types.
        - The classical data types, as sets, lists, stacks, and queues.
        - Programs which are specific to particular domain-specific applications.

2.2.2 Case Studies Applications

Case studies applications are directly linked to the teaching library. Along the specification activity, the teacher asks students to access the teaching library, execute some selected software units in order to report their description in separate specification files. Along the implementation activity, students access initial implementation texts related to the specified selected software units and modify them progressively and iteratively in order to achieve particular software qualities.

We justify the previous kinds of libraries by the following premises:

- The environment library is naturally the first one used by students; also, we want to help the student apprehend it and understand it using the same approach.

- The language library makes practical the idea that a programming language can be viewed as a set of programs: for this purpose, the predefined data types in this library are organised as accessible and independent units.

- The data structure library shows that there is no conceptual difference between data types and data structures and enables us to enrich and make more abstract the programming langage used.

- Finally, the domain oriented library constitutes a set of prototypes helping students understand more complex specifications.

2.3 Course Structure

The programming course is organised into three kinds of sessions:
- theoretical course session (36 hours),
- application course session (72 hours), and
- practical course session (108 hours).

These sessions are organised during 24 weeks with respectively the following credits: (1 x 1h30), (2 x 1h30), and (3 x 1h30). The course begins with practical sessions during 10 days (3 hours per day) in order to introduce students rapidly to the environment library. During these sessions, students organise their libraries to make them ready to accept specification and implementation files. We recall that all kinds of sessions are organised around the teaching library.

3 Teaching Strategies

In practice, we want students to build a software library similar to the teaching library with software units having particular qualities. Using Ada as a programming langage, each software unit is organised into separate specification and implementation files. Because it is difficult to understand specifications, we have decided to make them executable as Prolog programs. So, the work is organised following the two next sequential programming activities:

- specification activity, and
- implementation activity.

To learn specification and implementation, we use the following
sequential teaching activities:
- program execution, and
- program modification.

The aim of the next sections is to explain in more detail the
programming and teaching activities and their relationship.

3.1 Learning Specification by Program Execution

Given software units, the aim of this activity is to lead
students understand external program qualities. To this effect,
we follow two steps:
- defining program abstractions, and
- matching program abstractions against program
  specifications.

3.1.1 Defining Program Abstractions

The main question that we adress in this step is:
    Given a program P. What is the meaning of P?

Using the teaching library and external execution of its software
units, the aim of this step is to make students learn how to
approach program abstractions. In this step, we characterise each
program by its input space, output space, domain, codomain, and
relation between input and output spaces. We consider in   this
step two kinds of programs: non deterministic programs and
deterministic programs representing respectively specifications
and implementations. We recall that actually specifications are
Prolog programs [4] and implementations are Ada programs. Given
a selected program from the teaching library, this program is
first executed, and then its abstraction is written in a separate
Ada specification file.

3.1.2 Comparing Program Abstractions

The main question that we tackle in this step is:
    Given a program P defined by its specification T and its
    implementation I. When can we say that I is correct w.r.t.
    T?

Given the software library, we treat essentially the correctness
quality. Considering that a program is defined by its
specification and implementation, the correctness criteria is
adressed by comparing abstractions respectively associated to the
specification and implementation of each selected program.

Illustrative   examples   processes   defineetness,   partial
correctness, total correctness, empty and full specifications,
implementations having larger domains than specifications, and
specifications having several implementations.

3.2 Learning Implementation by Program Execution and Modification

To guide students in implementing specifications, we consider two steps: solving specifications by external program use and solving specifications by internal program use.

3.2.1 Solving Specifications by Program Execution

The main question addressed in this step is:

Given a software library L and a specification T. Is there a program P in L having an implementation I that is correct w.r.t. T? If not, is it possible to find a set of implementations doing the same thing by external user synchronisation and communication?

Hence, in this step, we introduce students to use the library to solve specifications. When a student is looking for an implementation, he has to compare his specification to actual specifications in the library to be able to determine whether he can associate to it a given implementation. When there is no implementation satisfying a given specification, students look for a set of implementations and try to find an external sequence, choice, or iteration use.

In this activity, the student has to synchronize the communication between different units: each time he uses a unit, he compares his intended specification with the unit's specification. In this processes, he learns some elements about specification decomposition and program composition.

3.2.2 Satisfying Specifications by Program Modification

The main question addressed in this step is:

Given a software library L and a specification T. Is there in L a program P having an implementation I that is correct w.r.t. T? If not, is it possible to find a set of implementations doing the same thing by internal synchronisation and communication or modification?

This question is made harder by some constraints such as software internal qualities. We answer it by considering a set of parameters that we change alternatively during the course, applying them to data types and data structures.

3.2.2.1 Modification Parameters

The set of parameters we consider is defined by the following elements related to a considered data type or data structure:

- specification,
- implementation style,
- representation type, and
- test procedure.

The specification can be defined:
- without exceptions, or
- with exceptions.

Operations are defined as
- procedures,
- functions, or
- pocedures and functions.

These operations can be:
- binary having two arguments, or
- n-ary having more than two arguments.

They can also be:
- non generic, or
- generic.

Implementations have styles in
- the functional style using recursion, or in
- the imperative style using iteration and assignment.

A representation type can be:
- a predefined data type, or
- a new data type.

And it can be:
- not private, or
- private.

A test procedure uses a data type or data structure package to be tested.

All the activity is conducted by combining these parameters going from one version to another. We are guided by the idea of program modification and the interest of program qualities.

A particular attention is given to a data structure list. This data structure is lisp oriented and it introduces the following operations: init, cons, first, and empty. Also when this structure is implemented, we use it to implement the other recursive data structure implementations.

3.2.2.2 Programming Steps

The following activities are followed by students and teachers:
- Understanding specification by execution.
- Designing an implementation version.
- Maintaining this version by modification.

4 Illustrative Example

The aim of this example is to illustrate the student work when he is defining the function of a particular software unit and comparing abstractions.

For that, let me consider that each software unit P is caracterised by specification T and implementation I. Because specifications and implementations are executable, we caracterise them respectively by (Xt,Yt,[T]), and (Xi,Yi,[I]) where Xt, Yt, [T] denote respectively the input space, the output space, and the function of the specification; and Xi, Yi, [I] denote respectively the input space, the output space, and the function of the implementation.

Consider now that the student is asked to execute the algorithmic specification add1 and the implementation add2 defined on the same and equal input and output spaces. His report should be as follows:

For specification add1

```
S = integer x integer x integer
add1 = (S, S, [add1])

[add1] = {((0,0,-),(-,-,0)),
          (0,1,-),(-,-,1)),
          (1,0,-),(-,-,1))}.
```

For implementation add2

```
S = integer x integer x integer
add2 = (S, S, [add2])

[add2] = {((0,0,-),(0,0,0)),
          (0,1,-),(0,1,1)),
          (1,0,-),(1,0,1))}
          (1,1,-),(1,1,2))}.
```

So, we introduce progressively a mathematical logic notation to describe the link between the input and output data. The descriptions given above can also be denoted in closed form by the following formulas:

$$S = \{(x,y,z)/ \ (x,y,z) \ \text{in (integer x integer x integer)}\}$$

$$[add1] = \{((x,y,z),(x',y',z'))/ \ x \ \text{in} \ \{0,1\} \ \text{and} \ y \ \text{in} \ \{0,1\}$$
$$\text{and} \ z'=x+y \ \text{and} \ x'=x \ \text{and} \ y'=y\}$$

$$[add2] = \{((x,y,z),(x',y',z'))/ \ x \ \text{in} \ \{0,1\} \ \text{and} \ y \ \text{in} \ \{0,1\}$$
$$\text{and} \ z'=x+y\}.$$

This enables us to verify that students are able to evaluate predicates and understand what they are representing.

In the begining of program execution activity, we choose software units having small spaces and domains. In the other cases we determine only partially the program function.

When we are concerned by the data type specification, each element of the input space is a sequence made up of some operations of the data type. For example, the following elements belong to the abstraction [stack]:

```
(init.push(a).push(b).push(c).top,c)
(init.top,error).
```

Considering the preceding abstractions related to add1 and add2. To verify that add2 is correct w.r.t. add1, we execute add1 and add2 for each add1 input data and compare their associated set of outputs. We obtain the following results:

Let me define the domain of add1 by:

$d = \{(0,0,-),(0,1,-),(1,0,-)\}.$

For the input data $(0,0,-)$
    add2 computes the output data set O1= $\{(0,0,0)\}$
    add1 computes the output data set O2= $\{(-,-,0)\}.$
We note that O1 is included in O2.

For the input data $(0,1,-)$
    add2 computes the output data set O1=$\{(0,1,1)\}$
    add1 computes the output data set O2=$\{(-,-,1)\}.$
We note that O1 is included in O2.

For the input data $(1,0,-)$
    add2 computes the output data set O1=$\{(1,0,1)\}$
    add1 computes the output data set O2=$\{(-,-,1)\}.$
We note that O1 is included in O2.

So the student concludes that add2 is correct (totally) w.r.t. add1. The reader can note that the verification algorithm interpretes the following correctness formula:

Implementation I is correct w.r.t. specification T if and only if for each input data s of T, I defines an output data s' defined by T.

Given a software unit P, when its associated specification T is executed and its abstraction determined, the student creates for it an Ada separate specification file, then compiles it and catalogues it.

For example, the following specification file is created for the software unit add:

```
with types; use types;
procedure add(s1: in S; s2: out S);
-- begin specification
    -- prec: x in {0,1} and y in {0,1}
    -- posc: z' = x + y
-- end specification;
```

The reader can note that the preconditions and postconditions formulas are directly extracted from the relation representing the abstraction of add1. The unit types is here a package containing the declaration of the type S.

Also, because during program execution activity, students manipulate data spaces, we have found that they are more prepared to make the transition from graphical and mathematical description of a program unit to its Ada representation, accept the langage syntax, and understand more easily the semantic. For space S, e.g., the following description is used in package types:

```
type S = record
        x: integer;
        y: integer;
        z: integer;
    end record;
```

246

5 Interests

The execution phase is made necessary by the fact that with the recent advent of microcomputers, access to computing facilities is growing more wide-spread. This is causing a myriad of problems ranging from heterogeneity of students'backgrounds to ill-conseived first contacts with programming [2].

It becomes possible to teach all the data types operations of the language by executing these data types as separate programs. When the data types of the language are executed externally, we describe this execution and assimilate it to a specification. Because programs are considered as black boxes, we expect that students will refer to them in their problem solving activity on the basis of their abstraction.

Also, students learn data abstraction because they are asked to find a unit declaration: they have to find the parameters, their names, and types; all the declaration is application oriented and is not influenced by the names of the primitive data types.

Students also learn some elements of specification decomposition and program composition because they are asked to solve specifications by external communication between program units.

Solving specifications by execution evoques also the hierarchy between abstractions and prepares the later explanation that implementations are more specific than specifications which can be interpreted that they contain more details. Hence the student library is reorganised as a set of units, each unit being characterised by one specification (program) and one or more than one implementation (program). So, the basic programming culture of the student is updated at the same time. This means that we expect students to use specifications in program design activity.

Hence, it becomes possible to enrich the student culture by virtual specifications. The student is invited to imagine specifications, write their corresponding abstractions, and catalogue the description in a separate specification file. When later he recognises the specification, he can use it.

By giving the syntactic declaration of each operation in one data type, and using the specification coming from the specification step using external execution, it becomes easy to reimplement the langage operations using various parameters as operation name, and operation form. This work introduces naturally the import export notion, the subroutine call, and the sequence control structure. Also, it completes the first programming culture related to the programming language.

External use of program units will surely raise exception messages, then the previous implementations are naturally updated: the exception mechanism is introduced along with the conditional control structure.

Hiding information and using program abstractions during implementation is learned using different versions of the test procedure of the data structure. When a data structure is not private, students observe that they can directly access the representation structure and must change their programs when the implementation uses another representation structure. When a data structure is private, they observe that the compiler prevents them from accessing the representation structure and observe that they do not have to change the procedure test even though the representation structure changes.

The inheritance concept is introduced first by using any defined data structure as a new representation structure and next by adding new operations to the data structure. The following operations are used to enrich the data structure:
- make full
- make empty
- insert by position or value after or before an element determined by position or value.
- delete by position or value after or before an element determined by position or value.
- modify by position or value after or before an element determined by position or value.
- list all elements.

The genericity concept is introduced after developing specialised particular versions.

Functional programming style is learned using the following recursive unit model:

```
with operations; use operations;
function iter_recursively(x: in T1) return T2 is
  begin -- iter_recursively
    if p(x)
      then return it(x)
      else return
            cons(tr(first(x)),iter_recursively(rest(x)));
    end if;
  end iter_recursively;
```

where c, it, cons, tr, first, and rest are functions depending on the considered specification at hand, and separately developped and tested.

A particular attention is given to the list data structure. This data structure is lisp oriented and introduces the following operations: init, cons, first, and empty. Also when this structure is implemented, we use it to implement the other recursive data structure implementations.

The logic programming style and specification writing is introduced first by authorizing the reading access of Prolog file texts and next by asking students to formalise specifications they have written during execution activity. But this step is not yet experimented. Following the same idea, we can also organise the teaching of specification validation as we have organised the teaching of verification.

248

The iteration technique is introduced later in the course using the following unit model:

```
with operations; use operations;
procedure iter(x: in T1; y: out T2) is
  x1: T1 := x;
  y1: T2;
  stop: boolean;
  begin -- iter
    it(y1)
    iv(x1)
    ir(stop);
    while (not stop)
      loop
        tr(x1,y1)
        av(x1);
        ar(x1,y1,stop);
      end loop;
      y := y1;
  end iter;
```

where operations depend on the specification.

When we are faced with an iterative specification, we make its implementation equivalent to the problem of finding the following three pairs of subroutines (tr,it), (av,iv), (ar,ia) respectively related to the definition of the output y, the process of the input x, and the definition of the iteration test. Our conviction is that students can learn a great deal about how to do implementations by using abstractions and how to import and export program units before to teach them iteration, as it is done in most introductory programming courses.

6. Conclusion

Including multi-programming paradigms in first programming courses becomes a necessity on one hand and constitutes a special challenge for teachers on the other hand. In this paper we have proposed an approach to handle this problem.

Overall, we feel fairly satisfied with the course as it is now, though we are seeking to improve it through interactions with other teachers of similar courses.

Acknowledgement

The author gratefully acknowledge Pr. R. Mittermeir (Klagenfurt University) and Pr. A. Mili (Tunis University) for previous discussions on the subject. This work is supported by a grant from FRST (The National Foundation for Scientific and Technical Research).

References

1. Boehm, B. Software Engineering Economics. Prentice-Hall, 1981.

2. Dijkstra, E.W. Selected Writing on Computing: A Personal

Perspective. Springer Verlag, 1982.

3. Ferchichi, A., and A. Jaoua. Teaching First Year Programming: A Proposal. _SIGCSE Bulletin_, September, 1987.

4. Ferchichi, A., et A. Mili. Spécification Relationrelle Assistée par Prolog. Département d'Informatique, Université d'Ottawa, Mars 1992.

5. Liskov, B., and J. Guttag. _Abstraction and Specification in Program Development_. Mass., MIT Press, 1986.

6. Meyer, B. _Object-oriented Software Construction_. Prentice Hall International, New York, 1988.

7. Mili, A., N. Boudriga, and F. Mili. _Towards Structured Specifying: Theory, Practice and Applications_. Chichester, Ellis Horwood Ltd., 1989.

8. Wiener, R., and R. Sincovec. _Software Engineering With Modula-2 and Ada_. New York, John Wiley and Sons Inc., 1984.

TEACHING AND TRAINING IN THE CASE TOOL ENVIRONMENT

Tatjana Welzer, Jozsef Györkös
University of Maribor
Faculty of Technical Sciences
SLO-62000 MARIBOR, Slovenia
Smetanova 17
Tel. + 038 62 25 461, Fax + 030 62 212 013
e-mail: welzer@uni-mb.ac.mail.yu
gyorkos@uni-mb.ac.mail.yu

Our contribution focuses on the experiences gained while training different groups of users in the CASE tool environment. Most of these tools are based on the classical design methodos like the Chen E-R diagram, or the DeMarco-Yourdan and Gane&Sarson techniques [2], which are reasonably well known to users.

An effective use of any CASE tool should be supported by a basic knowledge of the chosen structured methods [1,3]. This fact leads to a division of users into different groups: users experienced in software development but with little knowledge of structured methodos, users experienced both in software development and in structured methods and inexperienced users who are usually experts in structured methods.

The intention of our presentation is not to draw a general conclusion about which group of users is more successfuler in teaching and training, but only to highlight a problem of basic knowledge as well as of experience in the CASE tool environment.

The first group that is involved in our experiment is assembled from young engineers inexperienced in software development, who gained quite a lot of knowledge about structutred methods at the university , while in the second and the third groups, users experienced in the development of different projects are involved. They have a lot of experience and expert knowledge about software development and in addition they are not (the third group) or just partly (the second group) familiar with the basic knowledge of the techniques mentioned above. Because of this they are sometimes intolerant towards the new way of work supported by the CASE tool. Therefore we try to combine training in the CASE tool environment with teaching of some of the skills needed in the relevant structured methods [4].

References

1. J.M. Clifton: An Industry approach to the Software Engineering Course, ACM SIGCSE BULLETIN Vol. 23, No. 1, March 1991, pp.296-299.

2. C. Finkelstein: An Introduction to Information Engineering, Addison Wesley, 1989.

3. J.E. Tomayako: Teaching Software Development in a Studio Environment, ACM SIGCSE BULLETIN Vol. 23, No1., March 1991 pp.300-303.

4. T.Welzer,J.Györkös:Teaching structured techniques supported by CASE tool,CASE 2,Rijeka,1990, pp.2/1-5.

SCIENCE POLICY

Chair: G. Haring

Research Policy in Information Technologies
for Small European Countries

The dynamism in research and in industrial development in Information Technology as well as concentrated efforts to boost R&D in this discipline on national and supranational levels poses the special question of how to meet this challenge from the perspective of a small country.

In Europe, the various programs to foster information technology have already a solid tradition. Special schemes have been developed by the EEC-Commission for establishing programs, soliciting and evaluating proposals as well as monitoring the progress of sponsored projects. The high volume of research money thus available and the possibility for setting trends poses special challenges for such Central-European countries as Austria - just seeking EEC-membership -, Hungary - being in the process of change in its economic, and hence also research policy system -, and Slovenia - a country which obtained independence just recently.

The following distinguished IT-policy leaders are invited to address under the chairmenship of G. Haring, President of the Austrian Computer Society, the consequences to be drawn from the technical, economical, and political circumstances we currently witness in central Europe:

P. Lepape (CEC, Directorate-General XIII, Brussels);
C. Bašković (Ministrstvo za Znanost in Tehnologijo, Ljubljana);
L. Nyíri (National Committee for Technological Development, Budapest);
N. Roszenich (Bundesministerium f. Wissenschaft und Forschung, Wien)

A Min Tjoa, Isidro Ramos (eds.)

Database and Expert Systems Applications

Proceedings of the International Conference
in Valencia, Spain, 1992

1992. 324 figures. XIV, 541 pages.
Soft cover DM 148,-, öS 1036,-
ISBN 3-211-82400-6

Prices are subject to change without notice

The Database and Expert Systems Applications (DEXA) conferences are
mainly oriented to establish a state-of-the-art forum on database and expert
systems applications. But practice without theory has no sense, as Leonardo
said five centuries ago. Therefore, as presented in this book, a compromise
has been aimed at these two complementary aspects. Five sessions are ap-
plication-oriented, ranging from classical applications to more unusual ones
in software engineering. Actual research aspects in databases, such as activity, deductivity and/or object orientation are also presented in DEXA '92, as
well as the implications of the new "data models" such as OO-model, deductive model, etc. are included in the modelling sessions.

Other areas of interest, such as hypertext and multimedia applications, together with the classical field of information retrieval are also considered.
Finally, implementation aspects are reflected in very concrete fields.

Springer-Verlag Wien New York

J. Forslin and P. Kopacek (eds.)

Cultural Aspects of Automation

Proceedings of the 1st IFAC Workshop on Cultural Aspects of Automation,October 1991, Krems, Austria

(Schriftenreihe der Wissenschaftlichen Landesakademie für Niederösterreich)

1992. 21 figures. VIII, 113 pages.
Soft cover DM 39,-, öS 275,-
ISBN 3-211-82362-X

Prices are subject to change without notice

In October of last year experts from different research disciplines, like control engineering, systems engineering, sociology, art, philosophy, and politics met in Krems (Austria) to discuss the interplay between recent developments in automation and the culture and social framework, with special emphasis on the approaches in the East and the West.

Main topics of these intensive discussions were technology design, automation software and culture, social conditions, education, computer and art, design of man-machine-systems, CIM and culture as well as appropriate methods for interdisciplinary research.

A selection of papers presented at this conference can be found in this volume.

Springer-Verlag Wien New York

Reactivity and Structure
Concepts in Organic Chemistry

Volume 14

Editors:

Klaus Hafner   Jean-Marie Lehn
Charles W. Rees P. von Rague Schleyer
Barry M. Trost   Rudolf Zahradník

William P. Weber

Silicon Reagents
for Organic Synthesis

Springer-Verlag
Berlin Heidelberg New York 1983

William P. Weber

Department of Chemistry, University of Southern California
University Park
Los Angeles, CA 90007/USA

ISBN-13:978-3-642-68663-4   e-ISBN-13:978-3-642-68661-0
DOI: 10.1007/978-3-642-68661-0

Library of Congress Cataloging in Publication Data.

Weber, William P., 1940–
Silicon reagents for organic synthesis. (Reactivity and structure; v. 14)
Bibliography: p. Includes index. 1. Chemistry, Organic–Synthesis. 2. Organo-
silicon compounds. 3. Chemical tests and reagents. 1. Title. II. Series.
QD262.W35 1982 547 .2 82-5890 AACR2

2152/3020-543210

To Heather and our sons: Edward, Robert and Justin

Preface

The application of silicon reagents in organic synthesis has grown at an increasingly rapid rate over the last twenty years. This has been the result of truly international interest. Significant contributions have been made by Japanese, Russian, German, French, English, American, Swiss and Canadian as well as by chemists from many other countries. This monograph attempts to comprehensively cover this field. Some seventeen hundred articles reporting contributions by over eighteen hundred scientists are summarized. Nevertheless, I have no doubt that interesting and important work has been left out. I welcome comments about such results which should be included in any future editions of this monograph.

I would like to thank Robert Damrauer who first stimulated my interest in organosilicon chemistry. In addition, I thank a number of chemists who have shared my enthusiasm for silicon chemistry over the years: A Chihi, M.E. Childs, R.A. Felix, H. Firgo, T.Y. Gu, T.I. Ito, I.N. Jung, K.E. Koenig, H. Okinoshima, M.M. Radcliffe, B.I. Rosen, H.S.D. Soysa, K.P. Steele, R.E. Swaim, D. Tzeng, P.B. Valkovich, A.K. Willard, S. Wunderly, and present members of my research group. The opportunity to spend a quiet sabbatical leave at U.C.L.A greatly assisted in the preparation of this book. Finally, I am indebted to Michelle Dea who typed the entire manuscript, to Jennifer L. Teller who prepared camera ready copies of all equations and figures and to John Carpenter who assisted in collecting literature references.

Los Angeles, California U.S.A.
August 1982

William P. Weber

Table of Contents

Table of Contents

Table of Contents

Abbreviations

AIBN	azo-isobutyronitrile
$AlCl_3$	aluminium trichloride
aq.	aqueous
$BF_3 \cdot OEt_2$	boron trifluoride etherate
BF_3	boron trifluoride
BF_4^-	tetrafluoroborate
Cl_3SiH	trichlorosilane
CCl_4	carbon tetrachloride
DBU	1,8-diazabicyclo[5,4,0]undec-7-ene
DBN	1,5-diazabicyclo[4,3,0]non-5-ene
DC-18-C-6	dicyclohexyl-18-crown-6
DCC	dicyclohexylcarbodiimide
DDQ	2,3-dichloro-5,6-dicyanoquinone
DIBAL	diisobutyl aluminium hydride
DIOP, (+) or (−)	(+) or (−) 2,3-0-isopropylidene-2,3-dihydroxy-1,4-*bis*(diphenylphosphino)butane
Disiamyl borane	$\left((CH_3)_2CH-\underset{CH_3}{CH} \right)_2 B-H$
DME	dimethoxyethane
DMF	dimethyl formamide
DMSO	dimethyl sulfoxide
e.e.	enantiomeric excess
eq.	equation
e.u.	entropy unit
HBr	hydrobromic acid
HCl	hydrochloric acid
HI	hydriodic acid
HMPT	hexamethylphosphorous triamide
IR	infrared
KCN	potassium cyanide
$KHSO_4$	potassium hydrogen sulfate
LDA	lithium diisopropyl amide
$LiAlH_4$	lithium aluminium hydride
MCPBA	*meta*-chloroperbenzoic acid
NBS	*N*-bromosuccinimide
NCS	*N*-chlorosuccinimide
$NaBH_4$	sodium borohydride

Abbreviations

Pd	palladium
PTC	phase transfer catalysis
SnCl$_4$	stannic chloride
TBAF	tetra-*n*-butylammonium fluoride
TCNE	tetracyanoethylene
Th	thymidine
TiCl$_4$	titanium tetrachloride
THF	tetrahydrofuran
THP	tetrahydropyranyl ether
TMEDA	N,N,N′,N′-tetramethylethylenediamine
TMS-Br	trimethylsilyl bromide
TMS-CN	trimethylsilyl cyanide
TMS-Cl	trimethylsilyl chloride
TMS-F	trimethylsilyl fluoride
TMS-I	trimethylsilyl iodide
TMS-N$_3$	trimethylsilyl azide
TMS-X	trimethylhalosilane
TMU	tetramethylurea
TsOH	*p*-toluene sulfonic acid
UV	ultraviolet
18-C-6	18-crown-6
9-BBN	9-borabicyclo[3,3,1]nonane

1 Fundamental Considerations

The goal of this monograph is to review the use of silicon reagents in organic synthesis. Activity in this area has grown by leaps and bounds in the past decade. The commercial availability of many of these silicon reagents should further encourage development of new chemistry in this area [1–6]. This topic has been the subject of several previous reviews [7–13]. In the present monograph, I have attempted to comprehensively cover this field with the exception of silylation, the protection of O–H, N–H, and S–H bonds as silyl ethers [11, 12]. This choice was dictated by the vast number of examples of the use of silylation whose comprehensive coverage would have easily doubled the length of this already sizeable monograph.

Before beginning, a short summary of some of the physical bases underlying all silicon chemistry is in order. These data will be compared to those for carbon since organic chemists are the intended audience of this book.

The ground electronic configuration of silicon is $1s^2 2s^2 2p^6 3s^2 3p^2$ whereas carbon is $1s^2 2s^2 2p^2$. Both are usually tetracoordinate in their stable compounds and silicon, like carbon, uses four sp^3 hydridized orbitals in its bonding. Suitable organosilicon compounds are capable of optical activity. Chiral compounds such as α-naphthylphenylmethylsilane have proved useful for the study of reaction mechanisms at silyl centers [14].

Silylenes are divalent silicon species, and like carbenes, are highly reactive intermediates. While research is active in this area [15], the use of silylenes in organic synthesis has yet to be reported.

Unlike carbon, silicon shows little tendency to form stable compounds possessing multiple bonds. No reagents which possess multiple bonds between silicon and carbon or any other elements have yet been developed. This situation may change, however, since chemists interested in reactive intermediates have intensively studied this area for the past dozen years [16].

Because silicon forms bonds with orbitals of principle quantum number 3 rather than 2, its bonds will be longer than the comparable ones of carbon. The atomic radius of silicon is 1.17 Å while that for carbon is 0.77 Å. In single bonds, carbon and silicon nuclei are 1.87–1.89 Å apart while the carbon-carbon separation in ethane is 1.54 Å [17]. This may reduce the steric bulk of a trimethylsilyl group, making it appear smaller than might be anticipated. For example, chloromethyltrimethylsilane undergoes S_n2 substitution reactions with greater facility than do neopentyl halides [18].

$$(CH_3)_3SiCH_2Cl \xrightarrow[\text{Acetone}]{\text{NaI}} (CH_3)_3SiCH_2I \qquad (1.1)$$

1

Silicon, unlike, carbon, possesses comparatively low lying vacant 3d orbitals. Nucleophiles may associate with these empty orbitals and thus affect the regiochemistry observed in their reactions with organosilicon compounds. For example, α-trimethylsilyl epoxides undergo nucleophilic attack by dialkyl cuprate reagents at the carbon bearing the silyl group. This contrasts with the usual nucleophilic attack on epoxides at the less hindered carbon [19].

$$(CH_3)_3Si\underset{O}{\diagdown\!\!\!\triangle} \quad \xrightarrow{(n\text{-}Bu)_2CuLi} \quad (CH_3)_3Si\underset{n\text{-}Bu}{\overset{OH}{\diagup\!\!\!\diagdown_H}} \tag{1.2}$$

3d Orbitals may stabilize transition states as well as pentacoordinate reaction intermediates. These orbitals may provide low energy pathways for nucleophilic displacements in which bond making preceeds bond breaking. Compounds of the type R_3SiX (X = halogen, etc.) undergo facile S_n2 nucleophilic displacement and solvolysis, while similar tertiary alkyl halides generally react by S_n1 pathways.

Several types of compounds in which silicon is penta- and even hexacoordinate are known. These possess electronegative ligands which may cause contraction of the 3d orbitals [20—22]. Recently, dipotassium alkyl or alkenyl pentafluorosilicates have been extensively employed in organic synthesis [23] (See Chapter 10).

Although many electronegativity scales exist and have minor differences in absolute values between them, all agree that silicon is more electropositive than either carbon or hydrogen. In all silicon is relatively close in electronegativity to hydrogen. On Pauling's scale carbon is at 2.5 while silicon is at 1.8. Hydrogen at 2.1 is intermediate [24]. The reactions of methyl lithium with triphenylsilane and triphenylmethane illustrate this difference [25].

$$Ph_3Si\text{-}H + CH_3Li \longrightarrow Ph_3Si\text{-}CH_3 + Li^+ H^- \tag{1.3}$$

$$Ph_3C\text{-}H + CH_3Li \longrightarrow Ph_3C^- Li^+ + CH_3\text{-}H \tag{1.4}$$

The success of ionic hydrogenation in which silanes serve as hydride donors to carbocations reflects these differences [26].

$$Ph_3C^+ BF_4^- + Et_3Si\text{-}H \longrightarrow Ph_3C\text{-}H + Et_3Si\text{-}F + BF_3 \tag{1.5}$$

On the other hand, silanes, which possess Si–H bonds, may be compared to hydrogen. Hydrosilation and hydrogenation reactions have many common features [27] (see Chapter 10).

$$R\text{-}C{\equiv}C\text{-}H \xrightarrow[H_2PtCl_6]{HSiCl_3} \underset{H}{\overset{R}{\diagdown}}C{=}C\underset{SiCl_3}{\overset{H}{\diagup}} \tag{1.6}$$

Trimethylsilyl groups often react in a manner analogous to a proton. For example, HCN adds to the carbonyl group of aldehydes and ketones to form cyanohydrins, while trimethylsilyl cyanide in similar reactions yields tri-methylsilyloxynitriles. (See Chapter 2)

$$\text{>=0} \quad \xrightarrow{\quad HCN \quad} \quad NC\text{>}OH \qquad (1.7)$$

$$\text{>=0} \quad \xrightarrow{\quad (CH_3)_3SiCN \quad} \quad NC\text{>}OSi(CH_3)_3 \qquad (1.8)$$

Recent work has determined many silicon bond dissociation energies. Substitution appears to have much less effect on both Si—H and Si—C bond energies than it does on C—H and C—C bond energies. Most Si—H bond dissociation energies (kcal/mole) are about 89.5 whereas C—H bond dissociation energies vary from 104.8 for methane to 87.9 for the alpha C—H bonds of toluene. Silicon-carbon bonds are close to 88.5 kcal/mole in strength, whereas C—C bond energies vary from 88 in ethane to 82 for the C—C bond of neopentane [28]. Silicon forms very strong bonds with electronegative elements such as fluorine and oxygen (see Table for Bond Energies). This has considerable synthetic implications (see Chapter 25).

The strength of Si—O bonds may result from partial double bond character; oxygen 2p lone pairs can overlap with empty 3d orbitals on adjacent silicon. Consistent with this view, the Si—O—Si bond angle of disiloxane is observed to be 144° [29, 30].

$$H_3Si \overset{\displaystyle O}{\diagup \diagdown} SiH_3 \qquad\qquad (1.9)$$
$$\underset{144°}{\diagdown \diagup}$$

The fact that carbanions alpha to silicon are formed both by metallation of tetraalkylsilanes [31] and by addition of organometallics to vinyl silanes [32, 33] may reflect stabilization of such anions by overlap of the filled 2p orbital on carbon with the adjacent empty 3d orbitals on silicon (see Chapter 6).

$$Ph_3Si\diagdown\diagup \cdot + PhLi \longrightarrow Ph_3Si—CH-CH_2-Ph \qquad (1.10)$$

However, the importance of 3d orbitals has been questioned [34, 35].

Finally, silicon has a definite stabilizing effect on beta carbocations in cases where the Si—C bond can achieve a *trans*-coplanar arrangement with the vacant 2p orbital of the carbocation center. β-Bromoethyltrimethylsilane undergoes solvolytic elimination to yield ethylene and the elements of TMS-Br. This reaction is as sensitive to solvent polarity as is the ionization of *t*-butyl chloride [36]. This is unusual reactivity results from stabilization of the carbocation by hyperconjugation [37] with the Si—C bond or by bridging of the trimethylsilyl group [38].

$$
(CH_3)_3Si \overset{+\delta}{\diagdown} \underset{Br^{-\delta}}{} \xrightarrow{\quad EtOH \quad} (CH_3)_3SiOEt \ + \ CH_2=CH_2 \ + \ HBr \qquad (1.11)
$$

Bond Dissociation Energies (kcal/mole) [28]

$H_3Si-SiH_3$	74		
$(CH_3)_3Si-CH_3$	89,4	H_3C-CH_3	88
$(CH_3)_3Si-H$	90.3		
$(CH_3)_3Si-Cl$	113	$(CH_3)_3C-Cl$	80
$(CH_3)_3Si-Br$	96	$(CH_3)_3C-Br$	64
$(CH_3)_3Si-I$	77	$(CH_3)_3C-I$	51
F_3Si-F	160	CF_3-F	130
$(CH_3)_3Si-OH$	128	$(CH_3)_3C-OH$	91
$(CH_3)_3Si-NHCH_3$	100	$(CH_3)_3C-NHCH_3$	80
$(CH_3)_3Si-SC_4H_9$	99	$(CH_3)_3C-S-C_4H_9$	71

These values are in general considerably higher than those for average bond energies given by Ebsworth [39].

Average Bond Energies (kcal/mole) [39]

	C	Si
H	98.7	76.5
C	82.6	73.2
N	72.8	87.3 $(CH_3)_3Si-NEt_2$
O	85.5	106
F	116	142
Cl	81	97.2
Br	68	75.6
I	51	56

In particular chapters where it is pertinent, this minimal information will be supplemented.

References

1. Petrach Systems Inc., Bristol, Pennsylvania, USA.
2. PCR Research Chemicals Inc., Gainesville, Florida, USA.
3. Pierce Chemical Co., Rockford, Illinois, USA.
4. Silar Laboratories, Inc., Scotia, New York, USA.
5. Aldrich Chemical Co., Milwaukee, Wisconsin, USA.
6. Fluka AG CH-9470, Buchs, Switzerland.
7. Hudrilik, P.F. "Organosilicon Compounds in Organic Synthesis", in J. Organometal. Chem. Libr., *1*, 127, Seyferth, D. Ed., Amsterdam, Elsevier, 1976.
8. Colvin, E.W. "Silicon in Organic Synthesis", Chem. Soc. Rev., *7*, 15 (1978)
9. Fleming, I. "Organic Silicon Chemistry" in Comprehensive Organic Chemistry, Barton, D.H.R. and Ollis, W.D. Eds., Vol. 3, 539, Oxford, Pergamon, 1979.

10. Birkofer, L. and Stuhl, O. "Silylated Synthons", Topics Current Chemistry, *88*, 33, Heidelberg, Springer Verlag (1980).
11. Klebe, J. "Silylation in Organic Synthesis", Adv. Org. Chem., *8*, 97 (1972).
12. Pierce, A.F. "Silylation of Organic Compounds", Pierce Chemical Co., Rockford, Ill. 1968.
13. Colvin, E.W. "Silicon in Organic Synthesis", London, Butterworth, 1981.
14. Sommer, L.H.: "Stereochemistry, Mechanism, and Silicon". New York: McGraw Hill 1965
15. For a recent review of silylene chemistry see Gaspar, P.P., in "Reactive Intermediates" (M. Jones, Jr. and R.A. Moss, Eds.). Vol. I, p. 229–277. New York: Wiley-Interscience 1978
16. "Formation and Properties of Unstable Intermediates Containing Multiple P_π-P_π Bonded Group 4B Metals;" Gusel'nikov, L.E., Nametkin, N.S.: Chem. Rev. *79*, 529–577 (1979)
17. Ebsworth, E.A.V.: "Physical Basis of the Chemistry of the Group IV Elements" in "Organometallic Compounds of the Group IV Elements", MacDiarmid, A.G., Ed. p. 1–104, New York: Marcel Dekker, 1968
18. Bott, R.W., Eaborn, C., Swaddle, T.W.: J. Organometal. Chem. *5*, 233 (1966)
19. Hudrlik, P.F., Peterson, D., Rona, R.J.: J. Org. Chem. *40*, 2263 (1975)
20. Frye, C.L.: J. Am. Chem. Soc. *86*, 3170 (1964)
21. Boer, F.R., Flynn, J., Turley, J.: J. Am. Chem. Soc. *90*, 6973 (1968)
22. Perozzi, E.F., Martin, J.C.: J. Am. Chem. Soc. *101*, 1591 (1979)
23. Müller, R., Organometal: Chem. Rev. *1*, 359 (1966)
24. Pauling, L., "The Nature of the Chemical Bond", 3rd Ed., p. 90. Cornell: 1960
25. Gilman, H., Melvin, Jr., H.W.: J. Am. Chem. Soc. *71*, 4050 (1949)
26. Kursanov, D.N., Parnes, Z.N., Loim, N.M.: Synthesis 633 (1974)
27. Benkeser, R.A.: Pure and Applied Chemistry *13*, 133 (1966)
28. Walsh, R.: Accts. of Chem. Res. *14*, 246 (1981)
29. Mauret, P., Abadie, A., Calas, R., Valade, J.: Bull. Chem. Soc. Fr. 1221 (1967)
30. Almenningen, A., Bastiansen, O., Ewing, V., Hedberg, K., Traetteberg, M.: Acta Chem. Scand. *17*, 2455 (1963)
31. Peterson, D.J.: J. Organometal. Chem. *9*, 373 (1967)
32. Cason, L.F., Brooks, H.G.: J. Am. Chem. Soc. *74*, 4582 (1952)
33. Mulvaney, J.E., Gardlund, Z.G.: J. Org. Chem. *30*, 917 (1965)
34. Baechler, R.D., Andose, J.D., Stackhouse, J., and Mislow, K.: J. Am. Chem. Soc. *94*, 8060 (1972).
35. Baechler, R.D., Casey, J.P., Cook, R.J., Senkler, Jr., G.H., and Mislow, K.: J. Am. Chem. Soc., *94*, 2859 (1972).
36. Sommer, L.H., Braughman, G.A.: J. Am. Chem. Soc. *83*, 3346 (1961)
37. Traylor, T.G., Hanstein, W., Berwin, H.J., Clinton, N.A., Brown, R.S.: J. Am. Chem. Soc. *93*, 5715 (1971)
38. Jarvie, A.W.P., Holt, A., Thompson, J.: J. Chem. Soc. *B*, 852 (1969)
39. Reference 17, p. 46.

2 Chemistry of Trimethylsilyl Cyanide

2.1 Introduction

Some of the fundamentals of silicon chemistry have been presented in Chapter One. We now consider one of the most versatile of the silicon reagents: trimethylsilyl cyanide (TMS-CN). Its reactivity effectively illustrates one of the fundamentals of silicon chemistry. Specifically, the trimethylsilyl group often reacts as if it were a proton. One might therefore expect TMS-CN to approximate the reactions and toxicity of hydrogen cyanide.

2.2 Addition of Trimethylsilyl Cyanide to Polar Multiple Bonds

TMS-CN reacts with ketones or aldehydes to yield trimethylsilyl ethers of the corresponding cyanohydrins [1–8]. Even sterically congested systems such as camphor and diaryl ketones, which fail to form cyanohydrins under normal conditions, react readily with TMS-CN [4].

$$\text{(2.1)}$$

A problem with the reagent is that it will also react with acidic hydrogens such as OH [9], SH, and NH [10] to yield the trimethylsilyl derivative and HCN. This dual reactivity of TMS-CN was used to advantage in a prostaglandin synthesis in which a ketone was converted to a trimethylsilyloxy nitrile group with simultaneous protection of an alcohol as its trimethylsilyl ether [9].

$$\text{(2.2)}$$

As might be predicted, dimethyldicyanosilane reacts exothermically with enolizable β-diketones to yield six-membered heterocycles [11].

6

$$\text{(2.3)}$$

Trimethylsilyloxy nitriles have previously been prepared by the sulfuric acid catalyzed addition of HCN to trimethylsilyl enol ethers [12, 13] or by reaction of TMS-Cl with a cyanohydrin in the presence of tertiary amines [14]. These earlier methods suffered from experimental difficulties and limitations. The two most important advantages of the TMS-CN reaction with ketones or aldehydes are its generality, and high yields [4, 7].

$$\text{(2.4)}$$

The increased reactivity of TMS-CN toward carbonyl groups compared to HCN has been attributed to the greater heat of reaction [4]. This results primarily from the fact that the Si−C (76 kcal/mole) or Si−N bond (76 kcal/mole) [15] of TMS-CN is weaker than the H−C bond of HCN (111 kcal/mole) [16], rather than from differences in strength of the Si−O (106 kcal/mole) [15], and H−O (110 kcal/mole) [16] bonds. Si−C and Si−N bond strengths must both be considered since TMS-CN is known to exist as an equilibrium mixture of cyanide and isocyanide forms [17–19]. Cyanosilylation may be initiated by alpha [3] addition of the isocyano form to the carbonyl group [4].

$$(CH_3)_3Si-C\equiv N \quad \rightleftharpoons \quad (CH_3)_3Si-N=C: \qquad \text{(2.5)}$$

Both electrophilic (zinc iodide) [4, 5, 7] and nucleophilic catalysis by cyanide anion effectively promote the reaction between TMS-CN and ketones or aldehydes [1, 3, 9]. Zinc iodide catalysis presumably involves coordination of the zinc cation with the carbonyl oxygen. The resulting increase in electrophilic character at the carbonyl carbon facilitates nucleophilic attack by the isonitrile form of TMS-CN. This may be followed by transfer of the trimethylsilyl group to oxygen.

$$\text{(2.6)}$$

Zinc iodide catalyzed addition of TMS-CN to 4-*t*-butyl cyclohexanone yields a 9:1 ratio of stereoisomers in which the axial cyano group predominates. This results from kinetic rather than thermodynamic control [4].

$$\text{(2.7)}$$

Nucleophilic catalysis requires an organic soluble form of cyanide ion. Both potassium cyanide/18-C-6 complex [1] and tetrabutylammonium cyanide are effective [1]. Cyanide catalysis is thought to occur by addition of cyanide to the carbonyl group. The resulting alkoxide ion reacts at silicon to yield the trimethylsilyloxy nitrile and regenerate cyanide ion. Consistent with this mechanism, azide ion is also an effective catalyst [1].

$$\text{(2.8)}$$

TMS-CN also undergoes Lewis acid catalyzed addition to the C$-$N double bond of imines. α-Amino nitriles are obtained after hydrolysis. Ojima has shown that if the imine is formed from a chiral amine, such as α-phenethyl amine, asymmetric induction in the addition of TMS-CN occurs 22–58% e.e. [20, 21].

$$\text{(2.9)}$$

In the presence of triethylamine, TMS-CN will also add to the C$-$N triple bond of electron deficient nitriles to yield N-trimethylsilyl-α-cyano imines [22].

$$\text{(2.10)}$$

2.3 Utility of Trimethylsilyl Ethers of Cyanohydrins

Cyanohydrin trimethylsilyl ethers are extremely versatile intermediates. Cyanohydrins of ketones which are inaccessible by usual synthetic methods can be formed by use of TMS-CN. Acidic hydrolysis (3 N HCl) of trimethylsilyl ethers of cyanohydrins affords the corresponding cyanohydrin in excellent yields [23–25, 75, 76].

$$(2.11)$$

$$(2.12)$$

Hydrolysis with conc. sulfuric acid, on the other hand, gives the corresponding α-hydroxy amides [6].

$$(2.13)$$

Dehydration of cyanohydrins is a practical way to transform ketones into α,β-unsaturated nitriles. Likewise, the trimethylsilyl ethers of ketone cyanohydrins may be converted into α,β-unsaturated nitriles by treatment with phosphorous oxychloride and pyridine [26].

$$(2.14)$$

The trimethylsilyl ethers of cyanohydrins can be reduced with LiAlH$_4$ to yield β-aminomethyl alcohols [4, 27, 28]. These can be used in the Tiffeneau-Demjanov reaction [29]. For example, 2,4-bis-homobrendan-2-one was prepared from 4-homobrendan-2-one as outlined below (Eq. 2.15) [30].

$$(2.15)$$

In a similar manner, 7,8,9,10-tetrahydro-6-(5 H)-benzocyclooctenone was prepared from benzosuberone [31]. This methodology was also utilized in the preparation of 8,9:13,14-diseco-18-norestradiol [32]. 2-Amino-1-o-bromo-phenylethanols, which can be converted to indoles, have been prepared from o-bromo-acetophenones (Eq. 2.16) [5].

$$\text{(2.16)}$$

β-Aminomethyl alcohols have been previously prepared by reduction of cyanohydrins or β-hydroxy nitroalkanes [33].

In the presence of a catalytic amount of Lewis acid, TMS-CN adds regio-specifically in a 1,2 sense to α,β-unsaturated ketones or aldehydes (Eq. 2.17) [4, 34, 35]. Hydrogen cyanide, nitromethane anion and TMS-CN with two equivalents of triethylaluminium [Eq. 2.18] give Michael addition products on reaction with α,β-unsaturated ketones or aldehydes [36].

$$\text{(2.17)}$$

$$\text{(2.18)}$$

Organolithium reagents add twice to the cyano group of trimethylsilyl ethers of cyanohydrins to yield substituted β-amino alcohols [37].

$$\text{(2.19)}$$

Trimethylsilyl ethers of cyanohydrins can also be used to protect carbonyl groups. For example, TMS-CN adds in a 1,2-sense to the more electrophilic carbonyl group of both benzo- [3, 39] and naphthoquinones [38]. Selective protection of one of the two quinone carbonyl groups is thus achieved. Organometallic reagents such as Grignards, lithium alkyls [38] (Eq. 2.20) and lithium enolates [39, 40] (Eq. 2.21) add in a regiospecific 1,2-manner to the unprotected carbonyl group of the mono-cyanosilylated benzoquinone. Removal of the trimethylsilyloxy nitrile protecting group by treatment with silver fluoride [38] or aq. sodium fluoride [39] yields *p*-quinols. The driving force for this reaction is the strength of the Si−F bond [15].

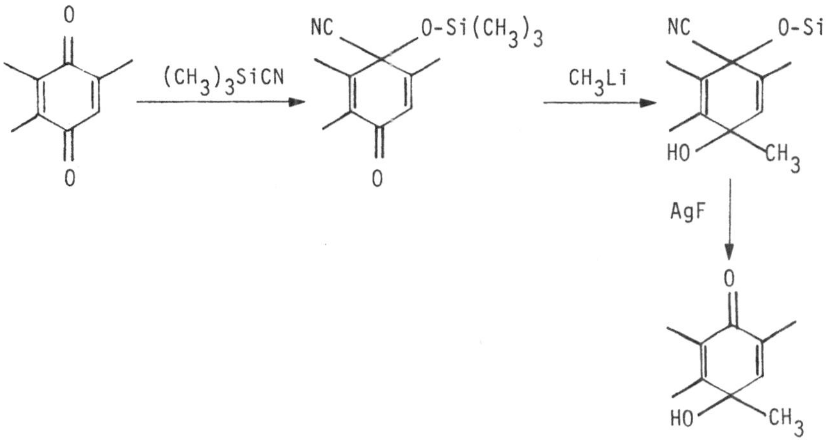

(2.20)

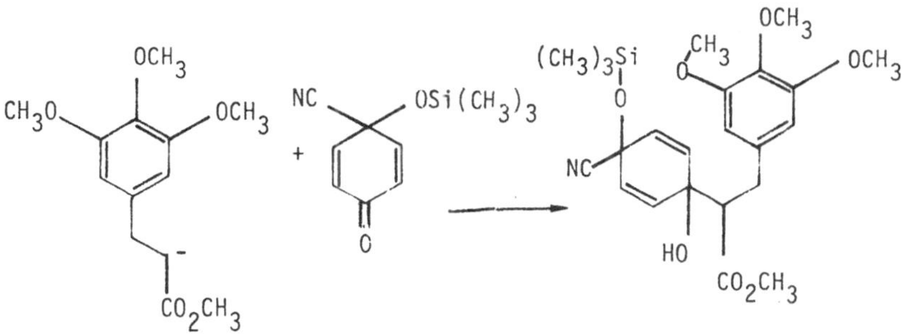

(2.21)

1,2-Addition of allylic Grignard reagents to the unprotected carbonyl group of mono-cyanosilylated benzo- or naphthoquinones yields masked quinols. These then undergo a [3 + 3]-sigmatropic (Cope) rearrangement concurrent with removal of the trimethylsilyloxy protecting group [41, 42].

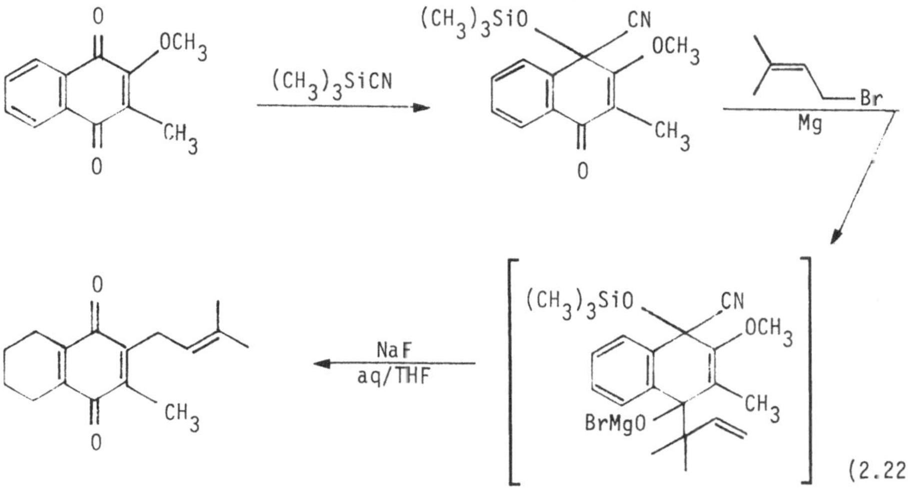

(2.22)

11

Trimethylsilyl ether derivatives of aldehyde cyanohydrins are particularly useful intermediates due to the acidity of the former aldehydic proton. This proton can be removed by sterically hindered, non-nucleophilic bases such as LDA. The cyano-stabilized carbanion thus formed is an acyl anion equivalent which can be alkylated to yield ketones [34, 35, 43, 44]. It reacts with ketones or aldehydes to afford trimethylsilyl ether derivatives of α-hydroxy ketones via rearrangement of the trimethylsilyl group and loss of lithium cyanide [45, 46] (Eq. 2.23). α-Cyano-α-trimethylsilyloxy allylic anions, formed by deprotonation of the trimethylsilyl ethers of α,β-unsaturated aldehyde cyanohydrins, react with alkyl halides regiospecifically at the α-position to yield trimethylsilyl ethers of α,β-unsaturated ketone cyanohydrins [47] (Eq. 2.24). A particular advantage of these acyl anion equivalents compared to 1,3-dithianes is the ease with which the trimethylsilyloxy nitrile protecting group may be removed.

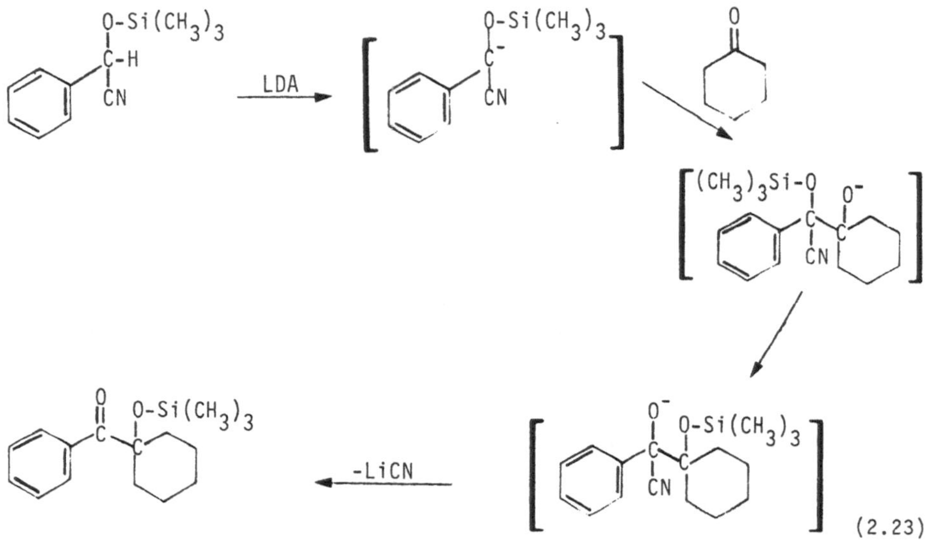

(2.23)

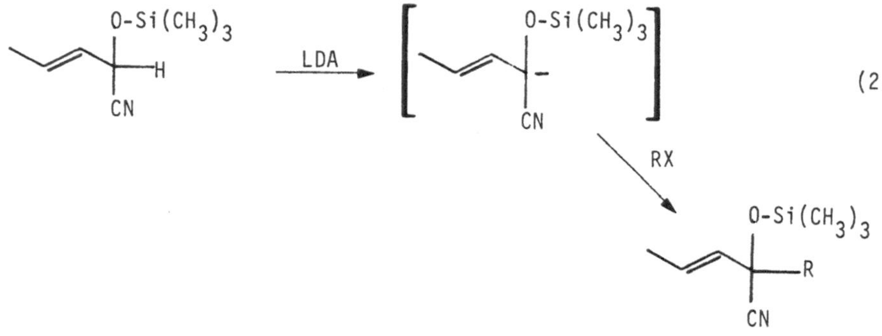

(2.24)

3-Cyano-3-trimethylsilyloxy-1,5-hexadienes undergo Claisen rearrangement on pyrolysis to yield 1-cyano-1-trimethylsilyloxy-1,5-hexadienes. These react with methanol to yield methyl hex-5-enoates [48].

$$(2.25)$$

2.4 Acyl Substitution Reactions of Trimethylsilyl Cyanide

Acyl nitriles can be prepared by reaction of TMS-CN with acid chlorides [49, 50]. These reactions may occur by addition of TMS-CN to the carbonyl group of acid chlorides to form unstable adducts which lose TMS-Cl. This results in acyl substitution rather than addition.

$$(2.26)$$

In the presence of pyridine, addition of a second molecule of TMS-CN to the carbonyl group of the acyl nitrile occurs to yield 1,1-dicyano-1-trimethylsilyl-oxyalkanes [50].

$$(2.27)$$

A similar sequence of reactions of TMS-CN with phosgene, oxalyl chloride and trifluoroacetylchloride yields respectively tricyanotrimethylsilyloxy-methane, 1,1,2,2-tetracyano-1,2-*bis*-(trimethylsilyloxy)ethane and 2,2-dicyano-1,1,1-trifluoro-2-trimethylsilyloxyethane [2].

$$(2.28)$$

$$(NC)_3C-O-Si(CH_3)_3$$

13

In the case of carbonyl fluoride the initial product is stable [2]. TMS-CN also reacts with methyl and ethyl chloroformate to yield the corresponding alkyl cyanoformates [50, 51].

$$
\text{CH}_3\text{O}-\overset{\overset{\text{O}}{\|}}{\text{C}}\diagdown\text{Cl} \quad \xrightarrow{(\text{CH}_3)_3\text{SiCN}} \quad \text{CH}_3\text{O}-\overset{\overset{\text{O}}{\|}}{\text{C}}\diagdown\text{CN} \quad + \quad (\text{CH}_3)_3\text{SiCl} \qquad (2.29)
$$

2.5 Reactions of Trimethylsilyl Cyanide with Polar Cumulenes

TMS-CN reacts with the carbonyl group of ketenes to yield 1-cyano-1-tri-methylsilyloxy-1-alkenes. Ketenes can be generated *in-situ* in the presence of TMS-CN by dehydrohalogenation of the corresponding acid halides by triethylamine [52].

$$
\text{CH}_3-\text{C}\diagup^{\text{O}}_{\diagdown\text{Cl}} \quad \xrightarrow{\text{Et}_3\text{N}} \quad \text{CH}_2\text{=C=O} \quad \xrightarrow{(\text{CH}_3)_3\text{SiCN}} \quad \text{H}_2\text{C=C}\diagup^{\text{O-Si(CH}_3)_3}_{\diagdown\text{CN}} \qquad (2.30)
$$

Alternatively, 1-cyano-1-trimethylsilyloxy-1-alkenes can be prepared by base catalyzed isomerization of 1-cyano-1-trimethylsilyloxy-2-alkenes with amines [53].

$$
(2.31)
$$

The reaction of TMS-CN with isocyanates [54, 55], isothiocyanates and carbodiimides [56, 57] results in formation of five-membered heterocycles by reaction of one equivalent of TMS-CN with two equivalents of the reactive cumulene. In the case of reactions of TMS-CN with carbodiimides, inter-mediates formed by addition of TMS-CN across one of the C−N double bonds of the carbodiimides can be isolated. These species will react further with a second equivalent of carbodiimide to yield the five-membered heterocycles.

$$
\begin{array}{c}
\text{R-N=C=N-R} \\
\xrightarrow{\quad \text{AlCl}_3 \quad} \\
(\text{CH}_3)_3\text{SiCN}
\end{array}
\quad
\begin{array}{c}
\text{CN} \\
| \\
\text{R-N-C=N-R} \\
| \\
(\text{CH}_3)_3\text{Si}
\end{array}
\quad
\xrightarrow{\text{R'-N=C=N-R'}}
\qquad (2.32)
$$

2.6 Substitution Reactions of Trimethylsilyl Cyanide

TMS-CN reacts with epoxides under $AlCl_3$ catalysis to yield 3-trimethyl-silyloxy propionitriles [50, 78].

$$(2.33)$$

TMS-CN reacts with α-methoxyamides to yield α-cyanoamides and meth-oxytrimethylsilane. The reaction is catalyzed by Lewis acids, such as $SnCl_4$ or $BF_3 \cdot OEt_2$ [58].

$$(2.34)$$

TMS-CN and compounds which possess S–Cl single bonds undergo chloride-cyanide exchange. This leads to TMS-Cl and thiocyanates, which are uncontaminated by isomeric isothiocyanates [2, 50].

$$Cl-S-S-Cl \ + \ 2(CH_3)_3SiCN \longrightarrow NCS-SCN \ + \ 2(CH_3)_3SiCl \qquad (2.35)$$

This exchange reaction is useful for the preparation of aryl thiocyanates [61].

$$Ph-S-Cl \ + \ (CH_3)_3SiCN \longrightarrow Ph-SCN \ + \ (CH_3)_3SiCl \qquad (2.36)$$

Several phosphorothiocyanatidates and phosphinothiocyanatidates have been prepared in a similar fashion. Such thiocyanatidates rearrange easily to the thermodynamically more stable isothiocyanatidates [59, 60].

$$(2.37)$$

TMS-CN also undergoes exchange with the methoxy group of methyl benzene sulfenate to yield phenyl thiocyanate and methoxytrimethylsilane [62].

15

Chloride cyanide exchange also occurs between N-trichloroisocyanuric acid and TMS-CN to yield *tris*-trimethylsilyl cyanurate and cyanogen chloride [63].

$$+ \; 3(CH_3)_3SiCN \qquad\qquad (2.38)$$

$$+ \; 3ClCN$$

2.7 Synthesis of Trimethylsilyl Cyanide

As the synthetic versatility and potential of TMS-CN has become evident over the last ten years, the methods available for its preparation have dramatically improved. One of the early preparations of TMS-CN involved the reaction of TMS-Cl with silver cyanide [64]. Dimethyldicyanosilane has also been prepared by this procedure [65]. The cost of silver is a problem.

$$(CH_3)_2SiCl_2 \; + \; 2AgCN \; \longrightarrow \; (CH_3)_2Si(CN)_2 \; + \; 2AgCl\!\downarrow \qquad (2.39)$$

High yields of TMS-CN (88%) result from the reaction of TMS-Cl with thallium (I) cyanide. The toxicity of thallium salts limits the utility of this reaction [66].

Evans found that lithium cyanide would react with TMS-Cl in ether to yield TMS-CN [4, 77]. However, lithium cyanide is not commercially available and must be prepared by reaction of HCN with lithium hydride or *n*-butyl lithium or by reaction of lithium hydride with acetone cyanohydrin [77].

Durst's report that TMS-CN could be prepared (40–50%) by reaction of TMS-Cl with potassium cyanide in acetonitrile catalyzed by 18-C-6 is an example of solid/liquid PTC and the first really economical synthesis of this reagent [67].

$$(CH_3)_3SiCl \; \xrightarrow[\substack{18-C-6 \\ CH_3CN}]{KCN} \; (CH_3)_3SiCN \qquad\qquad (2.40)$$

For those who do not mind working with quantities of HCN, the report of Uznanski that TMS-Cl and HCN will react to yield TMS-CN (70%) in the presence of triethylamine and ether may be a useful synthetic method [68].

Anhydrous HCN will also react with *p*-dimethylamino phenyltrimethylsilane via a protodesilylation reaction to yield TMS-CN (89%) and N,N-dimethylaniline [69].

$$(2.41)$$

Cyanogen bromide reacts with trimethylsilyl enol ethers to yield the corresponding α-bromo ketone and TMS-CN [70]. The reaction involves addition of a bromonium ion to the C−C double bond of the trimethylsilyl enol ether to yield a carbocation stabilized by both the lone pairs of electrons of the adjacent oxygen and by hyperconjugation of the trimethylsilyl group. Attack by cyanide on the silyl center of this carbocation leads to fragmentation and formation of products.

$$(2.42)$$

The simultaneous reports of Hünig [71] and Rasmussen [72] that TMS-Cl will react with sodium or potassium cyanide in dry N-methylpyrrolidone to give a 70% yield of TMS-CN constitutes an excellent procedure. The reaction with sodium cyanide requires catalysis by a small amount of quarternary alkyl ammonium salt (Adogen 1%) while that with potassium cyanide does not.

$$(2.43)$$

bis-Trimethylsilyl sulfate also reacts with potassium cyanide in dry N-methylpyrrolidone to yield TMS-CN in 96% yield [73].

Finally, both Evans and Rasmussen have developed methods to cyanosilylate ketones and aldehydes which do not involve independent preparation of TMS-CN. *trans*-Cyanosilylation of α-trimethylsilyloxy isobutyronitrile [1] with a less volatile ketone or aldehyde catalyzed by KCN/18-C-6, yields a new trimethylsilyloxy nitrile and acetone. Removal of acetone from the reaction

17

by distillation shifts the equilibrium to yield the desired trimethylsilyloxy nitrile.

$$H_3C \overset{\overset{\displaystyle O-Si(CH_3)_3}{|}}{\underset{\underset{\displaystyle C\equiv N}{|}}{-}} CH_3 \quad + \quad R-\overset{\overset{\displaystyle O}{\|}}{C}-R' \quad \underset{\overline{18-C-6}}{\overset{NaCN}{\rightleftharpoons}} \quad R-\overset{\overset{\displaystyle O-Si(CH_3)_3}{|}}{\underset{\underset{\displaystyle C\equiv N}{|}}{C}}-R' \quad + \quad CH_3-\overset{\overset{\displaystyle O}{\|}}{C}-CH_3 \quad (2.44)$$

Aromatic aldehydes react directly with TMS-Cl and potassium cyanide in acetonitrile or DMF to yield the corresponding trimethylsilyloxy nitriles. In the case of ketones, the formation of trimethylsilyl enol ethers is a significant side reaction [74].

Less than ten years ago TMS-CN was known only as an inorganic pseudo-halide of unusual structure (cyanide or isocyanide). In the intervening years this compound has rapidly found a valuable place in synthetic organic chemistry. Further utility of this reagent is probably only limited by our imagination and creativity.

References

1. Evans, D.A., Truesdale, L.K.: Tetrahedron Lett. 4929 (1973)
2. Lidy, W., Sundermeyer, W.: Chem. Ber. *106*, 587 (1973)
3. Evans, D.A., Truesdale, L.K., Carroll, G.L.: J. C. S. Chem. Commun. 55 (1973)
4. Evans, D.A., Carroll, G.L., Truesdale, L.K.: J. Org. Chem. *39*, 914 (1974)
5. Fleming, I., Woolias, M.: J. Chem. Soc. Perkin *I*, 829 (1979)
6. Grunewald, G.L., Brouillette, W.J., Finney, J.A.: Tetrahedron Lett. 1219 (1980)
7. Corey, E.J., Tius, M.A., Das, J.: J. Am. Chem. Soc. *102*, 1742 (1980)
8. Demina, M.M., Medvedeva, A.S., Protsuk, N.I., Vyazankin, N.S.: Zhur. Obsh. Khim. *48*, 1563 (1978)
9. Stork, G., Kraus, G.: J. Am. Chem. Soc. *98*, 6747 (1976)
10. Voronkov, M.G., Keiko, N.A., Kuznetsova, T.A., Tsetlina, E.O.: Zhur. Obsh. Khim. *48*, 2138 (1978)
11. Ryu, I., Murai, S., Shinonaga, A., Horiike, T., Sonoda, N.: J. Org. Chem., *43*, 780 (1978)
12. Parham, W.E., Roosevelt, C.S.: Tetrahedron Lett. 923 (1971)
13. Parham, W.E., Roosevelt, C.S.: J. Org. Chem. *37*, 1975 (1972)
14. Frisch, K.C., Wolf, M.: J. Org. Chem. *18*, 657 (1953)
15. Ebsworth, E.A.V., in "Organometallic Chemistry of the Group IV Elements" Vol. I, part I, (MacDiarmid, A.G., Ed.) p. 46. New York: Marcel Dekker, 1968
16. Cottrell, T.L., "The Strength of Chemical Bonds", London: Butterworths 1958
17. Booth, M.R., Frankiss, S.G.: Spectrochim. Acta. Part A, *26*, 859 (1970)
18. Seckar, J.A., Thayer, J.S.: Inorganic Chem. *15*, 501 (1976)
19. Seyferth, D., Kahlen, N.: J. Am. Chem. Soc. *82*, 1080 (1960)
20. Ojima, I., Inaba, S.I., Nagai, Y.: Chem. Lett 737 (1975)
21. Ojima, I., Inaba, S.I., Nakatsugawa, K., Nagai, Y.: Chem. Lett. 331 (1975)
22. Lazukina, L.A., Kukhar, V.P.: Synthesis, 747 (1979)
23. Gassman, P.G., Talley, J.J.: Tetrahedron Lett., 3773 (1978)
24. Boutte, D., Auronx, A., Demande, Fr.: 2, 321, 484 Chem. Abst. *88*, P37454i
25. Gassman, P.G., Talley, J.J.: J. Am. Chem. Soc. *102*, 4138 (1980)
26. Oda, M., Yamamuro, A., Watabe, T.: Chem. Lett. 1427 (1979)
27. Takadate, A., Fishman, J.: J. Org. Chem. *44*, 67 (1979)

28. Bartholow, R.M., Walaszek, E.J.: J. Med. Chem. *19*, 189 (1976)
29. Smith, P.A.S., Baer, D.R.: Org. React. *11*, 157 (1960)
30. Takaishi, N., Fujikura, Y., Inamoto, Y., Aigami, K.: J. Org. Chem. *42*, 1737 (1977)
31. Thies, R.W., Seitz, E.P.: J. Org. Chem. *43*, 1050 (1978)
32. Thies, R.W., Yue, S.: J.C.S. Chem. Commun. 950 (1980)
33. Dauben, Jr., H.J., Ringold, H.J., Wade, R.H., Anderson, A.G. Jr.: J. Am. Chem. Soc. *73*, 2359 (1951)
34. Deuchert, K., Hertenstein, U., Hünig, S.: Synthesis, 777 (1973)
35. Hertenstein, U., Hünig, S., Öller, M.: Synthesis, 416 (1976)
36. Utimoto, K., Obayashi, N., Shishiyama, Y., Inoue, M., Nozaki, H.: Tetrahedron Lett. 3389 (1980)
37. Amouroux, R., Axiotis, G.P.: Synthesis, 270 (1981)
38. Evans, D.A., Hoffman, J.M., Truesdale, L.K.: J. Am. Chem. Soc. *95*, 5822 (1973)
39. Evans, D.A., Wong, R.Y.: J. Org. Chem. *42*, 350 (1977)
40. Evans, D.A., Cain, P.A., Wong, R.Y.: J. Am. Chem. Soc. *99*, 7083 (1977)
41. Evans, D.A., Hoffman, J.M.: J. Am. Chem. Soc. *98*, 1983 (1976)
42. Hegedus, L.S., Evans, B.R.: J. Am. Chem. Soc. *100*, 3461 (1978)
43. Hünig, S., Wehner, G.: Synthesis, 180 (1975)
44. Deuchert, K., Hertenstein, U., Hünig, S., Wehner, G.: Chem. Ber. *112*, 2045 (1979)
45. Hünig, S., Wehner, G.: Synthesis, 391 (1975)
46. Hünig, S., Öller, M.: Chem. Ber. *114*, 959 (1981)
47. Hertenstein, U., Hünig, S., Öller, M.: Chem. Ber. *113*, 3783 (1980)
48. Ziegler, F.E., Nelson, R.V., Wong, T.F.: Tetrahedron Lett. 2125 (1980)
49. Heermann, K., Simchen, G.: Synthesis, 204 (1979)
50. Lidy, W., Sundermeyer, W.: Tetrahedron Lett. 1449 (1973)
51. Childs, M.E., Weber, W.P.: J. Org. Chem. *41*, 3486 (1970)
52. Hertenstein, U., Hünig, S.: Angew. Chem. Int. Ed. *14*, 179 (1975)
53. Voronkov, M.G., Keiko, N.A., Kuznetsova, T.A., Keiko, V.V., Tsetlina, E.O., Pestunovich, V.A.: Izv. Akad. Nauk. SSSR Ser. Khim. 906 (1978)
54. Ojima, I., Inaba, S.T., Nagai, Y.: J.C.S. Chem. Commun. 826 (1974)
55. Lutz, W., Sundermeyer, W.: Chem. Ber. *112*, 2158 (1979)
56. Ojima, I., Inaba, S.I.: Tetrahedron Lett. 817 (1979)
57. Ojima, I., Inaba, S.I., Nagai, Y.: J. Organometallic Chem. *99*, C5 (1975)
58. Asher, V., Becu, C., Anteunis, M.J.O., Callens, R.: Tetrahedron Lett. 141 (1981)
59. Łopusiński, A., Michalski, J., Stec, W.J.: Angew. Chem. Int. *14*, 108 (1975)
60. Łopusiński, A., Michalski, J., Stec, W.J.: Liebigs Ann. Chem. 924 (1977)
61. Harpp, D.N., Friedlander, B.T., Smith, R.A.: Synthesis, 181 (1979)
62. Harpp, D.N., Friedlander, B.T., Larsen, C., Steliou, K., Stockton, A.: J. Org. Chem. *43*, 3481 (1978)
63. Nachbaur, E., Kosmus, W., Krannich, H.J., Sundermeyer, W.: Monat. für Chem. *109*, 1211 (1978)
64. Evers, K.C., Freitag, W.O., Keith, J.N., Kriner, W.A., MacDiarmid, A.G., Sujishi, S.: J. Am. Chem. Soc. *81*, 4493 (1959)
65. Ryu, I., Murai, S., Horiike, T., Shinonaga, A., Sonoda, N.: Synthesis, 154 (1978)
66. Taylor, E.C., Andrade, J.G., John, K.C., McKillop, A.: J. Org. Chem. *43*, 2280 (1978)
67. Zubrick, J.W., Dunbar, B.I., Durst, H.D.: Tetrahedron Lett., 71 (1975)
68. Uznanski, B., Stec, W.J.: Synthesis, 154 (1978)
69. Häbich, D., Effenberger, F.: Synthesis, 755 (1978)
70. Lazukina, L.A., Kukhar, V.P., Pesotskaya, G.V.: Zhur. Obsh. Khim. *45*, 2100 (1975)

71. Hünig, S., Wehner, G.: Synthesis, 522 (1979)
72. Rasmussen, J.K., Heilmann, S.M.: Synthesis, 523 (1979)
73. Kantehner, W., Haug, E., Mergen, W.W.: Synthesis, 460 (1980)
74. Rasmussen J.K., Heilmann, S.M.: Synthesis, 219 (1978)
75. Gassman, P.G., Saito, K., Talley, J.J.: J. Am. Chem. Soc. *102*, 7613 (1980)
76. Gassman, P.G., Talley, J.J.: Org. Syn. *60*, 14 (1981)
77. Livinghouse, T.: Org. Syn. *60*, 126 (1981)
78. Mullis, J.C., Weber, W.P.: J. Org. Chem. *47*, 2873 (1982).

3 Trimethylsilyl Iodide and Bromide

3.1 Introduction

Both trimethylsilyl bromide [1] and iodide [2, 3] have been known since the late 1940's.

$$Ph-Si(CH_3)_3 \xrightarrow{\text{I}_2} Ph-I + (CH_3)_3Si-I \tag{3.1}$$

Nevertheless, it has only been in the last six years that their use as reagents in organic synthesis has been actively explored.

3.2 Cleavage of Ethers

TMS-I's greatest utility is in the removal of ether, ester, and carbamate protecting groups. Key requirements for a protecting group are ease of reaction with the functional group to be protected and mild reaction conditions for removal after its protective function has been fulfilled [4]. The difficulty of cleaving methyl and ethyl ethers has limited their use as protecting groups. The chemistry developed with TMS-I during the last five years has changed this situation. Between 1948 when Whitmore prepared TMS-I and 1976 when Jung and Olah simultaneously began work on its use in organic synthesis, there were at least three reports that TMS-I, would easily cleave ethers [5–7].

$$\text{(furan ring with O)} + (CH_3)_3Si-I \longrightarrow \text{(chain with I and O-Si(CH_3)_3)} \tag{3.2}$$

In 1976 this situation changed. Voronkov found that tetrahydropyran reacts with TMS-I to yield 1-iodo-5-trimethylsilyloxypentane [9]. Both Olah and Voronkov reported that TMS-I would cleave aryl methyl ethers under neutral conditions to yield methyl iodide and aryloxytrimethylsilanes [8]. The latter could be easily hydrolyzed to phenols [10, 11].

$$\qquad\qquad (3.3)$$

TMS-I, generated *in-situ* by reaction of trimethylphenylsilane with a 10% molar excess of iodine at 110°C, reacts with aryl methyl ethers to give high yields (90%) of cleavage products. In the proposed cyclic six-membered ring transition state the hard acid silicon interacts with the hard oxygen of the ether, while simultaneously, the soft iodine interacts with carbon. Free TMS-I may not be involved [12, 13].

$$\qquad\qquad (3.4)$$

This reactions is general. For example, TMS-I cleaves sterically congested aryl methyl ethers, such as 1,4-dimethoxyphenanthrene, to yield 1,4-dihydroxy-phenanthrene which is oxidized during work-up to 1,4-phenanthraquinone [14].

$$\qquad\qquad (3.5)$$

Likewise, treatment of 2,4-dimethoxy-6-substituted pyrimidines with TMS-I followed by work-up yields 6-substituted uracils. Other methods of hydrolysis often result in loss of the 6-substituent in this system [15].

$$\qquad\qquad (3.6)$$

Jung found that TMS-I would cleave trityl, benzyl, and *t*-butyl ethers much faster than methyl, ethyl, isopropyl or cyclohexyl ethers. The cleavage of unsymmetrical dialkyl ethers is often not regioselective.

$$R-O-CH_3 \xrightarrow{(CH_3)_3SiI} R-O-Si(CH_3)_3 + CH_3O-Si(CH_3)_3 + R-I + CH_3I \qquad (3.7)$$

However, methyl cyclohexyl ether reacts with TMS-I to yield predominantly methyl iodide and cyclohexanoxytrimethylsilane.

$$\text{(structure)} \xrightarrow{(CH_3)_3SiI} \text{(structure)}-OSi(CH_3)_3 \;+\; CH_3I \qquad (3.8)$$

An alternative mechanism has been proposed to account for this specificity. Transfer of a trimethylsilyl group to the ether oxygen may form a dialkyltrimethylsilyloxonium/iodide ion pair. S_n2 nucleophilic attack by iodide on a methyl carbon would be favored over attack on a cyclohexyl carbon [16]. C−C double and triple bonds, ketone carbonyls, and aryl halides are stable to the reaction conditions [17].

$$\text{(structure)}-OCH_3 \xrightarrow[50°]{(CH_3)_3SiI} \text{(structure)}-OH \qquad (3.9)$$

Among the problems associated with TMS-I are its extreme hydrolytic instability and sensitivity to light. Freshly distilled, TMS-I (bp 106°C) is almost water white. It rapidly develops a pink color and further darkens on exposure to light. Its ease of hydrolysis suggests that HI may often be involved in reactions of TMS-I.

Olah has found that TMS-Cl reacts with sodium iodide in acetonitrile to yield TMS-I. This reagent cleaves ethers at room temperature even more rapidly than TMS-I itself. Apparently, excess iodide acts as a catalyst [18].

TMS-I generated *in-situ* by reaction of TMS-Cl and sodium iodide in acetonitrile [18] cleaves enol and dienol methyl ethers [19]. Aq. work-up provides aldehydes or ketones in quantitative yield. This is noteworthy since such dienol methyl ethers are susceptible to acid catalyzed polymerization.

$$\text{(structure, SPh, OCH}_3\text{)} \xrightarrow[NaI,\; CH_3CN]{(CH_3)_3SiCl} \text{(structure, SPh, CHO)} \qquad (3.10)$$

β-Phenylseleno cyclic ethers react with TMS-I, generated as above, to yield ω-hydroxy alkenes [20] as outlined in Eq. 3.11.

$$\text{(structure, PhSe, O)} \xrightarrow{(CH_3)_3SiI} \left[\text{(structure, O-Si(CH}_3)_3,\; Ph\text{-}Se^+,\; I^-)} \right] \qquad (3.11)$$

$$\longrightarrow \text{(structure, O-Si(CH}_3)_3\text{)} \;+\; Ph\text{-}SeI$$

3.3 Cleavage of Acetals and Ketals

TMS-I reacts with dimethoxymethane to yield iodomethyl methyl ether [21].

$$CH_3OCH_2-OCH_3 \xrightarrow{(CH_3)_3SiI} \left[\begin{matrix} \overset{+}{CH_3O}-CH_2-\overset{..}{O}CH_3 \\ | \\ Si(CH_3)_3 \end{matrix} \right] I^- \tag{3.12}$$

$$CH_3OSi(CH_3)_3 + \overset{+}{CH_2}=OCH_3 \longrightarrow ICH_2OCH_3$$
$$I^-$$

Iodomethyl methyl ether is not only a viable substitute for chloromethyl methyl ether, a restricted carcinogen, but also a valuable synthetic intermediate [22].

$$Ph_3P + ICH_2OCH_3 \longrightarrow \overset{+}{Ph_3P}-CH_2OCH_3 \xrightarrow{PhLi} Ph_3P=CHOCH_3 \tag{3.13}$$
$$I^-$$

Ketones and aldehydes are frequently protected by conversion to dimethyl or diethyl acetals and ketals. Deprotection and regeneration of the ketone or aldehyde functionality is normally carried out by treatment with aq. acid. Jung has found that both dimethyl and diethyl acetals and ketals can be converted back to aldehydes and ketones under neutral conditions by treatment with TMS-I in chloroform or CCl$_4$ [23].

$$ \tag{3.14}$$

Unfortunately, TMS-I does not react cleanly with the ethylene ketal or the ethylene thioketal of cyclohexanone [23]. On the other hand, TMS-I reacts with 1,3-dioxolanes and 1,3-oxathiolanes to yield iodomethyl-2-trimethylsilyl-oxyethyl ether and iodomethyl-2-trimethylsilyloxyethyl sulfide respectively. Both of these are valuable alkylating agents [24, 25].

$$\underset{O \underset{}{\overset{}{\diagup}} S}{} \xrightarrow{(CH_3)_3SiI} (CH_3)_3Si-O\diagdown\diagup\diagdown S\diagdown CH_2-I \qquad (3.15)$$

The methyl ether of sesamol methyl ether is selectively cleaved by reaction with TMS-I in quinoline [26].

$$\xrightarrow[\text{2) } H_2O]{\text{1) } (CH_3)_3SiI} \qquad (3.16)$$

TMS-I reacts with *bis*(dimethylamino)methane to yield dimethyl(methylene)-ammonium iodide, a valuable synthetic intermediate [27, 28]. Other *bis*(dialkyl-amino)methanes react in a similar manner [27].

$$(CH_3)_2N-CH_2-N(CH_3)_2 \xrightarrow{(CH_3)_3SiI} \left[(CH_3)_2\overset{Si(CH_3)_3}{\underset{+}{N}}CH_2-\overset{..}{N}(CH_3)_2 \right] I^- \qquad (3.17)$$

$$\searrow$$

$$\underset{H_2C=N(CH_3)_2}{\overset{I^-}{+}}$$

$$(CH_3)_3Si-N(CH_3)_2$$

3.4 Conversion of Alcohols and Alkoxytrimethylsilanes to Alkyl Iodides

Red phosphorous and iodine or HI convert alcohols to alkyl iodides. TMS-I is also an excellent reagent for this purpose. TMS-I (2 equivalents) react with alcohols at 25 °C in methylene chloride, chloroform, or CCl₄ to yield alkyl iodides, HI, and hexamethyldisiloxane. The presence of HI makes this reaction unsuitable for alcohols which possess acid-sensitive functional groups [29].

$$\underset{}{\diagdown}OH + (CH_3)_3SiI \longrightarrow \underset{}{\diagdown}I + (CH_3)_3SiOH \qquad (3.18)$$

$$\xrightarrow{(CH_3)_3SiI} (CH_3)_3SiOSi(CH_3)_3 + HI$$

25

The reaction apparently proceeds largely by an S_n2 type process since treatment of optically active 2-octanol with TMS-I yields 2-octyl iodide whose configuration is 94% inverted.

$$(3.19)$$

Similar results have been obtained by treatment of primary, secondary, and tertiary, allylic and benzylic alcohols with TMS-Cl and sodium iodide in acetonitrile [18]. In fact, this *in-situ* method results in more rapid reaction. This acceleration may result from the difference in solvent. However, the reaction of TMS-I itself can be accelerated by the addition of sodium iodide.

Alkoxytrimethylsilanes are cleaved regiospecifically by TMS-I under neutral conditions to yield alkyl iodides and hexamethyldisiloxane [30, 31]. This reaction is general for primary, secondary, and tertiary alkoxytrimethylsilanes [29].

$$(3.20)$$

Similar results were obtained with TMS-I generated *in-situ* by reaction of TMS-Cl and sodium iodide in acetonitrile [32].

TMS-I and aldehydes react in a 1:1 ratio to yield iodohydrin trimethylsilyl ethers. Attempts to purify these compounds by distillation or chromatography led to regeneration of the starting aldehyde.

$$(3.21)$$

If a 2:1 ratio is used, the initial aldehyde iodohydrin trimethylsilyl ether is converted to a 1,1-diiodide and hexamethyldisiloxane [33]. This reaction is related to the cleavage of alkoxytrimethylsilanes by TMS-I to yield alkyl iodides. Phenylacetaldehyde is an exception. It undergoes slow reaction with excess TMS-I at 0°C to give 2,3,6,7-dibenzo-9-oxabicyclo[3,3,1]nona-2,6-diene [33].

O-Trimethylsilyl hemithioacetals and ketals react with TMS-I to form α-iodosulfides and hexamethyldisiloxane. α-Iodosulfides were previously virtually unknown. They undergo facile dehydrohalogenation on treatment with triethylamine or with sodium hydroxide under PTC conditions to yield vinyl sulfides [34].

$$CH_3CH_2CH_2-\underset{\underset{H}{|}}{\overset{\overset{OSi(CH_3)_3}{|}}{C}}-SCH_2Ph \xrightarrow{(CH_3)_3SiI} CH_3CH_2CH_2-\underset{\underset{I}{|}}{CH}-SCH_2Ph \quad (3.22)$$

$$\xrightarrow{Et_3N} CH_3-CH_2-C \overset{\underset{H}{|}}{=}C \diagup SCH_2Ph$$

α,α'-bis(Trimethylsilyloxy) sulfides react with TMS-I to give α,α'-diiodo sulfides as intermediates which undergo dehydrohalogenation with triethylamine to yield divinylsulfides [35].

$$(CH_3)_3Si-S-Si(CH_3)_3 + (CH_3)_2CH-C\overset{O}{\underset{H}{\diagup}} \xrightarrow[18-C-6]{KCN} (CH_3)_2CH-\underset{\underset{S-Si(CH_3)_3}{|}}{\overset{\overset{OSi(CH_3)_3}{|}}{C}}-H$$

$$(CH_3)_2CH-C\overset{O}{\underset{H}{\diagup}} \overset{KCN}{\underset{18-C-6}{\Big|}}$$

$$(CH_3)_2C=CH\diagdown_S\diagup CH=C(CH_3)_2 \xleftarrow[2) Et_3N]{1) (CH_3)_3SiI} (CH_3)_2CH-\underset{\underset{(CH_3)_3SiO}{|}}{CH}-S-\underset{\underset{OSi(CH_3)_3}{|}}{CH}-CH(CH_3)_2 \quad (3.23)$$

3.5 Reaction of TMS-Br with Alcohols

Unlike TMS-I, TMS-Br does not rapidly cleave esters of carboxylic acids, carbonates, ethers, or alkoxytrimethylsilanes under mild conditions. This difference has been attributed to the lower electrophilicity of TMS-Br. Alcohols are converted to bromides by reaction with two equivalents of TMS-Br. HBr is generated in the reaction. The reaction is rapid at 25°C for tertiary, allylic, and benzylic alcohols but slower for primary and secondary alcohols which require heating at 50°C for several hours to effect reaction. This

27

difference permits the conversion of these more reactive alcohols to bromides in the presence of primary and secondary alcohols [36].

$$(CH_3)_2C-CH_2-CH-CH_3 \xrightarrow{\substack{(CH_3)_3SiSi(CH_3)_3 \\ \\ \text{pyridine} \cdot H^+ \, Br_3^-}} (CH_3)_2C-CH_2-CH-CH_3 \qquad (3.24)$$

with OH groups on left becoming Br and OH on right.

The reaction of TMS-Br with optically active 2-octanol proceeds with 94% inversion of configuration via an S_n2 type process [37]. TMS-Br, generated *in-situ* by reaction of TMS-Cl and lithium bromide in acetonitrile, reacts faster with alcohols. This acceleration has been attributed to catalysis by bromide ion. TMS-Br may also be generated *in-situ* by reaction of hexamethyldisilane with pyridinium perbromide at 25 °C [36].

3.6 Reaction of Oxiranes with TMS-I — Conversion to Allylic Alcohols

Epoxides react with TMS-I, which was generated by reaction of hexamethyl-disilane with iodine, to give 2-iodoalkoxytrimethylsilanes. These can be converted to allylic alcohols by treatment with tertiary amine bases, such as DBU or DBN, followed by hydrolysis [38].

$$\text{epoxycyclohexane} \xrightarrow{(CH_3)_3SiI} \text{cyclohexane with I and O-Si(CH_3)_3} \xrightarrow{DBN} \text{cyclohexene with O-Si(CH_3)_3} \qquad (3.25)$$

Epoxides of terminal alkenes react with TMS-I to yield approximately a 4:1 ratio of 1-iodo-2-trimethylsilyloxyalkanes [39] and 2-iodo-1-trimethyl-silyloxyalkanes [38]. 1-Iodo-2-trimethylsilyloxyalkanes can be oxidized to yield α-iodo ketones.

$$CH_3-CH_2-CH\underset{O}{-}CH_2 \xrightarrow{(CH_3)_3SiI} CH_3-CH_2-\underset{O-Si(CH_3)_3}{CH}-CH_2-I \quad + \quad CH_3-CH_2-\underset{I}{CH}-CH_2-O-Si(CH_3)_3$$

$$84 \qquad : \qquad 16 \qquad (3.26)$$

TMS-I reacts with an oxirane in preference to a methyl ester or ethylene ketal functional groups [40]. Similar results have been obtained with *t*-butyl-dimethylsilyl iodide. The *t*-butyldimethylsilyl ethers of allylic alcohols are more stable to hydrolysis than the corresponding trimethylsilyl ethers. They can be hydrolyzed by treatment with tetraalkylammonium fluoride in moist

DMSO or THF or with potassium fluoride in the presence of a catalytic amount of 18-C-6 [41, 42].

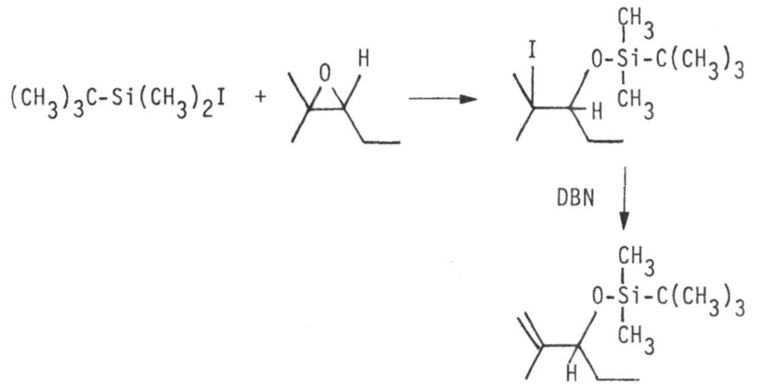
$(CH_3)_3C-Si(CH_3)_2I$
+
O
H
I
CH_3
$O-Si-C(CH_3)_3$
CH_3
H
DBN
CH_3
$O-Si-C(CH_3)_3$
CH_3
H

(3.27)

The conversion of oxiranes to allylic alcohols has previously been accomplished by a variety of methods [43]. This transformation can be accomplished by treatment of the oxirane with equimolar amounts of trimethylsilyl trifluoromethanesulfonate, DBU and 2,6-lutidine [44].

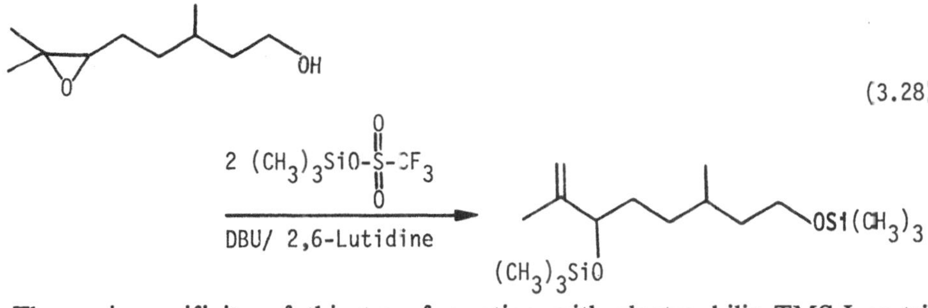
O
OH
2 $(CH_3)_3SiO-S(O_2)-CF_3$
DBU/ 2,6-Lutidine
$OSi(CH_3)_3$
$(CH_3)_3SiO$

(3.28)

The regiospecificity of this transformation with electrophilic TMS-I or trimethylsilyl trifluoromethanesulfonate is different than that with nucleophilic sodium phenylselenide [43].

Reaction of epoxides with two equivalents of TMS-I in CCl_4 results in deoxygenation of the epoxide to yield an alkene with retention of stereochemistry. Thus *cis*-9,10-octadecene oxide reacts with TMS-I to yield *cis*-9,10-octadecene. Similar results have been obtained with *trans*-9,10-octadecene oxide [45]. This reaction probably proceeds by initial formation of 9-iodo-10-trimethylsilyloxyoctadecane. Cleavage of the C−O single bond of this alkoxytrimethylsilane with a second equivalent of TMS-I yields 9,10-diiodooctadecane which is unstable relative to octadecene and iodine.

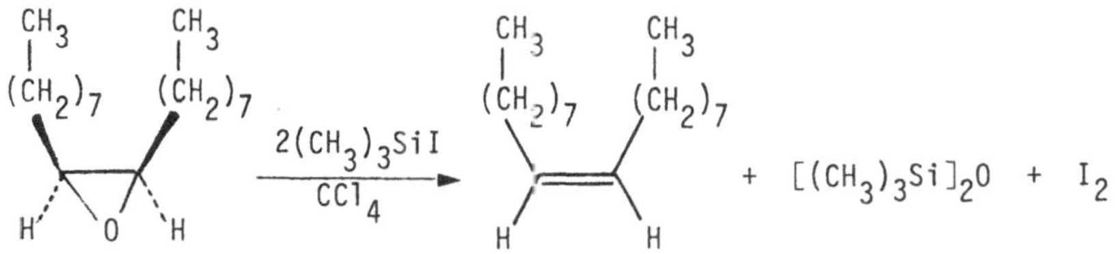
CH_3
$(CH_2)_7$
H
O
H
$2(CH_3)_3SiI$
CCl_4
CH_3
$(CH_2)_7$
H
H
+ $[(CH_3)_3Si]_2O$ + I_2

(3.29)

3.7 Hydrolysis of Esters

The hydrolysis of alkyl esters has been accomplished in a number of ways [46–49]. TMS-I rapidly cleaves methyl, ethyl, *i*-propyl, *t*-butyl, and benzyl esters in CCl_4 at 50°C to yield the corresponding trimethylsilyl esters and alkyl iodides. The wide generality of ester hydrolysis by TMS-I makes this method a major synthetic advance. Phenyl esters do not react. The reaction tolerates a large number of functional groups such as C−C double bonds.

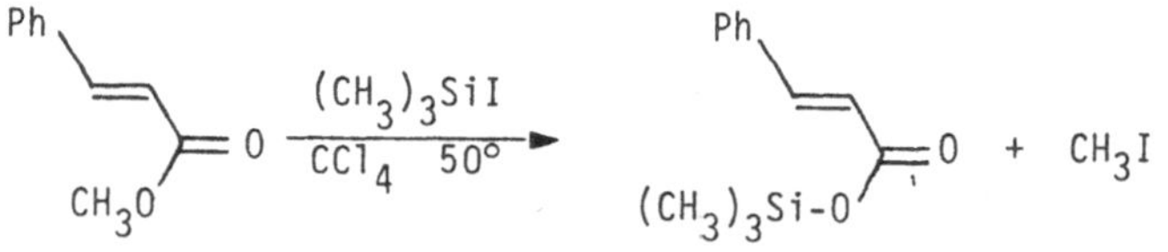

$$\text{(3.30)}$$

The following reaction mechanism has been proposed. TMS-I reacts in a rapid reversible reaction with the carbonyl oxygen of the ester to yield trimethylsilyloxy alkoxy-stabilized carbocation/iodide ion pair. Rate limiting nucleophilic attack by iodide on the α-carbon of the alkoxy group yields alkyl iodide and the trimethylsilyl ester. In the presence of excess TMS-I the trimethylsilyl ester is converted to an acyl iodide (IR C=O 1,830–1,800 cm^{-1}) and hexamethyldisiloxane [50]. The fact that TMS-I is usually contaminated by traces of HI acid may account for the hydrolysis of *t*-butyl esters, since nucleophilic attack on a *t*-butyl group is improbable.

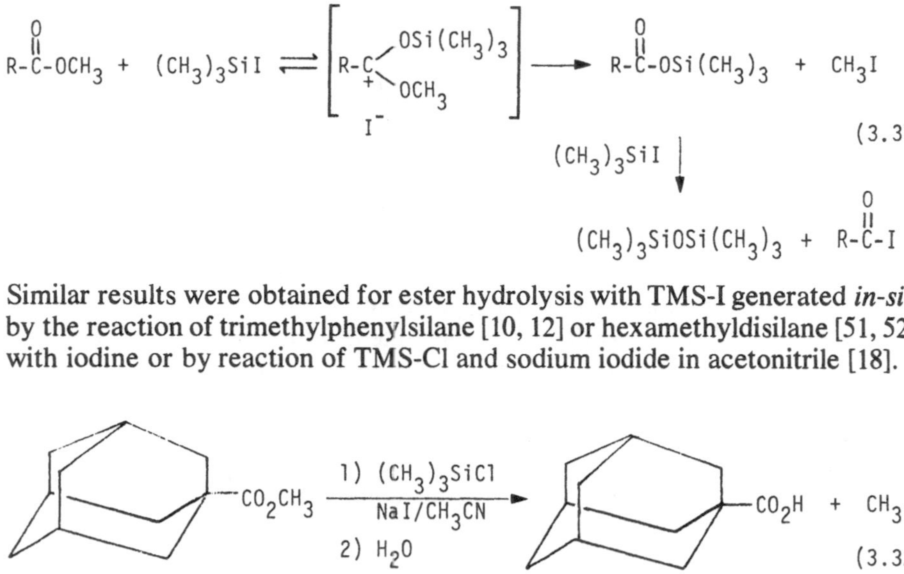

$$\text{(3.31)}$$

Similar results were obtained for ester hydrolysis with TMS-I generated *in-situ* by the reaction of trimethylphenylsilane [10, 12] or hexamethyldisilane [51, 52], with iodine or by reaction of TMS-Cl and sodium iodide in acetonitrile [18].

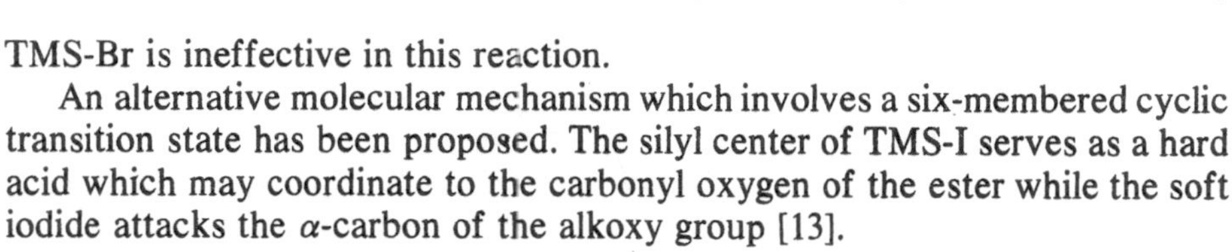

$$\text{(3.32)}$$

TMS-Br is ineffective in this reaction.

An alternative molecular mechanism which involves a six-membered cyclic transition state has been proposed. The silyl center of TMS-I serves as a hard acid which may coordinate to the carbonyl oxygen of the ester while the soft iodide attacks the α-carbon of the alkoxy group [13].

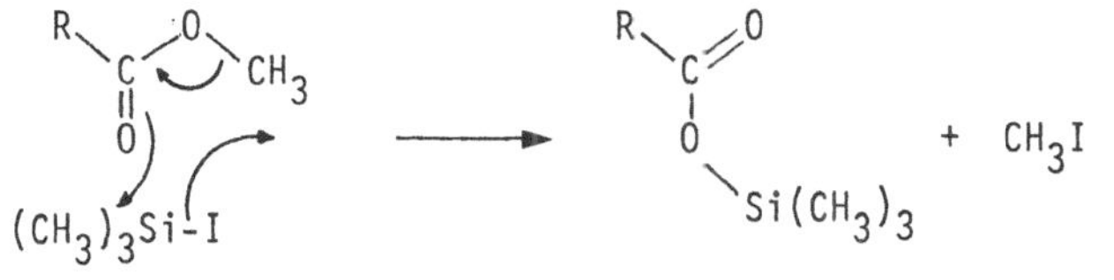

$$R-\underset{\underset{O}{\overset{\|}{C}}}{\overset{O}{\diagdown}}CH_3 \quad \longrightarrow \quad R-\underset{\underset{Si(CH_3)_3}{\overset{|}{O}}}{\overset{\diagup O}{\overset{\|}{C}}} \quad + \quad CH_3I \qquad (3.33)$$

$(CH_3)_3Si-I$

TMS-I and TMS-Br permit stereoselective iodination or bromination of anomeric glycosyl acetates. Under these conditions TMS-Br does not affect ether, ester, or acetal protecting groups [53, 54].

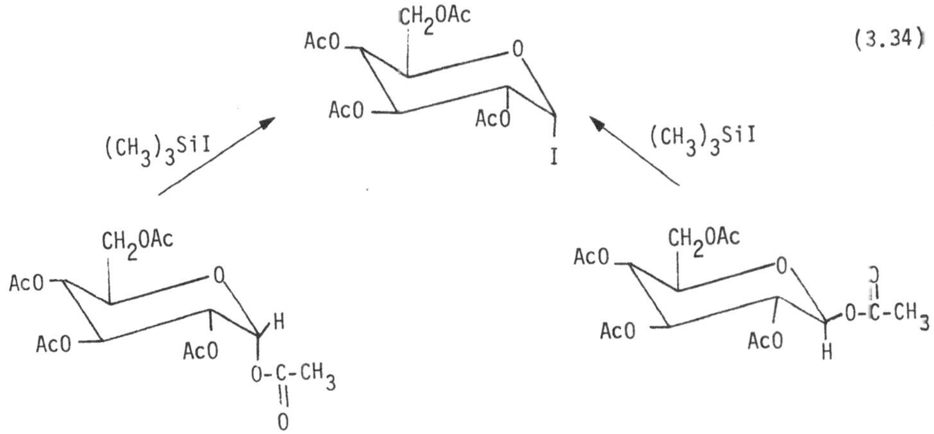

$$(3.34)$$

Trimethylsilyl esters of aromatic carboxylic acids can be reduced by trichlorosilane and tertiary aliphatic amines to benzyltrichlorosilanes which then can be cleaved by potassium hydroxide in methanol to yield the corresponding methyl aromatics. Alkyl esters of aromatic carboxylic acids, are not reduced under these conditions [55] (see Chapter 20).

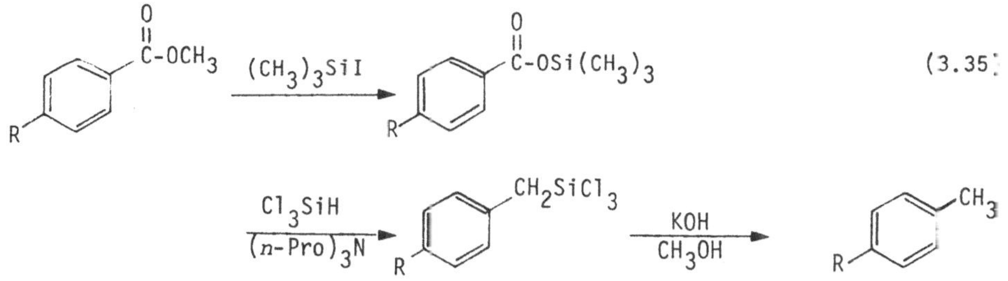

$$(3.35)$$

γ-Lactones are cleaved by both TMS-I and TMS-Br [18, 56, 57].

$$(3.36)$$

TMS-I generated *in-situ* by reaction of TMS-Cl and sodium iodide in acetonitrile reacts with β-phenylselenolactones to yield olefinic carboxylic acids [20].

31

$$(3.37)$$

TMS-Br reacts with ortho esters [37].

$$HC(OCH_3)_3 + (CH_3)_3SiBr \longrightarrow H-\overset{O}{\underset{}{C}}-OCH_3 + CH_3Br + CH_3OSi(CH_3)_3 \qquad (3.38)$$

Trimethylsilyl esters react with two equivalents of primary or secondary alcohols to yield the corresponding alkyl esters. This permits transesterification under neutral conditions [58].

$$Ph-\overset{O}{\underset{}{C}}-OCH_3 \xrightarrow{(CH_3)_3SiI} Ph-\overset{O}{\underset{}{C}}-OSi(CH_3)_3 \xrightarrow{CH_3CH_2OH} Ph-\overset{O}{\underset{}{C}}-OCH_2CH_3 \qquad (3.39)$$

Trimethylsilyl trifluoromethanesulfonate/triethylamine does not react with methyl or benzyl esters but selectively converts t-butyl esters into trimethylsilyl esters [59]. This reaction may occur as outlined (Eq. 3.40).

$$(3.40)$$

3.8 Hydrolysis of Carbamates

Alkyl carbamates have been utilized to protect primary and secondary amine groups. TMS-I preferentially cleaves carbamates under conditions which do not affect peptide amide bonds, alkyl esters, or benzyl ether protecting groups [18, 52, 60].

$$(CH_3)_3C-O-\overset{O}{\overset{||}{C}}-NH-CH_2-\overset{O}{\overset{||}{C}}-O-CH_2-Ph \xrightarrow{(CH_3)_3Si-Si(CH_3)_3/I_2} H_2N-CH_2-\overset{O}{\overset{||}{C}}-O-CH_2-Ph$$

$$(3.41)$$

Extensive work on the removal of carbamate protecting groups from dipeptides by TMS-I has been reported [61].

3.9 Hydrolysis of Dialkyl Phosphonates

Alkaline hydrolysis of dialkyl phosphonates to the corresponding phosphonic acids requires vigorous conditions which are not compatible with many functional groups. On the other hand, *bis*(trimethylsilyl) phosphonates are readily hydrolyzed by treatment with water. The problem of hydrolysis of dialkyl phosphonates hence becomes one of transesterification, converting a methyl or ethyl ester to a trimethylsilyl ester.

Rabinowitz found that dialkyl phosphonates react slowly (one week) with TMS-Cl at 120° to yield *bis*(trimethylsilyl) phosphonates. The reaction may proceed in a manner similar to the Arbuzov reaction as outlined [62].

$$(3.42)$$

Analysis by McKenna led to the suggestion that the rate limiting step might be reaction of the phosphonium cation/chloride ion pair. On this basis, TMS-Br might be a more reactive reagent due to the increased nucleophilicity of bromide compared to chloride [63]. In fact, TMS-Br rapidly converts dialkyl phosphonates into *bis*(trimethylsilyl) phosphonates at 25 °C [63, 64]. C–C double and triple bonds, esters, ethers, benzoyl, and diazo functionalities are compatible with the reaction conditions. No halogen exchange is observed when diethyl iodomethyl phosphonate is treated with TMS-Br.

$$CH_3CH_2O-\overset{\overset{O}{\|}}{C}-\overset{\overset{O}{\|}}{P}\overset{OCH_2CH_3}{\underset{OCH_2CH_3}{\big<}} \xrightarrow{\quad 2(CH_3)_3SiBr \quad} CH_3CH_2O-\overset{\overset{O}{\|}}{C}-\overset{\overset{O}{\|}}{P}\overset{OSi(CH_3)_3}{\underset{OSi(CH_3)_3}{\big<}} \qquad (3.43)$$

TMS-Br converts dialkyl phosphorochloridates, dialkyl phosphorobromidates, and dialkyl phosphoramidates to the corresponding *bis*(trimethylsilyl) esters [65].

$$Br-\overset{\overset{O}{\|}}{P}-(OCH_3)_2 \xrightarrow{\quad 2(CH_3)_3SiBr \quad} Br-\overset{\overset{O}{\|}}{P}-[OSi(CH_3)_3]_2 \qquad (3.44)$$

Transesterifications can also be achieved with TMS-I [66–69]. TMS-I reacts with dialkyl phosphonates in preference to dimethyl acetals, or methyl esters.

$$(CH_3O)_2CH-\overset{\overset{O}{\|}}{P}-(OCH_3)_2 \xrightarrow[\text{NaI/CH}_3\text{CN}]{2(CH_3)_3SiCl} (CH_3O)_2CH-\overset{\overset{O}{\|}}{P}-[OSi(CH_3)_3]_2 \qquad (3.45)$$

Neither TMS-Br nor TMS-I reacts with dialkyl phosphonates to yield alkyl trimethylsilyl phosphonate intermediates.

$$(CH_3O)_2\overset{\overset{O}{\|}}{P}-R \xrightarrow{(CH_3)_3SiBr} \overset{(CH_3)_3SiO}{\underset{CH_3O}{\big>}}\overset{\overset{O}{\|}}{P}-R \qquad (3.46)$$

While TMS-I reacts more rapidly than TMS-Br with dialkyl phosphonates, both yield *bis*(trimethylsilyl)phosphonates. However, only TMS-I permits transesterification of dialkyl thiophosphonates (P=S) to yield *bis*(trimethylsilyl)thiophosphonates (P=S) [65].

$$\xrightarrow{(CH_3)_3SiBr} (RO)_2\overset{\overset{S}{\|}}{P}-O-\overset{\overset{O}{\|}}{P}-[OSi(CH_3)_3]_2 \qquad (3.47)$$

$$\overset{RO}{\underset{RO}{\big>}}\overset{\overset{S}{\|}}{P}-O-\overset{\overset{O}{\|}}{P}\overset{OR}{\underset{OR}{\big<}}$$

$$\xrightarrow{(CH_3)_3SiI} [(CH_3)_3SiO]_2\overset{\overset{S}{\|}}{P}-O-\overset{\overset{O}{\|}}{P}-[OSi(CH_3)_3]_2 \qquad (3.48)$$

Reductions with TMS-I are considered in Chapter 20.

3.10 Preparation of β- and γ-Iodo Ketones

Zine iodide catalyzed reaction of TMS-I with cyclobutanones yields after hydrolysis ring opened β-iodoketones [70]. This may occur as outlined below.

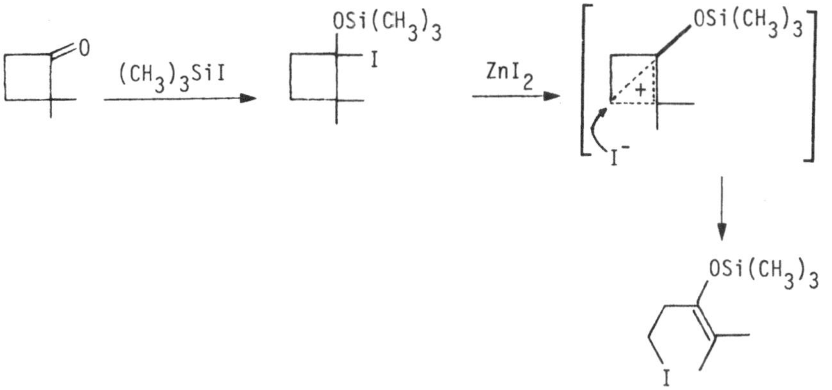

(3.49)

β-Iodoketones undergo facile reaction with various nucleophiles, such as cyanide and phenylthiolate ions. β-Iodoketones can also be prepared by Michael addition of TMS-I to α,β-unsaturated ketones [71].

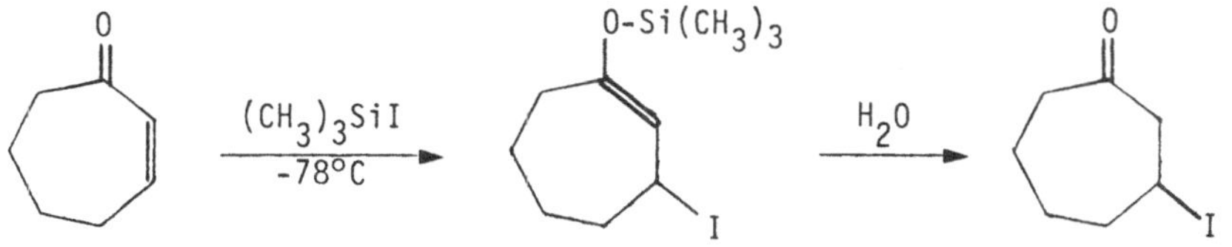

(3.50)

TMS-I reacts with α,β-cyclopropylketones to yield γ-iodoketones [71, 72].

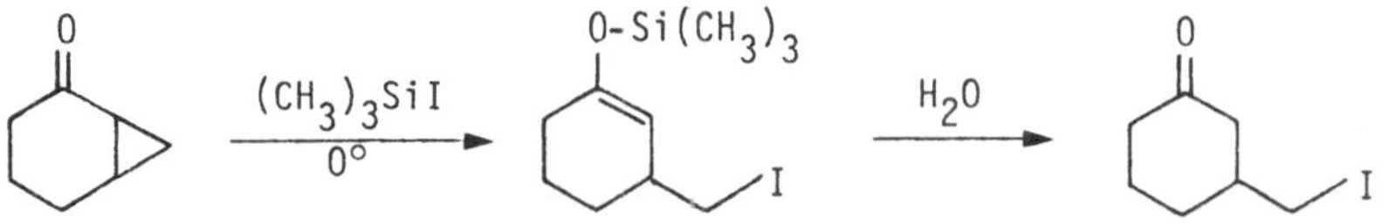

(3.51)

TMS-I and TMS-Br undergo halogen exchange with acyl chlorides to yield respectively, acyl iodides and acyl bromides [73].

$$\text{Ph-}\overset{\overset{O}{\|}}{C}\text{-Cl} \ + \ (CH_3)_3SiI \ \longrightarrow \ \text{Ph-}\overset{\overset{O}{\|}}{C}\text{-I} \ + \ (CH_3)_3SiCl \qquad (3.52)$$

3.11 Preparation of TMS-Br and TMS-I

TMS-Br, a water white liquid (bp 80 °C) has been prepared by the reaction of hexamethyldisiloxane with phosphorous tribromide catalyzed by ferric chloride [1]. It reacts immediately with moisture but is otherwise reasonably stable. Reaction of phenyltrimethylsilane with bromine at steam bath temperature for one hour, results in an 85% yield of TMS-Br. Reaction of bromine with a mixture of 1,2-bis(trimethylsilyl)-1,2-dihydronaphthalene and 1,4-bis-(trimethylsilyl)-1,4-dihydronaphthalene also yields TMS-Br [74]. TMS-Br has

35

also been generated *in-situ* by reaction of TMS-Cl with lithium bromide in acetonitrile solvent or by reaction of hexamethyldisilane with pyridinium perbromide [36].

$$(3.53)$$

TMS-I has been prepared by reaction of hexamethyldisiloxane with iodine and aluminum powder [5, 75]. Freshly distilled TMS-I is a colorless liquid (bp 107°C) which reacts rapidly with water. It is therefore usually contaminated with small amounts of HI. It rapidly darkens on standing in the light. TMS-I has been prepared by several *in-situ* reactions. Among these are the reaction of trimethylphenylsilane with iodine at 120°C [2, 12]. This reaction may be catalyzed by aluminium iodide [3, 76]. TMS-I results from *in-situ* reaction of allyltrimethylsilane with iodine. A problem is that allyl iodide is itself a reactive electrophile which may alkylate nucleophilic centers in the substrate or product. Further, only half the iodine atoms are productively utilized [77].

$$(3.54)$$

The reaction of iodine with 3,6-*bis*(trimethylsilyl)-1,4-cyclohexadiene yields two molecules of TMS-I and benzene which can easily be removed from the reaction mixture [77]. However, the preparation of 3,6-*bis*(trimethylsilyl)-1,4-cyclohexadiene is time consuming [78].

$$(3.55)$$

Reaction of a mixture of 1,2-*bis*(trimethylsilyl)-1,2-dihydronaphthalene and 1,4-*bis*(trimethylsilyl)-1,4-dihydronaphthalene with iodine also yields TMS-I. The precursor mixture is easily prepared [79].

$$\text{(3.56)}$$

TMS-I has also been generated *in-situ* by the reaction of iodine with phenyl-seleno-trimethylsilane [80]. Phenylseleno-trimethylsilane (bp 110–115 °C/18 mm) has been prepared by reaction of phenylselenol, TMS-Cl and triethyl-amine [81] or by the reaction of sodium phenylselenide and TMS-Cl in THF [82].

$$2 \ PhSe\text{-}Si(CH_3)_3 \xrightarrow{\ I_2\ } PhSe\text{-}SePh \ + 2\,(CH_3)_3SiI \qquad (3.57)$$

The reaction of iodine with hexamethyldisilane to yield TMS-I is most direct [38, 51, 52, 83, 84]. However, hexamethyldisilane is not easily prepared except by reaction of TMS-Cl with sodium-potassium alloy.

$$(CH_3)_3SiCl \xrightarrow{\ Na/K\ } (CH_3)_3SiSi(CH_3)_3 \xrightarrow{\ I_2\ } 2(CH_3)_3SiI \qquad (3.58)$$

t-Butyldimethylsilyl iodide may be prepared by reaction of iodine with phenylseleno-*t*-butyldimethylsilane [41, 42]. Phenylseleno-*t*-butyldimethyl-silane may be prepared by reaction of sodium or lithium phenylselenide with *t*-butyldimethylchlorosilane [41, 42]. *t*-Butyldiphenylsilyl iodide can be prepared in a similar manner.

In conclusion, it appears to us that for most reactions Olah's procedure which involves reaction of TMS-Cl with sodium iodide in acetonitrile is the most economical and facile [18]. For TMS-I it appears that the simplest method really is best.

$$(CH_3)_3SiCl \xrightarrow[CH_3CN]{NaI} (CH_3)_3SiI \qquad (3.59)$$

References

1. Gilliam, W.G., Meals, R.N., Sauer, R.D.: J. Am. Chem. Soc. 68, 1161 (1946)
2. Pray, B.O., Sommer, L.H., Goldberg, G.M., Kerr, G.T., DiGiorgio, P.A.. Whitmore, F.C.: J. Am. Chem. Soc. 70, 433 (1948)
3. Eaborn, C.: J. Chem. Soc. 2755 (1949)
4. Reese, C.B., "Protection of Alcoholic Hydroxyl Groups and Glycol Systems", in Protecting Groups in Organic Chemistry, (McOmie, J.F.W., Ed.) p. 95–143. New York: Plenum Press, 1973
5. Voronkov, M.G., Khudobin, Y.I.: Izv. Akad. Nauk. SSSR Otd. Khim. Nauk, 713 (1956)
6. Voronkov, M.G., Khudobin, Y.I.: Zh. Obsh. Khim. 26, 584 (1956)
7. Krürke, U.: Chem. Ber. 174 (1962)

8. Voronkov, M.G., Puzanova, V.E., Pavlov, S.F., Dubinskaya, E.I.: Izv. Akad. Nauk. SSSR Ser. Khim. 448 (1975)
9. Voronkov, M.G., Dubinskaya, E.I., Komarov, V.G., Pavlov, S.F.: Zh. Obsh. Khim. *46*, 1908 (1976)
10. Ho, T.L., Olah, G.A.: Angew. Chem. Int. Ed. *15*, 774 (1976)
11. Voronkov, M.G., Dubinskaya, E.I., Pavlov, S.F., Gorokhova, V.G.: Izv. Akad. Nauk SSSR Ser. Khim. 2355 (1976)
12. Ho, T.L., Olah, G.A.: Synthesis, 417 (1977)
13. Ho, T.L., Olah, G.A.: Proc. Natl. Acad. Sci. USA, *75*, 4 (1978)
14. Rosen, B.I., Weber, W.P.: J. Org. Chem. *42*, 3463 (1977)
15. Silverman, R.B., Radak, R.E., Hacker, N.P.: J. Org. Chem. *44*, 4970 (1979)
16. Jung, M.E., Lyster, M.A.: J. Org. Chem. *42*, 3761 (1977)
17. Seitz, D.E., Ferreira, L.: Syn. Commun. *9*, 931 (1979)
18. Olah, G.A., Narang, S.C., Gupta, B.G.B., Malhotra, R.: J. Org. Chem. *44*, 1247 (1979)
19. Kosarych, Z., Cohen, T.: Tetrahedron Lett., 3959 (1980)
20. Clive, D.L.J., Kalé, V.N.: J. Org. Chem. *46*, 231 (1981)
21. Jung, M.E., Mazurek, M.A., Lim, R.M.: Synthesis, 588 (1978)
22. Wittig, G., Schlosser, W.: Chem. Ber. *94*, 1373 (1961)
23. Jung, M.E., Andrus, W.A., Ornstein, P.L.: Tetrahedron Lett. 4175 (1977)
24. Keyser, G.E., Bryant, J.D., Barrio, J.R.: Tetrahedron Lett. 3263 (1979)
25. Bryant, J.D., Keyser, G.E., Barrio, J.R.: J. Org. Chem. *44*, 3733 (1979)
26. Minamikawa, J., Brossi, A.: Tetrahedron Lett. 3085 (1978)
27. Bryson, T.A., Bonitz, G.H., Reichel, C.J., Dardis, R.E.: J. Org. Chem. *45*, 524 (1980)
28. Schreiber, J., Maag, H., Hashimoto, N., Eschenmoser, A.: Angew. Chem. Int. Ed. *10*, 330 (1971)
29. Jung, M.E., Ornstein, P.L.: Tetrahedron Lett. 2659 (1977)
30. Voronkov, M.G., Pavlov, S.F., Dubinskaya, E.I.: Izv. Akad. Nauk. SSSR Ser. Khim. 657 (1975)
31. Voronkov, M.G., Pavlov, S.F., Dubinskaya, E.I.: Akad. Nauk. SSSR, *227*, 607 (1976)
32. Morita, T., Yoshida, S., Okamoto, Y., Sakurai, H.: Synthesis, 379 (1979)
33. Jung, M.E., Mossman, A.B., Lyster, M.A.: J. Org. Chem. *43*, 3698 (1978)
34. Aida, T., Harpp, D.N., Chan, T.H.: Tetrahedron Lett. 3247 (1980)
35. Aida, T., Chan, T.H., Harpp, D.N.: Tetrahedron Lett. 1089 (1981)
36. Olah, G.A., Gupta, B.G.B., Malhotra, R., Narang, S.C.: J. Org. Chem. *45*, 1638 (1980)
37. Jung, M.E., Hatfield, G.L.: Tetrahedron Lett. 4483 (1978)
38. Sakurai, H., Sasaki, K., Hosomi, A.: Tetrahedron Lett. 2329 (1980)
39. Denis, J.N., Krief, A.: Tetrahedron Lett. 1429 (1981)
40. Kraus, G.A., Fraiser, K.: J. Org. Chem. *45*, 2579 (1980)
41. Detty, M.R.: J. Org. Chem. *45*, 924 (1980)
42. Detty, M.R., Seidler, J.D.: J. Org. Chem. *46*, 1283 (1981)
43. Sharpless, K.B., Lauer, R.F.: J. Am. Chem. Soc. *95*, 2697 (1973)
44. Murata, S., Suzuki, M., Noyori, R.: J. Am. Chem. Soc. *101*, 2738 (1979)
45. Denis, J.N., Magnane, R., Eenoo, M.V., Krief, A.: Nouv. J. Chim. *3*, 705 (1979)
46. Haslam, E., "Protection of Carboxyl Groups" in Protecting Groups in Organic Chemistry, edited by (McOmie, J.F.W., Ed.) pp. 183–215. New York 1973, Plenum Press.
47. Woodward, R.B., Heusler, K., Gosteli, J., Naegeli, P., Oppolzer, W., Ramage, R., Ranganathan, S., Vorbruggen, H.: J. Am. Chem. Soc. *88*, 852 (1966)

48. Elsing, E., Schreiberg, J., Eschenmoser, A.: Helv. Chim. Acta. *43*, 113 (1960)
49. Bartlett, P.A., Johnson, W.S.: Tetrahedron Lett. 4459 (1970)
50. Jung, M.E., Lyster, M.A.: J. Am. Chem. Soc. *99*, 969 (1977)
51. Sakurai, H., Shirahata, A., Sasaki, K., Hosomi, A.: Synthesis, 740 (1979)
52. Olah, G.A., Narang, S.C., Gupta, B.G.B., Malhotra, R.: Angew. Chem. Int. Ed. *18*, 612 (1979)
53. Thiem, J., Meyer, B.: Chem. Ber. *113*, 3075 (1980)
54. Gillard, J.W., Israel, M.: Tetrahedron Lett. 513 (1981)
55. Benkeser, R.A., Mozdzen, E.C., Muth, C.L.: J. Org. Chem. *44*, 2185 (1979)
56. Voronkov, M.G., Komarov, V.G., Albanov, A.I., Kositsina, E.I., Dubinskaya, E.I. Izv. Akad. Nauk. SSSR Ser. Khim. 1692 (1978)
57. Kricheldorf, H.R.: Angew. Chem. Int. Ed. *18*, 689 (1979)
58. Olah, G.A., Narang, S.C., Salem, G.F., Gupta, B.G.B.: Synthesis, 142 (1981)
59. Borgulya, J., Bernauer, K.: Synthesis, 545 (1980)
60. Jung, M.E., Lyster, M.A.: J. Chem. Soc. Chem. Commun. 315 (1978)
61. Lott, R.S., Chauhan, V.S., Stammer, C.H.: J. Chem. Soc. Chem. Commun. 495 (1979)
62. Rabinowitz, R.: J. Org. Chem. *28*, 2975 (1963)
63. McKenna, C.E., Higa, M.T., Cheung, N.H., McKenna, M.C.: Tetrahedron Lett. 155 (1977)
64. McKenna, C.E., Schmidhauser, J.: J. Chem. Soc. Chem. Commun. 739 (1979)
65. Chojnowski, J., Cypryk, M., Michalski, J.: Synthesis, 777 (1978)
66. Blackburn, G.M., Ingleson, D.: J. Chem. Soc. Chem. Commun. 870 (1978)
67. Blackburn, G.M., Ingleson, D.: J. Chem. Soc. Perkin, *I*, 1150 (1980)
68. Zygmunt, J., Kafarski, P., Mastalerz, P.: Synthesis, 609 (1978)
69. Morita, T., Okamoto, Y., Sakurai, H.: Tetrahedron Lett. 2523 (1978)
70. Miller, R.D., McKean, D.R.: Tetrahedron Lett. 2639 (1980)
71. Miller, R.D., McKean, D.R.: Tetrahedron Lett. 2305 (1979)
72. Miller, R.D., McKean, D.R.: J. Org. Chem. *46*, 2412 (1981)
73. Schmidt, A.H., Russ, M., Grosse, D.: Synthesis, 216 (1981)
74. Birkofer, L., Krämer, E.: Chem. Ber. *100*, 2776 (1967)
75. Jung, M.E.: Org. Synthesis, in press
76. Eaborn, C., Walton, D.R.M., Young, D.J.: J. Chem. Soc. *B*, 15 (1969)
77. Jung, M.E., Blumenkopf, T.A.: Tetrahedron Lett. 3657 (1978)
78. Weyenberg, D.R., Toporcer, L.H.: J. Am. Chem. Soc. *84*, 2843 (1960)
79. Weyenberg, D.R., Toporcer, L.H.: J. Org. Chem. *30*, 943 (1965)
80. Detty, M.R.: Tetrahedron Lett. 4189 (1979)
81. Derkach, N.Y., Pasmurtseva, N.A., Levchenko, E.S.: Zhur. Org. Khim. *7*, 1543 (1971)
82. Detty, M.R.: Tetrahedron Lett. 5087 (1978)
83. Kumada, M., Shiina, K., Yamaguchi, M.: Kogyo, Hagakn Zasshi, *57*, 230 (1954)
84. Bundel, Y.G., Bobrovskii, S.I., Smirnov, V.V., Novikova, I.A., Sergeev, G.B., Reutov, O.A.: Izv. Akad. Nauk. SSSR Ser. Khim. 2129 (1979)

4 Silyl Azides

4.1 Introduction

Organosilyl azides have proved themselves useful as reagents in organic synthesis. On the basis of the analogy between a trimethylsilyl group and a proton, trimethylsilyl azide (TMS-N_3) might be expected to demonstrate reactivity and toxicity similar to that of hydrazoic acid.

4.2 Preparation and Properties of Organosilyl Azides

TMS-N_3, a colorless liquid boiling at 95–96°C/760 mm, is more convenient to handle than hydrazoic acid. Organosilyl azides are considerably more thermally stable than organic azides [1–4]. For example, triphenylsilyl azide does not decompose in the vapor phase at 590°C [5]. The thermal stability has been attributed to dative d_π–p_π bonding between silicon and nitrogen which increases the bond order for the Si–N bond [2, 3]. Nevertheless, these compounds should be handled with care, since diazidodimethylsilane is reported to explode unpredictably [6]. Organosilyl azides also react rapidly with water to release toxic hydrazoic acid [2].

TMS-N_3 has been prepared by reaction of TMS-Cl with lithium azide in 2,4-lutidine [5] or THF [4].

$$(CH_3)_3SiCl \ + \ LiN_3 \quad \xrightarrow[\text{or 2,4-Lutidine}]{\text{THF}} \quad (CH_3)_3SiN_3 \qquad (4.1)$$

TMS-N_3 can also be prepared by reaction of TMS-Cl with the more commonly available sodium azide in THF in the presence of AlCl$_3$ [7]. DMF [8], HMPT [8] or diethylene glycol dimethyl ether [1] can also be used as solvents for this reaction.

These procedures are quite general and permit the preparation of a variety of organosilyl azides [9, 10]. However, they do not permit preparation of organosilyl azides possessing Si–H, Si–NH$_2$ or C–C double bonds. Methylphenylsilyl azide has been prepared by an exchange reaction between TMS-N_3 and methylphenylchlorosilane [11, 12].

$$(CH_3)_3SiN_3 \ + \ \overset{\overset{\displaystyle CH_3}{\displaystyle |}}{\underset{\underset{\displaystyle H}{\displaystyle |}}{Ph-Si-Cl}} \quad \longrightarrow \quad (CH_3)_3SiCl \ + \ \overset{\overset{\displaystyle CH_3}{\displaystyle |}}{\underset{\underset{\displaystyle H}{\displaystyle |}}{Ph-Si-N_3}} \qquad (4.2)$$

A rather detailed comparison of synthetic methods for the preparation of organosilyl azides has been published [13]. A number of them are commercially available from Petrach [14].

4.3 Cycloaddition Reactions

TMS-N_3 undergoes [2 + 3] cycloaddition reactions with acetylenes to yield 2-trimethylsilyl-1,2,3-triazoles. These result from isomerization, via a 1,5-sigmatropic shift of the trimethylsilyl group, of the initially formed 1-trimethylsilyl 1,2,3-triazoles [15–18].

$$CH_3-C\equiv C-CH_3 \ + \ (CH_3)_3SiN_3 \longrightarrow \left[\begin{array}{c} CH_3 \\ CH_3 \end{array} \right] \longrightarrow \begin{array}{c} CH_3 \\ CH_3 \end{array} \quad (4.3)$$

The trimethylsilyl group of such 2-trimethylsilyl-1,2,3-triazoles can easily be removed by hydrolysis to yield 1,2,3-triazoles.

TMS-N_3 undergoes thermal [2 + 3] cycloaddition reaction with aryl nitriles to give mixtures of 5-aryl-2-trimethylsilyl tetrazoles [11], 3,5-diaryl-2-trimethylsilyl-1,2,4-triazoles and 3,6-diaryl-1,4-*bis*(trimethylsilyl)-1,2,4,5-tetrazines [19]. The latter two products result from thermal decomposition of the initial 5-aryl-2-trimethylsilyl tetrazole to give nitrogen and a N-trimethylsilyl substituted nitrile imine [20]. Such reactive 1,3-dipolar species react with an additional molecule of aryl nitrile to yield 3,5-diaryl-2-trimethylsilyl-1,2,4-triazoles or dimerize to yield 3,6-diaryl-1,4-*bis*(trimethylsilyl)-1,2,4,5-tetrazines.

$$ArC\equiv N \ + \ (CH_3)_3SiN_3 \longrightarrow \quad (4.4)$$

However, ferrocenyl nitrile reacts with TMS-N_3 under $AlCl_3$ catalysis to yield exclusively 2-trimethylsilyl-5-ferrocenyl tetrazole (75%) [19].

TMS-N_3 undergoes slow thermal [2 + 3] cycloaddition reactions with alkenes to yield 1-trimethylsilyl-Δ^2-1,2,3-triazoles. These lose nitrogen on heating at higher temperature or on photolysis to give N-trimethylsilyl aziridines [11, 21].

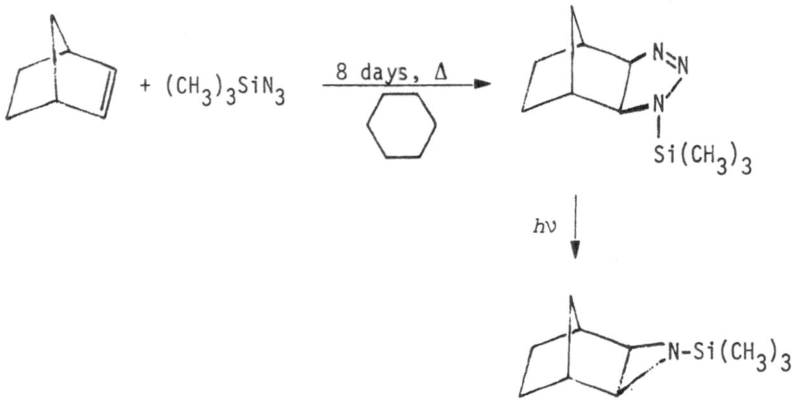

(4.5)

This reaction has been utilized in an unequivocal synthesis of N-substituted-1,4-dihydropyridines [22].

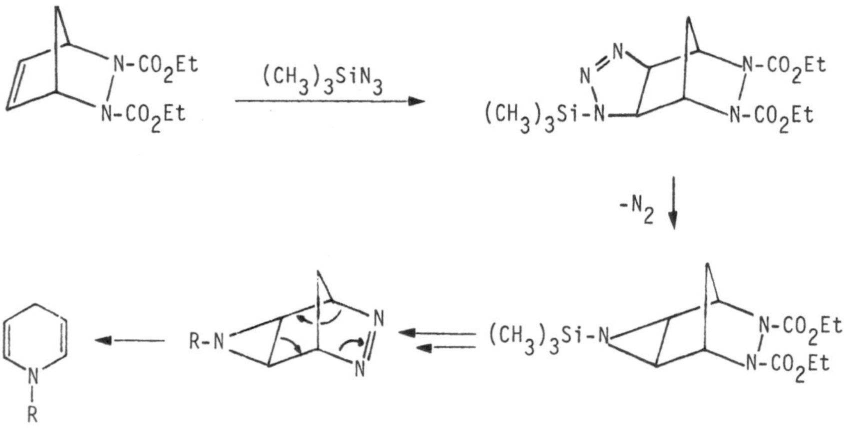

(4.6)

4.4 Reactions with Aldehydes or Ketones

TMS-N_3 reacts with aliphatic aldehydes under both electrophilic catalysis by zinc chloride [23, 24] or anionic activation by potassium azide and 18-C-6 [25] to yield α-trimethylsilyloxyalkyl azides. Catalysis by zinc chloride may involve coordination of zinc cation to the carbonyl oxygen increasing its electrophilicity.

$$\text{Zn}^{+2} \quad \text{Si(CH}_3)_3 \qquad \left[\begin{array}{c} \text{Zn}^{+2} \\ \text{(CH}_3)_2\text{CH-C-N-N}\equiv\text{N} \end{array} \right]$$

$$(CH_3)_2CH-\overset{O^{-\delta}}{\underset{\underset{H}{|}}{\overset{||}{\underset{|}{C^{+\delta}}}}} \qquad \overset{|}{\underset{-}{:N-N\equiv N}} \longrightarrow \left[(CH_3)_2CH-\overset{\overset{O^-}{|}}{\underset{\underset{H}{|}}{C}}-\overset{Si(CH_3)_3}{\underset{+}{N-N\equiv N}} \right]$$

$$\downarrow$$

$$(CH_3)_2CH-\overset{\overset{O-Si(CH_3)_3}{|}}{\underset{\underset{H}{|}}{C}}-N_3 \qquad + \; Zn^{+2} \qquad (4.7)$$

Anionic catalysis occurs by addition of azide ion to the carbonyl group to yield an alkoxide anion. This then reacts with TMS-N₃ to give the product and regenerate azide ion.

$$R-\overset{\overset{O}{||}}{C}-H \quad \xrightarrow[\text{18-C-6}]{KN_3} \quad R-\overset{\overset{O^-}{|}}{\underset{\underset{N_3}{|}}{C}}-H \quad \xrightarrow{(CH_3)_3SiN_3} \quad R-\overset{\overset{O-Si(CH_3)_3}{|}}{\underset{\underset{N_3}{|}}{C}}-H \quad + \; K\,N_3 \qquad (4.8)$$

Higher yields are obtained with anionic activation. Recently it has been shown that aliphatic aldehydes or ketones react with TMS-Cl and sodium azide in DMF to yield α-trimethylsilyloxyalkyl azides directly [26]. Although TMS-N₃ can be prepared under similar reaction conditions [8], it is not clear whether this reaction involves prior *in-situ* formation of TMS-N₃ or not.

$$\bigcirc\!\!=\!\!O \; + \; (CH_3)_3SiCl \; + \; NaN_3 \quad \xrightarrow{DMF} \quad \bigcirc\!\!\!\!\!\begin{array}{c} O-Si(CH_3)_3 \\ N_3 \end{array} \qquad (4.9)$$

α-Trimethylsilyloxyalkyl azides undergo pyrolysis at 280° to yield N-trimethylsilyl amides and nitrogen [11, 24].

$$(CH_3)_2CH-\overset{\overset{O-Si(CH_3)_3}{|}}{\underset{\underset{H}{|}}{C}}-N_3 \quad \xrightarrow{\Delta} \quad N_2 \; + \; \left[(CH_3)_2CH-\overset{\overset{O-Si(CH_3)_3}{|}}{\underset{\underset{H}{|}}{C}}-\overset{..}{N}: \right]$$

$$\downarrow$$

$$(CH_3)_2CH-\overset{\overset{O}{||}}{C}-N\overset{\diagup Si(CH_3)_3}{\diagdown H} \qquad (4.10)$$

α-Trimethylsilyloxyalkyl azides react with methanol to give the corresponding dimethyl acetal and hydrazoic acid [24].

$$(4.11)$$

α-Trimethylsilyloxyalkyl azides are reduced by LiAlH$_4$ to yield after hydrolysis, primary alkyl amines (Eq. 4.12)[27].

$$(4.12)$$

Finally, α-trimethylsilyloxyalkyl azides react as organic azides in thermal [2 + 3] cycloaddition reactions with polar acetylenes to yield substituted triazoles [24].

$$(4.13)$$

4.5 Reactions with Epoxides

Cyclohexene oxide reacts with TMS-N$_3$ in the presence of zinc chloride to yield *trans*-1-azido-2-trimethylsilyloxycyclohexane while styrene oxide yields 2-azido-1-trimethylsilyloxyphenylethane [24].

$$(4.14)$$

4.6 Reactions with Cumulenes

Phenyl isocyanate reacts with TMS-N$_3$ in a 1:1 ratio to give phenyl carbamoyl azide (32%) and 1-phenyl-5-(4H)-tetrazolinones (62%) after hydrolysis as outlined in Eq. 4.15. If a 1:2 ratio is used, only 1-phenyl-5-(4H)-tetrazolinone is obtained [55].

$$Ph-N=C=O \ + \ (CH_3)_3SiN_3 \longrightarrow Ph-N-C=O \xrightarrow{H_2O} PhNH-C-N_3 \qquad (4.15)$$

Benzoyl isocyanate reacts with TMS-N$_3$ in a similar manner to yield initially 1-benzoyl-5-trimethylsilyloxy-tetrazole. Loss of nitrogen yields a reactive 1,3-dipolar species which undergoes an intramolecular electrocyclic reaction with the carbonyl group to give 5-phenyl-3-trimethylsilyloxy-1,2,4-oxadiazole [55].

$$Ph-C-N=C=O \ + \ (CH_3)_3SiN_3 \longrightarrow \qquad (4.16)$$

Carbodiimides react with TMS-N$_3$ in an analogous manner [55].

$$Ph-N=C=N-Ph \ + \ (CH_3)_3SiN_3 \longrightarrow \qquad (4.17)$$

Phenyl isothiocyanate, on the other hand gives 5-anilino-1,2,3,4-thiotriazole [26].

4.7 Reactions with Phosphines

Organosilyl azides react with tertiary aliphatic and aromatic phosphines to yield N-organosilyl tertiary phosphineimines and nitrogen [9, 28]. These can be hydrolyzed to tertiary phosphineimines.

$$Et_3P \ + \ (CH_3)_3SiN_3 \longrightarrow Et_3P=N-Si(CH_3)_3 \xrightarrow{\ CH_3OH/H^+\ } Et_3P=N-H \qquad (4.18)$$
$$+ \ N_2$$

N-Trimethylsilyltriphenylphosphineimines react with acid chlorides or anhydrides to yield N-acyl triphenylphosphineimines [29].

$$Ph_3P=N-Si(CH_3)_3 \ + \ Ph-\overset{O}{\overset{\|}{C}}-Cl \longrightarrow Ph_3P=N-\overset{O}{\overset{\|}{C}}-Ph \qquad (4.19)$$

4.8 Reactions with Grignard Reagents

Aryl Grignard reagents react with triorganosilyl azides via two competing pathways. This first results in magnesium bromide N-silyl amides and nitrogen. These can be hydrolyzed to give primary amines (Eq. 4.20). The second gives magnesium azide bromide and a tetraorganosilane (Eq. 4.21) [30]. The ratio of these two processes depends on solvent, triorganosilyl azide, and the organometallic reagent. Addition is favored by less polar solvents, triphenylsilyl azide compared to TMS-N$_3$, and diphenyl magnesium rather than phenyl magnesium bromide. With phenyl lithium only substitution occurs [31, 32].

$$Ph_3SiN_3 \ + \ PhMgBr \ \begin{cases} Ph_3SiN\overset{Ph}{\underset{MgBr}{\diagdown}} \ + \ N_2 \xrightarrow{\ H_2O\ } PhNH_2 \qquad (4.20) \\[2em] Ph_4Si \ + \ BrMgN_3 \qquad\qquad\qquad (4.21) \end{cases}$$

4.9 Reactions with Acid Chlorides or Anhydrides

TMS-N$_3$ reacts rapidly with both aliphatic and aromatic acid chlorides to yield TMS-Cl and the corresponding acyl azide which undergoes loss of nitrogen. Rearrangement of the acyl nitrene intermediate thus formed gives high yields of isocyanate. TMS-N$_3$ thus permits the Curtis degradation to be carried out under mild neutral conditions (Eq. 4.22) [33, 34]. ω-Bromo aliphatic acid chlorides are readily converted to ω-bromo alkyl isocyanates [33, 35].

$$\text{(structure: benzene with two } \overset{O}{\underset{}{C}}\text{-Cl groups)} + 2(CH_3)_3SiN_3 \longrightarrow \text{(structure: benzene with two N=C=O groups)} + 2N_2 + 2(CH_3)_3SiCl$$

$$(4.22)$$

While alkenes undergo [2 + 3] cycloaddition reactions with TMS-N₃ [21, 22], TMS-N₃ reacts with acid chlorides more rapidly. This permits the conversion of unsaturated carboxylic chlorides to the corresponding isocyanates [33, 34].

$$CH_2=CH-(CH_2)_8-\overset{O}{\underset{}{C}}-Cl + (CH_3)_3SiN_3 \longrightarrow CH_2=CH-(CH_2)_8-N=C=O \qquad (4.23)$$

ω-Methoxycarbonyl alkanoyl chlorides can be converted to ω-methoxycarbonyl alkyl isocyanates in high yields [34]. On the other hand, reactive esters such as diketene and β-propiolactone react with TMS-N₃. Diketene yields a 1:1 mixture of 2-trimethylsilyloxy-2-propenyl isocyanate and 2-trimethylsilyloxy-1-propenyl isocyanate while β-propiolactone gives trimethylsilyl-3-azido propionate [36].

$$\text{(diketene structure)} + (CH_3)_3SiN_3 \longrightarrow CH_2=C\begin{cases} CH_2-N=C=O \\ O-Si(CH_3)_3 \end{cases}$$

$$\longrightarrow CH_3-C=CH-N=C=O \atop \underset{O-Si(CH_3)_3}{|} \qquad (4.24)$$

Cyclopropanoyl chloride reacts with diphenyldiazosilane to yield cyclopropyl isocyanate [37]. However, catalysis by potassium azide and 18-C-6 proved necessary in the reaction of 1-phenylcyclopropanoyl chloride with TMS-N₃ [38].

$$\text{(1-phenylcyclopropanoyl chloride structure)} + (CH_3)_3SiN_3 \xrightarrow[\text{18-C-6}]{KN_3} \text{(1-phenylcyclopropyl isocyanate structure)} \qquad (4.25)$$

Even perfluoroalkyl acid chlorides have been smoothly converted to the perfluoroalkyl isocyanates [39, 40]

$$CF_3(CF_2)_4-\overset{O}{\underset{}{C}}{\diagdown}_{Cl} + (CH_3)_3SiN_3 \longrightarrow CF_3-(CF_2)_4-N=C=O \qquad (4.26)$$

Aryl chloroformates react with TMS-N₃ in chloroform to yield aryl azido formates. Pyridine catalyzes the reaction at room temperature (Eq. 4.27). At higher temperatures (90°) aryl azido formates decompose to yield the corresponding nitrenes which react with solvent. Aryl azido formates react with triphenylphosphine as outlined below (Eq. 4.28) [29].

$$Ph-O-\overset{\overset{O}{\|}}{C}-Cl \ + \ (CH_3)_3SiN_3 \ \longrightarrow \ Ph-O-\overset{\overset{O}{\|}}{C}-N_3 \ + \ (CH_3)_3SiCl \qquad (4.27)$$

$$Ph-O-\overset{\overset{O}{\|}}{C}-N_3 \ + \ Ph_3P \ \longrightarrow \ Ph-O-\overset{\overset{O}{\|}}{C}-N=PPh_3 \qquad (4.28)$$

Anhydrides react with TMS-N$_3$ in a similar manner to acid chloride to give equal amounts of trimethylsilyl esters and isocyanates [34, 41, 42].

$$\left(CH_3-(CH_2)_2-\overset{\overset{O}{\|}}{C}\right)_2O \ + \ (CH_3)_3SiN_3 \ \overset{\displaystyle CH_3-(CH_2)_2-\overset{\overset{O}{\|}}{C}-O-Si(CH_3)_3}{\underset{\displaystyle CH_3-(CH_2)_2-N=C=O \ + \ N_2}{<}} \qquad (4.29)$$

Cyclic saturated anhydrides react with TMS-N$_3$ to give ω-trimethylsilyloxy-carbonyl alkyl isocyanates [42, 43].

$$+ \ (CH_3)_3SiN_3 \ \longrightarrow \ O=C=N-(CH_2)_2-CO_2-Si(CH_3)_3 \qquad (4.30)$$

α,β-Unsaturated cyclic anhydrides such as maleic and phthalic anhydride react with TMS-N$_3$ to yield N-trimethylsilyl-1,3-oxazine-2,6-diones [41] as outlined below (Eq. 4.31).

Halogen, alkyl and aryl substituted maleic anhydrides react with TMS-N₃ to yield mixtures of 4 and 5 substituted N-trimethylsilyl-1,3-oxazine-2,6-diones. Surprisingly, the 4-substituted isomers are always predominant [45-48].

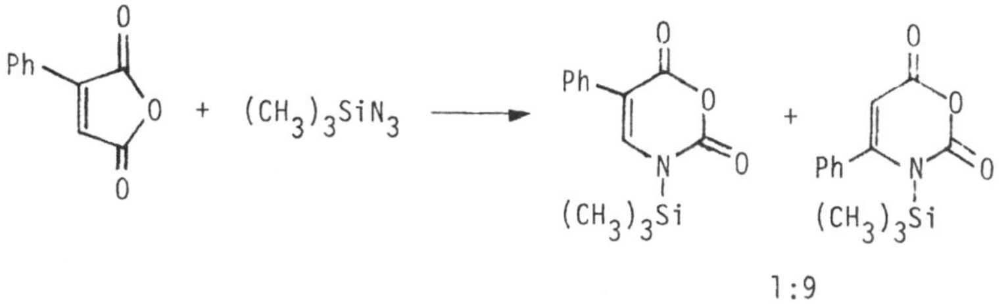

(4.32)

1:9

In a similar manner, *cis*-1,3-pentadienyl isocyanate, prepared by reaction of sorboyl chloride with TMS-N₃, undergoes intramolecular electrocyclic reaction to yield 3-methyl-2-pyridone [44].

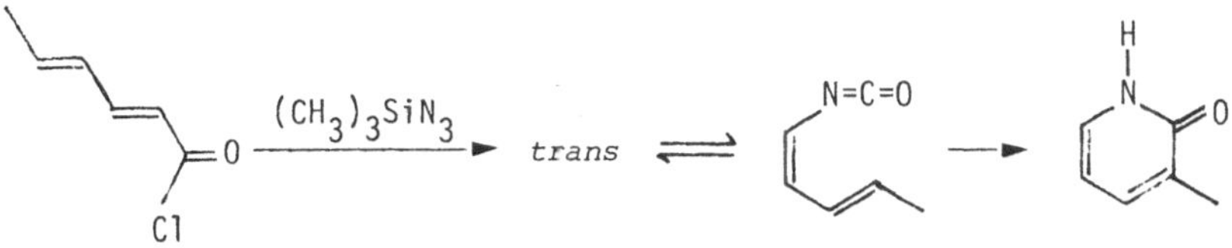

(4.33)

N-Butyl isomaleimide reacts with TMS-N₃ to yield 3-butyl uracil after hydrolysis [41].

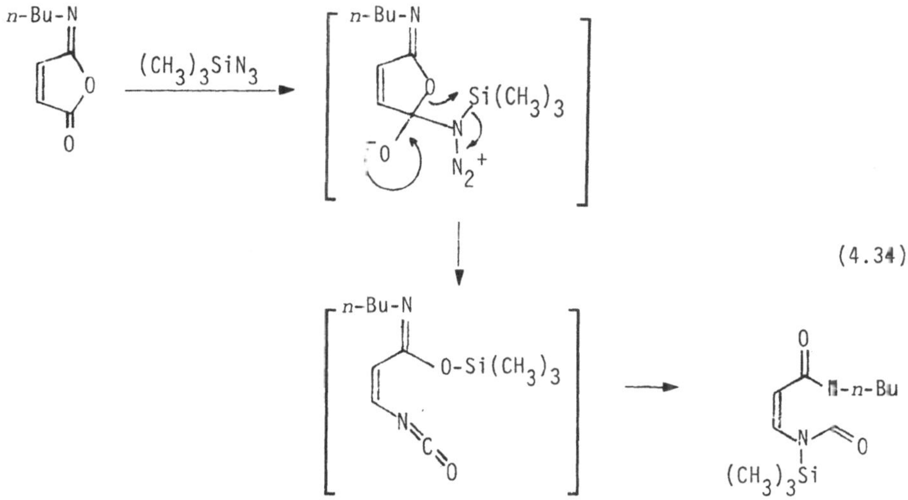

(4.34)

4.10 Reactions with Lead Tetraacetate or Phenyliodosodiacetate

The reactivity of lead tetraacetate has been modified by reaction with TMS-N₃ [56]. An exchange reaction results in formation of species, such as lead diacetate diazide and acetoxytrimethylsilane.

$$Pb(OAc)_4 + 2(CH_3)_3SiN_3 \longrightarrow Pb(OAc)_2(N_3)_2 + 2(CH_3)_3SiOAc \qquad (4.35)$$

This system reacts with activated alkenes, such as styrene, to yield mixtures of 1,2-diazido phenylethane, 1-acetoxy-2-azido phenylethane and α-azidomethyl phenyl ketone. This regiospecificity suggests an intermediate benzylic carbocation [49].

$$Ph-CH=CH_2 + Pb(OAc)_{4-n}(N_3)_n \qquad (4.36)$$

Oxidation of norbornene with this system yields 5-*exo*-acetoxy-7-*syn* azido-norbornane. This result is consistent with a carbocation intermediate [50].

$$(4.37)$$

With disubstituted steroidal alkenes this system regiospecifically yields α-azido ketones. A mechanism, in which the initial α-azido carbocation loses a proton to form a vinyl azide which is further oxidized, has been suggested [51].

$$(4.38)$$

Trisubstituted steroidal alkenes undergo oxidative cleavage of the C–C double bond to yield ε-keto nitriles. A mechanism involving ionic intermediates has been proposed. An azido epoxide intermediate may be involved in framentation of the C–C double bond [52].

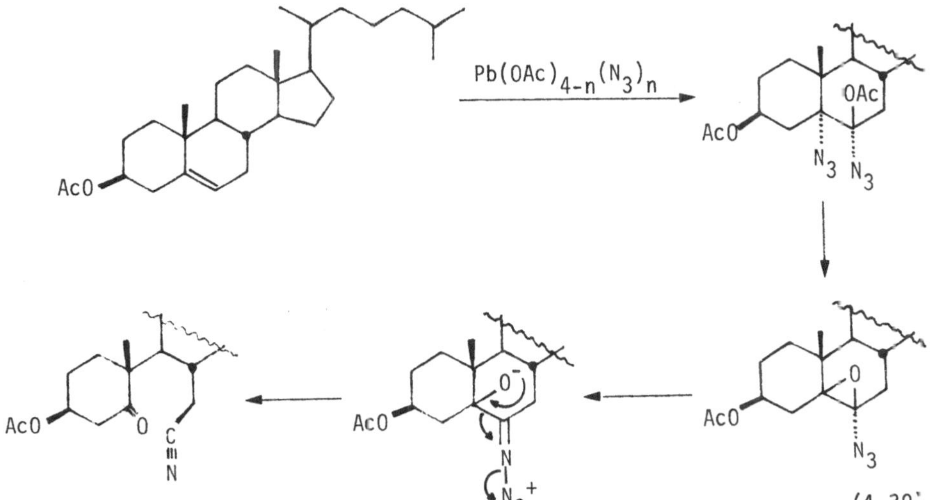

(4.39)

It should be noted that lead azides are explosive. This system has the obvious advantage of generating these species *in-situ*.

The reactivity of phenyliodosodiacetate has also been modified by equilibration with TMS-N$_3$. Phenyliodosodiacetate/TMS-N$_3$ reacts with disubstituted alkenes to give α-azido ketones [53].

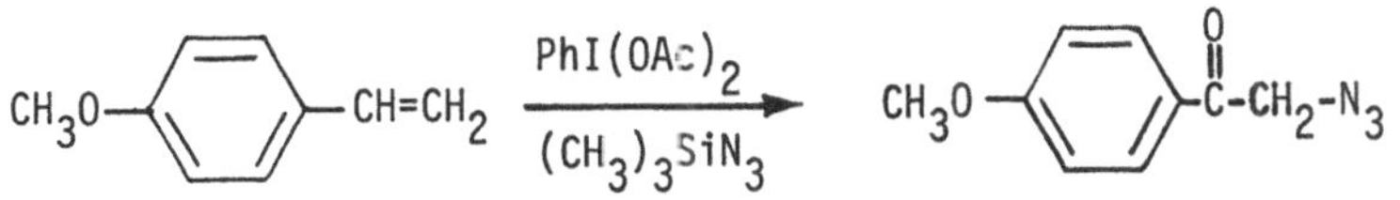

(4.40)

With phenyliodosodiacetate/TMS-N$_3$, trisubstituted alkenes undergo oxidative cleavage of the C–C double bond to give ε-keto nitriles in slightly lower yields than with lead tetraacetate/TMS-N$_3$ [54].

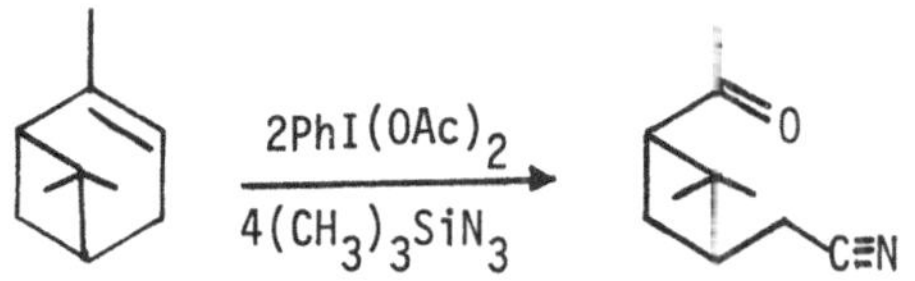

(4.41)

An advantage of phenyliodosodiacetate/TMS-N$_3$ is that it is potentially less hazardous since no explosive lead azides can be formed.

References

1. Birkofer, L., Wegner, P.: Org. Syn. *50*, 107 (1970)
2. West, R., Thayer, J.S.: J. Am. Chem. Soc. *87*, 1763 (1962)
3. Thayer, J.S., West, R.: Inorg. Chem. *3*, 889 (1964)
4. Wiberg, N., Raschig, F., Sustmann, R.: Angew. Chem. Int. Ed. *1*, 335 (1962)
5. Reichle, W.T.: Inorg. Chem. *3*, 402 (1964)
6. Wolfsberger, W., Schmidbauer, H.: J. Organometal. Chem. *28*, 301 (1971)
7. Thayer, J.S., West, R.: Inorg. Chem. *3*, 406 (1964)
8. Washburne, S.S., Peterson, Jr., W.R.: J. Organometal. Chem. *33*, 153 (1971)
9. Wiberg, N., Raschig, F., Sustmann, R.: Angew. Chem. Int. Ed. *1*, 335 (1962)
10. Wiberg, N., Raschig, F., Sustmann, R.: Angew. Chem. Int. Ed. *1*, 551 (1962)
11. Ettenhuber, E., Rühlmann, K.: Chem. Ber. *101*, 743 (1968)
12. Sundermeyer, W.: Angew. Chem. Int. Ed. *1*, 595 (1962)
13. Peterson, Jr., W.R.: Reviews on Silicon, Germanium, Tin and Lead Compounds *I*, 193 (1974)
14. Petrach Systems, Inc., Bristol Pennsylvania, 19007, USA.
15. Birkhofer, L., Wegner, P.: Chem. Ber. *99*, 2512 (1966)
16. Birkofer, L., Ritter, A., Uhlenbrauck, H.: Chem. Ber. *96*, 3280 (1963)
17. Tanaka, Y., Velen, S.R., Miller, S.I.: Tetrahedron, *29*, 3271 (1973)
18. Birkofer, L., Wegner, P.: Chem. Ber. *100*, 3485 (1967)
19. Washburne, S.S., Peterson, Jr. W.R.: J. Organometal. Chem. *21*, 427 (1970)
20. Birkofer, L., Ritter, A., Richter, P.: Chem. Ber. *96*, 2750 (1963)
21. Scheiner, P.: Tetrahedron, *24*, 2757 (1968)
22. Stout, D.M., Takaya, T., Meyers, A.I.: J. Org. Chem. *40*, 563 (1975)
23. Birkofer, L., Müller, F., Kaiser, W.: Tetrahedron Lett. 2781 (1967)
24. Birkofer, L., Kaiser, W.: J. Lieligs. Ann. *1975*, 266
25. Evans, D.A., Truesdale, L.K.: Tetrahedron Lett. 4929 (1973)
26. Vorbrüggen, H., Krolikiewicz, K.: Synthesis 35 (1979)
27. Kyba, E.P., John, A.M.: Tetrahedron Lett. 2737 (1977)
28. Birkofer, L., Kim, S.M.: Chem. Ber. *97*, 2100 (1969)
29. Kricheldorf, H.R.: Synthesis 695 (1972)
30. Wiberg, N., Schmid, K.H., Joo, W.C.: Angew. Chem. Int. Ed. *4*, 90 (1965)
31. Wiberg, N., Joo, W.C.: J. Organometal. Chem. *22*, 333 (1970)
32. Wiberg, N., Joo, W.C., Olbert, P.: J. Organometal. Chem. *22*, 341 (1970)
33. Kricheldorf, H.R.: Synthesis 551 (1972)
34. Washburne, S.S., Peterson, Jr., W.R.: Syn. Commun. *2*, 227 (1972)
35. Kricheldorf, H.R.: Angew. Chem. Int. Ed. *18*, 689 (1979)
36. Kricheldorf, H.R.: Chem. Ber. *106*, 3765 (1973)
37. Kricheldorf, H.R., Regel; W.: Chem. Ber. *106*, 3757 (1973)
38. Warren, J.D., Press, J.B.: Syn. Commun. *10*, 107 (1980)
39. Peterson, Jr., W.R., Radell, J., Washburne, S.S.: J. Flourine Chem. *2*, 437 (1972/1973)
40. Lutz, W., Sundermeyer, W.: Chem. Ber. *112*, 2158 (1979)
41. Washburne, S.S., Peterson, Jr., W.R., Berman, D.A.: J. Org. Chem. *37*, 1738 (1972)
42. Kricheldorf, H.R.: Chem. Ber. *105*, 3958 (1972)
43. Kricheldorf, H.R., Regel, W.: Chem. Ber. *106*, 3753 (1973)
44. MacMillan, J.H., Washburne, S.S.: J. Org. Chem. *38*, 2982 (1973)
45. Warren, J.D., MacMillan, J.H., Washburne, S.S.: J. Org. Chem. *40*, 743 (1975)
46. Washburne, S.S., Lee, H.: J. Org. Chem. *43*, 2719 (1978)

47. Farkas, J., Fliegerova, O., Skoda, J.: Collect. Czech. Chem. Commun. *41*, 2059 (1976)
48. MacMillan, J.H., Washburne, S.S.: J. Heterocyclic Chem. *12*, 1215 (1975)
49. Zbiral, E., Kischa, K.: Tetrahedron Lett. 1167 (1969)
50. Zbiral, E., Stütz, A.: Tetrahedron, *27*, 4953 (1971)
51. Zbiral, E., Nestler, G.: Tetrahedron, *27*, 2293 (1971)
52. Zbiral, E., Nestler, G., Kischa, K.: Tetrahedron, *26*, 1427 (1970)
53. Ehrenfreund, E., Zbiral, E.: Tetrahedron, *28*, 1697 (1972)
54. Zbiral, E., Nestler, G.: Tetrahedron, *26*, 2945 (1970)
55. Tsuge, O., Urano, S., Oe, K.: J. Org. Chem. *45*, 5130 (1980)
56. Zbiral, E.: Synthesis, 285 (1972)

5 Silyl Nitronates

5.1 Introduction — Physical and Spectroscopic Properties

A limited amount of synthetic work has been carried out with silyl nitronates (silyl esters of nitronic acids). IR, UV, and variable temperature NMR spectra, as well as, a low temperature X-ray structure of a silyl nitronate have been reported [2]. The concentration independent variable temperature NMR behavior of these species is consistent with fast intramolecular migration of the silyl group between the two oxygens of the nitronate [2]. Although

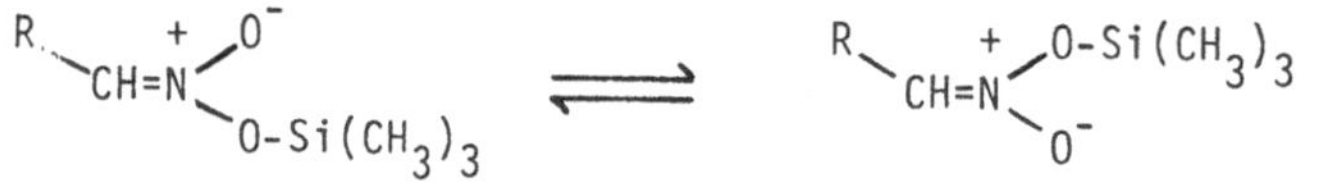

$$
\begin{array}{c}
R \\
\diagdown CH=N^+ \diagup O^- \\
\diagdown O-Si(CH_3)_3
\end{array}
\rightleftharpoons
\begin{array}{c}
R \\
\diagdown CH=N^+ \diagup O-Si(CH_3)_3 \\
\diagdown O^-
\end{array}
\tag{5.1}
$$

silyl nitronates are more thermally stable than the corresponding alkyl nitronates [1, 2], they readily undergo hydrolysis to regenerate the nitroalkanes. *t*-Butyldimethylsilyl nitronates are less susceptible to hydrolysis than trimethylsilyl nitronates [2].

5.2 Cycloaddition Reactions

Silyl nitronates undergo thermal [2 + 3] cycloaddition reactions with alkenes substituted by electron withdrawing groups to yield regiospecifically 5-substituted-2-N-silyloxyisoxazolidines [1, 3, 4].

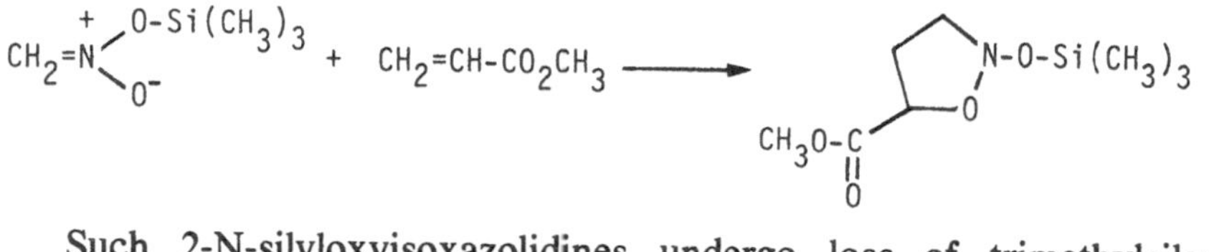

$$
\begin{array}{c}
CH_2=N^+ \diagup O-Si(CH_3)_3 \\
\diagdown O^-
\end{array}
+ CH_2=CH-CO_2CH_3 \longrightarrow
\begin{array}{c}
\\
N-O-Si(CH_3)_3 \\
O \\
CH_3O-C \\
\| \\
O
\end{array}
\tag{5.2}
$$

Such 2-N-silyloxyisoxazolidines undergo loss of trimethylsilanol on treatment with acid (HCl or TsOH [3]) or heat [4] to yield 2-isoxazolines [1, 3].

$$
\begin{array}{c}
H \diagup CH_2CH_3 \\
\\
N-O-Si(CH_3)_3 \\
O \\
Ph
\end{array}
\xrightarrow{\text{HCl}}
\begin{array}{c}
CH_2CH_3 \\
\\
N \\
O \\
Ph
\end{array}
\tag{5.3}
$$

Treatment of 2-N-trimethylsilyloxyisoxazolidines with potassium methoxide in benzene, followed by acidic work-up, gives γ-hydroxy oximes [1, 4]. 2-N-Trimethylsilyloxyisoxazolidines have been converted to 3-substituted isoxazoles and 1,3-substituted pyrazoles [3].

5.3 Nitro-Aldol Reactions

Silyl nitronates react with aliphatic and aromatic aldehydes under nucleophilic catalysis by TBAF to yield 2-silyloxy nitroalkanes [5]. The reaction may proceed by fluoride ion attack on the silyl group to yield the nitro stabilized carbanion. This adds to the aldehyde carbonyl group to give an alkoxide anion which attacks the silyl center of another silyl nitronate molecule. Transfer of the silyl group yields the product and regenerates the nitro stabilized carbanion.

$$(5.4)$$

Fluoride ion catalyzed nitro-Aldol reactions of *t*-butyldimethylsilyl nitronates with aliphatic aldehydes proceed diastereoselectively to yield practically pure *erythro* isomers. Lower diastereoselectivity is observed with benzaldehyde. The preferential formation of one diastereomer is consistent with a chair transition state which minimizes steric interactions [6].

$$(5.5)$$

Unfortunately the reaction fails with ketones. 2-Silyloxy nitroalkanes are successfully reduced with LiAlH$_4$ to 2-amino alcohols [5].

$$\text{(5.6)}$$

5.4 Oxidation

Secondary silyl nitronates undergo oxidative cleavage by ceric ammonium nitrate in acetonitrile to yield the corresponding ketones [7].

$$\text{(5.7)}$$

Nitroalkanes have been converted into the corresponding aldehydes or ketones by treatment with basic silica gel, followed by elution of the carbonyl compound with ether. The reaction may occur by interaction of the nitronate ion with the surface siloxane functionality of the silica gel to yield a surface bound silyl nitronate. Attack by absorbed hydroxide or silanoate on the silyl nitronate, converts it to the carbonyl compound and nitrogen oxides [8].

$$\text{(5.8)}$$

5.5 Preparation

Trimethylsilyl nitronates have been prepared by reaction of primary and secondary nitroalkanes with N,O-*bis*(trimethylsilyl)acetamide [1,3].

$$CH_3-CH_2-NO_2 \xrightarrow[\substack{\displaystyle CH_3-C=N-Si(CH_3)_3 \\ \displaystyle OSi(CH_3)_3}]{} CH_3-CH=\overset{+}{N}\overset{\nearrow O^-}{\underset{\diagdown O-Si(CH_3)_3}{}} \qquad (5.9)$$

Nitromethane, -ethane and -propane can be converted to the corresponding trimethylsilyl nitronates by treatment with TMS-Cl and triethylamine [3]. Reaction of TMS-Cl with nitrocyclohexanes and lithium sulfide in acetonitrile provides an efficient route to the corresponding trimethylsilyl nitronates [9].

$$\xrightarrow[CH_3CN]{(CH_3)_3SiCl/Li_2S} \qquad (5.10)$$

Perhaps the most general method involves reaction of the lithium nitronates, generated by treatment of primary and secondary nitroalkanes with LDA in THF at −78°, with the desired trialkylchlorosilane. *t*-Butyldimethylsilyl nitronates, as well as trimethylsilyl nitronates, have been prepared by this method [2].

$$(5.11)$$

$$\xrightarrow[\substack{THF \\ -78°}]{LDA} \qquad \xrightarrow[]{\substack{CH_3 \\ t-Bu-Si-Cl \\ CH_3}}$$

Since silyl nitronates are now readily available, new chemistry with these interesting compounds may be forthcoming.

References

1. Kashutina, M.V., Ioffe, S.L., Tartakovskii, V.A.: Dokl. Akad. Nauk. SSSR, *218*, 109 (1974)
2. Colvin, E.W., Beck, A.K., Bastani, B., Seebach, D., Kai, Y., Dunitz, J.D.: Helv. Chim. Acta. *63*, 697 (1980)
3. Sharma, S.C., Torssell, K.: Acta, Chem. Scand. *B33*, 379 (1979)
4. Torssell, K., Zeuthen, O.: Acta. Chem. Scand. *B32*, 118 (1978)
5. Colvin, E.W., Seebach, D.: J. Chem. Soc. Chem. Commun. 689 (1978)
6. Seebach, D., Beck, A.K., Lehr, F., Weller, T., Colvin, E.: Angew. Chem. Int. Ed. *20*, 397 (1981)
7. Olah, G.A., Gupta, B.G.B.: Synthesis, 44 (1980)
8. Keinan, E., Mazur, Y.: J. Am. Chem. Soc. *99*, 3861 (1977)
9. Olah, G.A., Gupta, G.B.G., Narang, S.C., Malhotra, R.: J. Org. Chem. *44*, 4272 (1979)

6 Peterson Reaction

6.1 Introduction

The Silyl-Wittig or Peterson reaction involves addition of a stoichiometric quantity of an α-silyl carbanion to the carbonyl group of a ketone or aldehyde. This yields a β-silyl alkoxide which decomposes by alkoxide attack on silicon to yield an alkene and a silanoate. The ease of this decomposition is dependent on the cation. Potassium and sodium alkoxides decompose far more readily than the more covalent magnesium alkoxides [1].

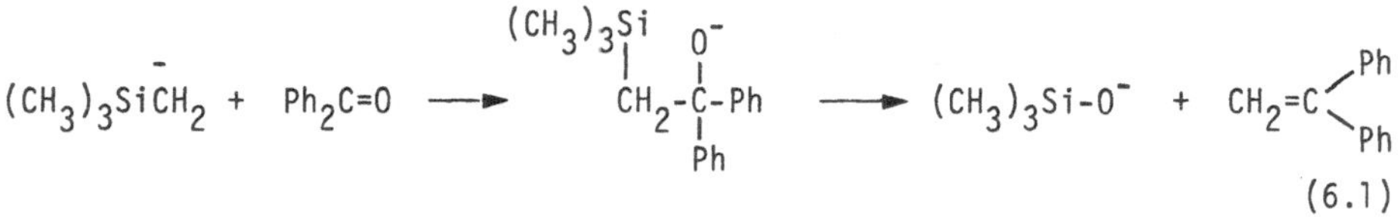

$$(CH_3)_3SiCH_2^- + Ph_2C=0 \longrightarrow \underset{\underset{Ph}{|}}{\overset{\overset{(CH_3)_3Si}{|}}{CH_2-\overset{\overset{O^-}{|}}{C}-Ph}} \longrightarrow (CH_3)_3Si-O^- + CH_2=C\overset{Ph}{\underset{Ph}{\diagdown}} \tag{6.1}$$

The similarity of this reaction sequence to the Wittig reaction is apparent: α-trimethylsilyl carbanions are analogous to ylids, while β-trimethylsilyl alkoxides are similar to betaines. Finally the trimethylsilanoate may be compared to triphenylphosphine oxide. The driving force for this reaction results from the formation of a strong Si$-$O single bond. In fact, given a choice the alkoxide oxygen prefers to attack silicon rather than phosphorous. The Peterson reaction occurs in preference to both the Wittig [2] (Eq. 6.2) and the Wittig-Horner-Emmons reactions (Eq. 6.3) [3]. This permits synthesis of vinyl phosphonates.

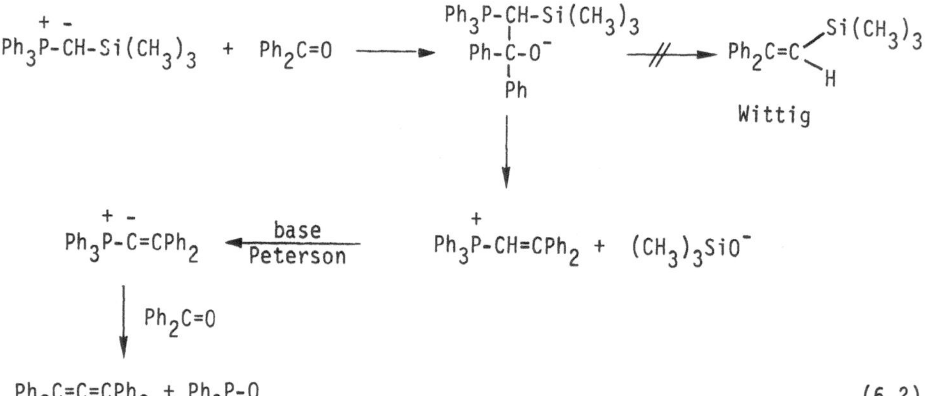

$$Ph_3\overset{+}{P}-\overset{-}{C}H-Si(CH_3)_3 + Ph_2C=0 \longrightarrow \underset{\underset{Ph}{|}}{\overset{\overset{Ph_3P-CH-Si(CH_3)_3}{|}}{Ph-C-O^-}} \overset{/\!/}{\longrightarrow} Ph_2C=C\overset{Si(CH_3)_3}{\underset{H}{\diagdown}}$$

Wittig

$$Ph_3\overset{+}{P}-\overset{-}{C}=CPh_2 \xrightarrow[\text{Peterson}]{\text{base}} Ph_3\overset{+}{P}-CH=CPh_2 + (CH_3)_3SiO^-$$

$$\downarrow Ph_2C=0$$

$$Ph_2C=C=CPh_2 + Ph_3P-O \tag{6.2}$$

58

The Peterson reaction is successful with enolizable ketones while the Wittig reaction often fails. This is because alkylidenetriphenylphosphoranes may react as strong bases with enolizable ketones rather than undergoing nucleophilic addition to form betaines. α-Trimethylsilyl carbanions, on the other hand, add to such ketones as nucleophiles [4].

6.2 α-Silyl Organometallics

The synthetic utility of the Peterson reaction has generated interest in α-silyl organometallics [5]. These have been generated in a number of ways. The ease of formation and the stability of carbanions alpha to silicon have been attributed to delocalization of the extra electron density centered in a 2p orbital on carbon into an empty 3d orbital on silicon.

$$(6.5)$$

A. α-Silyl Grignard and Organolithium Reagents

α-Haloalkyltrimethylsilanes or α-haloalkyltriphenylsilanes can be converted to Grignard or organolithium reagents [9, 10].

$$(CH_3)_3Si-CH_2Cl \xrightarrow{Mg/Et_2O} (CH_3)_3SiCH_2-MgCl \xrightarrow[2) \ H_2O]{1) \ CH_3-\overset{O}{\overset{||}{C}}-H} (CH_3)_3SiCH_2-\overset{OH}{\underset{}{CH}}-CH_3 \tag{6.6}$$

α-Trimethylsilyl Grignard reagents will add to ketones or aldehydes to yield after hydrolysis β-hydroxyalkyltrimethylsilanes. This occurs because the intermediate magnesium β-trimethylsilyl alkoxides do not easily undergo elimination [1]. Treatment of β-hydroxyalkyltrimethylsilanes with sodium or potassium hydride converts them to sodium or potassium β-trimethylsilyl alkoxides which lose trimethylsilanoate and form alkenes.

B. Halogen-Metal Exchange

Halogen-metal exchange between bromomethyltriphenylsilane and n-butyl lithium yields triphenylsilylmethyl lithium [11].

$$Ph_3SiCH_2Br \xrightarrow{n\text{-}BuLi} Ph_3SiCH_2Li \tag{6.7}$$

Halogen-metal exchange has also been used to generate bromo-*bis*(trimethylsilyl)methyl lithium [12] and *tris*(trimethylsilyl)methyl lithium [13].

$$[(CH_3)_3Si]_2C\overset{Br}{\underset{Br}{<}} \xrightarrow{n\text{-}BuLi} [(CH_3)_3Si]_2C\overset{Br}{\underset{Li}{<}} \tag{6.8}$$

C. Addition of Organometallics to Vinyl Silanes

While Grignard reagents and organolithium compounds will not, in general, add to isolated C$-$C double bonds, they will add to the C$-$C double bond of vinyl silanes to form a carbanion adjacent to silicon [14–18].

$$Ph_3Si\diagup\!\!\!\diagdown \ + \ PhLi \longrightarrow Ph_3Si\diagup\!\!\diagdown\!\!\overset{Li^+}{\underset{-}{\diagup}}\!\!\diagdown Ph \tag{6.9}$$

$$\underset{\underset{CH_3}{|}}{\overset{\overset{CH_3}{|}}{CH_2{=}CH{-}Si{-}O{-}CH_2CH_3}} \xrightarrow{i\text{ProMgBr}} \underset{\underset{Br}{\overset{|}{Mg}}}{\overset{\overset{CH_3}{|}}{(CH_3)_2CHCH_2{-}CH{-}Si{-}O{-}CH_2CH_3}}\ \ \overset{|}{CH_3} \tag{6.10}$$

D. Metallation

While tetramethylsilane can be metallated by *n*-butyl lithium/TMEDA [6–8], the reaction is more facile when a second carbanion stabilizing group is present. *bis*(Trimethylsilyl)methane [19] and *tris*(trimethylsilyl)methane [13, 19] are easily metallated to yield carbanions stabilized by two and three adjacent trimethylsilyl groups respectively.

$$[(CH_3)_3Si]_2CH_2 \xrightarrow[\substack{t-BuLi \\ -78°C}]{THF/HMPT} [(CH_3)_3Si]_2\overset{-}{C}HLi^+ \tag{6.11}$$

Adjacent aryl, ester and nitrile groups stabilize carbanions. Both benzyl-triphenylsilane [20] and benzyltrimethylsilane [21] are readily metallated by reaction with *n*-butyl lithium. 2-(Trimethylsilylmethyl)pyridine is easily deprotonated by LDA in THF at −78 °C [22, 23].

$$\text{(structure: pyridine-CH}_2\text{-Si(CH}_3)_3\text{)} \xrightarrow[THF]{LDA} \text{(structure: pyridine-}\overset{-}{C}\text{H-Si(CH}_3)_3\text{)} \tag{6.12}$$

t-Butyl and ethyl esters of trimethylsilylacetic acid [24–27] and trimethylsilyl-acetonitrile [28, 29] can be converted to α-silyl carbanions by treatment with LDA.

$$(CH_3)_3SiCH_2CO_2\text{-}t\text{-Bu} \xrightarrow[-78°]{LDA} (CH_3)_3Si\overset{-}{C}H\text{-}CO_2\text{-}t\text{-Bu} \quad Li^+ \tag{6.13}$$

2-Trimethylsilyl-1,3-dithiane and other such trimethylsilyl-substituted thioacetals are easily metallated [30].

$$\text{(dithiane structure, H, Si(CH}_3)_3\text{)} \xrightarrow{n\text{-BuLi}} \text{(dithiane structure, }^{-}\text{, Si(CH}_3)_3\text{)} \tag{6.14}$$

E. Displacement Reactions

α-Trimethylsilyl carbanions have been formed by displacement reactions. *tetrakis*(Trimethylsilyl)methane reacts with sodium methoxide in HMPT to form *tris*(trimethylsilyl)methyl sodium and methoxytrimethylsilane [31]. The driving force for this reaction may be the formation of the strong Si−O single bond of methoxytrimethylsilane. Similar reactions occur with *tris*(trimethyl-silyl)methane and *bis*(trimethylsilyl)methane, to yield the corresponding α-silyl carbanions via loss of one trimethylsilyl group as methoxytrimethylsilane [31].

$$[(CH_3)_3Si]_2CH_2 \xrightarrow[HMPT]{CH_3O^-Na^+} (CH_3)_3SiCH_2^-Na^+ + (CH_3)_3SiOCH_3 \tag{6.15}$$

Displacement of phenylthiolate from 1-phenylthio-1-trimethylsilylalkanes by reaction with lithium naphthalide yields α-trimethylsilyl alkyl lithium reagents [32].

$$(6.16)$$

Similarly, displacement of methyl selenide from methyl trimethylsilylmethyl selenide by n-butyl lithium yields trimethylsilylmethyl lithium [33].

$$CH_3SeCH_2Si(CH_3)_3 \xrightarrow{\text{n-BuLi}} n\text{-EuSeCH}_3 + Li^+ \,{}^-CH_2Si(CH_3)_3 \qquad (6.17)$$

6.3 Stereochemical Control of Elimination

The Peterson reaction is of synthetic interest, not only due to the wide variety of alkenes which can be prepared, but also because the reaction can be controlled to yield either *cis* or *trans* alkenes. Treatment of *threo* 5-trimethyl-silyloctan-4-ol with potassium hydride in THF yields exclusively *trans*-4-octene via a *syn*-elimination (Eq. 6.18). On the other hand, β-hydroxyalkylsila-nes also undergo elimination under acidic conditions [9]. Treatment of this diastereomer with a catalytic amount of sulfuric acid in THF or BF$_3 \cdot$ OEt$_2$ in methylene chloride, yields *cis*-4-octene via an *anti*-elimination (Eq. 6.19) [34, 35]. Trimethylsilyl groups stabilize developing beta carbocation centers when they can assume a *trans*-diaxial relationship to the leaving group (see Chapter 7).

$$(6.18)$$

$$(6.19)$$

The necessary *threo*-5-trimethylsilyloctan-4-ol is prepared by reducticn of 5-trimethylsilyloctan-4-one with DIBAL in pentane at $-120°C$. This stereo-selectivity is predicted by Cram's rule [36] and the assumption that the tri-methylsilyl group is larger than the *n*-propyl group.

6.4 Preparation of Substituted Alkenes

A. Ketene Thioacetals

The Peterson reaction has been used to prepare ketene thioacetals [37–39]. α-Trimethylsilyl carbanions stabilized by two adjacent sulfur atoms are easily formed by metallation reactions. For example, 2-trimethylsilyl-1,3-dithiane reacts with *n*-butyl lithium to yield 2-lithio-2-trimethylsilyl-1,3-dithiane [42, 43]. Reaction of this α-silyl carbanion with ketones or aldehydes yields ketene thioacetals. With α,β-unsaturated ketones and aldehydes, only 1,2-addition is observed (Eq. 6.20) [30, 40, 44, 45]. *bis*-(Methylmercapto)methane. *bis*-(phenylmercapto)methane, and *bis*(phenylseleno)methane react similarly [19, 40, 41].

$$\text{(6.20)}$$

Ketene thioacetals are valuable synthetic intermediates. They can be hydro-lyzed to yield carboxylic acids [39].

$$\xrightarrow[\text{Hg}^{++}]{\text{H}_2\text{O}} \quad \text{RCH}_2\text{-CO}_2\text{H} \tag{6.21}$$

The C—C double bond of ketene thioacetals can be reduced by treatment with triethylsilane and trifluoracetic acid to yield thioacetals [46] (see Chapter 17).

$$\xrightarrow{\text{CF}_3\text{CO}_2\text{H}} \quad \xrightarrow{\text{Et}_3\text{SiH}} \quad \xrightarrow[\text{Hg}^{++}]{\text{H}_2\text{O}} \quad \text{RCH}_2\text{-}\overset{\text{O}}{\overset{\|}{\text{C}}}\text{-H} \tag{6.22}$$

Ketene thioacetals can be metallated with *n*-butyl lithium to yield allylic carbanions [47, 48].

$$\xrightarrow{n\text{-BuLi}} \tag{6.23}$$

B. Vinyl Sulfoxides

Trimethylsilylmethyl phenyl sulfoxide can be metallated to yield 1-trimethyl-silyl-1-phenylsulfinylmethyl lithium which reacts with ketones or aldehydes to yield 1-phenylsulfinyl alkenes [49].

$$Ph_2C=O \ + \ (CH_3)_3Si\text{-}\overset{-}{C}H\text{-}\overset{\overset{\displaystyle O}{\|}}{S}\text{-}Ph \ \longrightarrow \ Ph_2C=C\overset{\overset{\displaystyle O}{\underset{\displaystyle S-Ph}{\|}}}{\underset{\displaystyle H}{}} \qquad (6.24)$$

The necessary sulfoxide was prepared by reaction of trimethylsilylmethyl magnesium chloride with methyl benzene sulfinate [50].

$$(CH_3)_3Si\text{-}CH_2\text{-}MgCl \ + \ Ph\text{-}\overset{\overset{\displaystyle O}{\|}}{S}\text{-}OCH_3 \ \longrightarrow \ Ph\text{-}\overset{\overset{\displaystyle O}{\|}}{S}\text{-}CH_2\text{-}Si(CH_3)_3 \qquad (6.25)$$

C. Thio Enol Ethers

Metallation of trimethylsilylmethyl methyl sulfide yields a carbanion which reacts with ketones or aldehydes to yield methyl vinyl sulfides [1, 3].

$$(CH_3)_3Si\text{-}CH_2\text{-}S\text{-}CH_3 \ \xrightarrow{n\text{-}BuLi} \ (CH_3)_3Si\text{-}\overset{-}{C}H\text{-}SCH_3 \ \xrightarrow[Ph_2C=O]{} \ Ph_2C=C\overset{SCH_3}{\underset{H}{}} \qquad (6.26)$$

Thio enol ethers can be hydrolyzed to ketones, albeit under vigorous conditions [51].

Phenylthio trimethylsilylmethyl lithium reacts with N,N-dialkyl benzamides to yield 2-phenylthio-1-dialkylamino alkenes [52]. This lithium reagent reacts with 2-cyclohexenone in THF to give the expected vinyl sulfide (Eq. 6.27). On the other hand, in HMPT or DME, 1,4-conjugate addition occurs (Eq. 6.28) [53].

$$(6.27)$$

$$(6.28)$$

D. Sulfines

The Peterson reaction has been used to prepare sulfines. α-Trimethylsilyl carbanions add to a S—O double bond of SO_2. Loss of trimethylsilanoate results in formation of a S—C double bond [54, 55].

$$(6.29)$$

N-Sulfinylamines have also been prepared by reaction of lithium N-aryl-N-trimethylsilylamides with SO_2 in THF [56].

$$(6.30)$$

E. Allenes

Allenes have also been prepared by the Peterson reaction. α-Bromotriphenyl-silylethylene undergoes halogen-metal exchange with n-butyl lithium to yield α-lithio-triphenylsilylethylene. This reacts with ketones and aldehydes to yield 2-triphenylsilyl substituted allylic alcohols. Unlike other β-hydroxyalkyl-silanes, these do not undergo facile elimination on treatment with either acid or base [57]. However, reaction of the alcohol with thionyl chloride gives an allylic chloride which loses the elements of triphenylchlorosilane when treated with tetraethylammonium fluoride in DMSO [58].

$$(6.31)$$

The driving force for this elimination is the formation of a strong Si—F bond. Similar results are obtained with α-lithio trimethylsilylethylene generated by halogen-metal exchange of α-bromo trimethylsilylethylene with t-butyl lithium at $-78°$ [59].

F. Vinyl Silanes (see Chapter 7)

Metallation of *tris*(trimethylsilyl)methane with methyl lithium yields a carbanion which reacts with formaldehyde to give 1,1-*bis*(trimethylsilyl)ethylene [19, 60].

$$[(CH_3)_3Si]_3C^-Li^+ \ + \ CH_2=O \ \longrightarrow [(CH_3)_3Si]_2C=CH_2 \qquad (6.32)$$

bis-(Trimethylsilyl)methyl sodium reacts with benzophenone to yield 1,1-diphenyl-2-trimethylsilyl ethylene [31].

One of the few cases where the Peterson reaction fails involves bromo-*bis*-(trimethylsilyl)methyl lithium. This reagent reacts normally with aldehydes to yield the expected α-bromo-trimethylsilylalkenes. However, it fails to add to enolizable ketones and reacts with benzophenone to give 1,1-*bis*-(trimethylsilyl)-2,2-diphenylethylene oxide [12].

$$(6.33)$$

G. Vinyl Boronic Esters

The Peterson reaction has been utilized to prepare vinyl boronic esters. Metallation of pinacol trimethylsilylmethane boronate with the sterically hindered base, lithium 2,2,6,6-tetramethylpiperidide, gives a carbanion which reacts with ketones or aldehydes to yield the desired pinacol alkenyl boronic esters [61].

$$(6.34)$$

H. Cross Aldol Reaction—α,β-Unsaturated Aldehydes

The formal "cross-aldol" coupling of two aldehydes, RCHO and $R'CH_2CHO$, to yield an α,β-unsaturated aldehyde $RCH=CR'-CHO$ has been achieved in several ways [62–64]. The Peterson reaction provides a general method to accomplish this transformation The necessary precursors, α-trimethylsilyl aldimines have been prepared by metallation of aldehyde-t-butylimines with LDA followed by addition of TMS-Cl.

$$CH_3CH_2-CH=N^{\diagup C(CH_3)_3} \xrightarrow[\text{2) } (CH_3)_3SiCl]{\text{1) LDA}} CH_3-\underset{\underset{Si(CH_3)_3}{|}}{CH}-CH=N^{\diagup C(CH_3)_3} \qquad (6.35)$$

Metallation of α-trimethylsilylaldehyde-t-butylimines with LDA occurs readily. This carbanion reacts with ketones or aldehydes to yield the desired α,β-unsaturated aldehydes after mild acidic hydrolysis of the t-butyl imine protecting group [65].

$$(6.36)$$

This methodology was recently utilized in Corey's synthesis of ($\pm$) N-methyl-maysenine [66, 67].

$$(6.37)$$

Metallation of 2-trimethylsilylmethyl-4,4,6-trimethyl-5,6-dihydro-1,3-oxazine with t-butyl lithium followed by reaction with ketones or aldehydes yields α,β-unsaturated oxazines [68]. These can be hydrolyzed to α,β-unsaturated aldehydes.

$$(6.38)$$

I. α,β-Unsaturated Carboxylic Acids

α,β-Unsaturated carboxylic acids can be prepared by reaction of the dianion of trimethylsilyl acetic acid with ketones or aldehydes [69].

$$(6.39)$$

J. α,β-Unsaturated Nitriles

α-Trimethylsilylnitriles have been prepared by [Ph$_3$P]$_3$RhCl catalyzed hydrosilation of α,β-unsaturated nitriles (Eq. 6.40) [28]. On the other hand, reaction of TMS-Cl with chloroacetonitrile and zinc in benzene/THF yields trimethylsilylacetonitrile (Eq. 6.41) [29].

$$(6.40)$$

$$(CH_3)_3SiCl \;+\; ClCH_2\text{-}CN \;\xrightarrow[C_6H_6/THF]{Zn}\; (CH_3)_3SiCH_2CN \qquad (6.41)$$

Deprotonation of these α-silylnitriles with LDA gives carbanions which react with both ketones and aldehydes to yield α,β-unsaturated nitriles.

$$(6.42)$$

K. α,β-Unsaturated Esters

The synthesis of α,β-unsaturated esters by the Peterson reaction requires α-trimethylsilyl esters as precursors. t-Butyl trimethylsilylacetate can be prepared by reaction of TMS-Cl with the lithium enolate of t-butyl acetate in THF at −78°C [70].

$$CH_3CO_2-t-Bu \quad + \quad \text{[cyclohexyl-N-isopropyl amide, Li}^+\text{]} \tag{6.43}$$

$$CH_2-CO_2-t-Bu \quad \xrightarrow{(CH_3)_3SiCl} \quad (CH_3)_3SiCH_2CO_2-t-Bu$$
$$Li^+$$

Ethyl trimethylsilylacetate has been prepared by a modified Reformatsky reaction of ethyl bromoacetate and TMS-Cl with zinc [71].

$$(CH_3)_3SiCl \quad + \quad BrCH_2-CO_2Et \quad \xrightarrow{Zn} \quad (CH_3)_3Si-CH_2-CO_2Et \tag{6.44}$$

Both t-butyl trimethylsilylacetate and ethyl trimethylsilylacetate are converted to α-trimethylsilyl lithium enolates by treatment at low temperature with LDA or lithium dicyclohexylamide. They react ketones or aldehydes to yield α,β-unsaturated esters [25–27, 72]. Lithio-t-butyl trimethylsilylacetate is quite stable.

$$(CH_3)_3SiCH_2CO_2Et \quad \xrightarrow{-78°} \quad (CH_3)_3SiCHCO_2Et$$
$$\text{[(cyclohexyl)}_2N^-Li^+\text{]} \qquad Li^+$$

$$\downarrow \text{[cyclohexanone, =O]}$$

$$\text{[cyclohexylidene]}\sim CO_2Et \tag{6.45}$$

LDA readily converts t-butyl *bis*(trimethylsilyl)acetate to an enolate which reacts with aldehydes but not ketones to yield α-trimethylsilyl-α,β-unsaturated esters. These are useful Michael acceptors [25].

$$
\text{Li}^+ \ ^- \underset{\underset{Si(CH_3)_3}{|}}{\overset{\overset{Si(CH_3)_3}{|}}{C}}\text{-CO}_2\text{-}t\text{-Bu} \quad + \quad CH_2{=}0 \tag{6.46}
$$

$$
H_2C{=}C\overset{Si(CH_3)_3}{\underset{CO_2\text{-}t\text{-Bu}}{}} \quad \xrightarrow[\text{2) } H_2O]{\text{1) } CH_3CH_2\text{-}\overset{\overset{Li^+}{|}\ \overset{O^-}{}}{C}{=}C\overset{H}{\underset{CH_3}{}}} \quad CH_3CH_2\text{-}\overset{O}{\overset{\|}{C}}\text{-}\underset{CH_3}{\overset{}{CH}}\text{-}CH_2\text{-}\overset{Si(CH_3)_3}{\underset{CO_2\text{-}t\text{-Bu}}{C}}\text{-H}
$$

t-Butyl trimethylsilylchloroacetate has been prepared by reaction of the lithium enolate of *t*-butyl chloroacetate with TMS-Cl. Deprotonation of this silyl reagent with LDA forms an ester enolate which reacts with ketones or aldehydes to yield α-chloro-α,β-unsaturated esters [24].

$$
Cl\text{-}\overset{\overset{Si(CH_3)_3}{|}}{\underset{CO_2\text{-}t\text{-Bu}}{C}} \quad + \quad (CH_3)_2CH\text{-}\overset{O}{\overset{\|}{C}}\text{-H} \quad \longrightarrow \quad (CH_3)_2CH\text{-}CH{=}C\overset{CO_2\text{-}t\text{-Bu}}{\underset{Cl}{}} \tag{6.47}
$$

L. α-Ylidene-γ-butyrolactones

α-Ylidene-γ-butyrolactones have been prepared by Peterson reaction of aldehydes with the enolate anion generated from α-trimethylsilyl γ-butyrolactones.

$$
\xrightarrow[\text{2) } CH_3\text{-}\overset{O}{\overset{\|}{C}}\text{-H}]{\text{1) } Ph_3C^-Li^+/THF} \tag{6.48}
$$

The necessary α-trimethylsilyl-γ-butyrolactones were prepared by reaction of epoxides with the dianion of trimethylsilyl acetic acid (Eq. 6.49) [69].

$$
(CH_3)_3Si\overset{-}{CH}\text{-}CO_2^- \quad + \quad \triangle\!\!\!\!\!\text{O} \tag{6.49}
$$

$$
(CH_3)_3Si\overset{CO_2^-}{\underset{O^-}{}} \quad \xrightarrow[\text{2) } TsOH/C_6H_6]{\text{1) } H_2O} \quad (CH_3)_3Si
$$

α-Ylidene-γ-lactones have also been prepared from γ-trimethylsilyloxy-propionitriles. These can be deprotonated with LDA to yield cyano-stabilized anions which react with aldehydes to give α-(1-hydroxyalkyl)-γ-trimethyl-silyloxy nitriles. These undergo acidic hydrolysis to α-(1-hydroxyalkyl)-γ-lactones which can be dehydrated to α-ylidene γ-lactones [92].

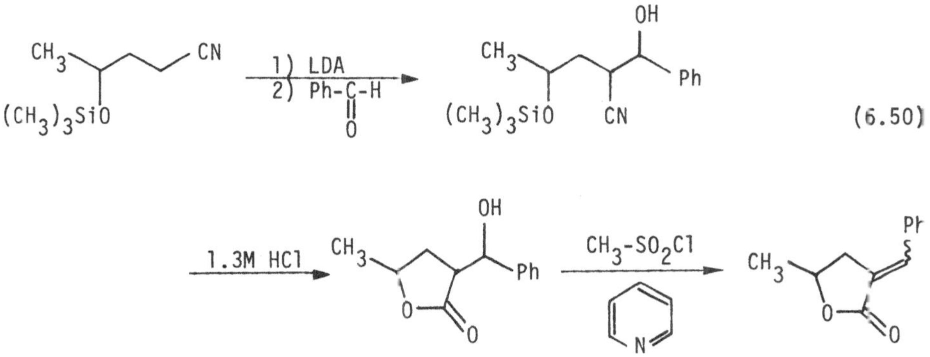

(6.50)

α-Lithio trimethylsilylacetonitrile reacts with epoxides to produce γ-trimethylsilyloxy propionitriles via a 1,4-shift of the trimethylsilyl group from carbon to the alkoxide oxygen [91].

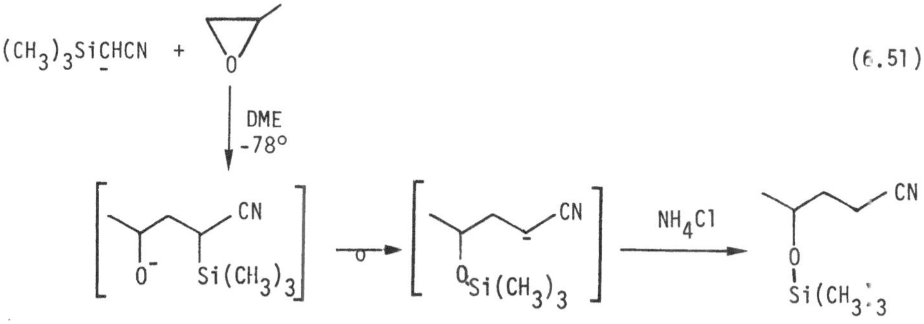

(6.51)

M. Silyl Reformatsky Reaction

The Peterson reaction is not catalytic in base but rather requires one equivalent of α-silyl carbanion. In the presence of a catalytic amount of sodium hydroxide at 160–180°, ethyl trimethylsilylacetate reacts with aromatic alde-hydes to yield ethyl β-aryl β-trimethylsilyloxy propionates (Eq. 6.52) [90].

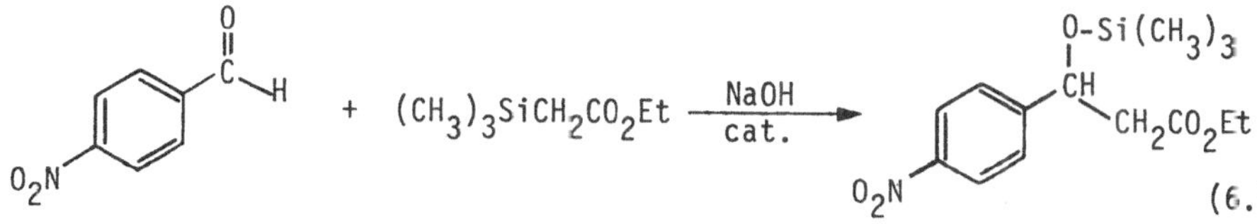

(6.52)

Likewise, trimethylsilylacetonitrile reacts with aromatic aldehydes in the presence of a catalytic amount of sodium hydroxide at 160–180° to give β-aryl-β-trimethylsilyloxy-propionitrile [90].

$$(CH_3)_3SiCH_2-CN \xrightleftharpoons{\text{cat. NaOH}} (CH_3)_3SiOH + \overset{-}{C}H_2-CN \qquad (6.53)$$

N. α,β-Unsaturated Thiol Esters

Deprotonation of *t*-butyl α-trimethylsilylthioacetate with LDA yields an ester enolate which reacts with both ketones and aldehydes to give α,β-unsaturated thio esters [73].

$$(6.54)$$

O. α,β-Unsaturated Amides

N-Phenyl-3-alkylidene azetidin-2-ones have been prepared by the Peterson reaction [74].

$$(6.55)$$

P. Imines

The reaction of the sodium salt of hexamethyldisilazane with non-enolizable ketones yields N-trimethylsilyl imines [75].

$$(6.56)$$

6.5 Related Reactions

There are several related reactions which involve formation of either β-hydroxyalkyltrimethylsilanes or β-trimethylsilyl alkoxide intermediates by alternative routes. For example, Hudrlik found that β-hydroxyalkyltrimethylsilanes can be prepared regio- and stereospecifically by the reaction of dialkyl cuprates with α-trimethylsilyl epoxides (see Chapter 7). Nucleophilic attack by dialkyl cuprates occurs on the backside of the carbon atom of the epoxide which bears the trimethylsilyl group and results in opening the epoxide ring.

$$(CH_3)_3Si \overset{}{\underset{O}{\triangle}} + (n\text{-Bu})_2Cu^- Li^+ \longrightarrow \underset{n\text{-Bu}}{\overset{(CH_3)_3Si}{\diagdown}}CH\text{-}CH_2OH \qquad (6.57)$$

Di-*n*-propyl copper lithium reacts with *cis*-1-trimethylsilylpentene oxide to yield *erythro*-5-trimethylsilyloctan-4-ol and with *trans*-1-trimethylsilylpentene oxide to yield *threo*-5-trimethylsilyloctan-4-ol. Both of these diastereomeric β-hydroxyalkyltrimethylsilanes can be converted to either *cis* or *trans*-4-octene by the appropriate choice of conditions for the elimination step [76].

(6.58)

The addition of Grignard or organolithium reagents to β-ketosilanes, also yields β-hydroxyalkyltrimethylsilanes [77].

$$(CH_3)_3SiCH_2-\overset{\overset{\displaystyle O}{\|}}{C}-CH_3$$

n-Pentyl-MgBr

$$(CH_3)_3SiCH_2\underset{HO}{\overset{(CH_2)_4CH_3}{\diagup}}\underset{CH_3}{\overset{}{\diagdown}} \quad \xrightarrow[NaOAc]{HOAc} \quad CH_2\!\!=\!\!\overset{(CH_2)_4CH_3}{\underset{CH_3}{\diagup}} \qquad (6.59)$$

Organolithium reagents add to β-keto silanes, such as 5-trimethylsilyldecan-4-one, to yield β-hydroxysilanes with high stereoselectivity as predicted by Cram's rule. These undergo *syn* elimination on treatment with potassium *t*-butoxide to yield tri-substituted alkenes of predominantly *E*-configuration whereas treatment with glacial acetic acid leads to alkenes of predominantly *Z* configuration via *trans* elimination [78, 79]. The necessary β-keto silanes are easily prepared by treatment of 2-trimethylsilyl-2,3-dialkyl oxiranes with HI followed by reaction of the iodohydrins with one equivalent of methyl lithium in ether [79] or *n*-butyllithium in hexane/ether [80].

$$CH_3(CH_2)_5\underset{}{\overset{H}{\diagup}}\!\!=\!\!\underset{(CH_2)_5CH_3}{\overset{Si(CH_3)_3}{\diagdown}} \quad \xrightarrow{MCPBA} \quad CH_3(CH_2)_5\underset{O}{\overset{H}{\diagup}\diagdown}(CH_2)_5CH_3^{Si(CH_3)_3}$$

$$\text{HI} \downarrow \qquad (6.60)$$

$$CH_3(CH_2)_5-\overset{\overset{\displaystyle O}{\|}}{C}-\underset{Si(CH_3)_3}{\overset{}{C}}H(CH_2)_5CH_3 \quad \xleftarrow{CH_3Li} \quad CH_3(CH_2)_5\underset{OH}{\overset{H}{\diagup}}\underset{(CH_2)_5CH_3}{\overset{I}{\diagdown}}{Si(CH_3)_3}$$

α-Trimethylsilyl epoxides react with Grignard reagents to yield β-hydroxyalkylsilanes. This reaction proceeds by initial rearrangement of the α-trimethylsilyl epoxides under the influence of magnesium bromide to α-bromo-β-hydroxysilanes which react with additional magnesium bromide to give β-silyl aldehydes or ketones [81]. α-Trimethylsilyl epoxides also rearrange to β-keto silanes on treatment with magnesium iodide [82, 93].

$$CH_3(CH_2)_2\underset{O}{\overset{H}{\diagup}\diagdown}(CH_2)_4CH_3^{Si(CH_3)_3} \quad \xrightarrow[Et_2O]{MgI_2} \quad CH_3(CH_2)_2-\overset{\overset{\displaystyle O}{\|}}{C}-\underset{Si(CH_3)_3}{\overset{}{C}}H(CH_2)_4CH_3 \qquad (6.61)$$

β-Silyl aldehydes react stereoselectively with Grignard reagents to yield β-hydroxyalkyl silanes [83]. The stereoselectivity of this addition is predicted by Cram's Rule. 2-Trimethylsilyl-1-pentene oxide reacts with *n*-propyl magnesium bromide to yield a β-hydroxyalkylsilane which undergoes a *syn* elimination on treatment with potassium hydride to yield *cis*-4-octene or *trans* elimination on treatment with $BF_3 \cdot Et_2O$ to yield *trans*-4-octene [83].

$$(5.62)$$

Dervan found that trimethylsilyl potassium would react with epoxides in a stereospecific manner to yield olefins of inverted geometry. For example, *trans*-3-hexene oxide reacts with trimethylsilyl potassium to yield *cis*-3-hexene. This result was explained as follows. Backside nucleophilic attack by trimethylsilyl potassium on the epoxide yields a β-trimethylsilyl alkoxide. This must rotate about the 3,4 C–C single bond by 180° in order to achieve the necessary geometry for *syn* elimination of potassium trimethylsilanoate [84].

$$(6.63)$$

The required trimethylsilyl potassium can be prepared by reaction of hexamethyldisilane with potassium methoxide in HMPT or THF/18-C-6 [85–87].

$$(CH_3)_3SiSi(CH_3)_3 \xrightarrow[THF/18\text{-}C\text{-}6]{K^+ \ ^-OCH_3} (CH_3)_3Si^-K^+ + (CH_3)_3SiOCH_3 \qquad (6.64)$$

Likewise, triethylsilyl potassium results from reaction of triethylsilane with potassium hydride in DME or HMPT [88].

$$Et_3SiH \xrightarrow[DME \ or \ HMPT]{KH} Et_3Si^- \ K^+ + H_2 \qquad (6.65)$$

The deoxygenation of epoxides on treatment with TMS-Cl and magnesium in HMPT may be related [89].

$$\xrightarrow[\substack{Mg/TiCl_4 \\ HMPT}]{(CH_3)_3SiCl} \qquad + \ (CH_3)_3SiOSi(CH_3)_3 \qquad (6.66)$$

References

1. Peterson, D.J.: J. Org. Chem. *33*, 780 (1968)
2. Gilman, H., Tomasi, R.A.: J. Org. Chem. *27*, 3647 (1962)
3. Carey, F.A., Court, A.S.: J. Org. Chem. *37*, 939 (1972)
4. Boeckman, Jr., R.K., Silver, S.M.: Tetrahedron Lett. 3497 (1973)
5. For a review see Peterson, D.J.: Organometal. Chem. Rev. *A, 7*, 295 (1972)
6. Peterson, D.J.: J. Organometal. Chem. *9*, 373 (1967)
7. Langer, Jr., A.W.: Trans. N.Y. Acad. Sci. *27*, 741 (1965)
8. Eberhardt, G.G., Butte, W.A.: J. Org. Chem. *29*, 2928 (1964)
9. Whitmore, F.C., Sommer, L.H., Gold, J., van Strien, R.E.: J. Am. Chem. Soc. *69*, 1551 (1947)
10. Hauser, C.R., Hance, C.R.: J. Am. Chem. Soc. *74*, 5091 (1952)
11. Brook, A.G., Duff, J.M., Anderson, D.G.: Can. J. Chem. *48*, 651 (1970)
12. Seyferth, D., Lefferts, J.L., Lambert, Jr., R.L.: J. Organometal. Chem. *142*, 39 (1977)
13. Cook, M.A., Eaborn, C., Jukes, A.E., Walton, D.R.M.: J. Organometal. Chem. *24*, 529 (1970)
14. Cason, L.F., Brooks, H.G.: J. Am. Chem. Soc. *74*, 4582 (1952)
15. Cason, L.F., Brooks, H.G.: J. Org. Chem. *19*, 1278 (1954)
16. Mulvaney, J.E., Gardlund, Z.G.: J. Org. Chem. *30*, 917 (1965)
17. Hudrlik, P.F., Peterson, D.: Tetrahedron Lett. 1133 (1974)
18. Buell, G.R., Corriu, R., Guerin, C., Spialter, L.: J. Am. Chem. Soc. *92*, 7424 (1970)
19. Gröbel, B.T., Seebach, D.: Chem. Ber. *110*, 852 (1977)
20. Brooks, A.G., Duff, J.M., Anderson, D.G.: Can. J. Chem. *48*, 561 (1970)
21. Chan, T.H., Chang, E., Vinokur, E.: Tetrahedron Lett. 1137 (1970)
22. Konakahara, T., Takagi, Y.: Synthesis, 192 (1979)
23. Konakahara, T., Takagi, Y.: Tetrahedron Lett. 2073 (1980)
24. Chan, T.H., Moreland, M.: Tetrahedron Lett. 515 (1978)
25. Hartzell, S.L., Rathke, M.W.: Tetrahedron Lett. 2757 (1976)
26. Hartzell, S.L., Sullivan, D.F., Rathke, M.W.: Tetrahedron Lett. 1403 (1974)
27. Shimoji, E., Taguchi, H., Oshima, K., Yamamoto, H., Nozaki, H.: J. Am. Chem. Soc. *96*, 1620 (1974)
28. Ojima, I., Kumagai, M., Nagai, Y.: Tetrahedron Lett. 4005 (1974)

29. Matsuda, I., Murata, S., Ishii, Y.: J. Chem. Soc. Perkin I, 26 (1979)
30. Carey, F.A., Court, A.S.: J. Org. Chem. *37*, 1926 (1972)
31. Sakurai, H., Nishiwaki, K., Kira, M.: Tetrahedron Lett. 4193 (1973)
32. Ager, D.J.: Tetrahedron Lett. 2923 (1981)
33. Dumont, W., Krief, A.: Angew. Chem. Int. Ed. *15*, 161 (1976)
34. Hudrlik, P.F., Peterson, D.: Tetrahedron Lett. 1133 (1974)
35. Hudrlik, P.F., Peterson, D.: J. Am. Chem. Soc. *97*, 1464 (1975)
36. Cram, D.J., Abd. Elhafez, F.A.: J. Am. Chem. Soc. *74*, 5828 (1952)
37. Larsson, F.C.V., Lawesson, S.O.: Tetrahedron, *28*, 5341 (1972)
38. Dalgaard, L., Kolind-Andersen, H., Lawesson, S.O.: Tetrahedron, *29*, 2077 (1973)
39. Corey, E.J., Markl, G.: Tetrahedron Lett. 3201 (1967)
40. Seebach, D., Gröbel, B.T., Beck, A.K., Braum, M., Geiss, K.H.: Angew. Chem. Int. Ed. *11*, 433 (1972)
41. Seebach, D., Kolb, M., Gröbel, B.T.: Chem. Ber. *106*, 2277 (1973)
42. Brook, A.G., Duff, J.M., James, P.F., Davis, N.R.: J. Am. Chem. Soc. *89*, 431 (1967)
43. Corey, E.J., Seebach, D., Freedman, R.: J. Am. Chem. Soc. *89*, 434 (1967)
44. Jones, P.F., Lappert, M.F.: J. Chem. Soc. Chem. Commun. 526 (1972)
45. Jones, P.F., Lappert, M.F., Szary, A.C.: J. Chem. Soc. Perkin I, 2272 (1973)
46. Carey, F.A., Neergaard, J.R.: J. Org. Chem. *36*, 2731 (1971)
47. Seebach, D.: Synthesis, 17 (1969)
48. Coffen, D.L., McEntee, Jr., T.E. Williams, D.R.: J. Chem. Soc. Chem. Commun. 913 (1970)
49. Carey, F.A., Hernandez, O.: J. Org. Chem. *38*, 2670 (1973)
50. Brook, A.G., Anderson, D.G.: Can. J. Chem. *46*, 2115 (1968)
51. Seebach, D., Bürstinghaus, R., Gröbel, B.T., Kolb, M.: Liebigs Ann., 830 (1977)
52. Agawa, T., Ishikawa, M., Komatsu, M., Ohshiro, Y.: Chem. Lett. 335 (1980)
53. Ager, D.J.: Tetrahedron Lett. 2803 (1981)
54. van der Leij, M., Porskamp, P.A.T., Lammerink, B.G.M., Zwanenburg, B.: Tetrahedron Lett. 811 (1978)
55. van der Leij, M., Zwanenburg, B.: Tetrahedron Lett. 3383 (1978)
56. Porskamp, P.A.T.W., Zwanenburg, B.: Synthesis, 368 (1981)
57. For a review of such elimination reactions see: Jarvie, A.W.P.: Organometal. Chem. Rev. *A*, *6*, 153 (1970)
58. Chan, T.H., Mychajlowskij, W.: Tetrahedron Lett. 171 (1974)
59. Chan, T.H., Mychajlowskij, W., Ong, B.S., Harpp, D.N.: J. Org. Chem. *43*, 1526 (1978)
60. Gröbel, B.T., Seebach, D.: Angew. Chem. Int. Ed. *13*, 83 (1974)
61. Matteson, D.S., Majumdar, D.: J. Chem. Soc. Chem. Commun. 39 (1980)
62. Wittig, G., Reiff, H.: Angew. Chem. Int. Ed. *7*, 7 (1968)
63. Trippett, S., Walker, D.M.: J. Chem. Soc. 2130 (1961)
64. Cresp, T.M., Sargent, M.J., Vogel, P.: J. Chem. Soc. Perkin *I*, 37 (1974)
65. Corey, E.J., Enders, D., Bock, M.G.: Tetrahedron Lett. 7 (1976)
66. Corey, E.J., Weigel, L.O., Floyd, D., Bock, M.G.: J. Am. Chem. Soc. *100*, 2916 (1978)
67. Corey, E.J., Weigel, L.O., Chamberlain, R.A., Lipshutz, B.: J. Am. Chem. Soc. *102*, 1439 (1980)
68. Sachdev, K.: Tetrahedron Lett. 4041 (1976)
69. Grieco, P.A., Wang, C.L.J., Burke, S.D.: J. Chem. Soc. Chem. Commun. 537 (1975)
70. Rathke, M.W., Sullivan, D.F.: Syn. Commun. *3*, 67 (1973)

71. Fessenden, R.J., Fessenden, J.S.: J. Org. Chem. *32*, 3535 (1967)
72. Taguchi, T., Shimoji, K., Yamamoto, Y.Y., Nozaki, H.: Bull. Soc. Chem. Japan, *47*, 2529 (1974)
73. Lucast, D.H., Wemple, J.: Tetrahedron Lett. 1103 (1977)
74. Kano, S., Ebata, T., Funaki, K., Shibuya, S.: Synthesis, 746 (1978)
75. Krüger, C., Rochow, E.G., Wannagat, U.: Chem. Ber. *96*, 2132 (1963)
76. Hudrlik, P.F., Peterson, D., Rona, R.J.: J. Org. Chem. *40*, 2263 (1975)
77. Hudrlik, P.F., Peterson, D.: Tetrahedron Lett. 1785 (1972)
78. Utimoto, K., Obayashi, M., Nozaki, H.: J. Org. Chem. *41*, 2940 (1976)
79. Obayashi, M., Utimoto, K., Nozaki, H.: Bull. Chem. Soc. Japan, *52*, 1760 (1979)
80. Obayashi, M., Utimoto, K., Nozaki, H.: Tetrahedron Lett. 1383 (1978)
81. Hudrlik, P.F., Misra, R.N., Withers, G.P., Hudrlik, A.M., Rona, R.J., Arcoleo, J.P.: Tetrahedron Lett. 1453 (1976)
82. Obayashi, M., Utimoto, K., Nozaki, H.: Tetrahedron Lett. 1807 (1977)
83. Hudrlik, P.F., Hudrlik, A.M., Misra, R.N., Peterson, D., Withers, G.P., Kulkarni, A.K.: J. Org. Chem. *45*, 4444 (1980)
84. Dervan, P.B., Shippey, M.A.: J. Am. Chem. Soc. *98*, 1265 (1976)
85. Sakurai, H., Okada, A., Kira, M., Yonezawa, K.: Tetrahedron Lett. 1511 (1971)
86. Sakurai, H., Okada, A.: J. Organometal. Chem. *35*, C13 (1972)
87. Sakurai, H., Kondo, F.: J. Organometal. Chem. *92*, C46 (1975)
88. Corriu, J.R.P., Guerin, C.: J. Chem. Soc. Chem. Commun. 168 (1980)
89. Dunoguès, J., Calas, R., Duffant, N., Picard, J.P.: J. Organometal. Chem. *26*, C13 (1971)
90. Birkofer, L., Ritter, A., Wieden, H.: Chem. Ber. *95*, 971 (1962)
91. Matsuda, I., Murata, S., Ishii, Y.: J. Chem. Soc. Perkin *I*, 26 (1979)
92. Matsuda, I., Murata, S., Izumi, Y.: Bull. Chem. Soc. Japan, *52*, 2389 (1979)
93. Obayashi, M., Utimoto, K., Nozaki, H.: Bull. Chem. Soc. Japan, *52*, 2646 (1979)

7 Vinyl Silanes

7.1 Introduction

The material of this chapter has been divided into seven parts. The first six are concerned with synthetically useful reactions of β-halosilanes, vinyl silanes, and α-silyl epoxides. The seventh deals with the preparation of vinyl silanes.

First will be elimination reactions of β-halosilanes. Second will be electrophilic substitution reactions of vinyl silanes and α-silyl epoxides. This often results in regio- and stereospecific formation of substituted alkenes. These reactions frequently proceed by electrophilic addition to the vinylsilane to yield a β-halosilane followed by loss of the elements of trimethylhalosilane (TMS-X) from the intermediate β-halosilane. Third will be regiospecific addition of carbanions to the C−C double bond of vinyl silanes to yield α-silyl carbanions. Touched on fourth will be vinyl silanes as masked carbonyl compounds. Fifth will be the 1,2-transposition of carbonyl groups and six cycloaddition reactions of vinyl silanes.

7.2 Elimination of Trimethylhalosilanes from β-Halosilanes

β-Halosilanes, such as β-bromoethyltrimethylsilane, undergo facile Sn1 solvolysis to yield alkenes with loss of the elements of TMS-X [1]. This may result from the stabilization of the developing primary carbocation by hyperconjugation with the C−Si sigma bond [2] or by bridging of the trimethylsilyl group.

$$(7.0)$$

This latter hypothesis [3] is supported by the fact that 2-trimethylsilylethanol 1,1-d$_2$ reacts with phosphorous tribromide to yield 2-bromoethyltrimethylsilane in which the deuterium is scrambled.

$$(7.1)$$

This elimination reaction of β-halosilanes has been exploited synthetically. Thus β-trimethylsilyl ketones can be converted to α,β-unsaturated ketones by α-bromination followed by loss of TMS-Br [4–6]. The loss of TMS-Br may be accelerated by fluoride ion attack on the silyl center.

$$(7.2)$$

β-Trimethylsilyl ketones can be prepared by C-alkylation of the enolate anions of β-keto-esters with iodomethyltrimethylsilane in HMPT.

$$(7.3)$$

Alternatively, β-phenyldimethylsilyl ketones can be prepared by the conjugate addition of phenyldimethylsilyl lithium [7] to α,β-unsaturated ketones under the influence of cuprous iodide [8].

$$(7.4)$$

This stabilizing effect of trimethylsilyl groups on a β-carbocation has been utilized to direct carbocation rearrangements. Treatment of 3-trimethylsilyl-2-phenylthio substituted alcohols with acid leads to specific allylic phenyl sulfides. The trimethylsilyl group encourages the migration of the phenylthio group to the initial carbocation center to form a new carbocation located *beta* to the trimethylsilyl group. Nucleophilic attack on the silyl center leads to regiospecific C–C double bond formation [9, 10].

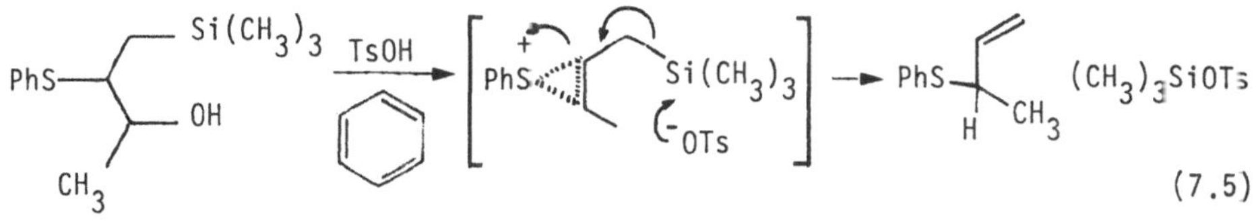

$$\text{[Scheme for equation 7.5]}$$

(7.5)

Likewise, 3-trimethylsilyl substituted undergo tertiary alcohols acid catalyzed rearrangement and loss of trimethylsilanol to yield particular alkenes [11].

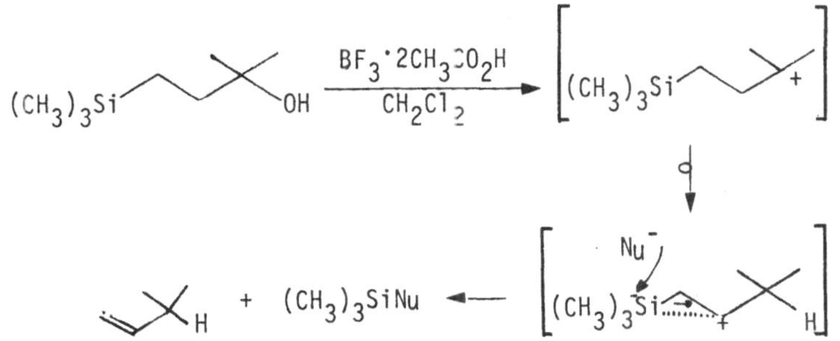

$$\text{[Scheme for equation 7.6]}$$

(7.6)

7.3 Stereospecificity of Elimination

Synthetic chemists were intrigued by the report that E-propenyltrimethylsilane reacts with bromine to yield a single diastereomeric dibromide which then undergoes solvolysis with loss of TMS-Br to yield predominantly Z-bromopropene. These results could be accounted for by a *trans*-addition of bromine to E-propenyltrimethylsilane to yield *erythro*-1,2-dibromopropyltrimethylsilane followed by *trans*-elimination of TMS-Br. The trimethylsilyl group must be *trans* coplanar to the bromide which is lost in order to stabilize the incipient primary carbocation. This causes stereospecific *trans*-elimination. Nucleophilic attack by solvent on the bridging trimethylsilyl group leads to products [3].

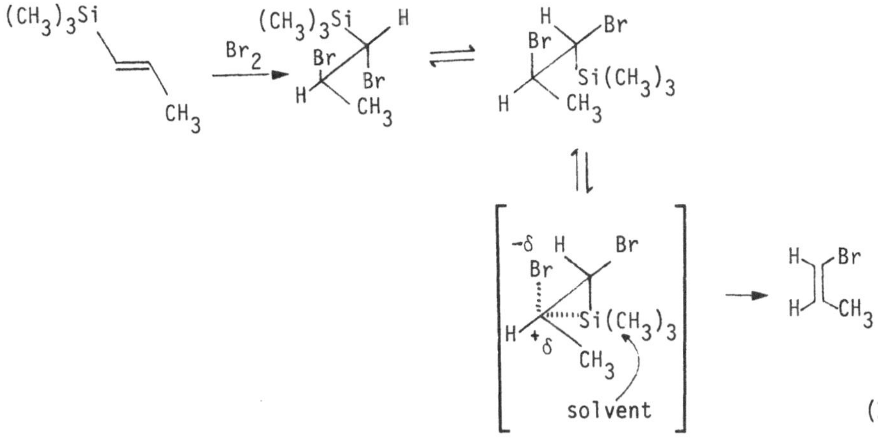

$$\text{[Scheme for equation 7.7]}$$

(7.7)

6-Substituted-1-trimethylsilyl cyclohexenes have been prepared by addition of iodine electrophiles (IN$_3$) to 1-trimethylsilylcyclohexene followed by dehydrohalogenation of the initial adducts with DBU in benzene. The success of the reaction is dependent on the inability of the trimethylsilyl to achieve a *trans* coplanar orientation with the adjacent azide group [12].

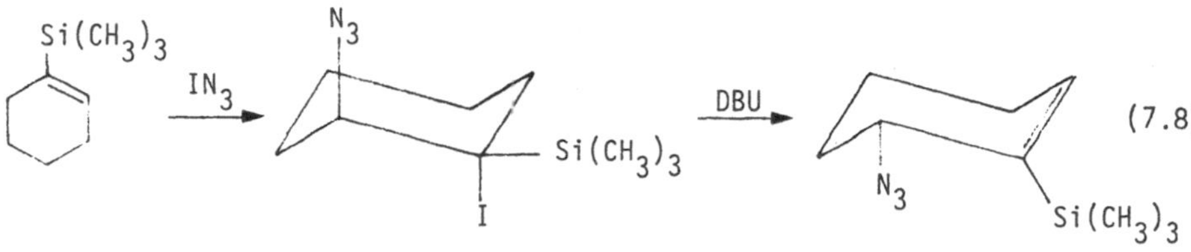

(7.8)

7.4 Electrophilic Substitution Reactions

A. Halogens

Stereospecific *trans* addition of electrophiles to vinyl silanes followed by *trans* elimination of the elements of TMS-X permits the stereospecific preparation of a variety of substituted alkenes. Z-1-trimethylsilyl hexene reacts with either chlorine or bromine at −78 °C to yield the respective *threo*-1-trimethylsilyl-1,2-dihalohexanes. These undergo *trans* elimination of the elements of TMS-X on treatment with sodium methoxide in methanol, potassium fluoride dihydrate in DMSO or alumina in pentane to yield E-1-bromohexene or E-1-chlorohexene. Lower stereoselectivity is observed with alumina. Likewise, E-1-trimethylsilyl hexene reacts with chlorine or bromine to yield the respective *erythro*-1-trimethylsilyl-1,2-dihalohexanes which undergo elimination under comparable conditions to yield Z-1-bromohexene or Z-1-chlorohexene [13, 15].

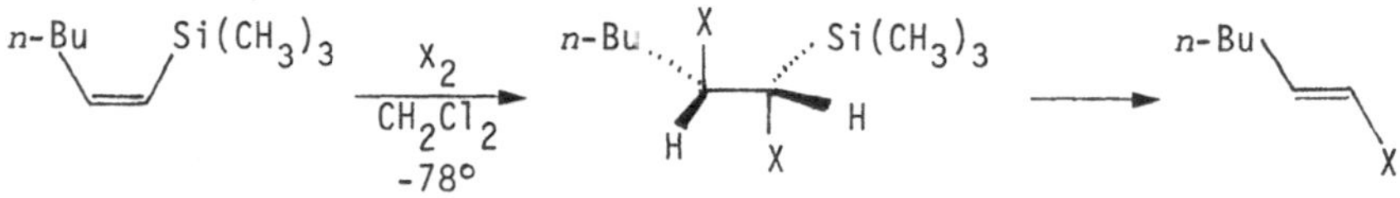

(7.9)

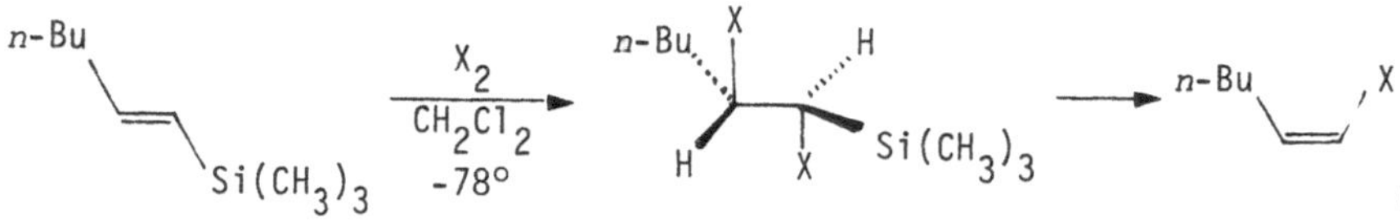

(7.10)

Similar stereospecificity has been observed with Z- and E-2-cyclohexyl-1-trimethylsilylethylene. Lower stereospecificity is observed with Z-2-t-butyl-1-trimethylsilylethylene.

E-1,2-*bis*(trimethylsilyl)ethylene also reacts with chlorine or bromine to yield *meso*-1,2-dihalo-1,2-*bis*(trimethylsilyl)ethanes. These undergo elimination of the elements of TMS-X on treatment with potassium fluoride in

DMSO to yield Z-1-chloro-2-trimethylsilylethylene or Z-1-bromo-2-trimethyl-silylethylene, respectively [16].

$$(7.11)$$

Trisubstituted alkenes have also been prepared in this manner. For example, Z-2-cyclohexyl-1-ethyl-1-trimethylsilylethylene reacts with bromine to yield a dibromide which loses TMS-Br in acetonitrile to give E-1-bromo-2-cyclo-hexyl-1-ethyl ethylene. Likewise, E-2-cyclohexyl-1-ethyl-1-trimethylsilyl ethy-lene reacts with bromine to yield Z-1-bromo-2-cyclohexyl-1-ethyl ethylene [17]. Similar results have been obtained with E- and Z-2-n-butyl-1-methyl-1-trimethylsilylethylene [18].

The reaction of iodine with vinyl trimethylsilanes followed by elimination of TMS-I to yield vinyl iodides is more complex. For example, E-1,2-bis(tri-methylsilyl)ethylene reacts with iodine in CCl_4 to give equal amounts of Z- and E-1-iodo-2-trimethylsilylethylene [16]. On the other hand, Z-1-trimethylsilyl-hexene reacts with iodine in methylene chloride to yield Z-1-iodohexene [14]. The stereoselectivity of this reaction can be controlled by the use of silver trifluoroacetate and iodine followed by elimination with potassium fluoride in DMSO. Under these conditions Z-1-trimethylsilylhexene yields E-1-iodo-hexene. However, iodine monochloride has proved more effective. E-1-Trimethylsilylhexene reacts with iodine monochloride in CCl_4 at 0° to give an adduct which loses the elements of TMS-Cl on treatment with potassium fluoride in DMSO to yield almost pure Z-1-iodohexene. While Z-1-trimethyl-silylhexene reacts with iodine monochloride to give predominantly E-1-iodo-hexene [19, 20].

$$(7.12)$$

$$(7.13)$$

B. Reactions of α-Trimethylsilyl Epoxides with Electrophiles

α-Trimethylsilyl epoxides undergo acid catalyzed opening of the epoxide with simultaneous nucleophilic attack on the carbon bearing the trimethylsilyl group. For example, treatment of 1-trimethylsilylcyclohexene oxide with aq. acid leads to 1-trimethylsilyl-*trans*-1,2-cyclohexanediol. This α,β-dihydroxy-alkyl trimethylsilane does not undergo acid catalyzed loss of trimethylsilanol since the trimethylsilyl group and the adjacent β-hydroxyl group cannot achieve a *trans*-coplanar arrangement [21].

$$(7.14)$$

On the other hand, mild acid catalyzed hydrolysis of 2-trimethylsilyl-1,2-octene oxide yields 2-trimethylsilyl-1,2-octanediol. Treatment with stronger mineral acids results in elimination of trimethylsilanol and formation of 2-octanone [22].

$$(7.15)$$

α-Trimethylsilyl epoxides also undergo acid catalyzed ring opening on treatment with HBr in ethyl ether to yield α-bromo-β-hydroxyalkyl trimethyl-silanes. These *trans*-bromohydrins undergo loss of trimethylsilanol on treatment with $BF_3 \cdot OEt_2$ in methylene chloride. Thus Z-1-trimethylsilylpentene oxide reacts with HBr to give a bromohydrin which reacts with $BF_3 \cdot OEt_2$ to yield E-1-bromopentene. A similar reaction sequence starting with E-1-tri-methylsilylpentene oxide gives Z-1-bromopentene [23].

$$(7.17)$$

The stereospecific formation of enol acetates occurs when α-trimethylsilyl epoxides are treated sequentially with acetic acid and then a catalytic amount of $BF_3 \cdot OEt_2$. Reaction of α-trimethylsilyl epoxides with methanol under acidic conditions permits the stereospecific preparation of methyl enol ethers [23].

C. β-Silyl Styrenes

trans-Addition of electrophiles to vinyl trimethylsilanes followed by *trans* elimination of TMS-X fails to account for the stereochemistry observed on reaction of Z and E-β-trimethylsilylstyrene with bromine. E and Z-β-trimethylsilylstyrene react with bromine to yield dibromo adducts. Subsequent addition of acetonitrile leads to stereospecific elimination of TMS-Br. Z-β-Bromostyrene from the dibromo adduct of results Z-β-trimethylsilylstyrene. Similarly the dibromo adduct of E-β-trimethylsilylstyrene gives E-β-bromostyrene [24]. This retention of stereochemistry may result from *cis* addition of bromine followed by a *trans* elimination of the elements of TMS-Br.

$$(7.18)$$

Similar results were obtained with Z and E-β-triphenylsilylstyrene. Evidence for *cis* addition of bromine to E-β-triphenylsilylstyrene was obtained by X-ray crystallography [25].

D. Protodesilylation of Vinyl Silanes

Vinyl silanes undergo protodesilylation on treatment with acids. In those cases where stereochemistry can be determined, substitution of the trimethylsilyl group by a proton occurs with retention. For example, Z and E-β-trimethylsilylstyrene react with DCl or DBr in dry acetonitrile to yield Z-β-deuteriostyrene and E-β-deuteriostyrene, [26] respectively. This may result from protonation of the double bond and simultaneous rotation about the developing C−C single bond in a direction which permits the trimethylsilyl group to continuously stabilize the incipient benzylic carbocation center [2, 27, 28]. Attack by the nucleophilic anion then occurs on silicon to yield products.

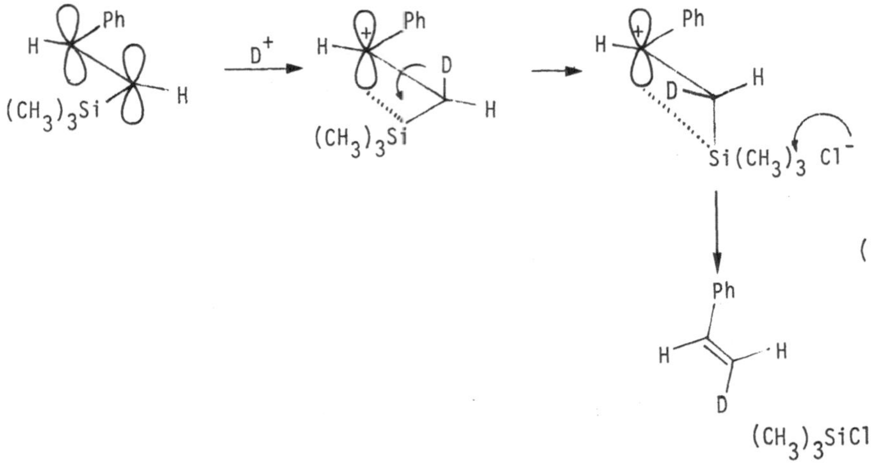

(7.19)

Similar results have been observed in the protodesilylation of E-7-trimethyl-silyl-7-tetradecene with HI [29].

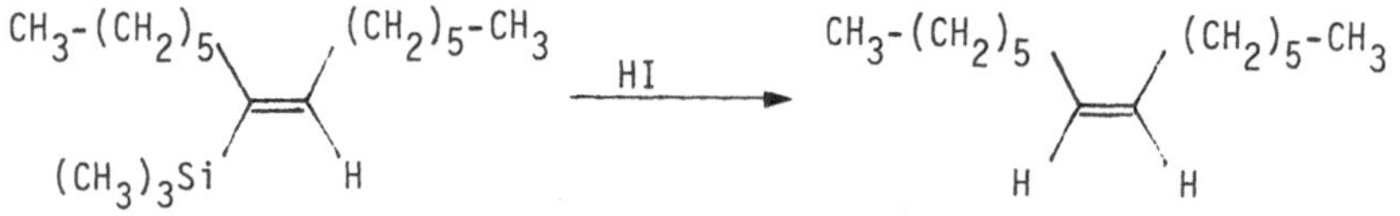

(7.20)

The selective protodesilylation of the terminal trimethylsilyl group of E-1,2-*bis*(trimethylsilyl)-1-octene with acetic acid-O-d$_1$ also proceeds with retention [30].

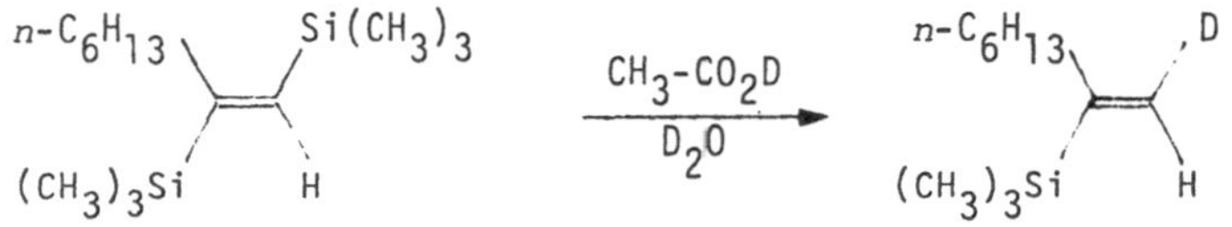

(7.21)

p-Toluenesulfonic acid is also effective for protodesilylation of vinyl silanes [31].

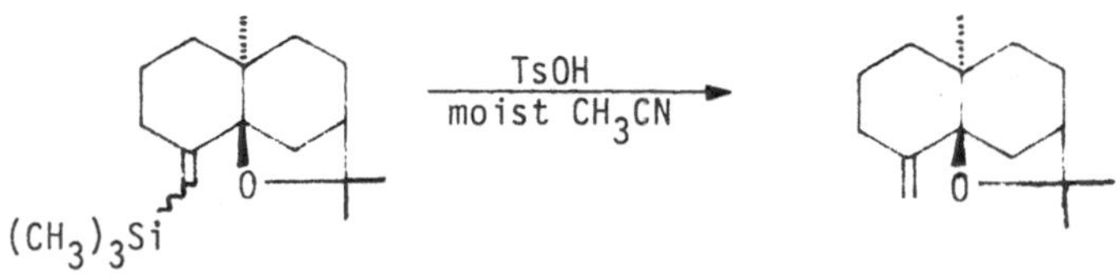

(7.22)

E. Friedel-Crafts Acylation Reactions

Vinyltrimethylsilanes also undergo Friedel-Crafts acylation reactions in which an acyl group replaces the trimethylsilyl group [32].

$$(CH_3)_3Si \quad \xrightarrow[\substack{AlCl_3 \\ -5^\circ}]{\underset{CH_3-\overset{\text{O}}{\overset{\|}{C}}-Cl}{}} \quad (CH_3)_3Si \qquad (7.23)$$

Friedel-Crafts acylation of cyclohexenyl-1-trimethylsilanes provides an efficient synthesis of 1-acetyl cyclohexenes [33–34].

$$(7.24)$$

Similar reactions of β-trimethylsilylstyrene with either benzoyl chloride or phenylacetyl chloride have been carried out. These electrophilic substitutions proceed with retention [17].

$$(7.25)$$

Friedel-Crafts acylation/desilylation of vinyl silanes is also successful with α,β-unsaturated acid chlorides [35]. This procedure has been combined with the termally allowed acid catalyzed cyclization of penta-1,4-dien-3-ones to yield cyclopentenones [36–38].

$$(7.26)$$

Vinyltrimethylsilane has been used as an ethylene equivalent in Nazarov-type reactions [39]. Thus, α,β-unsaturated carboxylic acid chlorides undergo Friedel-Crafts acylation/desilylation with vinyltrimethylsilane in the presence of SnCl₄ to yield cyclopentenones directly [40, 41].

$$(7.27)$$

F. Friedel-Crafts Alkylation

Chloromethyl methyl ether reacts with vinyltrimethylsilane and $AlCl_3$ to give allyl methyl ether.

$$(7.28)$$

α,α-Dichloromethyl methyl ether reacts with E-1,2-*bis*(trimethylsilyl)-ethylene to yield β-trimethylsilylacrolein [35]. This reaction permits the synthesis of α,β-unsaturated aldehydes from vinyl silanes. Unfortunately, this electrophilic substitution is *not* stereospecific [17].

$$(7.29)$$

Yields in this reaction are greatly improved if $TiCl_4$ is utilized in place of $AlCl_3$ [42]. This methodology has been used in an efficient synthesis of Nuciferal [43].

$$(7.30)$$

Intramolecular reaction of iminium ions with vinylsilanes provides a new method for forming unsaturated nitrogen heterocycles [143]. This electrophilic substitution proceeds with retention of the stereochemistry of the vinylsilane.

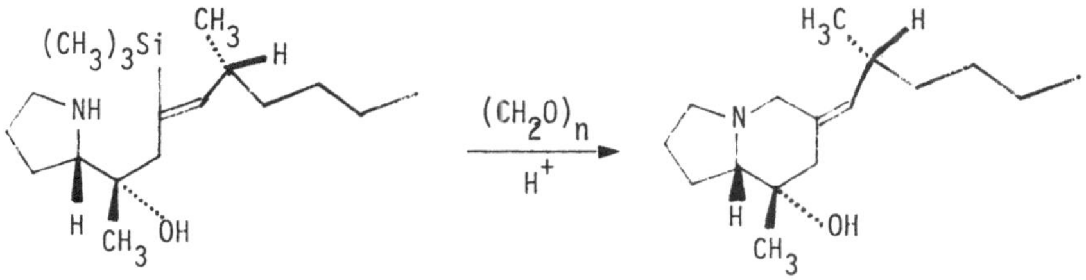

(7.31)

G. Sulfenyl Halides

Aryl sulfenyl halides add to vinyltrimethylsilane to give adducts. These undergo elimination of the elements of TMS-X on treatment with potassium fluoride dihydrate in DMSO to yield aryl vinyl sulfides [41]. On the other hand, treatment of these adducts with the tertiary amine bases such as DBU or DBN leads to 1-arylthio-1-trimethylsilylethylenes [41].

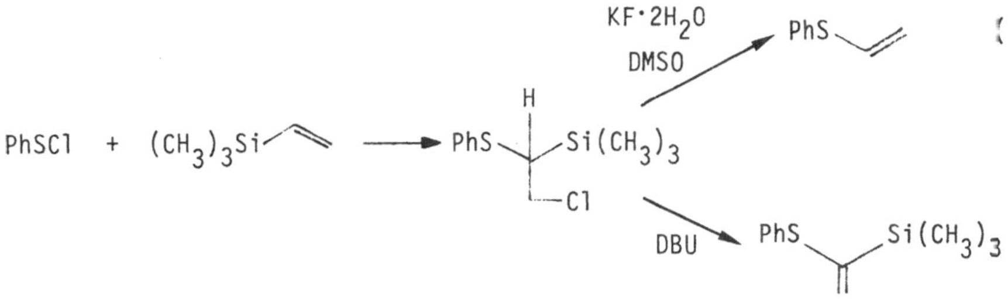

(7.32)

(7.33)

H. Palladium Chloride

E-β-Trimethylsilylstyrene undergoes reaction with palladium chloride in methanol to yield E,E-1,4-diphenylbutadiene. This reaction may involve E-β-palladiostyrene as a reactive intermediate (Eq. 7.34) [44].

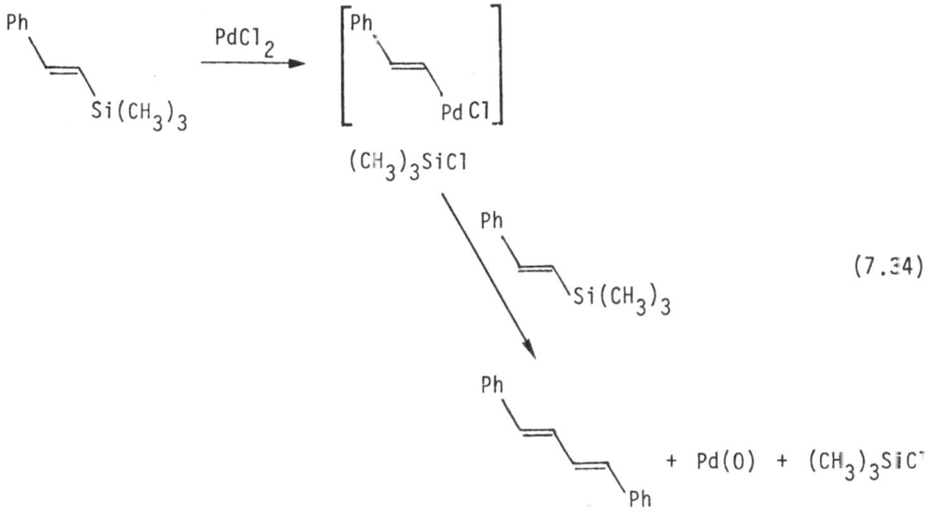

(7.34)

7.5 Addition of Carbanions to Vinyl Silanes

Many examples of the addition of organometallics to vinyl silanes were considered in Chapter Six. Silyl groups not only stabilize adjacent carbanions but may prevent undesired reactions. For example, treatment of phenyl β-styrenyl sulphone with n-butyl lithium does not result in addition to the C–C double bond to yield a sulphone stabilized carbanion, but rather in abstraction of the vinyl hydrogen adjacent to the sulphone group [45].

$$(7.35)$$

This problem can be solved by use of a trimethylsilyl protecting group. Reaction of phenyl α-trimethylsilylvinyl sulphones with methyl or n-butyl lithium results in addition of the alkyl lithium and formation of a carbanion stabilized by both the adjacent phenyl sulphone and trimethylsilyl groups. After protonation, the trimethylsilyl group can be removed by treatment with potassium fluoride [46].

$$(7.36)$$

Such phenyl α-trimethylsilylvinyl sulphones have been prepared by the Peterson reaction [46, 47].

Regiospecific addition of enolate anions to methyl vinyl ketone fails in aprotic solvents. This problem has been overcome by the use of methyl α-trimethylsilylvinyl ketone in place of methyl vinyl ketone. The enolate anion formed by the initial Michael addition is stabilized by the silyl group. With this reagent aprotic conditions can be applied successfully [48].

$$(7.37)$$

The silyl group is easily removed under the conditions of the subsequent cross-Aldol cyclization process.

Organo-copper enolates also undergo Michael addition with methyl α-trimethylsilyl vinyl ketone [49, 50].

$$(7.38)$$

This reaction sequence is also effective with α,β-unsaturated cyclopentenones [51].

$$(7.39)$$

Methyl α-trimethylsilylvinyl ketone has been prepared as outlined below. Addition of bromine at −78 °C to vinyltrimethylsilane yields the expected dibromide which undergoes dehydrohalogenation on treatment with diethyl-amine to yield α-bromovinyltrimethylsilane [52]. α-Bromovinyltriphenylsilane has been prepared in a similar manner [53]. Reaction of the Grignard reagent prepared from α-bromovinyltrimethylsilane with acetaldehyde yields 3-tri-methylsilyl-but-3-en-2-ol. Jones oxidation of this alcohol yields the desired methyl α-trimethylsilylvinyl ketone [54].

$$(7.40)$$

Bis-annelation reagents based on α-trimethylsilylvinyl ketones have been developed [55].

$$(7.41)$$

7.6 Masked Carbonyl Groups

Vinyl silanes are equivalent to masked carbonyl functionalities. Epoxidation of vinyl silanes with peracids, such as MCPBA, yields α-trimethylsilyl epoxides [56, 57].

$$(7.42)$$

These undergo acid catalyzed ring opening to generate a carbonyl functional group at the carbon which formerly bore the trialkylsilyl group [58]. This may occur as outlined.

$$(7.43)$$

This information may have led to the design of 1-iodo-3-trimethylsilyl-2-butene as an ketone annulation reagent. C-Alkylation of lithium enolates by this allylic iodide yields δ-trimethylsilyl-γ,δ-unsaturated ketones. Subsequent treatment with MCPBA yields δ-trimethylsilyl γ,δ-epoxy ketones which are converted to 1,5-diketones by m-chlorobenzoic acid with loss of the trimethylsilyl group [59].

$$(7.44)$$

1-Iodo-3-trimethylsilyl-2-butene has been prepared from 3-trimethylsilylpropyn-1-ol [60, 61].

Treatment of E-1-(2'-hydroxyalkyl)-2-trimethylsilylethylenes with MCPBA leads to α-trimethylsilyl epoxides. These react with $BF_3 \cdot OEt_2$ in methanol to yield lactol methyl ethers which can be oxidized with Jones reagents to the corresponding γ lactones [62].

$$(7.45)$$

The conjugate addition of *bis*(α-trimethylsilylvinyl)copper lithium to α,β-unsaturated ketones is synthetically equivalent to a Michael addition of an acyl anion. This results from the fact that vinyl trimethylsilanes can be readily oxidized by MCPBA to α-trimethylsilyl epoxides which undergo acid catalyzed hydrolysis to yield ketones or aldehydes. This synthetic sequence permits the generation of 1,4-dicarbonyl compounds. Due to the low reactivity of vinyl silanes toward MCPBA, it may be necessary to protect the ketone prior to epoxidation to prevent competitive Baeyer-Villiger oxidation [63, 64].

$$(7.46)$$

1,5-Keto aldehydes have been prepared as outlined below (Eq. 7.47) [65].

$$(7.47)$$

An alternative approach to the synthesis of α-trimethylsilyl epoxides involves the reaction of ketones or aldehydes with α-chloro-α-trimethylsilyl-ethyl lithium [66, 67].

$$(7.48)$$

This methodology has been exploited in an efficient synthesis of R(+)-Frontalin [69]. α-Chloro-α-trimethylsilylethyl lithium has been prepared by metallation of α-chloroethyltrimethylsilane by sec-butyl lithium in THF at $-78°$. α-Chloro-α-trimethylsilylethane has been prepared as outlined (Eq. 7.49). This provides an example of a limitation in the ability of silicon to stabilize a β-carbocation [68]. Thus HCl adds in an anti-Markovnikoff sense to vinyl-trimethylsilane but in a Markovnikoff sense to the vinyltrichlorosilane.

$$(7.49)$$

α-Trimethylsilyl epoxides have also been prepared by reaction of α-lithio-trimethylsilyldiazomethane with ketones. This reagent is formed by metallation of α-trimethylsilyldiazomethane with n-butyl lithium in THF/n-pentane at $-100°$ [70]. However, the preparation of α-trimethylsilyldiazomethane is rather difficult [71].

7.7 1,2-Transposition of Carbonyl Groups

Photochemically generated singlet oxygen undergoes regiospecific reaction with vinyl trimethylsilanes to yield 2-trimethylsilylallylic hydroperoxides. These can be reduced with NaBH$_4$ to yield 2-trimethylsilylallylic alcohols (Eq. 7.50) [72]. The adjacent hydroxyl functionality facilitates removal of the trimethylsilyl group by fluoride ion in DMSO or acetonitrile (Eq. 7.51) [73].

$$(7.50)$$

$$(7.51)$$

Combining these reactions with the efficient synthesis of vinyltrimethylsilanes from ketones (outlined below Eq. 7.52) permits the regiospecific conversion of ketones to allylic alcohols [72, 76]. The 1,2-transposition of the oxygen functionality in this process should be noted.

$$(7.52)$$

An adjacent hydroxyl functionality also facilitates removal of trimethylsilyl groups from α-trimethylsilyl epoxides by fluoride [74, 75].

$$(7.53)$$

By comparison neither vinyltriphenylsilane nor vinyltrimethylsilane are desilylated under these conditions [73].

1,2-Transposition of a ketone carbonyl functionality can be efficiently achieved by the use of vinyl silanes. Epoxidation of vinyl trimethyl silanes with MCPBA followed by treatment of the α-trimethylsilyl epoxides with LiAlH$_4$ yields β-hydroxyalkyltrimethylsilanes [21, 77]. This results from nucleophilic attack by the hydride at the silyl substituted carbon of the epoxide ring [77]. Oxidation of the β-hydroxyalkyltrimethylsilane with Jones reagent yields the desired ketone [76, 78]. Such 2-trimethylsilyl ketones easily suffer cleavage of the C–Si bond under acidic conditions [79, 80].

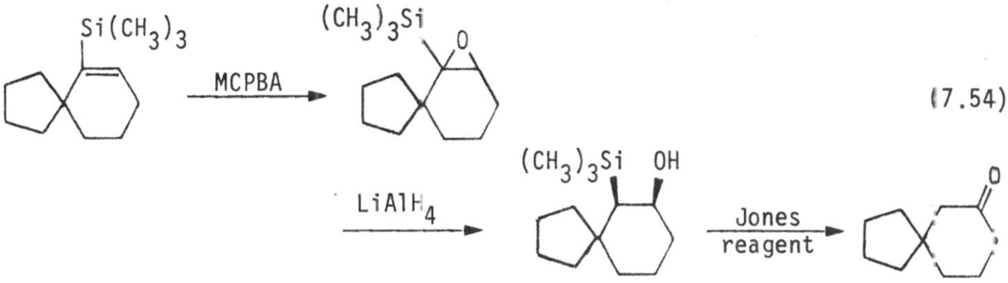

(7.54)

7.8 Cycloaddition Reactions

Limited work has been done on cycloaddition reactions of vinyl silanes. Diels-Alder reaction of trichlorosilylacetylene with cyclopentadiene provides an efficient route to 2-trichlorosilylnorbornadiene. Similar reaction of trimethylsilylacetylene with cyclopentadiene requires higher temperatures (270°) [81].

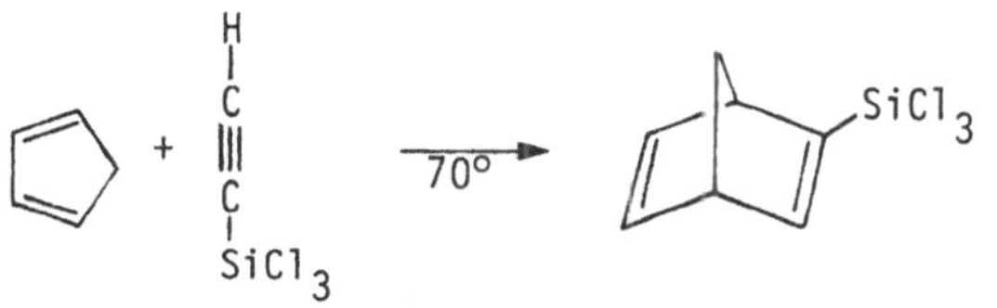

(7.55)

Vinyltrichlorosilane also undergoes ene reactions [82].

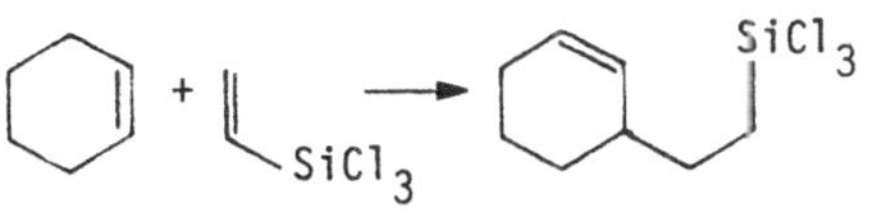

(7.55)

Ene reactions of allylic silanes with maleic anhydride, diethylazodicarboxylate, benzyne, formaldehyde, 4-phenyl-1,2,4-triazoline-3,5-dione and singlet oxygen provide efficient routes to functionally-substituted vinyl silanes [82–87].

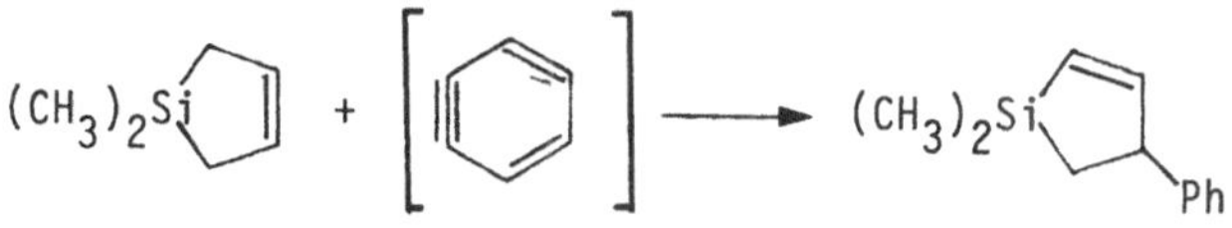

(7.57)

97

$$(CH_3)_2Si\diagdown + O_2' \xrightarrow[\text{Rose Bengal}]{h\nu} (CH_3)_2Si\diagdown_{OOH} \qquad (7.58)$$

2-Triethylsilyl-1,3-butadiene undergoes Diels-Alder reactions with a variety of dienophiles.

$$Et_3Si\diagdown + \begin{array}{c}CO_2CH_3\\ \|\\ C\\ \|\\ CO_2CH_3\end{array} \xrightarrow{\Delta} Et_3Si\diagdown\diagup^{CO_2CH_3}_{CO_2CH_3} \qquad (7.59)$$

Hydrosilation of 1,4-dichloro-2-butyne with triethylsilane catalyzed by chloroplatinic acid followed by dechlorination with zinc dust in ethanol yields 2-triethylsilyl-1,3-butadiene [88].

$$Et_3SiH + \begin{array}{c}CH_2Cl\\ \|\\ C\\ \|\\ C\\ \|\\ CH_2Cl\end{array} \xrightarrow{H_2PtCl_6} \begin{array}{c}H\diagup CH_2Cl\\ Et_3Si\diagup^{\diagdown}CH_2Cl\end{array} \xrightarrow[EtOH]{Zn} Et_3Si\diagdown \qquad (7.60)$$

Trimethylsilyl vinyl ketene also undergoes Diels Alder reactions with a variety of dienophiles [89].

$$(CH_3)_3Si\diagdown_{C=O} + \begin{array}{c}CO_2CH_3\\ CH_3O_2C\diagup\end{array} \xrightarrow[\text{toluene}]{\Delta} (CH_3)_3Si\diagdown\diagup^{O}_{CO_2CH_3}{}^{CO_2CH_3} \qquad (7.61)$$

This ketene was prepared by dehydrohalogenation of Z-2-trimethylsilyl-3-butenoyl chloride with triethylamine [89].

7.9 Preparation of Vinyl Silanes

The variety of stereo- and regiospecific transformations which can be accomplished by use of vinyl silanes has led to considerable interest in methods to prepare these compounds with specific substitution patterns and defined stereochemistry.

Industrially, vinyltrichlorosilane and vinylmethyldichlorosilane may be produced by heating either trichlorosilane, or methyldichlorosilane and vinyl chloride at 600° [90, 91]. A more convenient laboratory method is the atmospheric pressure hydrosilation of acetylene by trichlorosilane, triethoxysilane, methyldichlorosilane, or methyldiethoxysilane catalyzed by ruthenium, rhodium, or platinum complexes [92].

$$HC\equiv CH \ + \ HSiCl_3 \ \xrightarrow{\ RuCl_2(PPh_3)_2\ } \ \underset{H}{\overset{H}{>}}C=C\underset{SiCl_3}{\overset{H}{<}} \qquad (7.62)$$

tetrakis(Triphenylphosphine) palladium (O) catalyzes the reaction of vinyl chloride with either *sym*-dichlorotetramethyldisilane or *sym*-tetrachlorodimethyldisilane to yield vinyldimethylchlorosilane or vinylmethyldichlorosilane respectively [93].

$$\underset{\underset{CH_3}{|}}{\overset{\overset{CH_3}{|}}{Cl_2Si\text{-}SiCl_2}} \ + \ CH_2=CH\text{-}Cl \ \xrightarrow{\ [Ph_3P]_4Pd\ } \ CH_2=CH\text{-}\underset{\underset{Cl}{|}}{\overset{\overset{Cl}{|}}{Si}}\text{-}CH_3 \ + \ CH_3SiCl_3 \qquad (7.63)$$

Based on the similarities between catalytic hydrogenation and hydrosilation, a direct synthesis of vinyl silanes would involve a catalytic reaction of a silane with an alkene to yield an alkylsilane as an intermediate which would lose hydrogen and give a vinyl silane as a final product. This concept has been demonstrated in practice for a few cases. Trialkylsilanes react both thermally [94] and photochemically [95] with alkenes to give a mixture of vinyltrialkylsilanes and tetraalkylsilanes under catalysis by iron pentacarbonyl. Similar results have been obtained with a rhodium catalyst [96]. Triethylsilane reacts with α-olefins under catalysis by a dimeric rhodium complex to give mixtures of alkyltriethylsilanes, alkenyltriethylsilanes, and allylic triethylsilanes. The desired alkenyltrimethylsilane is the predominant product at high ratios of olefin to triethylsilane [97]. Most recently, encouraging results have been reported when a ruthenium carbonyl cluster is used as catalyst [98].

$$PhCH=CH_2 \ + \ Et_3SiH \ \xrightarrow{\ Ru_3(CO)_{12}\ } \ \underset{Ph}{\diagup}\!\!=\!\!\diagup^{SiEt_3} \ + \ H_2 \qquad (7.64)$$

A. E-1-Trimethylsilyl-1-alkenes

E-1-trimethylsilyl-1-alkenes are readily prepared by the chloroplatinic acid catalyzed hydrosilation of terminal alkynes with either trichlorosilane or methyldichlorosilane followed by addition of methylmagnesium bromide [99].

$$n\text{-}C_4H_9C\equiv CH \ \xrightarrow[\ H_2PtCl_6\ ]{\ CH_3SiCl_2H\ } \ \underset{\underset{CH_3}{|}}{\overset{n\text{-}C_4H_9}{\diagdown}}\!\!SiCl_2 \ \xrightarrow{\ 2CH_3MgBr\ } \ \underset{}{\overset{n\text{-}C_4H_9}{\diagdown}}\!\!Si(CH_3)_3 \qquad (7.65)$$

E-1-Lithio-2-trimethylsilylethylene, prepared form *E*-1-bromo-2-trimethylsilylethylene by halogen-metal exchange with *t*-butyl lithium [63] or by direct reaction with lithium [100, 101] permits the preparation of a variety of *E*-1-trimethylsilylethylene derivatives.

$$(CH_3)_3Si \diagup\diagdown \xrightarrow[\text{2) } H^+]{\text{1) } CO_2} (CH_3)_3Si \diagup\diagdown CO_2H \qquad (7.66)$$

Treatment of 1-trimethylsilylalkynes with DIBAL in hydrocarbon solvents followed by protonolysis leads to E-1-trimethylsilyl alkenes [102].

$$Ph-C{\equiv}C-Si(CH_3)_3 \xrightarrow[\text{heptane}]{\text{DIBAL}} \underset{H}{\overset{Ph}{>}}{=}\underset{Si(CH_3)_3}{\overset{Al(i\text{-}Bu)_2}{}} \xrightarrow{H_3O^+} \underset{H}{\overset{Ph}{>}}{=}\underset{Si(CH_3)_3}{\overset{H}{}} \qquad (7.67)$$

Metallation of allyltrimethylsilane with *sec*-butyl lithium in THF/TMEDA yields 1-trimethylsilylallyl lithium. This reagent reacts regiospecifically at its 3-position with ketones or aldehydes to yield E-1-(2′-hydroxyalkyl)-2-trimethylsilylethylenes [62, 103, 104].

$$(7.68)$$

E-1,2-*bis*(Trimethylsilyl)ethylene has been prepared by treatment of vinyltrimethylsilane with TMS-Cl and magnesium powder in HMPT [105].

$$(CH_3)_3Si-CH{=}CH_2 \xrightarrow[\substack{\text{Mg/HMPT}\\ \text{FeCl}_3}]{(CH_3)_3SiCl} (CH_3)_3Si\diagup\diagdown Si(CH_3)_3 \qquad (7.69)$$

E-1,2-*bis*(Trimethylsilyl)ethylene has also been prepared by hydrosilation of trimethylsilylacetylene with dimethylchlorosilane catalyzed by chloroplatinic acid followed by addition of methylmagnesium iodide [106]. Reaction of E-2-trimethylsilyl vinyl magnesium bromide with TMS-Cl also gives E-1,2-*bis*(trimethylsilyl)ethylene. E-1-Bromo-2-trimethylsilylethylene is readily available by the addition of dry HBr to trimethylsilylacetylene under free radical catalysis by di-t-butyl peroxide [107, 108].

$$(CH_3)_3Si-C{\equiv}CH \xrightarrow[(CH_3)_3CO-OC(CH_3)_3]{HBr} (CH_3)_3Si\diagup\diagdown Br \qquad (7.70)$$

B. *Z*-1-Trimethylsilyl-1-alkenes

A variety of methods permit preparation of *Z*-1-trimethylsilyl-1-alkenes. Among these is the low pressure catalytic hydrogenation of 1-trimethylsilyl alkynes over either Raney nickel [109] or a nickel boride catalyst (P-2-Ni) [15].

$$Ph-C\equiv C-Si(CH_3)_3 \xrightarrow[Pd]{H_2} \underset{H}{\overset{Ph}{\diagdown}}\!\!=\!\!\underset{H}{\overset{Si(CH_3)_3}{\diagup}} \tag{7.71}$$

Hydroboration of 1-trimethylsilyl alkynes with dicyclohexyl borohydride [14] or disiamyl borohydride, followed by protonolysis of the sp² hybridized C−B bond by acetic acid also yields *Z*-1-trimethylsilyl-1-alkenes.

$$n\text{-}C_4H_9C\equiv CSi(CH_3)_3 \;+\; \left(\bigcirc\right)_2 BH \tag{7.72}$$

Treatment of 1-trimethylsilyl alkynes with DIBAL in ether [15, 110] or in heptane in the presence of one equivalent of tertiary amines [102] leads to *Z*-1-trimethylsilyl alkenes after protonolysis of the sp² hybridized C−Al bond.

$$Ph-C\equiv C-Si(CH_3)_3 \xrightarrow[\text{or Et}_2O]{DIBAL} \tag{7.73}$$

Such *Z*-1-trimethylsilyl alkenes undergo facile isomerization on irradiation with a sunlamp in pyridine with a catalytic amount of NBS (5 mole %) to yield *E*-1-trimethylsilyl alkenes [110].

C. 2-Trimethylsilyl-1-alkenes

2-Trimethylsilyl-1-alkenes have been prepared by a variety of methods. Chloroplatinic acid catalyzed hydrosilation of 1-trimethylsilyl alkynes with methyldichlorosilane, followed by addition of methylmagnesium bromide generally yields *E*-1,2-*bis*(trimethylsilyl)alkenes [30]. 1-*t*-Butyl-2-trimethylsilyl acetylene is an exception [111]. Protodesilylation with acetic acid/water selectively removes the terminal trimethylsilyl group to yield 2-trimethyl-silyl-1-alkenes [30].

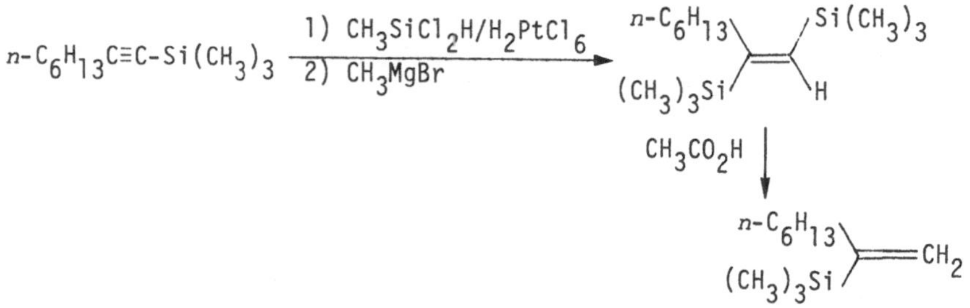

$$n\text{-}C_6H_{13}C{\equiv}C\text{-}Si(CH_3)_3 \xrightarrow[\text{2) } CH_3MgBr]{\text{1) } CH_3SiCl_2H/H_2PtCl_6}$$

(7.74)

α-Bromovinyltrimethylsilane is an extremely versatile precursor for the preparation of 2-trimethylsilyl-1-alkenes. Addition of bromine to vinyltrichloro-silane, followed by dehydrohalogenation with quinoline or N,N-diethylaniline yields α-bromovinyltrichlorosilane. This reacts with excess methyl Grignard reagent to yield α-bromovinyltrimethylsilane [112].

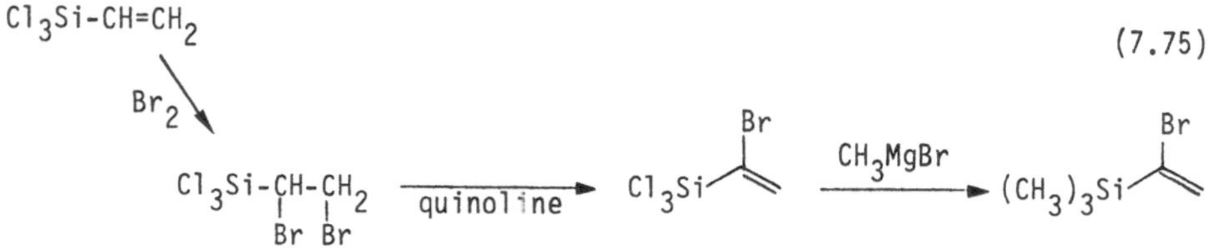

(7.75)

Alternatively, α-bromovinyltrimethylsilane can be prepared from vinyltri-methylsilane by addition of bromine, followed by dehydrohalogenation with diethylamine [52, 54]. The reaction of 1,1-*bis*-(trimethylsilyl)ethylene with bromine [113] also yields α-bromovinyltrimethylsilane.

α-Bromovinyltrimethylsilane undergoes coupling reactions with Grignard reagents catalyzed by *tetrakis*(triphenylphosphine) palladium (O) to yield 2-trimethylsilyl-1-alkenes [20].

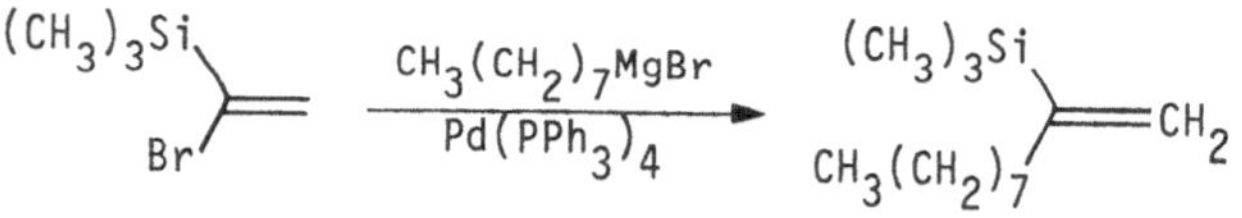

(7.76)

α-Bromovinyltrimethylsilane can be converted to a Grignard reagent which will couple with primary alkyl iodides or tosylates (Eq. 7.77), or undergo conjugate addition to α,β-unsaturated ketones in the presence of copper (I) salts (Eq. 7.78) [20].

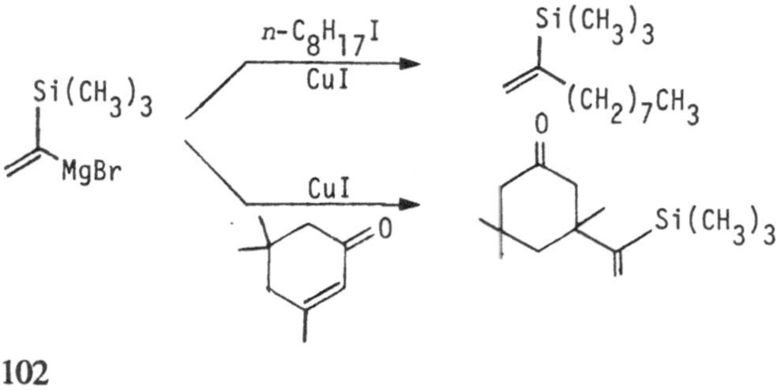

(7.77)

(7.78)

Halogen-metal exchange between α-bromovinyltrimethylsilane and t-butyl lithium at −78 °C gives the expected vinyl lithium reagent. Reaction of this with cuprous iodide yields *bis*(α-trimethylsilylvinyl)copper lithium which undergoes conjugate addition to α,β-unsaturated ketones [63, 64].

$$\left(\begin{array}{c} (CH_3)_3Si \\ \end{array} \right)_2 CuLi \quad + \quad \text{(cyclohexenone)} \quad \longrightarrow \quad \text{(product)} \quad Si(CH_3)_3 \qquad (7.79)$$

α-Ethoxy-α-trimethylsilyl ethylene has been prepared by reaction of α-ethoxy vinyl lithium with TMS-Cl [114].

$$CH_3CH_2O-CH=CH_2 \xrightarrow[-50°]{t-BuLi} \underset{Li}{\overset{OCH_2CH_3}{=\!\!<}} \xrightarrow{(CH_3)_3SiCl} \underset{Si(CH_3)_3}{\overset{OCH_2CH_3}{=\!\!<}} \qquad (7.80)$$

In a similar manner, reaction of 1-lithio-1-methoxy-1,3-butadiene with TMS-Cl yields 1-methoxy-1-trimethylsilyl-1,3-butadiene [115, 116]. 1-Methoxy-1-trimethylsilylallene, prepared from 1-methoxyallene, can be converted to 1-methoxy-1-trimethylsilyl-1,2-heptadiene (Eq. 7.81). This reacts with fluoride ion to yield E-2-heptenal [117].

$$H_2C=C=C\underset{Si(CH_3)_3}{\overset{OCH_3}{<}} \xrightarrow[2)\ n-C_4H_9I]{1)\ n-BuLi} \underset{H}{\overset{n-C_4H_9}{>}}C=C=C\underset{Si(CH_3)_3}{\overset{OCH_3}{<}} \qquad (7.81)$$

$$\xrightarrow[2)\ H_3O^+]{1)\ TBAF} \underset{H}{\overset{n-C_4H_9}{>}}C=C\underset{H}{\overset{}{<}}=O$$

D. 1-Cycloalkenyltrimethylsilanes

Cyclic ketones can easily be converted to 1-cycloalkenyltrimethylsilanes. The ketone is reacted with PCl_5 to give a 1-chlorocycloalkene, which undergoes a Wurtz type coupling with TMS-Cl in the presence of sodium [33, 118, 119].

$$\text{(cyclohexanone)} \xrightarrow{PCl_5} \text{(chlorocyclohexene)} \xrightarrow[Na]{(CH_3)_3SiCl} \text{(silylcyclohexene)} \qquad (7.82)$$

An alternative method involves conversion of the ketone to a benzene or p-toluene sulfonyl hydrazone. Such hydrazones react with excess n-butyl lithium/TMEDA to yield the least substituted vinyl lithium reagent. This can be quenched with TMS-Cl to yield the corresponding vinyl trimethylsilane [38, 78, 118, 120, 121].

$$(7.83)$$

Birch reduction (Eq. 7.84) or the related electrochemical reduction (Eq. 7.85) of aryltrimethylsilanes is not generally useful for the preparation of 1-trimethylsilylcyclohexene derivatives because trimethylsilyl groups are often lost under the reaction conditions. Nevertheless, in specific cases good to excellent yields are achieved [122, 123].

$$(7.84)$$

$$(7.85)$$

E. *E* and *Z*-1,2-Dialkyl-1-trimethylsilyl ethylenes

α-Lithiovinyl trimethylsilane reacts with aldehydes or ketones to yield 2-trimethylsilyl allylic alcohols. These can be converted to 2-trimethylsilyl allylic acetates which undergo S_N2' coupling with dialkyl copper lithium reagents to yield predominantly *E*-1,2-dialkyl-1-trimethylsilylethylenes [124].

$$(7.86)$$

On the other hand, treatment of 2-trimethylsilyl allylic alcohols with thionyl chloride yields rearranged 2-trimethylsilyl allylic chlorides [124, 125]. These undergo coupling with dialkyl copper lithium reagents to yield predominantly Z-1,2-dialkyl-1-trimethylsilylethylenes [124].

$$(7.87)$$

Z-1,2-dialkyl-1-trimethylsilylethylene can be prepared from 1-trimethyl-silylalkynes. Hydroboration of 1-trimethylsilyl alkynes with dicyclohexylborane proceeds in a *cis* manner regiospecifically to yield vinyl boranes in which both boron and silicon are bonded to the same carbon atom. Treatment of this intermediate sequentially with methyl lithium, cuprous iodide, triethyl phosphite in HMPT and finally a primary alkyl iodide yields the desired Z-1,2-dialkyl-1-trimethylsilylethylene [126].

$$(7.88)$$

Dialkylcopper magnesium halides add in a stereospecific *cis* manner to both trimethylsilylacetylene [127] and triphenylsilylacetylene [128] to yield regio-specifically intermediates in which both copper and silicon are bonded to the same carbon atom. These α-silyl vinyl cuprate reagents can be alkylated with primary alkyl iodides in HMPT (Eq. 7.89) [127, 128]. The vinyl-copper bond is cleaved stereospecifically with retention by cyanogen, bromine, iodine and *NBS* (Eq. 7.90) [128].

$$(7.89)$$

$$(7.90)$$

Both *Z*- and *E*-1,2-dialkyl-1-trimethylsilyl ethylenes can be prepared from 1-trimethylsilyl alkynes. Reaction of 1-trimethylsilyl alkynes with DIBAL in hydrocarbon solvent proceeds regiospecifically [102] in a *trans* manner (Eq. 7.91). On the other hand, in the presence of a donor solvent such as ether or one equivalent of tertiary amine, the addition proceeds in a *cis* manner (Eq. 7.92) [15, 102, 110]. These vinyl aluminum reagents can be converted to ate complexes by reaction with methyl lithium. Reaction with alkyl halides occurs with retention of stereochemistry [129, 130].

$$(7.91)$$

$$(7.92)$$

These *E*-vinyl aluminum species react with bromine to give *E*-1-bromo-1-trimethylsilyl-2-alkyl ethylenes. These will undergo photoisomerization in the presence of bromine to the corresponding Z-1-bromo-1-trimethyl-silyl-2-alkyl-ethylenes. Both of these vinyl bromides undergo halogenmetal exchange with retention of stereochemistry on treatment with *sec*-butyl lithium. Such *E*- or *Z*-1-lithio-1-trimethylsilyl-2-alkyl ethylenes couple efficiently with primary alkyl iodides to yield stereospecifically *E*- or *Z*-1,2-dialkyl-1-trimethylsilyl ethylenes [18] or Reaction with iodine yields similar results [75].

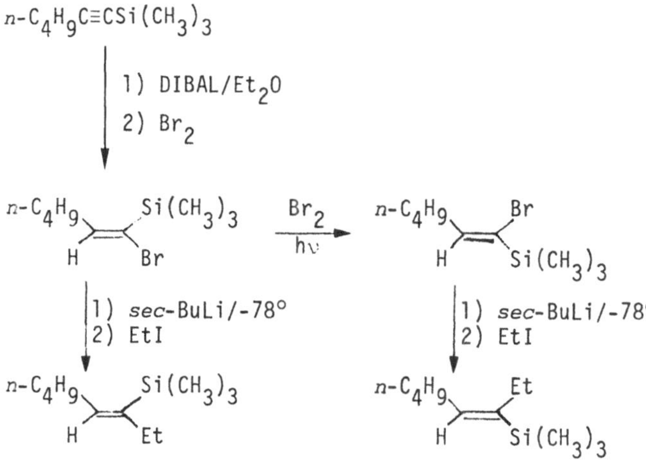

n-$C_4H_9C\equiv CSi(CH_3)_3$

1) DIBAL/Et$_2$O

2) Br$_2$

(7.93)

bis-Silyl lithium cuprate reagents add in a *cis* manner to terminal alkynes. The silyl substituted vinyl copper reagents thus formed are most versatile [131].
Some of their chemistry is summarized below [Eq. 7.94].

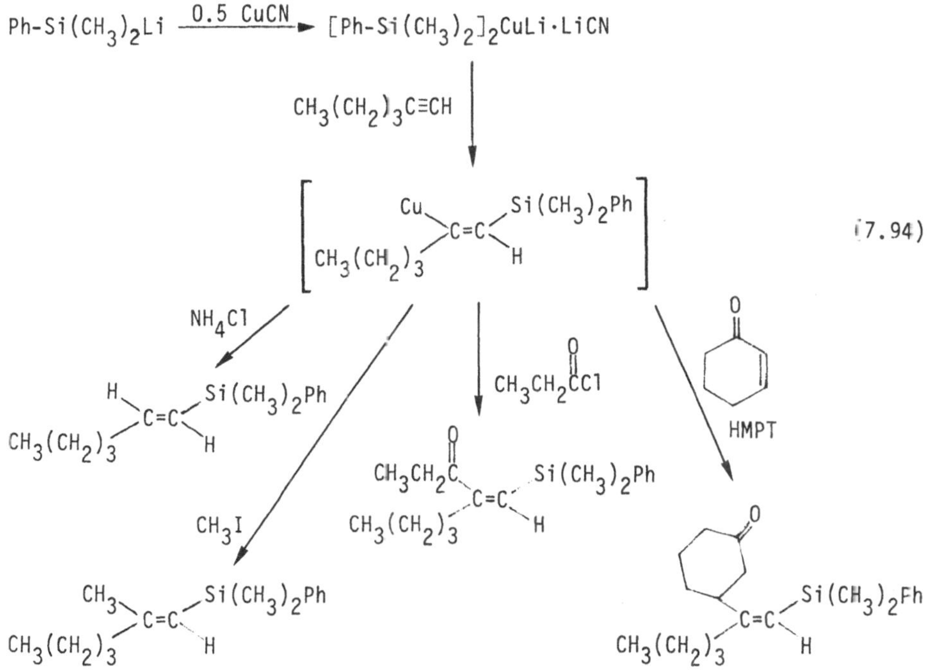

$Ph-Si(CH_3)_2Li \xrightarrow{\ 0.5\ CuCN\ } [Ph-Si(CH_3)_2]_2CuLi \cdot LiCN$

$CH_3(CH_2)_3C\equiv CH$

(7.94)

bis-Cyclopentadienyl titanium dichloride catalyzes the *cis*-addition of magnesium hydride across the C−C triple bond of 1-trimethylsilyl alkynes. Opposite regiospecificity is observed with aliphatic and aromatic 1-trimethyl-silyl substituted acetylenes (Eq. 7.95 and 7.96). It seems probable that the reaction proceeds by initial reaction of *iso*-butylmagnesium bromide with the *bis*-cyclopentadienyl titanium dichloride to yield an *iso*-butyl titanium species which undergoes β-hydride elimination. The titanium hydride species thus formed adds in a stereospecific *cis*-manner to the 1-trimethylsilyl alkyne to yield a vinyl titanium species which untergoes a metal-exchange with more *iso*-butylmagnesium bromide to yield the vinyl magnesium product and regenerate the *iso*-butyl titanium species [132].

$$n\text{-}C_4H_9C{\equiv}CSi(CH_3)_3 + (CH_3)_2CHCH_2MgBr \longrightarrow$$

$$(7.95)$$

$$PhC{\equiv}CSi(CH_3)_3 + (CH_3)_2CHCH_2MgBr \longrightarrow$$

$$(7.96)$$

F. 1,2-Disubstituted-1,2-*bis*(trimethylsilyl)ethylenes, 1,1-Disubstituted-2,2-*bis*(trimethylsilyl)ethylenes and 1,1,2-Trisubstituted-2-trimethyl-silyl ethylenes

Reductive silylation with magnesium in HMPT of diphenyl acetylene [133] or trimethylsilyl phenyl acetylene [134] is successful.

$$PhC{\equiv}CPh + Cl\text{-}Si\text{-}O\text{-}Si\text{-}Cl \xrightarrow{\text{Mg}}{\text{HMPT}} \qquad (7.97)$$

Bromine has been reported to add to *bis*(trimethylsilyl)acetylene to yield *E*-1,2-dibromo-1,2-*bis*(trimethylsilyl)ethylene [135]. Zinc chloride also catalyzes the *trans* addition of both chlorine and bromine to *bis*(trimethylsilyl)-acetylene [106].

1,1-*bis*(Trimethylsilyl) alkenes have been prepared by the Peterson reaction. Thus, reaction of *tris*(trimethylsilyl)methyl sodium with non-enoliz-able ketones yields 1,1-*bis*(trimethylsilyl)alkenes [136].

$$[(CH_3)_3Si]_3C^-Na^+ + Ph_2C{=}O \longrightarrow Ph_2C{=}C\begin{smallmatrix}Si(CH_3)_3\\Si(CH_3)_3\end{smallmatrix} \qquad (7.98)$$

The following reaction sequence based on the reaction of trialkyl(trimethylsilylethynyl)borates with electrophiles has been used to prepare 1,1,2-trialkyl-2-trimethylsilyl ethylenes [137, 139].

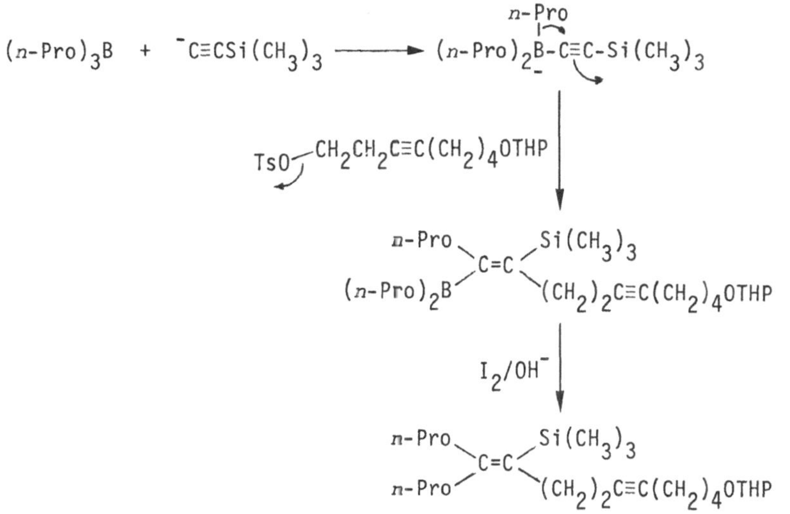

$$(n\text{-Pro})_3B \ + \ ^-C{\equiv}CSi(CH_3)_3 \longrightarrow (n\text{-Pro})_2\overset{\overset{\displaystyle n\text{-Pro}}{|}}{\underset{-}{B}}-C{\equiv}C-Si(CH_3)_3$$

$$TsO{-}CH_2CH_2C{\equiv}C(CH_2)_4OTHP$$

$$\begin{array}{c} n\text{-Pro} \\ \diagdown \\ C{=}C \\ \diagup \qquad\qquad \diagdown \\ (n\text{-Pro})_2B \qquad\qquad (CH_2)_2C{\equiv}C(CH_2)_4OTHP \end{array} \qquad (7.99)$$

$$I_2/OH^-$$

$$\begin{array}{c} n\text{-Pro} \qquad\qquad Si(CH_3)_3 \\ \diagdown \qquad\quad \diagup \\ C{=}C \\ \diagup \qquad\quad \diagdown \\ n\text{-Pro} \qquad\qquad (CH_2)_2C{\equiv}C(CH_2)_4OTHP \end{array}$$

Addition of TMS-Cl to sodium trialkylpropynylborates gives E-2-trimethylsilyl vinyl boranes [138].

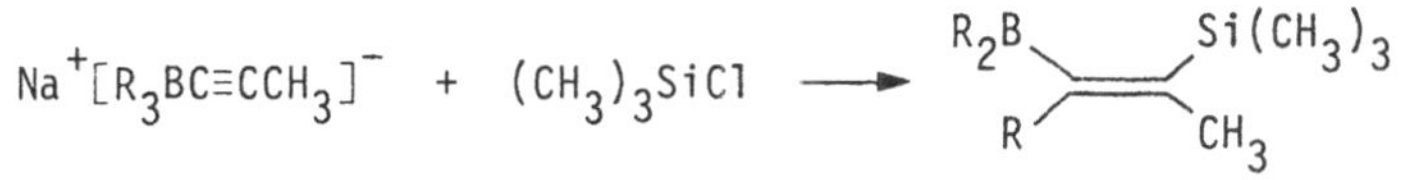

$$Na^+[R_3BC{\equiv}CCH_3]^- \ + \ (CH_3)_3SiCl \longrightarrow \begin{array}{c} R_2B \qquad\quad Si(CH_3)_3 \\ \diagdown \quad\; \diagup \\ \diagup \quad\; \diagdown \\ R \qquad\qquad CH_3 \end{array} \qquad (7.100)$$

Such vinyl boranes can be converted to E-1,2-dialkyl-2-trimethylsilylethylene by protonolysis.

A reactive methyl nickel species, generated by reaction of methylmagnesium bromide in the presence of a catalytic amount of nickel (II) acetylacetonate and trimethylaluminium, adds in a *cis* manner to 1-trimethylsilyl alkynes. The addition is both stereo and regiospecific such that nickel and silicon are bonded to the same carbon. This intermediate reacts with water (D$_2$O), aldehydes, carbon dioxide, iodine, vinyl bromide, and alkyl bromide to yield a variety of specific trimethylsilyl substituted alkenes [140].

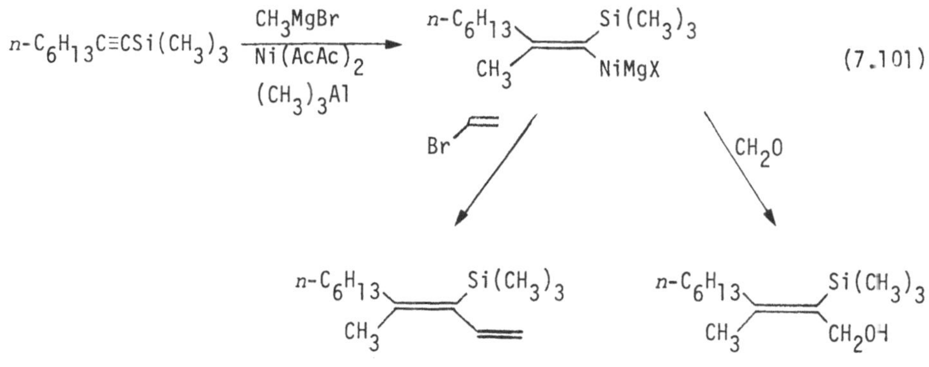

$$n\text{-}C_6H_{13}C{\equiv}CSi(CH_3)_3 \xrightarrow[\substack{Ni(AcAc)_2 \\ (CH_3)_3Al}]{CH_3MgBr} \begin{array}{c} n\text{-}C_6H_{13} \qquad Si(CH_3)_3 \\ \diagdown \quad\; \diagup \\ \diagup \quad\; \diagdown \\ CH_3 \qquad\quad NiMgX \end{array} \qquad (7.101)$$

$$Br\diagup$$

$$CH_2O$$

$$\begin{array}{c} n\text{-}C_6H_{13} \qquad Si(CH_3)_3 \\ \diagdown \quad\; \diagup \\ \diagup \quad\; \diagdown \\ CH_3 \end{array} \qquad\qquad \begin{array}{c} n\text{-}C_6H_{13} \qquad Si(CH_3)_3 \\ \diagdown \quad\; \diagup \\ \diagup \quad\; \diagdown \\ CH_3 \qquad\quad CH_2OH \end{array}$$

The reaction is limited to methylmagnesium bromide since with larger alkyl groups β-hydride elimination occurs [141].

Finally, α-lithiovinyltrimethylsilane reacts with ketones to yield 2-trimethylsilylallylic alcohols which can be converted to allylic acetates by treatment with acetyl chloride and silver cyanide. These will undergo S_N2' coupling with dialkylcopper lithium reagents to yield predominantly E-1,1,2-trialkyl-2-trimethylsilyl ethylenes [142].

$$(7.102)$$

References

1. Sommer, L.H., Braughman, G.A.: J. Am. Chem. Soc. *83*, 3346 (1961)
2. Traylor, T.G., Hanstein, W., Berwin, H.J., Clinton, N.A., Brown, R.S.: J. Am. Chem. Soc. *93*, 5715 (1971)
3. Jarvie, A.W.P., Holt, A., Thompson, J.: J. Chem. Soc. B, 852 (1969)
4. Fleming, I., Goldhill, J.: J. Chem. Soc. Chem. Comm. 176 (1978)
5. Fleming, I., Goldhill, J.: J. Chem. Soc. Perkin I, 1493 (1980)
6. Eberson, L.: Acta Chem. Scand. *10*, 633 (1956)
7. Gilman, H., Lichtenwalter, G.D.: J. Am. Chem. Soc. *80*, 608 (1958)
8. Ager, D.J. Fleming, I.: J. Chem. Soc. Chem. Comm. 177 (1978)
9. Brownbridge, P., Fleming, I., Pearce, A., Warren, S.: J. Chem. Soc. Chem. Comm. 751 (1976)
10. Fleming, I., Paterson, I., Pearce, A.: J. Chem. Soc. Perkin I, 256 (1981)
11. Fleming, I., Patel, S.K.: Tetrahedron Lett. 2321 (1981)
12. Thomas, E.J., Whitman, G.H.: J. Chem. Soc. Chem. Comm. 212 (1979)
13. Miller, R.B., McGarvey, G.: Syn. Comm. *7*, 475 (1977)
14. Miller, R.B., Reichenbach, T.: Tetrahedron Lett. 543 (1974)
15. Miller, R.B., McGarvey, G.: J. Org. Chem. *43*, 4424 (1978)

16. Pillot, J.P., Dunoguès, J., Calas, R.: Syn. Comm. *9*, 395 (1979)
17. Chan, T.H., Lau, P.W.K., Mychajlowskij, W.: Tetrahedron Lett. 3317 (1977)
18. Miller, R.B., McGarvey, G.: J. Org. Chem. *44*, 4623 (1979)
19. Miller, R.B., McGarvey, G.: Syn. Comm. *8*, 291 (1978)
20. Huynh, C., Linstrumelle, G.: Tetrahedron Lett. 1073 (1979)
21. Robbins, C.M., Whitman, G.H.: J. Chem. Soc. Chem. Comm. 697 (1976)
22. Hudrilik, P.F., Arcoleo, J.P., Schwartz, R.H., Misra, R.N., Rona, R.J.: Tetrahedron Lett. 591 (1977)
23. Hudrilik, P.F., Hudrilik, A.M., Rona, R.J., Misra, R.N., Withers, G.P.: J. Am. Chem. Soc. *99*, 1993 (1977)
24. Koenig, K.E., Weber, W.P.: Tetrahedron Lett. 2533 (1973)
25. Brook, A.G., Duff, J.M., Reynolds, W.F.: J. Organometal. Chem. *121*, 293 (1976)
26. Koenig, K.E., Weber, W.P.: J. Am. Chem. Soc. *95*, 3416 (1973)
27. Cook, M.A., Eaborn, C., Walton, D.R.M.: J. Organometal. Chem. *24*, 301 (1970)
28. Bourne, A.J., Jarvie, A.W.P.: J. Organometal. Chem. *24*, 335 (1970)
29. Utimoto, K., Kitai, M., Nozaki, H.: Tetrahedron Lett. 2825 (1975)
30. Hudrilik, P.F., Schwartz, R.H., Hogan, J.C.: J. Org. Chem. *44*, 155 (1979)
31. Büchi, G., Wüest, H.: Tetrahedron Lett. 4305 (1977)
32. Pillot, J.P., Dunoguès, J., Calas, R.: C.R. Acad. Sci, Paris, Ser. C, 789 (1974)
33. Fleming, I., Pearce, A.: J. Chem. Soc. Perkin I, 2485 (1980)
34. Fleming, I., Pearce, A.: J. Chem. Soc. Chem. Comm. 633 (1975)
35. Pillot, J.P., Dunoguès, J., Calas, R.: Bull. Soc. Chim. Fr. 2143 (1975)
36. Woodward, R.B., Hoffman, R., "The Conservation of Orbital Symmetry": Verlag. Chem. 58 (1971)
37. Fristad, W.E., Dime, D.S., Bailey, T.R., Paquette, L.A.: Tetrahedron Lett. 1999 (1979)
38. Paquette, L.A., Fristad, W.E., Dime, D.S., Bailey, T.R.: J. Org. Chem *45*, 3017 (1980)
39. Nazarov, I.N., Zaretskaya, I.I.: Zh. Obsh. Khim. *27*, 693 (1957)
40. Cooke, F., Schwindeman, J., Magnus, P.: Tetrahedron Lett. 1995 (1979)
41. Cooke, F., Moerck, R., Schwindeman, J., Magnus, P.: J. Org. Chem. *45*, 1046 (1980)
42. Yamamoto, K., Nunokawa, O., Tsuji, J.: Synthesis, 721 (1977)
43. Yamamoto, K., Yoshitake, J., Qui, N.T., Tsuji, J.: Chem. Lett., 859 (1978)
44. Weber, W.P., Felix, R.A., Willard, A.K., Koenig, K.E.: Tetrahedron Lett. 4701 (1971)
45. Isobe, M., Kitamura, M., Goto, T.: Chem. Lett. 331 (1980)
46. Isobe, M., Kitamura, M., Goto, T.: Tetrahedron Lett. 239 (1981)
47. Grobel, B.T., Seebach, D.: Chem. Ber. *110*, 852 (1977)
48. Stork, G., Ganem, B.: J. Am. Chem. Soc. *95*, 6152 (1973)
49. Boeckman, Jr., R.K.: J. Am. Chem. Soc. *95*, 6867 (1973)
50. Boeckman, Jr., R.K., Blum, D.M., Ganem, B.: Org. Syn. *58*, 158 (1978)
51. Boeckman, Jr., R.K.: J. Am. Chem. Soc. *96*, 6179 (1974)
52. Ottolenghi, A., Fridkin, M., Zilkha, A.: Can. J. Chem. *41*, 2977 (1963)
53. Brook, A.G., Duff, J.M., Legrow, G.E.: J. Organometal. Chem. *122*, 31 (1976)
54. Boeckman, Jr., R.K., Blum, D.M., Ganem, B., Halvey, N.: Org. Syn. *58*, 152 (1978)
55. Stork, G., Singh, J.: J. Am. Chem. Soc. *96*, 6181 (1974)
56. Eisch, J.J., Trainor, J.T.: J. Org. Chem. *28*, 487 (1963)
57. Sakurai, H., Hayashi, N., Kumada, M.: J. Organometal. Chem. *18*, 351 (1969)
58. Stork, G., Colvin, E.: J. Am. Chem. Soc. *93*, 2080 (1971)
59. Stork, G., Jung, M.E.: J. Am. Chem. Soc. *96*, 3682 (1974)

60. Stork, G., Jung, M.E., Colvin, E., Noei, Y.: J. Am. Chem. Soc. *96*, 3684 (1974)
61. Altnau, G., Rösch, L., Bohlmann, F., Lonitz, M.: Tetrahedron Lett. 4069 (1980)
62. Ehlinger, E., Magnus, P.: J. Am. Chem. Soc. *102*, 5004 (1980)
63. Boeckman, Jr., R.K., Bruza, K.J.: Tetrahedron Lett. 3365 (1974)
64. Boeckman, Jr., R.K., Bruza, K.J.: J. Org. Chem. *44*, 4781 (1979)
65. Han, Y.K., Paquette, L.A.: J. Org. Chem. *44*, 3731 (1979)
66. Cooke, F., Magnus, P.: J. Chem. Soc. Chem. Comm. 513 (1977)
67. Burford, C., Cooke, F., Ehlinger, E., Magnus, P.: J. Am. Chem. Soc. *99*, 4536 (1977)
68. Cook, M.A., Eaborn, C., Walton, D.R.M.: J. Organometal. Chem. *29*, 389 (1971)
69. Magnus, P., Roy, G.: J. Chem. Soc. Chem. Commun. 297 (1978)
70. Schollkopf, U., Scholz, H.U.: Synthesis, 271 (1976)
71. Seyferth, D., Dow, A.W., Menzel, H., Flood, T.C.: J. Am. Chem. Soc. *90*, 1080 (1968)
72. Fristad, W.E., Bailey, T.R., Paquette, L.A., Gleiter, R., Böhm, M.C.: J. Am. J. Am. Chem. Soc. *101*, 4420 (1979)
73. Chan, T.H., Mychajlowskij, W.: Tetrahedron Lett. 3479 (1974)
74. Chan, T.H., Lau, P.W.K., Li, M.P.: Tetrahedron Lett. 2667 (1976)
75. Hasan, I., Kishi, Y.: Tetrahedron Lett. 4229 (1980)
76. Fristad, W.E., Bailey, T.R., Paquette, L.A.: J. Org. Chem. *45*, 3038 (1980)
77. Eisch, J.J., Trainor, J.T.: J. Org. Chem. *28*, 2870 (1963)
78. Fristad, W.E., Bailey, T.R., Paquette, L.A.: J. Org. Chem. *43*, 1620 (1978)
79. Whitmore, F.C., Sommer, L.H., Gold, J., Van Strien, R.E.: J. Am. Chem. Soc. *69*, 1551 (1947)
80. Hauser, C.R., Hance, C.R.: J. Am. Chem. Soc. *74*, 5091 (1952)
81. Cunico, R.F.: J. Org. Chem. *36*, 929 (1971)
82. Laporterie, A., Dubac, J., Lesbre, M.: C. R. Acad. Sci. Paris, Ser. C, *278*, 375 (1974)
83. Laporterie, A., Dubac, J., Lesbre, M.: J. Organometal. Chem. *101*, 187 (1975)
84. Lesbre, M., Laporterie, A., Dubac, J., Manuel, G.: C. R. Acad. Sci. Paris, Ser. C, *280*, 787 (1975)
85. Laporterie, A., Dubac, J., Mazerolles, P.: J. Organometal. Chem. *202*, C89 (1980)
86. Laporterie, A., Dubac, J., Manuel, G., Déléris, G., Kowalski, J., Dunoguès, J., Calas, R.: Tetrahedron *34*, 2669 (1978)
87. Ohashi, S., Ruch, W.E., Butler, G.B.: J. Org. Chem. *46*, 614 (1981)
88. Batt, D.G., Ganem, B.: Tetrahedron Lett. 3323 (1978)
89. Danheiser, R.L., Sand, H.: J. Org. Chem. *45*, 4810 (1980)
90. Mironov, V.F., Petrov, A.D., Pisarenko, V.V.: Dokl. Akad. Nauk. SSSR, *124*, 102 (1959)
91. Weyenberg, D.R., German Federal Republic Patent 936, 445, December 15, 1955
92. Watanabe, H., Asami, M., Nagai, Y.: J. Organometal. Chem. *195*, 363 (1980)
93. Matsumoto, H., Nagashima, S., Kato, T., Nagai, Y.: Angew. Chem. Int. *17*, 279 (1978)
94. Nesmeyanov, A.N., Freidlina, R.K., Chukovskaya, E.C., Petrova, R.G., Belyavsky, A.B.: Tetrahedron, *17*, 61 (1962)
95. Schroeder, M.A., Wrighton, M.S.: J. Organometal. Chem. *128*, 345 (1977)
96. Schepinov, S.A., Khidekef, M.L., Lagodzinskaya, G.V.: Izv. Akad. Nauk. SSSR, Ser. Khim. 2165 (1968)
97. Millan, A., Towns, E., Maitlis, P.M.: J. Chem. Soc. Chem. Comm. 673 (1981)
98. Seki, Y., Takeshita, K., Kawamoto, K., Murai, S., Sonoda, N.: Angew. Chem. Int. *19*, 928 (1980)

99. Benkeser, R.A., Burraus, M.L., Nolse, L.E., Schisler, J.V.: J. Am. Chem. Soc. 83, 4385 (1961)
100. Husk, G.R., Vilitchko, A.M.: J. Organometal. Chem. 49, 85 (1973)
101. Cunico, R.F., Clayton, F.J.: J Org. Chem. 41, 1480 (1976)
102. Eisch, J.J., Foxton, M.W.: J. Org. Chem. 36, 3520 (1971)
103. Ayalon-Chass, D., Ehlinger, E., Magnus, P.: J. Chem. Soc. Chem. Comm. 772 (1977)
104. Ehlinger, E., Magnus, P.: J. Chem. Soc. Chem. Comm. 421 (1979)
105. Dunoguès, J., Pillot, J.P., Duffaut, N., Calas, R.: C. R. Acad. Sci. Paris, Ser. C. 467 (1974)
106. Birkofer, L., Kühn, T.: Chem. Ber. 111, 3119 (1978)
107. Yarosh, O.G., Voronkov, V.K., Komarov, N.V.: Izv. Akad. Nauk SSSR Ser. Khim. 875 (1971)
108. Komarov, N.V., Yarosh, O.G.: Izv. Akad. Nauk. SSSR Ser. Khim. 1573 (1971)
109. Weber, W.P., Willard, A.K., Boettger, H.G.: J. Org. Chem. 36, 1620 (1971)
110. Zwiefel, G., On, H.P.: Synthesis, 803 (1980)
111. Bock, M., Seidel, H.: J. Organometal. Chem. 13, 87 (1968)
112. Mironov, V.F., Petrov, A.D., Maksimova, N.G.: Izv. Akad. Nauk. SSSR, Otd. Khim. Nauk. 954 (1958)
113. Fritz, G., Grobe, J.: Z. Anorg. Allg. Chem. 309, 77 (1961)
114. Dexheimer, E.M., Spialter, L.: J. Organometal. Chem. 107, 229 (1976)
115. Soderquist, J.A., Hassner, A.: J. Am. Chem. Soc. 102, 1577 (1980)
116. Soderquist, J.A., Hassner, A.: J. Org. Chem. 45, 541 (1980)
117. Clinet, J.C., Linstrumelle, G.: Tetrahedron Lett. 3987 (1980)
118. Chan, T.H., Baldassarre, A., Massuda, D.: Synthesis, 801 (1976)
119. Nagendrappa, G.: Synthesis, 704 (1980)
120. Taylor, R.T., Degenhardt, C.R., Melega, W.P., Paquette, L.A.: Tetrahedron Lett. 159 (1977)
121. Chamberlin, A.R., Stemke, J.E., Bond, F.T.: J. Org. Chem. 43, 147 (1978)
122. Eaborn, C., Jackson, R.A., Pearce, R.: J. Chem. Soc. Perkin I, 2055 (1974)
123. Eaborn, C., Jackson, R.A., Pearce, R.: J. Chem. Soc. Perkin I, 470 (1975)
124. Mychajlowskij, W., Chan, T.H.: Tetrahedron Lett. 4439 (1976)
125. Chan, T.H., Mychajlowskij, W., Ong, B.S., Harpp, D.N.: J. Organometal. Chem. 107, C1 (1976)
126. Uchida, K., Utimoto, K., Nozaki, H.: J. Org. Chem. 41, 2941 (1976)
127. Obayashi, M., Utimoto, K., Nozaki, H.: Tetrahedron Lett. 1807 (1977)
128. Westmijze, H., Meijer, J., Vermeer, P.: Tetrahedron Lett. 1823 (1977)
129. Eisch, J.J., Damasevitz, G.A.: J. Org. Chem. 41, 2214 (1976)
130. Uchida, K., Utimoto, K., Nozaki, H.: J. Org. Chem. 41, 2215 (1976)
131. Fleming, I., Roessler, F.: J. Chem. Soc. Chem. Comm. 276 (1980)
132. Sato, F., Ishikawa, H., Sato, M.: Tetrahedron Lett. 85 (1981)
133. Calas, R., Dunoguès, J.: C.R. Acad. Sci. Paris, Ser. C, 554 (1971)
134. Dunoguès, J., Bourgeois, P., Pillot, J.P., Merault, G., Calas, R., Lapouyade, P.: J. Organometal. Chem. 87, 169 (1975)
135. Frisch, K.C., Young, R.B.: J. Am. Chem. Soc. 74, 4853 (1952)
136. Sakurai, H., Nishiwaki, K.I., Kira, M.: Tetrahedron Lett. 4193 (1973)
137. Utimoto, K., Kitai, M., Naruse, M., Nozaki, H.: Tetrahedron Lett. 4233 (1975)
138. Binger, P., Köster, R.: Synthesis, 309 (1973)
139. Köster, R., Hagelee, L.A.: Synthesis, 118 (1976)
140. Snider, B.B., Karras, M., Conn, R.S.E.: J. Am. Chem. Soc. 100, 4624 (1978)
141. Snider, B.B., Conn, R.S.E., Karras, M.: Tetrahedron Lett. 1679 (1979)
142. Amouroux, R., Chan, T.H.: Tetrahedron Lett. 4453 (1978)
143. Overman, L.E., Bell, K.L.: J. Am. Chem. Soc. 103, 1851 (1981)

8 Aryl Silanes

8.1 Introduction

Electrophilic cleavage of aryl silanes result, in general, in specific substituted aromatic compounds in which the electrophile occupies the position to which the silyl group was previously bonded. Unlike normal electrophilic substitution reactions which involve loss of a proton, mixtures of isomers are *not* obtained.

$$(8.1)$$

8.2 Protodesilylation

The first example of protodesilylation was reported by Kipping [1].

$$Ph_4Si \; + \; H_3O^+ \longrightarrow Ph_3SiOH \; + \; PhH \qquad (8.2)$$

The mechanism of this reaction has been extensively studied by Eaborn [2, 3]. The observations that protodesilylation of *p*-methoxyphenyltrimethylsilane occurs 1.55 times faster with HCl in H_2O/*p*-dioxane than with DCl in D_2O/*p*-dioxane [4] and 7.3 times [5] as fast in CF_3CO_2H/H_2O as in CF_3CO_2D/D_2O are consistent with a mechanism in which proton transfer to form the sigma complex is rate limiting.

$$(8.3)$$

Substituent effects on the rate of protodesilylation of aryltrimethylsilanes have been determined [6]. The effect of two methyl groups in 2,4-dimethyl-phenyltrimethylsilane and 2,5-dimethylphenyltrimethylsilane is additive. However, 2,6-dimethylphenyltrimethylsilane undergoes protodesilylation significantly faster (~ 10 times). This acceleration is consistent with a decrease of steric strain in the sigma complex [7, 8].

$$(8.4)$$

Although the C—Si bond is not broken in the rate determining step, phenyltrimethylsilane undergoes protodesilylation ten thousand times faster than benzene-d_1 undergoes dedeuteration in aq. sulfuric acid. This acceleration has been attributed to inductive electron release by the trimethylsilyl group [9].

From a synthetic viewpoint the reaction has been utilized to introduce deuterium into specific positions of aromatic nuclei [10, 11].

$$(8.5)$$

2-Trimethylsilylpyridine undergoes protodesilylation by water, methanol, or ethanol. The reaction has been proposed to occur by a four-center transition state which is stabilized by hydrogen bonding [12].

$$(8.6)$$

The large negative entropy of activation for the reaction ($\Delta H^+ = 16$, $\Delta S^+ = -29$ e.u.) is consistent with this proposal. This type of protodesilylation does not occur with 3 or 4-trimethylsilylpyridines.

8.3 Halodesilylation

Although benzene can not be directly iodinated to yield iodobenzene, phenyl-trimethylsilane reacts with iodine to yield TMS-I and iodobenzene [13].

$$(8.7)$$

Iodine and aluminium powder [14, 15] have also been utilized. Iodine monochloride has proved particularly effective. Aryl iodides and TMS-Cl are obtained. The reaction is successful even when the aromatic ring is substituted by strongly electron withdrawing groups. o-, m-, and p-Iodo nitrobenzenes, have been prepared [16].

$$(8.8)$$

o-, m-, and p-bis(Trimethylsilyl) benzenes have been converted to o-, m-, and p-diiodobenzenes, respectively, by reaction with iodine monochloride [17, 18].

[Hydroxy(tosyloxy)iodo]arenes react with aryltrimethylsilanes in acetonitrile to yield diaryl iodonium tosylates [19, 20].

$$(8.9)$$

The reaction of bromine with tetraphenylsilane [21] or phenyltrimethylsilane [13, 22] yields bromobenzene and triphenylbromosilane [21] or TMS-Br, respectively, [13, 22].

$$Ph_4Si + Br_2 \longrightarrow PhBr + Ph_3SiBr \qquad (8.10)$$

Reaction of bromine with optically active α-naphthyl p-methoxyphenyl-phenylmethylsilane leads predominantly to α-naphthylphenylmethylbromosilane and p-bromo anisole. Inversion of stereochemistry at the silyl center is observed. This is consistent with electrophilic attack by a bromonium ion on the carbon bearing the silyl group to form a sigma complex. Backside attack of bromide ion on the silyl center yields the products [23, 25]. A four-center mechanism, on the other hand, would be expected to result in retention of stereochemistry at the silyl center.

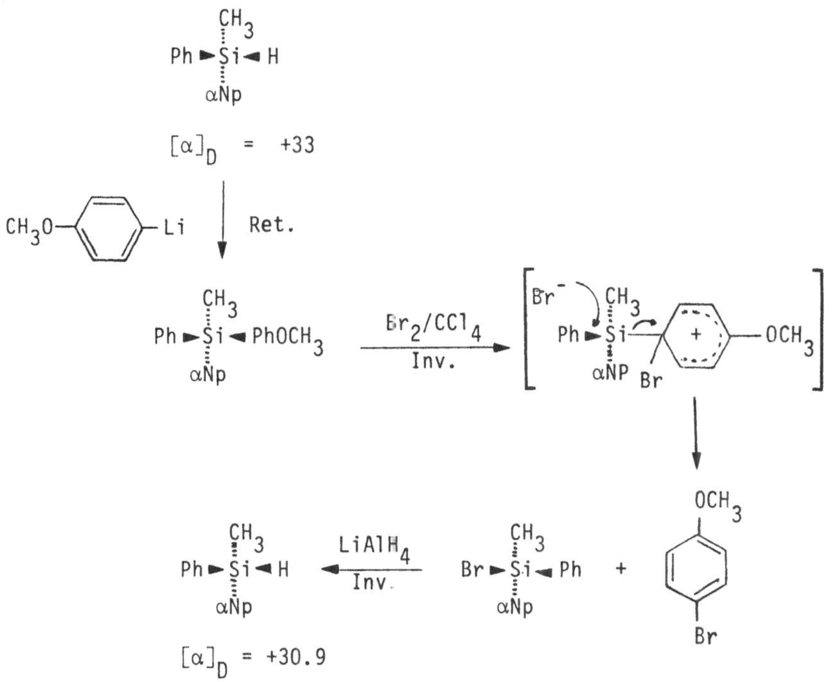

CH₃
Ph ► Si ◄ H
αNp

$[\alpha]_D$ = +33

CH₃O—⟨ ⟩—Li | Ret.

CH₃
Ph ► Si ◄ PhOCH₃   →(Br₂/CCl₄, Inv.)→   [Br⁻ ↷ CH₃ ; Ph ► Si ↱⟨ + ⟩—OCH₃ ; αNp Br]

↓

OCH₃
⟨ ⟩
Br

CH₃   CH₃
Ph ► Si ◄ H   ←(LiAlH₄, Inv.)—   Br ► Si ◄ Ph   +
αNp   αNp

(8.11)

$[\alpha]_D$ = +30.9

o-*bis*(Trimethylsilyl)benzene undergoes monobromo-desilylation to yield o-bromophenyltrimethylsilane [15].

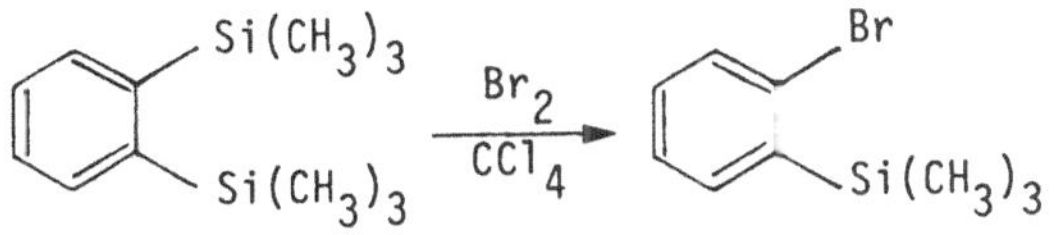

⟨ Si(CH₃)₃ / Si(CH₃)₃ ⟩ →(Br₂, CCl₄)→ ⟨ Br / Si(CH₃)₃ ⟩   (8.12)

Sequential electrophilic desilylations of 4,5- [10] and 3,4- [11] *bis*(trimethylsilyl)benzocyclobutenes, as well as 5,6-*bis*(trimethylsilyl)benzocyclopentene, and 6,7-*bis*(trimethylsilyl)benzocyclohexene [10] by bromine, followed by iodine monochloride, yield the corresponding *ortho* bromo iodo aromatics.

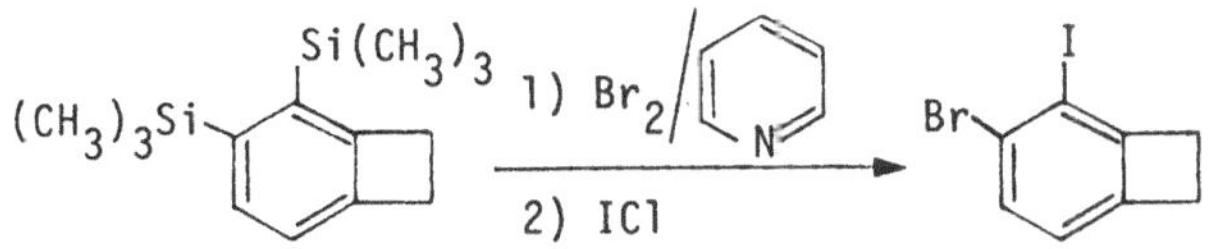

(CH₃)₃Si—⟨ Si(CH₃)₃ ⟩⊐   →(1) Br₂/pyridine; 2) ICl)→ Br—⟨ I ⟩⊐   (8.13)

With 3,4-*bis*(trimethylsilyl)benzocyclobutene, 4-bromo-3-iodo-benzocyclobutene is obtained. This regiospecificity results from the fact that desilylation occurs at the 4-position 500 times faster than at the 3-position [11]. *ortho*-*bis*(Trimethylsilyl)benzenes have a tendency to rearrange under acid catalysis to the corresponding *meta* isomers [26]. This results in relief of steric strain. Pyridine prevents this acid catalyzed rearrangement from competing with the bromodesilylation above.

117

$$(8.14)$$

93%   5%

Unexpectedly, bromination of 2-n-octyl-4-trimethylsilyl furan with pyridinium bromide perbromide in THF gives 2-bromo-3-trimethylsilyl-5-n-octyl furan. Electrophilic substition apparently occurs in preference to bromo-desilylation [27].

The mechanism of chlorodesilylation of aryltrimethylsilanes has been studied [18, 22].

8.4 Metallo-desilylation

Electrophilic desilylation of aryl silanes by mercuric was reported eighty-five years ago [28].

$$(8.15)$$

The reaction of mercuric acetate with aryltrimethylsilanes in glacial acetic acid has been thoroughly studied. The mercuric acetate group in the product unequivocally assumes the position occupied by the trimethylsilyl group in the starting material [29].

$$(8.16)$$

Aryltrimethylsilanes undergo regiospecific electrophilic desilylation on treatement with thallium (III) *tris*-trifluoroacetate in trifluoracetic acid to yield aryl thallium *bis*-trifluoroacetate derivatives. The reaction proceeds readily even with moderately electron withdrawing substituents on the aromatic ring [30–32].

$$(8.17)$$

Lead *tetrakis* trifluoroacetate affects electrophilic desilylation of aryltrimethylsilanes in trifluoracetic acid to yield regiospecifically aryl trifluoroacetates. The reaction may involve an aryl lead *tris*-trifluoroacetate as an intermediate [33].

Lead tetraacetate in acetic acid is not effective.

$$\text{(8.18)}$$

8.5 Sulfo-desilylation

The reaction of tetraphenylsilane with sulfuric acid to yield benzene sulfonic acid and silica was reported by Kipping [1]. Similarly the reaction of sulfur trioxide with aryltrimethylsilanes regiospecifically yields trimethylsilyl benzenesulfonates. This reaction permits introduction of a sulfonic acid group at a specific position of the aromatic ring [34, 35]. o- [15], m- [35], and p- [34] bis(Trimethylsilyl)benzenes react with sulfur trioxide to yield o-, m-, and p-trimethylsilyl trimethylsilylbenzenesulfonates, respectively.

$$\text{(8.19)}$$

Trimethylsilyl chlorosulfonate reacts with aryltrialkylsilanes to yield trialkylsilyl arylsulfonates and TMS-Cl [36].

o-, m-, and p-Nitrophenyltrimethylsilanes undergo electrophilic desilylation with trimethylsilyl chlorosulfonate to yield the corresponding o-, m-, and p-nitrobenzene sulfonic acids after aq. work-up [16].

$$\text{(8.20)}$$

Treatment of o-, m-, or p-trimethylsilyl acetanilide with trimethylsilyl chlorosulfonate followed by aq. work-up gives the corresponding N-acetyl amino-benzene sulfonic acids [16].

$$(8.21)$$

8.6 Acyl-desilylation

Aryltrimethylsilanes undergo acyl-desilylation on treatment with acid chlorides in the presence of $AlCl_3$ [10, 37].

$$(8.22)$$

Only one of the two trimethylsilyl groups of 1,2- [15] or 1,4-*bis*(trimethyl-silyl)benzene undergoes acyl-desilylation.

$$(8.23)$$

Phenyltrichlorosilane undergoes acyl-desilylation with acetyl chloride and $AlCl_3$ to yield acetophenone and tetrachlorosilane [38].

8.7 Alkyl-desilylation

A very limited number of alkyl-desilylation reactions have been reported. Phenyltrimethylsilane reacts with benzyl bromide and $AlCl_3$ to give diphenyl-methane [37]. While 1,2-*bis*(trimethylsilyl)benzene reacts with *t*-butyl chloride and $AlCl_3$ to give *o-t*-butylphenyltrimethylsilane [15].

$$\text{(8.24)}$$

8.8 Diazo-desilylation

Aryltrimethylsilane substituted by electron donating groups *ortho* or *para* to the trimethylsilyl group react regiospecifically with aryl diazonium salts via diazo-desilylation [39–41].

$$\text{(8.25)}$$

meta-Dimethylaminophenyltrimethylsilane, however, undergoes normal diazo coupling [42].

8.9 Nitrodesilylation

Nitration of aryltrimethylsilanes is rather complicated. The usual conditions (H_2SO_2/HNO_3) can not be used due to competition from protodesilylation. Nitric acid in acetic anhydride or cupric nitrate trihydrate in acetic acid are successful [43–45]. The course of the reaction is highly dependent on temperature and the conditions used to prepare the nitric acid/acetic anhydride mixture. For example, if nitric acid and acetic anhydride are mixed at low temperature and reacted with phenyltrimethylsilane between large 0°–10°, nitration principally occurs. Nitrodesilylation is the minor process. Similar results are obtained with cupric nitrate. From the distribution of o-, m-, and p-nitro-phenyltrimethylsilane products it appears that a trimethylsilyl group is a weak *ortho/para* director.

18%   24.7%   17.3%   23%

$$\text{(8.26)}$$

On the other hand, aryltrimethylsilanes have been reported to undergo nitrodesilylation on treatment with nitric acid (71%) and acetic anhydride at reflux [46]. Likewise, 1,4-*bis*(trimethylsilyl)benzene undergoes nitrodesilylation on treatment with nitric acid in acetic anhydride [47].

$$(8.27)$$

Formation of *p*-nitrophenyltrimethylsilane does not result from protodesilylation of 1,4-*bis*(trimethylsilyl)benzene, followed by nitration of phenyltrimethylsilane, because this would lead to a mixture of isomers. In a similar manner, *p*-tolyltrimethylsilane permits a clear distinction to be drawn between nitrodesilylation and protodesilylation followed by nitration.

$$(8.28)$$

When nitric acid/acetic anhydride are heated briefly to 100° and then reacted with *p*-tolyltrimethylsilane at 15°, nitrodesilylation is the predominant process. Nitrodesilylation results from initial nitrosodesilylation, followed by oxidation. On the other hand, when nitric acid and acetic anhydride are prepared at 15° and reacted with *p*-tolyltrimethylsilane at this temperature, nitration and nitrodesilylation occur with almost equal facility [48].

$$(8.29)$$

The electrophile involved in nitrosodesilylation is highly selective for the C−Si bond. Nitrosodesilylation can be achieved by treatment of aryltrimethylsilanes with isoamyl nitrite or sodium nitrite and trifluoroacetic acid. These nitroso aromatics can easily be oxidized to nitro aromatics with hydrogen peroxide [49, 74].

$$(8.30)$$

8.10 Aryl Silanes as Organometallic Reagents

On the basis of differences in electronegativity, the C−Si bond possesses 12% ionic character. Silicon is the positive end and carbon is the negative end of the dipole. In a limited number of cases, aryl silanes react with aldehydes as if they were aryl Grignard or aryl lithium reagents. Both penta-fluoro and pentachlorophenyltrimethylsilane react with benzaldehyde to give the corresponding α-pentahalophenyl benzyl trimethylsilyl ethers [50].

$$(8.31)$$

In a similar manner, 2-trimethylsilyl pyridine [51, 52], 1-methyl-2-trimethyl-silyl imidazole [53], and 2-trimethylsilyl benzthiazoles [54], react with benzaldehydes to give α-(2-pyridinyl), α-[2-(1-methylimidazolyl)] or α-(2-benzthiazolyl)benzyl trimethylsilyl ethers, respectively.

$$(8.32)$$

While phenyltrimethylsilane does not react thermally with benzaldehyde, aryltrimethylsilanes substituted with electron withdrawing groups in the *ortho* position react with benzaldehyde, under nucleophilic catalysis by potassium *t*-butoxide, potassium or cesium fluoride as outlined below [55].

$$(8.33)$$

Similar reactions occur with alkyl aryl ketones, acyl fluorides, anhydrides and CO_2. On the other hand, the reaction fails when the aryl nucleus is substituted by electron donating groups. This difficulty can be overcome by use of trimethylsilyl arene chromium tricarbonyl complexes. These undergo reaction with aldehydes or ketones under nucleophilic catalysis by cesium fluoride. Oxidative removal of the chromium tricarbonyl group by treatment with iodine followed by hydrolysis yields benzylic alcohols [75].

$$(8.34)$$

2-Trimethylsilyl pyridine undergoes acyl-desilylation on reaction with acid chlorides, anhydrides and ethyl chloroformate. These reactions do not require Lewis acids and presumably depend on the unusual polarity of the C−Si bond which is cleaved [52].

$$(8.35)$$

Similar results have been obtained with 1-methyl-2-trimethylsilyl imidazole and 2-trimethylsilyl benzthiazole [54, 56].

$$(8.36)$$

While 1-methyl-2-trimethylsilyl pyrrole fails to react with benzaldehyde, it undergoes acyl-desilylation with acid chlorides, and anhydrides in the absence of Lewis acids [53].

8.11 Preparation

The preparation of aryl silanes has been recently reviewed [57]. Benzene reacts with trichlorosilane under the influence of Lewis acid catalysts to yield phenyltrichlorosilane [58].

$$\text{C}_6\text{H}_6 + \text{Cl}_3\text{SiH} \xrightarrow[250\text{-}300°]{\text{BCl}_3} \text{C}_6\text{H}_5\text{-SiCl}_3 + \text{SiCl}_4 \tag{8.37}$$

Aryl chlorides undergo thermal reaction with trichlorosilane to yield aryltrichlorosilanes and HCl. In a side reaction, the aryl chloride is reduced by trichlorosilane to the corresponding aromatic hydrocarbon and tetrachloro-silane [59, 60].

$$\text{C}_6\text{H}_5\text{Cl} + \text{HSiCl}_3 \xrightarrow{600°} \text{C}_6\text{H}_5\text{-SiCl}_3 + \text{HCl} + \text{C}_6\text{H}_6 + \text{SiCl}_4 \tag{8.38}$$

Free radical chain processes have been proposed to account for these results.

Many aryltrimethylsilanes have been prepared by *in-situ* Grignard reactions. These are carried out by addition of the aryl halide to a mixture of TMS-Cl, ether and magnesium turnings [61].

$$\text{(pyridyl)Cl} \xrightarrow[\text{Mg/THF}]{(\text{CH}_3)_3\text{SiCl}} \text{(pyridyl)Si(CH}_3)_3 \tag{8.39}$$

o-, *m-*, and *p-bis*(Trimethylsilyl)benzene have been prepared by addition of the corresponding *o-*, *m-*, or *p-*dichlorobenzene to a mixture of TMS-Cl in HMPT and magnesium [62].

$$\text{C}_6\text{H}_4\text{Cl}_2 \xrightarrow[\text{Mg / THF}]{(\text{CH}_3)_3\text{SiCl}} \text{C}_6\text{H}_4(\text{Si(CH}_3)_3)_2 \tag{8.40}$$

1,3,5-*tris*(Trimethylsilyl)benzene and 2,4,6-*tris*(trimethylsilyl) anisole have been prepared by *in-situ* Grignard reactions [63, 64].

$$\text{C}_6\text{H}_3\text{Br}_3 \xrightarrow[\text{Mg/THF}]{(\text{CH}_3)_3\text{SiCl}} \text{C}_6\text{H}_3(\text{Si(CH}_3)_3)_3 \tag{8.41}$$

Aryl trimethylsilanes have also been prepared by *in-situ* formation of aryl lithium or sodium derivatives in the presence of TMS-Cl [65].

$$\text{(8.42)}$$

tetrakis(Triphenylphosphine) palladium (O) catalyzes the reaction of aryl chlorides and bromides with hexamethyldisilane to yield aryltrimethylsilanes. Of particular note, this reaction is successful with nitrohalobenzenes [66–69].

$$\text{(8.43)}$$

Trimethylsilyl lithium, sodium or potassium react with aryl halides to yield aryltrimethylsilanes. The necessary reagents may be prepared *in-situ* by reaction of hexamethyldisilane with methyl lithium, sodium methoxide or potassium methoxide in HMPT [70].

$$\text{(8.44)}$$

Aryltrimethylsilanes have also been prepared by transition metal catalyzed cycloaddition reactions of 1-trimethylsilyl alkynes (see Chapter 9).

$$\text{(8.45)}$$

Dissolving metal reduction of aromatic hydrocarbons in the presence of TMS-Cl yields 1,4-*bis*(trimethylsilyl)-1,4-dihydroaromatics. These can be oxidized by air to yield 1,4-*bis*(trimethylsilyl) aromatics [71–73].

$$\text{(8.46)}$$

126

References

1. Kipping, F.S., Lloyd, L.L.: J. Chem. Soc. 449 (1901)
2. Eaborn, C.: Pure and Applied Chemistry, *19*, 375 (1969)
3. Eaborn, C., Bott, R.W., "Synthesis and Reaction of the Silicon Carbon Bond" in Organometallic Compounds of the Group IV Element, Vol I, (MacDiarmid, A.G., Ed.), p. 407–435, New York: Marcel Dekker, 1968
4. Bott, R.W., Eaborn, C., Greasley, P.M.: J. Chem. Soc. 4804 (1964)
5. Eaborn, C., Jackson, P.M., Taylor, R.: J. Chem. Soc. *B*, 613 (1966)
6. See Ref. 3, p. 410–411 and 414.
7. Benkeser, R.A., Krysiak, H.R.: J. Am. Chem. Soc. *76*, 6353 (1954)
8. Eaborn, C., Moore, R.C.: J. Chem. Soc. 3640 (1959)
9. Eaborn, C., Pande, K.C.: J. Chem. Soc. 1566 (1960)
10. Hillard, III, R.L., Vollhardt, K P.C.: J. Am. Chem. Soc. *99*, 4058 (1977)
11. Hillard, III, R.L., Vollhardt, K P.C.: Angew. Chem. Int. *16*, 399 (1977)
12. Anderson, D.G., Bradney, M.A.M., Webster, D.E.: J. Chem. Soc. *B*, 450 (1968)
13. Pray, B.O., Sommer, L.H., Goldberg, G.M., Kerr, G.T., DiGiorgio, P.A., Whitmore, F.C.: J. Am. Chem. Soc. *70*, 433 (1948)
14. Eaborn, C.: J. Chem. Soc. 2755 (1949)
15. Eaborn, C., Walton, D.R.M., Young, D.J.: J. Chem. Soc. *B*, 15 (1969)
16. Félix, G., Dunoguès, J., Calas, R.: Angew. Chem. Int. Ed. *18*, 402 (1979)
17. Félix, G., Dunoguès, J., Pisciotti, F., Calas, R.: Angew. Chem. Int. Ed. *16*, 483 (1977)
18. Stock, L.M., Spector, A.R.: J. Org. Chem. *28*, 3272 (1963)
19. Koser, G.F., Wettach, R.H., Smith, C.S.: J. Org. Chem. *45*, 1543 (1980)
20. Beringer, F.M., Dehn, Jr., J.W., Winicov, M.: J. Am. Chem. Soc. *82*, 2948 (1960)
21. Ladenburg, A.: Chem. Ber. *40*, 2274 (1907)
22. Eaborn, G., Webster, D.E.: J. Chem. Soc. 179 (1960)
23. Eaborn, C., Steward, O.W.: Proc. Chem. Soc. 59 (1963)
24. Eaborn, C., Steward, O.W.: J. Chem. Soc. 521 (1965)
25. Sommer, L.H., Michael, K.W., Korte, W.D.: J. Am. Chem. Soc. *89*, 868 (1967)
26. Seyferth, D., White, D.L.: J. Am. Chem. Soc. *94*, 3132 (1972)
27. Nolan, S.M., Cohen, T.: J. Org. Chem. *46*, 2473 (1981)
28. Combes, C.: Compt. Rend. Acad. Sci. Paris, *122*, 622 (1896)
29. Benkeser, R.A., Hoke, D.I., Hickner, R.A.: J. Am. Chem. Soc. *80*, 5294 (1958)
30. Bell, H.C., Kalman, J.R., Pinhey, J.T., Sternhall, S.: Tetrahedron Lett. 3391 (1974)
31. Taylor, E.C., Kienzle, F., Robey, R.L., McKillop, A., Hunt, J.D.: J. Am. Chem. Soc. *93*, 4845 (1971)
32. McKillop, A., Fowler, J.S., Zeleska, M.J., Hunt, J.D., Taylor, E.C., McGillivray, G.: Tetrahedron Lett. 2423 (1969)
33. Kalman, J.R., Pinhey, J.T., Sternhall, S.: Tetrahedron Lett. 5369 (1972)
34. Eaborn, C., Hashimoto, T.: Chem. and Ind. 1081 (1961)
35. Bott, R.W., Eaborn, C., Hashimoto, T.: J. Organometal. Chem. *3*, 442 (1965)
36. Calas, R., Bourgeois, P., Duffaut, N.: Compt. Rend, Acad. Sci. Paris, *263*, C243 (1966)
37. Dey, K., Eaborn, C., Walton, D.R.M.: Organometal. Chem. Syn. *1*, 151 (1970/71)
38. Austin, J.D., Eaborn, C., Smith, J.D.: J. Chem. Soc. 4744 (1963)
39. Sunthankar, S.V., Gilman, H.: J. Org. Chem. *15*, 1200 (1950)
40. Sakata, Y., Hashimoto, T.: Yakugaku Zasshi, *80*, 728 (1960), CA *54*, 24480 (1960)
41. Sakata, Y., Hashimoto, T.: Yakugaku Zasshi, *79*, 878 (1959), CA *54*, 358a (1960)
42. Hashimoto, T., Seki, M.: Yakugaku Zasshi, *81*, 204 (1961), CA *55*, 14340 (1961)
43. Speier, J.L.: J. Am. Chem. Soc. *75*, 2930 (1953)

44. Benkeser, R.A., Brumfield, P.E.: J. Am. Chem. Soc. *73*, 4770 (1951)
45. Benkeser, R.A., Landesman, H.: J. Am. Chem. Soc. *76*, 904 (1954)
46. Chvalovsky, V., Bazant, V.: Collect. Czech. Chem. Commun. *16*, 580 (1951)
47. Deans, F.B., Eaborn, C.: J. Chem. Soc. 498 (1957)
48. Eaborn, C., Salih, Z.S., Walton, D.R.M.: J. Chem. Soc. Perkin II, 172 (1972)
49. Birkofer, L., Franz, M.: Chem. Ber. *104*, 3062 (1971)
50. Webb, A.F., Sethi, D.S., Gilman, H.: J. Organometal. Chem. *21*, P61 (1970)
51. Pinkerton, F.H., Thames, S.F.: J. Heterocyclic Chem. *6*, 433 (1969)
52. Pinkerton, F.H., Thames, S.F.: J. Organometal. Chem. *24*, 623 (1970)
53. Pratt, J.R., Pinkerton, F.H., Thames, S.F.: J. Organometal. Chem. *38*, 29 (1972)
54. Pinkerton, F.H., Thames, S.F.: J. Heterocyclic Chem. *8*, 257 (1971)
55. Effenberger, F., Spiegler, W.: Angew. Chem. Int. Ed. *20*, 265 (1981)
56. Pinkerton, R.H., Thames, S.F.: J. Heterocyclic Chem. *9*, 67 (1972)
57. Häbich, D., Effenberger, F.: Synthesis, 84 (1979)
58. Barry, A.J., Gilkey, J.W., Hook, D.E.: Ind. Eng. Chem. *51*, 131 (1959)
59. Chernyshev, E.A., Li, G.L., Petrov, A.D.: Dokl. Akad. Nauk. SSSR, *127*, 808 (1959)
60. Petrov, A.D., Mironov, V.F., Ponomarenko, V.A., Chernyshev, E.A., Synthesis of Organosilicon Monomers, p. 288, New York: Consultants Bureau, 1964
61. Anderson, D.G., Bradney, M.A.M., Webster, D.E.: J. Chem. Soc. *B*, 450 (1968)
62. Félix, G., Dunoguès, J., Pisciotti, F., Calas, R.: Angew. Chem. Int. Ed. *16*, 488 (1977)
63. Chaffee, R.G., Beck, H.N.: J. Chem. and Eng. Data, *8*, 453 (1963)
64. Beck, H.N., Chaffee, R.G.: J. Chem. and Eng. Data, *8*, 602 (1963)
65. Eaborn, C., Walton, D.R.M., Young, D.J.: J. Chem. Soc. *B*, 15 (1969)
66. Matsumoto, H., Shono, K., Nagai, Y.: J. Organometal. Chem. *208*, 145 (1981)
67. Matsumoto, H., Nagashima, S., Yoshihiro, K., Nagai, Y.: J. Organometal. Chem. *85*, C1 (1975)
68. Azarian, A., Dua, S.S., Eaborn, C., Walton, D.R.M.: J. Organometal. Chem. *117*, C55 (1976)
69. Matsumoto, H., Yoshihiro, K., Nagashima, S., Watanabe, H., Nagai, Y.: J. Organometal. Chem. *128*, 409 (1977)
70. Shippey, M.A., Dervan, P.B.: J. Org. Chem. *42*, 2654 (1977)
71. Laguerre, M., Dunoguès, J., Calas, R., Duffaut, N.: J. Organometal. Chem. *112*, 49 (1976)
72. Dunoguès, J., Calas, R., Ardoin, N.: J. Organometal. Chem. *43*, 127 (1972)
73. Laguerre, M., Dunoguès, J., Calas, R.: J. Chem. Res. *8*, 295 (1978)
74. Sakata, Y., Hashimoto, T.: Yakugaku Zasshi, *80*, 728 (1960), CA *54*, 24480 (1960)
75. Effenberger, F., Schöllkopf, K.: Angew. Chem. Int. Ed. *20*, 266 (1981)

9 Silyl Acetylenes

9.1 Introduction

Silyl acetylenes have proved to be versatile reagents in a number of reactions. This chapter will be organized into five major sections: first, addition reactions to 1-silyl alkynes; second, electrophilic substitution reactions; third, the use of 1-silyl alkynes as protecting groups for terminal alkynes; fourth, cycloaddition reactions; and fifth, the preparation of these compounds.

9.2 Addition Reactions

1-Trimethylsilylalkynes undergo a variety of addition reactions to yield vinyl silanes. These have been discussed in chapter 7. Nevertheless we will summarize them here since they were previously organized from a different viewpoint.

1-Trimethylsilylalkynes undergo both catalytic hydrogenation [1] and hydrosilation [2] reactions to yield vinyl silanes. HBr adds to trimethylsilyl

$$(CH_3)_3SiC\equiv CH \ + \ \overset{\overset{\displaystyle Cl}{|}}{HSi(CH_3)_2} \ \xrightarrow{\ H_2PtCl_6\ } \ (CH_3)_3Si \diagdown \diagup H \diagup \diagdown Si(CH_3)_2Cl \diagup H \qquad (9.1)$$

acetylene under the influence of peroxides to yield E-1-bromo-2-trimethylsilyl ethylene [3, 4]. Both chlorine and bromine add to bis(trimethylsilyl)-acetylene to yield E-1,2-dihalo-1,2-bis(trimethylsilyl)ethylene [2].

Dialkyl boranes undergo cis addition to 1-trimethylsilylalkynes to yield vinyl organometallic species in which the silicon and boron are bonded to the same carbon atom [5].

$$n\text{-}C_4H_9C\equiv CSi(CH_3)_3 \ \xrightarrow[\qquad 2\ BH\qquad]{} \ n\text{-}C_4H_9 \diagdown \diagup Si(CH_3)_3 \diagup \diagdown H \qquad B \qquad (9.2)$$

Such vinyl organometallics are useful intermediates for the preparation of acyl silanes. Oxidation of $tris$-vinyl borane intermediates with anhydrous trimethylamine oxide followed by hydrolysis affords acyl silanes in high yield [10].

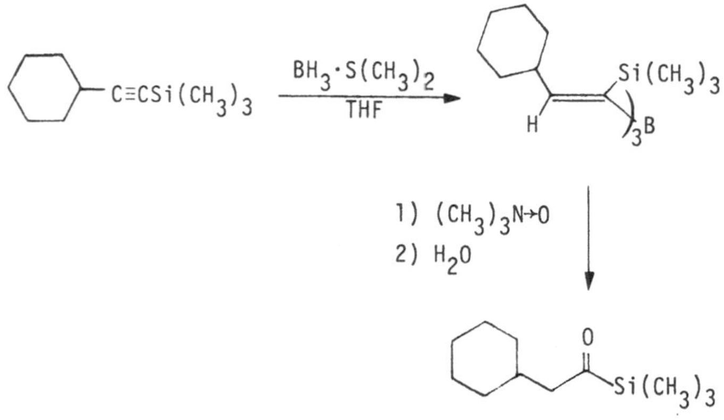
C≡CSi(CH3)3
BH3·S(CH3)2
THF
Si(CH3)3
H
3B
1) (CH3)3N→O
2) H2O
O
Si(CH3)3

(9.3)

Cis-addition of DIBAL to 1-trimethylsilylalkynes occurs in ether solvents [1, 6, 8, 9] or in the presence of one equivalent of a tertiary amine [7]. *Trans*-addition is observed in hydrocarbon solvent [7, 8]. These vinyl alumium-silanes have proved to be synthetically useful (see Chapter 7.9).

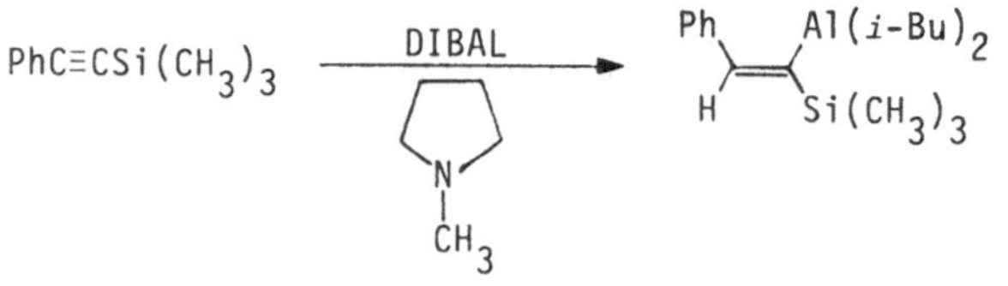
PhC≡CSi(CH3)3
DIBAL
N
CH3
Ph
Al(i-Bu)2
H
Si(CH3)3

(9.4)

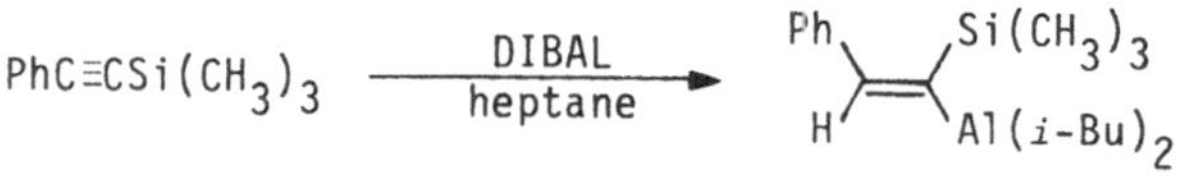
PhC≡CSi(CH3)3
DIBAL
heptane
Ph
Si(CH3)3
H
Al(i-Bu)2

(9.5)

The reaction of 1-trialkylsilylalkynes with isobutylmagnesium bromide catalyzed by *bis*(cyclopentadienyl)titanium dichloride results in *cis* addition of magnesium hydride. This reaction regiospecifically yields a vinyl magnesium species with both the magnesium and silicon bonded to the same carbon (see Vinyl Silanes 7.9) [11].

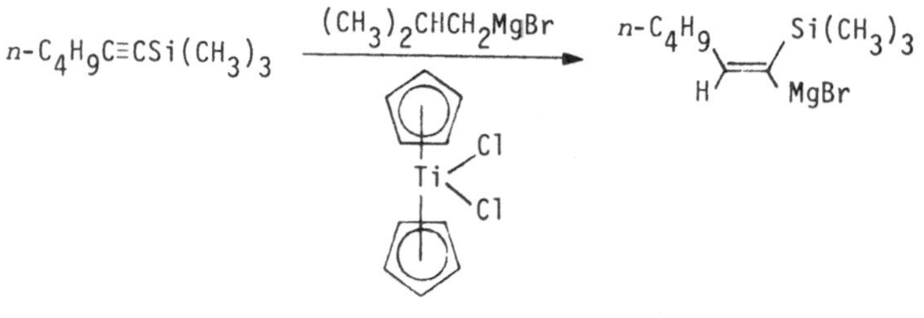
n-C4H9C≡CSi(CH3)3
(CH3)2CHCH2MgBr
Ti
Cl
Cl
n-C4H9
Si(CH3)3
H
MgBr

(9.5)

Magnesium dialkyl cuprate reagents also add in a *cis* manner to 1-trimethylsilylalkynes to yield vinyl cuprates [12, 13].

$$(CH_3)_3SiC{\equiv}CH \;+\; \underset{2\ CuMgBr}{\left(\bigcirc\right)} \longrightarrow \underset{H}{\overset{\bigcirc}{\diagdown}}C{=}C\underset{Si(CH_3)_3}{\overset{CuMgBr}{\diagup}} \qquad (9.7)$$

The same regiospecificity is observed in the nickel catalyzed addition of methyl Grignard reagent to 1-trimethylsilyl alkynes [14].

$$n\text{-}C_6H_{13}C{\equiv}CSi(CH_3)_3 \xrightarrow[\substack{Ni(AcAc)\\Al(CH_3)_3}]{CH_3MgBr} \underset{CH_3}{\overset{n\text{-}C_6H_{13}}{\diagdown}}C{=}C\underset{NiMgBr}{\overset{Si(CH_3)_3}{\diagup}} \qquad (9.8)$$

9.3 Electrophilic Substitution

The chemistry of 1-trimethylsilyl-1-alkynes, 2-alkynes, 1,2-dienes, and 2,3-dienes with electrophiles is similar in many respects and will therefore be considered together. All four types of compounds react with a variety of electrophiles. These reactions usually involve substitution of the trimethylsilyl group by an electrophile. The reactions are often accompanied by rearrangement.

$$HC{\equiv}CCH_2Si(CH_3)_3 \;+\; E^+X^- \longrightarrow H_2C{=}C{=}C\underset{E}{\overset{H}{\diagup}} \;+\; (CH_3)_3SiX \qquad (9.9)$$

A. Protic Acids

1-Trimethylsilyl-2-nonyne reacts with trifluoroacetic acid in methylene chloride to give 1,2-nonadiene [15].

$$CH_3(CH_2)_5C{\equiv}CCH_2Si(CH_3)_3 \xrightarrow[CH_2Cl_2]{CF_3CO_2H} CH_3(CH_2)_5CH{=}C{=}CH_2 \qquad (9.10)$$

1,3-bis(Trimethylsilyl)propyne reacts with methanesulfonic acid to yield trimethylsilyl methanesulfonate and the rearranged product, trimethylsilyl-allene [16]. This reaction may proceed by protonation of the C$-$C triple bond to yield a vinyl carbocation stabilized by a β-trimethylsilyl group. Attack by methanesulfonate ion on the stabilizing silyl center leads to products.

$$(CH_3)_3SiCH_2C{\equiv}CSi(CH_3)_3 \xrightarrow{CH_3SO_3H} \left[(CH_3)_3Si\underset{CH_2C{=}C}{\cdots}\overset{+}{\underset{Si(CH_3)_3}{}}\overset{H}{\diagup} \right] \qquad (9.11)$$

$$\downarrow$$

$$(CH_3)_3SiO{-}\underset{O}{\overset{O}{S}}{-}CH_3 \;+\; H_2C{=}C{=}C\underset{Si(CH_3)_3}{\overset{H}{\diagup}}$$

On the other hand, 1-trimethylsilyl-2-alkynes are stable to a variety of reagents and reaction conditions: mild acid hydrolysis (10% HCl/THF), propionic acid, basic hydrolysis (10% NaOH), alkylidenetriphenylphosphoranes, LiAlH$_4$, and methyl lithium. This stability permits incorporation of the propargyltrimethylsilane functionality into a variety of complex molecules [17].

1-Trimethylsilylalkynes are also stable to mild protic and Lewis acid conditions. For example, the diethyl acetal group of 5,5-diethoxy-1-trimethylsilyl-1-pentyne can be removed by hydrolysis with 1,5% HCl in THF without rearrangement to yield 5-trimethylsilylpent-4-yn-1-al [18].

$$(CH_3CH_2O)_2CHCH_2CH_2C{\equiv}CSi(CH_3)_3 \xrightarrow{\text{1.5\% HCl/THF-H}_2O} H-\overset{\overset{\text{O}}{\|}}{C}-CH_2CH_2C{\equiv}CSi(CH_3)_3$$

(9.12)

Likewise, the aldehyde functional group of 3-trimethylsilylprop-2-yn-1-al can be converted to a 1,3-dithiane by use of the Lewis acid BF$_3$·OEt$_2$ [19].

$$(CH_3)_3SiC{\equiv}C-\overset{\overset{\text{O}}{\|}}{C}-H \xrightarrow[\substack{\text{BF}_3\cdot\text{OEt}_2 \\ \text{HOAc}}]{\text{HS} \qquad \text{SH}} (CH_3)_3SiC{\equiv}C-\overset{\overset{\text{S} \quad \text{S}}{\frown}}{C}-H$$

(9.13)

1-Trimethylsilylalkynes are stable to thallium (III) nitrate in methanol, the conditions required to hydrolyze a 1,3-dithiane to the corresponding ketone [19].

(9.14)

B. Halogens

1-Iodo-2-trimethylsilylacetylene, formed by reaction of iodine monochloride with *bis*(trimethylsilyl)acetylene, is a valuable precursor for Castro coupling with aryl cuprate reagents [20, 21]. 1-Trimethylsilyl-2-nonyne reacts with bromine or iodine to yield 3-halo-1,2-nonadienes [15].

$$CH_3(CH_2)_5C{\equiv}CCH_2Si(CH_3)_3 \xrightarrow[\text{CH}_2\text{Cl}_2]{\text{Br}_2} \underset{\text{Br}}{\overset{CH_3(CH_2)_5}{\diagdown}}C{=}C{=}CH_2$$

(9.15)

1,3-*bis*(Trimethylsilyl)propyne reacts with bromine in CCl$_4$ to yield 1-bromo-1-trimethylsilylallene as the major product [16]. This reaction may occur as outlined below.

$$(CH_3)_3SiCH_2C\equiv CSi(CH_3)_3 \xrightarrow[\substack{CCl_4 \\ -78°}]{Br_2} \left[(CH_3)_3Si\overset{Br^-}{\underset{CH_2}{\cdots}}\overset{+}{C}=C\overset{Si(CH_3)_3}{\underset{Br}{}} \right] \quad (9.16)$$

$$\downarrow$$

$$H_2C=C=C\overset{Si(CH_3)_3}{\underset{Br}{}} + (CH_3)_3SiBr$$

3-Bromo-1-trimethylsilylpropyne has been prepared by reaction of 3-methoxy-1-trimethylsilylpropyne with boron tribromide [22].

$$CH_3OCH_2C\equiv CSi(CH_3)_3 \xrightarrow{BBr_3} BrCH_2C\equiv CSi(CH_3)_3 \quad (9.17)$$

C. Acyl Chlorides

1-Trimethylsilylalkynes react with acid chlorides and $AlCl_3$ to yield conjugated alkynones [23]. This reaction probably proceeds by addition of the acylium ion to the C–C triple bond to yield a β-trimethylsilyl stabilized vinyl carbocation. Attack by chloride on the silyl center causes loss of TMS-Cl and formation of product. The $AlCl_3$ catalyzed intramolecular electrophilic cyclization of 15-trimethylsilylpentadec-14-ynoyl chloride yields 2-cyclopentadecynone [24].

$$(CH_3)_3SiC\equiv C(CH_2)_{12}\overset{O}{\overset{\|}{C}}Cl \xrightarrow[CH_2Cl_2]{AlCl_3} \left(\overset{\overset{O}{\|}}{\underset{(CH_2)_{12}}{C-C\equiv C}} \right) \longrightarrow \longrightarrow muscone \quad (9.18)$$

When bis(trimethylsilyl)acetylene is subjected to similar conditions, only one of the two trimethylsilyl groups is replaced even in the presence of excess acid chloride [23, 25]. Apparently the electron withdrawing carbonyl group deactivates the triple bond toward further electrophilic attack by acylium ions. This difference provides a useful route to 1-trimethylsilyl alkyn-3-ones [23].

$$(CH_3)_3SiC\equiv CSi(CH_3)_3 + O_2N-\underset{}{\bigcirc}-\overset{O}{\overset{\|}{C}}-Cl \xrightarrow{AlCl_3} O_2N-\underset{}{\bigcirc}-\overset{O}{\overset{\|}{C}}-C\equiv CSi(CH_3)_3 \quad (9.19)$$

Similar electrophilic substitutions have been carried out with bis-1,4-(trimethylsilyl)-1,3-butadiyne and aromatic acid chlorides to give 1-aroyl-4-trimethylsilyl-1,3-butadiynes in moderate yield [26]. Isobutyryl chloride, 1,4-

bis(trimethylsilyl)-1,3-butadiyne, and AlCl₃ react to give 6-methyl-1-trimethyl-silyl-1,3-heptadiyn-5-one [27].

1-Trimethylsilyl-2-nonyne reacts with acetyl chloride and AlCl₃ to give 3-acetyl-1,2-nonadiene [15].

$$CH_3(CH_2)_5C\equiv CCH_2Si(CH_3)_3 \xrightarrow[\text{AlCl}_3]{\overset{\overset{O}{\parallel}}{CH_3-C-Cl}} \begin{array}{c} CH_3(CH_2)_5 \\ O=C \\ CH_3 \end{array} C=C=CH_2 \qquad (9.20)$$

Carbamyl chlorides react with 1-trimethylsilylalkynes in essentially the same way as acid chlorides [28].

$$n\text{-}C_4H_9C\equiv CSi(CH_3)_3 \ + \ \overset{O}{\underset{\parallel}{\bigcirc}}N\text{-}\overset{O}{\underset{\parallel}{C}}\text{-}Cl \xrightarrow{\text{AlCl}_3} n\text{-}C_4H_9C\equiv C\text{-}\overset{O}{\underset{\parallel}{C}}\text{-}N\bigcirc \qquad (9.21)$$

D. Sulfonyl Chlorides — Sulfur Trioxide

Arylsulfonyl halides react with *bis*(trimethylsilyl)acetylene under Friedel-Crafts conditions to yield 1-arylsulfonyl-2-trimethylsilylacetylenes [29].

$$(CH_3)_3SiC\equiv CSi(CH_3)_3 \ + \ CH_3 \text{—} \bigcirc \text{—} \overset{O}{\underset{O}{\overset{\parallel}{S}}}\text{-}Cl \xrightarrow{\text{AlCl}_3} CH_3 \text{—} \bigcirc \text{—} \overset{O}{\underset{O}{\overset{\parallel}{S}}}\text{-}C\equiv CSi(CH_3)_3$$

$$\downarrow \text{NaOH}$$

$$CH_3 \text{—} \bigcirc \text{—} \overset{O}{\underset{O}{\overset{\parallel}{S}}}\text{-}C\equiv CH \qquad (9.22)$$

Trimethylsilyl chlorosulfonate also reacts with 1-trimethylsilylalkynes to yield, in general, trimethylsilyl esters of ethynylsulfonic acids [30].

$$PhC\equiv CSi(CH_3)_3 \ + \ Cl\text{-}\overset{O}{\underset{O}{\overset{\parallel}{S}}}\text{-}OSi(CH_3)_3 \longrightarrow PhC\equiv C\text{-}\overset{O}{\underset{O}{\overset{\parallel}{S}}}\text{-}OSi(CH_3)_3 \ + \ (CH_3)_3SiCl \qquad (9.23)$$

Similar results are obtained from the reaction of trimethylsilylacetylenes with the sulfur trioxide complex of *p*-dioxane [31].

Propargyltrimethylsilanes react with either trimethylsilyl chlorosulfonate or the sulfur trioxide complex of *p*-dioxane to yield rearranged trimethylsilyl-allene sulfonates [32]. 1,3-*bis*(Trimethylsilyl)propyne reacts under these conditions as a propargylsilane rather than an alkynylsilane to yield the rearrangement product: trimethylsilyl 1-trimethylsilylallene-1-sulfonate [32].

$$(CH_3)_3SiCH_2C\equiv CSi(CH_3)_3 \xrightarrow[\text{(SO}_3\text{ dioxane)}]{SO_3} \left[\begin{array}{c} \overset{+}{C}\diagup Si(CH_3)_3 \\ CH_2 \diagdown C \\ (CH_3)_3Si \quad SO_2 \\ O \end{array} \right]$$

$$(9.24)$$

$$CH_2=C=C\begin{array}{c} Si(CH_3)_3 \\ O=S=O \\ | \\ OSi(CH_3)_3 \end{array}$$

The reaction of trimethylsilylallene with trimethylsilyl chlorosulfonate to yield trimethylsilyl propargylsulfonate may occur by a similar process [33].

$$H_2C=C=C\begin{array}{c} H \\ Si(CH_3)_3 \end{array} \xrightarrow{ClSO_3Si(CH_3)_3} HC\equiv CCH_2-\overset{O}{\underset{O}{\overset{||}{S}}}-OSi(CH_3)_3$$

$$(9.25)$$

E. Aldehydes and Ketones

Trimethylsilylacetylenes undergo Lewis acid catalyzed electrophilic substitution reactions with ketones and aldehydes to yield propargyl alcohols [34, 35].

$$PhC\equiv CSi(CH_3)_3 + Cl_3C-\overset{O}{\overset{||}{C}}-H \xrightarrow[\text{or GaCl}_3]{AlCl_3} PhC\equiv C-\overset{OH}{\underset{H}{\overset{|}{C}}}-CCl_3$$

$$(9.26)$$

The reaction may occur by Lewis acid coordination to the carbonyl group rending it sufficiently electrophilic to attack the silyl substituted acetylene.

$$n\text{-}C_4H_9C\equiv CSi(CH_3)_3 + H-\overset{O}{\overset{||}{C}}-CCl_3 \xrightarrow{AlCl_3} \left[\begin{array}{c} H\diagdown C \diagup CCl_3 \\ n\text{-}C_4H_9 \diagdown C=C \diagdown OAlCl_3 \\ \overset{+}{\diagup} \diagdown Si(CH_3)_3 \end{array} \right]$$

$$(9.27)$$

$$n\text{-}C_4H_9C\equiv C-\overset{OSi(CH_3)_3}{\underset{H}{\overset{|}{C}}}-CCl_3$$

When a similar reaction is attempted on *bis*(trimethylsilyl)acetylene only one of the trimethylsilyl groups undergoes reaction [36].

1-Trimethylsilylalkynes also react with aldehydes and ketones under nucleophilic catalysis by TBAF [37] or potassium fluoride/18-C-6 [38] to yield propargyl trimethylsilyl ethers. Presumably, these reactions are initiated by fluoride anion attack on the 1-trimethylsilylalkyne to form TMS-F. The resulting acetylide anion then reacts with the ketone. The alkoxide anion thus formed then attacks the 1-trimethylsilylalkyne affording the product and regenerating the acetylide anion [37].

$$PhC\equiv CSi(CH_3)_3 \quad + \quad (n\text{-}C_4H_9)_4N^+F^- \tag{9.28}$$

Propargylsilanes, on the other hand, undergo $AlCl_3$ catalyzed reactions with ketones and aldehydes to yield rearranged allenic alcohols [35].

$$HC\equiv CCH_2Si(CH_3)_3 \quad + \quad Cl_3C\overset{\overset{O}{\|}}{-}CH \xrightarrow{AlCl_3} H_2C=C=CH-\overset{\overset{OH}{|}}{C}H-CCl_3 \tag{9.29}$$

Propargyltrimethylsilanes react with aldehydes, ketones [39, 40] and acetals [41] in the presence of $TiCl_4$ at low temperature to yield respectively rearranged allenic carbinols or ethers. If the allenic carbinol is desired, these reactions must be hydrolyzed at low temperature ($-60°$). Warming prior to hydrolysis yields 2-chloro-1,3-butadiene derivatives by reaction of the initial allenic trimethylsilyl ethers with $TiCl_4$ [39, 40].

Reaction between propargyltrimethylsilanes and aldehydes may also be catalyzed by TBAF in THF. In the case of aliphatic aldehydes, the products are isomerically pure rearranged allenic carbinols. With benzaldehyde, however, a mixture of the expected allenic carbinol and the unrearranged propargyl alcohol are obtained in a 70:30 ratio [42].

$$HC\equiv CCH_2Si(CH_3)_3 \xrightarrow[(n\text{-}C_4H_9)_4N^+F^-]{Ph\overset{\overset{O}{\|}}{-}C-H} H_2C=C=C\overset{\overset{HO}{\diagup}CHPh}{\diagdown H} + HC\equiv CCH_2-\overset{\overset{OH}{|}}{C}H-Ph \tag{9.30}$$

Although *bis*-1,3-(trimethylsilyl)propyne undergoes electrophilic reaction with chloral as a silylacetylene (Eq. 9.30) [35], it reacts as a propargylsilane with acetals under catalysis by TMS-I to yield 1-alkoxy-2-trimethylsilyl-2,3-butadienes (Eq. 9.31) [43]. The reason for this difference is not clear at present.

$$(CH_3)_3SiCH_2C\equiv CSi(CH_3)_3$$

$$\xrightarrow[\text{AlCl}_3]{Cl_3C\text{-}\overset{\overset{\displaystyle O}{\|}}{C}\text{-}H} (CH_3)_3SiCH_2C\equiv C\text{-}\overset{\overset{\displaystyle OH}{|}}{\underset{\underset{\displaystyle H}{|}}{C}}\text{-}CCl_3 \tag{9.31}$$

$$\xrightarrow[\substack{(CH_3)_3SiI \\ -78°}]{PhCH(OCH_3)_2} Ph\text{-}CH\text{-}\overset{\overset{\displaystyle OCH_3}{|}}{\underset{\underset{\displaystyle Si(CH_3)_3}{|}}{C}}=C=CH_2 \tag{9.32}$$

1-Trimethylsilylallenes react with ketones or aldehydes in the presence of TiCl$_4$ to yield rearranged homopropargyl alcohols [44].

$$H_2C=C=C\overset{\displaystyle Si(CH_3)_3}{\underset{\displaystyle CH_3}{\big\langle}} + \text{(cyclohexanone)} \xrightarrow{TiCl_4} \text{(product)} \tag{9.33}$$

The TiCl$_4$ catalyzed reaction of 1-trimethylsilyl-2,3-dienes with aldehydes affords rearranged 2-(1'-hydroxyalkyl)-1,3-butadienes [45].

$$H_2C=C=C\overset{\displaystyle CH_2Si(CH_3)_3}{\underset{\displaystyle n\text{-}C_5H_{11}}{\big\langle}} \xrightarrow[n\text{-}C_8H_{17}CHO]{TiCl_4} \text{(product)} \tag{9.34}$$

1-Trimethylsilylallenes react with α,β-unsaturated ketones to yield trimethylsilylcyclopentene products. This approach to cyclopentenes by [2 + 3] cycloannulation provides a unique regiospecific synthesis of such compounds. The sequence of events outlined in Eq. 9.35 has been proposed to account for these results [46].

$$\text{(cyclohexenone)} + CH_2=C=C\overset{\displaystyle Si(CH_3)_3}{\underset{\displaystyle CH_3}{\big\langle}} \xrightarrow[\substack{-78° \\ CH_2Cl_2}]{TiCl_4} \text{(intermediate)} \tag{9.35}$$

1-Trimethylsilylallenes react with α,β-unsaturated acyl nitriles and TiCl$_4$ in a conjugate 1,4-Michael-type reaction to yield rearranged products [47].

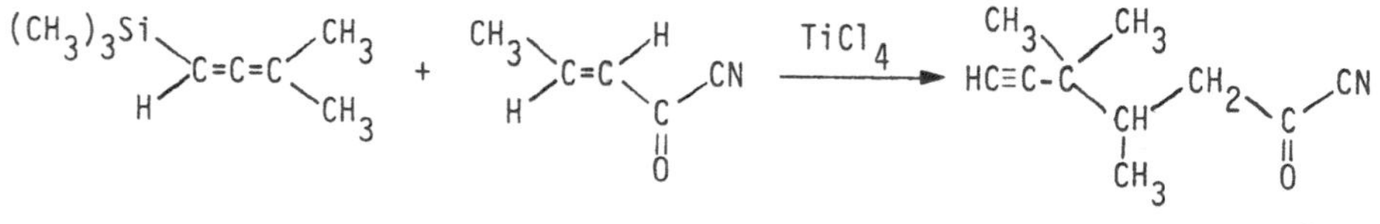

(9.36)

F. Carbocations

1-Trimethylsilylalkynes undergo intramolecular ring-closure with carbocations to yield cyclic ketones as outlined below [48].

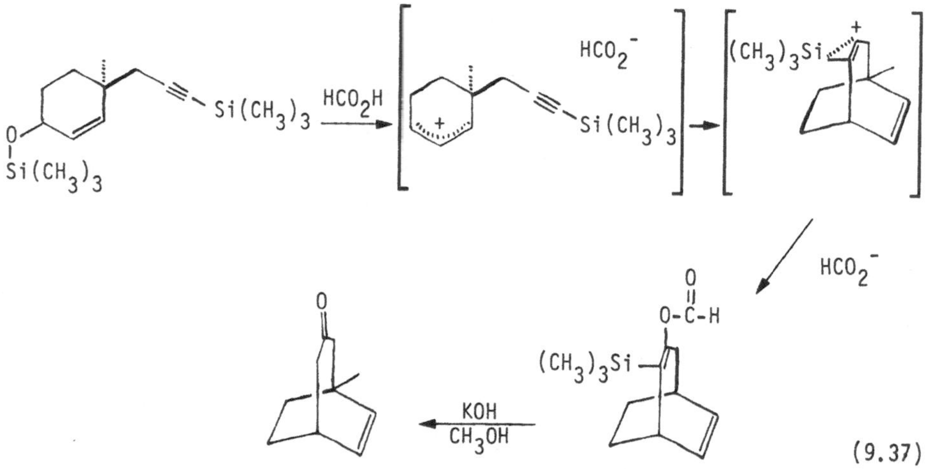

(9.37)

A 1-trimethylsilylalkyne has been used as a terminator in a biomimetic type cyclization to form D-homosteroids [18].

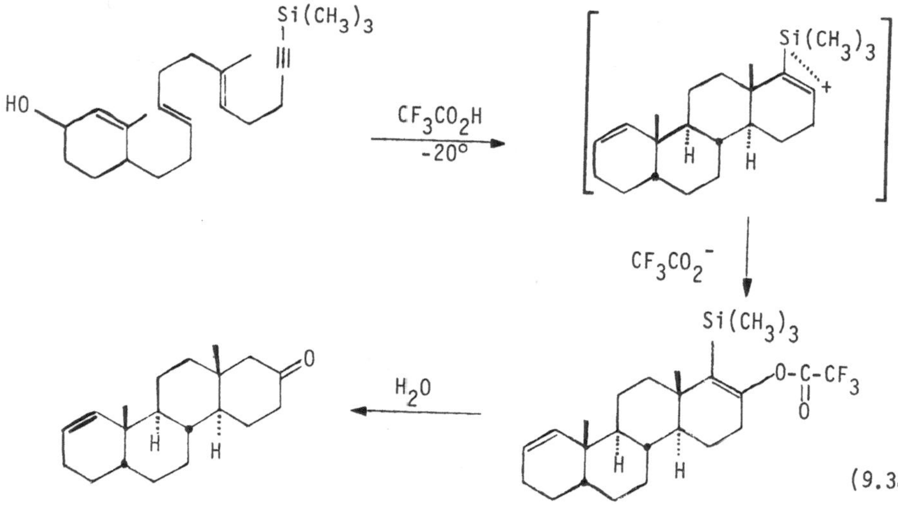

(9.38)

Methyl trimethylsilylacetylene N-carboethoxyglycinate has been prepared by reaction of *bis*(trimethylsilyl)acetylene with methyl-2-chloro-N-carboethoxy glycinate and $AlCl_3$ in methylene chloride [49].

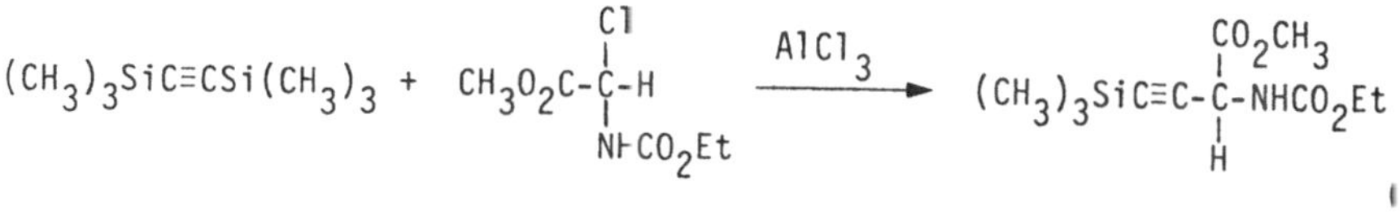
(CH3)3SiC≡CSi(CH3)3 + CH3O2C-C-H
Cl
NHCO2Et
AlCl3
(CH3)3SiC≡C-C-NHCO2Et
CO2CH3
H

(9.39)

Both trimethylsilyl groups of *bis*(trimethylsilyl)acetylene may be substituted by carbocations under electrophilic conditions [23].

Propargyltrimethylsilanes undergo intramolecular reaction with carbocations to yield vinylene cycloalkanes [50].

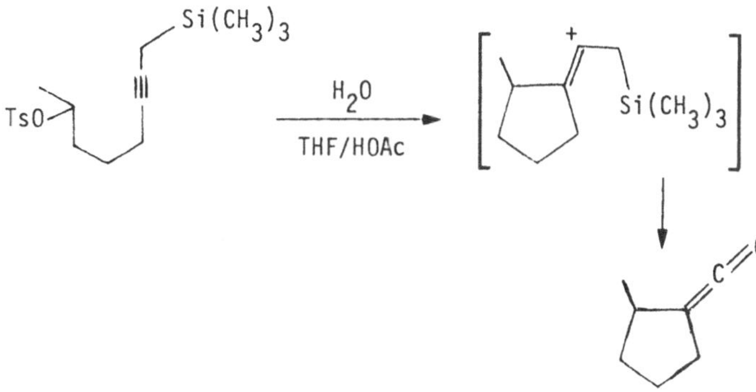
Si(CH3)3
TsO
H2O
THF/HOAc
+
Si(CH3)3
C
CH2

(9.40)

Propargyltrimethylsilanes have also proved effective as terminators in biomimetic carbocation cyclization reactions as outlined below [17].

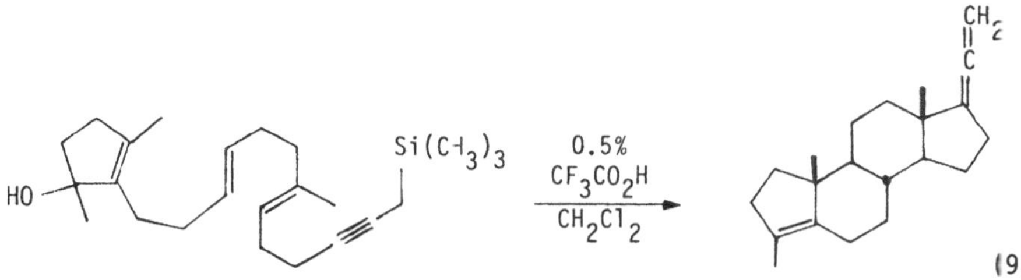
HO
Si(CH3)3
0.5%
CF3CO2H
CH2Cl2
CH2
C

(9.41)

9.4 Protection of Terminal Alkynes

Trimethylsilyl groups have been used to protect terminal alkynes from reduction during the hydrogenation of internal acetylenes to *cis*-alkenes [51].

$$(CH_3)_3Si\text{-}C\equiv C\text{-}C\equiv C\text{-}CH_3 \xrightarrow[Pd/CaCO_3]{H_2} (CH_3)_3Si\text{-}C\equiv C\text{-}\overset{H}{C}=\overset{H}{C}\text{-}CH_3 \qquad (9.42)$$

This approach has been utilized in a highly stereoselective synthesis of a terminal *cis*-enyne. After partial reduction of the internal acetylene by catalytic hydrogenation, the trimethylsilyl protecting group was removed by treatment with TBAF in THF [52].

$$(9.43)$$

The conversion of 4,9-dimethyl-3,9-dodecadien-1,6,11-triyne into 4,9-dimethyl-3,6,9-dodecatrien-1,11-diyne was achieved in a similar manner. The terminal acetylenic groups were protected by deprotonation with ethyl Grignard reagent followed by addition of TMS-Cl. The internal triple bond was then catalytically hydrogenated. Finally, the terminal trimethylsilyl groups were removed by treatment with silver nitrate in aq. ethanol followed by potassium cyanide in water [53].

$$(9.44)$$

It has been proposed that coordination of the silver cation with the triple bond facilitates attack by water on the silyl center which results in cleavage of the Si−C bond [53].

$$(9.45)$$

This deprotection technique may be the mildest method yet developed for the cleavage of Si−C sp hybridized bonds. This procedure has been utilized by Corey [54] in a stereospecific synthesis of *d,1*-C_{18}-Cecropia juvenile hormone, Eq. 9.46 [55], as well as in the preparation of α-Santalol [56].

$$\text{(9.46)}$$

Trimethylsilyl groups have been utilized to protect terminal acetylene not only from reduction but in a number of other reactions. For example, it is not possible to prepare a Grignard reagent from p-bromophenylacetylene due to the acidity of the sp hybridized C−H bond. This difficulty has been overcome by trimethylsilyl protection. Carbonation of the protected Grignard. followed by aq. alkaline cleavage of the Si−C bond yields 4-ethynylbenzoic acid [57].

$$\text{(9.47)}$$

The trimethylsilyl group has been used to protect terminal alkynes in the synthesis of α-acetylenic amines and α-acetylenic α-amino acids. Methyl trimethylsilylacetylene-N-carboethoxyglycinate can be deprotonated with LDA in HMPT to yield a reactive anion which can be alkylated with allylic and benzylic bromides or primary alkyl iodides. This anion can also undergo Michael addition with methyl acrylate α-Acetylene glutamic acid has been prepared as outlined. The trimethylsilyl protecting group is removed by treatment with aq. KOH [58].

$$\text{(9.48)}$$

The alidimine (I) has been used to prepare α-acetylenic α-amino acids and α-acetylenic amines. For example, an α-acetylenic DOPA derivative was prepared as outlined below [59].

$$(9.49)$$

The first example of basic cleavage of a Si−C sp hybridized bond was reported by Gilman. He observed that the base-catalyzed cleavage of the Si−C bond of phenyl triphenylsilyl acetylene was qualitatively fast compared to the cleavage of benzyltriphenylsilane [60]. Quantitative data shows that methanolic sodium hydroxide cleaves the Si−C bond of phenyl trimethylsilyl acetylene 2×10^7 times faster than the Si−C bond of benzyltrimethylsilane. This may reflect the greater stability of an acetylide anion compared to a benzylic anion [61, 62].

The Si−C bond of both 1-aroyl-2-trimethylsilylacetylenes and 1-aroyl-4-trimethylsilyl-1,3-butadiynes are cleaved on treatment with aq. borax and methanol to yield the corresponding aroyl acetylenes or 1-aroyl-1,3-butadiynes [26].

$$(9.50)$$

Potassium fluoride dihydrate in methanol will also cleave Si−C sp hybridized bonds [27].

$$(9.51)$$

Trimethylsilyl protecting groups permit the oxidative coupling of trimethylsilyl acetylenes to yield α,ω-bis(trimethylsilyl)polyacetylenes. The Hay modification [64] of the Glaser reaction has proved effective in this respect. For example, treatment of trimethylsilylacetylene with cuprous chloride,

TMEDA and oxygen yields 1,4-*bis*(trimethylsilyl)-1,3-butadiyne. Similar treatment of 1-trimethylsilyl-1,3-butadiyne yields, 1,8-*bis*(trimethylsilyl)-1,3,5,7-octatetrayne.

$$(CH_3)_3SiC \equiv C-C \equiv CH \xrightarrow[\text{O}_2]{\text{CuCl/TMEDA}} (CH_3)_3SiC \equiv C-C \equiv C-C \equiv CSi(CH_3)_3 \qquad (9.52)$$

Reaction of these products with aq. methanolic alkali yields 1,3-butadiyne and 1,3,5,7-octatetrayne respectively [65]. Triethylsilyl protecting groups have been used in the preparation of 1,3,7,9,13,15,19,21-octadehydro-24-annulene [67]. The rates of base catalyzed cleavage of Si−C bonds in trimethylsilyl-substituted polyacetylenes have been determined [66].

Likewise Cadiot-Chodkiewicz coupling [68] of 1-bromo-2-trialkylsilyl-acetylenes with terminal acetylenes yields 1-trialkylsilyl polyacetylenes [65, 69].

$$Br-\langle\bigcirc\rangle-C \equiv CH + Et_3SiC \equiv CBr \xrightarrow[\substack{EtNH_2 \\ DMF}]{H_2NOH, CuCl} Br-\langle\bigcirc\rangle-C \equiv C-C \equiv CSiEt_3 \qquad (9.53)$$

The reaction of phenylacetylene with 1-bromo-4-triethylsilyl-1,3-butadiyne yields 1-phenyl-6-triethylsilylhexatriyne. The necessary 1-bromo or 1-iodo-4-triethylsilyl-1,3-butadiyne was prepared from 1-triethylsilylbutadiyne. Reaction of 1-triethylsilylbutadiyne with N,N-dimethylamino-tri-*n*-butyltin gave 1-tri-*n*-butylstannyl-4-triethylsilyl-1,3-butadiyne which undergoes selective destannylation on treatment with bromine or iodine monochloride [70].

$$Et_3SiC \equiv C-C \equiv CH \xrightarrow{(n\text{-}Bu)_3SnN(CH_3)_2} Et_3SiC \equiv C-C \equiv CSn(n\text{-}Bu)_3 \xrightarrow{ICl} Et_3SiC \equiv C-C \equiv CI \qquad (9.54)$$

The inverse reaction of an α-bromoacetylene with a trimethylsilyl acetylene fails under Cadiot-Chodkiewicz conditions. However, aryl trimethylsilyl acetylenes can be efficiently prepared by *bis*(triphenylphosphine) palladium dichloride catalyzed coupling of aryl bromides or iodides with trimethylsilyl acetylene [71].

$$\langle\bigcirc\rangle-Br + HC \equiv CSi(CH_3)_3 \xrightarrow[\text{CuI, Et}_3\text{N}]{[Ph_3P]_2PdCl_2} \langle\bigcirc\rangle-C \equiv CSi(CH_3)_3 \qquad (9.55)$$
$$\quad NO_2 \qquad\qquad\qquad\qquad\qquad\qquad\qquad NO_2$$

The Castro coupling of aryl copper reagents with 1-iodo-2-trimethylsilyl-acetylene to yield 1-aryl-2-trimethylsilylacetylenes is closely related [20].

$$\langle\bigcirc\rangle-Cu + IC \equiv CSi(CH_3)_3 \longrightarrow \langle\bigcirc\rangle-C \equiv CSi(CH_3)_3 \qquad (9.56)$$
$$\quad CF_3 \qquad\qquad\qquad\qquad\qquad\qquad CF_3$$

143

Trimethylsilyl groups have been used to protect terminal acetylenes while Castro coupling was carried out between an aryl iodide and a terminal acetylenic copper reagent [72].

9.5 Cycloaddition Reactions

A. Diels-Alder Reactions

Silylacetylenes undergo a variety of cycloaddition reactions. Diels-Alder reactions of silylacetylenes are valuable for the preparation of certain silyl-substituted aromatic compounds [73].

$$(CH_3)_3SiC\equiv CH \quad + \qquad\qquad\qquad (9.57)$$

In a similar manner, *bis*(trimethylsilyl)acetylene undergoes a Diels-Alder reaction with α-pyrone in refluxing bromobenzene. The initial adduct decarboxylates to yield 1,2-*bis*(trimethylsilyl)benzene which readily undergoes acid catalyzed rearrangement to 1,3-*bis*(trimethylsilyl)benzene. The driving force for this rearrangement probably is relief of steric strain. Addition of 10 mole percent of triethylamine to the solvent prevents this rearrangement [74].

$$\qquad\qquad (9.58)$$

144

Both *mono-* and *bis-*(trimethylsilyl)acetylene undergo Diels-Alder reactions with 3,6-*bis*(carbomethoxy)-1,2,4,5-tetrazine to yield substituted pyridazines [75].

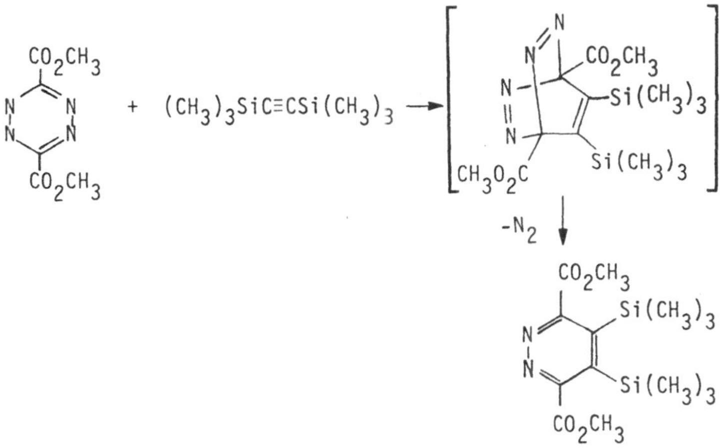

(9.59)

1-Arylsulfonyl-2-trimethylsilylacetylenes undergo Diels-Alder reactions with 1-methoxy-3-trimethylsilyloxy-1,3-butadiene to yield 2-arylsulfonyl-3-methoxy-1-trimethylsilyl-5-trimethylsilyloxy-1,4-cyclohexadienes. On treatment with acid in aq. THF, these lose methanol and hydrolyze to yield 4-arylsulfonyl-3-trimethylsilyl substituted phenols [76].

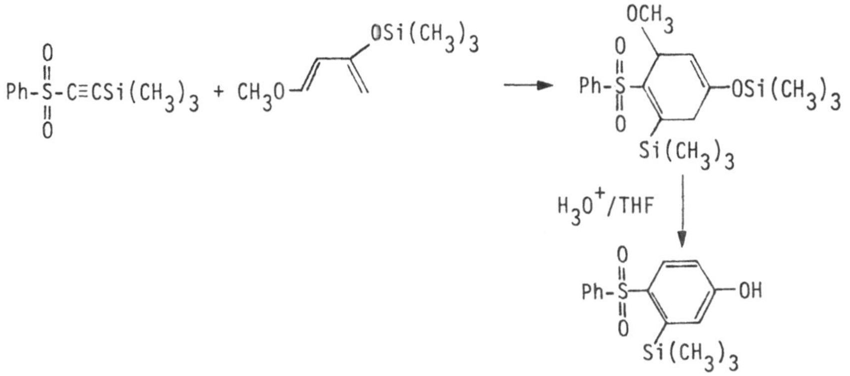

(9.60)

B. Silyl-ynamines

Silyl-ynamines are prepared by the reaction of 1-bromo-2-trimethylsilylacetylene with lithium amides. This reaction probably occurs by an addition – elimination sequence.

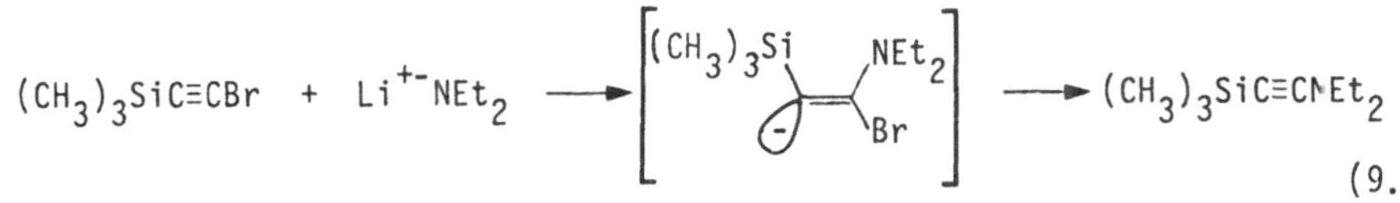

(9.51)

145

Silyl-ynamines undergo Diels-Alder reactions with α,β-usaturated ketones, to yield 2-dialkylamino-3-trimethylsilyl pyran derivatives. The regiospecificity observed may result from the zwitterionic intermediates formed by Michael addition of the nucleophilic carbon of the silyl-ynamine to the α,β-unsaturated ketone [77].

$$(9.62)$$

Silyl-ynamines react with diphenylketene to yield 3-silyloxy-3-buten-1-ynyl amines. Initial nucleophilic attack by the C-2 carbon of the silyl-ynamine on the carbonyl carbon of the ketene leads to a zwitterionic intermediate. Migration of the silyl group from carbon to the negatively charged oxygen yields the product [78].

$$(9.63)$$

On the other hand, silyl-ynamines react with ketene to yield 3-amino-2-silyl-2-cyclobuten-1-ones and 2-silyl-2,3-butadieneamides [79]. The reaction may proceed as indicated. The reason for the different behavior of the two ketenes is at present unknown.

$$(9.64)$$

The reaction of silyl-ynamines with dimethyl acetylenedicarboxylate probably involves a similar zwitterionic intermediate [80].

$$(9.65)$$

C. Cobalt-Catalyzed Cycloadditions

Dicobalt octacarbonyl catalyzed trimerization of trimethylsilylacetylene provides an efficient route to 1,2,4-*tris*-(trimethylsilyl)benzene [81].

$$(9.66)$$

A dicobalt hexacarbonyl complex of trimethylsilylacetylene, which is formed in the reaction, is also an effective catalyst [82].

$$(9.67)$$

η^5-Cyclopentadienyl cobalt dicarbonyl catalyzes cross-trimerization reactions between silylacetylenes and α,ω-diynes [83–85].

$$(9.68)$$

Benzocyclobutenes undergo thermal electrocyclic ring opening to reactive *ortho*-quinone methides which can participate in Diels-Alder reactions [84].

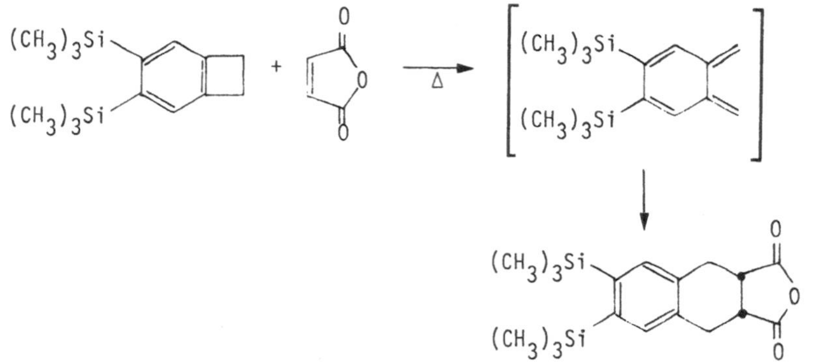

(9.69)

This approach has been utilized in the synthesis of 2,3-*bis*(trimethylsilyl)-estra-1,3,5-(10) trien-17-one as outlined below [86].

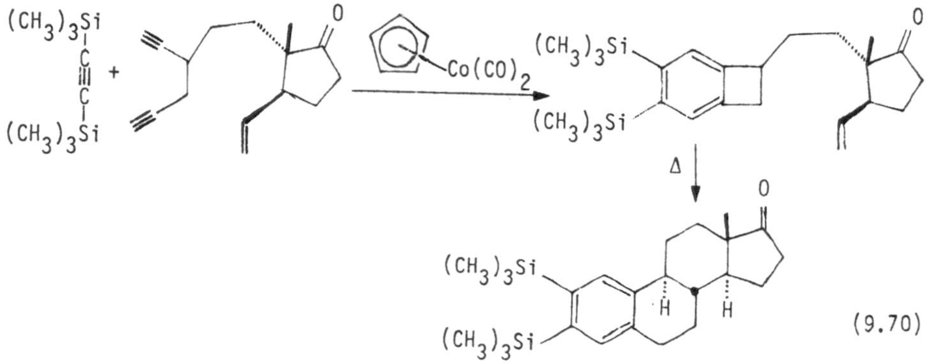

(9.70)

η^5-Cyclopentadienyl cobalt dicarbonyl catalyzes the reaction of 3-trimethyl-silyloxy-1,5-hexadiyne and an excess of *bis*(trimethylsilyl)acetylene to yield 2,3,6,7-*tetrakis*(trimethylsilyl)naphthalene [87].

D. [2 + 2] and [2 + 3] Cycloadditions

Trimethylsilylacetylene undergoes benzophenone triplet sensitized [2 + 2] photocycloaddition reaction with maleic anhydride to yield 1-trimethyl-silylcyclobutene-3,4-dicarboxylic acid anhydride [88].

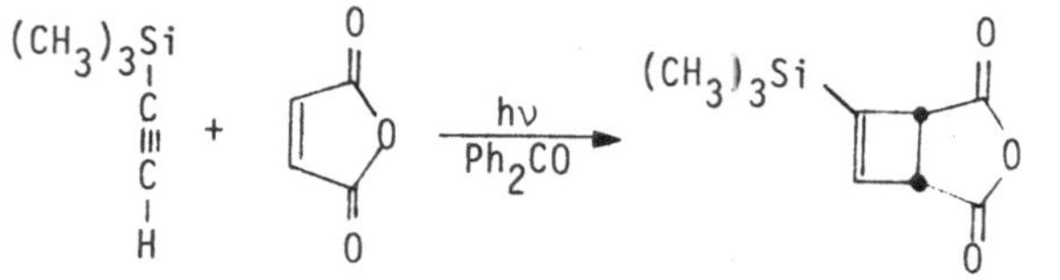

(9.71)

[2 + 3] Cycloaddition reactions between silylacetylenes and a variety of 1,3-dipolar species provide a reasonable synthetic route to silyl-substituted five-membered aromatic heterocycles.

For example, nitrile oxides react regiospecifically with silyl substituted acetylenes to yield 5-silyl isoxazoles [89].

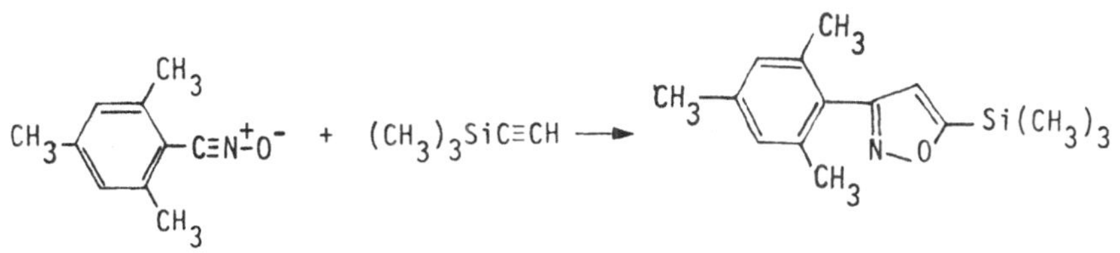

(9.72)

Likewise, diazomethane slowly reacts with silylacetylenes to yield 3-silylpyrazoles.

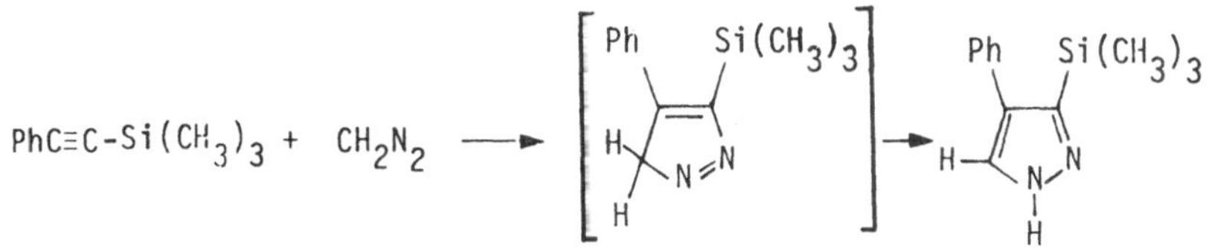

(9.73)

Ethyl diazoacetate reacts with *bis*(trimethylsilyl)acetylene to yield 3,4-*bis*-(trimethylsilyl)-5-carboethoxypyrazole [90, 91]. Although French workers have obtained similar results [92], they assign the N−H hydrogen to nitrogen-2. Which assignment is correct is not certain at this time.

On the other hand, reaction of diazomethane with methyl 2-trimethylsilyl-acetylenecarboxylate yields a mixture of 3- and 4-trimethylsilylpyrazole isomers. Similarly, a mixture of 3- and 4-trimethylsilylpyrazoles was obtained with 3-trimethylsilylpropynal [92]. Reaction of methyl 2-trimethylsilylacetyl-enecarboxylate with dimethyldiazomethane yields 5,5-dimethyl-3-trimethylsilyl-4-carbomethoxypyrazole, which loses nitrogen on photolysis to give 3,3-dimethyl-1-trimethylsilyl-2-carbomethoxycyclopropene [92].

The inverse reaction of *bis*(trimethylsilyl)diazomethane with dimethyl ace-tylenedicarboxylate initially yields dimethyl 5,5-*bis*(trimethylsilyl)-3,4-pyrazo-ledicarboxylate. Migration of a trimethylsilyl group from carbon to nitrogen results in the formation of either dimethyl 1,3-*bis*(trimethylsilyl)-4,5-pyrazole-dicarboxylate or dimethyl 1,5-*bis*(trimethylsilyl)-3,4-pyrazoledicarboxylate [93, 94]. N-Trimethylsilyl groups are easily removed by hydrolysis.

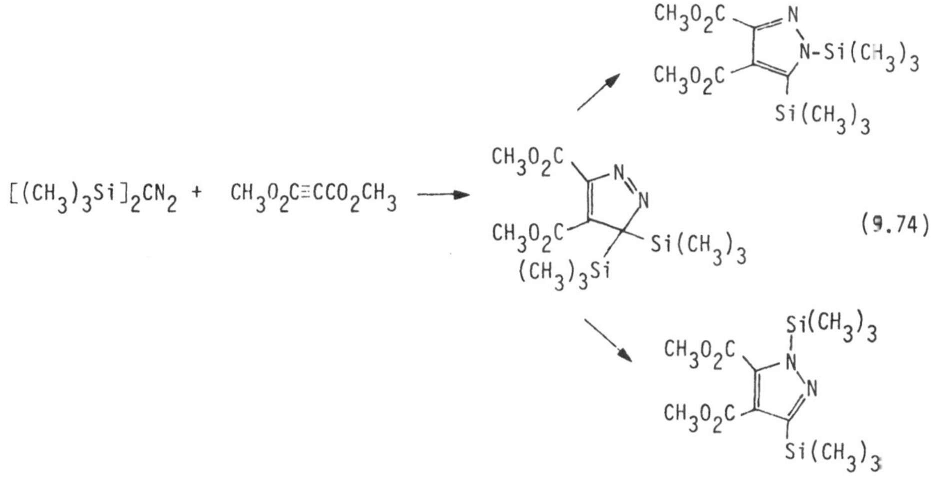

(9.74)

Silylacetylenes undergo [2 + 3] cycloaddition reactions with TMS-N_3 to yield initially 1,5 or 1,4-*bis*(trimethylsilyl)-1,2,3-triazoles which rearrange by a 1,2-shift of the trimethylsilyl group to yield 2,4-*bis*(trimethylsilyl)-1,2,3-triazoles [23, 95] (see 4.3).

$$PhC{\equiv}CSi(CH_3)_3 \ + \ (CH_3)_3SiN_3$$

$$(9.75)$$

Phenyl-2-trimethylsilylacetylene reacts with phenylazide to yield 1,5-diphenyl-4-trimethylsilyl-1,2,3-triazole. This regiospecificity is opposite that observed in the reaction of phenyl azide with phenylacetylene [23].

9.6 Preparation of Silylacetylenes

Since 1-trialkylsilyl-1,2-dienes, 2,3-dienes, 1-alkynes, and 2-alkynes are versatile synthetic intermediates, a variety of methods to prepare these compounds have been developed. Certain experimental conditions, such as high temperature lead to mixtures [96, 97].

A. 1-Trialkylsilylalkynes

1-Trimethylsilylalkynes may be prepared by reaction of alkali metal acetylides with TMS-Cl [54, 98].

$$CH_3C{\equiv}C^-Li^+ \ + \ (CH_3)_3SiCl \ \longrightarrow \ CH_3C{\equiv}CSi(CH_3)_3 \qquad (9.76)$$

The inverse reaction of trimethylsilyl-substituted acetylide anions with primary alkyl halides, is also effective. For example, 1,4-*bis*-(trimethylsilyl)-1,3-butadiyne reacts with methyl lithium to yield 1-lithio-4-trimethylsilyl-1,3-butadiyne and tetramethylsilane. This lithium reagent reacts efficiently with primary alkyl iodides to yield 1-trimethylsilyl-1,3-alkadiynes [38, 99].

$$(CH_3)_3SiC \equiv C-C \equiv CSi(CH_3)_3 \xrightarrow{CH_3Li} (CH_3)_3SiC \equiv C-C \equiv C^-Li^+$$

$$(CH_3)_4Si \qquad (9.77)$$

$$\xrightarrow{EtI/THF-HMPT} (CH_3)_3SiC \equiv C-C \equiv C-Et$$

1-Lithio-2-trimethylsilylacetylene reacts with ketones and aldehydes to yield 3-trimethylsilylprop-2-yn-1-ols. In the presence of the chiral chelating ligand (2S,2'S)-2-hydroxymethyl-1-[(1-methylpyrrolidin-2-yl)-methyl]pyrrolidine [100], this reaction gives propargyl alcohols of high e.e. [19, 101].

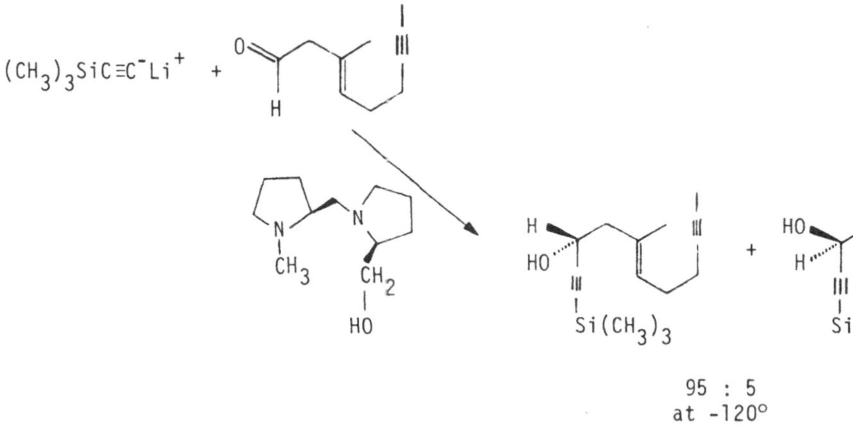

$$(CH_3)_3SiC \equiv C^-Li^+ \quad + \qquad\qquad\qquad (9.78)$$

95 : 5
at -120°

1-Alkyn-3-ols can be used to prepare 1-trimethylsilylalkynes. Deprotonation of 1-alkyn-3-ols with n-butyl lithium followed by addition of TMS-Cl yields after aq. work-up 1-trimethylsilylalkyn-3-ols. Treatment of these alkynols with acetic anhydride affords the corresponding propargyl acetates. These undergo S_n2 displacement with dialkyl copper lithium reagents [102, 103].

$$(CH_3)_3SiC \equiv CCH-n-C_5H_{11} \xrightarrow[\substack{2) \ (CH_3)_2CuLi}]{1) \ Ac_2O} (CH_3)_3SiC \equiv CCH-n-C_5H_{11} \qquad (9.79)$$
$$\underset{OH}{} \qquad\qquad\qquad\qquad\qquad\qquad \underset{CH_3}{}$$

Metallation of 1-trimethylsilylpropyne with n-butyl lithium/TMEDA followed by addition of primary alkyl iodides or allylic bromide gives 1-trimethylsilylalkynes [54–56, 104].

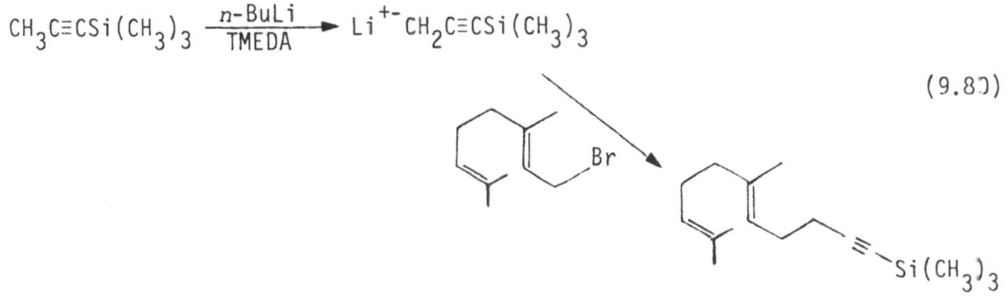

$$CH_3C \equiv CSi(CH_3)_3 \xrightarrow[TMEDA]{n-BuLi} Li^{+-}CH_2C \equiv CSi(CH_3)_3$$

$$(9.80)$$

151

3-Lithio-1-trimethylsilylpropyne reacts with epoxides to yield 5-trimethylsilyl pent-4-yn-1-ols. The reaction of this reagent with the mono-epoxide of cyclopentadiene was utilized in a general synthesis of prostaglandins [105].

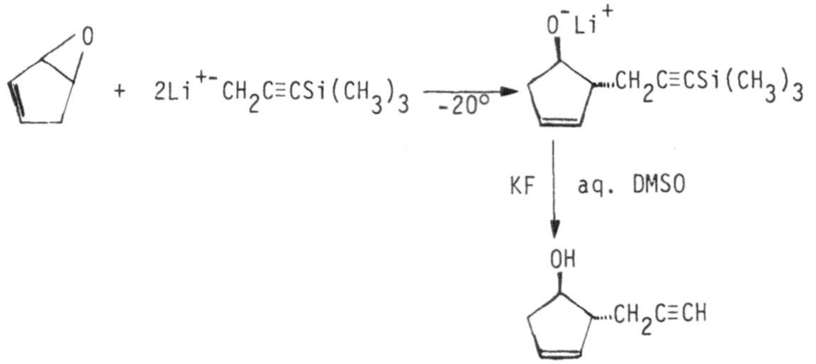
O
+ 2Li⁺⁻CH2C≡CSi(CH3)3
-20°
O⁻Li⁺
CH2C≡CSi(CH3)3
KF
aq. DMSO
OH
CH2C≡CH

(9.81)

Ketones and aldehydes react with 1-trimethylsilylpropargylzinc bromide [22] to yield 4-trimethylsilylbut-3-yn-1-ols [106].

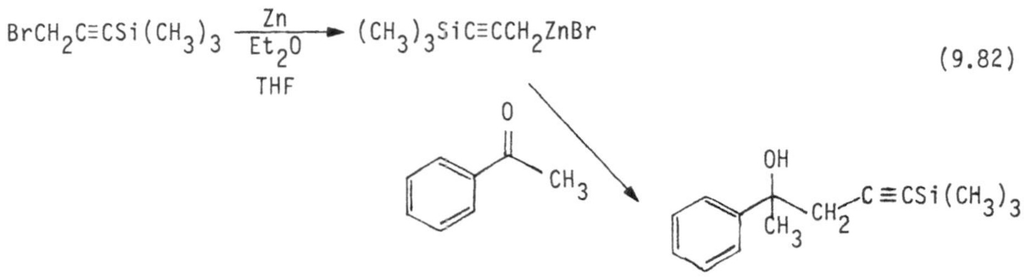
BrCH2C≡CSi(CH3)3
Zn
Et2O
THF
(CH3)3SiC≡CCH2ZnBr
O
CH3
OH
CH3
CH2
C≡CSi(CH3)3

(9.82)

Cuprous bromide dimethyl sulfide complex facilitates the conjugate addition of 1-trimethylsilylpropargylmagnesium bromide to α,β-unsaturated ketones [107].

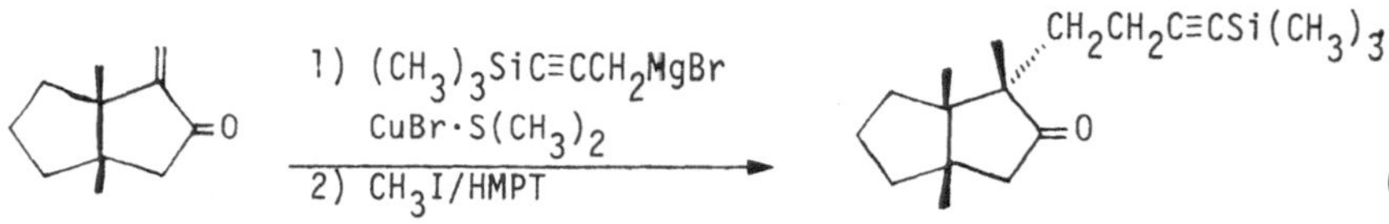
O
1) (CH3)3SiC≡CCH2MgBr
CuBr·S(CH3)2
2) CH3I/HMPT
CH2CH2C≡CSi(CH3)3
O

(9.83)

1-Trimethylsilylalkynes can be prepared from 3-phenoxy-1-trimethylsilylpropyne. Metallation with *n*-butyl lithium/TMEDA yields a propargyl lithium species which reacts with trialkylboranes to give propargyltrialkylborates. Treatment of these with acetic acid in HMPT yields 1-trimethylsilylalkynes. In this process, one of the alkyl groups migrates from boron to carbon [108].

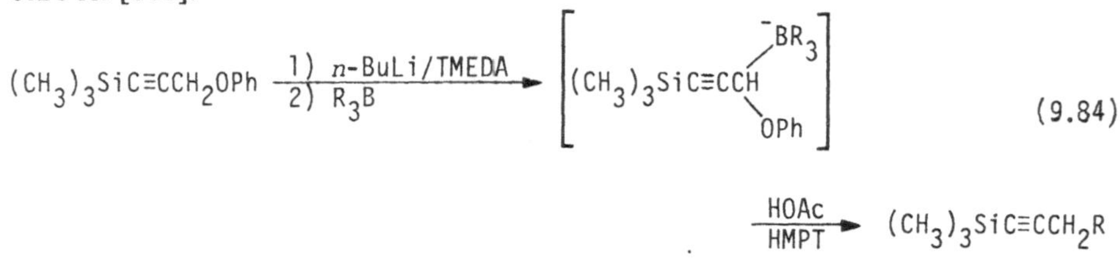
(CH3)3SiC≡CCH2OPh
1) n-BuLi/TMEDA
2) R3B
⁻BR3
(CH3)3SiC≡CCH
OPh
HOAc
HMPT
(CH3)3SiC≡CCH2R

(9.84)

B. 1-Trialkylsilyl-2-alkynes

1-Trimethylsilyl-2-alkynes can be prepared by reaction of 1-bromo-2-alkynes with magnesium in ether in the presence of TMS-Cl. Isomeric allenes are found in small yield in these reactions [109].

Reaction of lithium acetylides with either trimethylsilylmethyl trifluoro-methane sulfonate or chloromethyltrimethylsilane in HMPT [116] yields 1-tri-methylsilyl-2-alkynes [110]. The reaction of sodium acetylides with iodo-methyltrimethylsilane [17] is also effective.

$$\text{(9.85)}$$

1,3 bis(Trimethylsilyl)propyne can be easily prepared by a dissolving metal reaction of ether methyl or trimethylsilyl propargyl ethers with TMS-Cl and lithium in THF [111].

$$HC{\equiv}CCH_2OCH_3 \ + \ (CH_3)_3SiCl \ \xrightarrow[THF]{Li} \ (CH_3)_3SiC{\equiv}CCH_2Si(CH_3)_3 \qquad \text{(9.86)}$$

C. 1-Trialkylsilyl-1,2-dienes

1-Trialkylsilyl-1,2-dienes have been prepared by insertion of vinylidene carbenes into the Si−H bond of trialkylsilanes [96, 112].

$$\text{(9.87)}$$

Metallation of allene with one equivalent of n-butyl lithium in THF at −50° yields allenyl lithium which reacts with TMS-Cl to yield trimethyl-silylallene. On the other hand, treatment of allene with two equivalents of n-butyl lithium yields a dianion which reacts with TMS-Cl to yield 1,3-bis-(trimethylsilyl)-propyne [113].

$$\text{(9.88)}$$

1-Methoxy-1-trimethylsilylallene can be prepared by metallation of methoxyallene with n-butyl lithium followed by addition of TMS-Cl. Further metallation of 1-methoxy-1-trimethylsilylallene with *n*-butyl lithium followed by reaction with primary alkyl halides yields 1-methoxy-1-trimethylsilyl-1,2-dienes. These react with trifluoroacetic acid to yield α,β-unsaturated acyltrimethylsilanes or with TBAF to give α,β-unsaturated aldehydes [114].

$$\text{(9.89)}$$

Metallation of 3-phenoxy-1-trimethylsilylpropyne yields a propargyl anion which reacts with trialkylboranes to yield propargyltrialkylborates. Treatment of these with sodium methoxide gives 1-trimethylsilyl-1,2-dienes in which an alkyl group has migrated from boron to carbon [115].

$$\text{(9.90)}$$

Treatment of the methanesulfinate esters of 1-trimethylsilylalkyn-3-ols with magnesium dialkyl cuprates in THF [46, 116] yields 1-trimethylsilyl-1,2-dienes.

$$\text{(9.91)}$$

Conjugate 1,6-addition of 1-trimethylsilylpropargyl cuprates to alkyl 2,4-pentadienoates yields alkyl 6-trimethylsilyl-3,6,7-octatrienoates [117].

$$\text{(9.92)}$$

154

1-Trimethylsilyl-1,2-dienes result from treatment of the tosyl hydrazones of 3-trimethylsilyl alkynones with an excess of sodium cyanoborohydride in DMF/sulfolene [44].

$$\text{PhCH}_2\text{CH}_2\text{-}\overset{\overset{\text{N-NHTs}}{\|}}{\text{C}}\text{-C}\equiv\text{CSi(CH}_3)_3 \xrightarrow[\substack{\text{DMF} \\ \text{sulfolene}}]{\text{NaBH}_3\text{CN}} \left[\text{PhCH}_2\text{CH}_2\text{-}\overset{\overset{N^{\diagdown N\diagup H}}{|}}{\underset{H}{C}}\overset{\diagdown}{\underset{C}{}}\equiv\text{CSi(CH}_3)_3\right]$$

(9.93)

$$\text{PhCH}_2\text{CH}_2\text{CH=C=CHSi(CH}_3)_3$$

Reaction of 3-bromo-1-trimethylsilylpropyne with aluminum yields an organometallic reagent which reacts with ketones and aldehydes to yield rearranged products: 1-(1'-hydroxyalkyl)-1-trimethylsilylallenes [106].

$$(\text{CH}_3)_3\text{SiC}\equiv\text{CCH}_2\text{Br} \xrightarrow[\substack{2)}]{1) \text{ Al / Et}_2\text{O}} \quad (\text{CH}_3)_3\text{Si}\diagup\text{C=C=CH}_2$$

(9.94)

As previously mentioned, the corresponding zinc reagent reacts with ketones and aldehydes with no rearrangement (Eq 9.82). The reason for this difference in regiospecificity between the zinc and aluminum reagents is not clear.

D. 1-Trimethylsilyl-2,3-dienes

1-Trimethylsilyl-2,3-dienes can be prepared by reaction of trimethylsilyl-methylmagnesium cuprates with propargyl acetates or tosylates [45].

$$(\text{CH}_3)_2\overset{\overset{}{|}}{\underset{\underset{O}{\overset{\|}{\text{OCCH}_3}}}{\text{C}}}\text{C}\equiv\text{CH} \xrightarrow[\text{THF}]{(\text{CH}_3)_3\text{SiCH}_2\text{CuMgBr}} (\text{CH}_3)_2\text{C=C=C}\diagup\overset{\text{CH}_2\text{Si(CH}_3)_3}{\diagdown\text{H}}$$

(9.95)

References

1. Miller, J.B., McGarvey, G.: J. Org. Chem. *43*, 4424 (1978)
2. Birkofer, L., Kühn, T.: Chem. Ber. *111*, 3119 (1978)
3. Komarov, V.M., Yarosh, O.G.: Isv. Akad. Nauk. SSSR. Ser. Khim. 1573 (1971)
4. Yarosh, O.G., Vovenkov, V.K., Kamarov, N.V.: Izv. Akad. Nauk. SSSR Ser. Khim. 875 (1971)
5. Miller, R.B., Reichenbach, T.: Tetrahedron Lett. 543 (1974)
6. Zweifel, G., On, H.P.: Synthesis, 803 (1980)
7. Eisch, J.J., Foxton, M.W.: J. Org. Chem. *36*, 3520 (1971)
8. Uchida, K., Utimoto, K., Nozaki, H.: J. Org. Chem. *41*, 2941 (1976)
9. Hasan, I., Kishi, Y.: Tetrahedron Lett. 4229 (1980)

10. Miller, J.A., Zweifel, G.: Synthesis, 288 (1981)
11. Soto, F., Ishikawa, H., Soto, M.: Tetrahedron Lett. 85 (1981)
12. Obayashi, M., Utimoto, K., Nozaki, H.: Tetrahedron Lett. 1805 (1979)
13. Westmijze, H., Meijer, J., Vermeer, P.: Tetrahedron Lett. 1823 (1977)
14. Snider, B.B., Karras, M., Conn, R.S.E.: J. Am. Chem. Soc. *100*, 4624 (1978)
15. Flood, T., Peterson, P.E.: J. Org. Chem. *45*, 5006 (1980)
16. Bourgeois, P., Mérault, G.: J. Organometal. Chem. *39*, C44 (1972)
17. Schmid, R., Huesmann, P.L., Johnson, W.S.: J. Am. Chem. Soc. *102*, 5122 (1980)
18. Johnson, W.S., Yarnell, T.M., Myers, R.F., Morton, D.R.: Tetrahedron Lett. 2549 (1978)
19. Johnson, W.S., Frei, B., Gopalan, A.S.: J. Org. Chem. *46*, 1512 (1981)
20. Walton, D.R.M., Webb, M.J.: J. Organometal. Chem. *37*, 41 (1972)
21. Oliver, R., Walton, D.R.M.: Tetrahedron Lett. 5209 (1972)
22. Eiter, K., Lieb, F., Disselnkötter, H., Oediger, H.: Liebigs. Ann. Chem. *658*, (1978)
23. Birkofer, L., Ritter, A., Uhlenbrauck, H.: Chem. Ber. *96*, 3280 (1963)
24. Utimoto, K., Tanaka, M., Kitai, M., Nozaki, H.: Tetrahedron Lett. 2301 (1978)
25. Ladika, M., Stang, P.J.: J.C.S. Chem. Commun. 459 (1981)
26. Walton, D.R.M., Waugh, F.: J. Organometal. Chem. *37*, 45 (1972)
27. Stang, P.J., Ladika, M.: Synthesis, 29 (1981)
28. Bourgeois, P., Merault, G., Calas, R.: J. Organometal. Chem. *59*, C-4 (1973)
29. Bhattacharya, S.N., Josiah, B.M., Walton, D.R.M.: Organometal. Chem. Synthesis, *1*, 145 (1970/1971)
30. Bourgeois, P., Calas, R.: J. Organometal. Chem. *22*, 89 (1970)
31. Bourgeois, P., Mérault, G., Duffaut, N., Calas, R.: J. Organometal. Chem. *59*, 145 (1973)
32. Bourgeois, P., Mérault, G.: C.R. Acad. Sci. Paris Ser. C, *273*, 714 (1971)
33. Bourgeois, P., Calas, R., Mérault, G.: J. Organometal. Chem. *141*, 23 (1977)
34. Calas, R., Dunoguès, J., Deleris, G., Pisciotti, F.: J. Organometal. Chem. *69*, C15 (1974)
35. Deleris, G., Dunoguès, J., Calas, R.: J. Organometal. Chem. *93*, 43 (1975)
36. Deleris, G., Dunoguès, J., Calas, R.: Tetrahedron Lett. 2449 (1976)
37. Nakamura, E., Kuwajima, I.: Angew. Chem. Int. Ed. *15*, 498 (1976)
38. Holmes, A.B., Jennings-White, C.L.D., Schulthess, A.H., Akinde, B., Walton, D.R.M.: J. Chem. Soc. Chem. Commun. 840 (1979)
39. Pornet, J., Randrianoelina, B.: Tetrahedron Lett. 1327 (1981)
40. Pornet, J.: Tetrahedron Lett. 453 (1981)
41. Pornet, J.: Tetrahedron Lett. 2049 (1980)
42. Pornet, J.: Tetrahedron Lett. 455 (1981)
43. Sakurai, H., Sasaki, K., Hosomi, A.: Tetrahedron Lett. 745 (1981)
44. Danheiser, R.L., Carini, D.J.: J. Org. Chem. *45*, 3925 (1980)
45. Montury, M., Psaume, B., Gore, J.: Tetrahedron Lett. 163 (1980)
46. Danheiser, R.L., Carini, D.J., Basak, A.: J. Am. Chem. Soc. *103*, 1604 (1981)
47. Jellal, A., Santelli, M.: Tetrahedron Lett. 4487 (1980)
48. Kozar, L.G., Clark, R.D., Heathcock, C.H.: J. Org. Chem. *42*, 1386 (1977)
49. Casara, P., Metcalf, B.W.: Tetrahedron Lett. 1581 (1978)
50. Despo, A.D., Chiu, S.K., Flood, T., Peterson, P.E.: J. Am. Chem. Soc. *102*, 5120 (1980)
51. Shakhovskoi, B.G., Stadnichuk, M.D., Petrov, A.A.: J. Gen. Chem. USSR, *34*, 2646 (1964)
52. Holmes, A.B. Raphel, R.A., Welland, N.K.: Tetrahedron Lett. 1539 (1976)

53. Schmidt, H.M., Arens, J.F.: Rec. Trav. Chim de bas Pays, *86*, 1138 (1967)
54. Corey, E.J., Kirst, H.A.: Tetrahedron Lett. 5041 (1968)
55. Corey, E.J., Katzenellenbogen, J.A., Gilman, N.W., Roman, S.A., Erickson, B.W.: J. Am. Chem. Soc. *90*, 5618 (1968)
56. Corey, E.J., Kirst, H.A., Katzenellenbogen, J.A.: J. Am. Chem. Soc. *92*, 6314 (1970)
57. Eaborn, C., Thompson, A.R., Walton, D.R.M.: J. Chem. Soc. *C*, 1364 (1967)
58. Metcalf, B.W., Jund, K.: Tetrahedron Lett. 3689 (1977)
59. Metcalf, B.W., Casara, P.: Tetrahedron Lett. 3337 (1975)
60. Gilman, H., Brook, A.G., Miller, L.S.: J. Am. Chem. Soc. *75*, 4531 (1953)
61. Eaborn, C., Walton, D.R.M.: J. Organometal. Chem. *4*, 217 (1965)
62. Eaborn, C., Thompson, A.R., Walton, D.R.M.: J. Organometal. Chem. *17*, 149 (1969)
63. Newman, H.: J. Org. Chem. *38*, 2254 (1973)
64. Hay, A.S.: J. Org. Chem. *27*, 3320 (1962)
65. Eastmond, R., Walton, D.R.M.: J. Chem. Soc., Chem. Commun. 204 (1968)
66. Eastmond, R., Johnson, T.R., Walton, D.R.M.: J. Organometal. Chem. *50*, 87 (1973)
67. McQuilkin, R.M., Garrett, P.J., Sondheimer, F.: J. Am. Chem. Soc. *92*, 6682 (1970)
68. Eglinton, G., McCrae, W.: Adv. Org. Chem. *4*, 225 (1963)
69. Eaborn, C., Thompson, A.R., Walton, D.R.M.: J. Chem. Soc. *B*, 357 (1970)
70. Ghose, B.N., Walton, D.R.M.: Synthesis, 890 (1974)
71. Takahashi, S., Kuroyama, Y., Sonogashira, K., Hagihara, N.: Synthesis, 627 (1980)
72. Mitchell, R.H., Sondheimer, F.: Tetrahedron, *26*, 2141 (1970)
73. Seyferth, D., Sarafidis, C., Evnin, A.B.: J. Organometal. Chem. *2*, 417 (1964)
74. Seyferth, D., White, D.L.: J. Organometal. Chem. *34*, 119 (1972)
75. Birkofer, L., Stilke, R.: J. Organometal. Chem. *74*, C-1 (1974)
76. Kloek, J.A.: J. Org. Chem. *46*, 1951 (1981)
77. Shchukovskaya, L.L., Budakova, L.D., Pal'chik, R.I.: Zhur. Obsh. Khim. *43*, 1989 (1973)
78. Himbert, G.: Angew. Chem. *88*, 59 (1976)
79. Henn, L., Himbert, G.: Chem. Ber. *114*, 1015 (1981)
80. Sato, Y., Kobayashi, Y., Sugiura, M., Shirai, H.: J. Org. Chem. *43*, 199 (1978)
81. Hübel, W., Hoogzand, C.: Chem. Ber. *93*, 103 (1960)
82. Greenfield, H., Sternberg, H.W., Friedel, R.A., Wotiz, J.H., Markby, R., Wender, I.: J. Am. Chem. Soc. *78*, 120 (1965)
83. Hillard, III, R.L., Vollhardt, K.P.C.: Angew. Chem. Int. Ed. *14*, 712 (1975)
84. Aalbersberg, W.G.L., Barkovich, A.J., Funk, R.L., Hillard, III, R.L., Vollhardt, K.P.C.: J. Am. Chem. Soc. *97*, 5600 (1975)
85. Hillard, III, R.L., Vollhardt, K.P.C.: Angew. Chem. Int. Ed. *16*, 399 (1977)
86. Funk, R.L., Vollhardt, K.P.C.: J. Am. Chem. Soc. *99*, 5483 (1977)
87. Funk, R.L., Vollhardt, K.P.C.: J. Chem. Soc. Chem. Commun. 833 (1976)
88. Birkofer, L., Eichstädt, D.: J. Organometal. Chem. *145*, C29 (1978)
89. Birkofer, L., Stilke, R.: Chem. Ber. *107*, 3717 (1974)
90. Birkofer, L., Franz, M.: Chem. Ber. *100*, 2681 (1967)
91. Birkofer, L., Franz, M.: Chem. Ber. *105*, 17 (1972)
92. Guillerm, G., Honoré, A.L., Veniard, L., Pourcelot, G., Benaim, J.: Bull. Soc. Chem. Fr. 2739 (1973)
93. Seyferth, D., Dows, A.W., Menzel, H., Flood, T.C.: J. Am. Chem. Soc. *90*, 1080 (1968)

94. Seyferth, D., Flood, T.C.: J. Organometal. Chem. *29*, C25 (1971)
95. Birkofer, L., Wegner, P.: Chem. Ber. *99*, 2512 (1966)
96. Patrick, T.B., Haynie, E.C., Probst, W.J.: J. Org. Chem. *37*, 1553 (1972)
97. Slutsky, J., Kwart, H.: J. Am. Chem. Soc. *95*, 8678 (1973)
98. Eaborn, C., Walton, D.R.M.: J. Organometal. Chem. *4*, 217 (1965)
99. Holmes, A.B., Jones, G.E.: Tetrahedron Lett. 3111 (1980)
100. Mukaiyama, T., Soai, K., Sato, T., Shimizu, H., Suzuki, K.: J. Am. Chem. Soc. *101*, 1455 (1979)
101. Mukaiyama, T., Suzuki, K., Soai, K., Sato, T.: Chem. Lett. 447 (1979)
102. Brinkmeyer, R.S., MacDonald, T.L.: J. Chem. Soc. Chem. Commun. 876 (1978)
103. MacDonald, T.L., Reagan, D.R., Brinkmeyer, R.S.: J. Org. Chem. *45*, 4740 (1980)
104. Ireland, R.E., Dawson, M.I., Lipinski, C.A.: Tetrahedron Lett. 2247 (1970)
105. Stork, G., Kowalski, C., Garcia, G.: J. Am. Chem. Soc. *97*, 3258 (1975)
106. Daniels, R.G., Paquette, L.A.: Tetrahedron Lett. 1579 (1981)
107. Han, Y.K., Paquette, L.A.: J. Org. Chem. *44*, 3731 (1979)
108. Yogo, T., Koshino, J., Suzuki, A.: Syn. Commun. *9*, 809 (1979)
109. Masson, J.C., Quan, M.L., Cadiot, P.: Bull. Soc. Chim. Fr. 777 (1967)
110. Chiu, S.K., Peterson, P.E.: Tetrahedron Lett. 4047 (1980)
111. Laguerre, M., Dunoguès, J., Calas, R.: J. Organometal. Chem. *145*, C34 (1978)
112. Beard, C.D., Craig, J.C.: J. Am. Chem. Soc. *96*, 7950 (1974)
113. Jaffe, F.: J. Organometal. Chem. *23*, 53 (1970)
114. Clinet, J.C., Linstrumelle, G.: Tetrahedron Lett. 3987 (1980)
115. Yogo, T., Koshino, J., Suzuki, A.: Tetrahedron Lett. 1781 (1979)
116. Westmijze, H., Vermeer, P.: Synthesis, 390 (1979)
117. Ganem, B.: Tetrahedron Lett. 4467 (1974)

10 Tetraalkylsilanes, Alkylpentafluorosilicates and Alkenylpentafluorosilicates

10.1 Introduction

This chapter is concerned with the synthetically useful chemistry of tetraalkylsilanes and dipotassium alkyl-and alkenylpentafluorosilicates.

10.2 Electrophilic Cleavage of Tetraalkylsilanes

Like vinyl silanes many reactions of tetraalkylsilanes involve electrophilic cleavage of C−Si bonds.

A. Protic Acids

Reaction of chloromethyltrimethylsilane with sulfuric acid yields methane and chloromethyldimethylsilyl sulfate [1]. Similar reactions with 4-trimethylsilyl-2-butanone and 3-trimethylsilylpropionic acid yield methane and the corresponding silyl sulfate [2, 3].

$$(CH_3)_3SiCH_2CH_2CO_2H \xrightarrow{H_2SO_4} CH_4 + HO\underset{\underset{O}{\overset{\parallel}{}}}{\overset{\overset{O}{\parallel}}{S}}-O-\underset{\underset{CH_3}{\overset{\mid}{}}}{\overset{\overset{CH_3}{\mid}}{Si}}-CH_2CH_2CO_2H \qquad (10.1)$$

Cyclopropyltrimethylsilane reacts with HBr or sulfuric acid to yield cyclopropane [4].

$$\triangleright\!\!-Si(CH_3)_3 \xrightarrow{HBr} \triangleright + (CH_3)_3SiBr \qquad (10.2)$$

However, reaction of substituted cyclopropyltrimethylsilanes with HCl or TiCl$_4$ results in cleavage of a C−C bond of the cyclopropane rather a C−Si bond. The ratio of electrophilic cleavage of C−C bonds adjacent to the trimethylsilyl group compared to scission of the remote C−C bond of the cyclopropane varies with structure of the substrate and the electrophile [5].

$$14 : 86 \qquad (10.3)$$

$$(10.4)$$

B. Acylium Ions

Acylium ions formed by reaction of acid chlorides and AlCl$_3$ cleave terminal C$-$Si bonds of octamethyltrisilane and hexamethyldisilane to yield methyl ketones and 1,3-dichlorohexamethyltrisilane [6] and pentamethylchlorodisilane [7] respectively.

$$CH_3CH_2\text{-}\overset{O}{\overset{\|}{C}}\text{-}Cl + (CH_3)_3SiSi(CH_3)_3 \xrightarrow{AlCl_3} CH_3CH_2\text{-}\overset{O}{\overset{\|}{C}}\text{-}CH_3 + (CH_3)_3Si\text{-}\overset{CH_3}{\underset{CH_3}{\overset{|}{Si}}}\text{-}Cl \qquad (10.5)$$

This reaction was probably not widely appreciated due to the necessity to prepare either octamethyltrisilane or hexamethyldisilane. Recently, electrophilic cleavage of tetraalkylsilanes by acylium ions has been utilized in two related ketone syntheses [8, 9]. Unfortunately, only one of the four C$-$Si bonds of tetraalkylsilanes undergoes electrophilic cleavage by acylium ions [9]. Cyclopropyl alkyl ketones are efficiently prepared since the cyclopropyl group is selectively cleaved from cyclopropyltrimethylsilane [8]. The π-character of the cyclopropyl group may increase its susceptibility to electrophilic attack.

$$(10.6)$$

On the other hand, 2-methylcyclopropyltrimethylsilane reacts with acid chlorides and AlCl$_3$ via opening of the cyclopropyl ring and loss of the trimethylsilyl group to yield 2-butenyl ketones [10]. The reaction is stereospecific: *cis*-2-methylcyclopropyltrimethylsilane yields *E*-2-butenyl ketones while the *trans* isomer gives *Z*-2-butenyl ketones.

160

$$(CH_3)_3C\text{-}\overset{\overset{\displaystyle O}{\|}}{C}\text{-}Cl \;+\; \text{[cyclopropyl-Si(CH}_3)_3] \quad\xrightarrow{AlCl_3}\quad (CH_3)_3C\text{-}\overset{\overset{\displaystyle O}{\|}}{C}\diagdown\diagup \tag{10.7}$$

$$\text{[cyclohexyl-C(=O)-Cl]} \;+\; \text{[cyclopropyl-Si(CH}_3)_3] \quad\xrightarrow{AlCl_3}\quad \text{[cyclohexyl-C(=O)-CH}_2\text{-CH=CH-CH}_3] \tag{10.8}$$

Likewise, cyclopropylmethyltrimethylsilane reacts with aliphatic acid chlorides and AlCl₃ with cleavage of the cyclopropyl ring and loss of the trimethylsilyl group to yield β,γ-unsaturated ketones [11].

$$\text{[cyclopropyl]}\text{-}CH_2Si(CH_3)_3 \;+\; (CH_3)_2CH\text{-}\overset{\overset{\displaystyle O}{\|}}{C}\text{-}Cl \quad\xrightarrow{AlCl_3}\quad (CH_3)_2CH\text{-}\overset{\overset{\displaystyle O}{\|}}{C}\diagdown\diagup\diagdown \tag{10.9}$$

C. Carbocations

Carbocations also cleave C–Si bonds. Thus 3-bromopropyltrimethylsilane and a catalytic amount of AlCl₃ undergoes an intramolecular reaction to yield TMS-Br and cyclopropane [12].

$$(CH_3)_3SiCH_2CH_2CH_2Br \quad\xrightarrow{AlCl_3}\quad \text{[cyclopropane]} \;+\; (CH_3)_3SiBr \tag{10.10}$$

A related intramolecular electrophilic cleavage reaction provides a reasonable synthesis of 1,1-dimethylsilacyclopentane [13].

$$(CH_3)_3Si(CH_2)_3\text{-}\underset{\underset{\displaystyle CH_3}{|}}{\overset{\overset{\displaystyle CH_3}{|}}{Si}}\text{-}CH_2Cl \quad\xrightarrow{AlCl_3}\quad (CH_3)_3SiCl \;+\; \text{[silacyclopentane with } CH_3,CH_3] \tag{10.11}$$

Recently, intermolecular examples of carbocation cleavage of sp³ hybridized C–Si bonds have been observed. Protonation of tri- and tetra-substituted alkenes by trifluoroacetic acid yields tertiary carbocations. Tetramethylsilane reacts with these to transfer a methyl group from silicon to the tertiary carbocation centers [14].

$$\text{[methylcyclopentene]}\text{-}CH_3 \;+\; CF_3CO_2H \;\longrightarrow\; \left[\text{cyclopentyl cation}\text{-}CH_3\right]^+ \quad\xrightarrow[AlBr_3]{(CH_3)_4Si}\quad \text{[dimethylcyclopentane]} \tag{10.12}$$

D. Halogens

Tetraalkylsilanes undergo reaction with iodine catalyzed by aluminium iodide to yield trialkyliodosilanes and alkyl iodides [15]. Cyclopropyltrimethylsilane reacts with iodine monochloride to give cyclopropyl iodide and TMS-Cl [16].

$$\triangleright\text{-Si(CH}_3)_3 \ + \ \text{ICl} \ \longrightarrow \ \triangleright\text{-I} \ + \ \text{(CH}_3)_3\text{SiCl} \tag{10.13}$$

On the other hand, cyclopropyltrimethylsilane reacts with bromine with or without assistance from aluminium bromide to yield a mixture of products resulting from scission of C−C bonds of the cyclopropane ring [16].

E. Trimethylsilyl Chlorosulfonate

Tetraalkylsilanes react with trimethylsilyl chlorosulfonate to yield trimethylsilyl alkylsulfonates and trialkylchlorosilanes [17].

$$\text{Et}_4\text{Si} \ + \ \underset{\overset{\|}{O}}{\overset{\overset{O}{\|}}{\text{Cl-S}}}\text{-OSi(CH}_3)_3 \ \longrightarrow \ \text{Et}_3\text{SiCl} \ + \ \underset{\overset{\|}{O}}{\overset{\overset{O}{\|}}{\text{Et-S}}}\text{-OSi(CH}_3)_3 \tag{10.14}$$

Cyclopropyltrimethylsilane is cleaved by trimethylsilyl chlorosulfonate to yield trimethylsilyl cyclopropylsulfonate and TMS-Cl [18].

$$\triangleright\text{-Si(CH}_3)_3 \ + \ \underset{\overset{\|}{O}}{\overset{\overset{O}{\|}}{\text{Cl-S}}}\text{-OSi(CH}_3)_3 \ \longrightarrow \ \triangleright\underset{\overset{\|}{O}}{\overset{\overset{O}{\|}}{\text{-S}}}\text{-OSi(CH}_3)_3 \ + \ \text{(CH}_3)_3\text{SiCl}$$

$$\tag{10.15}$$

By contrast, 2-methylcyclopropyltrimethylsilane reacts with trimethylsilyl chlorosulfonate to yield trimethylsilyl 2-butenylsulfonate [10].

10.3 Preparation

Excellent methods exist to prepare alkyl silanes. Hydrosilation of alkenes can be carried out by a free radical chain process or by catalysis with chloroplatinic acid [19]. This latter method is generally regiospecific. For example, reaction of trichlorosilane with either 1- or 2-pentene catalyzed by chloroplatinic acid yields essentially pure 1-pentyltrichlorosilane [20]. This reacts with excess methyl Grignard reagent to yield n-pentyltrimethylsilane.

Cyclopropyltrimethylsilane is readily prepared by treatment of trimethylvinylsilane with Simmons-Smith reagent [21].

$$\text{(CH}_3)_3\text{Si}\diagup\!\!\!\diagdown \ + \ \text{CH}_2\text{I}_2 \ \xrightarrow{\text{Zn-Cu}} \ \text{(CH}_3)_3\text{Si-}\triangleleft \tag{10.16}$$

Alternatively, cyclopropyltrimethylsilanes may be prepared by addition of trimethylsilyl carbene to appropriate olefins.

α-Elimination of lithium chloride from α-chloro-α-lithiomethyltrimethyl-silane yields trimethylsilyl carbene, which reacts stereospecifically with alkenes, to give cyclopropyltrimethylsilanes [22]. Chloromethyltrimethyl-silane can be deprotonated by lithium 2,2,6,6-tetramethylpiperidide to yield α-chloro-α-lithiomethyltrimethylsilane.

$$(10.17)$$

Metallation of chloromethyltrimethylsilane with *sec*-butyl lithium in TMEDA/THF does not yield trimethylsilyl carbene [23, 24].

Copper (I) catalyzed addition of trimethylsilyldiazomethane [25, 26] to ole-fins also yields trimethylsilylcyclopropanes [25, 27, 28].

$$(10.18)$$

The ylid, dimethyltrimethylsilylmethylene sulphurane, reacts with α,β-un-saturated ketones to give trimethylsilylcyclopropyl ketones [29].

$$(10.19)$$

10.4 Alkylpentafluorosilicates

While the C$-$Si bond of alkyltrichlorosilanes is not easily cleaved by electrophiles, Kumada has found that the C$-$Si bond of the corresponding dipotassium alkylpentafluorosilicates is [30]. These are easily prepared by reaction of alkyltrichlorosilanes with potassium fluoride. Silicon can expand its coordination number beyond four by utilization of empty 3d orbitals to coordinate ligands such as fluoride. It is reasonable that alkylpentafluorosilicates which have a double negative charge should be readily attacked by electrophiles. One might, in fact, imagine that they would possess carbanionic character. However, unlike organolithium reagents or Grignard reagents, dipotassium alkylpentafluorosilicates are air stable, crystalline solids which can be isolated by filtration.

$$R\text{-}SiCl_3 \xrightarrow{\text{aq. KF}} K_2[R\text{-}SiF_5] \tag{10.20}$$

While the water solubility of dipotassium alkylpentafluorosilicates is very limited, the solubility of ammonium alkylpentafluorosilicates is considerably greater [31, 32]. PTC by quaternary alkyl ammonium salts or crown ethers capable of chelation to potassium tions might overcome this solubility problem.

10.5 Reaction of Alkylpentafluorosilicates with Halogens

1-Alkenes have been converted to 1-haloalkanes as outlined below. This constitutes a method to add the elements of HX to an alkene in a regiospecific anti-Markovnikoff manner. Such reactions are much less efficient with secondary alkylpentafluorosilicates.

$$n\text{-}C_6H_{13}CH{=}CH_2 \xrightarrow[\text{H}_2\text{PtCl}_6]{\text{HSiCl}_3} n\text{-}C_6H_{13}CH_2CH_2SiCl_3$$

$$\downarrow \text{KF}$$

$$K_2[n\text{-}C_6H_{13}CH_2CH_2SiF_5] \tag{10.21}$$

$$\underset{n\text{-}C_6H_{13}CH_2CH_2Cl}{\overset{Cl_2/Cl_4}{\swarrow}} \quad \underset{n\text{-}C_6H_{13}CH_2CH_2Br}{\overset{Br_2 / \text{or NBS}}{\downarrow}} \quad \underset{n\text{-}C_6H_{13}CH_2CH_2I}{\overset{I_2}{\searrow}}$$

The reaction of alkylpentafluorosilicates with NBS to yield 1-bromo alkanes tolerates esters, as well as C−C double bonds [33].

$$\tag{10.22}$$

This procedure permits efficient synthesis of R-(−)-α-curcumene (Eq. 10.23) It should be noted that NBS preferentially cleaves the primary sp³ C−Si bond rather than brominates the benzylic C−H bonds [34].

$$\tag{10.23}$$

Alkyl pentafluorosilicates also undergo electrophilic cleavage by anhydrous cupric chloride or bromide to yield respectively alkyl chlorides or bromides. The reaction is synthetically useful with primary alkyl and arylpentafluorosilicates; but not with secondary alkylpentafluorosilicates [35]..

Stereochemistry has been used to probe the mechanism of these reactions. Hydrosilation of 2-norbornene with trichlorosilane catalyzed by chloroplatinic acid yields exclusively *exo*-2-trichlorosilyl norbornane (Eq. 10.24). Preparation of *endo*-2-trichlorosilyl norbornane is more complicated. A Diels-Alder reaction of vinyltrichlorosilane and cyclopentadiene yields a mixture of *exo*- and *endo*-2-trichlorosilyl-5-norbornene, which can be separated by fractional distillation. Catalytic hydrogenation of *endo*-2-trichlorosilyl-5-norbornene over Pd/C yields *endo*-2-trichlorosilylnorbornane. Both *exo* and *endo*-2-trichlorosilylnorbornane react with potassium fluoride to yield the corresponding norbornylpentafluorosilicates with retention of configuration. These react with bromine or NBS in polar solvents such as methanol or THF to yield 2-norbornyl bromides of inverted (at least 95%) stereochemistry (Eq. 10.25 and 10.26). Reaction of *exo*-2-norbornylpentafluorosilicate with cupric bromide in methanol, on the other hand, yields 2-norbornyl bromide with predominant retention of configuration [36].

$$\text{(10.24)}$$

$$\text{(10.25)}$$

$$\text{(10.26)}$$

Asymmetric hydrosilation of prochiral olefins with trichlorosilane can be achieved by use of chiral catalysts such as menthyldiphenylphosphine, neomenthyldiphenylphosphine [37], or dichloro [(R)-N,N-dimethyl-1-(S)-2-(diphenylphosphine)ferrocenyl] ethyl amino Pd(II) [38]. Reaction of optically active *exo*-trichlorosilyl norbornane with potassium fluoride followed by NBS in methanol yields *endo*-norbornyl bromide $[\alpha]_D^{20} = -9.1{,}53\%$ e.e. [39].

$$\text{(10.27)}$$

^{1}H and ^{29}Si NMR chemical shifts indicate that organosilatranes and alkyl-pentafluorosilicates both have high charge density at the silyl center. Both primary alkyl and aryl organosilatranes react with NBS to yield the corresponding bromides [40].

$$n\text{-}C_8H_{17}S \xrightarrow[\text{CH}_2\text{Cl}_2]{\text{NBS}} n\text{-}C_8H_{17}Br \qquad \text{(10.28)}$$

While organosilatranes are readily prepared [41, 42] (see Eq. 10.29), they should be handled with care since certain of them have high mammalian toxicity [43].

$$RSiH_3 + Co_2(CO)_8 + (HOCH_2CH_2)_3N$$
$$RSi(OEt)_3 + (HOCH_2CH_2)_3N \longrightarrow R\text{-}Si \qquad \text{(10.29)}$$

10.6 Reaction with *m*-Chloroperbenzoic Acid

The following sequence permits the anti-Markovnikoff addition of water to 1-alkenes. Hydrosilation of 1-alkenes with trichlorosilane regiospecifically yields 1-alkyltrichlorosilanes which react with potassium fluoride to yield 1-alkylpentafluorosilicates. These undergo oxidative cleavage by MCPBA to yield alcohols.

$$K_2\left[n\text{-}C_6H_{13}CH_2CH_2SiF_5\right] \xrightarrow[\text{DMF}]{\text{MCPBA}} n\text{-}C_6H_{13}CH_2CH_2OH \qquad \text{(10.30)}$$

MCPBA reacts faster with the sp^3 hybridized C$-$Si bond of alkylpentafluoro-silicates than with disubstituted C$-$C double bonds to yield epoxides [44].

$$K_2\left[\quad\right] \xrightarrow{\text{MCPBA}} \qquad \text{(10.31)}$$

Oxidation of optically active *exo*-2-norbornylpentafluorosilicate, gives optically *exo*-2-norboranol in 50% e.e. with retention of configuration.

$$(10.32)$$

Primary alkyl and aryl organotriethoxysilanes and organosilatranes also undergo oxidation by MCPBA to yield primary alcohols or phenols [40].

10.7 Reaction with TCNE

Unlike the previous reactions, the reaction of alkylpentafluorosilicates with TCNE is not stereospecific. *exo*-2-Norbornylpentafluorosilicate reacts with TCNE to give a 1 : 1 ratio of *exo* and *endo* products [45]. This result has been accounted for in terms of an initial one electron transfer from the alkylpentafluorosilicate to TCNE to give an alkylpentafluorosilicate monoanion radical and the TCNE anion radical. Loss of configuration of the alkyl group in such a radical anion species is expected. In fact, on mixing *exo*-2-norbornylpentafluorosilicate and TCNE in acetonitrile at −40°C, the ESR spectra of the TCNE anion radical can be observed.

$$(10.33)$$

10.8 Reduction

Alkylpentafluorosilicates react with protic acids to yield alkyl trifluorosilanes. On the other hand, they react with cupric fluoride dihydrate in the solid state to yield the corresponding alkanes [46].

$$K_2[n\text{-}C_{12}H_{25}SiF_5] \xrightarrow[\Delta]{CuF_2 \cdot 2H_2O} n\text{-}C_{12}H_{26}$$

$$(10.34)$$

10.9 Exchange

Ammonium methylpentafluorosilicate reacts with mercuric chloride to yield methyl mercuric chloride or at higher temperatures dimethyl mercury [47, 48]. This reaction may occur by electrophilic attack of ^+HgCl on the $C-Si$ bond of methylpentafluorosilicate.

$$HgCl_2 \ + \ (NH_4)_2\left[CH_3SiF_5\right] \xrightarrow[25°C]{H_2O} CH_3HgCl \tag{10.35}$$

$$CH_3HgCl \ + \ (NH_4)_2\left[CH_3SiF_5\right] \xrightarrow[100°C]{H_2O} CH_3HgCH_3 \tag{10.36}$$

Alkylpentafluorosilicates react with cuprous chloride at 250 °C to yield virtually equal amounts of the corresponding alkene and alkane. These may result from disproportionation of an alkyl copper (I) species [46].

$$K_2\left[CH_3O_2C(CH_2)_{10}SiF_5\right] \xrightarrow[250°C]{CuCl} CH_3O_2C(CH_2)_{10}H \ + \ CH_3O_2C(CH_2)_8CH=CH_2$$

$$\phantom{K_2[CH_3O_2C(CH_2)_{10}SiF_5]}\quad 56\% \qquad\qquad 44\% \tag{10.37}$$

10.10 Alkenylpentafluorosilicates

Z or *E* alkenyltrichlorosilanes react with potassium fluoride to yield *Z* or *E* alkenylpentafluorosilicates. Hydrosilation of alkynes by trichlorosilane can be controlled to yield either *Z*- or *E*-alkenyltrichlorosilanes. Hydrosilation of terminal alkynes with trichlorosilane catalyzed by chloroplatinic acid yields *E*-1-alkenyltrichlorosilanes (Eq. 10.38). On the other hand, hydrosilation of terminal alkynes catalyzed by peroxides yields predominantly *Z*-1-alkenyltrichlorosilanes (Eq. 10.39). Finally, hydrosilation of internal alkynes with trichlorosilane catalyzed by chloroplantinic acid yields *E*-alkenyltrichlorosilanes (Eq. 10.40) [49–51].

$$\tag{10.38}$$

$$\tag{10.39}$$

$$\tag{10.40}$$

Most of the work so far has been done with *E*-1-alkenylpentafluorosilicates.

10.11 Electrophilic Cleavage of Alkenylpentafluorosilicates

E-1-alkenylpentafluorosilicates undergo electrophilic cleavage by NBS, cupric chloride or cupric bromide to yield the corresponding vinyl bromides or chlorides with retention of stereochemistry [52].

$$K_2 \left[\underset{H}{\overset{Ph}{>}} C=C \underset{SiF_5}{\overset{H}{<}} \right] \xrightarrow[\text{or NBS}]{CuBr_2} \underset{}{\overset{Ph}{>}} \underset{Br}{\diagdown} \qquad (10.41)$$

Alkenylpentafluorosilicates react with cupric thiocyanate to yield alkenyl thiocyanates, with retention of stereochemistry [53–56]. The reaction tolerates ether, cyano, and ester functional groups.

$$K_2 \left[\underset{H}{\overset{N\equiv C(CH_2)_2OCH_2}{>}} C=C \underset{SiF_5}{\overset{H}{<}} \right] \xrightarrow[DMF]{Cu(SCN)_2} \underset{H}{\overset{N\equiv C(CH_2)_2OCH_2}{>}} C=C \underset{SCN}{\overset{H}{<}} \qquad (10.42)$$

E-1-alkenylpentafluorosilicates are converted regio- and stereospecifically to the corresponding E-alkenyl ethers by treatment with a catalytic amount of cupric acetate in a primary alcohol solvent under an oxygen atmosphere. Cyano and ester functional groups are tolerated. Similarly, E-1-alkenyl pentafluorosilicates react with water in acetonitrile in the presence of a catalytic amount of cupric acetate to yield aldehydes [57].

$$K_2 \left[\underset{H}{\overset{CH_3O_2C(CH_2)_8}{>}} C=C \underset{SiF_5}{\overset{H}{<}} \right] \xrightarrow[Cu(OAc)_2]{CH_3OH} \underset{H}{\overset{CH_3O_2C(CH_2)_8}{>}} C=C \underset{OCH_3}{\overset{H}{<}} \qquad (10.43)$$

E-1-Alkenylpentafluorosilicates react with silver salts in homogeneous solution [31] or with cuprous chloride in the solid state [58] to yield symmetrical E,E-1,3-dienes. Thus, vinyl pentafluorosilicate yields 1,3-butadiene on treatment with silver fluoride. The highest yields are obtained with silver fluoride in acetonitrile or silver nitrate in water [59]. The heterogeneous reaction of E-1-alkenylpentafluorosilicate with cuprous chloride is carried out between 200° and 300°C under vacuum. The product, E,E-1,3-diene, distills out as it is formed [58]. Ether and ester functional groups are unaffected by this reaction.

$$K_2 \left[\underset{}{\overset{n\text{-}C_4H_9}{\diagup}} \underset{SiF_5}{\diagdown} \right] \xrightarrow[200-300°]{CuCl} \underset{}{\overset{n\text{-}C_4H_9}{\diagup}} \underset{n\text{-}C_4H_9}{\diagdown} \qquad (10.44)$$

169

E-1-Alkenylpentafluorosilicates react with palladium chloride and allyl chloride to yield 1,4-dienes [60–63]. The reaction probably occurs by transfer of the E-1-alkenyl group from silicon to Pd(II) as outlined.

$$(10.45)$$

Likewise, E-1-alkenylpentafluorosilicates react with CO (1 atm) in methanol under catalysis by palladium chloride to yield methyl-E-α,β-unsaturated esters [64]. The reaction may be analogous to that of vinyl mercurials with CO and methanol catalyzed by Pd(II) to yield acrylate esters [65]. While the chemistry may be similar, alkenylpentafluorosilicates are less toxic than organo-mercurial compounds.

$$(10.46)$$

References

1. Sommer, L.H., Baire, W.B., Gould, J.R.: J. Am. Chem. Soc. *75*, 3765 (1953)
2. Sommer, L.H., Marans, N.S., Goldberg, G.M., Rockett, J., Pioch, R.P.: J. Am. Chem. Soc. *73*, 882 (1951)
3. Sommer, L.H., Pioch, R.P., Marans, N.S., Goldberg, G.M., Rockett, J., Kerlin, J.: J. Am. Chem. Soc. *75*, 2932 (1953)
4. Mironov, V.F., Sheladyakov, V.D., Schcherbinin, V.V., Viktorov, E.A.: Zh. Obsh. Khim. *45*, 1796 (1975)
5. Daniels, R.G., Paquette, L.A.: J. Org. Chem. *46*, 2901 (1981)
6. Sakurai, H., Tominaga, K., Watanabe, T., Kumada, M.: Tetrahedron Lett. 5493 (1966)
7. Frainnet, E., Calas, R., Gerval, P., Dentone, Y., Bonastre, J.: Bull. Soc. Chim. Fr. 1259 (1965)
8. Grignon-Dubois, M., Dunoguès, J., Calas, R.: Synthesis, 737 (1976)
9. Olah, G.A., Ho, T.L., Prakash, G.K.S., Gupta, B.G.B.: Synthesis, 677 (1977)
10. Grignon-Dubois, M., Dunoguès, J., Calas, R.: Tetrahedron Lett. 2883 (1981)
11. Grignon-Dubois, M., Dunoguès, J., Calas, R.: Can. J. Chem. *59*, 802 (1981)
12. Sommer, L.H., Van Strien, R.E., Whitmore, F.C.: J. Am. Chem. Soc. *71*, 3056 (1949)
13. Nametkin, N.S., Vdovin, V.M., Pushchevaya, K.S.: Dokl. Akad. Nauk. SSSR, *150*, 562 (1963)

14. Parnes, Z.N., Bolestova, G.I., Akhrem, I.S., Vol'pin, M.E., Kursanov, D.N.: J. Chem. Soc. Chem. Commun. 748 (1980)
15. Eaborn, C.: J. Chem. Soc. 2755 (1949)
16. Grignon-Dubois, M., Dunoguès, J., Calas, R.: J. Chem. Res. Miniprint, 379 (1979)
17. Calas, R., Bourgeois, P., Duffant, N.: C.R. Acad. Sci. Ser. C., 263, 243 (1965)
18. Grignon-Dubois, M., Dunoguès, J., Calas, R.: Tetrahedron Lett. 1197 (1976)
19. Eaborn, C., Bott, R.W.: Synthesis and Reactions of the Silicon-Carbon Bond in "Organometallic Compounds of the Group IV Elements", Vol. 1, (MacDiarmid, A.G., Ed.), p. 213–278. New York: Marcel Dekker, 1968
20. Speier, J.L., Webster, J.A., Barnes, G.H.: J. Am. Chem. Soc. 79, 974 (1957)
21. Seyferth, D., Cohen, H.M.: Inorg. Chem. 1, 913 (1962)
22. Olofson, R.A., Hoskin, D.H., Lotts, K.D.: Tetrahedron Lett. 1677 (1978)
23. Burford, C., Cooke, F., Ehlinger, E., Magnus, P.: J. Am. Chem. Soc. 99, 4536 (1977)
24. Cooke, F., Magnus, P.: J. Chem. Soc. Chem. Commun. 513 (1977)
25. Seyferth, D., Dow, A.W., Menzel, H., Flood, T.C.: J. Am. Chem. Soc. 90, 1080 (1969)
26. Seyferth, D., Menzel, H., Dow, A.W., Flood, T.C.: J. Organometal. Chem. 44, 279 (1972)
27. Ashe, A.J.: J. Am. Chem. Soc. 95, 818 (1973)
28. Taylor, R.T., Paquette, L.A.: J. Org. Chem. 43, 242 (1978)
29. Cooke, F., Magnus, P., Bundy, G.L.: J. Chem. Soc. Chem. Commun. 714 (1978)
30. Tamao, K., Yoshida, J.I., Kumada, M.: J. Syn. Org. Chem. Japan, 38, 769 (1980)
31. Müller, R.: Organometal. Chem. Rev. 1, 359 (1966)
32. Müller, R., Dathe, Chr.: Z. Anorg. Allg. Chem. 341, 49 (1965)
33. Tamao, K., Yoshida, J.I., Takahashi, M., Yamamoto, H., Kakui, T., Matsumoto, H., Kurita, A., Kumada, M.: J. Am. Chem. Soc. 100, 290 (1978)
34. Tamao, K., Hayashi, T., Matsumoto, H., Yamamoto, H., Kumada, M.: Tetrahedron Lett. 2155 (1979)
35. Yoshida, J.I., Tamao, K., Kurita, A., Kumada, M.: Tetrahedron Lett. 1809 (1978)
36. Yoshida, J.I., Tamao, K., Kumada, M., Kawamura, T.: J. Am. Chem. Soc. 102, 3267 (1980)
37. Yamamoto, K., Kiso, Y., Ito, R., Tamao, K., Kumada, M.: J. Organometal. Chem. 210, 9 (1981)
38. Hayashi, T., Mise, T., Fukushima, M., Kagotani, M., Nagashima, N., Hamada, Y., Matsumoto, A., Kawakami, S., Konishi, M., Yamamoto, K., Kumada, M.: Bull. Chem. Soc. Japan, 53, 1138 (1980)
39. Hayashi, T., Tamao, K., Katsuro, Y., Nakae, I., Kumada, M.: Tetrahedron Lett. 1871 (1980)
40. Hosomi, A., Iijima, S., Sakurai, H.: Chem. Lett. 243 (1981)
41. Frye, C.L., Vogel, G.E., Hall, J.A.: J. Am. Chem. Soc. 83, 996 (1961)
42. Voronkov, M.G.: Pure and Applied Chem. 13, 35 (1966)
43. Voronkov, M.G., Biological Activity of Silatranes in Topics in Current Chem. Vol. 84, p. 78–88, Berlin: Springer, 1979
44. Tamao, K., Kakui, T., Kumada, M.: J. Am. Chem. Soc. 100, 2268 (1978)
45. Yoshida, J.I., Tamao, K., Kumada, M., Kawamura, T.: J. Am. Chem. Soc. 102, 3269 (1980)
46. Yoshida, J.I., Tamao, K., Kakui, T., Kumada, M.: Tetrahedron Lett. 1141 (1979)
47. Müller, R., Dathe, Chr.: J. Prakt. Chem. 22, 232 (1963)
48. Müller, R., Dathe, Chr.: Chem. Ber. 98, 235 (1965)
49. Benkeser, R.A.: Pure and Applied Chemistry, 13, 133 (1966)
50. Benkeser, R., Cunico, R.F.: J. Organometal. Chem. 4, 284 (1965)

51. Benkeser, R.A., Burrous, M.L., Nelson, L.E., Swisher, J.V.: J. Am. Chem. Soc. *83*, 4385 (1961)
52. Yoshida, J.I., Tamao, K., Kurita, A., Kumada, M.: Tetrahedron Lett. 1809 (1978)
53. Tamao, K., Kakui, T., Kumada, M.: Tetrahedron Lett. 111 (1980)
54. Reeves, W.P., White, M.R., Hilbrich, R.G., Biegert, L.L.: Syn. Commun. *6*, 509 (1976)
55. Liotta, C.L., Grisdale, E.E., Hopkins, H.P.: Tetrahedron Lett. 4205 (1975)
56. Guy, R.G., "The Chemistry of Cyanates and Their Thio Derivatives", (S. Patai, Ed.), Part 2, p. 819–886, New York: J. Wiley, 1977
57. Tamao, K., Kakui, T., Kumada, M.: Tetrahedron Lett. 4105 (1980)
58. Yoshida, J.I., Tamao, K., Kakui, T., Kumada, M.: Tetrahedron Lett. 1141 (1979)
59. Tamao, K., Matsumoto, M., Kakui, T., Kumada, M.: Tetrahedron Lett. 1137 (1979)
60. Yoshida, J.I., Tamao, K., Takahashi, M., Kumada, M.: Tetrahedron Lett. 2161 (1978)
61. Heck, R.F.: J. Am. Chem. Soc. *90*, 5518 (1968)
62. Heck, R.F.: J. Am. Chem. Soc. *90*, 5526 (1968)
63. Heck, R.F.: J. Am. Chem. Soc. *90*, 4431 (1968)
64. Tamao, K., Kakui, T., Kumada, M.: Tetrahedron, 619 (1979)
65. Larock, R.C.: J. Org. Chem. *40*, 3237 (1975)

11 Allylic Silanes

11.1 Introduction

Allylic trimethylsilanes are highly versatile synthetic intermediates. We will consider five aspects of their chemistry in this chapter. First will be electrophilic substitution reactions; second, cycloaddition reactions; third, synthesis of allylic silanes; fourth, reactions of silyl substituted allylic anions, and fifth, the chemistry of boron substituted allylic silanes.

11.2 Electrophilic Substitution

Many reactions of allylic trimethylsilanes involve electrophilic substitution with allylic rearrangement and loss of the trimethylsilyl group. These reactions often occur by addition of the electrophile to the $C-C$ double bond to yield a carbocation which is stabilized by a β-trimethylsilyl group. Nucleophilic attack on silicon by the associated anion or solvent results in loss of the silyl group and formation of products. On the other hand, addition of the anion to the carbocation center results in electrophilic addition.

$$(11.1)$$

A. Protic Acids

Both HBr and HI add to allyltrimethylsilane in an anti-Markovnikoff sense. On the other hand, HCl reacts with allyltrimethylsilane to yield TMS-Cl

$$(11.2)$$

and propene. Electrophilic substitution results from attack by chloride ion at the silyl center rather than at the carbocation center [1].

In such electrophilic-substitution reactions of allylic trimethylsilanes, the position of the C−C double bond shifts. For example, treatment of the Diels-Alder adduct of 1-trimethylsilyl-1,3-butadiene and maleic anhydride with TsOH results in loss of the trimethylsilyl group and a specific 1,2-shift of the C−C double bond [2].

$$\text{(11.3)}$$

In a similar manner, 4-methylene cyclohexanones have been prepared by treatment of 1-methoxy-4-trimethylsilylmethyl-1,4-cyclohexadienes with HCl in THF and methanol. Protodesilylation of the allylic trimethylsilane and hydrolysis of the methyl enol ether occurs simultaneously [3].

$$\text{(11.4)}$$

Protodesilylation of 2-methyl-1,4-bis-(trimethylsilyl)-2-butene with HCl yields 2-methyl-4-trimethylsilyl butene. This selectivity results from protonation of the C−C double bond to yield the more stable tertiary carbocation intermediate [4]. Boron trifluoride/acetic acid has proved highly effective for protodesilylation of allylic trimethysilanes [5].

$$\text{(11.5)}$$

Protodesilylation of 1,3-bis-(trimethylsilyl)-1-alkenes yields allylic trimethylsilanes. This selectivity results from the preferential reaction of the allylic trimethylsilane functionality [6].

$$\text{(11.6)}$$

Allyltrimethylsilane reacts with alcohols and a catalytic amount of TsOH to yield trimethylsilyl ethers and propene as outlined [7].

$$(11.7)$$

Allyltrimethylsilane and allyl-*t*-butyldimethylsilane react with primary or secondary alcohols under catalysis by HI to yield trimethylsilyl or *t*-butyldimethylsilyl ethers, respectively. Trimethylsilyl iodide or *t*-butyldimethylsilyl iodide are intermediates [8]. This provides a method to silylate alcohols under acidic conditions.

$$(11.8)$$

B. Halogens

Allyltrimethylsilane reacts with bromine to yield allyl bromide and TMS-Br [1]. This reaction has been used to prepare 1-bromo-indene, a previously poorly characterized compound [9, 10]. In a similar manner, allyltrimethylsilane reacts with iodine to yield allyl iodide and TMS-I [11].

$$(11.9)$$

C. Acid Chlorides

Allylic trimethylsilanes react with acid chlorides in the presence of Lewis acids to yield rearranged allylic ketones. For example, pivaloyl chloride reacts with allyltrimethylsilane in the presence of gallium trichloride, indium tri-chloride or AlCl$_3$ to yield allyl *t*-butyl ketone. While 1,4-*bis*-(trimethylsilyl)-2-cyclooctene, reacts with acetyl chloride and AlCl$_3$ to yield 3-acetyl-4-tri-methylsilyl cyclooctene [12].

$$(11.10)$$

Reaction of γ,γ-dimethylallyltrimethylsilane with γ,γ-dimethylacryloyl chlo-ride and AlCl$_3$ provides an efficient synthesis of L'Artemisia ketone [13].

$$(11.11)$$

The observation that α-pinenyltrimethylsilane reacts with acetyl chloride in the presence of AlCl$_3$ to yield acetyl-β-pinene [14], attests to the mild reaction conditions.

$$(11.12)$$

Similar regiospecific reactions of allylic trimethylsilanes with acid chlorides have been reported [5, 15]. 2,3-*bis*(Trimethylsilyl)cycloalkenes possess both allylic and vinylic trimethylsilane functionalities. Preferential electrophilic desilylation of the allylic trimethylsilane occurs with acetyl chloride and AlCl$_3$ [16].

$$(11.13)$$

Reaction of 2-trimethylsilylmethyl-1,3-butadiene with acid chlorides and TiCl$_4$ yields isopropenyl ketones [17].

$$ (CH_3)_3Si \diagdown\diagup + (CH_3)_2CH-\overset{O}{\overset{\|}{C}}-Cl \xrightarrow{TiCl_4} \diagup\diagdown \overset{O}{\diagup} \atop CH(CH_3)_2 \qquad (11.14) $$

A similar reaction of 5-trimethylsilyl-1,3-pentadiene with pivaloyl chloride leads to a mixture of products formed by electrophilic attack by the acylium ion on both the 1 and 3 carbons of the pentadienyl system [18].

$$ (CH_3)_3C-\overset{O}{\overset{\|}{C}}-Cl + (CH_3)_3Si\diagup\diagdown\diagup\diagdown\diagup \qquad (11.15) $$

$$ \xrightarrow{TiCl_4} (CH_3)_3C-\overset{O}{\overset{\|}{C}}\diagup\diagdown\diagup\diagdown\diagup + (CH_3)_3C-\overset{O}{\overset{\|}{C}}\diagup\diagdown $$

The reaction of 1-chloro-3-trimethylsilyl propene with acid chlorides catalyzed by AlCl$_3$ provides an efficient route to α-chloro-β,γ-unsaturated ketones. Reduction of these with NaBH$_4$ or LiAlH$_4$ followed by cyclization cf the chlorohydrin product with sodium hydroxide gives vinyl substituted epoxides [19].

$$ (CH_3)_3Si\diagdown\diagup\diagdown Cl + \underset{}{\overset{O}{\bigcirc\!\!-\!\!C}}Cl \xrightarrow[CH_2Cl_2]{AlCl_3} \underset{}{\overset{O}{\bigcirc}}\diagdown_{Cl} $$

$$ \begin{array}{c} 1) \ NaBH_4 \\ 2) \ NaOH \end{array} \Big\downarrow \qquad (11.16) $$

1-Trimethylsilyloxyallyltrimethylsilane reacts with acid chlorides under the influence of TiCl$_4$ to yield 4-keto trimethylsilyl enol ethers. These can be hydrolyzed to yield 4-keto aldehydes [20].

$$ \diagup\diagdown\overset{Si(CH_3)_3}{\underset{O\diagdown Si(CH_3)_3}{\diagup}} + (CH_3)_2CH-\overset{O}{\overset{\|}{C}}-Cl \xrightarrow{TiCl_4} (CH_3)_2CH\overset{O}{\diagup}\diagdown\diagup\diagdown_{O}^{Si(CH_3)_3} $$

$$ H_3O^+ \Big\downarrow \qquad (11.17) $$

$$ (CH_3)_2CH\diagdown\diagup\diagdown\overset{O}{\diagup}\diagdown^{H}_{O} $$

α-Trimethylsilylallyl phenyl sulfides undergo regiospecific acylation with acid chlorides and AlCl$_3$ to yield γ-phenylthio β,γ-unsaturated ketones [21].

177

$$(11.18)$$

Metallation of allyloxytrimethylsilane yields an organo-lithium reagent which reacts regiospecifically with ketones to yield 1,2-dihydroxy-3-alkenes [22].

$$(11.19)$$

Homoallylic trimethylsilanes react with acid chlorides under the influence of TiCl₄ to yield mixtures of β-chloro ketones, cyclopropyl carbinyl ketones, and homoallylic ketones. The β-chloro ketones result from secondary reaction of the cyclopropyl carbinyl ketones with TiCl₄ [23].

$$(11.20)$$

D. Sulfonyl Chlorides

Under catalysis by cuprous chloride, allyltrimethylsilane reacts with benzene sulfonyl chloride or methane sulfonyl chloride to yield TMS-Cl and allyl phenyl sulfone or allyl methyl sulfone, respectively.

$$(11.21)$$

In a similar manner, trimethylsilyl chlorosulfonate reacts with allylic silanes to yield trimethylsilyl allylsulfonates and TMS-Cl [25].

Reaction of trimethylsilyl chlorosulfonate with 1,3-*bis*-(trimethylsilyl) propene yields trimethylsilyl 1-trimethylsilylallylsulfonate. The product results from preferential electrophilic attack on the allylic silane [25].

$$(11.22)$$

E. Transition Metal Complexes

Allylic trimethylsilanes undergo electrophilic substitution reactions with certain transition metal complexes. For example, trimethylsilyl 3-trimethylsilyl-methyl-3-butenoate reacts with palladium chloride in methanol to yield the 1-carbomethoxy-2-methyl-π-allyl palladium chloride dimer [26].

$$(11.23)$$

Cyclohexadienyl iron tricarbonyl cations react with allylic trimethylsilanes regiospecifically at the least hindered end to yield an allyl substituted cyclohexadiene iron tricarbonyl complexes [27].

$$(11.24)$$

Propargyl $Co_2(CO)_6$ cations react with allylic trimethylsilanes to yield hex-1-en-5-yne $Co_2(CO)_6$ complexes. Removal of the $Co_2(CO)_6$ protecting group by oxidation with ferric nitrate yields hex-1-en-5-ynes [28]. No isomeric allenic by-products are formed.

$$(11.25)$$

179

F. Sulfenyl Halides

Low temperature reaction of benzene sulfenyl chloride with allylsilane (I) gives an addition product which undergoes fluoride induced elimination to yield the rearranged allyl phenyl sulfide [2, 10, 29].

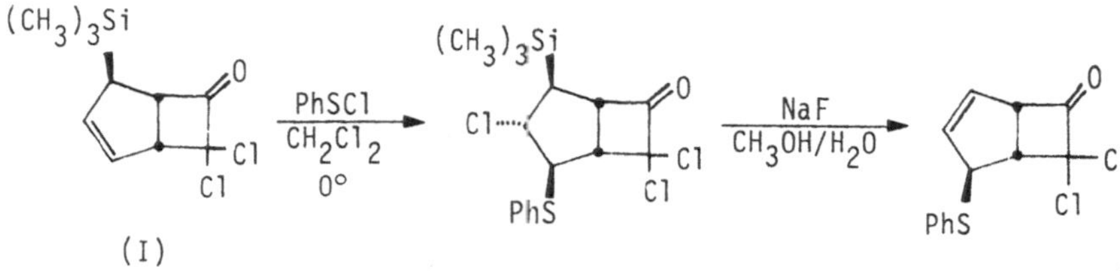

(11.26)

G. Carbocations

Carbocations react with allylic trimethylsilanes to yield rearranged allyl substituted alkanes. Thus adamantyl chloride reacts with allylic trimethylsilanes to yield 1-allyl adamantane derivatives [5, 30, 31].

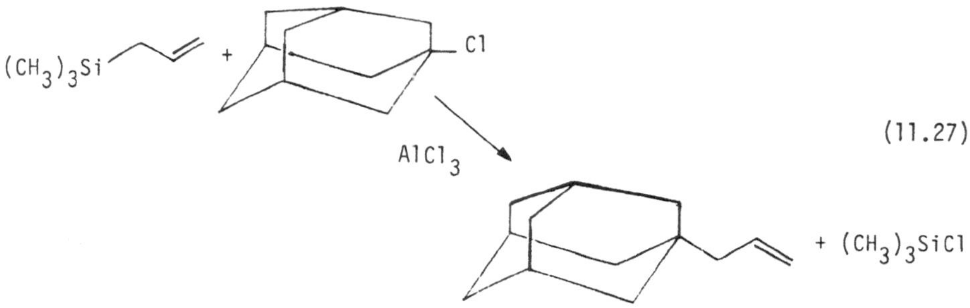

(11.27)

The use of allyl trimethylsilanes as terminators in biomimetic polyene cyclizations has been explored.

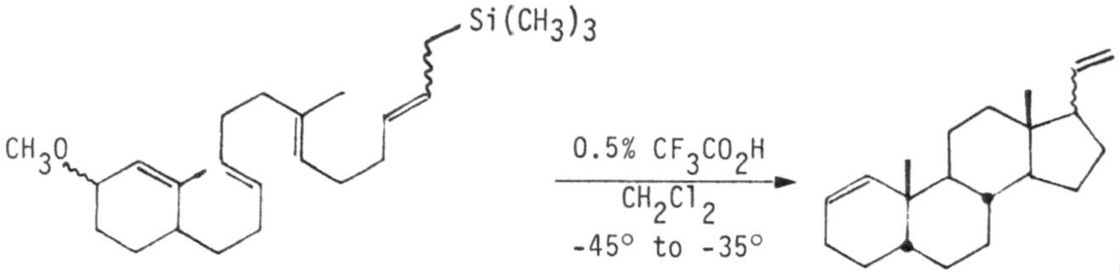

(11.28)

Mixtures of epimeric products at C-17 were obtained. The stability of the allylic trimethylsilane towards a variety of reaction conditions, permits its incorporation into complex molecutes [32].

Chloromethyl methyl ether reacts with allylic trimethylsilanes under SnCl$_4$ catalysis to yield rearranged homoallylic methyl ethers [10, 29]. This reaction has been used as a key step in the preparation of a precursor [33] to prostaglandin A and F.

$$(11.29)$$

The reaction of allyl trimethylsilanes with ethylene oxide under the influence of TiCl$_4$ provides an efficient route to 4-penten-1-ols [5].

$$(11.30)$$

H. Ketones, Aldehydes, Acetals, and Ketals

With AlCl$_3$ or gallium trichloride, allylic trimethylsilanes undergo regiospecific reaction with aldehydes or ketones to yield rearranged homoallylic alcohols [34–37]. These reactions probably proceed by coordination of the Lewis acid to the carbonyl oxygen rendering the carbonyl carbon sufficiently electrophilic to attack the nucleophilic C–C double bond of the allylic silane.

$$(11.31)$$

When an equivalent amount of TiCl$_4$ was used as Lewis acid in these reactions, significantly higher yields of homoallylic alcohols were obtained at lower temperatures [38].

$$(11.32)$$

Allylic trimethylsilanes also react with acetals or ketals under Lewis acid activation by TiCl$_4$ to yield homoallylic ethers [39]. Higher yields have often been obtained from comparable reactions of an allylic trimethylsilane with an acetal or ketal rather the corresponding aldehyde or ketone.

$$(11.33)$$

This reaction probably involves Lewis acid assisted heterolysis of a C−O bond of the ketal or acetal to yield an alkoxy stabilized carbocation which attacks the C−C double bond of the allylic trimethylsilane. A wide variety of ketones, aldehydes, acetals, or ketals react with allylic trimethylsilanes under these conditions [15].

Rearrangement of the allylic group occurs during the reaction. Thus α,α-dimethylallyltrimethylsilane reacts with aldehydes under Lewis acid catalysis by TiCl₄ to yield γ,γ-dimethylallyl (prenyl) carbinols [40].

$$(11.34)$$

In a similar manner, 2-trimethylsilyl methylene cyclobutane reacts with aldehydes, or ketones and TiCl₄ to yield cyclobutenylmethyl carbinols. The cyclobutene ring of such alcohols will undergo a thermally allowed electrocyclic conrotatory opening to yield isopropenyl substituted carbinols [41].

$$(11.35)$$

Intramolecular reactions of aldehydes or ketones with allylic silanes under Lewis acid catalysis yields cyclic homoallylic alcohols. 3-Trimethylsilylallyl alcohol undergoes acid catalyzed exchange with ethyl vinyl ethers to yield 3-trimethylsilylallyl vinyl ethers. On heating, Claisen rearrangement occurs to yield α-(1-trimethylsilylallyl) ketones. These undergo electrophilic cyclization/desilylation on treatment with TiCl₄ to yield cyclopent-3-en-1-ols [42].

$$(11.36)$$

3-Trimethylsilylallyl alcohol has been prepared from propargyl alcohol as outlined [42].

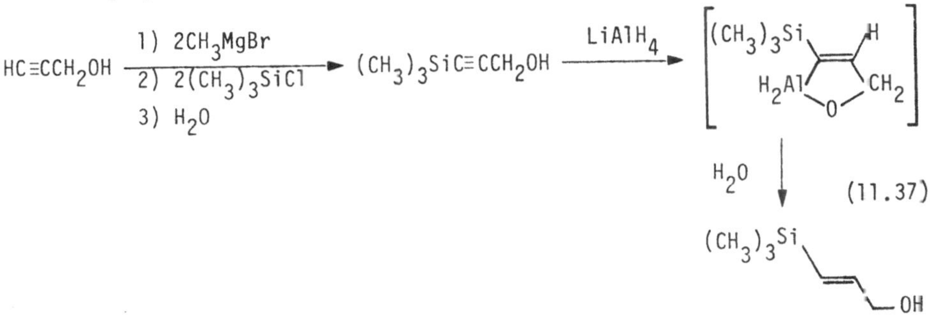
1) 2CH3MgBr
HC≡CCH2OH
2) 2(CH3)3SiCl
3) H2O
(CH3)3SiC≡CCH2OH
LiAlH4
(CH3)3Si
H
H2Al
CH2
O
H2O
(CH3)3Si
OH

(11.37)

Intramolecular cyclization reactions of 7-methyl-8-phenylthio-8-trimethylsilyl oct-6-en-1-al (II) have been carried out with $SnCl_4$, $BF_3 \cdot OEt_2$ or TBAF catalysis. With these catalysts both *Z* and *E* isomers of II yield mixtures of stereoisomeric 2-(3′-phenylthio-propenyl)cyclohexanols. On the other hand, stereospecific cyclization occurs with trifluoroacetic acid. *E*-II yields *cis*-2-(3′-phenylthio propenyl) cyclohexanol while the corresponding *Z*-II yields *trans*-2-(3′-phenylthio propenyl) cyclohexanol [43].

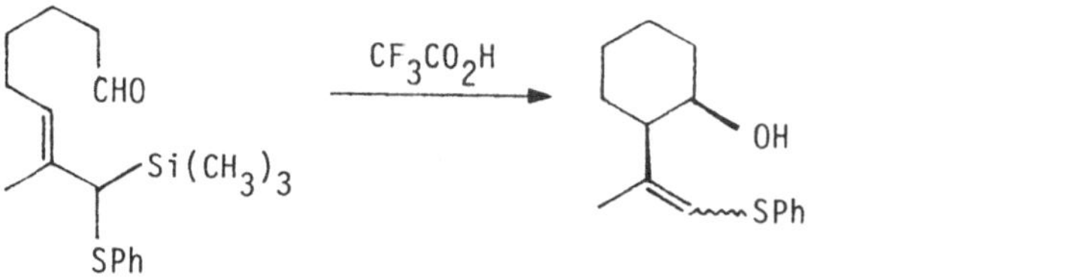
CHO
Si(CH3)3
SPh
CF3CO2H
OH
SPh

E-II

(11.38)

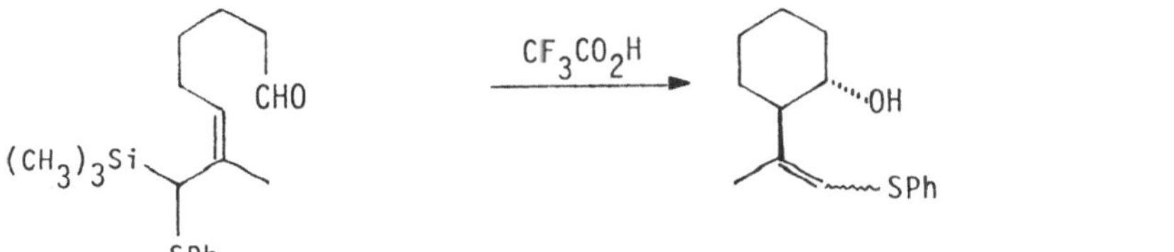
CHO
(CH3)3Si
SPh
CF3CO2H
OH
SPh

Z-II

(11.39)

Lewis acid facilitated intramolecular reactions of 5-trimethylsilylmethyl-hex-5-en-1-als provide an efficient route to 3-methylene cyclohexanols. The ratio of axial to equitorial alcohols depends on the catalyst [44].

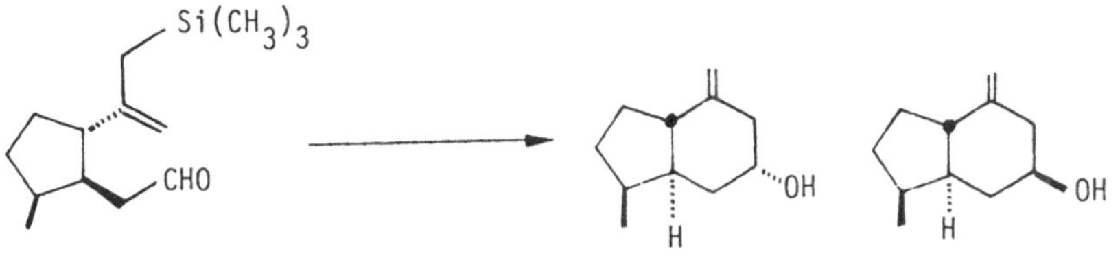
Si(CH3)3
CHO
OH
H
OH
H

$BF_3 \cdot OEt_2/CH_2Cl_2$	85%	15%
TBAF/THF	18%	82%

(11.40)

Catalysis by TBAF may occur as outlined below. The TBAF catalyzed

(11.41)

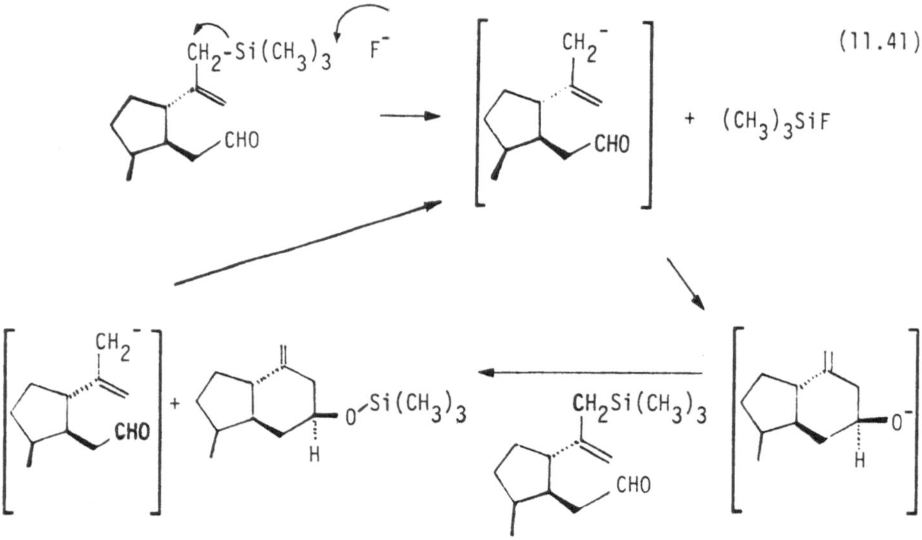

reaction of allylic trimethylsilanes with aldehydes or ketones to yield homoallylic alcohols is not regiospecific [45]. This reaction is probably related to the isomerization of allylic trimethylsilanes with this catalyst system [92].

(11.42)

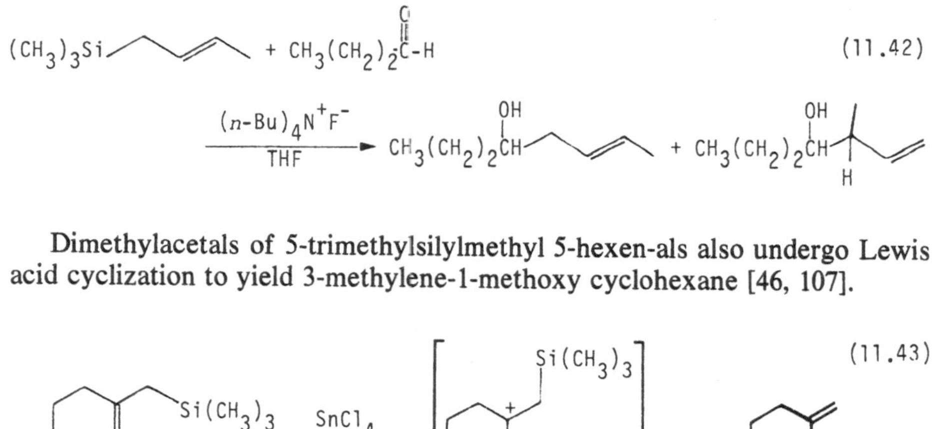

Dimethylacetals of 5-trimethylsilylmethyl 5-hexen-als also undergo Lewis acid cyclization to yield 3-methylene-1-methoxy cyclohexane [46, 107].

(11.43)

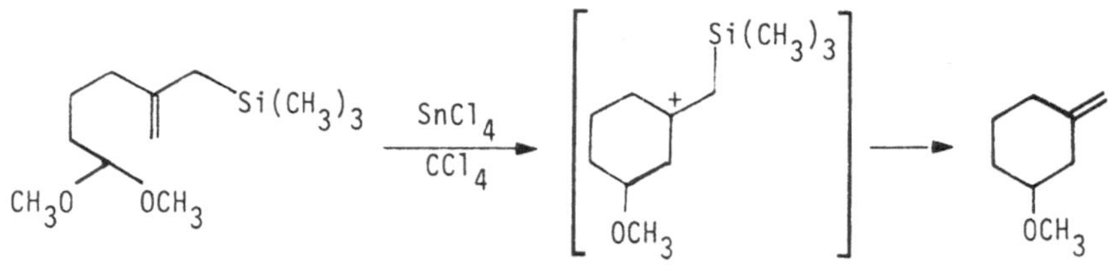

Trimethylsilyl-3-trimethylsilylmethyl-3-butenoate reacts with ketones under the influence of TiCl$_4$ to yield 5-hydroxy-3-methylene carboxylic acids. These can be cyclized to yield α,β-unsaturated-δ-lactones on treatment with HCl [47].

$$(11.44)$$

3-Trimethylsilylmethyl-3-butenoic acid has been prepared by a nickel chloride catalyzed addition of trimethylsilylmethyl magnesium chloride to diketene. Base catalyzed isomerization of this acid with lithium *bis*(trimethylsilyl) amide in TMEDA stereospecifically yields *E*-3-methyl-4-trimethylsilyl-2-butenoic acid. On the other hand, isomerization of trimethylsilyl ester with the same base yields predominantly *Z*-3-methyl-4-trimethylsilyl-2-butenoic acid after hydrolysis [48].

$$(11.45)$$

Lewis acid catalyzed reaction of trimethylsilyl-α-trimethylsilylmethyl acrylate with dimethyl acetals yields the corresponding γ-methoxy-α-methylene esters. These react with TMS-I to yield α-methylene-γ-lactones [49].

$$(11.46)$$

185

The necessary trimethylsilyl-α-trimethylsilylmethyl acrylate was prepared as outlined below.

$$(CH_3)_3SiCl \quad + \quad {}^-CH(CO_2Et)_2$$

$$(CH_3)_3SiCH_2CH(CO_2Et)_2 \xrightarrow[2) \ CH_2Br_2]{1) \ NaH} (CH_3)_3SiCH_2\underset{\underset{CH_2Br}{|}}{C}(CO_2Et)_2$$

$$\text{KOH/EtOH} \Big\downarrow \overset{H_2O}{\underset{\Delta}{}} \qquad (11.47)$$

$$(CH_3)_3SiCH_2-C\overset{\displaystyle CH_2}{\underset{\displaystyle \underset{O}{\overset{\|}{C}}-OSi(CH_3)_3}{\Big\langle}} \xleftarrow[\text{\includegraphics{pyridine}}]{(CH_3)_3SiCl} (CH_3)_3SiCH_2-C\overset{\displaystyle CO_2H}{\underset{\displaystyle CH_2}{\Big\langle}}$$

Isopropenyltrimethylsilane reacts with aldehydes or dimethylacetals under the influence of TiCl$_4$ to yield isopropenyl substituted carbinols or the corresponding methyl ethers, respectively (Eq. 11.48) [17]. Isopropenyltrimethylsilane has been prepared by a nickel catalyzed coupling of 2-chloro-1,3-butadiene with trimethylsilylmethyl magnesium chloride.

$$Ph(CH_2)_2\overset{\overset{O}{\|}}{C}-H \quad + \quad \underset{}{\diagup}\overset{CH_2Si(CH_3)_3}{} \xrightarrow{TiCl_4} \overset{OH}{\overset{|}{}}\quad CH_2\overset{|}{C}H(CH_2)_2Ph \qquad (11.48)$$

5-Trimethylsilyl-1,3-pentadiene reacts with dimethyl acetals under catalysis by BF$_3 \cdot$ OEt$_2$ or TiCl$_4$ as outlined [50, 51].

$$(CH_3)_3Si\diagdown\diagup\diagdown\diagup \quad + \quad PhCH(OCH_3)_2 \xrightarrow{BF_3 \cdot OEt_2} Ph\underset{\underset{OCH_3}{|}}{C}H\diagdown\diagup\diagdown\diagup \qquad (11.49)$$

Similar reactions with aldehydes or ketones [52] under catalysis by TiCl$_4$ yield 1,3-pentadienylic carbinols.

$$(CH_3)_3Si\diagdown\diagup\diagdown\diagup \quad + \quad (CH_3)_3C-\overset{\overset{O}{\|}}{C}-H \xrightarrow[\underset{-40°}{CH_2Cl_2}]{TiCl_4} \diagup\diagdown\diagup\diagdown\underset{\underset{H}{|}}{\overset{\overset{OH}{|}}{C}}C(CH_3)_3 \qquad (11.50)$$

The reaction of allylic trimethylsilanes with acetals as usually carried out requires a stoichiometric amount of TiCl$_4$. Recently, two new procedures have been reported which only require a catalytic amount of Lewis acid. Both trimethylsilyl trifluoromethanesulfonate [106] and TMS-I [53] have proved effective catalysts for such reactions. TMS-I is particularly convenient since it can be generated *in-situ* by addition of a small amount of iodine to a slight excess of the allylic trimethylsilane.

$$(11.51)$$

Allyltrimethylsilane reacts with p-quinone and $TiCl_4$ to yield 2-allyl hydroquinones. Allyl p-quinol is a probable intermediate [54].

$$(11.52)$$

I. α,β-Unsaturated Ketones and Aldehydes

Allylic trimethylsilanes react with α,β-unsaturated ketones and $TiCl_4$ to yield δ,ε-enones as outlined in Eq. 11.53. This is equivalent to a Michael addition of the rearranged allyl group.

$$(11.53)$$

This reaction permits the introduction of an allyl group at the angular position of a fused cyclic α,β-unsaturated enone [11, 55].

$$(11.54)$$

1-Acetyl-2-methyl cyclopentene reacts with allytrimethylsilane and TiCl$_4$ to give a 6:4 mixture of $Z:E$ 1-acetyl-2-allyl-2-methyl cyclopentanes.

[56] However, reaction with acetyl cyclohexene proved to be more complicated [52].

$$(11.55)$$

This regiospecific Michael addition of allylic groups to α,β-unsaturated ketones has been utilized in the synthesis of (+) Nootkatone [57, 58]. The key allylation step is outlined in Eq. 11.56.

$$(11.56)$$

Allylic trimethylsilanes also react with α,β-unsaturated ketones under catalysis by TBAF to yield both 1,2- and 1,4-addition products [45].

$$(11.57)$$

Reaction of 2-methylallyltrimethylsilane with α,β-unsaturated ketones which are activated by TiCl$_4$ or BF$_3 \cdot$ OEt$_2$ yields δ,ε-enones. The C$-$C double bond of these can be cleaved with ozone, followed by a reductive work-up to yield 1,5-dicarbonyl compounds [59].

$$(CH_3)_3Si \quad + \quad \text{(cyclohexenone)} \quad \xrightarrow[CH_2Cl_2]{TiCl_4} \quad \text{(product)} \qquad (11.58)$$

$$\xrightarrow[\substack{2)\ Zn \\ CH_3CO_2H}]{1)\ O_3} \quad \text{(product)}$$

2-Chloromethyl-allyltrimethylsilane undergoes TiCl$_4$ induced reaction with cyclohexenone to yield β-(2-chloromethyl allyl) cyclohexanone. Treatment of this with strong base results in an intramolecular C-alkylation of the ketone enolate by the allylic chloride. This sequence permits the [3 + 2] annulation of a five membered ring onto the C−C double bond of cyclic α,β-unsaturated ketones [60].

$$(CH_3)_3Si \underset{CH_2Cl}{\diagup} \quad + \quad \text{(cyclohexenone)} \quad \xrightarrow[\substack{CH_2Cl_2 \\ -78°}]{TiCl_4} \quad \text{(product, } CH_2Cl) \qquad (11.59)$$

$$\xrightarrow{K^+ \ {}^-O\text{-}C(CH_3)_3} \quad \text{(product)}$$

The necessary reagent, 2-chloromethyl-allyltrimethylsilane has been prepared from iodomethyltrimethylsilane as outlined in Eq. 11.60.

$$(CH_3)_3SiCH_2I \quad + \quad Na^{+-}CH(CO_2Et)_2 \quad \longrightarrow \quad (CH_3)_3SiCH_2CH(CO_2Et)_2 \qquad (11.60)$$

$$\xrightarrow[\substack{1)\ NaH \\ 2)\ LiAlH_4}]{} (CH_3)_3SiCH_2CH(CH_2OH)_2 \xrightarrow[\substack{1)\ CH_3SO_2Cl/Et_3N \\ 2)\ LiCl/DMF \\ 3)\ collidine}]{} (CH_3)_3SiCH_2\text{-}C\underset{CH_2Cl}{\overset{CH_2}{\diagup}}$$

[2+3] Annulation of a five membered ring onto ketones has also been achieved by use of allylic silane reagents. The reaction of the enolate anion of cyclic-β-keto sulfones with 2-trimethylsilylmethyl prop-2-enyl methanesulfonate yields α-phenylsulfonyl-α-(2-trimethylsilylmethylpropenyl) ketones. Treatment of these with TBAF in THF results in cyclization. This involves an allylic anion intermediate formed by fluoride ion attack on the silyl center [108]. The initial product often undergoes fragmentation under these conditions to yield a three carbon ring expanded product.

$$(11.61)$$

Allylic trimethylsilanes react with α,β-unsaturated ketones under the influence of $TiCl_4$ to yield δ,ε-unsaturated trimethylsilyl enol ether or δ,ε-unsaturated titanium trichloride enolates as the initial reaction products. These can be utilized synthetically, since such enol ethers react with electrophiles (acetals, aldehydes, or ketones) un the presence of $TiCl_4$ to yield α substituted δ,ε-unsaturated ketones [61] (see Chapter 12).

$$(11.62)$$

By comparison, α,β-unsaturated dimethylacetals react at the acetal carbon with allylic trimethylsilanes under the influence of TMS-I [53].

$$(11.63)$$

α,β-Unsaturated acyl cyanides undergo reactions with allylic trimethyl-silane and TiCl$_4$ to yield δ,ε-unsaturated acyl cyanides [62].

$$(11.64)$$

J. α-Nitro Alkenes

In the presence of AlCl$_3$, allylic trimethylsilanes undergo a Michael reaction with α-nitro olefins to yield reactive γ,δ-unsaturated nitronic acids. Treatment of these with titanium trichloride yields γ,δ-unsaturated ketones [63].

$$(11.65)$$

K. α- and β-Keto Acetals and α-Keto Esters

Reaction of allylic trimethylsilanes with β-keto acetals and TiCl$_4$ occurs preferentially at the acetal carbon [64].

$$(11.66)$$

With α-keto acetals the site of reaction is determined by the particular Lewis acid chosen. Thus, with AlCl$_3$ reaction occurs exclusively at the carbonyl carbon, while with TiCl$_4$ reaction occurs at both the carbonyl carbon and the acetal carbon [64].

$$(11.67)$$

Allyltrimethylsilane reacts with the ketone carbonyl of pyruvate esters in the presence of TiCl$_4$ to yield γ,δ-unsaturated-α-hydroxyvalerates [65]. 3-Trimethylsilyl cyclopentene reacts similarly with ethyl pyruvate and ethyl phenyl glyoxalate [15].

$$(11.68)$$

(−)Menthyl pyruvate reacts with allyltrimethylsilane at −75°C to yield (−)menthyl 2-hydroxy-2-methyl-pent-4-enoate. Asymmetric induction results in a 55% e.e. (S) at the new chiral center [65].

11.3 Cycloaddition Reactions of Allylic Silanes

A. [2 + 2] Cycloaddition Reactions

[2 + 2] Cycloaddition reaction of 5-trimethylsilylcyclopentadiene with dichloroketene yield exclusively 7,7-dichloro-4-exo-trimethylsilylbicyclo[3,2,0]hept-2-en-6-one (Eq. 11.69) [10, 29]. On the other hand, TCNE reacts with allyltrimethylsilane to yield a mixture of 1,1,2,2-tetracyano-3-trimethylsilylmethyl cyclobutane and 1,1,2,2-tetracyano-4-pentene [66].

$$(11.69)$$

Hexafluoroacetone reacts with allyltrimethylsilane to yield a mixture of 2,2-*bis*-(trifluoromethyl)-4-trimethylsilylmethyloxetane and 1,1-*bis*-(trifluoromethyl)-4-trimethylsilyl-3-buten-1-ol [34].

$$(11.70)$$

Allyltrimethylsilane undergoes [2 + 2] photocycloaddition with naphthoquinone [67].

$$(11.71)$$

Chlorosulfonyl isocyanate undergoes a [2 + 2] cycloaddition reaction with γ,γ-dimethylallyltrimethylsilane at 0° to yield 4,4-dimethyl-3-trimethylsilyl-methyl-N-chlorosulfonyl β lactam. At 25° this compound rapidly rearranges to α,α-dimethylallyl trimethylsilyloxy-N-chlorosulfonyl imine [68].

$$(11.72)$$

Treatment of these adducts with pyridine yields the corresponding nitriles [68].

$$(11.73)$$

Such allylic trimethylsilyloxy-N-chlorosulfonyl imines can also be converted to allylic esters [69].

B. [3 + 2] Cycloadditions

2-Acetoxymethyl-3-allyltrimethylsilane undergoes Pd(O) catalyzed reaction with alkenes substituted with electron withdrawing groups to yield methylene cyclopentane derivatives. These reactions may involve formation of a tri-methylene methane palladium complex as an intermediate [70].

$$(11.74)$$

2-Trimethylsilylmethyl π-allyl palladium L_2^+ complexes, can be trapped by nucleophiles [71].

$$(11.75)$$

2-Acetoxymethyl-3-allyltrimethylsilane can be prepared from α-methylallyl alcohol by metallation with two equivalents of *n*-butyl lithium/TMEDA followed by the addition of TMS-Cl. Hydrolysis of the trimethylsilyl ether, followed by acetylation gives the desired reagent.

C. Diels-Alder Reactions

Isopropenyltrimethylsilane undergoes Diels-Alder reactions with various dienophiles to yield 1-trimethylsilylmethyl cyclohexenes [41, 72].

$$(11.76)$$

Isopropenyltrimethylsilane has been prepared by thermally allowed conrotatory electrocyclic ring opening of—trimethylsilylmethyl cyclobutene [17, 41, 73].

1-Trimethylsilylbutadiene undergoes Diels-Alder reactions with dienophiles to give mixtures of regioisomers. The *ortho* adducts are usually predominant [74].

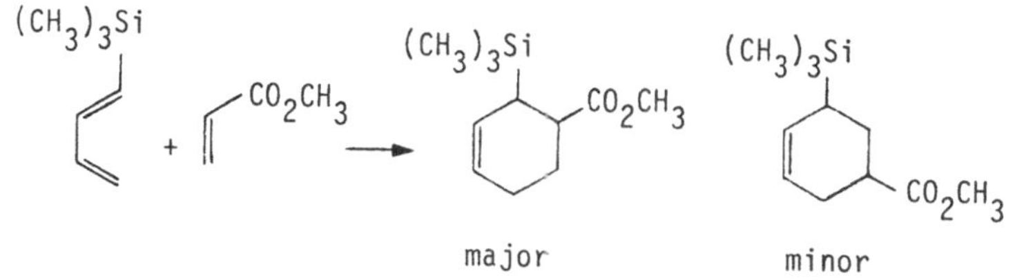

(11.77)

major   minor

11.4 Preparation

A. Direct Synthesis

Allyltrichlorosilane has been prepared by the direct synthesis. Thus reaction of allyl chloride with copper-silicon powder (10:90) at 250° yields a mixture of allyldichlorosilane, diallyldichlorosilane, and allyltrichlorosilane in which the latter product is predominant [75]. Allylic trichlorosilanes can be converted to allylic trimethylsilanes by reaction with an excess of methyl magnesium bromide [75] or by reaction with methyl chloride and zinc in N-methyl pyrrolidone [76].

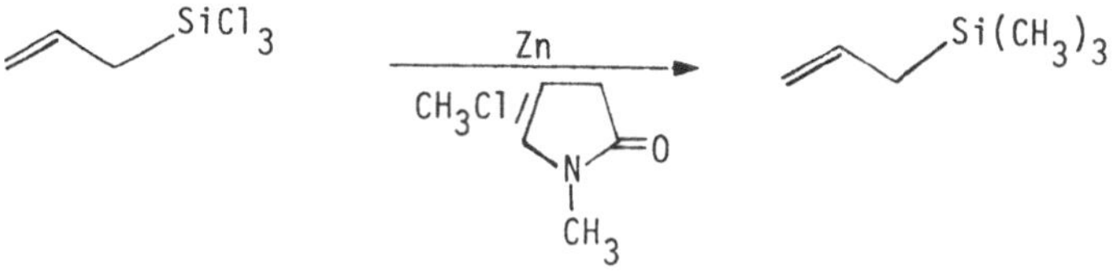

(11.78)

A more practical laboratory synthesis of allyltrichlorosilane involves the room temperature reaction of trichlorosilane with allyl chloride and triethyl-amine catalyzed by cuprous chloride [77].

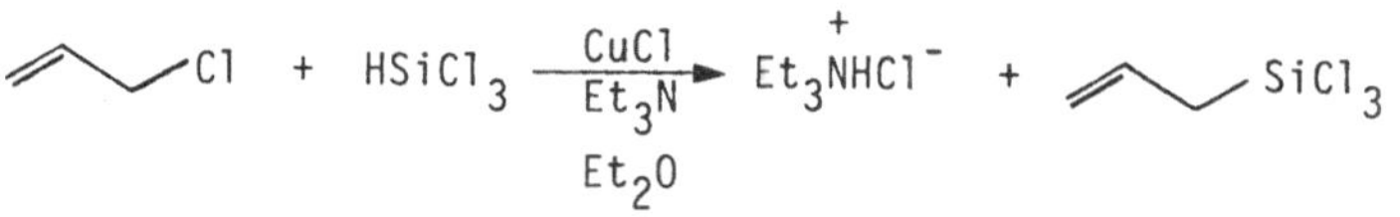

(11.79)

B. Catalytic Reactions of Disilanes

Nickelocene catalyzes the reaction of allylic chlorides, silicon tetrachloride and a mixture of *sym*-tetrachlorodimethyldisilane and 1,1,2-trichloro-1,2,2-trimethyldisilane to yield methyltrichlorosilane and allylic trichlorosilanes [78]. Unfortunately the reaction is not regiospecific. Both γ,γ-dimethylallyl-chloride and α,α-dimethylallylchloride yield γ,γ-dimethylallyltrichlorosilane.

195

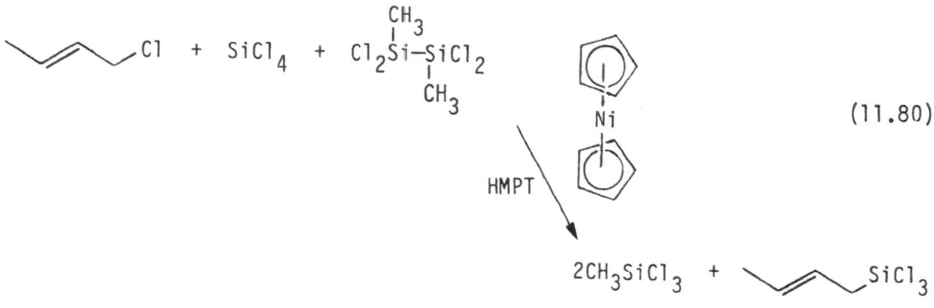

$$\text{CH}_3\text{-CH=CH-CH}_2\text{Cl} + \text{SiCl}_4 + \text{Cl}_2\overset{\overset{\displaystyle \text{CH}_3}{|}}{\underset{\underset{\displaystyle \text{CH}_3}{|}}{\text{Si}}}\text{-SiCl}_2 \xrightarrow[\text{HMPT}]{\text{Ni}} 2\text{CH}_3\text{SiCl}_3 + \text{CH}_3\text{-CH=CH-CH}_2\text{SiCl}_3$$

(11.80)

Hexamethyldisilane, *sym*-dichlorotetramethyldisilane or *sym*-tetra-chlorodimethyldisilane react with allyl chloride under catalysis by *tetrakis*-(triphenylphosphine) palladium (O) to yield allyltrimethylsilane, allyldimethyl-chlorosilane, or allylmethyldichlorosilane, respectively [79].

Hexamethyldisilane, as well as methoxy and chloro substituted disilanes undergo palladium (O) catalyzed addition to allene to yield 2,3-*bis*(silyl)-propene [80].

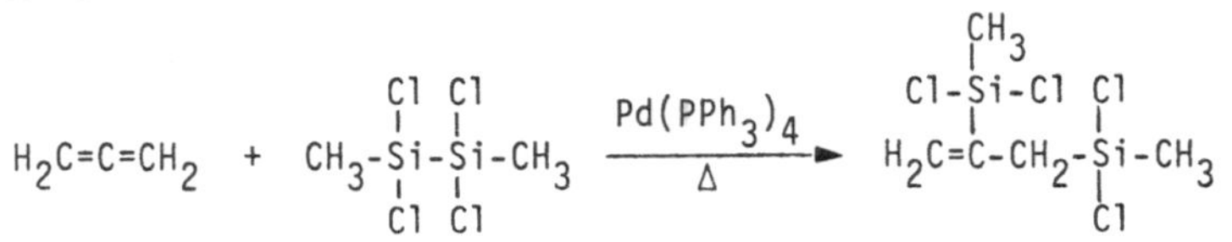

$$\text{H}_2\text{C=C=CH}_2 + \underset{\underset{\displaystyle \text{Cl Cl}}{|\ |}}{\overset{\overset{\displaystyle \text{Cl Cl}}{|\ |}}{\text{CH}_3\text{-Si-Si-CH}_3}} \xrightarrow[\Delta]{\text{Pd(PPh}_3)_4} \text{H}_2\text{C=C-CH}_2\text{-Si-CH}_3$$

(11.81)

C. Pyrolysis

Allyltrimethylsilane has been prepared by the flash vacuum pyrolysis of cyclopropyltrimethylsilane [81].

D. Hydrosilation Reactions

Hydrosilation of alkenes usually yields alkyl silanes. However, free radical catalyzed hydrosilation of β-pinene with trichlorosilane yields 4-isopropyl-1-trichlorosilylmethyl cyclohexene [14].

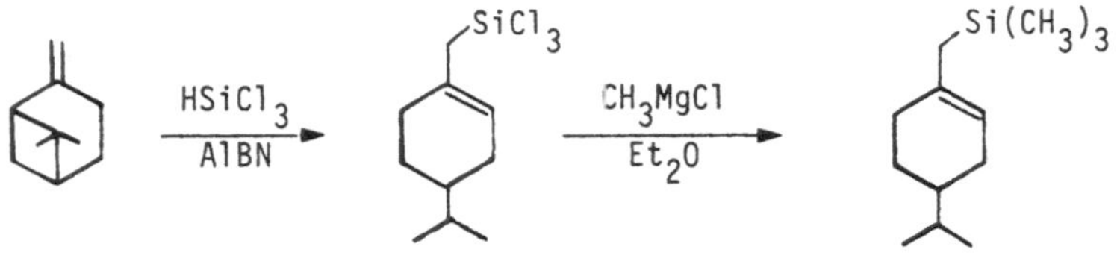

$$\xrightarrow[\text{AIBN}]{\text{HSiCl}_3} \quad \xrightarrow[\text{Et}_2\text{O}]{\text{CH}_3\text{MgCl}}$$

(11.82)

Transition metal catalyzed hydrosilations of 1,3-dienes occurs predominantly in a 1,4-manner to yield allylic silanes [15].

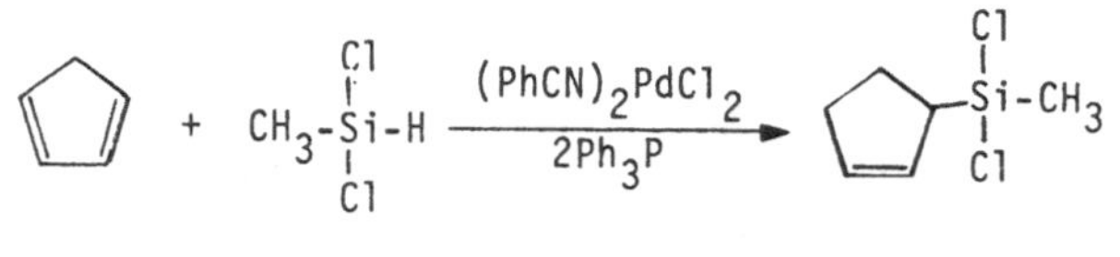

$$+ \text{CH}_3\text{-Si-H} \xrightarrow[2\text{Ph}_3\text{P}]{\text{(PhCN)}_2\text{PdCl}_2} \text{Si-CH}_3$$

(11.83)

Under the catalytic influence of *tetrakis*-(triphenylphosphine) palladium(o), chloro substituted disilanes react with alicyclic 1,3-dienes to yield Z-1,4-*bis*-(silyl)-2-butenes [82].

$$Cl_3Si-SiCl_3 \ + \ \diagup\!\!\!\diagdown\!\!\!\diagup \ \xrightarrow{(Ph_3P)_4Pd} \ Cl_3Si \diagup\!\!\!\diagdown SiCl_3 \qquad (11.84)$$

E. Dissolving Metal Reductions

Dissolving metal reductions of aromatic hydrocarbons [83], 1,3- [4] and 1,2-dienes [16], allylic methyl ethers [84, 85], allylic trimethylsilyl sulfides [14, 86] α,β-unsaturated ethylene thioacetals or ketals [6] with TMS-Cl have proved useful for the synthesis of allylic trimethylsilanes (see Chapter 19).

$$\text{(benzene)} \ \xrightarrow[\ (CH_3)_3SiCl\ ]{Li/THF} \ \text{(product with } H,\ Si(CH_3)_3) \qquad (11.85)$$

F. Wittig Reactions

The Wittig reaction of 2-trimethylsilylethylidene triphenylphosphorane with aldehydes or ketones [5, 87] regiospecifically yields allylic trimethylsilanes. The precursor phosphonium salt, 2-trimethylsilylethyl triphenylphosphonium iodide, is prepared by reaction of iodomethyltrimethylsilane 88–90] with methylene triphenylphosphorane.

$$Ph_3P=CH_2 \ + \ (CH_3)_3SiCH_2I \ \longrightarrow \ Ph_3\overset{+}{P}-CH_2CH_2Si(CH_3)_3\ I^-$$

$$\xrightarrow{PhLi/Et_2O}$$

$$\text{(cyclohexylidene-CH}_2\text{-Si(CH}_3)_3) \ \xleftarrow{} \ Ph_3P=CHCH_2Si(CH_3)_3 \qquad (11.86)$$

With sterically hindered ketones better yields are obtained with 2-dimethyl-silylethylidene triphenylphosphorane [87].

2-Cyano-3-trimethylsilyl alkenes have been prepared by a Wittig-Horner-Emmons reaction [91].

$$(EtO)_2\overset{O}{\underset{\underset{CN}{|}}{P}}CHCH_2Si(CH_3)_3 \ \xrightarrow[\ 2)\ \text{(cyclohexanone)}\ ]{1)\ NaH/THF} \ \text{(product, CN, Si(CH}_3)_3) \qquad (11.87)$$

G. Allylic Organometallics

Generally, unsymmetrical allylic organometallic reagents react with TMS-Cl to yield both possible isomeric allylic trimethylsilanes [41].

$$40 \quad : \quad 60 \qquad (11.88)$$

Treatment of isomeric mixtures of allylic trimethylsilanes with a catalytic amount of TBAF in THF at reflux results in isomerization of the mixture to the more thermodynamically stable isomer. Allylic anions may be intermediates in this equilibration [92].

$$(11.89)$$

In certain cases, the regiospecificity of reaction of allylic organometallic reagents with chlorosilanes can be determined by the choice of the chlorosilane. For example, 3-methylbut-2-enyl magnesium chloride reacts with TMS-Cl to yield γ,γ-dimethylallyltrimethylsilane (Eq. 11.90), while it reacts with trichlorosilane to yield α,α-dimethylallyldichlorosilane (Eq. 11.91). This latter product can be converted to α,α-dimethyallyltrimethylsilane [40].

$$(11.90)$$

$$(11.91)$$

The particular metal cation associated with an allylic anion may also determine the regiospecificity of coupling with TMS-Cl. Pentadienyl lithium, reacts with TMS-Cl to yield 5-trimethylsilyl-1,3-pentadiene [52]. On the other hand, pentadienyl potassium reacts with TMS-Cl to yield a mixture of 5-trimethylsilyl-1,3-pentadiene and 3-trimethylsilyl-1,4-pentadiene [18].

$$(11.92)$$

$$2 \; : \; 1$$

$$(11.93)$$

Substituted allylic anions may react regiospecifically with TMS-Cl For example, α,α-dichloroallyl lithium reacts with TMS-Cl to yield 1,1-dichloro-1-trimethylsilyl-2-propene [93].

$$Cl_3C-CH=CH_2 \xrightarrow[THF]{n-BuLi} \quad \xleftarrow{n-BuLi} \quad Cl_2C=\overset{\overset{H}{|}}{C}-CH_2PbPh_3$$

(11.94)

$$\downarrow (CH_3)_3SiCl$$
$$(CH_3)_3Si-\overset{\overset{Cl}{|}}{\underset{\underset{Cl}{|}}{C}}$$

α-(N-methyl-N-phenylamino) allyl anion reacts with TMS-Cl to give 3-trimethylsilylpropenyl-N-methyl aniline [94].

$$\underset{CH_3}{\overset{Ph}{}}N\diagdown \diagup \quad \xrightarrow[(CH_3)_3CO^-K^+]{n-BuLi} \quad \underset{CH_3}{\overset{Ph}{}}N\diagdown \diagup^-$$

(11.95)

$$(CH_3)_3SiCl \searrow \quad \underset{CH_3}{\overset{Ph}{}}N\diagdown \diagup Si(CH_3)_3$$

Metallation of allyloxytrimethylsilane with sec-butyl lithium in THF/HMPT yields α-trimethylsilyloxyallyl lithium. This undergoes a Brook rearrangement where the trimethylsilyl group migrates from oxygen to the adjacent carbon. This rearrangement converts the allyl anion to an alkoxide anion. Quenching the reaction with TMS-Cl yields α-trimethylsilyloxyallyl trimethylsilane [20].

$$\diagup\diagdown OSi(CH_3)_3 \xrightarrow[\substack{(CH_3)_3CO^-K^+ \\ THF/HMPT}]{sec-BuLi} \left[\underset{OSi(CH_3)_3}{\diagup\diagdown} \rightleftharpoons \underset{O^-}{\diagup\diagdown Si(CH_3)_3} \right]$$

$$(CH_3)_3SiCl \downarrow$$

$$\underset{OSi(CH_3)_3}{\diagup\diagdown Si(CH_3)_3}$$

(11.96)

11.5 Silyl Substituted Allylic Anions

The regiospecificity of reactions of silyl substituted allylic anions is influenced by the associated cation. α-Triphenylsilylallyl lithium reacts regiospecifically at the γ position with aldehydes [95, 96], ketones [76–78], methyl iodide [76, 77], or TMS-Cl (Eq. 11.97) [95–97]. However, it reacts at both the α and γ position with carbon dioxide, ethylene oxide, or water [95, 96].

Similar regiospecificity has been observed in the reactions of α-trimethylsilyl-allyl lithium with ketones [98, 99].

(11.97)

α-Triphenylsilylallyl Grignard reagent reacts with either carbon dioxide or ethylene oxide, predominantly at the α-position but with either benzophenone or TMS-Cl at the γ position.

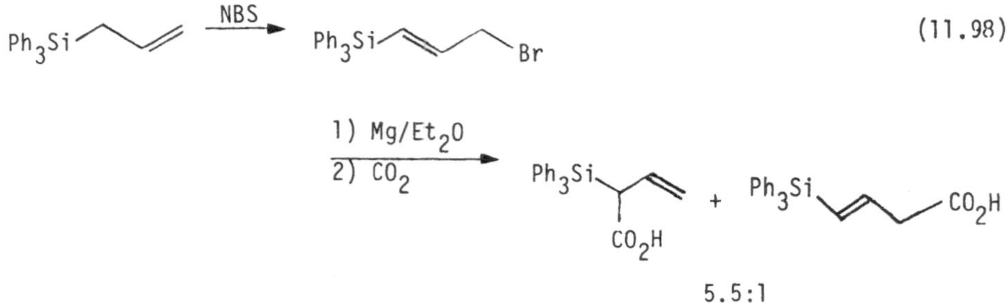

(11.98)

5.5:1

Addition of magnesium bromide to α-trimethylsilylallyl lithium prior to reaction with ketones or aldehydes at −78° alters the regiospecificity of this reagent. The predominant reaction at the α position occurs with ketones to yield 2-trimethylsilylbut-3-en-1-ols. These can be converted to 1,3-dienes by reaction with thionyl chloride. 1,3-Dienes also result from treatment of the corresponding acetate with fluoride ion [100].

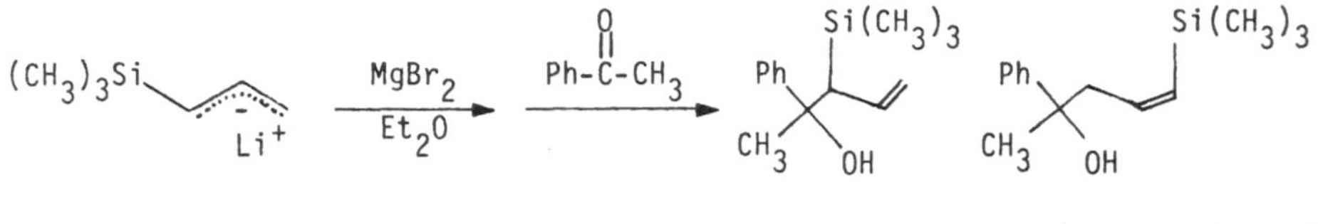

92 : 8   (11.99)

α-Chloro-α-trimethylsilylallyl lithium shows a delicate balance between α and γ reactivity with various substrates. It reacts with methyl iodide at both the α and γ positions to yield a mixture of 2-chloro-2-trimethylsilyl-3-butene and 1-chloro-1-trimethylsilyl-1-butene (4:1). Likewise, it reacts with ketones or aldehydes to yield a mixture of products. Reaction at the α-position yields 2-chloro-1,3-dienes via a Peterson reaction, while reaction at the γ-position yields 4-chloro-4-trimethylsilyl-but-3-en-1-ols [101].

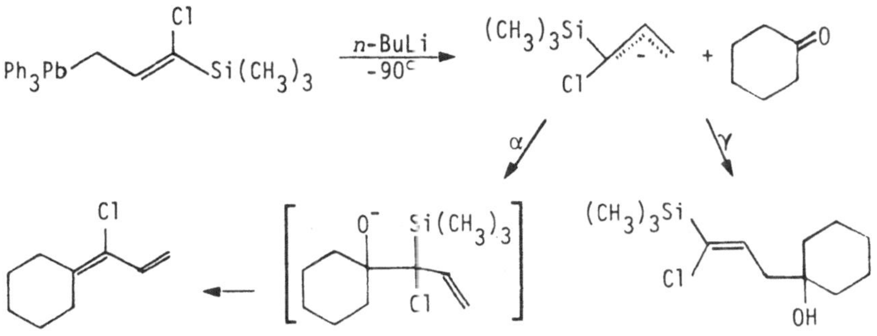

(11.100)

11.6 Boron Substituted Allylic Silanes

1 Alkynes can be converted specifically either to 3-trimethylsilyl-1-alkenes or to Z-2-alkenyltrimethylsilanes. Hydroboration of 1-alkynes with disiamyl borane yields a vinyl borane which can be metallated with lithium 2,2,6,6-tetramethyl-piperidide. This boron stabilized allylic anion reacts regiospecifically with TMS-Cl at the γ-position. This may be due to steric hinderance at the α-position from the bulky disiamyl group (Eq. 11.101) [102]. Likewise, hydro-boration of 1-alkynes with 9-BBN yields a vinyl borane. This can be metallated as above to give a boron stabilized allylic anion which reacts specifically with TMS-Cl at the α position, possibly due to the smaller steric size of 9-BBN group (Eq. 11.102) [103]. These vinyl boron bonds can be cleaved by hydrolysis to give allylic silane regiospecifically.

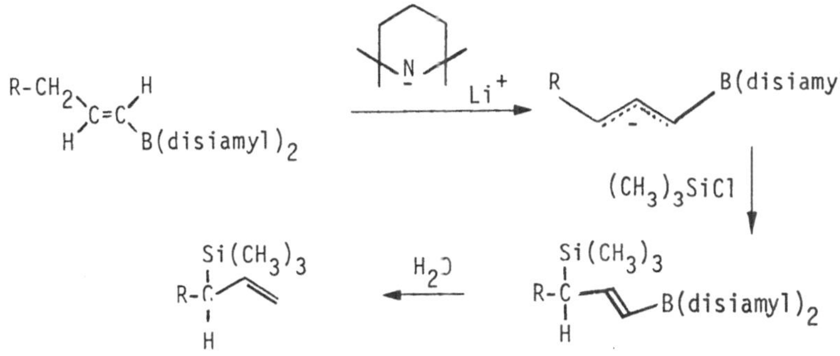

(11.101)

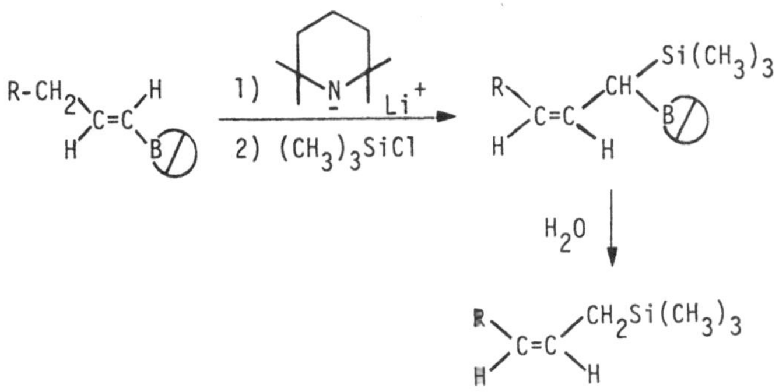

(11.102)

α-Trimethylsilyl crotyl 9-BBN reacts with aldehydes under the influence of pyridine or n-butyl lithium to yield homoallylic alcohols in which the stereochemistry of the four consecutive carbon atoms is controlled. This may result from the favored geometry of the six membered cyclic transition state [104].

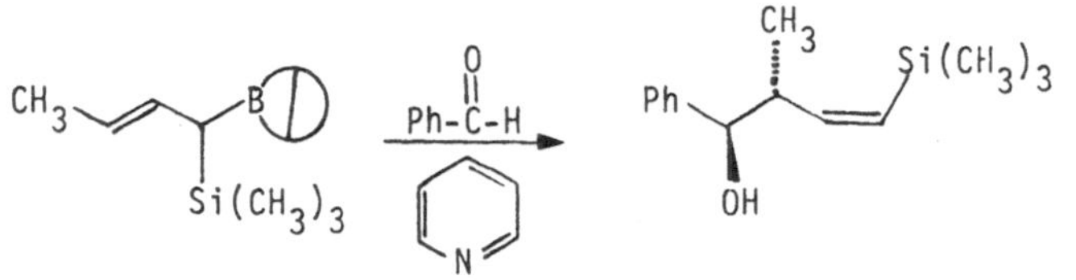

(11.103)

Alternatively, reaction of pinacol-E-1-trimethylsilyl-1-propenyl boronate with aldehydes diastereoselectively yields (±)-(R*, S*) 3-trimethylsilyl 4-hydroxy-1-alkenes. These can be converted selectively to Z or E dienes [105].

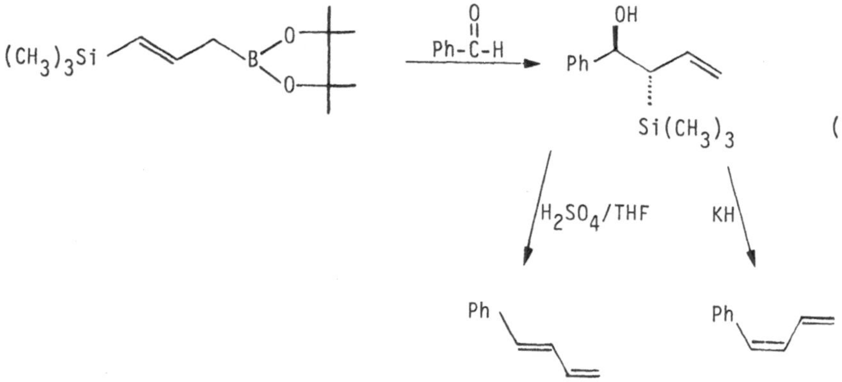

(11.104)

Dimethyl E-1-trimethylsilyl-1-propenyl-3-boronate was prepared by reaction of α-trimethylsilylallyl lithium with trimethylborate at −78°. This was converted to pinacol-E-1-trimethylsilyl-1-propenyl-3-boronate by treatment with pinacol hydrate.

References

1. Sommer, L.H., Tyler, L.J., Whitmore, F.C.: J. Am. Chem. Soc. 70, 2872 (1948)
2. Carter, M.J., Fleming, I.: J. Chem. Soc. Chem. Commun. 679 (1976)
3. Coughlin, D.J., Salomon, R.G.: J. Org. Chem. 44, 3784 (1979)
4. Dunoguès, J., Arréguy, B., Biran, C., Calas, R., Pisciotti, F.: J. Organometal. Chem. 63, 119 (1973)
5. Fleming, I., Paterson, I.: Synthesis, 446 (1979)
6. Pandy-Szekeres, D., Déléris, G., Picard, J.P., Pillot, J.P., Calas, R.: Tetrahedron Lett. 4267 (1980)
7. Moritz, T., Okamoto, Y., Sakurai, H.: Tetrahedron Lett. 835 (1980)
8. Hosomi, A., Sakurai, H.: Chem. Lett. 85 (1981)
9. Woell, J.B., Boudjouk, P.: J. Org. Chem. 45, 5213 (1980)
10. Fleming, I., Au-Yeung, B.W.: Tetrahedron, 37, 13 (1981)

11. Jung, M.E., Blumenkopf, T.A.: Tetrahedron Lett. 3657 (1978)
12. Calas, R., Dunoguès, J., Pillot, J.P., Biran, C., Pisciotti, F., Arréguy, R.: J. Organometal. Chem. *85*, 149 (1975)
13. Pillot, J.P., Dunoguès, J., Calas, R.: Tetrahedron Lett. 1871 (1976)
14. Pillot, J.P., Déléris, G., Dunoguès, J., Calas, R.: J. Org. Chem. *44*, 3397 (1979)
15. Ojima, I., Kumagai, M., Miyazawa, Y.: Tetrahedron Lett. 1385 (1980)
16. Laguerre, M., Dunoguès, J., Calas, R.: Tetrahedron Lett. 57 (1978)
17. Hosomi, A., Saito, M., Sakurai, H.: Tetrahedron Lett. 429 (1979)
18. Hosomi, A., Saito, M., Sakurai, H.: Tetrahedron Lett. 3783 (1980)
19. Ochiai, M., Fujita, E.: Tetrahedron Lett. 4369 (1980)
20. Hosomi, A., Hashimoto, H., Sakurai, H.: J. Org. Chem. *43*, 2551 (1978)
21. Hiroi, K., Chen, L.M.: J. Chem. Soc. Chem. Commun. 377 (1981)
22. Still, W.C., MacDonald, T.L.: J. Org. Chem. *41*, 3620 (1976)
23. Sakurai, H., Imai, T., Hosomi, A.: Tetrahedron Lett. 4045 (1977)
24. Pillot, J.P., Dunoguès, J., Calas, R.: Synthesis, 469 (1977)
25. Grignon-Dubois, M., Pillot, J.P., Dunoguès, J., Duffaut, N., Calas, R.: J. Organometal. Chem. *124*, 135 (1977)
26. Itoh, K., Fukui, M., Kurachi, Y.: J. Chem. Soc. Chem. Commun. 500 (1977)
27. Kelly, L.F., Narula, A.S., Birch, A.J.: Tetrahedron Lett. 871 (1980)
28. O'Boyle, J.E., Nicholas, K.M.: Tetrahedron Lett. 1595 (1980)
29. Au-Yeung, B.W., Fleming, I.: J. Chem. Soc. Chem. Commun. 81 (1977)
30. Sasaki, T., Usuki, A., Ohno, M.: Tetrahedron Lett. 4925 (1978)
31. Sasaki, T., Usuki, A., Ohno, M.: J. Org. Chem. *45*, 3559 (1980)
32. Hughes, L.R., Schmid, R., Johnson, W.S.: Bioorganic Chem. *8*, 513 (1979)
33. Raganathan, S., Raganathan, D., Mehrotra, A.K.: J. Am. Chem. Soc. *96*, 5261 (1974)
34. Abel, E.W., Rowley, R.J.: J. Organometal. Chem. *84*, 199 (1975)
35. Déléris, G., Dunoguès, J., Calas, R.: J. Organometal. Chem. *93*, 43 (1975)
36. Calas, R., Dunoguès, J., Déléris, G., Pisciotti, F.: J. Organometal. Chem. *69*, C15 (1974)
37. Déléris, G., Dunoguès, J., Calas, R.: Tetrahedron Lett. 2449 (1976)
38. Hosomi, A., Sakurai, M.: Tetrahedron Lett. 1295 (1976)
39. Hosomi, A., Endo, M., Sakurai, H.: Chem. Lett. 941 (1976)
40. Hosomi, A., Sakurai, H.: Tetrahedron Lett. 2589 (1978)
41. Wilson, S.R., Phillips, L.R., Natalie, Jr., K.J.: J. Am. Chem. Soc. *101*, 3340 (1979)
42. Kuwajima, I., Tanaka, T., Atsumi, K.: Chem. Lett. 779 (1979)
43. Itoh, A., Oshima, K., Nozaki, M.: Tetrahedron Lett. 1783 (1979)
44. Sarkar, T.K., Andersen, N.H.: Tetrahedron Lett. 3513 (1978)
45. Hosomi, A., Shirahata, A., Sakurai, H.: Tetrahedron Lett. 3043 (1978)
46. Fleming, I., Pearce, A., Snowden, R.L.: J. Chem. Soc. Chem. Commun. 182 (1976)
47. Itoh, K., Fukui, M., Kurachi, Y.: J. Chem. Soc. Chem. Commun. 500 (1977)
48. Itoh, K., Yogo, T., Ishii, Y.: Chem. Lett. 103 (1977)
49. Hosomi, A., Hashimoto, H., Sakurai, H.: Tetrahedron Lett. 951 (1980)
50. Hosomi, A., Saito, M., Sakurai, M.: Tetrahedron Lett. 3783 (1980)
51. Pornet, J.: Tetrahedron Lett. 2049 (1980)
52. Seyferth, D., Pornet, J.: J. Org. Chem. *45*, 1721 (1980)
53. Sakurai, H., Sasaki, K., Hosomi, A.: Tetrahedron Lett. 745 (1981)
54. Hosomi, A., Sakurai, H.: Tetrahedron Lett. 4041 (1977)
55. Hosomi, A., Sakurai, H.: J. Am. Chem. Soc. *99*, 1673 (1977)
56. Pardo, R., Zahra, J.P., Santelli, M.: Tetrahedron Lett. 4557 (1979)

203

57. Yanami, T., Miyashita, M., Yoshikoshi, A.: J. Chem. Soc. Chem. Commun. 525 (1979)
58. Yanami, T., Miyashita, M., Yoshikoshi, A.: J. Org. Chem. *45*, 607 (1980)
59. Hosomi, A., Kobayashi, M., Sakurai, H.: Tetrahedron Lett. 955 (1980)
60. Knapp, S., O'Connor, U., Mobilio, D.: Tetrahedron Lett. 4557 (1980)
61. Hosomi, A., Hashimoto, H., Sakurai, H.: Chem. Lett. 245 (1979)
62. Jellal, A., Santelli, M.: Tetrahedron Lett. 4487 (1980)
63. Ochiai, M., Arimoto, M., Fujita, E.: Tetrahedron Lett. 1115 (1981)
64. Ojima, I., Kumagai, M.: Chem. Lett. 575 (1978)
65. Ojima, I., Miyazawa, Y., Kumagai, M.: J. Chem. Soc. Chem. Commun. 927 (1976)
66. Hartman, G.D., Traylor, T.G.: Tetrahedron Lett. 939 (1975)
67. Ochiai, M., Arimoto, M., Fujita, E.: J. Chem. Soc. Chem. Commun. 460 (1981)
68. Déléris, G., Dunoguès, J., Calas, R.: J. Organometal. Chem. *116*, C45 (1976)
69. Au-Yeung, B.W., Fleming, I.: J. Chem. Soc. Chem. Commun. 81 (1977)
70. Trost, B.M., Chan, D.M.T.: J. Am. Chem. Soc. *101*, 6429 (1979)
71. Trost, B.M., Chan, D.M.T.: J. Am. Chem. Soc. *101*, 6432 (1979)
72. Hosomi, A., Saito, M., Sakurai, H.: Tetrahedron Lett. 355 (1980)
73. Slutsky, J., Kwart, H.: J. Am. Chem. Soc. *95*, 8678 (1973)
74. Fleming, I., Percival, A.: J. Chem. Soc. Chem. Commun. 681 (1976)
75. Hurd, D.T.: J. Am. Chem. Soc. *67*, 1813 (1945)
76. Rhone-Poulenc, French Patent 2,051,903 (1969)
77. Furuya, N., Sukawa, T.: J. Organometal. Chem. *96*, C-1 (1975)
78. Lefort, M., Simmonet, C., Birot, M., Déléris, G., Dunoguès, J., Calas, R.: Tetrahedron Lett. 1857 (1980)
79. Matsumoto, H., Yako, T., Nagashima, S., Motegi, T., Nagai, Y.: J. Organometal. Chem. *148*, 97 (1978)
80. Watanabe, H., Saito, M., Sutou, N., Nagai, Y.: J. Chem. Soc. Chem. Commun. 617 (1981)
81. Sakurai, H., Hosomi, A., Kumada, M.: Tetrahedron Lett. 2469 (1968)
82. Matsumoto, H., Shono, K., Wada, A., Matsubara, I., Watanabe, H., Nagai, Y.: J. Organometal. Chem. *199*, 185 (1980)
83. Laguerre, M., Dunoguès, J., Calas, R., Duffaut, N.: J. Organometal. Chem. *112*, 49 (1976)
84. Biran, C., Duffaut, N., Dunoguès, J., Calas, R.: J. Organometal. Chem. *91*, 279 (1975)
85. Tzeng, D.J., Weber, W.P.: J. Org. Chem. *46*, 281 (1981)
86. Déléris, G., Kowalski, J., Dunoguès, J., Calas, R.: Tetrahedron Lett. 4211 (1977)
87. Seyferth, D., Wursthorn, K.R., Lim, T.F.O., Sepelak, D.J.: J. Organometal. Chem. *181*, 293 (1979)
88. Whitmore, F.C., Sommer, L.H.: J. Am. Chem. Soc. *68*, 481 (1946)
89. Cooper, G.D., Prober, M.: J. Am. Chem. Soc. *76*, 3943 (1954)
90. Eaborn, C., Jeffrey, J.C.: J. Chem. Soc. 4266 (1954)
91. Gopalan, A., Moerck, R., Magnus, P.: J. Chem. Soc. Chem. Commun. 548 (1979)
92. Hosomi, A., Shirahata, A., Sakurai, H.: Chem. Lett. 901 (1978)
93. Seyferth, D., Murphy, G.J., Woodruff, R.A.: J. Organometal. Chem. *141*, 71 (1977)
94. Ahlbrecht, H., Eichler, J.: Synthesis, 672 (1974)
95. Corriu, R.J.P., Massé, J., Samate, D.: J. Organometal. Chem. *93*, 71 (1975)
96. Corriu, R.J.P., Massé, J.: J. Organometal. Chem. *57*, C5 (1973)

97. Corriu, R.J.P., Lanneau, G.F., Leclercq, D., Samate, D.: J. Organometal. Chem. *144*, 155 (1978)
98. Ayalon-Chass, D., Ehlinger, E., Magnus, P.: J. Chem. Soc. Chem. Commun. 772 (1977)
99. Ehlinger, E., Magnus, P.: Tetrahedron Lett. 11 (1980)
100. Lau, P.W.K., Chan, T.H.: Tetrahedron Lett. 2383 (1978)
101. Seyferth, D., Mammarella, R.E.: J. Organometal. Chem. *156*, 279 (1978)
102. Kow, R., Rathke, M.W.: J. Am. Chem. Soc. *95*, 2715 (1973)
103. Yatagi, H., Yamamoto, Y., Maruyama, K.: J. Am. Chem. Soc. *102*, 4548 (1980)
104. Yamamoto, Y., Yatagai, H., Maruyama, K.: J. Am. Chem. Soc. *103*, 3229 (1981)
105. Tsai, D.J.S., Matteson, D.S.: Tetrahedron Lett. 2751 (1981)
106. Tsunoda, T., Suzuki, M., Noyori, R.: Tetrahedron Lett. 71 (1980)
107. Fleming, I., Pearce, A.: J. Chem. Soc. Perkin *I*, 251 (1981)
108. Trost, B.M., Vincent, J.E.: J. Am. Chem. Soc. *102*, 5680 (1980)

12 Electrophilic Reactions of Silyl Enol Ethers

12.1 Introduction

The electron rich C−C double bond of silyl enol ethers is extremely susceptible to attack by electrophiles. Electrophiles regiospecifically attack the C−C double bond of trimethylsilyl enol ethers to yield a trimethylsilyloxy stabilized carbocation. Usually, the nucleophilic anion associated with the electrophile attacks the silyl center of this intermediate to yield a substituted ketone in which the electrophile is bonded to the α position.

$$(12.1)$$

12.2 Carbocations

Tertiary alkyl halides which ionize to carbocations on treatment with a Lewis acid, such as $TiCl_4$, react regiospecifically with trimethylsilyl enol ethers to yield α-t-alkyl ketones and TMS-X [1].

$$(12.2)$$

$$(12.3)$$

If one considers the problems associated with alkylation α to a carbonyl group, trimethylsilyl enol ethers and enolate anions compliment each other. Enolate anions react efficiently with primary alkyl halides whereas trimethyl-

206

silyl enol ethers react with tertiary alkyl halides [2, 3, 4]. Enolate anions usually react with alkyl halide by an S_n2 process and hence yield products with inversion of configuration. By comparison, reactive alkyl halides, which are known to solvolyze stereoselectively by S_n1 processes due to anchimeric assistance, react with silyl enol ethers in the presence of $TiCl_4$ with retention of configuration [5].

$$(12.4)$$

Secondary benzylic and allylic halides react with trimethylsilyl enol ethers in the presence of zinc bromide [6].

$$(12.5)$$

Cumyl chloride and trimethylsilyl enol ethers react in the presence of zinc chloride to yield α-cumyl ketones [7].

The formation of 2,2,5-trimethylcyclohept-4-en-1-one by intramolecular electrophilic cyclization of an allylic carbocation with a trimethylsilyl enol ether is an interesting example. The trimethylsilyl enol ether was generated regiospecifically by reduction of the corresponding α- bromo ketone with zinc dust in the presence of TMS-Cl [8].

$$(12.6)$$

Alkyl trimethylsilyl ketene acetals also react with tertiary alkyl halides in the presence of $TiCl_4$ to yield α-t-alkyl esters [9, 10].

$$(12.7)$$

Trimethylsilyl enol ethers react regiospecifically with 1,3-dithienium tetra-fluoroborate to yield α-(1,3-dithianyl) ketones [19].

$$(12.8)$$

The 1,3-Dithienium cation also reacts with 1-trimethylsilyloxy-1,3-dienes or 1-alkoxy-1-trimethylsilyloxy-1,3-dienes predominantly at the 4-position. This procedure permits the introduction of a masked carbonyl functional group [20].

Regiospecific uriedoalkylation of ketones has been achieved by reaction of methyl (N-chloromethyl, N-methyl) carbamate with trimethylsilyl enol ethers in the presence of $TiCl_4$ [21].

$$(12.9)$$

12.3 α-Methylene Ketones

There has been considerable interest in the preparation of α-methylene carbonyl compounds since many of these have high biological activity. Three methods to prepare such compounds based on silyl enol ethers have been reported.

Electrophilic attack by chloromethyl methyl ether, in the presence of an activated zinc couple (Zu−Cu) [11] or $TiCl_4$ [6], on trimethylsilyl enol ethers yields the corresponding α-methoxymethyl ketone. Pyrolysis of these with $KHSO_4$ at 160–180 °C gives the α methylene ketone.

$$(12.10)$$

Likewise, trimethylsilyl enol ethers react regiospecifically with dimethyl-(methylene)ammonium iodide [12] to yield α-dimethylaminomethyl ketones [13, 14]. Similar results have been obtained by treating silyl enol ethers with a combination of chloroiodomethane and N,N,N',N'-tetraethyldiaminomethane in DMSO [15]. Further reaction with methyl iodide converts the tertiary amine to an alkyl trimethylammonium iodide which undergoes elimination on treatment with DBU to yield the desired α-methylene ketone [14]. 1-Trimethyl-silyloxy-1,3-dienes react regiospecifically with dimethyl(methylene)ammonium iodide at the γ rather than the α position.

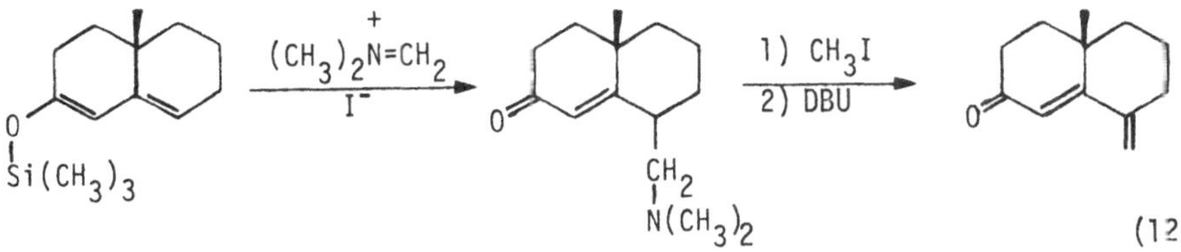

(12.11)

We have previously compared enolate anions, which react readily with primary alkyl halides by S_n2 displacement reactions, with trimethylsilyl enol ethers, which react easily with benzylic, allylic and tertiary alkyl halides. The use of α-chloroalkyl phenyl sulfides overcomes this limitation of trimethyl-silyl enol ethers. α-Chloroalkyl phenyl sulfide reacts with trimethylsilyl enol ethers, in the presence of $TiCl_4$ or zinc bromide, to yield α-(α'-phenylthio-alkyl) ketones. Raney nickel desulfurization removes the phenylthio group to yield an α-alkyl ketone [16, 17].

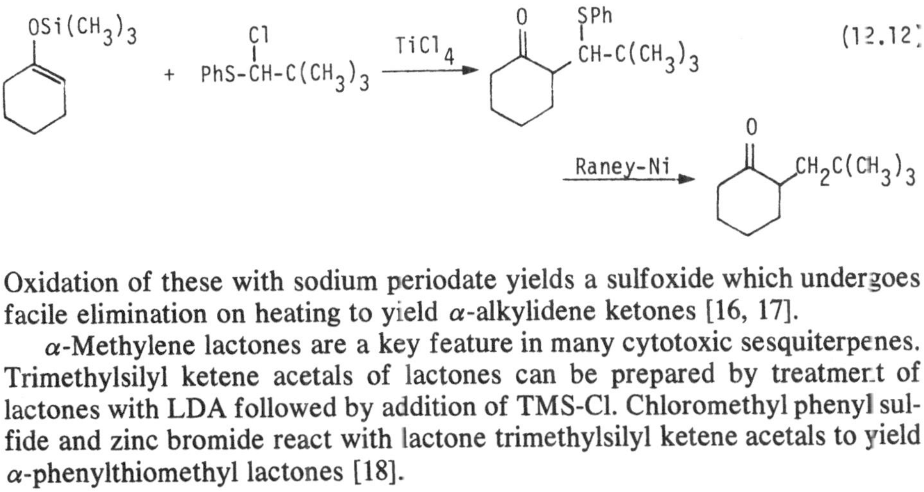

(12.12)

Oxidation of these with sodium periodate yields a sulfoxide which undergoes facile elimination on heating to yield α-alkylidene ketones [16, 17].

α-Methylene lactones are a key feature in many cytotoxic sesquiterpenes. Trimethylsilyl ketene acetals of lactones can be prepared by treatment of lactones with LDA followed by addition of TMS-Cl. Chloromethyl phenyl sul-fide and zinc bromide react with lactone trimethylsilyl ketene acetals to yield α-phenylthiomethyl lactones [18].

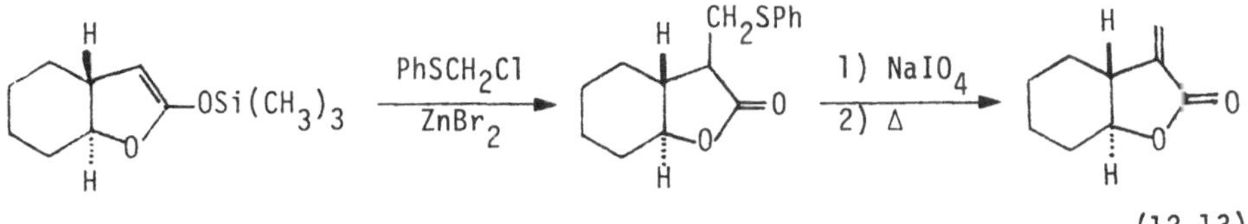

(12.13)

12.4 Cationic Iron Tricarbonyl Complexes

Trimethylsilyl enol ethers react with cationic cyclohexadienyl iron tricarbonyl iron complexes as outlined below. Removal of the iron tricarbonyl group by treatment with ferric chloride and dehydrogenation with DDQ gives α-aryl ketones [22].

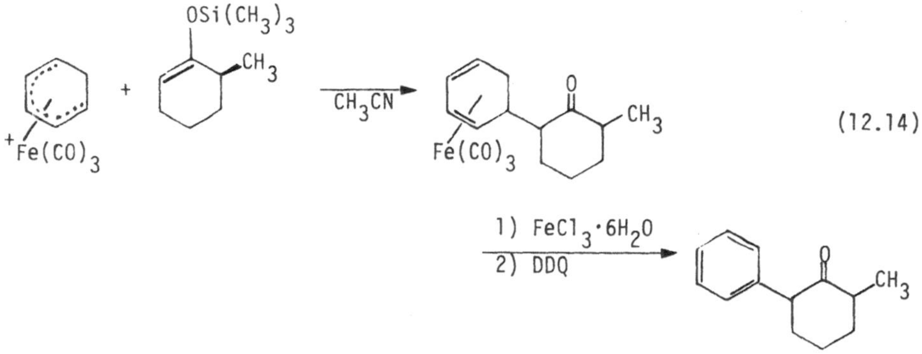

(12.14)

1,2 *bis*(Trimethylsilyloxy) cyclopentene reacts with the cationic 3-methoxy-cyclohexa-2,4-dien-1-yl iron tricarbonyl hexafluorophosphate complex to yield after oxidation 5-(2'-cyclopentenone) cyclohex-2-enone [23].

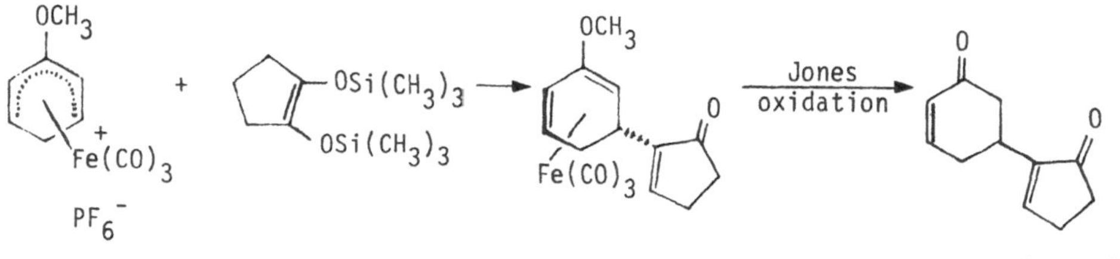

(12.15)

12.5 Halogens

Halogens react regiospecifically with trimethylsilyl enol ethers to yield α-halo ketones and TMS-X. Trimethylsilyloxycyclohexene reacts with chlorine, [24, 25] anhydrous cupric chloride or ferric chloride [26] to yield α-chloro cyclohexanone. Bromine [24, 25], cyanogen bromide [24], or NBS [27, 28] reacts with trimethylsilyloxycyclohexene to yield α-bromo cyclohexanone.

(12.16)

2-Trimethylsilyloxy-1,3-dienes react with bromine preferentially at the C−C double bond of the trimethylsilyl enol ether [29].

$$(12.17)$$

α-Bromo aldehydes can be prepared by reaction of appropriate trimethylsilyl enol ethers with bromine in CCl$_4$ [28, 29].

$$(12.18)$$

1,3-bis(Trimethylsilyloxy)-1-methoxy-1,3-butadiene reacts with one equivalent of bromine to yield methyl-4-bromo-3-keto butanoate. Apparently, a trimethylsilyl enol ether is more reactive than the alkyl trimethylsilyl ketene acetal [30].

Bromine reacts with 1,2-bis(trimethylsilyloxy)alkenes to yield 1,2-diketones [31]. 1,2-bis(Trimethylsilyloxy)cyclobutenes react with bromine to yield 1,2-cyclobutanediones which undergo a spontaneous benzylic acid rearrangement to give α-hydroxy cyclopropane acids [32].

$$(12.19)$$

Treatment of trimethylsilyl enol ethers sequentially with silver acetate and iodine followed by triethylammonium fluoride yields α-iodo ketones. Direct reaction of trimethylsilyl enol ethers with iodine is not successful [38].

$$(12.20)$$

12.6 α-Halo Acyl Silanes

α-Trimethylsilyl trimethylsilyl enol ethers react with bromine or chlorine in CCl$_4$ to yield α-bromo or α-chloro acylsilanes respectively [33].

$$(12.21)$$

α-Halo acylsilanes can also be prepared by treatment of 1,1-bis(trimethylsilyl) alkan-1-ols with NBS or NCS [34].

$$\underset{\substack{\text{Si(CH}_3)_3 \\ | \\ \text{PhCH}_2\text{CH}_2\text{-C-OH} \\ | \\ \text{Si(CH}_3)_3}}{} \xrightarrow{\text{NCS}} \underset{\substack{\text{O} \\ \| \\ \text{PhCH}_2\text{-CH-C-Si(CH}_3)_3 \\ | \\ \text{Cl}}}{} \qquad (12.22)$$

α-Halo acyltrimethylsilanes react with Grignard reagents to yield β-keto-alkyltrimethylsilanes. These undergo reduction to β-hydroxyalkyltrimethyl-silanes if the Grignard reagent possesses a β-hydrogen [35].

$$\underset{\substack{\text{O} \\ \| \\ \text{PhCH}_2\text{-CH-C-Si(CH}_3)_3 \\ | \\ \text{Cl}}}{} \xrightarrow{\text{CH}_3\text{MgBr}} \left[\underset{\substack{\text{O}^- \text{MgBr}^+ \\ \diagdown\diagup \\ \text{PhCH}_2\text{-CH-C-CH}_3 \\ | \quad | \\ \text{Cl} \quad \text{Si(CH}_3)_3}}{} \right] \longrightarrow \underset{\substack{\text{O} \\ \| \\ \text{PhCH}_2\text{-CH-C-CH}_3 \\ | \\ \text{(CH}_3)_3\text{-Si}}}{} \qquad (12.23)$$

In a similar manner, α-halo acyltrimethylsilanes react with lithium alkoxides to yield α-trimethylsilyl esters [36].

$$\underset{\substack{\text{O} \\ \| \\ \text{PhCH}_2\text{-CH-C-Si(CH}_3)_3 \\ | \\ \text{Cl}}}{} \xrightarrow[\substack{-78° \\ \text{THF}}]{\text{EtO}^- \text{Li}^+} \underset{\substack{\text{O} \\ \| \\ \text{PhCH}_2\text{-CH-C-OEt} \\ | \\ \text{Si(CH}_3)_3}}{} \qquad (12.24)$$

α-Chloro acyltrimethylsilanes react with lithium enolates of ketones to yield α-trimethylsilyl 1,3-diketones [37].

12.7 Pseudo Halogens, Sulfenyl and Selenyl Halides

A variety of pseudo halogens react with trimethylsilyl enol ethers. Thiocyano-gen reacts with 3,3-dimethyl-2 trimethylsilyloxy-1-butene to yield 3,3-dimethyl-1-thiocyanoto-2-butanone [24]. Phenylsulfenyl chloride reacts with trimethyl-silyl enol ethers to yield α-phenylthio ketones [39, 40].

$$\xrightarrow[\substack{\text{CH}_2\text{Cl}_2 \\ -78°}]{\text{PhSCl}} \qquad (12.25)$$

Phenylselenyl chloride or bromide reacts with trimethylsilyl enol ethers to ethers to yield α-phenylthio acyltrimethylsilanes. Oxidation of the sulfide to a sulfoxide with MCPBA followed by heating gives α,β-unsaturated acyltri-methylsilanes [41].

PhCH$_2$CH=C / OSi(CH$_3$)$_3$ \ Si(CH$_3$)$_3$ →[PhSCl][CCl$_4$][−20°] PhCH$_2$-CH-C / Ph-S / O \ Si(CH$_3$)$_3$ →[1) MCPBA][2) Δ] Ph / \ =O / (CH$_3$)$_3$Si

$$(12.26)$$

Phenylselenyl chloride or bromide reacts with trimethylsilyl enol ethers to yield α-phenylseleno ketones. Oxidation of the selenium to a selenoxide by MCPBA or hydrogen peroxide leads to facile *syn*-elimination of phenyl selenous acid. This converts the trimethylsilyl enol ether into an α,β-unsaturated ketone [42, 43] (see Chapter 13).

→[PhSeCl][CH$_2$Cl$_2$] →[MCPBA]

$$(12.27)$$

Carbon tetrachloride, carbon tetrabromide, trichloroacetonitrile or ethyl trichloroacetate add to trimethylsilyl enol ethers under catalysis by cuprous chloride [44].

12.8 Nitrosonium and Nitronium Cations

Nitrosyl chloride reacts with trimethylsilyl enol ethers to yield TMS-Cl and an α-nitroso carbonyl intermediate. 1,3-Tautomerization of a proton from carbon to oxygen yields α-oximino ketones. In those cases where there is no α-hydrogen, α-nitroso ketones are obtained [45].

Ph / OSi(CH$_3$)$_3$ + NOCl → [Ph / O / N=O] + (CH$_3$)$_3$SiCl → Ph

$$(12.28)$$

Alkyl trimethylsilyl ketene acetals also react with nitrosyl chloride to yield α-oximino esters which may be converted to α-amino acids.

OSi(CH$_3$)$_3$ →[NOCl] OH O / N

$$(12.29)$$

Nitronium tetrafluoroborate reacts at low temperature with trimethylsilyl enol ethers to yield α-nitroketones [46].

$$\text{(12.30)}$$

12.9 Mercuric Salts

A mixture of mercuric acetate and mercuric oxide reacts with trimethyl silyl enol ethers to yield α-mercuri-ketones [47, 48].

$$\text{(12.31)}$$

12.10 Acid Chlorides

The combination of an acid chloride and TiCl$_4$ reacts with trimethylsilyl enol ethers to yield 1,3-diketones. In some cases TiCl$_4$ is not necessary [30, 49, 50].

$$\text{(12.32)}$$

The reaction of trimethylsilyl enol ethers with oxalyl chloride provides the first general synthesis of 2,3-furandiones [51].

$$\text{(12.33)}$$

3-Carboethoxy-1-ethyl-1-trimethylsilyl ketene acetal reacts readily with acid chlorides to yield diethyl acul malonates [52].

214

$$(12.34)$$

Ethyl *t*-butyldimethylsilyl ketene acetal reacts with acid chlorides in the presence of triethylamine to yield *t*-butyldimethylsilyl enol ethers of β-keto esters [53, 54].

31%   58%   (12.35)

tris-(Trimethylsilyloxy)ethylene reacts with acid chlorides under $SnCl_4$ catalysis or heat to yield trimethylsilyl α-trimethylsilyloxy-β-keto esters. These can be hydrolyzed to α-hydroxy-β-keto acids which undergo decarboxylation to yield α-hydroxy ketones. This transformation has been previously carried out by reaction of acid chlorides with an excess of diazomethane. *tris*-(Trimethylsilyloxy)ethylene has been prepared from α-hydroxy acetic acid [55].

$$(12.36)$$

2-Hetero substituted *bis*(trimethylsilyl)ketene acetals react similarly with acid chlorides to yield α-hetero methyl ketones. For example, 2-methylthio-1,1-*bis*(trimethylsilyloxy)ethylene reacts with acid chlorides to yield after hydrolysis and decarboxylation, α-methylthiomethyl ketones [56].

1,3-*bis*(Trimethylsilyloxy)-1-methoxy-1,3-butadiene reacts with acetyl chloride to yield methyl hexa-3,5-dionoate [30].

215

$$(12.37)$$

Acetyl cyanide reacts with trimethylsilyl enol ethers and TiCl$_4$ to yield β-cyano-β-hydroxy ketones [57].

Sulfonyl chlorides [58] or carbomethoxylsulfamoyl chlorides [59] react with trimethylsilyl enol ethers to yield β-keto sulfones or β-keto carbomethoxy sulfonamides, respectively.

$$(12.38)$$

12.11 Aldehydes and Ketones

The specific cross Aldol condensation of two different aldehydes or ketones is potentially an extremely valuable synthetic reaction [60, 61]. Unfortunately, the formation of self-condensation, as well as, di- and polycondensation products frequently limits the utility of this reaction. The reaction of trimethylsilyl enol ethers with ketones or aldehydes, facilitated by TiCl$_4$ reported by Mukaiyama, provides a solution to this problem. The reaction requires a stoichiometric amount of TiCl$_4$ and methylene chloride as solvent.

Other Lewis acids, such as SnCl$_4$, BF$_3 \cdot$ OEt$_2$, or boron trichloride, are less effective. The reaction proceeds extremely rapidly with aldehydes at $-78°$, whereas with ketones the reaction is best run at 0°. This reaction may occur by interaction of TiCl$_4$ with the silyl enol ether to yield TMS-Cl and a trichloro titanium enol ether, which in turn reacts with the ketone or aldehyde to give the cross Aldol product [62].

$$(12.39)$$

An alternative possibility is that TiCl$_4$ coordinates to the carbonyl oxygen of ketone or aldehyde making it highly susceptible to nucleophillic attack by the electron rich C$-$C double bond of the trimethylsilyl enol ether. A cyclic transition state leading directly to products has been suggested.

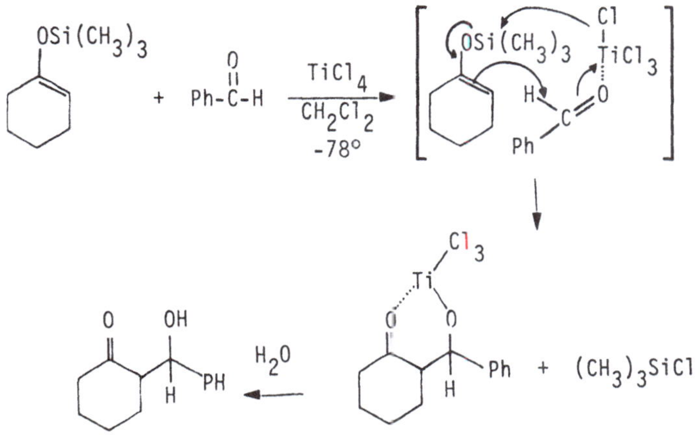

(12.40)

Cross Aldol condensation reactions between silyl enol ethers and formalde-hyde (trioxane) are successful.

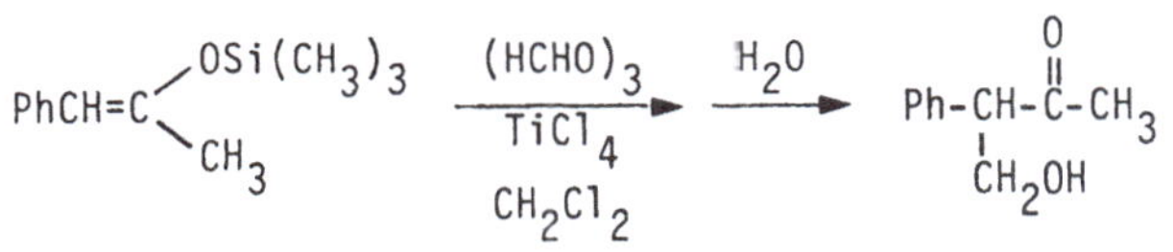

(12.41)

Isomeric trimethylsilyl enol ethers undergo regiospecific cross Aldol conden-sation reactions [63].

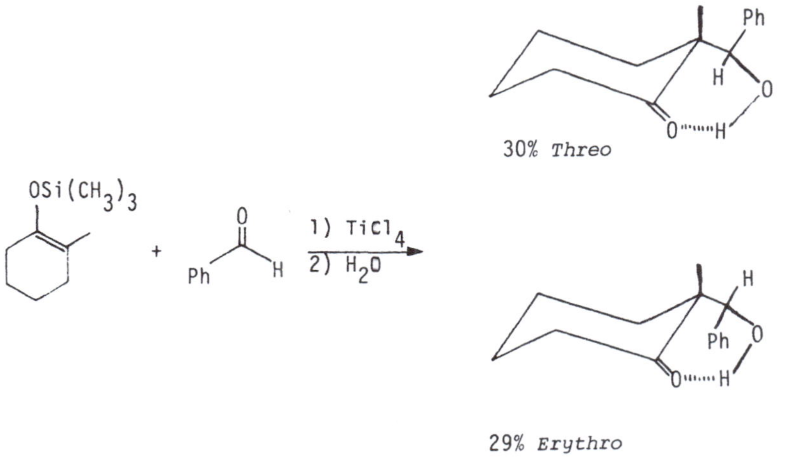

30% Threo

(12.42)

29% Erythro

In cross Aldol reactions zirconium enolates give a higher *erythro* to *threo* ratio of β-hydroxy ketones than do trimethylsilyl enol ethers [64].

Dialkyl boron enolates also provide greater stereo and regiochemical control than do silyl enol ethers [65]. Z-Trimethylsilyl enol ethers react with di-*n*-butyl boranyl trifluoromethane sulfonate to yield trimethylsilyl trifluoromethane sulfonate and the corresponding di-*n*-butyl boron enolate stereospecifically. Removal of solvent and the volatile trimethylsilyl trifluoro-

2% Axial *Erythro*   55% Axial *Threo*

$$\text{(12.43)}$$

20% Equitorial *Threo*   % Equitorial *Erythro*

methane sulfonate prior to reaction of the di-*n*-butyl boron enolate with benzaldehyde at $-78°$ yields cross Aldol products with high stereospecificity (*erythro* : *threo* 95 : 5) [66, 67].

$$\text{(12.44)}$$

1-Trimethylsilyloxycyclohexene reacts with 9-bromo-9-borabicyclo [3,3,1] nonane to yield the corresponding boron enolate and TMS-Br. Such dialkyl boron enolates react with benzaldehyde to yield cross Aldol products [68].

12.12 Silyl-Reformatsky

Alkyl trimethylsilyl ketene acetals and *bis*-(trimethylsilyl)ketene acetals undergo a slow thermal reaction with aromatic aldehydes to yield β-trimethyl-silyloxy esters [69, 70].

$$\text{(12.45)}$$

Silyl-Reformatsky reactions can be carried out under much milder conditions with TiCl$_4$ catalysis [71].

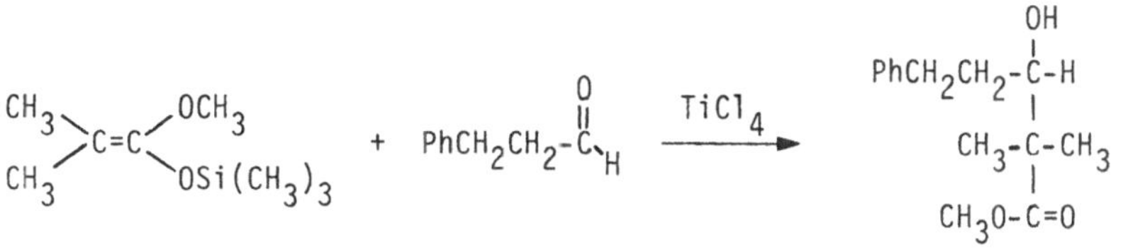

$$CH_3 \quad OCH_3 \atop CH_3 \diagdown C=C \diagup OSi(CH_3)_3 \quad + \quad PhCH_2CH_2-\underset{\underset{}{\overset{\overset{O}{\parallel}}{C}}}{}-_H \quad \xrightarrow{TiCl_4} \quad \begin{array}{c} OH \\ PhCH_2CH_2-\overset{|}{\underset{|}{C}}-H \\ CH_3-\overset{|}{\underset{|}{C}}-CH_3 \\ CH_3O-C=O \end{array} \qquad (12.46)$$

The reaction of 2-trimethylsilyloxy furans with aldehydes under the influence of SnCl$_4$ has been utilized in the synthesis of the macrolide antibiotic (±) -A26771B [72].

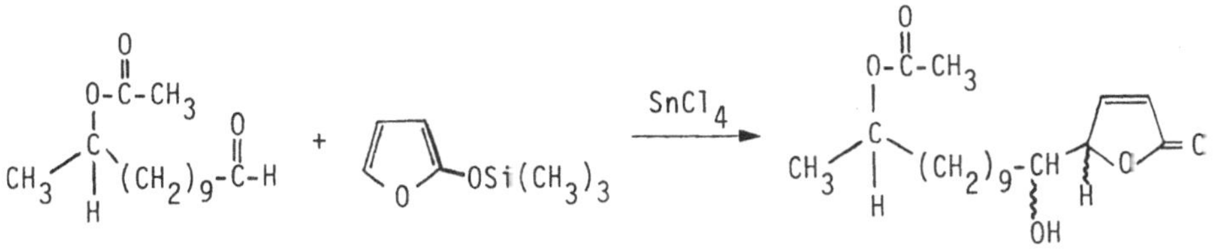

(12.47)

The cross Aldol reaction of 2,5-*bis*(trimethylsilyloxy) furan with ketones or aldehydes permits the facile synthesis of *bis*-lactone ligands [73].

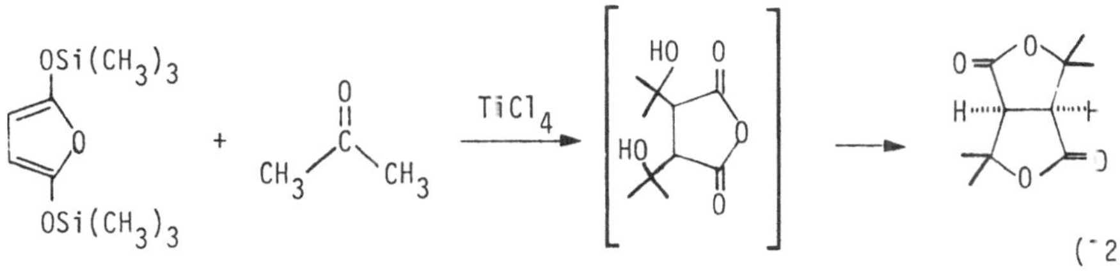

(12.48)

12.13 Acetals and Ketals

Trimethylsilyl enol ethers also undergo cross Aldol reactions with acetals, ketals, or trimethyl ortho formate activated by TiCl$_4$ to yield β-alkoxy ketones or β-keto acetals, respectively. It seems probable that these reactions proceed by TiCl$_4$ promoted ionization of a C−O bond of the acetal to yield an alkoxy stabilized carbocation which attacks the trimethylsilyl enol ether [74].

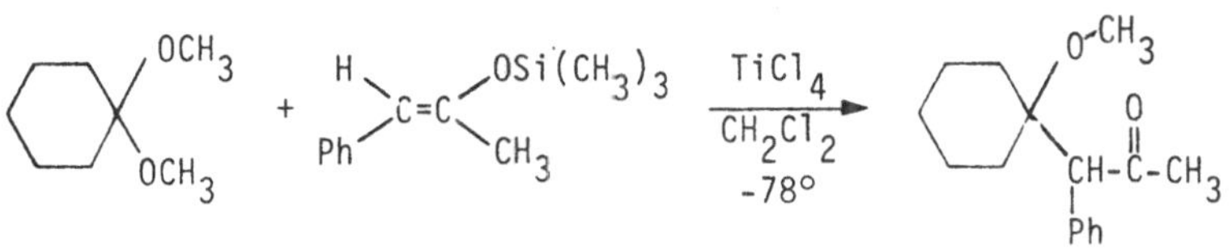

(12.49)

2-Trimethylsilyloxy furan reacts as a silyl enol ether with ketals or triethyl ortho acetate under Lewis acid activation to yield 4-substituted-2-buten-4-olides [75].

Similarly, reactions of trimethylsilyl enol ethers with acetals have been carried out with catalysis by trimethylsilyl trifluoromethane sulfonate [76–78].

$$(12.50)$$

93:7
Erythro:Threo

Reaction of α-bromo acetals or ketals with trimethylsilyl enol ethers promoted by $TiCl_4$ yields β-alkoxy-γ-bromo ketones. On heating, these undergo cyclization and elimination to yield furans [79, 80].

$$(12.51)$$

Trimethylsilyloxyallenes also react with acetals and $TiCl_4$ to yield α-(1-alkoxyalkyl) α,β-unsaturated ketones [81].

α-Trimethylsilyl trimethylsilyl enol ethers react with acetals and $BF_3 \cdot OEt_2$ at $-78°$ to yield β-alkoxy acylsilanes. On treatment with a catalytic amount of tetra-n-butylammonium hydroxide in acetonitrile these are converted to α,β-unsaturated aldehydes [82].

$$(12.52)$$

Such behavior is expected since acylsilanes yield aldehydes under mild basic conditions [83, 84].

$$(12.53)$$

Cross Aldol reactions of 1-trimethylsilyloxy-1,3-butadiene [85] with acetals activated by a mixture of $TiCl_4$ and titanium tetraisopropoxide, occur exclusively at the 4-position to yield δ-alkoxy-α,β-unsaturated aldehydes [85, 87].

12.14 α,β-Unsaturated Ketones, Ketals and Acetals

Trimethylsilyl enol ethers undergo Michael type reactions with α,β-unsaturated ketones activated by $TiCl_4$ to yield 1,5-dicarbonyl compounds [88].

$$(12.54)$$

Trimethylsilyl enol ethers also undergo Michael reactions with α,β-unsaturated acetals or ketals on activation by $TiCl_4$ [89].

$$(12.55)$$

Michael reaction of 1-trimethylsilyloxy-1-cyclopropyl ethylene [90, 91] with α,β-unsaturated ketones activated by $TiCl_4$ yields 1-cyclopropyl-1,5-diketones. These undergo an intramolecular Aldol condensation and dehydration on treatment with potassium hydroxide in methanol to yield β-cyclopropyl α,β-unsaturated ketones.

$$(12.56)$$

An intramolecular Michael reaction of a trimethylsilyl enol ether with an α,β-unsaturated ketone activated by TiCl₄ is a key step in an efficient synthesis of Seychellene [92].

$$(12.57)$$

Alkyl trimethylsilyl ketene acetals undergo TiCl₄ promoted Michael reactions with α,β-unsaturated ketones to yield δ-keto esters [93].

$$(12.58)$$

Such Michael reactions of α,β-unsaturated ketones with alkyl trimethylsilyl ketene acetals can also be carried out thermally in acetonitrile at 55° to yield the trimethylsilyl enol ether of the δ-keto esters [94].

$$(12.59)$$

12.15 α-Nitro Alkenes

Trimethylsilyl enol ethers also undergo Michael type reactions with α-nitro-alkenes under the influence of SnCl₄ or TiCl₄ to yield derivatives of nitronic acids. These can be hydrolyzed to yield 1,4-diketones [95].

$$(12.60)$$

12.16 Relative Reactivities

Phenyl glyoxal undergoes selective cross Aldol condensation with silyl enol ethers at the more reactive aldehyde carbonyl group.

$$(12.61)$$

Similarly, ketone carbonyl groups react in preference to ester carbonyl groups [96].

The cross Aldol reaction of trimethylsilyl enol ethers with α-keto esters cf optically active alcohols such as (−)menthyl pyruvate and (−)menthyl phenyl-glyoxylate gives 2-hydroxy-4-oxo-butyrates. High asymmetric induction (50% e.e.) at the new chiral center is observed [97].

$$(12.62)$$

Alkyl trimethylsilyl ketene acetals react with the keto group of α-keto esters of optically active alcohols to yield α-hydroxy succinic acid derivatives in which the new chiral center is generated with high e.e. [98].

12.17 Hydroboration

Hydroboration of cyclic trimethylsilyl enol ethers leads to cyclic *trans-β-*trimethylsilyloxy organoboranes. The trimethylsilyloxy group directs the boron almost exclusively to the β carbon. Oxidation of these with alkaline hydrogen peroxide followed by hydrolysis leads to cyclic *trans*-1,2-glycols [99, 100].

$$\text{(12.63)}$$

On the other hand, hydroboration of alicyclic trimethylsilyl enol ethers leads to β-trimethylsilyloxy organoboranes which undergo facile *syn*-elimination of trimethylsilyloxyborane to yield alkenes. Thus, an excess of *Z*-1-phenyl-2-trimethylsilyloxypropene reacts with borane to yield predominantly *z-β*-methylstyrene [100, 101].

$$\text{(12.64)}$$

Apparently, the reason cyclic *trans-β*-trimethylsilyloxy organoboranes are stable is that they cannot achieve the necessary geometry for spontaneous *syn*-elimination of trimethylsilyloxyborane. Nevertheless, cyclic-*trans-β*-trimethylsilyloxy organoboranes will undergo regiospecific elimination on treatment with acids, such as $BF_3 \cdot OEt_2$ or aq. HCl to yield specific alkenes [102].

$$\text{(12.65)}$$

References

1. Chan, T.H., Paterson, I., Pinsonnault, J.: Tetrahedron Lett. 4183 (1977)
2. Reetz, M.T., Maier, W.F.: Angew. Chem. Int. Ed. *17*, 48 (1978)
3. Reetz, M.T., Chatziiosifidis, I., Löwe, U., Maier, W.F.: Tetrahedron Lett. 1427 (1979)
4. Reetz, M.T., Maier, W.F., Chatziiosifidis, I., Giannis, A., Heimbach, H., Löwe, U.: Chem. Ber. *113*, 3741 (1980)
5. Reetz, M.T., Sauerwald, M., Walz, P.: Tetrahedron Lett. 1101 (1981)
6. Paterson, I.: Tetrahedron Lett. 1519 (1979)
7. Reetz, M.T., Hüttenhain, S.H.: Synthesis, 941 (1980)
8. Hashimoto, S., Itoh, A., Kitagawa, Y., Yamamoto, H., Nozaki, H.: J. Am. Chem. Soc. *99*, 4192 (1977)
9. Reetz, M.T., Maier, W.F., Schwellnus, K., Chatziiosifidis, I.: Angew. Chem. Int. Ed. *18*, 72 (1979)

10. Reetz, M.T., Schwellnus, K.: Tetrahedron Lett. 1455 (1978)
11. Shono, T., Nishiguchi, I., Komamura, T., Sasaki, M.: J. Am. Chem. Soc. *101*, 984 (1979)
12. Schreiber, J., Maag, H., Hashimoto, N., Eschenmoser, A.: Angew. Chem. Int. Ed. *10*, 330 (1971)
13. Danishefsky, S., Kitahara, T., McKee, R., Schuda, P.F.: J. Am. Chem. Soc. *98*, 6715 (1976)
14. Danishefsky, S., Prisbylla, M., Lipisko, B.: Tetrahedron Lett. 805 (1980)
15. Miyano, S., Hokari, H., Mori, A., Hashimoto, N.: Chem. Lett. 1213 (1980)
16. Paterson, I., Fleming, I.: Tetrahedron Lett. 995 (1979)
17. Paterson, I., Fleming, I.: Tetrahedron Lett. 2179 (1977)
18. Paterson, I., Fleming, I.: Tetrahedron Lett. 993 (1979)
19. Paterson, I., Price, L.G.: Tetrahedron Lett. 2829 (1981)
20. Paterson, I., Price, L.G.: Tetrahedron Lett. 2833 (1981)
21. Danishefsky, S., Guingant, A., Prisbylla, M.: Tetrahedron Lett. 2033 (1980)
22. Kelly, L.F., Narula, A.S., Birch, A.J.: Tetrahedron Lett. 4107 (1979)
23. Kelly, L.F., Dahler, P., Narula, A.S., Birch, A.J.: Tetrahedron Lett. 1433 (1981)
24. Lazukina, L.A., Kukhar, V.P., Pesotskaya, G.V.: Zhur. Obsh. Khim. *45*, 2100 (1975)
25. Jung, M.E., McCombs, C.A.: Tetrahedron Lett. 2935 (1976)
26. Ito, Y., Nakatsuka, M., Saegusa, T.: J. Org. Chem. *45*, 2022 (1980)
27. Nakamura, E., Murofushi, T., Shimizu, M., Kuwajima, I.: J. Am. Chem. Soc. *98*, 2346 (1976)
28. Reuss, R.H., Hassner, A.: J. Org. Chem. *39*, 1785 (1974)
29. Blanco, L., Amice, P., Conia, J.M.: Synthesis, 194 (1976)
30. Chan, T.H., Brownbridge, P.: J. Chem. Soc. Chem. Comm. 578 (1979)
31. Conia, J.M., Barnier, J.P.: Tetrahedron Lett. 4981 (1971)
32. Heine, H.G., Wendisch, D.: Liebigs Ann. Chem. 463 (1976)
33. Sato, T., Abe, T., Kuwajima, I.: Tetrahedron Lett. 259 (1978)
34. Kuwajima, I., Abe, T., Minami, N.: Chem. Lett. 993 (1976)
35. Sato, T., Abe, T., Kuwajima, I.: Tetrahedron Lett. 259 (1978)
36. Kuwajima, I., Matsumoto, K., Inoue, T.: Chem. Lett. 41 (1979)
37. Kuwajima, I., Matsumoto, K.: Tetrahedron Lett. 4095 (1979)
38. Rubottom, G.M., Mott, R.C.: J. Org. Chem. *44*, 1731 (1979)
39. Murai, S., Kuroki, Y., Hasegawa, K., Tsutsumi, S.: J. Chem. Soc. Chem. Comm. 946 (1972)
40. Trost, B.M., Curran, C.P.: J. Am. Chem. Soc. *102*, 5699 (1980)
41. Minami, N., Abe, T., Kuwajima, I.: J. Organometal. Chem. *145*, C1 (1978)
42. Ryu, I., Murai, S., Niwa, I., Sonoda, N.: Synthesis, 874 (1977)
43. Kita, Y., Segawa, J., Harata, J., Fujii, T., Tamura, Y.: Tetrahedron Lett. 3779 (1980)
44. Murai, S., Koroki, Y., Aya, T., Sonoda, N., Tsutsumi, S.: J. Chem. Soc. Chem. Comm. 741 (1972)
45. Rasmussen, J.K., Hassner, A.: J. Org. Chem. *39*, 2558 (1974)
46. Shvarts, I.S., Yarovenko, V.N., Krayushkin, M.M., Novikov, S.S., Sevost'yanova, V.V.: Izv. Akad. Nauk SSSR, Ser. Khim. 1674 (1976)
47. House, H.O., Auerbach, R.A., Gall, M., Peet, N.P.: J. Org. Chem. *38*, 514 (1973)
48. Kitching, W., Drew, G.M.: J. Org. Chem. *46*, 2695 (1981)
49. Murai, S., Koroki, Y., Hasegawa, K., Tsutsumi, S.: J. Chem. Soc. Chem. Comm. 946 (1972)
50. Donaldson, R.E., Fuchs, P.L.: J. Org. Chem. *42*, 2032 (1977)
51. Murai, S., Hasegawa, K., Sonoda, N.: Angew. Chem. Int. Ed. *14*, 636 (1975)

52. Schmidt, U., Schwochau, M.: Tetrahedron Lett. 4491 (1967)
53. Rathke, M.W., Sullivan, D.F.: Tetrahedron Lett. 1297 (1973)
54. Purlachenko, G.S., Mal'tsev, V.V., Baukov, Yu.I., Lutsenko, I.F.: Zhur. Obsh. Khim. *43*, 1724 (1973)
55. Wissner, A.: Tetrahedron Lett. 2749 (1978)
56. Wissner, A.: J. Org. Chem. *44*, 4617 (1979)
57. Kraus, G.A., Shimagaki, M.: Tetrahedron Lett. 1171 (1981)
58. Koroki, Y., Murai, S., Sonoda, N., Tsutsumi, S.: Organometal. Chem. Syn. *1*, 465 (1972)
59. Rasmussen, J.K., Hassner, A.: Tetrahedron Lett. 2783 (1973)
60. Wittig, G., Hess, A.: Org. Syn. *50*, 66 (1977)
61. House, H.O., Crumrine, O.S., Teranishi, A.Y., Olmstead, H.D.: J. Am. Chem. Soc. *95*, 3310 (1973)
62. Mukaiyama, T., Narasaka, K., Banno, K.: Chem. Lett. 1011 (1973)
63. Mukaiyama, T., Banno, K., Narasaka, K.: J. Am. Chem. Soc. *96*, 7503 (1974)
64. Yamamoto, Y., Maruyama, K.: Tetrahedron Lett. 4607 (1980)
65. Evans, D.A., Vogel, E., Nelson, J.V.: J. Am. Chem. Soc. *101*, 6120 (1979)
66. Kuwajima, I., Kato, M., Mori, A.: Tetrahedron Lett. 2745 (1980)
67. Kuwajima, I., Kato, M., Mori, A.: Tetrahedron Lett. 4291 (1980)
68. Wada, M.: Chem. Lett. 153 (1981)
69. Creger, P.L.: Tetrahedron Lett. 79 (1972)
70. Rathke, M.W., "The Reformatsky Reaction" in Organic Reactions, Vol. 22, J. Wiley, New York, New York: 1975
71. Saigo, K., Osaki, M., Mukaiyama, T.: Chem. Lett. 989 (1975)
72. Asaoka, M., Yanagida, N., Takei, H.: Tetrahedron Lett. 4611 (1980)
73. Brownbridge, P., Chan, T.H.: Tetrahedron Lett. 3427 (1980)
74. Mukaiyama, T., Hayashi, M.: Chem. Lett. 15 (1974)
75. Asaoka, M., Sugimura, N., Takei, H.: Bull. Chem. Soc. Japan, *52*, 1953 (1979)
76. Murata, S., Suzuki, M., Noyori, R.: J. Am. Chem. Soc. *102*, 3248 (1980)
77. Murata, S., Suzuki, M., Noyori, R.: Tetrahedron Lett. 2527 (1980)
78. Murata, S., Suzuki, M., Noyori, R.: Tetrahedron Lett. 2527 (1980)
79. Mukaiyama, T., Ishihara, H., Inomata, K.: Chem. Lett. 527 (1975)
80. Ishihara, H., Inomata, K., Mukaiyama, T.: Chem. Lett. 531 (1975)
81. Kuwajima, I., Kato, M.: Tetrahedron Lett. 623 (1980)
82. Sato, T., Arai, M., Kuwajima, I.: J. Am. Chem. Soc. *99*, 5827 (1977)
83. Brook, A.G.: J. Am. Chem. Soc. *79*, 4373 (1957)
84. Brook, A.G., Vandersar, T.J.D., Limburg, W.: Can. J. Chem. *56*, 1758 (1958)
85. Cazeau, P., Frainnet, E.: Bull. Soc. Chim. Fr. 1658 (1972)
86. Mukaiyama, T., Ishida, A.: Chem. Lett. 319 (1975)
87. Ishida, A., Mukaiyama, T.: Chem. Lett. 1167 (1975)
88. Narasaka, K., Soai, K., Mukaiyama, T.: Chem. Lett. 1223 (1974)
89. Narasaka, K., Soai, K., Aikawa, Y., Mukaiyama, T.: Bull. Soc. Chem. Japan, *49*, 779 (1976)
90. Fitjer, L., Conia, J.M.: Angew. Chem. Int. Ed. *12*, 332 (1972)
91. Greico, P.A., Ohfune, Y.: J. Org. Chem. *43*, 2720 (1978)
92. Jung, M.E., Pan, Y.G.: Tetrahedron Lett. 3127 (1980)
93. Saigo, K., Osaki, M., Mukaiyama, T.: Chem. Lett. 163 (1976)
94. Kita, Y., Segawa, J., Haruta, J., Fujii. T., Tamura, Y.: Tetrahedron Lett. 3779 (1980)
95. Miyashita, M., Yanami, T., Yoshikoshi, A.: J. Am. Chem. Soc. *98*, 4679 (1976)
96. Banno, K., Mukaiyama, T.: Chem. Lett. 741 (1975)
97. Ojima, I., Yoshida, K., Inaba, S.I.: Chem. Lett. 429 (1977)

98. Ojima, I., Yoshida, K., Inaba, S.I.: Chem. Lett. 429 (1979)
99. Klein, J., Levene, R., Dunkelblum, E.: Tetrahedron Lett. 2845 (1972)
100. Larson, G.L., Hernandez, D., Hernandez, A.: J. Organometal. Chem. *76*, 6 (1974)
101. Larson, G.L., Hernandez, A.: J. Organometal. Chem. *102*, 123 (1975)
102. Larson, G.L., Hernandez, E., Alonso, C., Nieves, I.: Tetrahedron Lett. 4005 (1975)

13 Oxidation of Silyl Enol Ethers

13.1 Introduction

A number of useful synthetic transformations are based on the selective oxidation of the electron rich C−C double bond of trimethylsilyl enol ethers.

13.2 Preparation of α,β-Unsaturated Ketones

Several methods have been developed to regiospecifically convert trimethylsilyl enol ethers into α,β-unsaturated ketones. For example, treatment of trimethylsilyl enol ether with DDQ and collidine yields α,β-unsaturated ketones. This reaction may proceed by hydride abstraction from the silyl enol ether to yield a trimethylsilyloxy stabilized allylic carbocation/DDQ hydroquinone anion pair. Nucleophilic attack on the silyl center by the hydroquinone anion yields the α,β-unsaturated ketone [1, 2].

$$(13.1)$$

The reaction of trityl tetrafluoroborate (BF_4^-) with trimethylsilyl enol ethers to yield α,β-unsaturated ketones is mechanistically closely related. Presumably, the trityl carbocation abstracts a hydride from the trimethylsilyl enol ether to yield triphenylmethane and a trimethylsilyloxy stabilized allylic carbocation/BF_4^- pair. Nucleophilic attack by the BF_4^- ion on the silyl center yields TMS-F, the α,β-unsaturated ketone and BF_3 [3]. Jung has used trityl BF_4^- to oxidize trimethylsilyl ethers of secondary alcohols to ketones [3, 4, 5].

$$(13.2)$$

Oxidation of trimethylsilyl enol ethers with palladium acetate in acetonitrile gives high yields of α,β-unsaturated ketones [6]. The reaction may occur by formation of an intermediate oxo-π-allyl Pd(II) complex. β-Elimination of hydride from this complex yields the α,β-unsaturated ketone, Pd(O) and acetic acid. Unfortunately, reoxidation of Pd(O) to Pd(II) is a problem. The highest yields are achieved with stoichiometric amounts of palladium acetate. Conceptually, this reaction may be considered to be the reverse of the transition metal catalyzed 1,4-hydrosilation of α,β-unsaturated ketones to yield trimethylsilyl enol ethers [7].

$$(13.3)$$

13.3 Preparation of 1,4-Diketones

Trimethylsilyl enol ethers react with silver oxide in DMSO to yield symmetrical 1,4-diketones [8]. This reaction may involve a silver (I) enolate intermediate. One electron transfer from the enolate anion to silver (I) would lead to an enol radical and silver (O). Dimerization of such enol radicals would yield the 1,4-diketone products.

$$(13.4)$$

13.4 Preparation of α-Acyloxy and α-Hydroxy Ketones

Oxidation of trimethylsilyl enol ethers with lead tetraacetate yields 1,2-diacetoxy-1-trimethylsilyloxy alkanes which hydrolyze to yield α-acetoxy ketones [9].

$$(13.5)$$

Oxidation of trimethylsilyl enol ethers with lead tetrabenzoate permits the preparation of α-benzoyloxy aldehydes, as well as α-benzoyloxy ketones. The initial 1,2-dibenzoyloxy-1-trimethylsilyloxy alkanes are converted to α-benzoyloxy aldehydes by treatment with triethylammonium fluoride [10].

Treatment of five and six-membered cyclic trimethylsilyl enol ethers with silver carboxylates and iodine in a 2 : 1 ratio, followed by addition of triethylammonium fluoride regiospecifically yields α-acyloxy ketones. With larger cyclic trimethylsilyl enol ethers the formation of 2-iodo ketones becomes important [28].

$$(13.6)$$

Oxidation of 2-methyl-5-trimethylsilyloxyfuran with lead tetraacetate yields 4-acetoxy-2-penten-4-olide which can be hydrolyzed to 4-oxo-2-pentenoic acid [11].

$$(13.7)$$

Oxidation of trimethylsilyl enol ethers with MCPBA yields α-trimethylsilyloxy ketones which can be hydrolyzed to α-hydroxy ketones [12–14].

$$(13.8)$$

Oxidation of trimethylsilyl enol ethers with a catalytic amount of osmium tetraoxide with N-methyl morpholine oxide [29] as a stoichiometric reoxidant regiospecifically yields α-hydroxy ketones [30].

$$(13.9)$$

2-Trimethylsilyloxy-1,3-dienes are oxidized by MCPBA to yield α'-hydroxy-α,β-unsaturated ketones. This regiospecificity results from the preferential oxidation of the trimethylsilyloxy substituted C−C double bond of the diene system [15].

$$(13.10)$$

Similarly oxidation of *bis*-trimethylsilyl ketene acetals with MCPBA yields α-hydroxy carboxylic acids after hydrolysis [16].

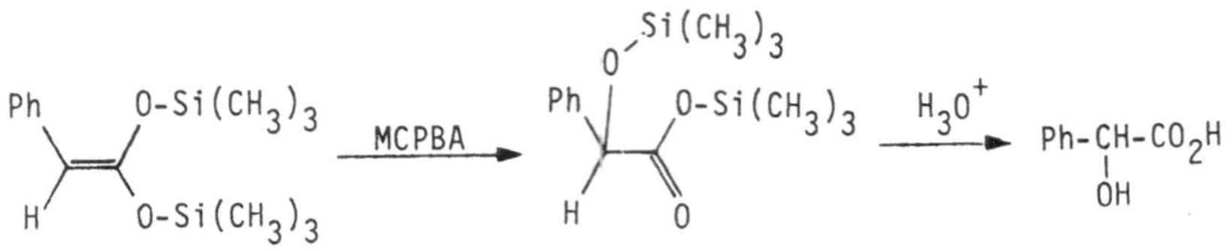

$$
\text{(13.11)}
$$

13.5 Baeyer-Villiger Oxidation of α-Trimethylsilyloxy Ketones

Treatment of trimethylsilyl enol ethers with two equivalents of MCPBA in ether solvent results in a Baeyer-Villiger oxidation of the initial α-trimethylsilyloxy ketone. The trimethylsilyloxy-substituted carbon selectively migrates to the electron-deficient oxygen generated in this reaction [17].

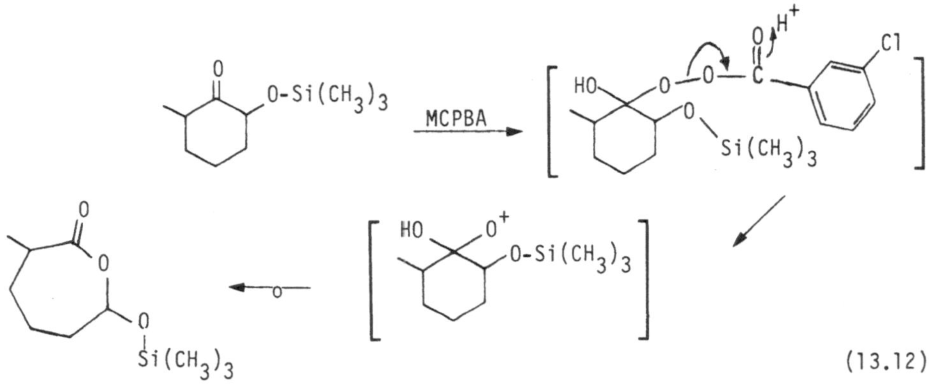

$$
\text{(13.12)}
$$

13.6 Ozonolysis of Silyl Enol Ethers

Trimethylsilyl enol ethers undergo regiospecific ozonolysis (Eq. 13.13). This can be explained if fragmentation of the primary ozonide to a ketone or aldehyde and a carbonyl ylid occurs so that the positive end of the 1,3-dipolar carbonyl ylid is stabilized by the trimethylsilyloxy group.

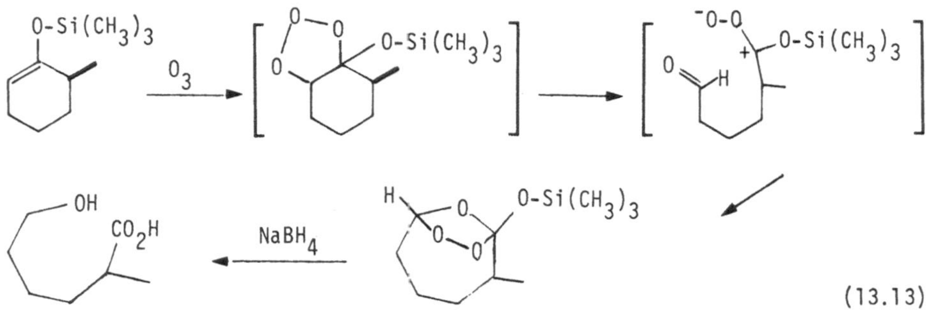

$$
\text{(13.13)}
$$

The high reactivity of the C−C double bond of trimethylsilyl enol ethers toward electrophilic reagents compared to other C−C double bonds has been utilized in a synthesis of Vernolepin. At −78°C, selective ozonolysis of a trimethylsilyl enol ether in the presence of a terminal vinyl group has been achieved [18–20].

$$ (CH_3)_3Si-O- \quad \xrightarrow[\text{2) NaBH}_4]{\text{1) O}_3, -78°} \quad (13.14) $$
3) H$_3$O$^+$

The C−C double bond of silyl enol ethers can be selectively cleaved by MoO$_2$(acac)$_2$ and t-butyl hydroperoxide [31].

$$ \xrightarrow[\text{(CH}_3)_3\text{C-OOH}]{\text{MoO}_2\text{(AcAc)}_2} \quad (13.15) $$

13.7 Reaction of Singlet Oxygen with Silyl Enol Ethers

Trimethylsilyl enol ethers react with photochemically generated singlet oxygen *via* two competing ene reactions. The first is a normal ene reaction in which an allylic hydrogen becomes bonded to oxygen to yield an allylic hydroperoxide. The other involves transfer of a trimethylsilyl group from one oxygen to another to yield an α-trimethylsilylperoxy ketone [21–23].

$$ \xrightarrow{} \quad \xrightarrow{Ph_3P} \quad (13.16) $$

$$ \xrightarrow{} \quad \xrightarrow{H_2/Pd} \quad (13.17) $$

This reaction has been utilized to prepare α-peroxy-α-lactones, which are synthetically inaccessible by other routes. α-t-Butyl-1-peroxy-α-lactone emits light on decomposition to carbon dioxide and pivaldehyde [24–27].

233

(13.18)

References

1. Ryu, I., Murai, S., Hatayama, Y., Sonoda, N.: Tetrahedron Lett. 3455 (1978)
2. Fleming, I., Paterson, I.: Syn. 736 (1979)
3. Jung, M.E., Pan, Y.G., Rathke, M.W., Sullivan, D.F., Woodbury, R.P.: J. Org. Chem. 42, 3961 (1977)
4. Jung, M.E.: J. Org. Chem. 41, 1479 (1976)
5. Jung, M.E., Speltz, L.M.: J. Am. Chem. Soc. 98, 7882 (1976)
6. Ito, Y., Hirao, H., Saegusa, T.: J. Org. Chem. 43, 1011 (1978)
7. Ojima, I., Nihonyanagi, N., Kogure, T., Kumagai, M., Horiuchi, S., Nakatsu-gawa, N., Nagai, Y.: J. Organometal. Chem. 94, 449 (1975)
8. Ito, Y., Konoike, T., Saegusa, T.: J. Am. Chem. Soc. 97, 649 (1975)
9. Rubottom, G.M., Gruber, J.M., Kincaid, K.: Syn. Commun. 6, 59 (1976)
10. Rubottom, G.M., Gruber, J.M., Mong, G.M.: J. Org. Chem. 41, 1673 (1976)
11. Asaoka, M., Yanagida, N., Sugimura, N., Takei, H.: Bull. Chem. Soc. Japan, 53, 1061 (1980)
12. Rubottom, G.M., Vazquez, M.A., Pelegrina, D.R.: Tetrahedron Lett. 4319 (1974)
13. Brook, A.G., MacRae, D.M.: J. Organometal. Chem. 77, C19 (1974)
14. Hassner, A., Reuss, R.H., Pinnick, H.W.: J. Org. Chem. 40, 3427 (1975)
15. Rubottom, G.M., Gruber, J.M.: J. Org. Chem. 43, 1599 (1978)
16. Rubottom, G.M., Marrero, R., I. Org. Chem. 40, 3783 (1975)
17. Rubottom, G.M., Gruber, J.M., Boeckman, Jr.R.K., Ramaiah, M., Medwid, J.B., Tetrahedron Lett. 4603 (1978)
18. Clark, R.D., Heathcock, C.H.: Tetrahedron Lett. 1713 (1974)
19. Clark, R.D., Heathcock, C.H.: Tetrahedron Lett. 2027 (1974)
20. Clark, R.D., Heathcock, C.H.: J. Org. Chem. 41, 1396 (1976)
21. Rubottom, G.M., Nieves, M.I.L.: Tetrahedron Lett. 2423 (1972)
22. Friedrich, E., Lutz, W.: Angew. Chem. Int. Ed. 16, 413 (1977)
23. Jefford, C.W., Rimbault, C.G.: Tetrahedron Lett. 2375 (1977)
24. Kuo, Y.N., Chen, F., Ainsworth, C., Bloomfield, J.J.: J. Chem. Sec. D, 135 (1971)
25. Adam, W., Liu, J.C.: J. Am. Chem. Soc. 94, 2894 (1972)
26. Adam, W., Steinmetzer, H.C.: Angew. Chem. Int. Ed. 11, 540 (1972)
27. Adam, W., Alzérreca, A., Liu, J.C., Yany, F.: J. Am. Chem. Soc. 99, 5768 (1977)
28. Rubottom, G.M., Mott, R.C., Juve, Jr., H.D.: J. Org. Chem. 46, 2717 (1981)
29. Van Rheenan, Kelly, R.C., Cha, D.Y.: Tetrahedron Lett. 1973 (1976)
30. McCormick, J.P., Tomasik, W., Johnson, M.W.: Tetrahedron Lett. 607 (1981)
31. Kaneda, K., Kii, N., Jitsukawa, K., Teranishi, S.: Tetrahedron Lett. 2595 (1981)

14 Cyclopropanation of Silyl Enol Ethers, Chemistry of Trimethylsilyloxycyclopropanes

14.1 Introduction

The electron rich C−C double bond of silyl enol ethers readily reacts with electrophilic carbenes to yield silyloxycyclopropanes. These are highly reactive compounds due to the cyclopropyl ring strain.

14.2 Preparation of Trimethylsilyloxycyclopropanes, Regiospecific Conversion to Methyl Ketones

The electron rich C−C double bond of trimethylsilyl enol ethers readily undergoes cyclopropanation with the Simmons-Smith reagent [CH_2I_2/Zn-Cu] [1, 2], or with methylene iodide and the more reactive zinc-silver couple in ethyl ether to yield trimethylsilyloxycyclopropane derivatives [3]. Trimethyl-silyloxycyclopropanes can be hydrolyzed in acidic methanol to yield cyclo-propanols (Eq. 14.1) [4, 5]. Treatment of these with methanolic sodium hydroxide yields α-methyl ketones (Eq. 14.2) [6].

The fact that trimethylsilyl enol ethers can be prepared regiospecifically from unsymmetrical ketones permits specific mono-methylation at either the α or α' position of the ketone [6].

$$(14.3)$$

$$(14.4)$$

Pyridine, which is added during work-up of the reaction, precipitates the Lewis acid zinc iodide from the ethyl ether solution as a *bis*-pyridine complex.

Trimethylsilyloxycyclopropanes can be converted to the corresponding cyclopropyl acetates by reaction with acetyl chloride and zinc iodide [7].

$$(14.5)$$

Trimethylsilyloxy substituted dienes can be prepared from α,β-unsaturated ketones. For example, methyl vinyl ketone can be converted to 2-trimethylsilyloxy-1,3-butadiene by treatment with TMS-Cl/triethylamine in DMF [8]. 2-Trimethylsilyloxy-1,3-cyclohexadiene can be prepared from 2-cyclohexenone by treatment with LDA followed by TMS-Cl. The trimethylsilyloxy substituted C–C double bond of these dienes is much more nucleophilic than the other C–C double bond and hence undergoes selective cyclopropanation [9].

$$(14.6)$$

Treatment of testosterone with TMS-Cl/triethylamine in DMF yields a 3-trimethylsilyloxy-3,5-diene derivative, whereas treatment with LDA and TMS-Cl yields a 3-trimethylsilyloxy-2,4-diene derivative. Cyclopropanation of both derivatives occurs from the less hindered α face of the steroid nucleus. Subsequent treatment with methanolic sodium hydroxide yields 4-methyl-testosterone and 2-α-methyltestosterone, respectively [9].

14.3 Acid Catalyzed Rearrangement of 1-Vinyl-1-trimethylsilyloxycyclopropanes

1-Vinyl-1-trimethylsilyloxycyclopropanes, formed by cyclopropanation of 2-trimethylsilyloxy-1,3-dienes undergo rearrangement to yield alkyl substituted cyclobutanones on treatment with HCl in THF [10, 11].

237

14.4 Pyrolysis of 1-Vinyl-1-trimethylsilyloxycyclopropanes

1-Vinyl-1-trimethylsilyloxycyclopropanes rearrange on pyrolysis to 1-trimethylsiloxycyclopentenes [11–13].

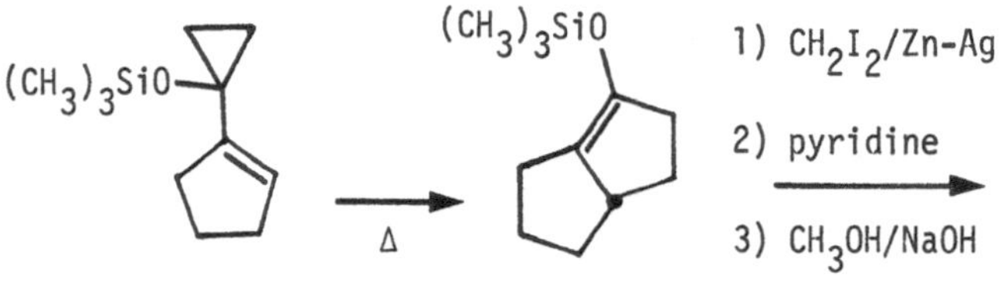

(14.10)

Alternatively, 1-vinyl-1-trimethylsilyloxycyclopropanes have been prepared by the sequential reaction of oxaspiropentanes with lithium diethylamide and TMS-Cl [11].

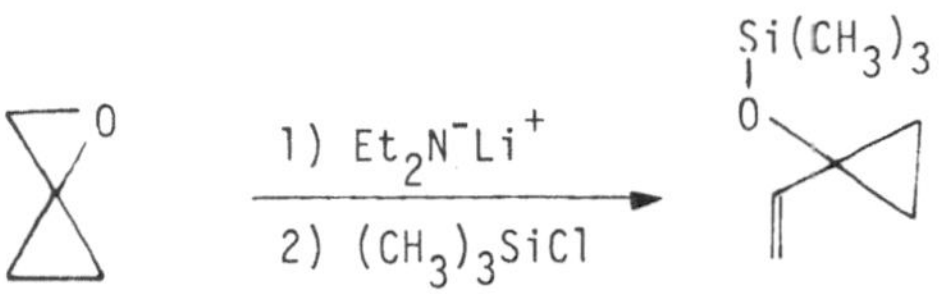

(14.11)

1-Cyclopropyl-1-trimethylsilyloxyethylenes undergo pyrolysis to yield, after acidic hydrolysis, cyclopentanones [14].

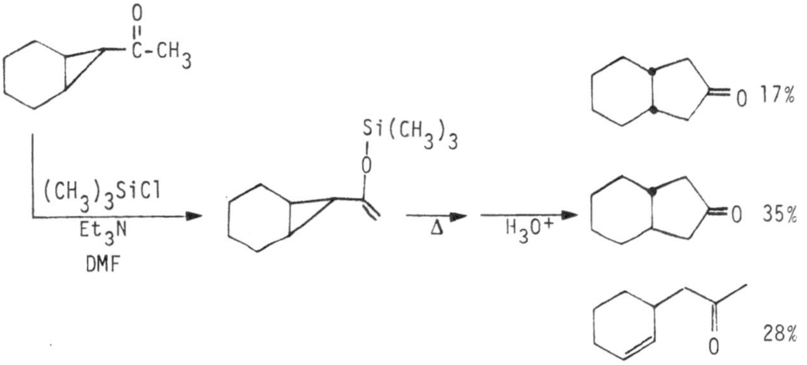

(14.12)

14.5 Reaction of Electrophiles with Trimethylsilyloxycyclopropanes

Trimethylsilyloxycyclopropanes are isomerized to α-methylene trimethylsilyloxyalkanes by zinc iodide [15, 16]. Diethyl zinc and methylene iodide can be used to achieve cyclopropanation of silyl enol ethers in aromatic solvents. Zinc-copper or zinc-silver couples are only effective in ether solvents. Cyclopropanation of trimethylsilyl enol ethers in benzene leads to extensive rearrangement of the initial trimethylsiloxycyclopropane due to the greater Lewis acidity of zinc iodide in hydrocarbon solvents [17].

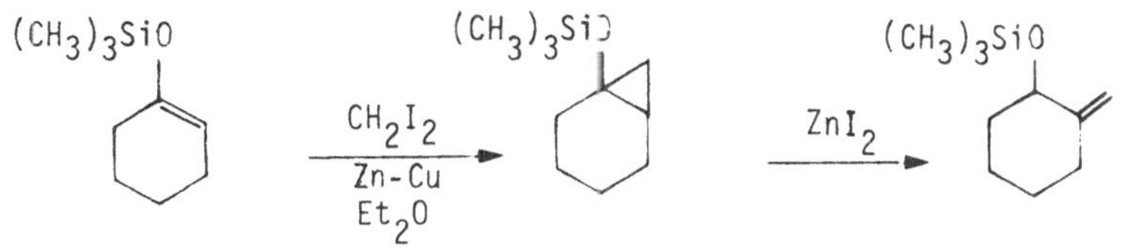

(14.13)

Trimethylsilyloxycyclopropanes react with bromine in methylene chloride at $-78°$ to yield β-bromo ketones. Electrophilic attack by bromine on the cyclopropane ring probably leads to C-Br bond formation, cyclopropane ring opening, and formation of trimethylsilyloxy stabilized carbocation. Attack by bromide at the silyl center leads to TMS-Br and the β-bromo ketone [19].

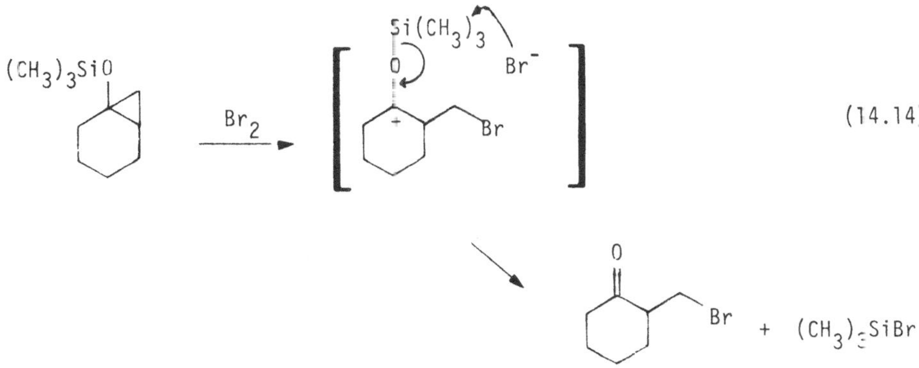

(14.14)

Trimethylsilyloxycyclopropanes react with mercuric acetate and $PdCl_2$ to yield α,β-unsaturated ketones. The following sequence of reactions may explain this result. Trimethylsilyloxycyclopropanes react with mercuric acetate to yield β-acetoxy mercuric ketones and acetoxytrimethylsilane. Metal interchange with Pd(II) gives β-palladio-ketones which undergo reductive elimination of Pd(O)/HCl to yield α,β-unsaturated ketones. The reaction can be made catalytic in Pd by reoxidation of Pd(O) to Pd(II) with cupric chloride [20].

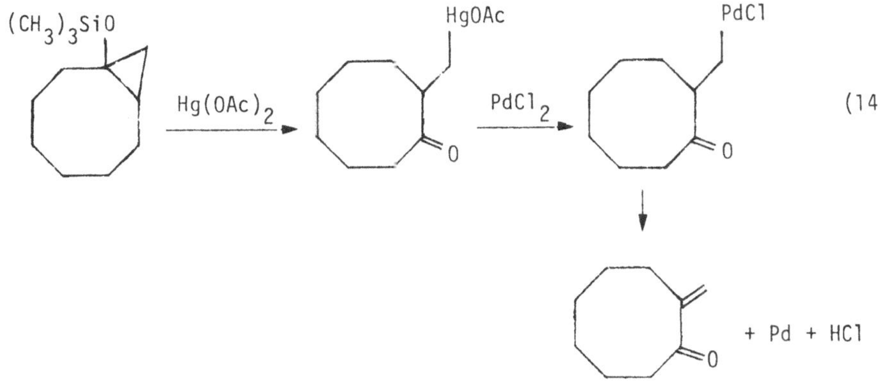

(14.15)

1-Trimethylsilyloxybicyclo[n,1,0] alkanes react with lead tetraacetate in acetic acid to yield ω-unsaturated carboxylic acids [21].

$$(14.16)$$

1-Trimethylsilyloxybicyclo[n,1,0] alkanes react with ferric chloride, by a series of one electron transfers, to yield 3-chlorocycloalkanones. These undergo dehydrohalogenation on treatment with sodium acetate to yield 2-cycloalkenones [22].

$$(14.17)$$

Cyclopropanation of 1,2-*bis*(trimethylsilyloxy) cyclotetradecene with diethyl zinc and methylene iodide gave 1,14-*bis*(trimethylsilyloxy) bicyclo-[12,1,0]pentadecane. Reaction of this with ferric chloride in DMF gave cyclopentadecan-1,3-dione [18].

$$(14.18)$$

14.6 Reaction of Silyl Enol Ethers with Other Carbenes

Silyl enol ethers react with other electrophilic carbenes. For example, 1-triethylsilyloxycyclotetradecene reacts with dichlorocarbene to give a 1,1-dichloro-2-triethylsilyloxycyclopropane derivative. Treatment of this with acid yields α-chlorocyclopentadecanone [23]. The precursor triethylsilyl enol ether was prepared by hydrosilation of a mixture of 2-cyclotetradecenone and 3-cyclotetradecenone. Isomerization of the β,γ-unsaturated ketone to the α,β-unsaturated ketone occurs faster than the 1,4-hydrosilation reaction.

$$(14.19)$$

In a similar manner, dibromocarbene reacts with trimethylsilyl enol ethers to yield 1,1-dibromo-2-trimethylsilyloxycyclopropanes. These undergo reaction with methanolic HCl to yield α-bromo-α,β-unsaturated ketones or aldehydes [24].

Chloromethylcarbene adds to both cyclic [25] and alicyclic [26] trimethylsilyl enol ethers to give 1-chloro-1-methyl-2-trimethylsilyloxycyclopropanes. On heating, these lose TMS-Cl to yield α-methyl-α,β-unsaturated ketones [27].

$$(14.20)$$

Copper salts catalyze the cyclopropanation of trimethylsilyl enol ethers by methyl diazoacetate to yield 1-carbomethoxy-2-trimethylsilyloxycyclopropanes. Treatment of these with triethylammonium fluoride results in ring opening and formation of γ-keto esters, or γ-aldehydo esters [28].

$$(14.21)$$

References

1. Simmons, H.E., Smith, R.D.: J. Am. Chem. Soc. *80*, 5223 (1958)
2. Simmons, H.E., Smith, R.D.: J. Am. Chem. Soc. *81*, 4256 (1959)
3. Denis, J.M., Girard, C., Conia, J.M.: Syn. 549 (1972)
4. Murai, S., Aya, T., Sonoda, N.: J. Org. Chem. *38*, 4354 (1973)
5. Rubottom, G.M., Lopez, M.I.: J. Org. Chem. 38, 2097 (1973)
6. Conia, J.M., Girard, C.: Tetrahedron Lett. 2767 (1973)
7. Ryu, I., Murai, S., Otani, S., Sonoda, N.: Chem. Lett. 93, (1976)
8. Girard, C., Conia, J.M.: Tetrahedron Lett. 3333 (1974)
9. Girard, C., Conia, J.M.: Tetrahedron Lett. 3327 (1974)
10. Girard, C., Amice, P., Barnier, J.P., Conia, J.M.: Tetrahedron Lett. 3329 (1974)
11. Trost, B.M., Bogdanowicz, M.J.: J. Am. Chem. Soc. *95*, 5311 (1973)
12. Trost, B.M., Scudder, P.H.: J. Org. Chem. *46*, 506 (1981)
13. For a review of the rearrangement of vinyl cyclopropanes to cyclopentenes see: Rearrangements in Small Ring Compounds by Breslow, R., in Molecular Rear-

rangements (de Mayo, P., Ed.) Vol. I. pp. 234–245, New York: Interscience Publishers, 1963

14. Monti, S., Cowherd, F.G., McAninch, T.W.: J. Org. Chem. *40*, 858 (1975)
15. Ryu, I., Murai, S., Otani, S., Sonoda, N.: Tetrahedron Lett. 1995 (1977)
16. Murai, S., Aya, T., Renge, T., Ryu, I., Sonoda, N.: J. Org. Chem. *39*, 858 (1974)
17. Ryu, I., Murai, S., Sonoda, N.: Tetrahedron Lett. 4611 (1977)
18. Ito, Y., Saegusa, T.: J. Org. Chem. *42*, 2326 (1977)
19. Murai, S., Seki, Y., Sonoda, N.: J. Chem. Soc., Chem. Commun. 1032 (1974)
20. Ryu, I., Matsumoto, K., Ando, M., Murai, S., Sonoda, N.: Tetrahedron Lett. 4283 (1980)
21. Rubottom, G.M., Marrero, R., Krueger, D.S., Schreiner, J.L.: Tetrahedron Lett. 4013 (1977)
22. Ito, Y., Fujii, S., Saegusa, T.: J. Org. Chem. *41*, 2073 (1976)
23. Stork, G., MacDonald, T.L.: J. Am. Chem. Soc. *97*, 1264 (1975)
24. Amice, P., Blanco, L., Conia, J.M.: Syn. 196 (1976)
25. Blanco, L., Amice, P., Conia, J.M.: Syn. 289 (1981)
26. Blanco, L., Amice, P., Conia, J.M.: Syn. 291 (1981)
27. Blanco, L., Slougui, M., Rousseau, G., Conia, J.M.: Tetrahedron Lett. 645 (1981)
28. Reissig, H.U., Hirsch, E.: Angew. Chem. Int. Ed. *19*, 813 (1980)

15 Cycloaddition and Electrocyclic Reactions of Silyl Enol Ethers

15.1 Introduction

The electron rich double bonds of silyl enol ethers and silyloxy dienes undergo a variety of cycloaddition and electrocyclic reactions.

15.2 [2 + 2] Cycloaddition

Trimethylsilyl enol ethers undergo regiospecific [2 + 2] cycloaddition with dichloroketene [1–3]. The regiospecificity results from a 1,4-zwitterionic intermediate comprised of trimethylsilyloxy stabilized carbocation and an α,α-dichloro enolate anion.

(15.1)

Consistent with this proposal, α-trimethylsilyloxy styrene reacts with dichloroketene to yield 1,1-dichloro-2-trimethylsilyloxy-4-phenyl-but-1-en-4-one [1].

1-Trimethylsilyloxy-1,3-butadiene undergoes regiospecific [2 + 2] cycloaddition with dichloroketene to yield 2,2-dichloro-3-[2'-(trimethylsilyloxy)-vinyl cyclobutanone [4].

$$(15.2)$$

On the other hand, dichloroketene reacts with 2-trimethylsilyloxy-1,3-cyclo-pentadiene to yield two products. Both result from an initial 1,4-zwitterionic intermediate [4]. The reason for the difference between the two systems is not clear.

$$(15.3)$$

Trimethylsilyl enol ethers of α-tetralone and α-indanone undergo regio-specific triplet sensitized $[2+2]$ photo-cycloaddition reactions with α,β-unsaturated carbonyl compounds such as ethyl acrylate, acrylonitrile and methyl vinyl ketone, to yield 1-trimethylsilyloxy-2-substituted cyclobutanes. These undergo ring opening on treatment with aq. acid to yield products of Michael addition of the trimethylsilyl enol ethers to the α,β-unsaturated carbonyl compounds [5, 41].

$$(15.4)$$

Photo-reaction of trimethylsilyl ethers of 1- and 2-naphthol with acrylo-nitrile yields similar results [6].

TiCl$_4$ causes silyl enol ethers to undergo [2+2] cycloaddition reactions with alkynes and alkenes which are substituted with electron withdrawing groups [7].

$$(15.5)$$

E and Z-1-trimethylsilyl propene undergo stereospecific [3+2] cyclo-addition reactions with acetonitrile oxide to yield stereoisomeric 5-trimethyl-silyl isoxazolines. These undergo vacuum pyrolysis with loss of acetonitrile and formation of trimethylsilyl enol ethers with retention of stereochemistry [8].

$$(15.6)$$

15.3 Diels-Alder, [4+2] Cycloaddition

Enolizable 1,3-dicarbonyl compounds, such as acetyl acetone, are readily converted into 1,3-bis-(trimethylsilyloxy)-1,3-dienes by reaction with TMS-Cl and triethylamine in the presence of a catalytic amount of zinc chloride [9, 10]. Such dienes readily undergo Diels-Alder reactions with suitable dienophiles [9].

$$(15.7)$$

α,β-Unsaturated ketones can be converted to 2-trimethylsilyloxy-1,3-dienes by reaction with TMS-Cl and triethylamine in DMF [11], TMS-I and hexamethyldisilazane [12], or with LDA in THF, followed by addition of TMS-Cl [13]. 2-Trimethylsilyloxy-1,3-cyclohexadiene has been prepared from 2-cyclohexenone by treatment with TMS-Cl and triethylamine in DMF or with LDA and TMS-Cl in THF. These dienes have proved useful in Diels-Alder reactions [11, 13].

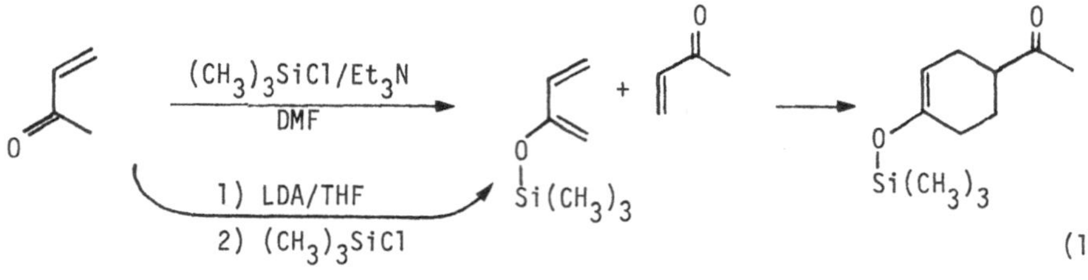

(15.8)

trans-1-Methoxy-3-trimethylsilyloxy-1,3-butadiene has been prepared by reaction of trans-4-methoxy but-3-en-2-one with TMS-Cl, triethylamine and zinc chloride [14].

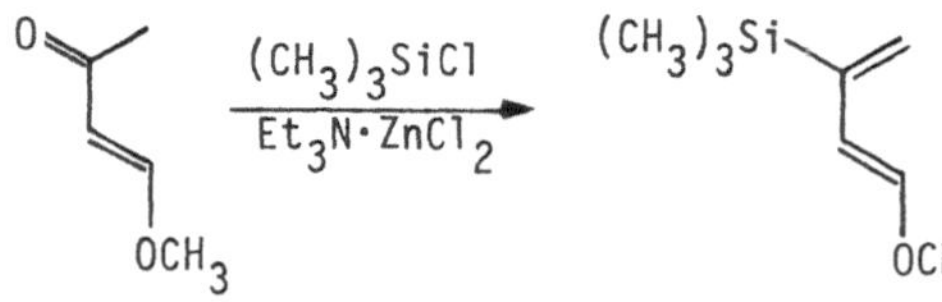

(15.9)

This diene undergoes Diels Alder reactions with a variety of dienophiles, and has been utilized in the synthesis of complex molecules.

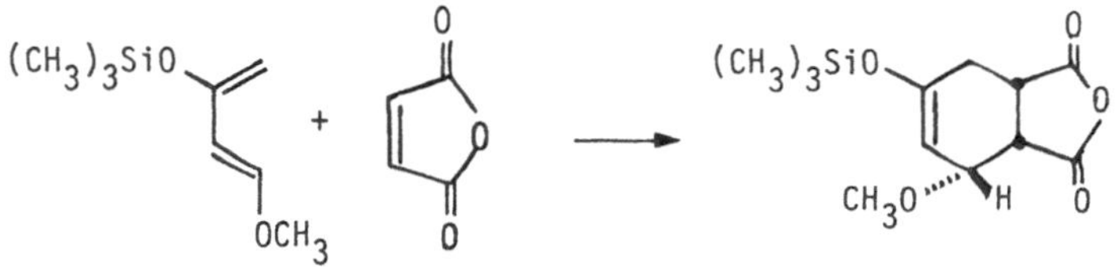

(15.10)

Reaction of this diene with methacrolein provides a one-step synthesis of 4-methyl-4-formyl cyclohex-2-en-1-one.

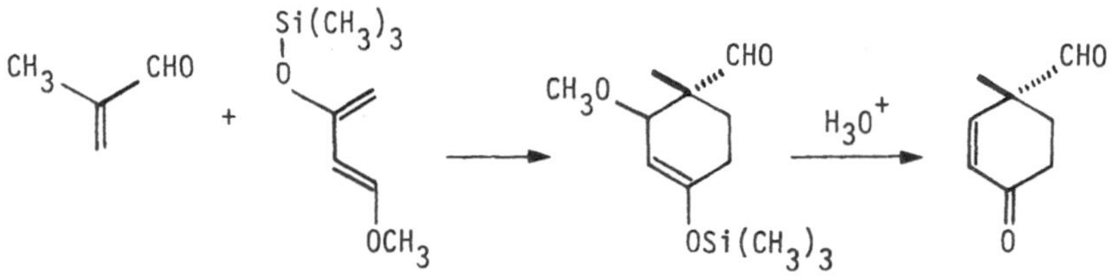

(15.11)

Reaction of trans-1-methoxy-3-trimethylsilyloxy-1,3-butadiene with methyl cyclohexene carboxylate leads to cis-10-carbomethoxy-1-Δ^1-3-octalone after work-up [15]

246

$$(15.12)$$

4-Methyl-4-carbomethoxy-2,5-cyclohexadienone has been efficiently prepared by a Diels-Alder reaction of *trans*-1-methoxy-3-trimethylsilyloxy-1,3-butadiene with β-phenylsulfinyl methyl methacrylate [16, 17].

$$(15.13)$$

1-Phenylseleno-2-trimethylsilyloxy-4-methoxy-1,3-butadiene undergoes a Diels-Alder reaction with methacryloyl chloride. Treatment of the adduct with methanol in pyridine followed by oxidation with hydrogen peroxide gives 4-methyl-4-carbomethoxy-2,5-cyclohexadienone.

$$(15.14)$$

The necessary diene was prepared by reaction of 1-methoxy-3-trimethylsilyl-oxy-1,3-butadiene with phenylselenyl chloride to give 1-phenylseleno-4-methoxy-but-3-en-2-one. This was silylated by treatment with TMS-Cl, triethyl-amine and zinc chloride [18].

$$(15.15)$$

1,1-Dimethoxy-3-trimethylsilyloxy-1,3-butadiene has also proved useful as a diene for the construction of complex molecules [19, 20].

$$(15.16)$$

The preparation and Diels-Alder reactions of E-1-methoxy-2-methyl-3-trimethylsilyloxy-1,3-butadiene, E-1-methoxy-3-trimethylsilyloxy-1,3-penta-diene, and E,Z-trans-1-methoxy-3-trimethylsilyloxy-4-phenylseleno-1,3-buta-diene have been described [21].

$$(15.17)$$

Intramolecular Diels-Alder reactions of 5-(3'-butenyl)-2-trimethylsilyl-oxycyclopentadiene and related systems have been studied [22, 23].

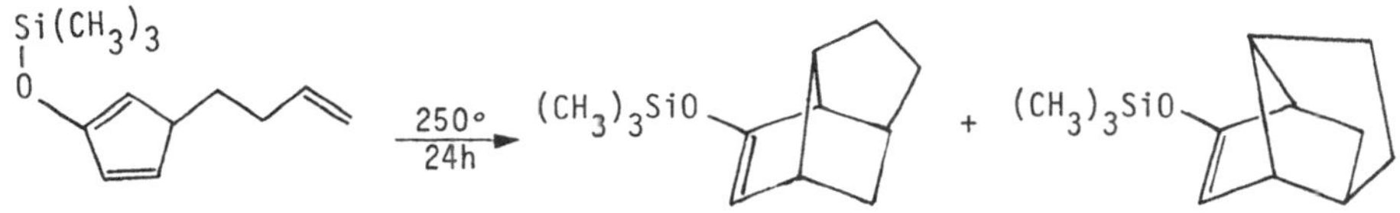

(15.18)

Retro Diels-Alder reactions of trimethylsilyl enol ethers of 2-norbornanones provide an efficient route to cyclopentenones [24].

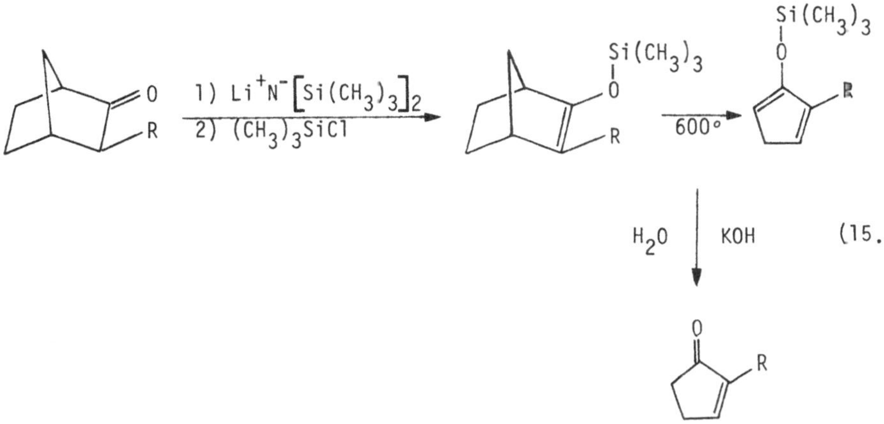

(15.19)

β,γ-Unsaturated γ-lactones can be converted into 2-trimethylsilyloxy furans by treatment with TMS-Cl and triethylamine. The Diels-Alder reaction of 5-methyl-2-trimethylsilyloxyfuran with maleic anhydride yields an adduct which can be converted regiospecifically to 7-hydroxyphthalide [26].

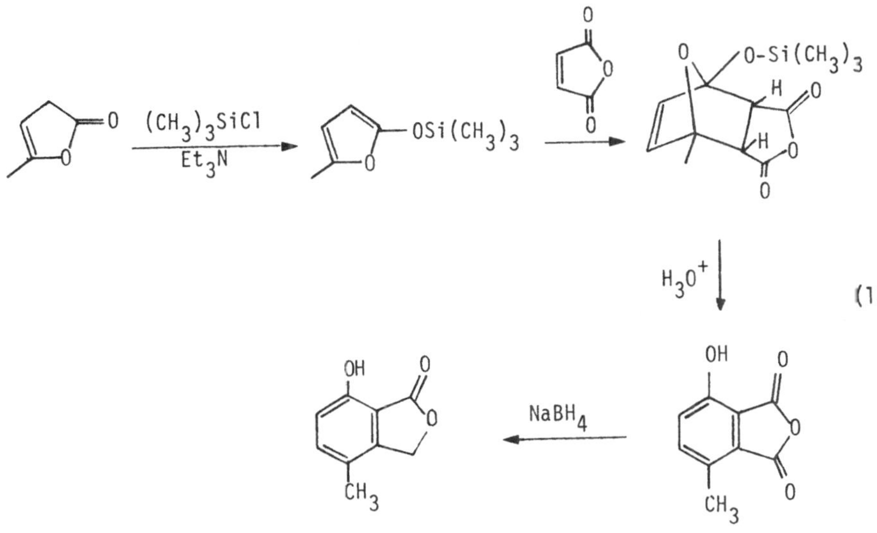

(15.21)

Succinic anhydride reacts with TMS-Cl and triethylamine in the presence of zinc chloride catalyst in acetonitrile to yield 2,5-*bis*-(trimethylsilyloxy) furan. Diels-Alder reaction of this furan with dimethylacetylene dicarboxylate yields, after hydrolysis, 3,6-dihydroxydimethylphthalate [27].

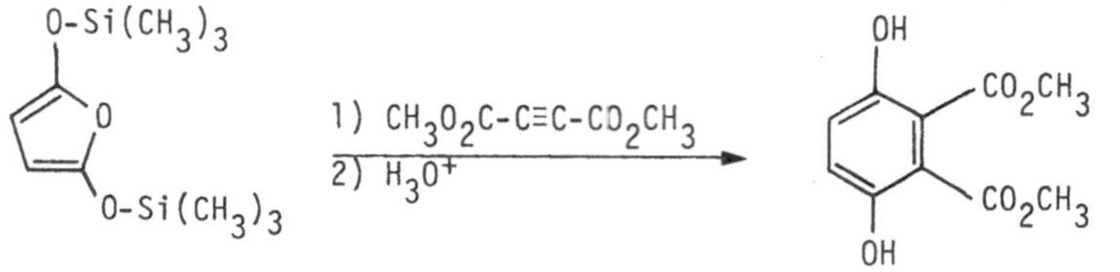

(15.22)

Silyl enol ethers can also serve as the dienophile component in Diels-Alder reactions. 3-Trimethylsilyloxy-3-buten-2-one undergoes Diels-Alder reactions with a number of dienes [25].

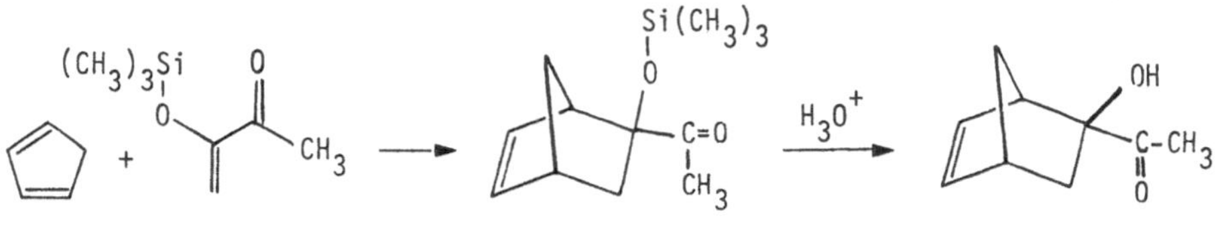

(15.20)

15.4 [3 + 4] and [3 + 2] Cycloaddition Reactions

Reaction of 2,4-dibromo-2,4-dimethyl-3-pentanone with a zinc-copper couple and TMS-Cl in the presence of anthracenes yields 12-oxo-9,10-propano anthracenes [28]. This reaction may occur as outlined (Eq. 15.23).

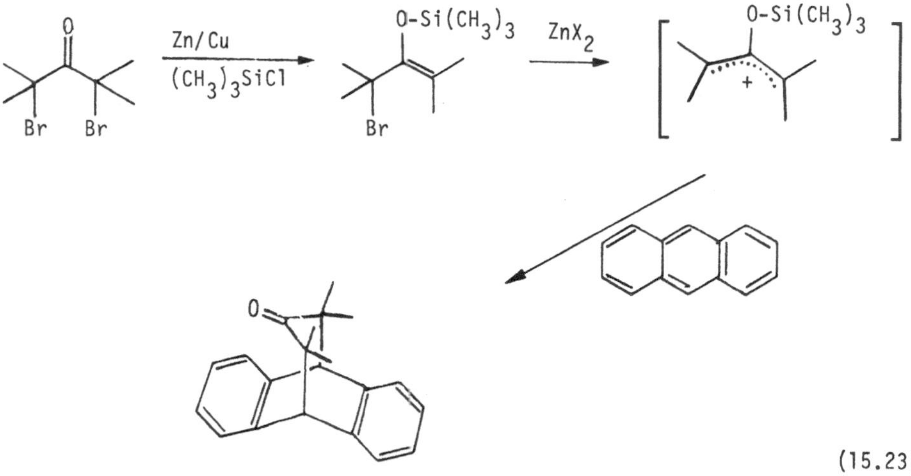

(15.23)

In a similar manner, 3-bromo-3-methyl-2-trimethylsilyloxy-1-butene under-goes zinc chloride assisted ionization to a 2-trimethylsilyloxy substituted allylic carbocation which reacts with 1,3-dienes [42] and α-methyl styrene [42].

$$(15.24)$$

3-Bromo-3-methyl-2-trimethylsilyloxy-1-butene was prepared by reaction of 3-bromo-3-methyl-2-butanone with LDA in THF followed by addition of TMS-Cl.

Likewise, 3-chloro-3-methyl-2-trimethylsilyloxy-1-butene undergoes silver ion assisted ionization to yield a 2-trimethylsilyloxy substituted allylic carbo-cation which undergoes cycloaddition with 1,3-diene [43].

$$(15.25)$$

3-Chloro-3-methyl-2-trimethylsilyloxy-1-butene was prepared by reaction of 3-chloro-3-methyl-2-butanone with TMS-Cl and triethylamine in DMF.

15.5 Electrocyclic Reactions of Silyl Enol Ethers

Allyl t-butyldimethylsilyl ketene acetals undergo Claisen [3,3]-sigmatropic rearrangement under mild conditions to yield t-butyldimethylsilyl γ,δ-unsaturated esters [29, 30, 31].

$$(15.26)$$

Allylic acetates can be converted to allyl t-butyldimethylsilyl ketene acetals by treatment with LDA at $-78°C$ followed by addition of t-butyldimethyl-chlorosilane.

2,3-*bis*(Trimethylsilyloxy)-1,3-butadiene can be prepared by a conrotatory electrocyclic ring opening of 1,2-*bis*(trimethylsilyloxy)-cyclobutene [12]. Alternatively, this interesting diene can be prepared by treatment of 2,3-butanedione with trimethylsilyl trifluoromethane sulfonate [12].

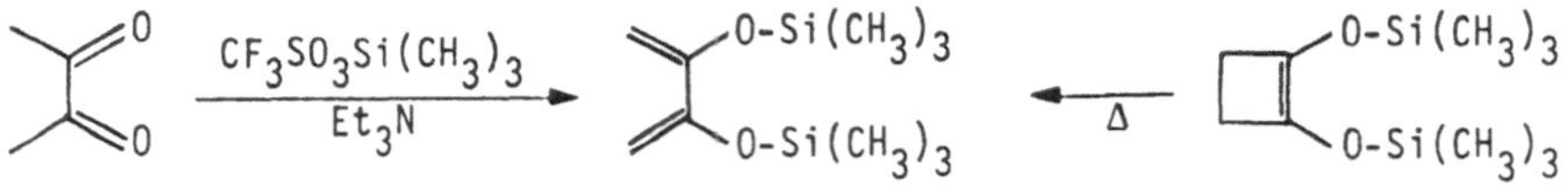

(15.27)

1,2-*bis*(Trimethylsilyloxy) cyclobutene is prepared by the silyl acyloin reaction with diethyl succinate [32].

There are several regiospecific methods to prepare trimethylsilyl enol ethers based on rearrangement reactions. For example trimethylsilyl β-keto carboxylates undergo pyrolysis with transfer of the trimethylsilyl group from the ester to the keto functional group with simultaneous decarboxylation to yield trimethylsilyl enol ethers [33–35]. This is analogous to the thermal decarboxylation of β-keto acids.

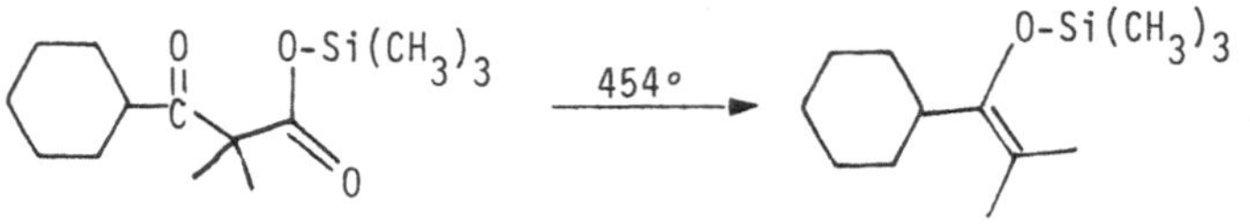

+ CO_2 (15.28)

Trimethylsilyl enol ethers of β-keto allyl carboxylates undergo a silyl-Carrol reaction on gas phase pyrolysis to yield specific allyl substituted trimethylsilyl enol ethers and carbon dioxide [33].

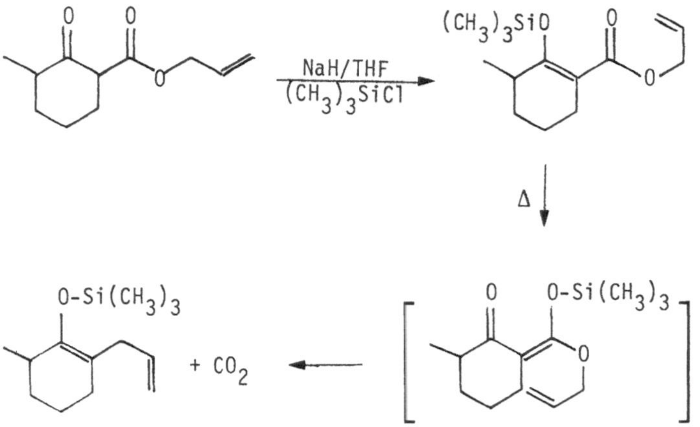

(15.29)

Thies has developed a valuable two carbon ring expansion reaction based on the silyloxy-Cope rearrangement [36–40]. Cyclic β,γ-unsaturated ketones react with vinyl Grignard reagent to yield a magnesium alkoxide which reacts with TMS-Cl to give the expected trimethylsilyl ether. Pyrolysis of such compounds largely occurs via a [1,3]-sigmatropic silyloxy-Cope rearrangement to yield a cyclic trimethylsilyl enol ether which possesses two additional carbon atoms [36–40]. The competing [3,3] sigmatropic process is less important.

major

minor

(15.30)

References

1. Krepski, L.R., Hassner, A.: J. Org. Chem. *43*, 3173 (1978)
2. Brady, W.T., Lloyd, R.M.: J. Org. Chem. *44*, 2560 (1979)
3. Brady, W.T., Lloyd, R.M.: J. Org. Chem. *45*, 2025 (1980)
4. Brady, W.T., Lloyd, R.M.: J. Org. Chem. *46*, 1322 (1981)
5. Mizuno, K., Okamoto, H., Pac, C., Sakurai, H., Murai, S., Sonoda, N.: Chem. Lett. 237 (1975)
6. Akhtar, I.A., McCullough, J.J.: J. Org. Chem. *46*, 1447 (1981)
7. Clark, R.D., Untch, K.G.: J. Org. Chem. *44*, 253 (1979)
8. Cunico, R.F.: J. Organometal. Chem. *212*, C51 (1981)
9. Ibuka, I., Ito, Y., Mori, Y., Anoyama, T., Inubushi, Y.: Syn. Comm. *7*, 131 (1977)
10. Hengge, E., Pletka, H.D.: Monat. für Chem. *104*, 1071 (1973)
11. Jung, M.E., McCombs, C.A.: Tetrahedron Lett. 2935 (1976)
12. Simchen, G., Kober, W.: Synthesis, 259 (1976)
13. Wunderly, S.W., Weber, W.P.: J. Org. Chem. *43*, 2277 (1978)
14. Danishefsky, S., Kitahara, T.: J. Am. Chem. Soc. *96*, 7807 (1974)
15. Danishefsky, S., Kitahara, T.: J. Org. Chem. *40*, 538 (1975)
16. Danishefsky, S., Singh, R.K., Harayama, T.: J. Am. Chem. Soc. *99*, 5810 (1977)
17. Danishefsky, S., Harayama, T., Singh, R.K.: J. Am. Chem. Soc. *101*, 7008 (1979)
18. Danishefsky, S., Yan, C.F., McCurry, Jr., P.M.: J. Org. Chem. *42*, 1819 (1977)
19. Danishefsky, S., Walker, F.J. J. Am. Chem. Soc. *101*, 7018 (1979)
20. Danishefsky, S., Singh, R.K., Gammill, R.B.: J. Org. Chem. *43*, 379 (1978)
21. Danishefsky, S., Yan, C.F., Singh, R.K., Gammill, R.B., McCurry, Jr., P.M., Fritsch, N., Clardy, J.: J. Am. Chem. Soc. *101*, 7001 (1979)
22. Snowden, R.L.: Tetrahedron Lett. 97 (1981)
23. Snowden, R.L.: Tetrahedron Lett. 101 (1981)
24. Bloch, R.: Tetrahedron Lett. 3945 (1979)
25. Ardecky, R.J., Kerdesky, F.A.J., Cava, M.P.: J. Org. Chem. *46*, 1483 (1981)
26. Asaoka, M., Miyake, K., Takei, H.: Chem. Lett. 167 (1977)
27. Brownbridge, P., Chan, T.H.: Tetrahedron Lett. 3423 (1980)
28. Giguere, R.J., Hoffmann, H.M.R., Hursthouse, M.B., Trotter, J.: J. Org. Chem. *46*, 2868 (1981)
29. Ireland, R.E., Mueller, R.H., Willard, A.K.: J. Am. Chem. Soc. *98*, 2868 (1976)
30. Ireland, R.E., Mueller, R.H.: J. Am. Chem. Soc. *94*, 5897 (1972)
31. Katzenellenbogen, J.A., Christy, K.J.: J. Org. Chem. *39*, 3315 (1974)
32. Bloomfield, J.J.: Tetrahedron Lett. 587 (1968)

33. Coates, R.M., Sandefur, L.O., Smillie, R.D.: J. Am. Chem. Soc. *97*, 1619 (1975)
34. Bloch, R., Boivin, F., Bortolussi, M.: J. Chem. Soc. Chem. Commun. 371 (1976)
35. Bloch, R., Denis, J.M.: J. Organometal. Chem. *90*, C9 (1975)
36. Thies, R.W., Bolesta, R.W.: J. Org. Chem. *41*, 1233 (1976)
37. Thies, R.W.: J. Am. Chem. Soc. *94*, 7074 (1972)
38. Thies, R.W., Wills, M.T., Chin, A.W., Schick, L.E., Walton, E.S.: J. Am. Chem. Soc. *95*, 5281 (1973)
39: Thies, R.W., Billigmeier, J.E.: J. Am. Chem. Soc. *96*, 200 (1974)
40. Thies, R.W.: J. Chem. Soc. Chem. Commun. 237 (1971)
41. Pak, C., Okamoto, H., Sakurai, H.: Synthesis, 589 (1978)
42. Sakurai, H., Shirahata, A., Hosomi, A.: Angew. Chem. Int. Ed. *18*, 163 (1979)
43. Shimizu, N., Tsuno, Y.: Chem. Lett. 103 (1979)

16 Preparation of Silyl Enol Ethers

16.1 Introduction

Due to the wide range of useful reactions which silyl enol ether undergo, numerous methods have been developed to prepare them. We will consider these methods in this chapter. Certain of these have been previously discussed (see Chapter 14 and 15).

16.2 Rearrangement of β-Silyl Ketones

β-Trimethylsilyl ketones have been prepared by reaction of trimethylsilyl-methyl magnesium chloride with anhydrides [1], or by reaction of diazomethane with α-silyl ketones [2].

$$(CH_3)_3SiCH_2MgCl \;+\; \left(CH_3\text{-}\overset{\overset{O}{\|}}{C}\right)_2O \;\longrightarrow\; (CH_3)_3SiCH_2\text{-}\overset{\overset{O}{\|}}{C}\text{-}CH_3 \qquad (16.1)$$

β-Trimethylsilyl ketones easily rearrange to the isomeric trimethylsilyl enol ethers. This rearrangement can be catalyzed by Lewis acids such as mercuric iodide or bromide. Under these conditions, the rearrangement is not completely intramolecular [3]. On the other hand, the rearrangement can also be carried out by heating β-trialkylsilyl ketones to between 160–200 °C. Under these conditions, the rearrangement is strictly intramolecular. The thermal rearrangement of an optically active β-silyl ketone to the corresponding silyl enol ether occurs with complete retention of configuration at the silyl center [4–6].

$$(16.2)$$

Lithium dialkyl cuprates undergo regiospecific S_n2' coupling with 1-chloro-2-trimethylsilyloxy propene to give trimethylsilyl enol ethers as outlined [7].

$$(CH_3)_3SiCH_2MgCl \; + \; \left(ClCH_2-\overset{\overset{\displaystyle O}{\|}}{C}\right)_2 O \; \longrightarrow \; (CH_3)_3SiCH_2-\overset{\overset{\displaystyle O}{\|}}{C}-CH_2Cl \qquad (16.3)$$

$$\xrightarrow{\;MgI_2\;} \;\; H_2C\overset{\displaystyle O-Si(CH_3)_3}{\underset{\displaystyle CH_2Cl}{\diagup\!\!\!\!C\diagdown}} \;\; \xrightarrow{\;(CH_3)_2CuLi\;} \;\; H_2C\overset{\displaystyle (CH_3)_3SiO}{\underset{\displaystyle CH_2CH_3}{\diagup\!\!\!\!C\diagdown}}$$

The reaction of β-trialkyltin ketones or esters with trialkylhalosilanes yields trialkylsilyl enol ethers or alkyl trialkylsilyl ketene acetals, respectively and trialkyltin halides [8].

16.3 Brook Rearrangement, α-Silyl Ketones

α-Silyl ketones react with diazomethane via a 1,4-dipolar intermediate to yield mixtures of silyl enol ethers and β-silyl ketones [2]. The rearrangement of silicon from carbon to the negatively charged oxygen with formation of a carbanion is related to the Brook rearrangement [9].

$$Ph_3Si-\overset{\overset{\displaystyle O}{\|}}{C}-Ph \; + \; CH_2N_2 \; \longrightarrow \; \left[Ph_3Si-\overset{\overset{\displaystyle O^-}{|}}{\underset{\underset{\displaystyle CH_2N_2^+}{|}}{C}}-Ph\right] \; \xrightarrow{\;\sigma\;} \; \left[\overset{\displaystyle Ph_3SiO}{\underset{\underset{\displaystyle CH_2N_2^+}{|}}{\overset{|}{-}C-Ph}}\right]$$

$$\downarrow{\scriptstyle d} \hspace{6cm} \downarrow \hspace{2cm} (16.4)$$

$$Ph_3SiCH_2-\overset{\overset{\displaystyle O}{\|}}{C}-Ph \; + \; N_2 \hspace{2cm} H_2C\overset{\displaystyle OSiPh_3}{\underset{\displaystyle Ph}{\diagup\!\!\!\!C\diagdown}} \; + \; N_2$$

The addition of methylene triphenylphosphorane to α-silyl ketones yields a similar 1,4-dipolar intermediate. Aryl α-silyl ketones yield silyl enol ethers, while alkyl α-silyl ketones yield vinyl silanes via a Wittig reaction. The stabilizing effect of an aryl group on an adjacent carbanion may account for this difference [10].

$$Ph_3Si-\overset{\overset{\displaystyle O}{\|}}{C}-Ph \; + \; Ph_3P=CH_2 \; \longrightarrow \; \left[Ph_3Si-\overset{\overset{\displaystyle O^-}{|}}{\underset{\underset{\displaystyle CH_2PPh_3^+}{|}}{C}}-Ph\right] \; \xrightarrow{\;\sigma\;} \; \left[\overset{\displaystyle Ph_3SiO}{\underset{\underset{\displaystyle Ph \;\;\; ^+PPh_3}{|\hspace{1.2cm}|}}{-C\!\!-\!\!\!-\!\!\!-CH_2}}\right]$$

$$\downarrow \hspace{3cm} (16.5)$$

$$\overset{\displaystyle Ph_3SiO}{\underset{\displaystyle Ph}{\diagdown\hspace{1mm}\diagup}}C=CH_2 \; + \; PPh_3$$

Benzyl-trimethylsilyl ketone reacts with α-lithioethyl phenyl sulphone to yield 1-phenyl-2-trimethylsilyloxy-2-butene and lithium phenyl sulfinate. This trimethylsilyl enol ether cannot be prepared from benzyl ethyl ketone either under the normal kinetic (LDA/TMS-Cl) or thermodynamic (TMS-Cl/Et₃N) conditions [11].

$$
\text{PhCH}_2\text{-}\overset{\text{O}}{\underset{\|}{\text{C}}}\text{-Si(CH}_3)_3 + \text{Ph-}\overset{\text{O}}{\underset{\overset{\|}{\underset{\text{Li}^+}{}}}{\text{S}}}\text{-}\overset{-}{\text{CH}}\text{-CH}_3 \longrightarrow
\left[\begin{array}{c} \text{PhCH}_2 \quad \overset{\text{O}^-}{\underset{\overset{|}{\text{C}}}{}}\quad\text{Si(CH}_3)_3 \\ \overset{\text{O}}{\underset{\overset{\|}{\text{Ph-S}}}{}}\quad\overset{\text{CH}}{\underset{\text{CH}_3}{}} \end{array} \right]
$$

(16.6)

$$
\text{PhSO}_2^-\ \text{Li}^+ + \quad \overset{(\text{CH}_3)_3\text{Si}\diagdown\text{O}}{\underset{\text{PhCH}_2-\text{C}}{}}=\overset{\text{H}}{\underset{\text{CH}_3}{\text{C}}} \longleftarrow
\left[\begin{array}{c} \text{PhCH}_2-\overset{\text{O}\diagup\text{Si(CH}_3)_3}{\underset{\overset{|}{\text{C}}\text{ Li}^+}{}} \\ \overset{\text{O}}{\underset{\overset{\|}{\text{Ph-S}}}{}}\quad\overset{\text{CH}}{\underset{\text{CH}_3}{}} \end{array} \right]
$$

The addition of vinyl magnesium bromide to α-trimethylsilyl ketones yields α-trimethylsilyl allylic alcohols. The corresponding these lithium alkoxides undergo the Brook rearrangement. Reaction of these trimethylsilyloxy substituted allylic anions with alkyl iodides occurs stereo- and regiospecifically at the γ-position to yield Z-trimethylsilyl enol ethers [12, 13].

$$
\text{CH}_3(\text{CH}_2)_2\text{-}\overset{\text{O}}{\underset{\|}{\text{C}}}\text{-Si(CH}_3)_3 \xrightarrow{\diagup\diagdown\text{MgBr}} \text{CH}_3(\text{CH}_2)_2\text{-}\overset{\text{O}^-}{\underset{\overset{|}{\text{C}}}{\underset{\text{Si(CH}_3)_3}{}}}\diagup\diagdown
$$

(16.7)

$$
\xrightarrow{} \text{CH}_3(\text{CH}_2)_2\text{-}\overset{\text{OSi(CH}_3)_3}{\underset{|}{\text{C}}}\diagup\diagdown
$$

$$
\xrightarrow{n\text{-BuI}} \overset{(\text{CH}_3)_3\text{SiO}\diagdown}{\underset{\text{CH}_3(\text{CH}_2)_2\diagup}{}}\text{C=C}\overset{\diagup n\text{-Bu}}{\underset{\diagdown\text{H}}{}}
$$

The addition of 2-lithio furans to α-trimethylsilyl ketones yields α-lithio-α-trimethylsilyloxy furans via a Brook rearrangement. Ring opening gives an enolate anion which reacts with TMS-Cl to give 1,5-bis(trimethylsilyloxy)-1,2,4-trienes [14].

257

$$\text{(16.8)}$$

1-Trimethylsilyl propargyl alcohols undergo Brook rearrangement on treatment with a catalytic amount of n-butyl lithium to yield trimethylsilyloxy allenes. These undergo hydrolysis to yield α,β-unsaturated aldehydes (Eq. 16.9). If a stoichiometric amount of n-butyl lithium is used, 1-lithio-3-trimethylsilyloxy allenes result. These will react with alkyl iodides specifically at the 1-position [15].

$$\text{(16.9)}$$

16.4 Preparation of α-Silyl Ketones

These methods obviously depend on the availability of α-silyl ketones. One of the best methods to prepare α-silyl ketones utilizes 1,3-dithiane. A major problem is hydrolysis of the 2-alkyl-2-trimethylsilyl-1,3-dithiane to the α-trimethylsilyl ketone [16, 17]. Chloramine T[3] may be a more effective hydrolysis catalyst than mercuric chloride [11].

$$(16.10)$$

α-Silyl ketones have also been prepared by reaction of 1-ethoxyvinyl lithium with chlorosilanes. The resulting 1-ethoxyvinyl silanes are relatively easy to hydrolyze [18].

$$(16.11)$$

In a similar manner, α-trimethylsilyl-α',β'-unsaturated ketones have been prepared from 1-methoxy-1,3-butadiene [75, 76], or 1-methoxy allene [77].

$$(16.12)$$

Triphenylsilyl lithium reacts with aliphatic acid chlorides and a stoichiometric amount of cuprous iodide to yield α-triphenylsilyl ketones [19].

$$(16.13)$$

Lithium 1,1-*bis*(trimethylsilyl) alkoxides react with benzophenone in nonpolar solvents to yield lithium diphenylmethoxide and α-trimethylsilyl trimethylsilyl enol ethers. These can be easily hydrolyzed to α-trimethylsilyl ketones [20].

$$PhCH_2CH_2-\overset{\overset{\displaystyle Si(CH_3)_3}{|}}{\underset{\underset{\displaystyle Si(CH_3)_3}{|}}{C}}-O^-Li^+ \quad + \quad Ph_2C=O \rightleftharpoons \left[\begin{array}{c} (CH_3)_3SiO \\ (CH_3)_3Si-C \\ PhCH_2CH \\ H \end{array} \overset{Li}{\underset{\underset{Ph}{\diagdown}}{\overset{O}{\diagup}}} \overset{O}{\underset{}{C-Ph}} \right] \qquad (16.14)$$

$$\longrightarrow \quad \underset{(CH_3)_3Si}{\overset{(CH_3)_3SiO}{\diagdown}} C=C \overset{H}{\underset{CH_2Ph}{\diagup}} \quad + \quad Ph_2CHO^-Li^+ \quad \xrightarrow{H_3O^+} \quad (CH_3)_3Si\overset{O}{\overset{||}{-C}}-CH_2CH_2Ph$$

Oxidation of 1,1-*bis*(trimethylsilyl)alkan-1-ols with *t*-butyl hypochlorite also yields acyl silanes [21].

$$PhCH_2CH_2-\overset{\overset{\displaystyle (CH_3)_3 \cdot Si}{|}}{\underset{\underset{\displaystyle (CH_3)_3}{\diagup Si}}{C}}-OH \quad \xrightarrow{(CH_3)_3COCl} \quad PhCH_2CH_2-\overset{\overset{\displaystyle (CH_3)_3 \cdot Si}{|}}{\underset{\underset{\displaystyle (CH_3)_3}{\diagup Si}}{C}}-OCl \qquad (16.15)$$

$$\downarrow$$

$$(CH_3)_3SiCl \quad + \quad PhCH_2CH_2\overset{O}{\overset{||}{-C}}-Si(CH_3)_3$$

Acyl silanes can also be prepared from α-trimethylsilyloxy allyl silanes. These undergo Pd/C catalyzed isomeration to yield α-trimethylsilyloxy vinyl silanes. These are easily hydrolyzed to acyl silanes [22]. α-Trimethylsilyloxy allyl silanes can be prepared by metallation of trimethylsilyl allyl ethers with *sec*-butyl lithium followed by reaction with chlorosilanes [23].

$$\diagup\diagdown\diagup OSi(CH_3)_3 \quad \xrightarrow[2)\ (CH_3)_3SiCl]{1)\ sec\text{-}BuLi} \quad \diagup\diagdown\underset{OSi(CH_3)_3}{\overset{\diagup Si(CH_3)_3}{\diagdown}} \qquad (16.16)$$

$$\xrightarrow[2)\ CH_3OH]{1)\ Pd/C} \quad CH_3CH_2\overset{O}{\overset{||}{-C}}-Si(CH_3)_3$$

α-Phenylthio trimethylsilyl enol ethers undergo reductive silylation to yield α-trimethylsilyl trimethylsilyl enol ethers [24] (see Chapter 19).

$$(16.17)$$

Methyl benzoate undergoes reductive silylation to yield α-methoxy-α-trimethylsilyl-α-trimethylsilyloxytoluene which can be hydrolyzed to yield benzoyltrimethylsilane [25] (see Chapter 19).

$$(16.18)$$

N-Phenyl pivalimidoyl chloride reacts with magnesium and TMS-Cl in THF/HMPT to yield the C-trimethylsilylimine. On hydrolysis this gives pivaloyltrimethylsilane [26].

$$(16.19)$$

Benzoyltrimethylsilane has been prepared by reaction of benzoyl chloride with hexamethyldisilane catalyzed by a palladium complex [79].

$$(16.20)$$

16.5 Conjugate Addition/Generation of Specific Lithium Enolates from Silyl Enol Ethers

Conjugate addition of organo cuprate reagents to α,β-unsaturated ketones yields specific enolate anions which can be quenched with TMS-Cl to give trimethylsilyl enol ethers [27, 28].

$$(16.21)$$

Analysis of the substitution pattern of prostaglandins suggests that such compounds might be prepared from appropriate cyclopentenone derivatives by conjugate addition of a vinyl cuprate reagent to the α,β-unsaturated ketone followed by alkylation of the enolate anion. The low reactivity of copper enolate anions in alkylation reactions constitutes a problem. However, copper enolates react with TMS-Cl to yield specific trimethylsilyl enol ethers. These can be converted to reactive lithium [29] enolates by reaction with methyl lithium or lithium amide in liquid ammonia [30, 31]. 11-Desoxyprostaglandins have been prepared by such a sequence.

$$(16.22)$$

A similar sequence was used by Stork in the syntheses of lycopodine [32].

The generation of lithium enolates by reaction of methyl lithium with trimethylsilyl enol ethers has been extensively studied [33].

$$(16.23)$$

Formaldehyde has been condensed with regiospecifically generated lithium enolates formed by reaction of methyl lithium with trimethylsilyl enol ethers [34].

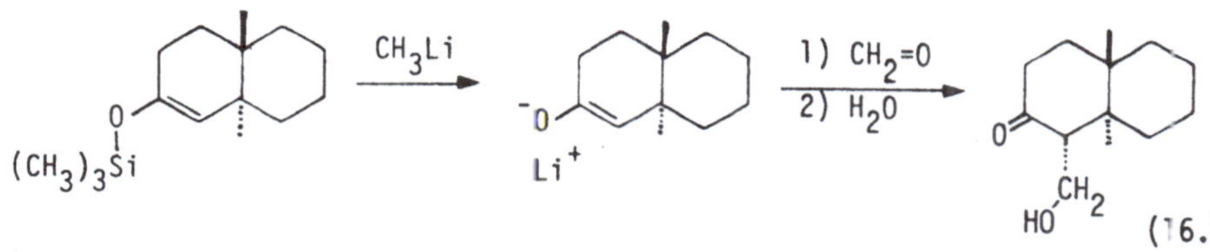

(16.24)

16.6 Hydrosilation of Ketones

Ketones can be catalytically hydrosilated to yield silyl ethers. (See Chapter 18.)
Nevertheless, ketones and aldehydes react with silanes in the presence of
certain catalysts to yield silyl enol ethers and hydrogen rather than silyl
ethers. Ketones [35] and aldehydes [36] react with triethylsilane and a catalyst
prepared from nickel chloride and diethyl sulfide or nickel sulfide to give
a mixture of triethylsilyl enol ether and alkyl triethylsilyl ether.

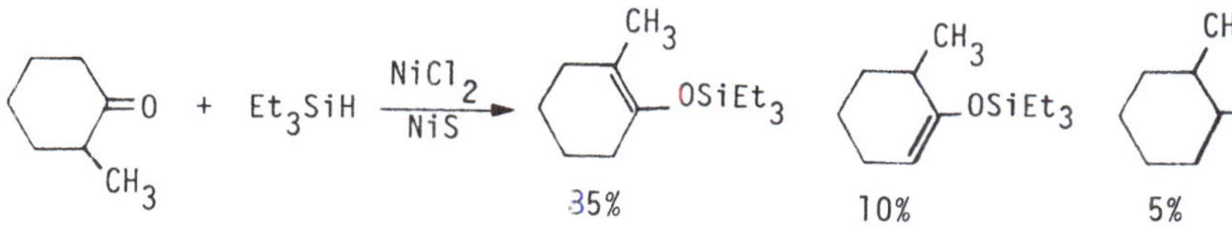

(16.25)

Similarly, ketones react with phenyldimethylsilane in the presence of
a catalytic amount of $Co_2(CO)_8$ and triethylamine or other bases to yield an
equilibrium mixture [27] of phenyldimethylsilyl enol ethers [37].

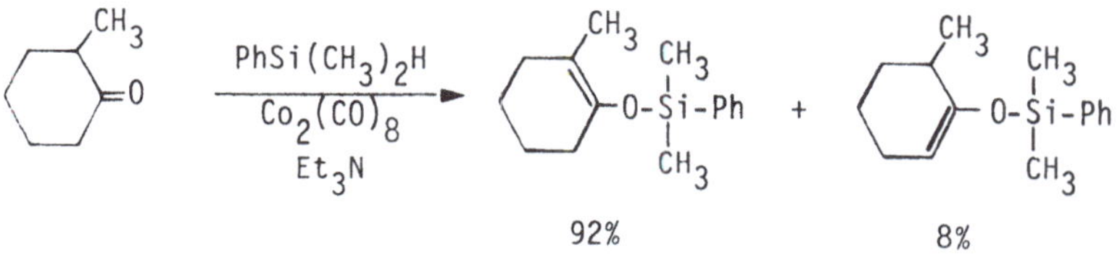

(16.26)

β-Keto esters or β-keto nitriles react with triethylsilane under catalysis
by $[Ph_3P]_3RhCl$ and a small amount of phenylthiotriethylsilane to yield the
corresponding triethylsilyl enol ethers and hydrogen [38].

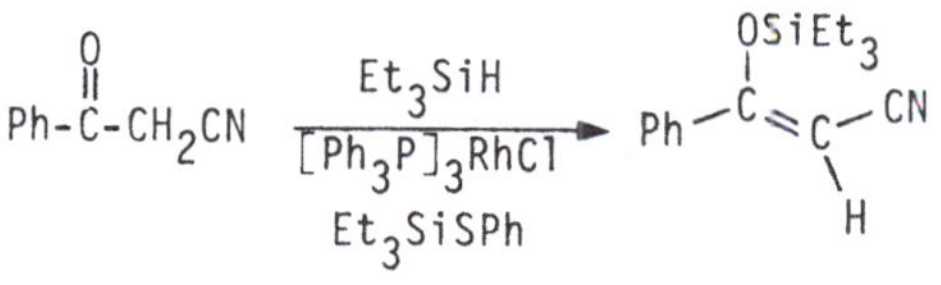

(16.27)

16.7 Silyl-Hydroformylation

The silyl-hydroformylation reaction of cycloalkenes with CO and triethyl-silane catalyzed by $Co_2(CO)_8$ yields triethylsilyloxymethylene cycloalkanes [39, 40].

$$\text{(cyclohexene)} + CO + HSiEt_3 \xrightarrow{Co_2(CO)_8} \text{(cyclohexane-CH-OSiEt}_3) \qquad (16.28)$$

While all the steps in this catalytic reaction are not certain, it is well known that trialkylsilanes react with $Co_2(CO)_8$ to yield tetracarbonylcobalt hydride and trialkylsilylcobalt tetracarbonyl [41].

$$HSiEt_3 + Co_2(CO)_8 \longrightarrow HCo(CO)_4 + Et_3SiCo(CO)_4 \qquad (16.29)$$

The catalytic reaction of 1-alkenes, CO, and diethylmethylsilane unfortunately yields mixtures of isomeric silyl enol ethers [42]. Similar product mixtures are obtained with $Co_2(CO)_8$ and triphenylphospine or with $(Ph_3P)_2RhCl$ and triethylamine as catalysts.

$Co_2(CO)_8$ catalyzes the reaction of aldehydes with diethylmethylsilane and CO to yield mixtures of E and Z 1,2-*bis*(diethylmethylsilyloxy)-1-alkenes [43].

$$CH_3(CH_2)_4\text{-}\overset{O}{\overset{\|}{C}}\text{-}H + 2Et_2\overset{CH_3}{\underset{CH_3}{SiH}} \xrightarrow[CO]{Co_2(CO)_8 \; PPh_3} \overset{CH_3}{Et_2SiO}\underset{CH_3(CH_2)_4}{\diagup}C=C\overset{OSiEt_2}{\underset{H}{\diagup}} + E\text{- isomer} \qquad (16.30)$$

16.8 1,4-Hydrosilation of α,β-Unsaturated Carbonyl Compounds

A particularly useful method to prepare specific silyl enol ethers is the catalytic 1,4-hydrosilation of α,β-unsaturated ketones or aldehydes. *bis*(Cyclo-octadienyl)nickel, $[Ph_3P]_3RhCl$ as well as a diplatinum complex are effective catalysts. The 1,4-hydrosilation of citral is outlined below. Hydrolysis of the triethylsilyl enol ether gives an aldehyde [44–46]. In this sense, the reaction is not only a synthesis of silyl enol ethers but also a selective reduction procedure.

$$\text{(citral-CHO)} \xrightarrow[{[Ph_3P]_3RhCl}]{Et_3SiH} \text{(OSiEt}_3) \xrightarrow[CH_3OH]{H_2O} \text{(CHO)} \qquad (16.31)$$

With certain α,β-unsaturated ketones, both 1,2-and 1,4-hydrosilation are observed. The ratio of these two processes depends on the particular silane [44–46].

$$\text{(16.32)}$$

R3SiH	1,4	1,2
Ph(CH3)2SiH	91	9
Et3SiH	44	56
Et2SiH2	0	100

Hydrosilation of α,β-unsaturated ketones with a chiral cationic rhodium complex-Rh[(R)-benzylmethylphenylphosphine]$_2$H$_2$S$_2^+$ ClO$_4^-$ yields after hydrolysis ketones which possess a chiral beta carbon. Only moderate asymmetric induction is observed (e.e. 15% or less) [78].

$$\text{(16.33)}$$

bis-(Cyclooctadienyl) nickel is particulary effective for the 1,4-hydrosilation of α,β-unsaturated aldehydes with trialkoxysilanes [47].

$$\text{(16.34)}$$

bis-Platinium complexes catalyze the 1,4-hydrosilation of α,β-unsaturated ketones or aldehydes. No competing 1,2-addition is observed [48].

$$\text{(16.35)}$$

265

16.9 Catalytic Isomerization of Allyloxyltrimethylsilanes

Allyloxytrimethylsilanes may be prepared by the reaction of allylic alcohols with TMS-Cl in the presence of pyridine. Both Pd/C [49] and ruthenium complexes, such as $H_2Ru(PPh_3)_4$, [50] are effective for the catalytic isomerization of allyloxytrimethylsilanes to trimethylsilyl enol ethers.

$$\text{(structures)} \quad \xrightarrow{H_2Ru(PPh_3)_4} \quad \text{(structure)} \quad OSi(CH_3)_3 \quad + \quad \text{(structure)} \quad OSi(CH_3)_3$$

$$\approx 1:1$$

$$(16.36)$$

16.10 Dissolving Metal Reduction (see Chapter 19)

Dissolving metal reductions are useful for the preparation of silyl enol ethers. Esters are reduced with TMS-Cl and sodium in toluene to yield alkoxyltrimethylsilanes and 1,2-*bis*(trimethylsilyloxy)alkenes [51].

$$\text{(structure)} \begin{array}{c} CO_2Et \\ CO_2Et \end{array} \quad \xrightarrow[\text{Toluene}]{Na/(CH_3)_3SiCl} \quad \text{(structure)} \begin{array}{c} OSi(CH_3)_3 \\ OSi(CH_3)_3 \end{array} \quad + \quad 2(CH_3)_3SiOEt \qquad (16.37)$$

Dissolving metal reduction of α,β-unsaturated ketones with lithium in ammonia and *t*-butanol yields specific lithium enolates which can be quenched with TMS-Cl and triethylamine to generate trimethylsilyl enol ethers [52].

$$\text{(structure)} \quad \xrightarrow[\text{2) }(CH_3)_3SiCl/Et_3N]{\text{1) }Li/NH_3-t-BuOH} \quad (CH_3)_3SiO-\text{(structure)} \qquad (16.38)$$

Birch reduction of dimethylisopropylphenoxysilanes or *t*-butyldimethylphenoxysilanes with lithium in liquid ammonia, THF, and *t*-butanol yields the corresponding isopropyl or *t*-butyldimethylsilyloxy-1,4-cyclohexadienes. Hydrolysis of these with THF and TBAF gives the corresponding cyclohex-3-en-1-ones [53].

$$CH_3-\text{(structure)}-O-\underset{\underset{CH_3}{|}}{\overset{\overset{CH_3}{|}}{Si}}-t-Bu \quad \xrightarrow[t-BuOH]{Li/NH_3-THF} \quad CH_3-\text{(structure)}-O-\underset{\underset{CH_3}{|}}{\overset{\overset{CH_3}{|}}{Si}}-t-Bu \qquad (16.39)$$

$$\xrightarrow[(n-Bu)_4N^+F^-]{H_2O/THF} \quad CH_3-\text{(structure)}=O$$

Dissolving metal reduction of α-bromo ketones yields specific enolate anions which react with TMS-Cl to give trimethylsilyl enol ethers [54, 55].

$$\text{(16.40)}$$

Reduction of dialkyl disubstituted malonates in the presence of TMS-Cl yields alkyl trimethylsilyl ketene acetals and CO [56].

$$\text{(16.41)}$$

16.11 Non-Nucleophilic Bases

Trimethylsilyl enol ethers can be prepared by the treatment of ketones with strong non-nucleophilic bases to generate the corresponding enolate anions which can be quenched with TMS-Cl. In order to prevent Aldol condensations, the ketone must be instantaneously converted to its enolate anion. This is achieved by the slow addition of the ketone to a solution of strong base. Sodium bis(trimethylsilyl)amide [57] or LDA in DME, have been frequently used. Kinetic trimethylsilyl enol ethers are formed in this way. Treatment of 2-methylcyclohexanone with LDA followed by TMS-Cl yields exclusively 1-trimethylsilyloxy-6-methylcyclohexene [58]. Similar results can be achieved by reaction of 2,6-dibromocyclohexanone with lithium dialkyl cuprates followed by addition of TMS-Cl [59]. Reaction of 1-trimethylsilyloxy-6-methylcyclohexene with TMS-Cl and triethylamine in DMF [58], or with a catalytic amount of TsOH [27] yields a 4:1 mixture of 1-trimethylsilyloxy-2-methylcyclohexene and 1-trimethylsilyloxy-6-methylcyclohexene.

$$\text{(16.42)}$$

When 4-testosterone-17-tetrahydropyrannyl ether is treated with lithium bis(trimethylsilyl)amide, a 2,4-dienolate anion is formed which can be trapped by TMS-Cl [60]

$$\text{(16.43)}$$

Non-nucleophilic strong bases, such as lithium cyclohexylisopropylamide, have been used to generate ester enolates which subsequently react with chlorosilanes to yield alkyl silyl ketene acetals. A significant problem is that C-silylation can occur in competition with the desired O-silylation. For example, reaction of methyl acetate with lithium cyclohexylisopropylamide at $-78°$ followed by addition of TMS-Cl yields methyl trimethylsilyl ketene acetal (65 %) and methyl trimethylsilylacetate (35 %). Selectivity for O-silylation can be achieved by use of t-butyldimethylchlorosilane and a mixed solvent system of THF and HMPT [61].

$$(16.44)$$

Treatment of ketones with sodium or potassium hydride in p-dioxane [62] or potassium hydride in THF [63] and TMS-Cl yields predominantly trimethylsilyl enol ethers.

$$(16.45)$$

The reaction of ethyl trimethylsilylacetate with ketones catalyzed by TBAF yields trimethylsilyl enol ethers and ethyl acetate as outlined below. This procedure can be carried out at $-78°C$ in which case, the kinetic trimethylsilyl enol ether is obtained. This method is extremely convenient since the by-product, ethyl acetate, is highly volatile [64]. Ethyl trimethylsilylacetate can be easily prepared by reaction of ethyl bromoacetate with TMS-Cl and zinc [65]

$$(CH_3)_3SiCH_2CO_2Et + (n-Bu)_4N^+F^- \longrightarrow (CH_3)_3SiF + [^-CH_2CO_2Et]\ ^+N(n-Bu)_4$$

$$(16.46)$$

E-trimethylsilyl enol ethers may be obtained by treatment of ketones with non-nucleophilic amide bases followed by TMS-Cl, while yields *Z*-trimethyl-silyl and ethers the reaction of ketones with ethyl trimethylsilylacetate and TBAF [66].

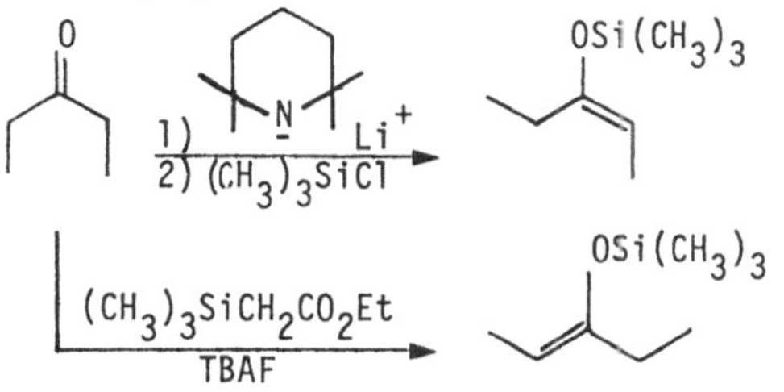

(16.47)

16.12 TMS-Cl/Triethylamine/DMF and Related Systems

Perhaps the most widely used method to prepare trimethylsilyl enol ethers is the reaction of ketones with TMS-Cl and triethylamine in DMF. Under these conditions, mixtures which approach the thermodynamic equilibrium of silyl enol ethers are formed [27, 58, 67]. *t*-Butyldimethylsilyl enol ethers, which are hydrolytically more stable than trimethylsilyl enol ethers can be prepared in this manner [27].

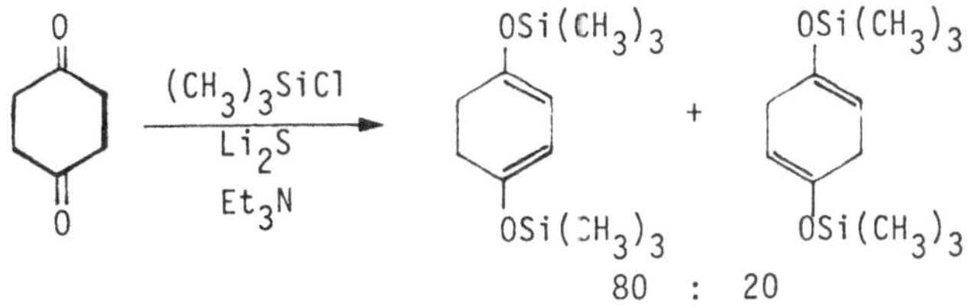

(16.48)

The combination of TMS-Cl, lithium sulfide and triethylamine is particularly effective [68].

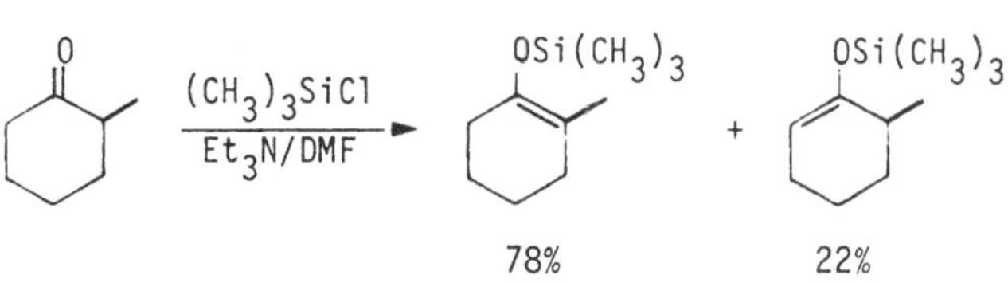

(16.49)

Treatment of ketones with TMS-I and hexamethyldisilazane directly yields the thermodynamic equilibrium mixture of trimethylsilyl enol ethers [69].
Reaction of dimethylaminotrimethylsilane with ketones yields the corresponding trimethylsilyl enol ethers [73].
α-Trimethylsilyl epoxides can also be converted to trimethylsilyl enol ethers [74].

Trimethylsilyl enol ethers of aldehydes can be prepared by reaction with TMS-Cl and triethylamine [70] or TMS-I and hexamethyldisilazane [69].

While TMS-Cl and triethylamine fail to convert camphor to its trimethylsilyl enol ether [54], trimethylsilyl trifluoromethane sulfonate and triethylamine are effective [55].

$$(16.50)$$

Esters and S-alkyl thioesters react with trimethylsilyl trifluoromethane sulfonate and triethylamine tŏ yield alkyl trimethylsilyl ketene acetals [71] and 1-alkylmercapto-1-trimethylsilyloxy alkenes [72], respectively.

$$(16.51)$$

References

1. Hauser, C.R., Hance, C.R.: J. Am. Chem. Soc. *71*, 5091 (1952)
2. Brook, A.G., Limburg, W.W., MacRae, D.M., Fieldhouse, S.A.: J. Am. Chem. Soc. *89*, 704 (1967)
3. Lutsenko, I.F., Baukov, Y.I., Dudukina, O.V., Kramarova, E.N.: J. Organometal. Chem. *11*, 35 (1968)
4. Brook, A.G., Fieldhouse, S.A.: J. Organometal. Chem. *10*, 235 (1967)
5. Brook, A.G., MacRae, D.M., Bassindale, A.R.: J. Organometal. Chem. *86*, 185 (1975)
6. Larson, G.L., Fernandez, Y.V.: J. Organometal. Chem. *86*, 193 (1975)
7. Sakurai, H., Shirahata, A., Araki, Y., Hosomi, A.: Tetrahedron Lett. 2325 (1980)
8. Baukov, J.I., Burlachenko, G.S., Lutsenko, I.F.: J. Organometal. Chem. *3*, 478 (1965)
9. Brook, A.G.: Accounts of Chem. Research, *7*, 77 (1974)
10. Brook, A.G., Fieldhouse, S.A.: J. Organometal. Chem. *10*, 235 (1967)
11. Reich, H.J., Rusek, J.J., Olson, R.E.: J. Am. Chem. Soc. *101*, 2225 (1979)
12. Kuwajima, I., Kato, M.: J. Chem. Soc. Chem. Commun. 708 (1979)
13. Kuwajima, I., Kato, M., Mori, A.: Tetrahedron Lett. 2745 (1980)
14. Kuwajima, I., Atsumi, K., Tanaka, T., Inoue, T.: Chem. Lett. 1239 (1979)
15. Kuwajima, I., Kato, M.: Tetrahedron Lett. 623 (1980)
16. Brook, A.G., Duff, J.M., Jones, P.F., Davis, N.R.: J. Am. Chem. Soc. *89*, 431 (1967)
17. Corey, E.J., Seebach, D., Freedman, R.: J. Am. Chem. Soc. *89*, 434 (1967)
18. Dexheimer, E.M., Spialter, L.: J. Organometal. Chem. *107*, 229 (1976)
19. Duffant, N., Dunoguès, J., Biran, C., Calas, R., Gerval, J.: J. Organometal. Chem. *101*, C23 (1978)
20. Kuwajima, I., Arai, M., Sato, T.: J. Am. Chem. Soc. *99*, 4181 (1977)

21. Kuwajima, I., Abe, T., Minami, N.: Chem. Lett. 993 (1976)
22. Hosomi, A., Hashimoto, H., Sakurai, H.: J. Organometal. Chem. *175*, Cl (1979)
23. Lau, P.W.K., Chan, T.H.: J. Organometal. Chem. *179*, C24 (1979)
24. Kuwajima, I., Kato, M., Sato, T.: J. Chem. Soc. Chem. Commun. 478 (1978)
25. Picard, J.D., Calas, R., Dunoguès, J., Duffaut, N.: J. Organometal. Chem. *26*, 183 (1971)
26. Bourgeois, P.: J. Organometal. Chem. *76*, C1 (1974)
27. Stork, G., Hudrlik, P.F.: J. Am. Chem. Soc. *90*, 4462 (1968)
28. Stotter, P.L., Hill, K.A.: J. Org. Chem. *38*, 2576 (1973)
29. Tanaka, T., Kurozumi, S., Toru, T., Kobayashi, M., Miuri, S., Ishimoto, S.: Tetrahedron Lett. 1535 (1975)
30. Kluge, A.F., Untch, K.G., Fried, J.H.: J. Am. Chem. Soc. *94*, 2827 (1972)
31. Patterson, Jr., J.W., Fried, J.H.: J. Org. Chem. *39*, 2506 (1974)
32. Stork, G.: Pure and Applied. Chem. *17*, 383 (1968)
33. House, H.O., Auerbach, R.A., Gall, M., Peet, N.P.: J. Org. Chem. *38*, 514 (1973)
34. Stork, G., d'Angelo, J.: J. Am. Chem. Soc. *96*, 7114 (1974)
35. Frainnet, E., Martel-Siegfried, V., Brousse, E., Dedier, J.: J. Organometal. Chem. *85*, 297 (1975)
36. Frainnet, E., Bourhis, R.: J. Organometal. Chem. *93*, 309 (1975)
37. Sakurai, H., Miyoshi, K., Nakadaira, Y.: Tetrahedron Lett. 2671 (1977)
38. Ojima, I., Nagai, Y.: J. Organometal. Chem. *57*, C42 (1973)
39. Seki, Y., Hadaka, A., Murai, S., Sonoda, N.: Angew. Chem. Int. Ed. *16*, 174 (1977)
40. Seki, Y., Hidaka, A., Makino, S., Murai, S., Sonoda, N.: J. Organometal. Chem. *140*, 361 (1977)
41. Chalk, A.J., Harrod, J.F.: J. Am. Chem. Soc. *89*, 1640 (1967)
42. Seki, Y., Murai, S., Hidaka, A., Sonoda, N.: Angew. Chem. Int. Ed. *16*, 881 (1977)
43. Seki, Y., Murai, S., Sonoda, N.: Angew. Chem. Int. Ed. *17*, 119 (1978)
44. Ojima, I., Kogure, T., Nagai, Y.: Tetrahedron Lett. 5085 (1972)
45. Ojima, I., Nihonyanagi, M., Kogure, T., Kumagai, M., Horiuchi, S., Nakatsugama, K.: J. Organometal. Chem. *94*, 449 (1975)
46. Ojima, I., Kogure, T., Nihonyanagi, M., Nagai, Y.: Bull. Chem. Soc. Japan, *45*, 3506 (1972)
47. Lappert, M.F., Nile, T.A.: J. Organometal. Chem. *102*, 543 (1975)
48. Barlow, A.P., Boag, N.M., Stone, F.G.A.: J. Organometal. Chem. *191*, 39 (1980)
49. Bourhis, R., Frainnet, E.: J. Organometal. Chem. *28*, C11 (1971)
50. Suzuki, H., Koyama, Y., Moro-Oka, Y., Ikawa, T.: Tetrahedron Lett. 1415 (1979)
51. Bloomfield, J.J.: Tetrahedron Lett. 587 (1968).
52. Stork, G., Singh, J.: J. Am. Chem. Soc. *96*, 6181 (1974)
53. Donaldson, R.E., Fuchs, P.L.: J. Org. Chem. *42*, 2032 (1977)
54. Pande, G.C., Pande, L.M.: Synthesis, 450 (1975)
55. Hashimoto, S., Itoh, A., Kitagawa, Y., Yamamoto, H., Nozaki, H.: J. Am. Chem. Soc. *99*, 4192 (1977)
56. Kuo, Y.N., Chen, J., Ainsworth, C., Bloomfield, J.J.: J. Chem. Soc. Chem. Commun. 136 (1971)
57. Krüger, C.R., Rochow, E.G.: J. Organometal. Chem. *1*, 476 (1964)
58. House, H.O., Czuba, L.J., Gall, M., Olmstead, H.D.: J. Org. Chem. *34*, 2324 (1969)
59. Posner, G.H., Sterling, J.J., Whitten, C.E., Lentz, C.M., Brunelle, D.J.: J. Am. Chem. Soc. *97*, 107 (1975)

60. Tanabe, M., Crowe, D.F.: J. Chem. Soc. Chem. Commun. 564 (1973)
61. Rathke, M.W., Sullivan, D.F.: Syn. Commun. *3*, 67 (1973)
62. Hudrlik, P.F., Takacs, J.M.: J. Org. Chem. *43*, 3861 (1978)
63. Brown, C.A.: J. Org. Chem. *39*, 1324 (1974)
64. Nakamura, E., Murofushi, T., Shimizu, M., Kuwajima, I.: J. Am. Chem. Soc. *98*, 2346 (1976)
65. Fessenden, R.J., Fessenden, J.S.: J. Org. Chem. *32*, 3535 (1967)
66. Nakamura, E., Hashimoto, K., Kuwajima, I.: Tetrahedron Lett. 2079 (1978)
67. House, H.O., Gall, M., Olmstead, H.D.: J. Org. Chem. *36*, 2361 (1971)
68. Olah, G.A., Gupta, B.G.B., Narang, S.C., Malhotra, R.: J. Org. Chem. *44*, 4272 (1979)
69. Miller, R.D., McKean, D.R.: Synthesis, 730 (1979)
70. Reuss, R.H., Hassner, A.: J. Org. Chem. *39*, 1785 (1974)
71. Simchen, G., Kober, W.: Synthesis, 259 (1976)
72. Simchen, G., West, W.: Synthesis, 247 (1977)
73. Hellberg, L.H., Juarez, A.: Tetrahedron Lett. 3553 (1974)
74. Hudrlik, P.F., Schwartz, R.H., Kulkarni, A.K.: Tetrahedron Lett. 2233 (1979)
75. Soderquist, J.A., Hassner, A.: J. Am. Chem. Soc. *102*, 1577 (1980)
76. Soderquist, J.A., Hassner, A.: J. Org. Chem. *45*, 451 (1980)
77. Clinet, J.C., Linstrumelle, G.: Tetrahedron Lett. 3987 (1980)
78. Hayashi, T., Yamamoto, K., Kumada, M.: Tetrahedron Lett. 3 (1975)
79. Yamamoto, K., Suzuki, S., Tsuji, J.: Tetrahedron Lett. 1653 (1980)

17 Ionic Hydrogenations

17.1 Introduction

Many reactions of silicon reagents may be classified as reductions. In this Chapter we will consider reactions in which hydrogen is added to an unsaturated functional group stepwise as a proton and a hydride ion. Major contributions to our understanding of this reaction have been made by Kursanov's group.

$$H_2C=CH_2 \ + \ H^+ \ \longrightarrow \ \left[H_3\overset{+}{C}-CH_2 \right] \ \overset{H^-}{\longrightarrow} \ H_3C-CH_3 \qquad (17.1)$$

It should be noted that the hydrosilation reaction of alkenes and alkynes which bears a strong analogy to catalytic hydrogenation has been previously considered (see Chapters 7 and 10).

17.2 Ionic Hydrogenation of Alkenes – Reduction of Carbocations

The reaction of methylcyclohexene, trifluoroacetic acid and triethylsilane in methylene chloride to yield methylcyclohexane and trifluoroacetoxytriethylsilane is an example of an ionic hydrogenation [1].

$$\text{(structure)} + Et_3SiH \ \xrightarrow{CF_3CO_2H} \ \text{(structure)} + Et_3SiO-\overset{\overset{\displaystyle O}{\|}}{C}-CF_3 \qquad (17.2)$$

Similarly, methylcyclopentene, 2-methyl-2-butene, 2-methyl-1-butene, 2-methyl-1-pentene [2], $\Delta^{9,10}$ octalin and 3-methyl-2-chloestene [3] are reduced under these conditions. Whereas, cyclohexene, 1-hexene, and 2-hexene are not. The reaction is a two-step process. The first step is the formation of a carbocation center. This can be accomplished by protonation of a substituted alkene by trifluoroacetic acid. The stability of triethylsilane to acid limits the reaction conditions. Triethylsilane is stable to trifluoroacetic acid, ($H_0 = -3.15$) but not to stronger mineral acids such as sulfuric, or conc. HCl. Hence the reaction is limited to alkenes which can be protonated to yield carbocations by

273

trifluoroacetic acid. Substituted alkenes which yield tertiary carbocations on protonation are reduced, whereas alkenes which yield secondary carbocations ions are, in general, not. Alternatively, the carbocation center can be generated by ionization of a covalent precursor. The second step involves transfer of a hydride from a silane, usually triethylsilane, to the carbocation center [4]. This affects the addition of a molecule of hydrogen to a $C-C$ double bond, as a proton and a hydride ion. The anion associated with the carbocation ion, often trifluoroacetate becomes covalently bonded to silicon.

Ionic hydrogenation permits the facile specific mono or di-deuteration of alkenes, by the use of either triethylsilane-d_1, or trifluoroacetic acid-d_1 or a combination of these reagents [5, 6].

$$\text{(17.3)}$$

The thermodynamic driving force for the transfer of a hydride from a silane to a carbocation results not only from the greater strength of the $C-H$ bond formed compared to the $Si-H$ bond broken [7] but also from the formation of a strong $Si-O$ bond [8]. The reaction of trimethylsilane with t-butyl carbocation is exothermic by 8 kcal/mol on the basis of appearance potential data [7].

The first examples of transfer of hydride from a silane to a carbocation were reported by Whitmore over thirty years ago. He found that when n-hexyl chloride was treated with triethylsilane and a catalytic amount of AlCl$_3$, n-hexane and triethylchlorosilane were formed. The fact that neopentyl chloride gave isopentane under these conditions provides additional evidence that carbocation intermediates are involved [9].

$$\text{(17.4)}$$

Reduction of secondary carbocations by silanes is competitive with their rearrangement to tertiary carbocations. Thus reaction of cycloheptyl bromide with triethylsilane and a catalytic amount of AlCl$_3$ yields a mixture of cycloheptane and methylcyclohexane. A similar reaction with the less reactive n-butylsilane yields methylcyclohexane and only a trace of unrearranged cycloheptane [10].

$$\left[\bigcirc + \right] \xrightarrow{\text{Et}_3\text{SiH}} \bigcirc$$

$$\xrightarrow{\hspace{3cm}} \left[\bigcirc + \right] \xrightarrow{\text{Et}_3\text{SiH}} \bigcirc \qquad (17.5)$$

Alkyl halides which ionize to carbocation/halide ion pairs are reduced by silanes in the absence of AlCl$_3$. Thus, triphenylmethyl chloride is reduced by either triphenylsilane or triethylsilane to triphenylmethane in methylene chloride, a solvent in which triphenylmethyl chloride dissociates to a triphenylmethyl carbocation/chloride ion pair. On the other hand, the reduction does not occur in solvents such as benzene or cyclohexane in which triphenylmethyl chloride does not dissociate. The rate of this reaction depends to the first order on both the concentration of the silane and triphenylmethyl chloride [11]. Although a four-center transition state in which the triphenylmethyl carbocation/chloride ion pair reacts with a silane to simultaneously form new Si–Cl and C–H bonds is attractive, careful study with optically active α-naphthylphenylmethylsilane does not support this suggestion. Retention of configuration at the chiral silicon center is predicted for such a four-center transition state. However, in a variety of solvents significant racemization of α-naphthylphenylmethylchlorosilane is observed [12, 13].

$$\left[\begin{array}{c} {}^{-\delta} \quad {}^{+\delta} \\ \text{Cl}\cdots\text{CPh}_3 \\ \alpha\text{-Np}\!\!-\!\!\text{Si}\cdots\text{H} \\ \diagup\quad\diagdown \\ \text{Ph}\quad\text{CH}_3 \end{array} \right] \xrightarrow{\hspace{2cm}} \begin{array}{c} \text{Cl} \\ | \\ \alpha\text{-Np}\!\!-\!\!\text{Si} \\ \diagup\quad\diagdown \\ \text{Ph}\quad\text{CH}_3 \end{array} + \text{Ph}_3\text{CH} \qquad (17.6)$$

Prochiral carbocations are reduced by chiral silanes to optically active alkanes (2–3 % e.e.). For example, the 2-phenyl-2-butyl carbocation, generated from either R, or S-2-phenyl-2-butanol or from 2-phenyl-1-butene by treatment with trifluoroacetic acid, is reduced by R-α-naphthylphenylmethylsilane to optically active 2-phenylbutane (2–3 % e.e. R). Likewise, this carbocation is reduced by S-α-naphthylphenylmethylsilane to optically active 2-phenylbutane (2–3 % e.e. S). This is consistent with a tight transition state for transfer of hydride from the chiral silane to the symmetrical prochiral carbocation [14, 15].

Carey has studied the reduction, by triethylsilane, of a wide range of triarylmethyl, diphenylmethyl and benzyl carbocations. These have been generated by treatment of the corresponding alcohols with trifluoroacetic acid. Carbocations whose stability is between that of tris-(2,6-dimethoxyphenyl)methyl carbocation (pK$_R$ 6.5) and 2,4,6-trimethylbenzyl carbocation (pK$_R$– 17.4) are reduced. The rate of these reductios depends on the concentration of both the silane and the carbocation. As might be expected, triarylsilanes substituted with electron donating groups are more reactive reducing agents than those substituted with electron withdrawing groups [Ar$_3$Si–H, p = – 1.84, Ar(CH$_3$)$_2$Si–H, p = – 1.01]. The small isotope effect observed for breaking the Si−H bond (Ph$_3$Si−H/Ph$_3$Si−D = 1.5 to 1.89) in these reactions [16] is consistant with a non-linear transition state [17]. While benzyl and cinnamyl alcohols are not reduced under these conditions [18], compounds which ionize to form secondary benzylic carbocations are reduced. Thus treatment of 1-trifluoroacetoxy-1-phenylethane with trifluoroacetic and triethylsilane leads to phenylethane [19, 20]. The triethylsilane reduction of a diphenylmethyl carbocation formed by ionization of a phthalide ester has been recently reported [21].

$$\xrightarrow[\text{Et}_3\text{SiH}]{\text{CF}_3\text{CO}_2\text{H}}$$

(17.7)

In the case of ionic hydrogenation of alkenes in which two stereoisomeric products can be formed, the product or ratio of products obtained does not depend on the stereochemistry of the precursor. For example, *exo* and *endo* 2-phenyl-2-norbornanol as well as 2-phenyl norbornene yield *endo*-2-phenyl norbornane on treatment with trifluoroacetic acid and triethylsilane in methylene chloride. Apparently, *exo* addition of hydride to the 2-phenyl norbornyl carbocation (pK$_R$ = −13) is highly favored [22].

(17.8)

This is consistent with a reaction which involves a common carbocation intermediate. On the other hand, the stereochemistry of the product or the ratio of stereoisomers produced depends on the nature of the silane reducing agent, in particular on its steric bulk. For example, reduction of the 4-*t*-butyl-1-phenylcyclohexyl carbocation (generated from either *cis* or *trans*-4-*t*-butyl-1-phenylcyclohexanol or 4-*t*-butyl-1-phenylcyclohexene) gives a mixture of *cis* and *trans*-4-*t*-butyl-1-phenylcyclohexane which depends on the silane reducing agent. The ratio of *trans* to *cis* is 2 for triethylsilane while it is 4.5 for diethylsilane [23]. The steric effect of a series of alkyl silanes on a ratio of *cis* to *trans* decalin produced by ionic hydrogenation of $\Delta^{9,10}$ octalin has been studied. Sterically hindered trialkylsilanes favor formation of *cis*-decalin [24].

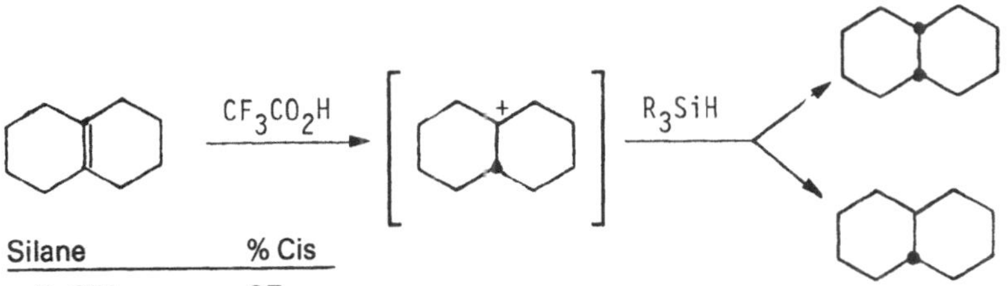

(17.9)

Silane	% Cis
n-BuSiH3	27
Et3SiH	42
(sec-Bu)3SiH	72
(t-Bu)3SiH	93

17.3 Stability of Functional Groups to Ionic Hydrogenation

Ionic hydrogenation tolerates a variety of functional groups. Carboxylic acids, esters, amides, nitriles, nitro groups, sulfonic esters, as well as most aromatic nuclei are not reduced under ionic hydrogenation conditions [4]. This permits the selective reduction of substituted C–C double bonds in the presence of a variety of functional groups [6, 25, 26].

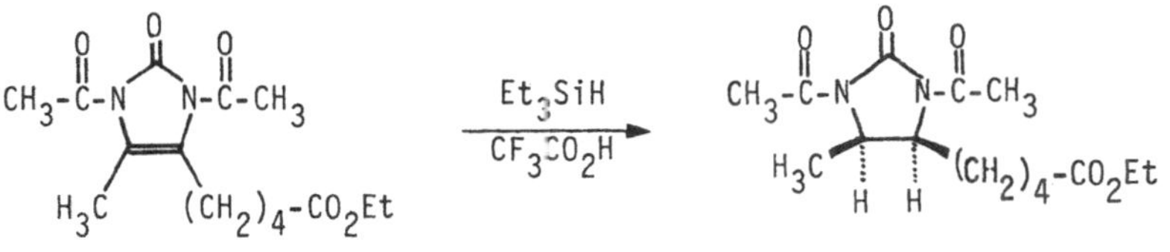

(17.10)

While both C–C double bonds of alkyl substituted conjugated 1,3-dienes are reduced under ionic hydrogenation conditions, it is possible to selectively reduce a non-conjugated tri-substituted alkene in the presence of a mono-substituted alkene [27].

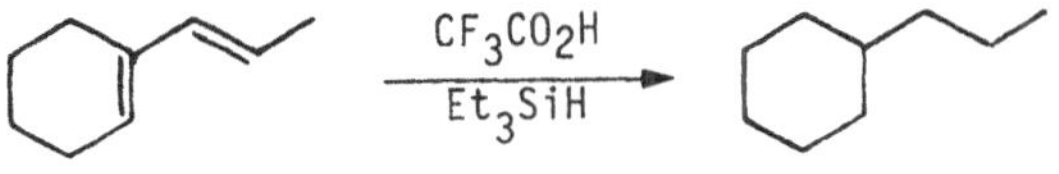

(17.11)

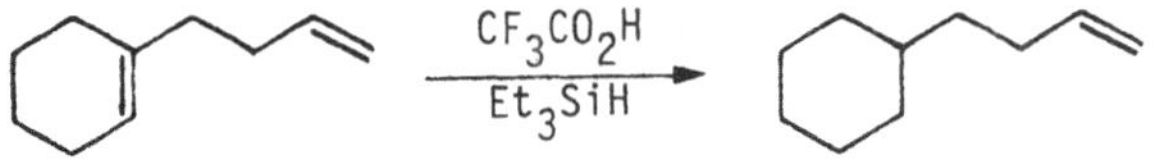

(17.12)

17.4 Ionic Hydrogenation — Reduction of Non-Classical Carbocations

2-Norbornene is reduced, albeit, in poor yield (3.5%) on treatment with triethylsilane and trifluoroacetic acid. This probably results from the unusual stability of the 2-norboryl carbocation. Treatment of *exo*-6-methyl-2-norbornene with trifluoroacetic acid gave *endo*-2-methylnorbornane. Deuterium labeling was used to determine the nature of the carbocation reduced. Treatment of *exo*-6-methyl-2-norbornene with triethylsilane-d$_1$, gave *endo*-2-methyl-norbornane-2-d$_1$. Clearly, the initial secondary carbocation is converted to a tertiary carbocation, probably by a 1,6-hydride shift prior to reduction [28].

$$(17.13)$$

The unusual stability of the cyclopropyl carbinyl carbocation permits the reduction of vinyl cyclopropane under ionic hydrogenation conditions to yield ethylcyclopropane [29, 30]. Ring opened products have been observed only with cyclopropyl carbinyl carbocations which possess multiple carbocation stabilizing groups [31].

$$(17.14)$$

17.5 Ionic Hydrogenation of Sigma Bonds

There are a few types of sigma bonds which are protonated by trifluoroacetic acid. These undergo heterolysis to yield carbocations which are reduced under the conditions of ionic hydrogenation. For example, alkyl substituted cyclopropanes which can open on protonation to yield tertiary carbocations are reduced on treatment with trifluoroacetic acid and triethylsilane [32, 33].

$$(17.15)$$

Ethylcyclopropane is not, however, reduced under these conditions since it can only form secondary carbocations on protonation and ring opening [34]. Isopropylcyclopropane, however, undergoes reduction to yield 2-methylpentane. Reduction with triethylsilane-d_1 has served to clarify this apparent contradiction. With triethylsilane-d_1, 2-methylpentane-2-d_1 is formed exclusively. Opening of the cyclopropane ring and 1,2-hydride migration to form a tertiary carbocation may occur simultaneously [35–37].

(17.16)

Aliphatic and many aromatic disulfides can be reduced to the corresponding thiols under ionic hydrogenation conditions. The reaction may proceed by initial protonation of one of the sulfur atoms. Cleavage of the S−S sigma bond then yields a thiol and a sulfenium cation which is reduced by hydride transfer from triethylsilane [38].

$$n\text{-BuS-S-}n\text{-Bu} \xrightarrow{\text{CF}_3\text{CO}_2\text{H}} n\text{-BuSH} + \left[n\text{-BuS}^+\right] \xrightarrow{\text{Et}_3\text{SiH}} n\text{-BuSH} \quad (17.17)$$

Similarly, ethers, which on protonation of oxygen, can undergo C−O bond heterolysis to yield stable carbocations, undergo reduction. For example, t-butyl ethyl ether reacts with trifluoroacetic acid and triethylsilane to yield isobutane and ethanol. bis-Diphenylmethyl ether is reduced to diphenylmethane [39, 40].

17.6 Reduction of Ketones

Kursanov's also reported the ionic hydrogenation of ketones [2, 41]. Thus cyclohexanone reacts with triethylsilane in the presence of trifluoroacetic acid to yield trifluoroacetoxycyclohexane. The reaction most probably proceeds by initial protonation of the oxygen of the carbonyl group to yield a hydroxy stabilized carbocation which reacts with triethylsilane to yield cyclohexanol. Cyclohexanol does not undergo further reduction. On the other hand, acetophenone and benzophenone are reduced initially to 1-phenylethanol and diphenylmethanol, respectively. These undergo further reduction under the reaction conditions to phenylethane and diphenylmethane [41, 42].

(17.18)

$$Ph-\overset{O}{\overset{\|}{C}}-CH_3 \xrightarrow{CF_3CO_2H} \left[Ph-\overset{OH}{\underset{+}{\overset{|}{C}}}-CH_3 \right] \xrightarrow{Et_3SiH} Ph-\overset{OH}{\underset{H}{\overset{|}{C}}}-CH_3 \qquad (17.19)$$

$$\xrightarrow{CF_3CO_2H} \left[Ph-\overset{+}{\underset{H}{\overset{|}{C}}}-CH_3 \right] \xrightarrow{Et_3SiH} PhCH_2CH_3$$

The reduction of 1,1-dibenzoylethane to 2-methyl-1,3-diphenyl propane, however, proved complicated [43].

17.7 Reduction of Aldehydes

Treatment of aldehydes with triethylsilane and trifluoroacetic acid yields a mixture of alcohols and symmetrical ethers. For example, benzaldehyde yields dibenzyl ether. The formation of ethers occurs by reaction of the initially formed alcohol with additional aldehyde to yield a hemi-acetal. Protonation of the hemi-acetal leads to loss of water and formation of a stabilized carbocation which is reduced by triethylsilane, to yield the ether. Consistent with this hypothesis, treatment of a mixture of *n*-pentanal and *n*-butanol with trifluoroacetic acid and triethylsilane yields *n*-amyl *n*-butyl ether [44, 45].

$$CH_3(CH_2)_3-\overset{O}{\overset{\|}{C}}-H + CH_3(CH_2)_2CH_2OH \xrightarrow{CF_3CO_2H} CH_3(CH_2)_3-\overset{OH}{\underset{O(CH_2)_3CH_3}{\overset{|}{C}}}-H \qquad (17.20)$$

$$\xrightarrow[Et_3SiH]{CF_3CO_2H} CH_3(CH_2)_3\overset{CH_2}{\underset{O(CH_2)_3CH_3}{\overset{|}{C}}}$$

The diethylketal of cyclohexanone undergoes reduction with triethylsilane in trifluoroacetic acid to yield cyclohexyl ethyl ether [46].

$$(17.21)$$

Ketals and acetals can also be reduced to ethers by treatment with trimethylsilane and a catalytic amount of trimethylsilyl triflate [47].

17.8 Reduction of N-Alkyl Nitrilium and N-Acyliminium Salts

N-Alkyl nitrilium ions are reduced by triethylsilane to yield N-alkylaldimines which can be hydrolyzed to aldehydes [48, 49].

$$(17.22)$$

Evidence for the intermediacy of N-acyliminium ions in a 2-aza Cope rearrangement has been obtained by their reduction *in-situ* with triethylsilane and trifluoroacetic acid [50].

$$(17.23)$$

17.9 Reduction of α,β-Unsaturated Ketones

Ionic hydrogenation of α,β-unsaturated ketones and aldehydes results in preferential reduction of the C—C double bond. Reaction of methyl vinyl ketone or benzalacetophenone with one equivalent of triethylsilane in the presence of a large excess of trifluoroacetic acid yields 2-butanone or 1,3-diphenyl-1-propanone, respectively [51]. Likewise, 2-benzylidene -1,3-indanediones are reduced to 2-benzyl-1,3-indanediones on treatment with triethylsilane and trifluoroacetic acid [52].

$$(17.24)$$

With excess triethylsilane, α,β-unsaturated ketones under further reduction to saturated alcohols. For example, mesityl oxide is reduced to 4-methyl-2-pentanol while benzalacetophenone yields 1,3-diphenylpropane [53].

The reduction of quinones is related to the ionic hydrogenation of α,β-unsaturated ketones. Treatment of benzoquinone with triethylsilane and trifluoroacetic acid yields hydroquinone. On the other hand, naphthoquinone and 9,10-anthraquinone are reduced to tetralin and 9,10-hydroanthracene, respectively [54]. The extent of reduction may depend on the stability of the initially formed hydroquinones.

The ionic hydrogenation of mixed carboxylic trifluoroacetic anhydrides yields trifluoroacetoxyalkanes [55].

$$(CH_3)_3C-\overset{O}{\overset{\|}{C}}\diagdown_{O}\diagup\overset{O}{\overset{\|}{C}}-CF_3 \xrightarrow[CF_3CO_2H]{Et_3SiH} (CH_3)_3CCH_2O-\overset{O}{\overset{\|}{C}}-CF_3 \qquad (17.25)$$

17.10 Reduction of Heteroaromatic Nuclei-Thiophenes

While aromatic nuclei are not *in general* reduced under ionic hydrogenation conditions, certain heterocyclic aromatic nuclei are reduced. The reduction of substituted thiophenes is important. Thiophenes cannot be reduced to tetrahydrothiophenes or thiophanes under usual catalytic hydrogenation conditions because the product sulfide poisons the Nobel catalyst. The reduction may occur by initial protonation of the thiophene ring at the two or the five positions. The delocalized allylic carbocation thus produced is reduced by hydride transfer from triethylsilane. The product, a 2,3-dihydrothiophene, then undergoes further reduction to the thiophane [56].

$$CH_3-\underset{S}{\diagdown\diagup}-CH_3 \xrightarrow[AlCl_3]{HCl} \left[CH_3-\underset{S}{\overset{+}{\diagdown\diagup}}\underset{H}{\diagdown}CH_3 \right] \xrightarrow{Et_3SiH} CH_3-\underset{S}{\diagdown\diagup}\underset{CH_3}{\diagdown}H \qquad (17.26)$$

$$\xrightarrow[Et_3SiH]{CF_3CO_2H} CH_3-\underset{S}{\diagdown\diagup}-CH_3$$

A number of phenyl substituted thiophenes have been reduced under ionic hydrogenation conditions to phenyl substituted tetrahydrothiophanes [57]. 2,2'-*bis*-Thiophene [1] has been reduced to 2,2'-octahydro-*bis*-thiophane [1] on treatment with triethylsilane and trifluoroacetic acid [58], while 2-acetyl thiophene yields 2-ethyltetrahydrothiophane [59].

$$\underset{S}{\diagdown\diagup}-\overset{O}{\overset{\|}{C}}-CH_3 \xrightarrow[CF_3CO_2H]{Et_3SiH} \left[\underset{S}{\diagdown\diagup}-\overset{OH}{\overset{\|}{CH}}-CH_3 \right] \xrightarrow[CF_3CO_2H]{Et_3SiH} \underset{S}{\diagdown\diagup}-CH_2\diagdown_{CH_3} \qquad (17.27)$$

$$\xrightarrow[CF_3CO_2H]{Et_3SiH} \underset{S}{\diagdown\diagup}-CH_2\diagdown_{CH_3}$$

The reduction of thiophenes under the usual ionic hydrogenation conditions is quite slow. The addition of a catalytic amount of $BF_3 \cdot OEt_2$ accelerates the reaction [59–61].

$$(17.28)$$

Reduction of the C–C double bond of 3-(β-methylallyl) benzothiophene occurs in preference to reduction of the thiophene nucleus.

$$(17.29)$$

On the other hand, the thiophene nucleus of 2-allyl-benzothiophene and the furan nucleus of 2-allyl-benzofuran are preferentially reduced [62].

$$(17.30)$$

In a similar manner, the pyrrole nucleus of indole is selectively reduced under ionic hydrogenation conditions [63, 64].

$$(17.31)$$

17.11 Reduction of Organometallic Complexes

Ionic hydrogenation has been utilized to reduce a number of transition metal organometallic complexes. α-Ferrocenyl alcohols, acetyl ferrocenes and vinyl ferrocenes are reduced under ionic hydrogenation conditions to yield alkyl substituted ferrocene derivatives. The rate of these reduction depends on the concentrations of both the α-ferrocenyl carbocation and triethylsilane [65–68].

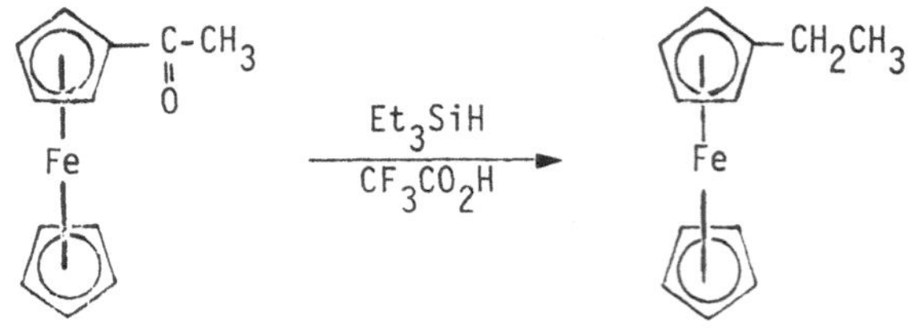

(17.32)

In a similar manner, acetyl, benzoyl, and formyl cyclopentadienyl manganese tricarbonyl complexes are reduced respectively to ethyl, benzyl, and methyl cyclopentadienyl manganese tricarbonyl complexes [69].

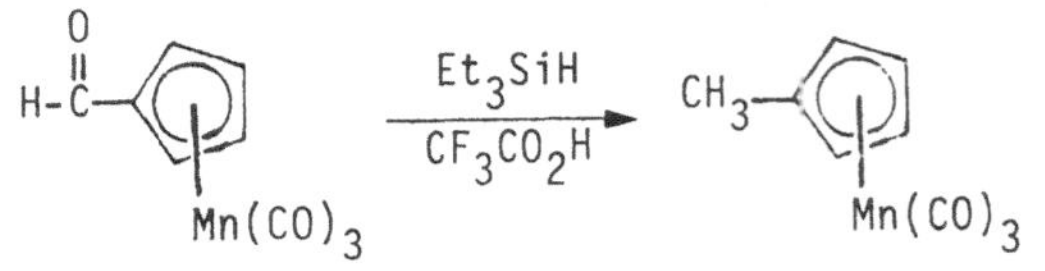

(17.33)

Acylidynetricobalt nonacarbonyl complexes are reduced under ionic hydrogenation conditions to alkyltricobalt nona carbonyl complexes [70, 71].

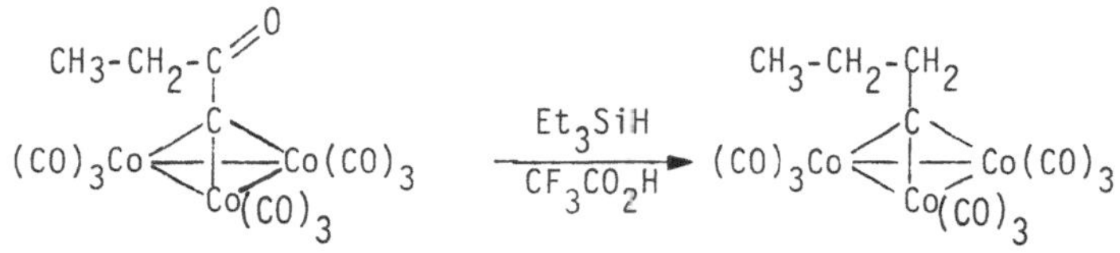

(17.34)

A benzylic alcohol π-anisole chromium tricarbonyl complex has been reduced to an alkyl π-anisole chromium tricarbonyl complex [72].

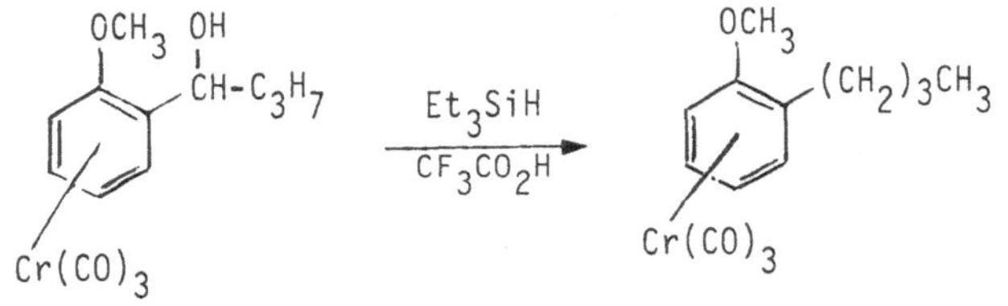

(17.35)

With the exception of the formyl manganese tricarbonyl complex just discussed, primary alcohols are not reduced under ionic hydrogenation conditions. However, N-hydroxymethyl groups are reduced on treatment with trifluoroacetic acid and triethylsilane to N-methyl groups [73].

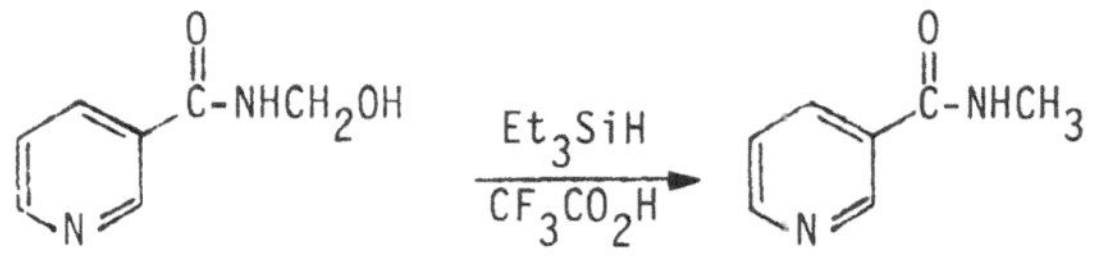

(17.36)

17.12 Improved Procedures

The rate accelerating effect of $BF_3 \cdot OEt_2$ on ionic hydrogenation of thiophene has been mentioned. It has been reported that $BF_3 \cdot H_2O$ can be substituted for trifluoroacetic acid to yield a more powerful reducing system. The acidity of $BF_3 \cdot H_2O$ may comparable to anhydrous sulfuric acid. Ketones such as 2-admantanone are reduced to adamantane, while polycyclic aromatic hydrocarbons such as anthracene are reduced to 9,10-dihydroanthracene by this new system [74]. The use of BF_3 in place of trifluoroacetic acid permits the reduction of aromatic [75] as well as aliphatic ketones [75], and secondary alcohols [76] to the corresponding alkanes.

$$CH_3(CH_2)_5 - \overset{OH}{\underset{|}{CH}} - CH_3 \quad \xrightarrow[BF_3]{Et_3SiH} \quad CH_3(CH_2)_6CH_3 \qquad (17.37)$$

Another practical improvement involves the use of polymethylsiloxane or polyethylsiloxane in place of triethylsilane. This may facilitate separation of the product [77].

$$Et_3SiO\left(\underset{\overset{|}{Et}}{\overset{\overset{H}{|}}{Si}}-O\right)_n SiEt_3 \quad \text{or} \quad (CH_3)_3SiO\left(\underset{\overset{|}{CH_3}}{\overset{\overset{H}{|}}{Si}}-O\right)_n Si(CH_3)_3 \qquad (17.38)$$

References

1. Parnes, Z.N., Zdanovich, V.I.. Kugucheva, E.E., Basova, G.I., Kursanov, D.N.: Dokl. Akad. Nauk. SSSR, *166*, 122 (1966)
2. Kursanov, D.N., Parnes, Z.N., Bassova, G.I., Loim, N.M., Zdanovich. V.I : Tetrahedron, *23*, 2235 (1967)
3. Carey, F.A., Tremper, H.S.: J. Org. Chem. *36*, 758 (1971)
4. Kursanov, D.N., Parnes, Z.N., Loim, N.M.: Synthesis, 633 (1974)
5. Parnes, Z.N., Khotimskaya, G.A., Lyakhovestskii, Y.I., Petrovskii, P.V.: Izv. Akad. Nauk. SSSR Ser. Khim 1562 (1972)
6. Guillerm, G., Frappier, F., Tabet, J.C., Marquet, A.: J. Org. Chem. *42*, 3776 (1977)
7. Hess, G.G., Lampe, F.W., Sommer, L.H.: J. Am. Chem. Soc. *87*, 5327 (1965)
8. Ebsworth, E.A.V., Physical Basis of the Chemistry of the Group IV Elements in Organometallic Compounds of the Group IV Elements, (MacDiarmid, A.G., Ed.), p. 46, New York: M. Dekker, 1968
9. Whitmore, F.C., Pietrusza, E.W., Sommer, L.H.: J. Am. Chem. Soc. *69*, 2108 (1947)
10. Doyle, M.P., McOsker, C.C., West, C.T.: J. Org. Chem. *41*, 1393 (1976)
11. Corey, J.Y., West, R.: J. Am. Chem. Soc. *85*, 2430 (1963)
12. Austin, J.D., Eaborn, C.: J. Chem. Soc. 2279 (1964)
13. Sommer, L.H., Bauman, D.L.: J. Am. Chem. Soc. *91*, 7076 (1969)
14. Fry, J.L.: J. Am. Chem. Soc. *93*, 3558 (1971)
15. Fry, J.L., Adlington, M.G.: J. Am. Chem. Soc. *100*, 7641 (1978)
16. Carey, F.A., Hsu, C.L.W.: J. Organometal. Chem. *19*, 29 (1969)

17. Lewis, E.S., Grinstein, R.H.: J. Am. Chem. Soc. *84*, 1158 (1962)
18. Carey, F.A., Tremper, H.S.: J. Am. Chem. Soc. *90*, 2578 (1968)
19. Parnes, Z.N., Kalinkin, M.I., Tsyryapkin, V.A., Khamitova, R.F., Kursanov, D.N.: Dokl. Akad. Nauk. SSSR, *203*, 600 (1972)
20. Serebryakova, T.A., Parnes, Z.N., Zakharychev, A.V., Ananchenko, S.N., Torgov, I.V.: Izv. Akad. Nauk. SSSR Ser. Khim. 725 (1969)
21. Newman, M.S., Kanakarajan, K.: J. Org. Chem. *45*, 2301 (1980)
22. Carey, F.A., Tremper, H.S.: J. Org. Chem. *34*, 4 (1969)
23. Carey, F.A., Tremper, H.S.: J. Am. Chem. Soc. *90*, 2578 (1968)
24. Doyle, M.P., McOsker, C.C.: J. Org. Chem. *43*, 693 (1978)
25. Kursanov, D.N., Kalinkin, M.I., Gridchin, S.A., Shatalov, G.V., Parnes, Z.N.: Izv. Akad. Nauk. SSSR Ser. Khim. 803 (1979)
26. Akhrem, A.A., Moiseenkov, A.M., Krivoruchko, V.A.: Izv. Akad. Nauk. SSSR, 1800 (1973)
27. Kursanov, D.N., Parnes, Z.N., Bolestova, G.I.: Dokl. Akad. Nauk. SSSR, *181*, 1132 (1968)
28. Bolestova, G.I., Parnes, Z.N., Belikova, N.A., Kursanov, Z.D.: Izv. Akad. Nauk. SSSR Ser. Khim. 798 (1979)
29. Parnes, Z.N., Khotimskaya, G.A., Lukina, N.Y., Kursanov, D.N.: Dokl. Akad. Nauk. SSSR, *178*, 620 (1968)
30. Mazur, R.H., White, W.N., Semenow, D.A., Lee, C.C., Silver, M.S., Roberts, J.D.: J. Am. Chem. Soc. *81*, 4390 (1959)
31. Carey, F.A., Tremper, H.S.: J. Am. Chem. Soc. *91*, 2967 (1969)
32. Parnes, Z.N., Khotimskaya, G.A., Lukina, N.Y., Kursanov, D.N.: Dokl. Akad. Nauk. SSSR, *178*, 620 (1968)
33. Parnes, Z.N., Khotimskaya, G.A., Kudryavtsev, R.V., Kursanov, D.N.: Izv. Akad. Nauk. SSSR Ser. Khim. 901 (1972)
34. Khotimskaya, G.A., Kudryavtsev, R.V., Mil'vitskaya, E.M., Plate, A.F., Parnes, Z.N.: Izv. Akad. Nauk. SSSR Ser. Khim. 1989 (1972)
35. Parnes, Z.N., Khotimskaya, G.A., Lukina, M.Y., Kursanov, D.N.: Dokl. Akad. Nauk. SSSR, *178*, 620 (1968)
36. Parnes, Z.N., Khotimskaya, G.A., Kudryavtsev, R.V., Lukina, N.Y., Kursanov, D.N.: Dokl. Akad. Nauk. SSSR, *184*, 615 (1969)
37. Kursanov, D.N., Khotimskaya, G.A., Fedin, E.I., Lukina, M.Y., Parnes, Z.N.: Izv. Akad. Nauk. SSSR, Ser. Khim., 746 (1969)
38. Kalinkin, M.I., Parnes, Z.N., Kursanov, D.N.: Dokl. Akad. Nauk. SSSR, *180*, 1370 (1968)
39. Zdanovich, V.I., Kudryavtsev, R.V., Kursanov, D.N.: Dokl. Akad. Nauk. SSSR, *182*, 593 (1968)
40. Verheyden, J.P.H., Richardson, A.C., Bhatt, R.S., Grant, B.D., Fitch, W.L., Moffatt, J.G.: Pure and Applied Chem. *50*, 1363 (1978)
41. Kursanov, D.N., Parnes, Z.N., Loim, N.M.: Izv. Akad. Nauk. SSSR Ser. Khim. 1289 (1966)
42. West, C.T., Donnelly, S.J., Kooistra, D.A., Doyle, M.P.: J. Org. Chem. *38*, 2675 (1973)
43. Mozhaev, G.M., Parnes, Z.N., Zalukaeva, L.P., Kursanov, D.N.: Zhur. Org. Khim. *14*, 1657 (1978)
44. Kursanov, D.N., Parnes, Z.N., Loim, N.M., Bakalova, G.V.: Dokl. Akad. Nauk. SSSR, *179*, 1106 (1968)
45. Loim, N.M., Parnes, Z.N., Vasil'eva, S.P., Kursanov, D.N.: Zhur. Org. Khim. *8*, 896 (1972)
46. Doyle, M.P., DeBruyn, D.J., Kooistra, D.A.: J. Am. Chem. Soc. *94*, 3659 (1972)

47. Tsunoda, T., Suzuki, M., Noyori, R.: Tetrahedron Lett. 4679 (1979)
48. Fry, J.L., Ott, R.A.: J. Org. Chem. *46*, 602 (1981)
49. Meerwein, H., Laasch, P., Mersch, R., Spille, J.: Chem. Ber. *89*, 209 (1956)
50. Hart, D.J., Tsai, Y.M.: Tetrahedron Lett. 1567 (1981)
51. Kursanov, D.N., Loim, N.M., Baranova, V.A., Moiseeva, L.V., Zalukaev, L.P., Parnes, Z.N.: Synthesis, 420 (1973)
52. Loim, N.M., Baranova, V.A., Moiseeva, L.V., Zalukaev, L.P., Parnes, Z.N., Kursanov, D.N.: Izv. Akad. Nauk. SSSR Ser. Khim. 843 (1974)
53. Parnes, Z.N., Loim, N.M., Baranova, V.A., Kursanov, D.N.: Zhur. Org. Khim. *7*, 2066 (1971)
54. Loim, N.M., Parnes, Z.N., Brunovlenskaya, I.I., Kursanov, D.N.: Dokl. Akad. Nauk. SSSR, *196*, 1361 (1971)
55. Kalinkin, M.I., Kolomnikova, G.D., Parnes, Z.N., Kursanov, D.N.: Izv. Akad. Nauk. SSSR Ser. Khim. 1902 (1976)
56. Parnes, Z.N., Lyakhovetsky, Y.I., Kalinkin, M.I., Kursanov, D.N., Belenkii, L.I.: Tetrahedron, *34*, 1703 (1978)
57. Parnes, Z.N., Bolestova, G.I., Dolgova, S.P., Udre, V.E., Voronkov, M.G., Kursanov, D.N.: Izv. Akad. Nauk. SSSR Ser. Khim. 1834 (1974)
58. Rudakov, E.S., Parnes, Z.N., Osipov, A.M., Lyakhovetskii, Y.I., Kursanov, D.N.: Izv. Akad. Nauk. SSSR Ser. Khim. 1173 (1976)
59. Kursanov, D.N., Parnes, Z.N., Bolestova, G.I., Belenkii, L.I.: Tetrahedron, *31*, 311 (1975)
60. Parnes, Z.N., Bolestova, G.I., Kursanov, D.N.: Izv. Akad. Nauk. SSSR, 478 (1976)
61. Parnes, Z.N., Bolestova, G.I., Kursanov, D.N.: Zhur. Org. Khim. *13*, 476 (1977)
62. Anisimov, A.V., Luzikov, Y.N., Nikolaeva, V.M., Viktorova, E.A.: Zhur. Org. Khim. *15*, 172 (1979)
63. Parnes, Z.N., Budylin, V.A., Beilinson, E.Y., Kost, A.N.: Zhur. Org. Khim. *8*, 2564 (1972)
64. Lanzilotti, A.E., Littell, R., Fanshawe, W.J., McKenszie, T.C., Lovell, F.M.: J. Org. Chem. *44*, 4809 (1979)
65. Kazakova, L.I., Loim, N.M., Perevalova, E.G., Parnes, Z.N.: Zhur. Obsh. Khim. *43*, 2306 (1973)
66. Nesmeyanov, A.N., Rybinskaya, M.I., Shul'pin, G.B., Tolstaya, M.V.: Dokl. Akad. Nauk. SSSR, *229*, 1124 (1976)
67. Nesmeyanov, A.N., Shul'pin, G.B., Rybinskaya, M.I.: Izv. Akad. Nauk. SSSR Ser. Khim. 2824 (1975)
68. Kazakova, L.I., Loim, N.M., Parnes, Z.N.: Zhur. Obsh. Khim. *43*, 1577 (1973)
69. Kursanov, D.N., Anisimov, K.N., Parnes, Z.N., Loim, N.M., Zlotina I.B, Valueva, Z.P.: Izv. Akad. Nauk. SSSR Ser. Khim. 713 (1972)
70. Seyferth, D., Hung, P.L.K., Hallgren, J.E.: J. Organometal. Chem. *44*, C66 (1972)
71. Seyferth, D., Williams, G.H., Eschbach, C.S., Nestle, M.O., Merola, J.S. Hallgren, J.E.: J. Am. Chem. Soc. *101*, 4867 (1979)
72. Semmelhack, M.F., Bisaha, J., Czarny, M.: J. Am. Chem. Soc. *101*, 768 (1979)
73. Auerbach, J., Zamore, M., Weinreb, S.M.: J. Org. Chem. *41*, 725 (1976)
74. Larson, J.W., Chang, L.W.: J. Org. Chem. *44*, 1168 (1979)
75. Fry, J.L., Orfanopoulos, M., Adlington, M.G., Dittman, Jr., W.R., Silverman, S.B: J. Org. Chem. *43*, 374 (1978)
76. Adlington, M.G., Orfanopoulos, M., Fry, J.L.: Tetrahedron Lett. 2955 (1976)
77. Parnes, Z.N., Bolestova, G.I., Intyakova, E.I., Kursanov, D.N.: Zhur. Org. Khim. *9*, 1704 (1973)

18 Reduction of Polar Multiple Bonds by Hydrosilation

18.1 Introduction

The reduction of ketones to alcohols by heterogeneous catalytic hydrogenation over noble metal catalysts is well-known. The discovery that olefins could be hydrogenated in the presence of the homogeneous catalyst [Ph$_3$P]$_3$RhCl, stimulated the search for similar catalysts which would permit the reduction of ketones [1]. While homogeneous catalytic hydrogenation of ketones has not developed, the homogeneous catalytic hydrosilation of ketones to yield alkyl silyl ethers has blossomed. These can be easily hydrolyzed to alcohols.

18.2 Hydrosilation of Ketones and Aldehydes

Platinum, ruthenium, rhodium, and nickel catalysts have all proved effective for the hydrosilation of ketones and aldehydes. A catalyst formed by reaction of nickel (II) chloride and triethylsilane facilitates the hydrosilation of aliphatic aldehydes. A mixture of alkyl triethylsilyl ethers, dialkyl ethers, and hexaethyldisiloxane is obtained [2].

$$(CH_3)_2CH\text{-}\overset{\overset{\text{O}}{\|}}{C}\text{-}H$$

$$Et_3SiH \downarrow NiCl_2$$

$$(CH_3)_2CH\text{-}CH_2OSiEt_3 \ + \ (CH_3)_2CHOCH(CH_3)_2 \ + \ Et_3SiOSiEt_3 \qquad (18.1)$$

The ratio of triethylsilane to aldehyde as well as the reaction temperature effects the ratio of products. Hydrosilation of ketones with triethylsilane with this catalyst yields predominantly alkyl triethylsilyl ethers. Modification of the catalyst by addition of phenyl thiol yields principally triethylsilyl enol ethers [3].

$$Et_3SiH + \text{[cyclohexanone]} \xrightarrow{NiCl_2} \text{[OSiEt}_3\text{ cyclohexyl] } 84\% \quad \text{[OSiEt}_3\text{ cyclohexenyl] } 11\% \quad (18.2)$$

$$\xrightarrow[PhSH]{NiCl_2} \quad 11\% \quad 84\%$$

Wilkinson's catalyst, [Ph₃P]₃RhCl, has proved exceptionally active for the hydrosilation of aliphatic ketones with triethylsilane. The reaction is complete in minutes at 0 °C. Hydrosilation of alkyl aryl ketones is slower, acetophenone requires heating at 60 °C for 15 minutes [4].

$$\text{[cyclohexanone]} + Et_3SiH \xrightarrow{[Ph_3P]_3RhCl} \text{[OSiEt}_3\text{ cyclohexyl]} \quad (18.3)$$

The reaction is fast with dihydro- and trihydrosilanes. Thus, the reaction of diethylsilane with acetophenone is exothermic at 0 °C [5, 6]. In the hydrosilation reaction of aldehydes or ketones, the analogous ruthenium complex RuCl₂(PPh₃)₂ is less active than Wilkinson's catalyst [7, 8]. With Wilkinson's catalyst, dihydrosilanes such as diphenylsilane, or α-naphthylphenylsilane yield only diarylalkoxysilanes [7].

$$Ph_2SiH_2 + (CH_3)_2C=O \xrightarrow{[Ph_3P]_3RhCl} \begin{array}{c} CH_3 \\ | \\ H-C-O-SiPh_2 \\ | \quad\quad | \\ CH_3 \quad H \end{array} \quad (18.4)$$

A yellow complex, (Ph₃P)₂RhHCl(SiEt₃) is formed on mixing triethylsilane and [Ph₃P]₃RhCl. This may result from oxidative addition of triethylsilane to coordinately unsaturated *bis*(triphenylphosphine)rhodium chloride formed by dissociation of a bulky triphenylphosphine ligand in solution [4, 6]. This complex has been suggested to be critical in the catalytic reaction sequence.

[Ph₃P]₃RhCl catalyzes the 1,4-hydrosilation of α,β-unsaturated ketones and aldehydes to yield silyl enol ethers. These undergo hydrolysis with methanolic potassium hydroxide to the corresponding ketones (see 16.8).

$$\text{[octalone]} + Et_3SiH \xrightarrow{[Ph_3P]_3RhCl} \text{[Et}_3SiO\text{ enol ether]} \quad (18.5)$$

A number of studies have been done to elucidate the mechanism of hydrosilation of ketones by [Ph₃P]₃RhCl. Hydrosilation of acetone with optically active α-naphthylphenylmethylsilane catalyzed by [Ph₃P]₃RhCl gave optically active isopropoxy-α-naphthylphenylmethylsilane. This was reduced with

LiAlH$_4$ to yield α-naphthylphenylmethylsilane of almost identical rotation to that of starting silane. Since LiAlH$_4$ reduction of alkoxysilanes is known to proceed with retention of configuration, the rhodium catalyzed hydrosilation of ketones must also proceed largely with retention of configuration at the silyl center [9].

$$\text{(18.6)}$$

The steric requirements of the transition state have been explored by hydrosilation of stereochemically rigid ketones such as camphor and menthone. The ratio of diastereomeric alkyl silyl ethers formed in these reactions depends on the silane used [10].

R$_3$SiH				(18.7)
Et$_2$SiH$_2$	91	:	9	
PhCH$_3$SiH$_2$	75	:	25	
Et$_3$SiH	30	:	70	

Hydrosilation of alkyl substituted cyclohexanones has been studied with [Ph$_3$P]$_3$RhCl and an analogus heterogeneous rhodium catalyst [11].

$$\text{(18.8)}$$

Similar stereoselectivities were observed with both heterogeneous and homogeneous catalysts [11].

Dichloro-*bis*(dimethylphenylphosphino) di-μ-chloro diplatinum is also effective for the hydrosilation of alkyl aryl ketones with methyldichlorosilane or dimethylchlorosilane [12, 13].

$$\underset{Ph}{\overset{O}{\underset{\|}{C}}}\!\!-\!CH_3 \;+\; (CH_3)_2SiHCl \;\xrightarrow[{[PhP(CH_3)_2PtCl_2]_2}]{} \; \underset{H}{\overset{O-Si(CH_3)_2Cl}{\underset{|}{Ph-\overset{|}{C}-CH_3}}} \qquad (18.9)$$

18.3 Catalytic Asymmetric Hydrosilation of Aldehydes and Ketones

A variety of transition metal complexes with chiral tertiary phosphine ligands have proved effective for the catalytic asymmetric hydrosilation of prochiral ketones. These reactions permit the preparation of chiral alcohols. Kumada, found that both dichloro *bis* [R(+)benzylmethylphenylphosphine]-di-μ-chloro diplatinum [R(+)BMPPt] and dichloro *bis*[R(−)methyl-*n*-propylphenylphosphine] di-μ-chloro diplatinum [R(−)MPPPt] were effect asymmetric hydrosilation catalysts for alkyl aryl ketones. However, the optical yields (e.e.) of the product alcohols were relatively low [12, 13].

$$R-\overset{O}{\overset{\|}{C}}-Ph \;+\; CH_3SiCl_2H \;\xrightarrow{[RR'R''P*PtCl_2]_2}\; R\!\!\blacktriangleright\!\!\underset{Ph}{\overset{OSiCH_3Cl_2}{C}}\!\!\blacktriangleleft\!\! H$$

$$\downarrow \begin{array}{l} 1)\; 2CH_3Li \\ 2)\; H_2O \end{array} \qquad (18.10)$$

$$R\!\!\blacktriangleright\!\!\underset{Ph}{\overset{OH}{C}}\!\!\blacktriangleleft\!\! H$$

R	Catalyst	Chemical Yield	Optical Yield	Configuration
CH₃	R(+)BMPPt	81	7.6	S
t-Bu	R(+)BMPPt	33	18.6	S
CH₃	R(−)MPPPt	71	5.5	R

A chiral cationic rhodium complex prepared from optically active R(+)ben-zylmethylphenylphosphine R(+)BMP is effective for the asymmetric hydro-silation of prochiral ketones with dialkyl or trialkylsilanes [14]. The extent of the asymmetric induction as well as the configuration of the predominant alcohol produced are dependent not only on the structure of the prochiral ketone but also on the particular silane used. The different alkyl groups of the silane may effect the asymmetric reduction process due to differences in stability of the two diastereomeric α-silyloxyalkyl rhodium intermediates Reductive elimination by transfer of hydrogen from rhodium to carbon in this intermediate yields the product [15].

$$R-\overset{O}{\overset{\|}{C}}-Ph \;\xrightarrow[{Rh[R(+)BMP]_2H_2S_2^+ClO_4^-}]{R'_3SiH}\; R\!\!\blacktriangleright\!\!\underset{Ph}{\overset{OSiR'_3}{C}}\!\!\blacktriangleleft\!\! H \qquad (18.11)$$

R	Silane	Chemical Yield	Optical Yield	Configuration
CH_3-	$PhSi(CH_3)_2H$	97	31.6	S
$(CH_3)_3C-$	$PhSi(CH_3)_2H$	84	61.8	S
CH_3-	$(CH_3)_3SiH$	100	5.1	S
$(CH_3)_3C-$	$(CH_3)_3SiH$	70	28.0	R

Chiral rhodium (I) complexes related to Wilkinson's catalyst have also proved effective. These have been prepared by substitution of R(+)benzyl-methylphenylphosphine R(+)BMP or S(−)benzylmethylphenylphosphine S(−)BMP for triphenylphosphine. The optical yield and configuration of the product alcohol are dependent on the structure of the prochiral ketone as well as on the silane utilized. Prochiral dialkyl ketones as well as alkyl aryl ketones undergo asymmetric reduction. Analysis of the relative size of the various groups in the diastereomeric α-silyloxyalkyl rhodium intermediates permits prediction of the configuration of the predominant silyl ether product [16–18].

$$(18.12)$$

Catalyst	R'	R''	Silane	Chemical Yield	Opt. Yield	Config.
S(−)BMP	Ph	CH_3	$PhSi(CH_3)_2H$	92	44	R
	Ph	$(CH_3)_2CH$		95	56	R
	Ph	$(CH_3)_2CH$	Et_2SiH_2	98	23	S
R(+)BMP	Ph	$(CH_3)_3C$	$EtSi(CH_3)_2H$	97	56	R
	Ph	$(CH_3)_3C$	$PhSi(CH_3)_2H$	92	54	S
	Ph	⬡—	$PhSi(CH_3)_2H$	90	58	S

Catalytic asymmetric hydrosilation reactions have also been carried out with chiral rhodium complexes prepared from (−) or (+) 2,3-O-isopropylidene-2,3-dihydroxy-1,4-bis(diphenylphosphino)butane, (−) or (+) DIOP. Hydrosilation of unsymmetrical ketones with prochiral silanes leads to asymmetric induction at both carbon and silicon of the alkoxysilane product. Hydrosilation of methyl ethyl ketone with α-naphthylphenylsilane catalyzed by a (−) DIOP rhodium complex leads to a chiral alkoxysilane. Reaction of this alkoxy silane with methyl Grignard yields both optically active (−) α-naphthylphenylmethylsilane (40% e.e.) and (−) 2-butanol (42% e.e.) [19, 20].

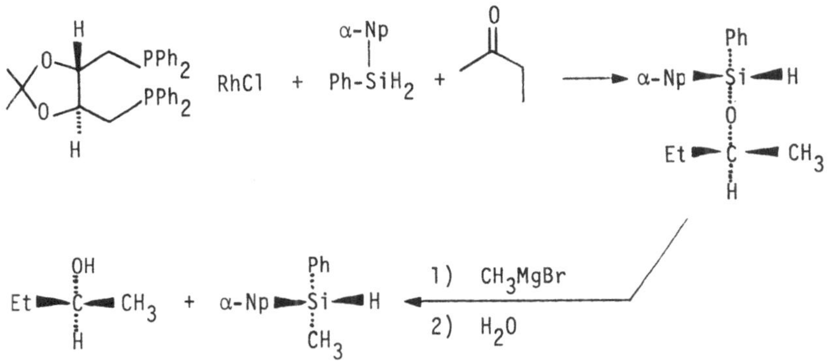

(18.13)

Both soluble chiral DIOP rhodium complexes and the analogous polymer bound chiral DIOP rhodium complexes yield similar results in catalytic asymmetric hydrosilation reactions of prochiral ketones [21, 22].

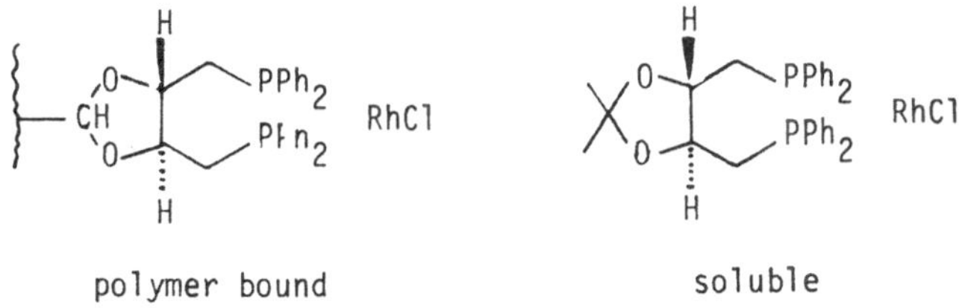

(18.14)

polymer bound   soluble

Catalyst	Silane	Ketone	Chemical Yield	Optical Yield
polymer	H_2SiPh_2	$Ph-C-CH_3$	90	29% S(−)
soluble	H_2SiPh_2	‖	100	28% S(−)
soluble	H_2Si-Ph $\alpha-Np$	O	76	53% S(−)

Catalytic hydrosilation of optically active ketones [(+) camphor and (−) menthone] with prochiral dihydrosilane such as α-naphthylphenylsilane has been studied. Both chiral and achiral rhodium complexes have been used as catalysts. The optically active diarylalkoxysilanes products were reacted with Grignard reagents to yield chiral silanes in up to 80% optical purity [23].

293

$$(18.15)$$

Chiral 2,2'-*bis*(diphenylphosphinomethyl)-1,1'-binaphthyl rhodium (I) complexes have also proved effective in the catalytic asymmetric hydrosilation of prochiral ketones [24].

$$(18.16)$$

18.4 Asymmetric Hydrosilation of α-Keto Esters

Catalytic asymmetric hydrosilation of α-keto esters such as *n*-propyl pyruvate or ethyl phenylglyoxylate, have been carried out with chiral rhodium complexes. The keto carbonyl group is preferentially reduced to yield chiral α-hydroxy esters. High asymmetric induction is observed [25].

$$(18.17)$$

Catalytic asymmetric hydrosilation of (−) menthyl benzoylformate with chiral rhodium catalysts yields chiral α-hydroxy menthyl esters (Eq. 18.18 and 18.19). The asymmetric induction results from both the chiral rhodium complex and the chiral menthyl group. To estimate the contribution of each, two experiments were done. First chiral menthyl α-keto esters were hydrosilated with Wilkinson's catalyst (Eq. 18.20). Second hydrosilation of cyclohexyl benzoylformate was catalyzed by the chiral rhodium complex (Eq. 18.21) [26, 27].

$$\text{Ph-C-C-O-[menthyl*]} \xrightarrow[\text{(+)DIOP-Rh}]{Ph_2SiH_2} \xrightarrow{\text{hydrolysis}} \text{HO}_2\text{C-C(OH)(H)-Ph} \quad 60\% \text{ e.e. } S \quad (18.18)$$

$$\text{Ph-C-C-O-[menthyl*]} \xrightarrow[\text{(-)DIOP-Rh}]{Ph_2SiH_2} \xrightarrow{\text{hydrolysis}} \text{Ph-C(OH)(H)-CO}_2\text{H} \quad 37\% \text{ e.e. } R \quad (18.19)$$

$$\text{Ph-C-C-O-[menthyl*]} \xrightarrow[\text{[Ph}_3\text{P]}_3\text{RhCl}]{Ph_2SiH_2} \xrightarrow{\text{hydrolysis}} \text{HO}_2\text{C-C(OH)(H)-Ph} \quad 32\% \text{ e.e. } S \quad (18.20)$$

$$\text{Ph-C-C-O-[cyclohexyl]} \xrightarrow[\text{(+)DIOP-Rh}]{Ph_2SiH_2} \xrightarrow{\text{hydrolysis}} \text{HO}_2\text{C-C(OH)(H)-Ph} \quad 42.5\% \text{ e.e. } S \quad (18.21)$$

While the rationalization of these results is complex, nevertheless, catalytic asymmetric hydrosilation of α keto ester provides a new method to prepare chiral α-hydroxy acids.

18.5 Hydrosilation of Imines and Pyridines

Imines can also be reduced to N-silyl amines by catalytic hydrosilation. [Ph₃P]₃RhCl is most effective with dihydrosilanes, while PdCl₂ works well with trimethylsilane [28].

$$\text{Ph-CH=N}^{CH_3} \xrightarrow[\text{[Ph}_3\text{P]}_3\text{RhCl}]{Et_3SiH_2} \text{PhCH}_2\text{N}(CH_3)(SiEt_2H) \quad (18.22)$$

Catalytic hydrosilation of prochiral imines with chiral rhodium complexes such as (+) DIOP Rh(I) yields after hydrolysis chiral secondary amines [29].

$$\underset{CH_3}{\overset{Ph}{>}}{=}\text{N}^{CH_2Ph} \xrightarrow[\text{2) H}_2\text{O}]{\text{1) Ph}_2\text{SiH}_2 \text{ (+) DIOP-Rh}} \text{Ph-C(H)(CH}_3)\text{-NH-CH}_2\text{Ph} \quad S \; 50\% \text{ e.e.} \quad (18.23)$$

Trimethylsilane adds to pyridine in the presence of Pd/C to yield a mixture of N-trimethylsilyl-1,2 and 1,4-dihydropyridines and N,N′-*bis*(trimethylsilyl)-1,1-dihydro-4,4′-bipyridine. The ratio of products is dependent on time and other reaction conditions [37, 38].

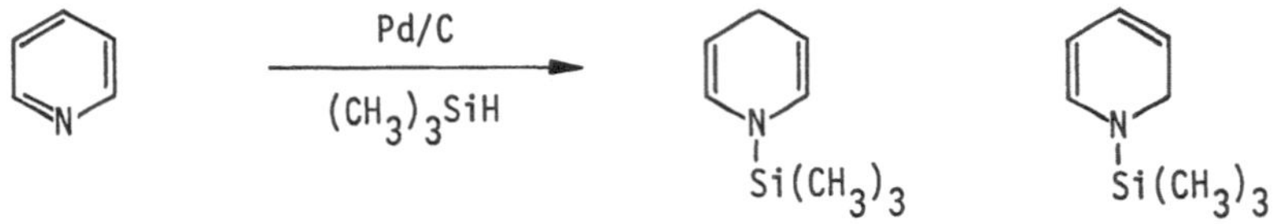

(18.24)

18.6 Hydrosilation of Isocyanates and Carbodiimides

Catalytic hydrosilation of aryl isocyanates with triethylsilane over Pd/C or with $PdCl_2$ gives N-α-aryl-α-silyl formamides. The opposite regiospecificity is observed with aliphatic isocyanates.

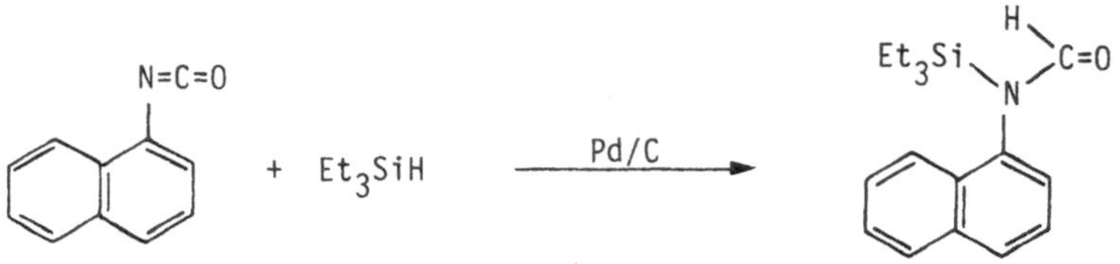

(18.25)

Both products react with methanol to yield formamides or with acetyl chloride to give N-acetyl formamides [30, 31]. Similar catalytic hydrosilation of dialkyl carbodiimides by $PdCl_2$ or $[Ph_3P]_3RhCl$ gives N,N′-dialkyl-N-silyl formamidines [32].

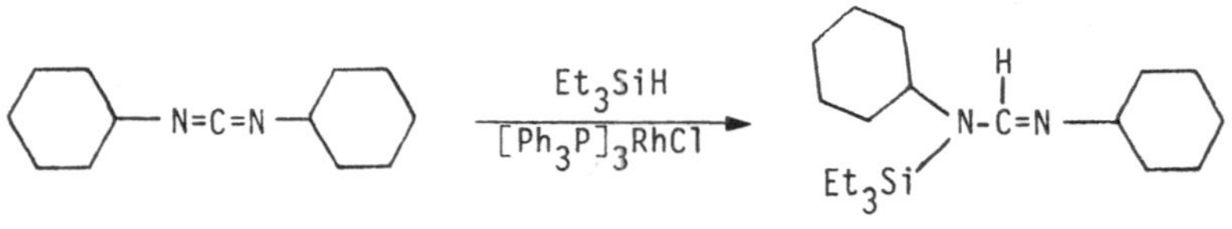

(18.26)

18.7 Silyl-Rosenmund Reduction

Like the Rosenmund reduction of acid chlorides by hydrogen over Pd [33], silanes react with acid chlorides over Pd/C [34] or in the presence of rhodium (I) complexes [35] to yield aldehydes and chlorosilanes. Yields are often higher than are obtained with lithium aluminum tri-*t*-butoxy hydride [36].

$$Et_3SiH + n\text{-}C_7H_{15}\text{-}C(=O)Cl \xrightarrow{Pd/C} n\text{-}C_7H_{15}\text{-}C(=O)H + Et_3SiCl \qquad (18.27)$$

References

1. Schrock, R.R., Osborn, J.A.: J. Chem. Soc. Chem. Commun. 567 (1970)
2. Bourhis, R., Frainnet, E.: J. Organometal. Chem. *86*, 205 (1975)

3. Frainnet, E., Martel-Siegfried, V., Brousse, E., Dedier, J.: J. Organometal. Chem. *85*, 297 (1975)
4. Ojima, I., Nihonyanagi, M., Nagai, Y.: J. Chem. Soc. Chem. Commun. 938 (1972)
5. Ojima, I., Kogure, T., Nihonyanagi, M., Nagai, Y.: Bull. Chem. Soc. Japan, *45*, 3506 (1972)
6. Ojima, I., Nihonyanagi, M., Kogure, T., Kumagai, M., Horiuchi, S., Nakatsugama, K.: J. Organometal. Chem. *94*, 449 (1975)
7. Corriu, R.J.P., Moreau, J.J.E.: J. Chem. Soc. Chem. Commun. 38 (1973)
8. Eaborn, C., Odell, K., Pidcock, A.: J. Organometal. Chem. *63*, 93 (1973)
9. Corriu, R.J.P., Moreau, J.J.E.: J. Organometal. Chem. *85*, 19 (1975)
10. Ojima, I., Nihonyanagi, M., Nagai, Y.: Bull. Chem. Soc. Japan, *45*, 3722 (1972)
11. Ishiyama, J.I., Senda, Y., Shinoda, I., Imaizumi, S.: Bull. Chem. Soc. Japan, *52*, 2353 (1979)
12. Yamamoto, K., Hayashi, T., Kumada, M.: J. Organometal. Chem. *46*, C65 (1972)
13. Hayashi, T., Yamamoto, K., Kumada, M.: J. Organometal. Chem. *112*, 253 (1976)
14. Yamamoto, K., Hayashi, T., Kumada, M.: J. Organometal. Chem. *54*, C45 (1973)
15. Hayashi, T., Yamamoto, K., Kasuga, K., Omizu, H., Kumada, M.: J. Organometal. Chem. *113*, 127 (1976)
16. Ojima, I., Kogure, T., Nagai, Y.: Chem. Lett. 541 (1973)
17. Ojima, I., Nagai, Y.: Chem. Lett. 223 (1974)
18. Ojima, I., Kogure, T., Kumagai, M., Horiuchi, S., Sato, T.: J. Organometal. Chem. *122*, 83 (1976)
19. Corriu, R.J.P., Moreau, J.J.E.: J. Organometal. Chem. *64*, C51 (1974)
20. Corriu, R.J.P., Moreau, J.J.E.: J. Organometal. Chem. *85*, 19 (1975)
21. Poulin, J.C., Dumont, W., Dang, T.P., Kagan, H.B.: Compt. Rend. Acad. Sci. Paris, *277*, C41 (1973)
22. Dumont, W., Poulin, J.C., Dang, T.P., Kagan, H.B.: J. Am. Chem. Soc. *95*, 8295 (1973)
23. Corriu, R.J.P., Moreau, J.J.E.: Nouv. J. de Chim. *1*, 71 (1977)
24. Tamao, K., Yamamoto, H., Matsumoto, H., Miyake, N., Hayashi, T., Kumada, M.: Tetrahedron Lett. 1389 (1977)
25. Ojima, I., Kogure, T., Nagai, Y.: Tetrahedron Lett. 1889 (1974)
26. Ojima, I., Nagai, Y.: Chem. Lett. 191 (1975)
27. Ojima, I., Kogure, T., Kumagai, M.: J. Org. Chem. *42*, 1671 (1977)
28. Ojima, I., Kogure, T., Nagai, Y.: Tetrahedron Lett. 2475 (1973)
29. Langlois, N., Dang, T.P., Kagan, H.B.: Tetrahedron Lett. 4865 (1973)
30. Ojima, I., Inaba, S.I.: Tetrahedron Lett. 4363 (1973)
31. Ojima, I., Inaba, S.I.: J. Organometal. Chem. *140*, 97 (1977)
32. Ojima, I., Inaba, S.I., Nagai, Y.: J. Organometal. Chem. *72*, C11 (1974)
33. The Rosenmund Reduction of Acid Chlorides to Aldehydes by Mosettig, E., Mozingo, R.: in Organic Reactions IV.
34. Citron, J.D.: J. Org. Chem. *34*, 1977 (1969)
35. Coutis, B., Dent, S.P., Eaborn, C., Pidock, A.: J. Chem. Soc. Dalton, 2460 (1975)
36. Brown, H.C., Subba Rao, B.C.: J. Am. Chem. Soc. *80*, 5377 (1958)
37. Cook, N.C., and Lyons, J.E.: J. Am. Chem. Soc. *87*, 3283 (1963)
38. Cook, N.C., and Lyons, J.E.: J. Am. Chem. Soc. *88*, 3396 (1966)

19 Dissolving Metal Reductions

19.1 Introduction

The products formed in dissolving metal reductions are often determined by the presence or absence of a proton source, as well as by other experimental conditions such as the particular metal and solvents used [1–3]. These differences may result from protonation of the initial anion radicals to yield radical intermediates, as well as from the ability of the proton source to limit the basicity of the media. Based on the analogy between a trimethylsilyl group and a proton, it is not surprising that TMS-Cl is able to influence the course of dissolving metal reductions.

This chapter will be organized by functional groups. Often several different combinations of reagents and solvents have been applied to reduce a single functional group. These may lead to diverse results. Solvent, metal, temperature, as well as the ratio of substrate to TMS-Cl influence the course of these reductions. Despite this number of variables, a coherent picture of these reductions may be possible.

French workers have made major contributions to our knowledge of dissolving metal reductions of unsaturated functional groups in the presence of TMS-Cl. They have utilized TMS-Cl with either lithium in THF (A) or magnesium in HMPT (B) as reduction systems.

19.2 Ketones and Aldehydes

Ketones and aldehydes undergo dissolving metal reduction in the presence of a proton source to yield alcohols, while in the absence of a proton source pinacol dimers are the usual products [4]. Reduction of ketones which have α-hydrogens with magnesium in HMPT or TMU and TMS-Cl leads to a mixture of products: *bis*-1,2-(trimethylsilyloxy)alkanes, and equal amounts of alkoxytrimethylsilanes and trimethylsilyl enol ethers. Formation of these products can be accounted for as follows. Initial electron transfer to the ketone forms a ketyl (anion radical) which reacts with TMS-Cl to yield a α-trimethylsilyloxyalkyl radical. Dimerization of such radicals yields *bis*-1,2-(trimethylsilyloxy)alkanes, while radical disproportionation results in equal amounts of alkoxytrimethylsilanes and trimethylsilyl enol ethers [5].

$$\text{(19.1)}$$

17%   17% $(CH_3)_3SiO \quad OSi(CH_3)_3$

With cyclohexanone only the disproportionation products, cyclohexanoxy-trimethylsilane and trimethylsilyloxycyclohexene are found [5].

On the other hand, benzophenone and *t*-butyl phenyl ketone react with B to yield diphenyl trimethylsilyl trimethylsilyloxymethane and *t*-butyl phenyl trimethylsilyl trimethylsilyloxymethane, respectively. These products result from a second electron transfer to the initial diphenyltrimethylsilyloxymethyl or *t*-butyltrimethylsilyloxybenzyl radicals to yield the corresponding carbanions which react with a second equivalent of TMS-Cl. Carbanion formation is probably favored by the phenyl groups. Dimerization of these radicals to form pinacol products may also be disfavored due to steric hinderance [6, 7].

$$Ph_2C=O \xrightarrow[HMPT]{Mg} \left[Ph_2\overset{.}{C}-O^-\right] \xrightarrow{(CH_3)_3SiCl} \left[Ph_2\overset{.}{C}-OSi(CH_3)_3\right] \qquad (19.2)$$

$$\xrightarrow{Mg} \left[Ph_2\overset{-}{C}-OSi(CH_3)_3\right] \xrightarrow{(CH_3)_3SiCl} \begin{array}{c} Si(CH_3)_3 \\ | \\ Ph-C-Ph \\ | \\ O \\ Si(CH_3)_3 \end{array}$$

Addition of THF to the HMPT or TMU solvent favors formation of pinacol products with benzophenone. Electron transfer to the silyloxy radicals may be slower in THF due to its decreased cation solvating ability [8].

With the reduction system (B), the ratio of benzaldehyde to TMS-Cl influences the distribution of products. A 1:1 ratio favors 1,2-diphenyl-1,2-*bis*(trimethylsilyloxy)ethane whereas a 2:1 ratio of TMS-Cl to benzaldehyde favors formation of α-trimethylsilyl-α-trimethylsilyloxytoluene [9].

$$\underset{O}{\overset{Ph-C-H}{||}} \xrightarrow[HMPT]{\overset{Mg}{(CH_3)_3SiCl}} \left[\underset{OSi(CH_3)_3}{\overset{Ph-\overset{-}{C}-H}{|}}\right] \xrightarrow{(CH_3)_3SiCl} \underset{OSi(CH_3)_3}{\overset{Si(CH_3)_3}{\underset{|}{Ph-C-H}}} \qquad (19.3)$$

$$\overset{O}{\underset{Ph-C-H}{||}}$$

$$\left[\begin{array}{c} H \\ Ph\diagdown C \diagup OSi(CH_3)_3 \\ | \\ Ph \diagup C \diagdown O^- \\ H \end{array}\right] \xrightarrow{(CH_3)_3SiCl} \begin{array}{c} H \\ Ph\diagdown C \diagup OSi(CH_3)_3 \\ | \\ Ph \diagup \underset{H}{C} \diagdown OSi(CH_3)_3 \end{array}$$

299

Chloral reacts with B to yield predominantly 1-chloro-1-trimethylsilyl-2-trimethylsilyloxy ethylene. Electron transfer to the trichloromethyltrimethyl-silyloxy methyl radical may yield a carbanion which loses chloride to give 1,1-dichloro-2-trimethylsilyloxy ethylene as an intermediate. Under similar conditions hexachloroacetone gives 1,1,3,3,3-pentachloro-2-trimethylsilyloxy propene [10].

Reduction of ketones or aldehydes with A yields a mixture of 1,2-*bis*-(trimethylsilyloxy) alkanes, alkoxytrimethylsilanes, trimethylsilyl enol ethers, and α-trimethylsilyl-α-trimethylsilyloxy alkanes [11–13].

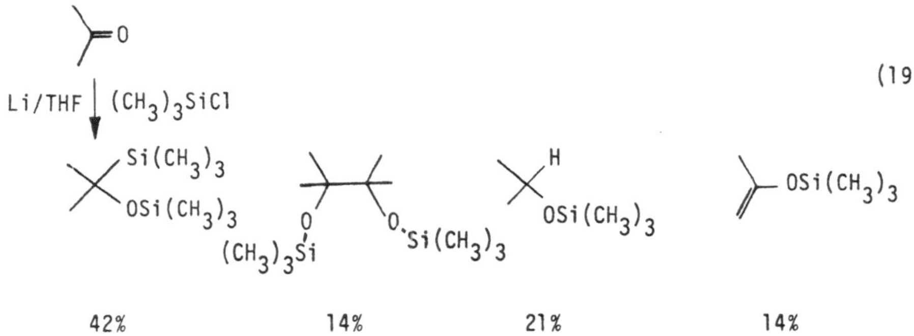

(19.4)

Apparently lithium in THF is a more powerful reducing agent than magnesium in HMPT. Reduction of the α-trimethylsilyloxy radical yields a carbanion which reacts with TMS-Cl to give C-silylated product. Formaldehyde is reduced by A at −50° to yield trimethylsilyloxytrimethylsilylmethane [14].

$$H_2C=O \xrightarrow[\substack{(CH_3)_3SiCl \\ -50°}]{Li/THF} (CH_3)_3SiCH_2OSi(CH_3)_3$$

(19.5)

The Clemmensen reduction of ketones to alkanes utilizes zinc-amalgam and HCl. Based on the analogy between a proton and a trimethylsilyl group, it is not surprising that the combination of TMS-Cl and zinc amalgam in ether reduce aliphatic cyclic ketones to cyclic alkenes. Cyclohexanone gave cyclohexene, while cyclooctanone gave cyclooctene and bicyclo [3.3.0] octane [15]. This latter product may indicate that a carbene intermediate is involved.

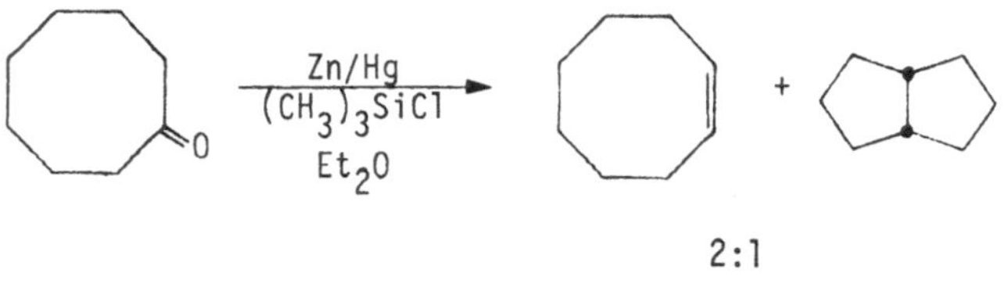

(19.6)

2:1

The reaction is quite selective, 3-keto groups are reduced in preference to keto groups in other positions of steroid nuclei [16]. Thus 5-α-cholestan-3-

one was reduced to 5-α-cholest-2-ene, while 5-α-cholestan-3,6-dione gave 5-α-cholest-2-en-6-one under these conditions.

$$(19.7)$$

On the other hand, aromatic ketones, such as acetophenone, gave *bis*(trimethylsilyl) ethers of the pinacol dimers [15].

A zinc-copper couple and dimethyldichlorosilane react with ketones to yield products which may arise from carbene intermediates. For example, benzaldehyde gives benzyl phenyl ketone and diphenylacetaldehyde. These products may result from zinc chloride catalyzed rearrangement of stilbene oxide, formed by reaction of phenyl carbene with benzaldehyde. Evidence in favor of this intriguing proposal is the observation that reaction of benzaldehyde with these reagents in the presence of cyclohexene yields phenylnorcarane [17]. Carbene intermediates have been previously proposed in the Clemmensen reduction of ketones to hydrocarbons [18].

Aliphatic ketones undergo reductive condensation in the presence of dimethyldiiodosilane and zinc in methylene chloride [19].

$$(19.8)$$

19.3 α,β-Unsaturated Ketones and Aldehydes

α,β-Unsaturated ketones or aldehydes undergo reduction by A or B to yield mixtures of products. Initial electron transfer to the α,β-unsaturated carbonyl compound yields an anion radical which reacts with TMS-Cl to give an α-trimethylsilyloxyallylic radical. This can undergo symmetrical dimerization at the α position to yield 3,4-*bis*(trimethylsilyloxy)-1,5-dienes (pinacol dimer). Symmetrical dimerization of the α-trimethylsilyloxy allylic radical at the γ-position gives 1,6-*bis*(trimethylsilyloxy)-1,5-dienes (3,3-dimer). Surprisingly no unsymmetrical dimer products have been detected. Further reduction of the α-trimethylsilyloxyallylic radical yields an α-trimethylsilyloxyallylic anion which reacts with TMS-Cl to yield predominantly 1-trimethylsilyloxy-3-trimethylsilyl-1-alkenes (1,4 product) and 1-trimethylsilyloxy-1-trimethylsilyl-2-alkenes (1,2 product). Product distribution data for reduction of a number of α,β-unsaturated ketones and aldehydes is given in Table 1. In these examples pinacol dimers are not found.

Table 1.

α,β-Unsaturated Ketone or Aldehyde	1,4	1,2	Pinacol Dimer	3,3-Dimer	Reduction System	Reference
(structure)	70%				A	13, 21
(structure)	20%	21%			A	13, 21
(structure)	65%				B	20, 22
(structure)	60%				B	24
(structure)	86%			5%	B	20, 22
(structure)	48%			25%	B	23
(structure)	70%			15%	B	23
(structure)	55%			30%	B	22
(structure)	33%	38%			A	12
(structure)	60%				A	12
(structure)	60%				A	12

$$(19.9)$$

Hydrolysis of 1-trimethylsilyloxy-3-trimethylsilyl-1-alkenes yields β-trimethylsilyl substituted ketones or aldehydes.

α- and β-Ionone both give unusual product distributions on reductive silylation. Reduction of α-ionone with B gives a 50% yield of pinacol dimer, while with β-ionone the 1,4-reduction product is predominant [20, 25].

$$(19.10)$$

In a similar manner, 2-alkynones undergo reduction by B to yield 1-trimethylsilyl-3-trimethylsilyloxy-allenes as the major products. These undergo hydrolysis to yield β-trimethylsilyl α,β-unsaturated ketones [26, 27].

303

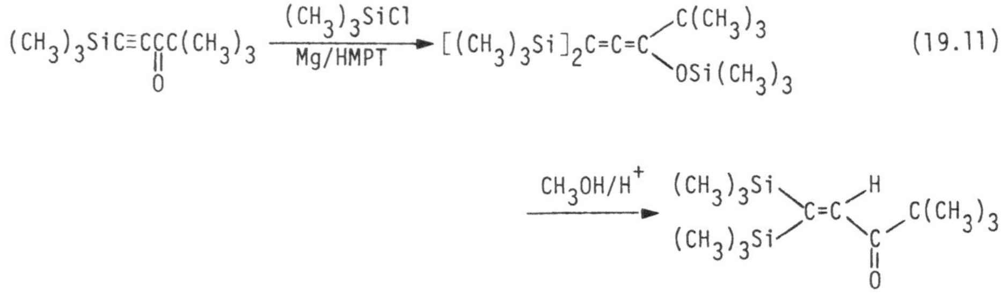

(19.11)

19.4 Esters/Silyl-Acyloin Reactions

Esters are reduced with TMS-Cl and sodium in toluene to yield alkoxytrimethylsilanes and 1,2-*bis*(trimethylsilyloxy) alkenes [28, 29]. These latter compounds undergo hydrolysis to yield α-hydroxy ketones (acyloins).

There are a number of advantages to the silyl acyloin reaction compared to the usual acyloin reaction. In the conventional acyloin reaction the media becomes increasingly basic as the reaction progresses due to formation of sodium alkoxides (Eq. 19.12). This permits competitive Claisen and Dieckman condensations to occur. In the silyl acyloin reaction, on the other hand, the reaction media remains neutral. Alkoxytrimethylsilanes and sodium chloride are formed instead of sodium alkoxides (Eq. 19.13).

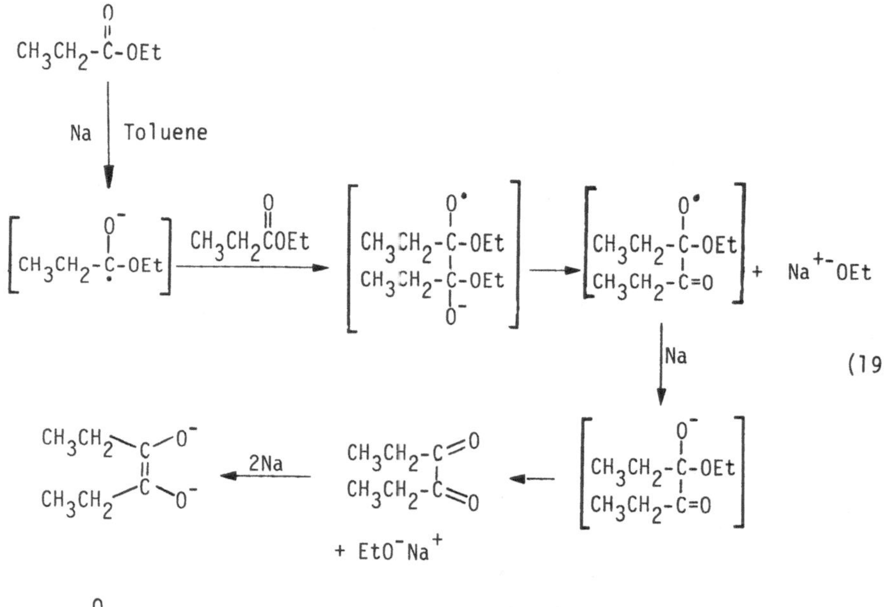

(19.12)

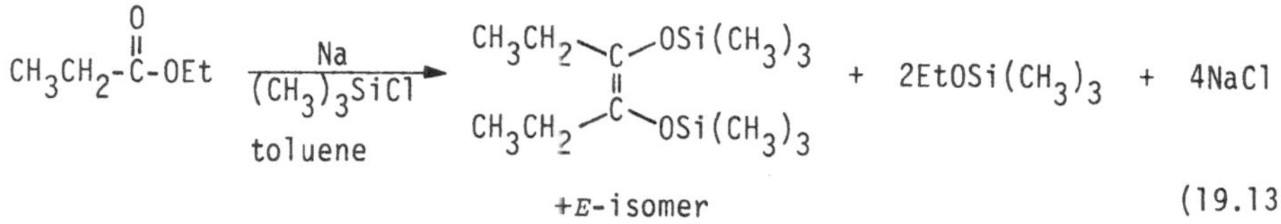

(19.13)

For example, treatment of diethyl pimelate with sodium under conventional acyloin conditions gives a mixture of Dieckman and acyloin products (Eq. 19.14). Whereas, under silyl acyloin conditions only 1,2-*bis*(trimethylsilyloxy)cycloheptene is formed (Eq. 19.15) [30].

$$(19.14)$$

$$(19.15)$$

The silyl acyloin reduction conditions eliminate competitive β-elimination reactions. β-Alkoxy, β-alkylmercapto and β-dialkylamino esters undergo the silyl acyloin reaction successfully [31].

$$(19.15)$$

E-isomer

Medium sized 1,2-*bis*-trimethylsilyloxy alkenes possessing β heteroatoms such as oxygen, sulfur, nitrogen, or phosphorous can be prepared. The normal acyloin reaction fails in these cases [32].

$$(19.17)$$

However, with ethyl β-chloropropionate reduction of the C−Cl bond apparently occurs preferentially. This leads to 1-ethoxy-1-trimethylsilyloxycyclopropane [29].

The neutral conditions of the silyl acyloin reaction permit successful reaction with ethyl phenylacetate [29]. In general the silyl acyloin reaction provides higher yields with alicyclic esters than the conventional acyloin reaction [33, 34]. With α,ω-diesters higher yields of cyclic products are obtained in the silyl acyloin reaction [28]. This is particularly useful for the preparation of medium and large sized cyclic compounds.

$$(CH_2)_8 \underset{CO_2Et}{\overset{CO_2Et}{<}} \quad \xrightarrow[\text{Toluene}]{Na/(CH_3)_3SiCl} \quad (CH_2)_8 \underset{OSi(CH_3)_3}{\overset{OSi(CH_3)_3}{<}} \qquad (19.18)$$

The silyl acyloin reaction has also proved useful for the preparation of 1,2-*bis*(trimethylsilyloxy) cyclobutenes [30, 35, 36].

$$\xrightarrow[\text{Toluene}]{Na/(CH_3)_3SiCl} \qquad (19.19)$$

The sequence of reactions, proposed by Bloomfield, outlined below accounts for most of the experimental results. Of particular note, this sequence does not involve an α-diketone intermediate [37].

$$2 \; CH_3O^- + 2 \; (CH_3)_3SiCl \longrightarrow 2 \; (CH_3)_3Si-OCH_3 \qquad (19.20)$$

Treatment of diethyl disubstituted malonates with sodium and TMS-Cl yields alkyl trimethylsilyl ketene acetals as outlined below [38].

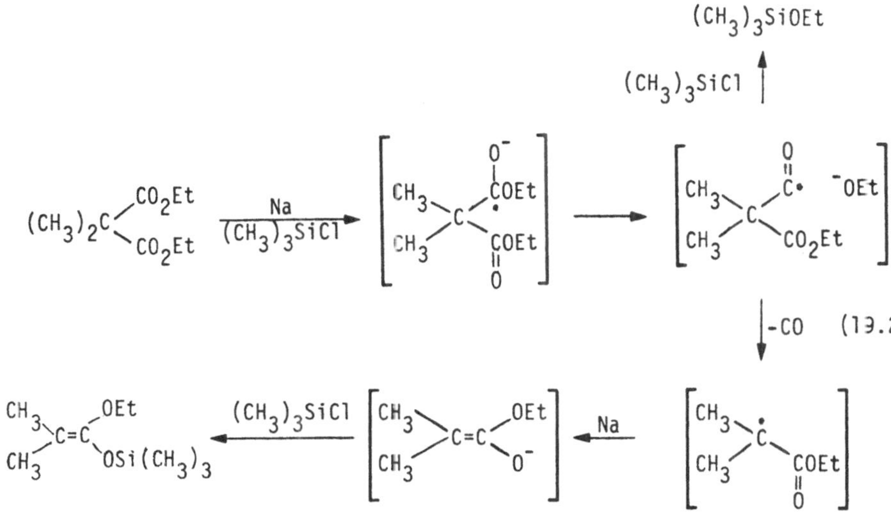
(CH3)3SiOEt
(CH3)3SiCl
(CH3)2C(CO2Et)2
Na
(CH3)3SiCl
-CO
Na
(CH3)3SiCl

(19.21)

On the other hand, in solvents like THF or DME, the reduction of esters with lithium or sodium and TMS-Cl yields 1-trimethylsilyloxy-1,1-*bis*(trimethylsilyl) alkanes [13, 39, 40]. This has been attributed to reaction of the initial ester anion radical with TMS-Cl rather than another molecule of ester. TMS-Cl reacts more efficiently with ketyls in more polar solvents. The α-alkoxy-α-trimethylsilyloxy alkyl radical undergoes further reduction to the corresponding anion which then reacts with TMS-Cl to yield 1-alkoxy-1-trimethylsilyl-1-trimethylsilyloxy alkanes. At low temperature these are relatively stable (Eq. 19.22) [13]. However, at higher temperature (refluxing THF), they undergo loss of alkoxytrimethylsilane and formation of acyltrimethylsilanes. These undergo further reductive silylation to yield 1-trimethylsilyloxy-1,1-*bis*(trimethylsilyl) alkanes (Eq. 19.23) [39, 40].

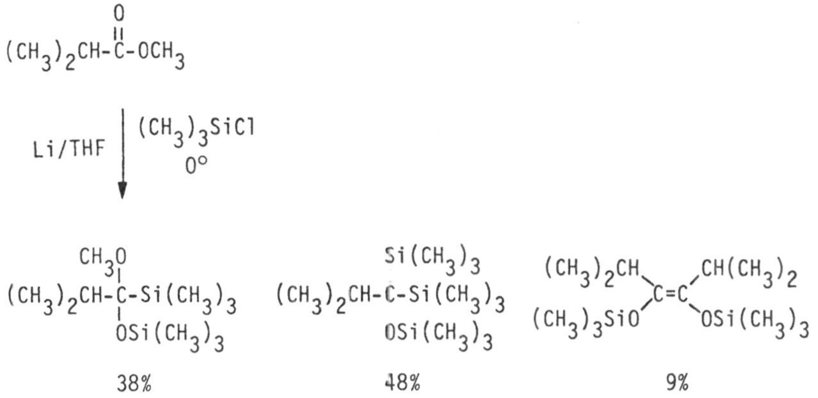
Li/THF
(CH3)3SiCl
0°
38%
48%
9%

(19.22)

$$(CH_3)_2CH\text{-}\overset{O}{\overset{\|}{C}}\text{-}OEt \xrightarrow[\text{THF}\quad\Delta]{Na/(CH_3)_3SiCl} \left[(CH_3)_2CH\text{-}\overset{O^-}{\overset{|}{\underset{\cdot}{C}}}\text{-}OEt\right] \xrightarrow{(CH_3)_3SiCl}$$

$$\left[(CH_3)_2CH\text{-}\overset{OSi(CH_3)_3}{\overset{|}{\underset{\cdot}{C}}}\text{-}OEt\right]$$

$$(CH_3)_2CH\text{-}\overset{OSi(CH_3)_3}{\overset{|}{\underset{\underset{Si(CH_3)_3}{|}}{C}}}\text{-}OEt \xleftarrow{(CH_3)_3SiCl} \left[(CH_3)_2CH\text{-}\overset{OSi(CH_3)_3}{\overset{|}{\underset{\cdot}{C}}}\text{-}OEt\right] \xleftarrow{Na/THF}$$

$$\Delta \Bigg| -(CH_3)_3\overline{SiO}Et \qquad\qquad (19.23)$$

$$(CH_3)_2CH\text{-}\overset{O}{\overset{\|}{C}}\text{-}Si(CH_3)_3 \xrightarrow[(CH_3)_3SiCl]{Na} (CH_3)_2CH\text{-}\overset{OSi(CH_3)_3}{\overset{|}{\underset{\underset{Si(CH_3)_3}{|}}{C}}}\text{-}Si(CH_3)_3$$

Consistent with this proposed mechanism, acyltrimethylsilanes are reduced under these conditions to 1-trimethylsilyloxy-1,1-*bis*(trimethylsilyl)alkanes [41]. These can be hydrolyzed to 1,1-*bis*(trimethylsilyl) alkanols. Alkoxides of these sterically hindered tertiary alcohols have proved to be highly selective bases (see Chapter 24).

Reductive silylation of ethyl-2-furoate by sodium and TMS-Cl in THF yields 1-trimethylsilyloxy-3,5-*bis*(trimethylsilyl) pent-4-yn-1-ene as outlined below [42].

$$(19.24)$$

19.5 α,β-Unsaturated Esters, Amides, and Acid Chlorides

α,β-Unsaturated esters undergo reduction with B [20, 43, 44] or A [45] to give 1-alkoxy-1-trimethylsilyloxy-3-trimethylsilyl-1-alkenes and 1,6-dialkoxy-1,6-*bis*(trimethylsilyloxy)-1,5-hexadienes. These dimers result from combination of the α-alkoxy-α-trimethylsilyloxy allylic radicals at the sterically less congested γ-end.

$$\text{(19.25)}$$

The ratio of these products formed with A depends on reaction temperature. Dimer products are favored by higher temperatures [46]. Methyl crotonate, on the other hand, is reduced by A to yield 1,3-*bis*(trimethylsilyl)-1-trimethyl-silyloxy-1-butene [45].

$$\text{(19.26)}$$

The electrochemical reduction of α,β-unsaturated esters in the presence of aliphatic ketones or aldehydes and TMS-Cl leads to formation of γ-lactones [47].

$$(19.27)$$

The presence of TMS-Cl is essential for the reaction although its exact role is not clear. Similar reactions occur with α,β-unsaturated nitriles to yield γ-hydroxynitriles.

The reductions of *n*-butanoic anhydride, dimethyl carbonate and methyl cyclopropanecarboxylate with B have been studied [46].

N,N-Dialkyl α,β-unsaturated amides undergo reduction by B to yield 1-dialkyl-amino-1-trimethylsilyloxy-3-trimethylsilyl-1-alkenes as major products [20, 48].

$$(19.28)$$

α,β-Unsaturated acid chlorides react with B to yield 1,3-*bis*(trimethylsilyl)-1-trimethylsilyloxy-1-alkenes. An α,β-unsaturated acyltrimethylsilane may be involved as an intermediate which undergoes further reduction [49, 50]. As predicted, the reaction requires three equivalents of TMS-Cl and two of magnesium for every mole of α,β-unsaturated acid chloride reduced. Such 1,3-*bis*-trimethylsilyl-1-trimethylsilyloxy-1-alkenes undergo hydrolysis to β-trimethylsilyl acyltrimethylsilanes [20].

19.6 Amides

N,N-Dimethylbenzamide reacts with B to yield a mixture of deoxygenated products. The ratio of these products varies with solvent. HMPT, TMU, and THF have been studied. Initial electron transfer yields an anion radical which reacts with TMS-Cl to give the α-dimethylamino α-trimethylsilyloxy-benzyl radical. Further electron transfer to this radical yields the anion which reacts with TMS-Cl to yield α-dimethylamino α-trimethylsilyloxybenzyltrimethylsilane. This undergoes fragmentation to a trimethylsilanoate anion/iminium cation pair. All products may arise from further reduction of the iminium cation [51].

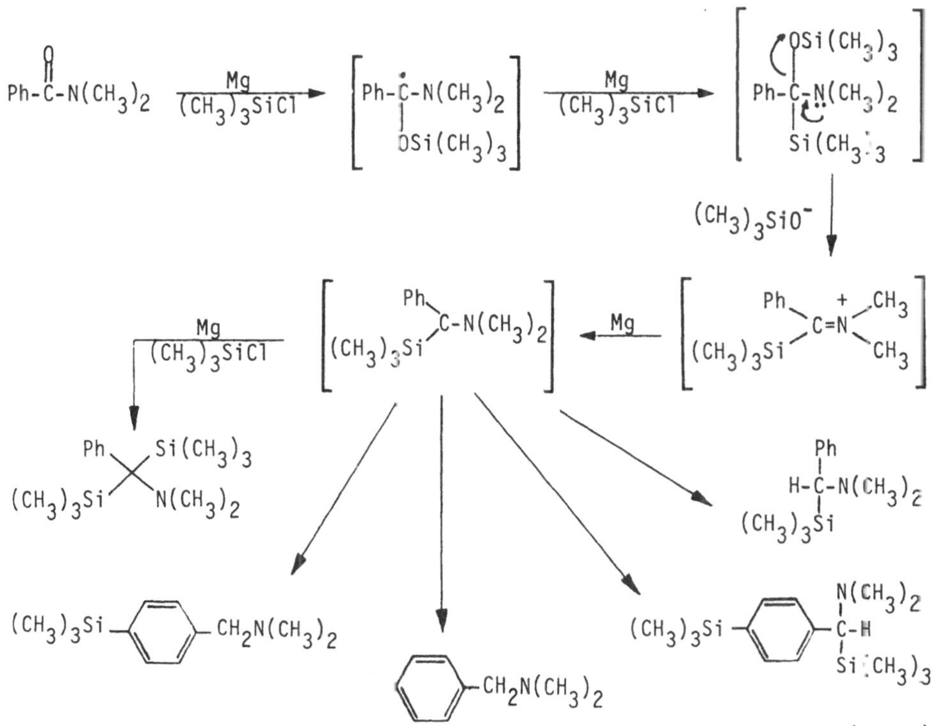

(19.29)

19.7 α,β-Unsaturated Nitriles

α,β-Unsaturated nitriles are reduced by B [50, 52] or A [46] to yield 1,2-*bis*(trimethylsilyl)alkylnitriles.

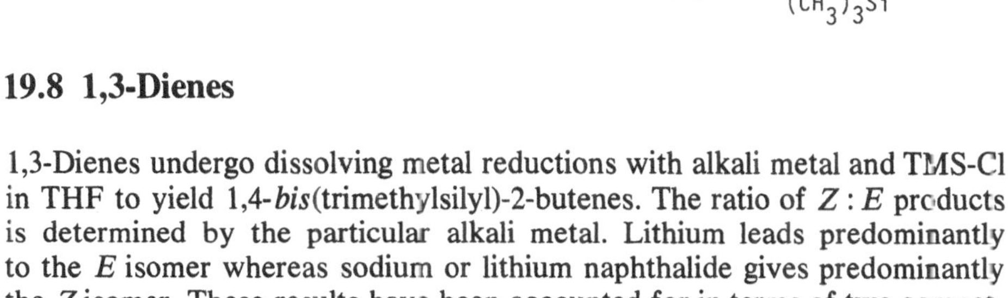

(19.30)

19.8 1,3-Dienes

1,3-Dienes undergo dissolving metal reductions with alkali metal and TMS-Cl in THF to yield 1,4-*bis*(trimethylsilyl)-2-butenes. The ratio of $Z:E$ products is determined by the particular alkali metal. Lithium leads predominantly to the E isomer whereas sodium or lithium naphthalide gives predominantly the Z isomer. These results have been accounted for in terms of two competing reaction pathways. An allylic anion radical prefers a cisoid conformation due to tight ion pairing and leads to Z isomer. Whereas an allylic dianion adopts a conformation to minimize repulsion between the two negative charges and gives E isomer [53].

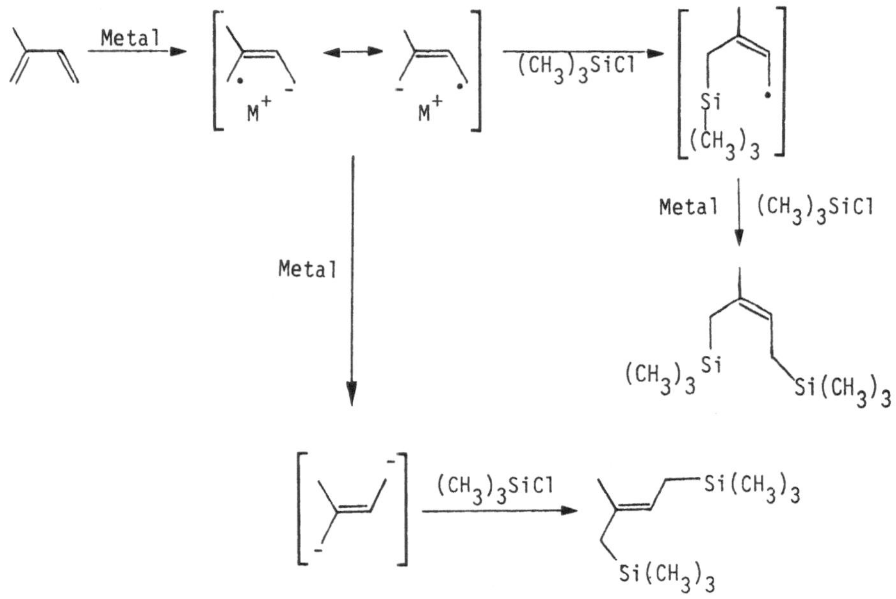

	Metal	%Z 1,4	%E 1,4
Isoprene	Na	95	5
	Li	15	85
	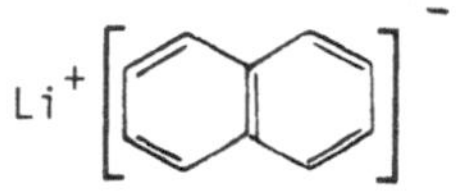 Li$^+$ [naphthalene]$^-$	81	19

(19.31)

Similar reduction of 1,3-dienes with B leads to both Z and E 1,4-*bis*(trimethylsilyl)-2-butenes in a 60:40 ratio [54]. Cyclic 1,3-dienes have also been reduced with B [55].

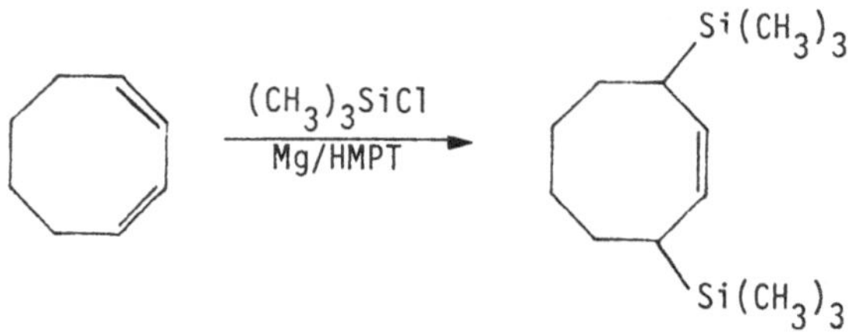

(19.32)

Dissolving metal reduction of cyclic allenes with A yields 2,3-*bis*(trimethylsilyl) cycloalkenes [56].

19.9 Acetylenes

Aryl acetylenes are reduced by B to E-1,2-*bis*(trimethylsilyl) alkenes. A silicon analogue of diethyl stilbesterol was prepared by treatment of *bis*(p-methoxyphenyl)acetylene with B [57].

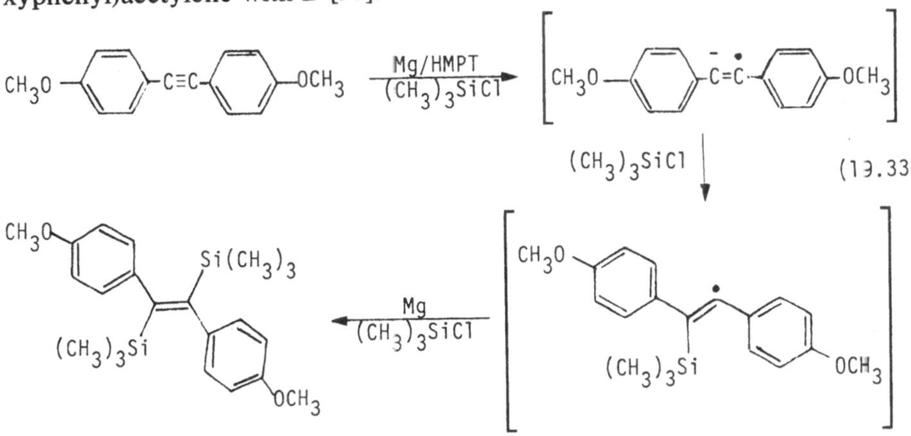

(19.33)

1-Phenyl-2-trimethylsilyl acetylene was reduced, in a similar manner, to yield 1-phenyl-1,2,2-*tris*(trimethylsilyl)ethylene [58].

On the other hand, treatment of aryl acetylenes with lithium in THF without TMS-Cl leads to dimerization of the initial anion radical intermediate to give 1,4-dilithio-1,3-butadienes [59].

19.10 Styrenes

Aryl substituted alkenes undergo reduction with B to yield aryl substituted 1,2-*bis*(trimethylsilyl) alkanes [60].

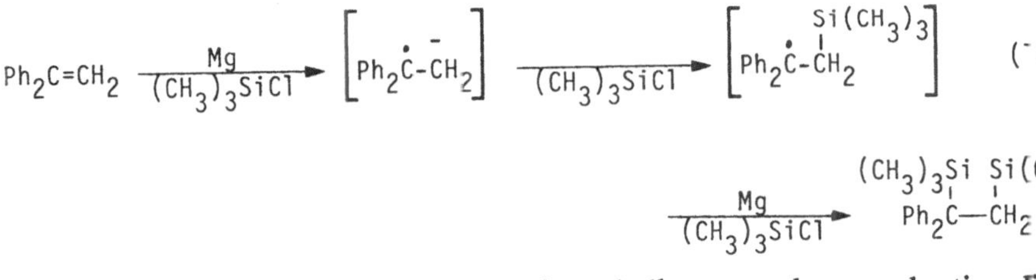

(19.34)

In the absence of TMS-Cl, aryl substituted alkenes undergo reductive dimerization to yield 1,4-diaryl-1,4-dilithio butanes [61].

19.11 Aromatics-Silyl Birch Reduction

Reduction of anisole with A gives 1-methoxy-3,6-*bis*(trimethylsilyl)-1,4-cyclohexadiene. On hydrolysis, this gives 5-trimethylsilyl-cyclohex-3-enone [62, 63].

The trimethylsilyl group adjacent to a carbonyl group is easily lost under either acidic or basic conditions by processes related to enol or enolate anion formation.

$$(19.35)$$

Reductions of benzene with A slowly yields 3,6-*bis*(trimethylsilyl)-1,4-cyclohexadiene [64].

$$(19.36)$$

Similar reductions of benzene [65], toluene [66], xylene isomers [66] or tetralin [67] have been reported.

Dissolving metal reduction of naphthalene with sodium and TMS-Cl occurs more rapidly to yield a mixture of 1,2-*bis*(trimethylsilyl)-1,2-dihydronaphthalene and 1,4-*bis*(trimethylsilyl)-1,4-dihydronaphthalene [68, 69]. Similar reduction of 1-trimethylsilyloxynaphthalene and 2-trimethylsilyloxynaphthalene yields 1-trimethylsilylnaphthalene and 2-trimethylsilylnaphthalene, respectively. The formation of 1-trimethylsilylnaphthalene may involve 1,2-*bis*(trimethylsilyl)-1-trimethylsilyloxy-1,2-dihydronaphthalene as an intermediate which loses hexamethyldisiloxane to yield the product [70].

$$(19.37)$$

Similarly, 1,5-*bis*(trimethylsilyl)naphthalene has been prepared by reduction of 1,5-*bis*(trimethylsilyloxy)naphthalene [71].

Treatment of acenaphthylene with B gives 1,2-dihydro-1,2-*bis*(trimethylsilyl)acenaphthylene [72]. Oxidation of this with DDQ yields 1-trimethylsilylacenaphthylene. While treatment of this compound with *n*-butyl lithium, TMEDA yields a dianion which can be oxidized with cadmium chloride [73, 74] to give 1,2-*bis*(trimethylsilyl)acenaphthylene (see 8.11).

Dissolving metal reduction of aryl nitriles with B appears to involve simultaneous reduction of the nitrile and the aromatic system [15, 76].

19.12 Allylic and Benzylic Ethers

Benzylic and allylic trimethylsilyl ethers undergo dissolving metal reduction with B or sodium, TMS-Cl/toluene to yield benzylic or allylic trimethylsilanes. With B, transition metal salt (TiCl$_4$, FeCl$_3$) catalysis may be necessary. Allylic trimethylsilyl ethers are also reduced by A to allylic trimethylsilanes. Reductive silylation is favored by TiCl$_4$ or dicyclopentadienyl titanium dichloride catalysis. The reaction probably occurs by initial electron transfer to the benzylic or allylic trimethylsilyl ether resulting in scission of a C–O bond to yield a benzylic or allylic radical and a trimethylsilanoate anion. Trimethylsilanoate anions react with TMS-Cl to yield hexamethyldisiloxane. Subsequent electron transfer to the benzylic or allylic radical yields the corresponding anion which reacts with TMS-Cl to yield product. Consistent with this mechanism, both α- or γ-methylallyl trimethylsilyl ethers yield similar mixtures of *E*- and *Z*-γ-methylallyltrimethylsilanes and α-methylallyltrimethylsilane [77–81].

$$(19.38)$$

19.13 Epoxides

Epoxides undergo deoxygenation on treatment with B to yield alkenes [82].

$$(19.39)$$

Styrene oxide yields 1-phenyl-1,2-*bis*(trimethylsilyl)ethane under these conditions. This product may result from initial deoxygenation to styrene which then is further reduced [60].

19.14 Carbon-Sulfur Bonds

Scission of C−S bonds under dissolving metal reduction conditions is well-known. α-Phenylthio trimethylsilyl enol ethers undergo dissolving metal reduction with sodium and TMS-Cl in benzene to yield α-trimethylsilyl trimethylsilyl enol ethers [83].

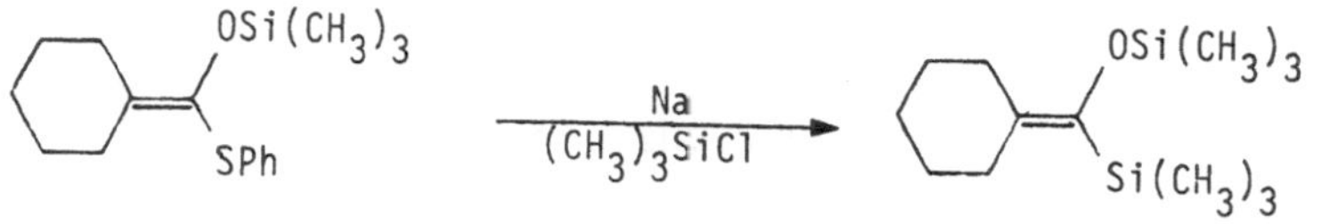

(19.40)

These undergo facile hydrolysis to acyltrimethylsilanes.

Allylic trimethylsilyl sulfides undergo reductive silylation on treatment with A to yield allylic trimethylsilanes [84, 85].

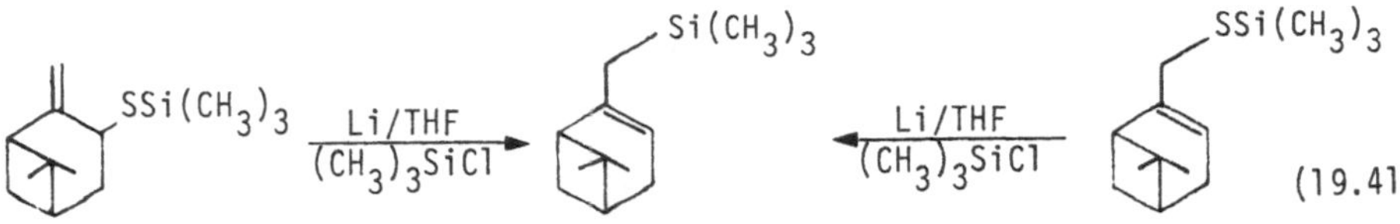

(19.41)

α,β-Unsaturated ethylene thioacetals or ketals undergo reductive silylation to yield mixtures of 3,3-*bis*(trimethylsilyl)-1-alkenes and 1,3-*bis*(trimethylsilyl) alkenes [86]. In certain cases selectivity is observed.

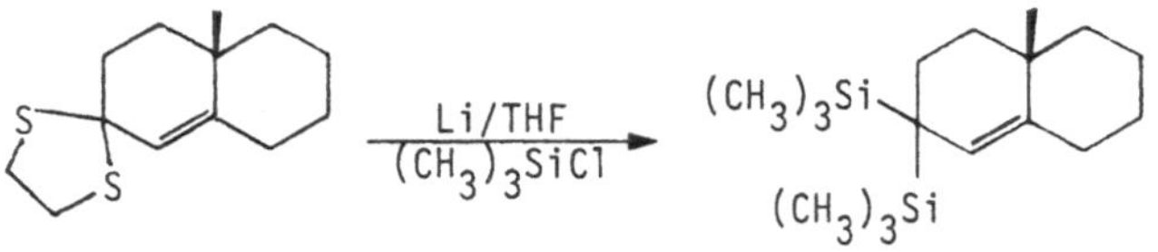

(19.42)

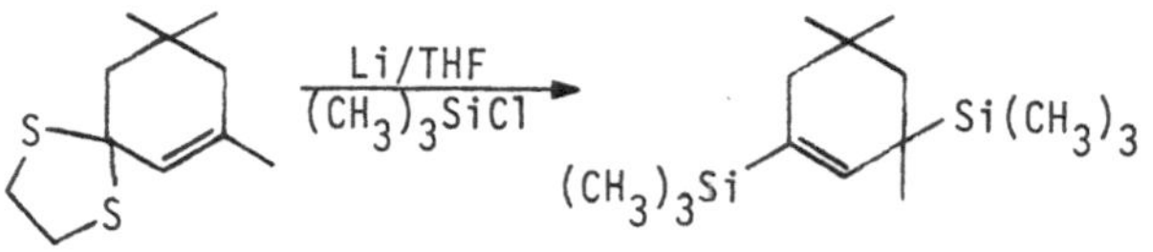

(19.43)

The combination of TMS-Cl and zinc in *moist* ether has been used to remove α-phenylthio groups from ketones. Apparently the phenylthio group is more easily reduced than the ketone carbonyl under these conditions [87].

$$(19.44)$$

Reduction of disulfides with sodium in the presence of TMS-Cl yields alkylthiotrimethylsilanes [88].

$$RS-SR \xrightarrow[\text{(CH}_3)_3\text{SiCl}]{\text{Na}} 2RS-Si(CH_3)_3 \qquad (19.45)$$

19.15 α-Nitroalkenes and Oximes

Steroidal nitroalkenes and oximes are converted to the corresponding ketones by reaction with zinc and TMS-Cl in ether [89].

References

1. Benkeser, R.A., Robinson, R.E., Sauve, D.M., Thomas, O.H.: J. Am. Chem. Soc. *77*, 3230 (1955)
2. Benkeser, R.A., Burrous, M.L., Hazdra, J.J., Kaiser, E.M.: J. Org. Chem. *28*, 1094 (1963)
3. Benkeser, R.A., Agnihotri, R.K., Burrous, M.L., Kaiser, E.M., Mallan, J.M., Ryan, P.W.: J. Org. Chem. *29,* 1313 (1964)
4. House, H.O., Modern Synthetic Reactions, 2nd Edition, Benjamin, W.A , Inc. 1972, p. 145–227.
5. Calas, R., Dunoguès, J., Duffaut, N., Biran, C.: C. R. Acad. Sci. *C, 267,* 494 (1968)
6. Calas, R., Dunoguès, J., Pillot, J.P., Biran, C., Duffaut, N.: J. Organometal. Chem. *25,* 43 (1970)
7. Calas, R., Biran, C., Dunoguès, J., Duffaut, N.: C. R. Acad. Sci. *C, 269,* 412 (1969)
8. Calas, R., Duffaut, N., Biran, C., Bourgeois, P., Pisciotti, F., Dunoguès, J.: C. R. Acad. Sci. *C, 267,* 322 (1968)
9. Chan, T.H., Vinokur, E.: Tetrahedron Lett. 75 (1972)
10. Dunoguès, J., Jousseaume, E., Pillot, J.P., Calas, R.: J. Organometal. Chem. *52,* C11 (1973)
11. Dunoguès, J., Calas, R., Duffaut, N., Lapouyade, P.: J. Organometal. Chem. *49,* C9 (1973)
12. Dunoguès, J., Ekouya, A., Calas, R., Duffaut, N.: J. Organometal. Chem. *87,* 151 (1975)
13. Picard, J.P., Ekouya, A., Dunoguès, J., Duffaut, N., Calas, R.: J. Organometal. Chem. *93,* 51 (1972)
14. Ekouya, A., Dunoguès, J., Duffaut, N., Calas, R.: J. Organometal. Chem. *142,* C35 (1977)
15. Motherwell, W.B.: J. Chem. Soc. Chem. Commun. 935 (1973)
16. Hodge, P., Khan, M.N.: J. Chem. Soc. Perkin, *1,* 809 (1975)

17. Smith, C.L., Arnett, J., Ezike, J.: J. Chem. Soc. Chem. Commun. 653 (1980)
18. Elphimoff-Felin, I., Sanda, P.: J. Chem. Soc. Chem. Commun. 1065 (1969)
19. Ando, W., Ikeno, M.: Chem. Lett. 1255 (1980)
20. Dunoguès, J., Calas, R., Bolourtchian, M., Biran, C., Duffaut, N., Barbe, B.: J. Organometal. Chem. 57, 55 (1973)
21. Dunoguès, J., Ekouya, A., Duffaut, N., Calas, R.: J. Organometal. Chem. 66, C36 (1974)
22. Calas, R., Dunoguès, J., Bolourtchian, M.: J. Organometal. Chem. 26, 195 (1971)
23. Bolourtchian, M., Saednya, A.: Bull. Chim. Soc. Fr. II 170 (1978)
24. Calas, R., Dunoguès, J.: C. R. Acad. Sci. C, 270, 855 (1970)
25. Calas, R., Bolourtchian, M., Dunoguès, J., Duffaut, N., Barbe, B.: J. Organometal. Chem. 34, 269 (1972)
26. Merault, G., Picard, J.P., Bourgeois, P., Dunoguès, J., Duffaut, N.: J. Organometal. Chem. 42, C80 (1972)
27. Merault, G., Bourgeois, P., Dunoguès, J., Duffaut, N.: J. Organometal. Chem. 76, 17 (1974)
28. Schräpler, U., Rühlmann, K.: Chem. Ber. 97, 1383 (1964)
29. Rühlmann, K.: Syn. 236 (1971)
30. Bloomfield, J.J.: Tetrahedron Lett. 591 (1968)
31. Rühlmann, K., Seefluth, M., Becker, M.: Chem. Ber. 100, 3820 (1967)
32. Von Reijenden, J.W., Baardmam, F.: Tetrahedron Lett. 5181 (1972)
33. Schräpler, U., Rühlmann, K.: Chem. Ber. 96, 2780 (1963)
34. Cookson, C.M., Whitman, H.: J. Chem. Soc. Perkin, 1, 806 (1975)
35. Bloomfield, J.J.: Tetrahedron Lett. 587 (1968)
36. Bloomfield, J.J., Martin, R.A., Nelke, J.M.: J. Chem. Soc. Chem. Commun. 96 (1972)
37. Bloomfield, J.J., Owsley, D.C., Ainsworth, C., Robertson, R.E.: J. Org. Chem. 40, 393 (1975)
38. Kuo, Y.N., Chen, F., Ainsworth, C., Bloomfield, J.J.: J. Chem. Soc. Chem. Commun. 136 (1971)
39. Kuwajima, I., Sato, T., Minami, N., Abe, T.: Tetrahedron Lett. 1591 (1976)
40. Kuwajima, I., Minami, N., Abe, T., Sato, T.: Bull. Chem. Soc. Japan, 51, 2391 (1978)
41. Picard, J.P., Calas, R., Dunoguès, J., Duffaut, N.: J. Organometal Chem. 26, 183 (1971)
42. Kuwajima, I., Atsumi, K., Azegami, I.: J. Chem. Soc. Chem. Commun. 76 (1977)
43. Picard, J.P.: J. Organometal. Chem. 34, 279 (1972)
44. Picard, J.P., Dunoguès, J., Calas, R.: J. Organometal. Chem. 77, 167 (1974)
45. Dunoguès, J., Ekouya, A., Calas, R., Picard, J.P., Duffaut, N.: J. Organometal. Chem. 66, C39 (1974)
46. Picard, J.P., Ekouya, A., Dunoguès, J., Duffaut, N., Calas, R.: J. Organometal. Chem. 93, 51 (1972)
47. Shono, T., Ohmizu, M., Kawakami, S., Sugiyama, M.: Tetrahedron Lett. 5029 (1980)
48. Bolourtchian, M., Bourgeois, P., Dunoguès, J., Duffaut, N., Calas, R.: J. Organometal. Chem. 43, 139 (1972)
49. Dunoguès, J., Bolourtchian, M., Calas, R., Duffaut, N., Picard, J.P.: J. Organometal. Chem. 43, 157 (1972)
50. Bolourtchian, M., Saednya, A.: Bull. Chim. Soc. Fr. II 170, (1978)
51. Bourgeois, P., Calas, R., Duffaut, N., Dunoguès, J.: J. Organometal. Chem. 32, 79 (1971)

52. Bolourtchian, M., Calas, R., Dunoguès, J., Duffaut, N.: J. Organometal. Chem. *33*, 303 (1971)
53. Weyenberg, D.R., Toporcer, L.H., Nelson, L.E.: J. Org. Chem. *33*, 1975 (1968)
54. Dunoguès, J., Arréguy, B., Biran, C., Calas, R., Pisciotti, F.: J. Organometal. Chem. *63*, 119 (1973)
55. Dunoguès, J., Calas, R., Dedier, J., Pisciotti, F., Lapouyade, P.: J. Organometal. Chem. *25*, 51 (1970)
56. Laguerre, M., Dunoguès, J., Calas, R.: Tetrahedron Lett. 57 (1978)
57. Calas, R., Bourgeois, P.: C. R. Acad. Sci. *C, 275,* 1117 (1972)
58. Dunoguès, J., Bourgeois, P., Pillot, J.P., Merault, G., Calas, R., Lapouyade, P.: J. Organometal. Chem. *87,* 169 (1975)
59. Nakadaira, Y., Sakurai, H.: J. Organometal. Chem. *47,* 61 (1973)
60. Dunoguès, J., Calas, R., Duffaut, N., Lapouyade, P., Gerval, J.: J. Organometal. Chem. *20,* P20 (1969)
61. Weyenberg, D.R., Toporcer, L.H., Bey, A.E.: J. Org. Chem. *30,* 4096 (1965)
62. Laguerre, M., Dunoguès, J., Calas, R., Duffaut, N.: J. Organometal. Chem *93,* C17 (1975)
63. Laguerre, M., Dunoguès, J., Duffaut, N., Calas, R.: J. Organometal. Chem. *149,* 49 (1978)
64. Weyenberg, D.R., Toporcer, L.H.: J. Am. Chem. Soc. *84,* 2843 (1960)
65. Dunoguès, J., Calas, R., Ardoin, N.: J. Organometal. Chem. *43,* 127 (1972)
66. Laguerre, M., Dunoguès, J., Calas, R., Duffaut, N.: J. Organometal. Chem *112,* 49 (1976)
67. Calas, R., Dunoguès, J., Pillot, J.P., Ardoin, N.: J. Organometal. Chem. *73,* 211 (1974)
68. Birkofer, L., Ramadan, N.: Chem. Ber. *104,* 138 (1971)
69. Weyenberg, D.R., Toporcer, L.H.: J. Org. Chem. *30,* 943 (1965)
70. Birkofer, L., Ramadan, N.: J. Organometal. Chem. *44,* C41 (1972)
71. Birkofer, L., Ramadan, N.: J. Organometal. Chem. *92,* C41 (1975)
72. Laguerre, M., Felix, G., Dunoguès, J., Calas, R.: J. Organometal. Chem. *44,* 4275 (1979)
73. Harvey, R.G., Cho, H.: J. Am. Chem. Soc. *96,* 2434 (1974)
74. Harvey, R.C., Cho, H.: J. Org. Chem. *40,* 3097 (1976)
75. Biran, C., Calas, R., Dunoguès, J., Duffaut, N.: J. Organometal. Chem. *22,* 557 (1970)
76. Biran, C., Dédier, J., Dunoguès, J., Calas, R., Duffaut, N., Gerval, J.: J. Organometal. Chem. *35,* 263 (1972)
77. Calas, R., Dunoguès, J., Biran, C., Duffaut, N., Pisciotti, F., Lapouyade, P.: J. Organometal. Chem. 20, P22 (1969)
78. Duffaut, N., Biran, C., Dunoguès, J., Calas, R., Lapouyade, P.: J. Organometal. Chem. *24,* C51 (1970)
79. Biran, C., Duffaut, N., Dunoguès, J., Calas, R.: J. Organometal. Chem. *91,* 279 (1975)
80. Tzeng, D., Weber, W.P.: J. Org. Chem. *46,* 265 (1981)
81. Biran, C., Dunoguès, J., Calas, R., Garvel, J., Tskhorrebachvili, T.: Syn. 220 (1981)
82. Dunoguès, J., Calas, R., Duffaut, N., Picard, J.P.: J. Organometal. Chem. *26,* C13 (1971)
83. Kuwajima, I., Kato, M., Sato, T.: J. Chem. Soc. Chem. Commun. 478 (1978)
84. Pillot, J.P., Déléris, G., Dunoguès, J., Calas, R.: J. Organometal. Chem. *44,* 3397 (1979)
85. Déléris, G., Kowalski, J., Dunoguès, J., Calas, R.: Tetrahedron Lett. 4211 (1977)

86. Pandy-Szekers, D., Déléris, G., Picard, J.P., Pillot, J.P., Calas, R.: Tetrahedron Lett. 4267
87. Kurozumi, S., Torù, T., Kobayashi, M., Ishimoto, S.: Syn. Commun. *7,* 427 (1977)
88. Kuwajima, I., Abe, T.: Bull. Chem. Soc. Japan, *51,* 2183 (1978)
89. Husain, M., Khan, N.H.: Syn. Commun. *11,* 185 (1981)

20 Miscellaneous Reductions

20.1 Introduction

In addition to ionic hydrogenations, dissolving metal reductions and hydrosilation reactions which we have previously considered, there are a number of reduction reactions which utilize organosilicon reagents. These have been divided into seven sections: 1) tin hydride mediated reductions, 2) reductions which utilize silyl radicals, 3) reductions with trichlorosilane (Cl_3SiH)/tertiary amines, 4) reductions of phosphine oxides, 5) reductions of sulfoxides, 6) reductions of amine oxides, and 7) reductions of α-halo ketones. The organizing principle of the first three sections is the combination of reagents used or the reactive intermediates involved. The latter four sections are concerned with reductions of specific functional groups.

20.2 Tin-Hydride Mediated Reductions

Trialkyltin hydrides, such as tri-n-butyltin hydride have been utilized to carry out a number of reduction reactions [1]. Tri-n-butyltin hydride has been prepared by treatment of tri-n-butyltin chloride or *bis*(tri-n-butyltin) oxide with $LiAlH_4$ [2]. One of the problems is that tin hydrides are air sensitive and hence difficult to store. Polymethylsiloxane will reduce *bis*(tri-n-butyltin)oxide as well as polymeric di-n-butyltin oxide to yield tri-n-butyltin hydride and di-n-butyltin dihydride, respectively (IR: Sn$-$H $1\,814\,cm^{-1}$) [3]. Monomeric silanes will also reduce tri-n-butyltin alkoxides [4].

$$Ph_3SiH + (n\text{-}Bu)_3SnOCH_3 \longrightarrow Ph_3SiOCH_3 + (n\text{-}Bu)_3SnH \qquad (20.1)$$

The mechanism of this reaction has been studied. Optically active α-naphthylphenylmethylsilane reacts with tri-n-butyltin methoxide to give tri-n-butyltin hydride and optically active α-naphthylphenylmethylmethoxysilane with 99% retention of configuration at the silyl center. Further, the rate of reaction depends on the concentration of both the silane and the tin alkoxide. The effect of isotopic substitution of a Si$-$D bond for Si$-$H bond on the reaction rate was determined by use of triphenylsilane-d_1 in place of triphenylsilane: $k_H/k_D = 1.64 \pm 0.08$ at $25\,°C$ [5–8]. These facts as well as the activation parameters for the reaction: $\Delta H^+ = 16.2\,kcal/mol$

and $\Delta S^+ = -32 \pm 3.6$ e.u. are consistent with a four-center S_N1-Si reaction mechanism.

$$(20.2)$$

The combination of polymethylsiloxane and *bis*(tri-*n*-butyltin)oxide is effective for the reduction of alkyl or aryl bromides to the corresponding hydrocarbons. *n*-Heptyl bromide yields *n*-heptane, while *ortho*-bromotoluene gives toluene. 1,1-Dibromocyclopropanes are reduced to bromocyclopropanes [9], while 1-chloro-1-nitroethane is reduced to nitroethane [10]. These reactions can be carried out thermally or photochemically [9].

$$(20.3)$$

Polymethylsiloxane reacts with *bis*(tri-*n*-butyltin)oxide to yield tri-*n*-butyltin hydride which in turn is involved in reducing the carbon-halogen bonds.

Lipowitz and Bowman have utilized a polymethylsiloxane to generate tin hydrides by *in-situ*-reduction of tin oxides. They found that *bis*(dibutylacetoxytin)oxide was reduced in protic solvents. The tin hydride thus formed reduces ketones or aldehydes to the corresponding alcohols [11]. 4-Methylcyclohexanone was reduced to a 3:1 mixture of *cis* and *trans*-4-methylcyclohexanol [9]. Only a catalytic amount (2%) of *bis*(dibutylacetoxytin)oxide is needed since a tin alkoxide which can be reduced again by polymethylsiloxane is formed in the reaction.

$$(20.4)$$

On the other hand, nitrobenzene, benzonitrile, benzyl chloride, ethyl acetate, δ-butyrolactone, 2-ethyl hexanoic acid, and DMF were not reduced under these conditions [11].

The combination of *bis*(tri-*n*-butyltin) oxide and polymethylsiloxane reacts with propargyl sulfides to yield allenic tin compounds [12].

20.3 Silyl Radicals

Silyl radicals have often been generated by homolytic cleavage of Si−H bonds. This can be accomplished by photolysis, gamma radiation or hydrogen abstraction from silanes by alkoxy radicals such as *t*-butoxy radicals [13]. Industrially, the free radical hydrosilation of alkenes is an extremely valuable method to form C−Si bonds. The free radical catalyzed addition of Cl_3SiH to styrene is outlined below.

$$Cl_3SiH \; + \; In\cdot \; \longrightarrow \; Cl_3Si\cdot \; + \; InH$$

$$Cl_3Si\cdot \; + \; CH_2=CHPh \; \longrightarrow \; Cl_3SiCH_2\dot{C}HPh \qquad\qquad (20.5)$$

$$Cl_3SiCH_2\dot{C}HPh \; + \; Cl_3SiH \; \longrightarrow \; Cl_3SiCH_2CH_2Ph \; + \; Cl_3Si\cdot$$

A. Reduction of Alkyl Halides

The high affinity of silyl radicals for halogen atoms is the basis of a number of useful reduction reactions. For example, the benzoyl peroxide catalyzed reaction of triethylsilane with CCl_4 yields chloroform and triethylchlorosilane [14]. Silyl radicals abstract chlorine from sp^2 as well as sp^3 hybridized carbons. For example, triphenylsilyl radicals react with chlorobenzene to yield triphenylchlorosilane and biphenyl [15]. A detailed kinetic study of such reactions in the gas phase indicates that abstraction of chlorine from the alkyl chloride by a silyl radical is the rate limiting step [16, 17].

Considerable selectivity is observed in the reduction of alkyl halides by silyl radicals. The ease of reduction of alkyl halides: $RBr > RCl > RF$ is consistent with increasing C−X bond energies. The order of reduction $-CCl_3 > CHCl_2 > -CH_2Cl$ results from the known stabilizing effect of chlorine atoms on carbon radical centers to which they are bonded [18].

$$ClCH_2CHCl_2 \xrightarrow[\text{benzoyl peroxide}]{Et_3SiH} ClCH_2CH_2Cl \qquad 100\% \qquad (20.6)$$

$$Cl_2HCCCl_3 \xrightarrow[\text{benzoyl peroxide}]{Et_3SiH} CHCl_2CHCl_2 \; + \; CH_2ClCCl_3$$

$$98\% : 2\% \qquad\qquad (20.7)$$

$$FCl_2CCF_2Cl \xrightarrow[\text{benzoyl peroxide}]{PhSi(CH_3)_2H} FClHCCF_2Cl \qquad 100\% \qquad (20.8)$$

$$Br(CH_2)_4Cl \xrightarrow[\text{benzoyl peroxide}]{PhSi(CH_3)_2H} CH_3(CH_2)_4Cl \;+\; CH_3(CH_2)_4Br \qquad (20.9)$$

$$98\% : 2\%$$

This selectivity permits the reduction of 1-bromo-1-fluorocyclopropanes to the corresponding fluorocyclopropanes. With di-*n*-butylsilane complete retention of configuration is observed.

$$(20.10)$$

Apparently the rate of hydrogen abstraction from di-*n*-butylsilane is fast relative to inversion of the cyclopropyl radical [19].

B. Reduction of Chloroformates

Primary and secondary chloroformates are reduced to alkanes by reaction with tri-*n*-propylsilane and a catalytic amount of di-*t*-butyl peroxide at 140 °C. Since primary and secondary chloroformates are readily prepared by reaction of corresponding alcohols with phosgene, this reaction provides a method to reduce these alcohols to the corresponding alkanes. The reaction may occur as outlined below [20].

$$(20.11)$$

C. Reduction of Acyl Fluorides

The reduction of acyl fluorides to esters with triethylsilane catalyzed by the radical initiator AIBN may result from the following sequence of reactions. A triethylsilyl radical abstracts a fluorine atom from the acyl fluoride to yield triethylfluorosilane and an acyl radical. This reacts with triethylsilane to yield an aldehyde and regenerate the triethylsilyl radical. After sufficient aldehyde has been formed, the acyl radical reacts competitively with it to yield a carbon radical, which abstracts a hydrogen atom from triethylsilane to yield the ester product and regenerate the silyl radical. Consistent with this proposal, a mixture of pentanoyl fluoride and hexanal are reduced by triethylsilane to yield n-hexyl pentanoate [21].

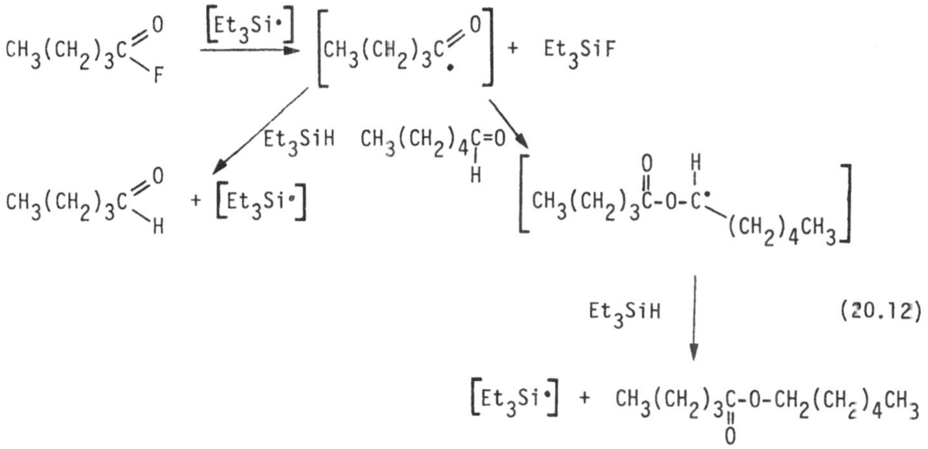

(20.12)

Reduction of perfluoroacyl fluorides with trimethylsilane gives 1,1-dihydroperfluoroalkyl perfluorocarboxylates [95].

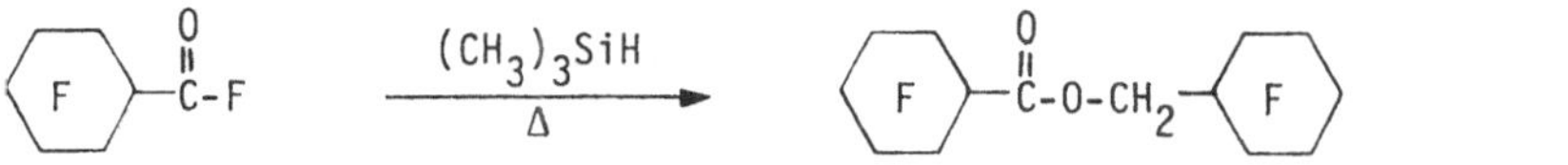

(20.13)

D. Reduction of Esters and Lactones

Esters and lactones are reduced to ethers by Cl_3SiH. This free radical reaction can be initiated by gamma, UV irradiation or di-t-butyl peroxide. The overall reaction involves two radical chain processes (Eq. 20.14 and 20.16) and a thermal exchange reaction (Eq. 20.15). Alkyl trichlorosilyl acetals undergo exchange with Cl_3SiH to yield pentachlorodisiloxane and α-chloro ethers (Eq. 20.15) [22–24].

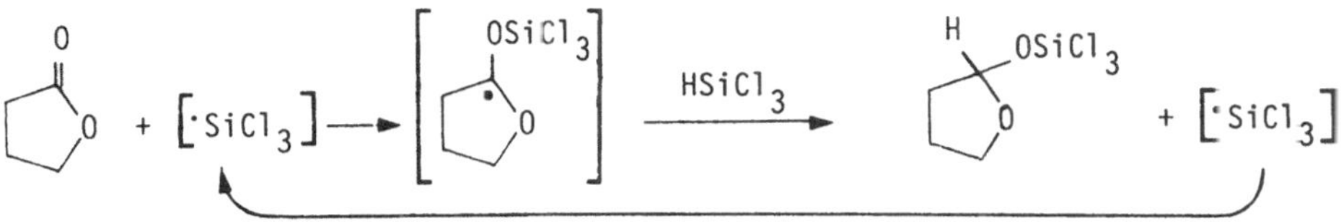

(20.14)

$$(20.15)$$

$$(20.16)$$

20.4 Reduction with Trichlorosilane and Tertiary Amines

Benkeser's work [25] has elucidated much of the chemistry of Cl_3SiH and tertiary aliphatic amines. Polyhalogenated alkanes are selectively reduced on treatment with Cl_3SiH in the presence of tertiary aliphatic amines, such as triethylamine. For example, CCl_4 is reduced to chloroform while methyl trichloroacetate yields methyl dichloroacetate [26]. The related reaction of *sym*-tetrachlorodimethyldisilane with CCl_4 has been reported [27]. When the reduction of CCl_4 with Cl_3SiH was carried out with dicyclohexylmethylamine, trichloromethyltrichlorosilane was obtained along with dicyclohexylmethyl-ammonium chloride. Trichloromethyltrichlorosilane reacts with tri-*n*-butylam-monium chloride to yield chloroform and tetrachlorosilane. These results led to the proposal that the reaction involves deprotonation of Cl_3SiH by the tertiary amine to form a trichlorosilyl anion/trialkylammonium cation pair. Nucleophilic attack by the trichlorosilyl anion, on CCl_4 yields trichloro-methyltrichlorosilane and chloride ion. Chloride attack on the silyl center of trichloromethyltrichlorosilane yields silicon tetrachloride and a trichloro-methyl anion which is protonated by the trialkylammonium ions to give chloroform and regenerate the tertiary amine.

$$(20.17)$$

This combination of reagents reacts with benzylic chlorides to yield benzylic trichlorosilanes and trialkylammonium chlorides. Benzyl chloride gives ben-zyltrichlorosilane while benzal chloride gives α,α-*bis*(trichlorosilyl) toluene [28].

Tertiary amine/chlorosilane complexes are well-known [29]. Spectroscopic evidence in support of the intermediacy of the trichlorosilyl anion in these reactions has been obtained. Thus the ^1H nmr resonance of Cl_3SiH occurs at δ 6.25 in acetonitrile. On addition of tri-*n*-propylamine, this resonance disappears, and a new resonance at δ 11.03, consistent with a N−H resonance of the tri-*n*-propylammonium cation grows in. In the presence of excess Cl_3SiH, rapid exchange between the Si−H of Cl_3SiH and the N−H of tri-*n*-propylammonium cation occurs. Consistent with the intermediacy of the trichlorosilyl anion, Cl_3SiH undergoes isotopic exchange of Si−H for Si−D in the presence of tri-*n*-propylammonium-N-d_1 chloride [30, 31].

Cl_3SiH and tertiary aliphatic amines have been utilized to reduce germanium tetrachloride to tertiary amine complexes of germanium trichloride These exist as trichlorogermanyl anion trialkylammonium cation pairs. These react with primary alkyl halides to yield alkyltrichlorogermanium compounds. This constitutes a valuable Ge−C bond-forming reaction [32, 33].

Of more general synthetic interest, aromatic ketones, aldehydes, and acid chlorides react with Cl_3SiH and aliphatic tertiary amines to yield deoxygenated products. A hydrogen and a trichlorosilyl group are bonded to the carbon in place of the double bonded oxygen of the starting material. Reaction of benzophenone with this pair of reagents yields diphenylmethyltrichlorosilane [34]. N,N-dialkyl benzamides are also reduced [35].

(20.18)

C−Si bonds of such benzylic-trichlorosilanes are readily cleaved by aq. alcoholic base [36]. Thus treatment of α-(N,N-dimethylamino)benzyltrichlorosilane with ethanolic potassium hydroxide yields N,N-dimethylbenzylamine [35].

The reduction of aromatic carboxylic acids to methyl aromatics is a general reaction. The first step involves reaction of the aromatic carboxylic acid with Cl_3SiH to yield a silyl ester. Treatment of the ester with additional Cl_3SiH and an aliphatic tertiary amine yields a benzylic trichlorosilane [37]. Finally, cleavage of the benzylic C−Si bond with base yields a methyl-substituted aromatic. This one-pot reaction sequence constitutes a unique procedure to convert aromatic carboxylic acids to methyl groups [38].

(20.19)

Consistent with this reaction sequence, alkyl benzoates are not reduced, whereas trimethylsilyl benzoates are reduced [39]. The reaction tolerates ether, aliphatic esters, and dimethylamino functional groups [39]. A number of methyl substituted aromatic compounds have been prepared by this method: 4-methylfluorene [40], 2-fluoro-8-methylnaphthalene [41], 1-fluoro-5-methyl-naphthalene [42], and 2-methylnaphtho [1,2,b] thiophene [43].

20.5 Reduction of Phosphine Oxides

Optically active tertiary phosphines are important not only for mechanistic studies but also as chiral ligands for catalytic asymmetric reactions. Optically active tertiary phosphine oxides can be prepared by reaction of Grignard or organolithium reagents with optically active dialkyl menthyl phosphinates [44]. The critical step in the preparation of chiral tertiary phosphines is the stereospecific reduction of the corresponding chiral tertiary phosphine oxides. Several silicon reagents are effective for the reduction of tertiary phosphine oxides to tertiary phosphines. By the appropriate choice of silane these reductions can be carried out stereoselectively either with retention or inversion of configuration at phosphorous.

$$(20.20)$$

Fritzsche showed that a variety of triaryl phosphine oxides, trialkyl phosphine oxides, and cyclic phosphine oxides could be reduced to the corresponding tertiary phosphines by treatment with polymethylsiloxane or phenylsilane [45].

$$(20.21)$$

A. Trichlorosilane-tertiary amines/hexachlorodisilane

The combination of Cl_3SiH and triethylamine reduces optically active acyclic tertiary phosphine oxides to the corresponding tertiary phosphines with net inversion of configuration. On the other hand, Cl_3SiH and pyridine or N,N-dimethylaniline reduces optically active tertiary phosphine oxides to tertiary phosphines with net retention of configuration [46]. These results were explained in terms of initial coordination of the Cl_3SiH to the oxygen of the phosphine oxide to yield a 1,3-zwitterionic species. In the presence of weak bases such as pyridine, this zwitterion undergoes an intramolecular transfer of hydride from silicon to the phosphonium center with simultaneous scission of the P−O bond to yield a trichlorosilyloxy anion/tertiary phosphonium cation pair. Proton transfer from the phosphonium cation to the silyloxy anion is the final step.

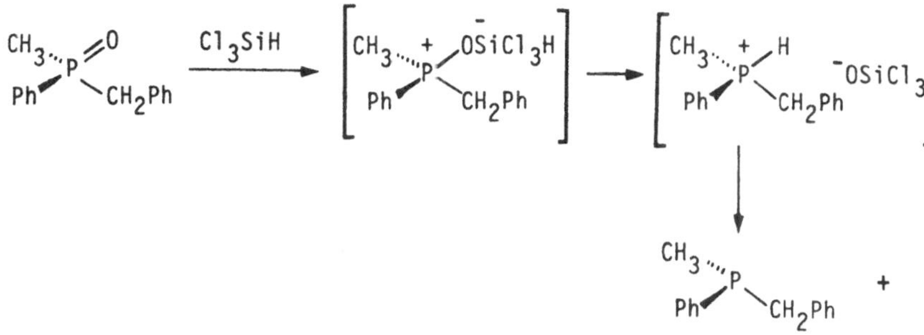

$$\text{CH}_3 \cdots\!\!\underset{\text{Ph}}{\overset{}{\text{P}}}\!\!\overset{\text{O}}{\diagdown}\text{CH}_2\text{Ph} \xrightarrow{\text{Cl}_3\text{SiH}} \left[\text{CH}_3 \cdots\!\!\underset{\text{Ph}}{\overset{+}{\text{P}}}\!\!\overset{\text{OSiCl}_3\text{H}}{\diagdown}\text{CH}_2\text{Ph} \right] \longrightarrow \left[\text{CH}_3 \cdots\!\!\underset{\text{Ph}}{\overset{+}{\text{P}}}\!\!\overset{\text{H}}{\diagdown}\text{CH}_2\text{Ph} \quad {}^-\text{OSiCl}_3 \right]$$

(20.22)

$$\downarrow$$

$$\text{CH}_3 \cdots\!\!\underset{\text{Ph}}{\overset{}{\text{P}}}\!\!\diagdown\text{CH}_2\text{Ph} \quad + \quad \text{HOSiCl}_3$$

In the presence of triethylamine, backside attack by hydride on the initial 1,3-zwitterionic complex occurs. This causes inversion at phosphorous.

$$\left[\underset{\text{Cl}_3\text{SiH}}{\overset{\text{O}}{\text{P}}}\!\!\!\!\underset{\text{CH}_2\text{Ph}}{\overset{\text{CH}_3}{\text{Ph}}} \quad \overset{\frown}{\text{H-SiCl}_3}\cdots\text{NEt}_3 \right] \longrightarrow \left[\text{CH}_3 \cdots\!\!\underset{\text{Ph}}{\overset{+}{\text{P}}}\!\!\overset{\text{H}}{\diagdown}\text{CH}_2\text{Ph} \quad {}^-\text{OSiCl}_3 \right]$$

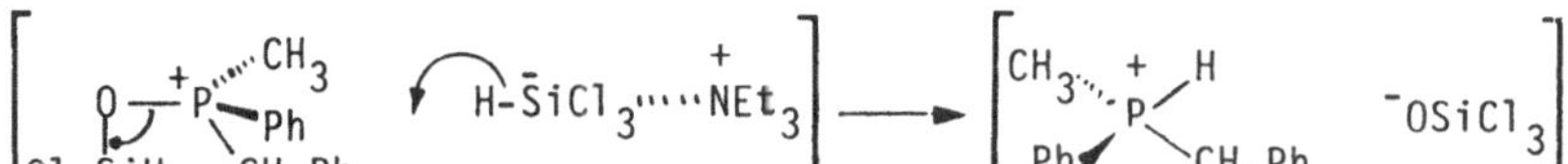

(20.23)

The mechanism of these reductions with Cl_3SiH was studied in detail by Mislow. He found that with strong tertiary nitrogen bases ($pK_b \leqq 5$) inversion of configuration at phosphorous occurs. Whereas with weaker tertiary amine bases ($pK_b > 7$), retention at phosphorous was observed. In the presence of triethylamine, Cl_3SiH undergoes equilibration to form perchloropolysilanes. These were proposed to be the active reducing agents [47]. In support of this proposal, Mislow found that hexachlorodisilane and octachlorotrisilane reduce chiral tertiary phosphine oxides with complete inversion of configuration. The reduction may occur by the following reaction sequence. Attack by the oxygen of the phosphine oxide on hexachlorodisilane yields a trichlorosilyl anion/trichlorosilyloxy-substituted phosphonium cation pair. Nucleophilic backside attack by the trichlorosilyl anion on the phosphonium cation leads to inversion at phosphorous and formation of trichlorosilyloxy anion/trichlorosilyl-substituted phosphonium cation. Attack by the trichlorosilyloxy anion on the silyl center yields hexachlorodisiloxane and the inverted tertiary phosphine [48].

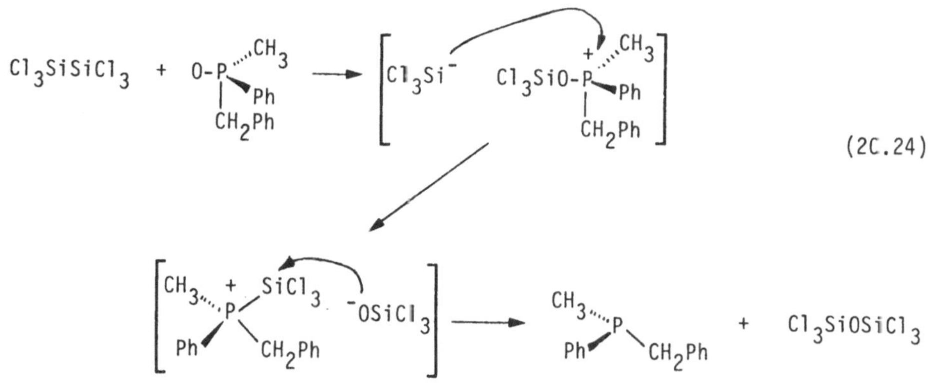

$$\text{Cl}_3\text{SiSiCl}_3 \quad + \quad \underset{\text{CH}_2\text{Ph}}{\overset{\text{CH}_3}{\text{O-P}}}\!\!\overset{}{\diagdown}\text{Ph} \longrightarrow \left[\text{Cl}_3\text{Si}^- \quad \text{Cl}_3\text{SiO-}\underset{\text{CH}_2\text{Ph}}{\overset{+}{\text{P}}}\!\!\overset{\text{CH}_3}{\diagup}\text{Ph} \right]$$

(20.24)

$$\left[\text{CH}_3 \cdots\!\!\underset{\text{Ph}}{\overset{+}{\text{P}}}\!\!\overset{\text{SiCl}_3}{\diagdown}\text{CH}_2\text{Ph} \quad {}^-\text{OSiCl}_3 \right] \longrightarrow \text{CH}_3 \cdots\!\!\underset{\text{Ph}}{\overset{}{\text{P}}}\!\!\diagdown\text{CH}_2\text{Ph} \quad + \quad \text{Cl}_3\text{SiOSiCl}_3$$

329

By comparison, hexachlorodisilane reduces chiral tertiary phosphine sulfides with retention of configuration [67].

Optically active *bis*(*o*-anisyl phenylphosphinyl) ethane has been reduced with Cl₃SiH and tri-*n*-butylamine in acetonitrile solvent to give the chiral *bis*-tertiary phosphine. Inversion at both asymmetric phosphorous atoms occurs during reduction [49]. This chiral ligand has been used in rhodium catalyzed asymmetric hydrogenation of α-acylamido acrylic acids. Commercially this chemistry is critical to the synthesis of L-Dopa.

$$(20.25)$$

Optically active 2,2′*bis*(diphenylphosphinomethyl)-1,1′-binaphthyl, a chiral tertiary phosphine possessing an axial element of chirality [50] has been prepared by reduction of the corresponding *bis*-phosphine oxide with Cl₃SiH and triethylamine.

$$(20.26)$$

However, Cl₃SiH and triethylamine or hexachlorodisilane reduce four membered cyclic phosphine oxides to cyclic phosphines with retention of configuration at phosphorous. This may be consistent with Mislow's mechanistic proposals, since S$_n$2 displacement at phosphorous in a four membered ring is expected to be disfavored by angle strain [51, 52].

$$(20.27)$$

On the other hand, phenylphosphahomocubane oxide, a compound in which phosphorous is in five membered rings, is reduced by hexachlorosilane or Cl₃SiH and triethylamine to phenylphosphahomocubane with inversion at phosphorous [53–55]. Reduction of diazaphospholene oxide with Cl₃SiH and triethylamine is not stereospecific. This results from stereomutation of the starting material by hexachlorodisiloxane [56].

$$\text{(20.28)}$$

A series of macrocyclic *bis*-phosphine oxides were reduced by treatment with Cl_3SiH. *cis-bis*-Phosphine oxides were reduced to *cis-bis*-phosphines while *trans-bis*-phosphine oxides gave the corresponding *trans-bis*-phosphines [57]. Hexachlorodisilane reduces 1-halophospholene oxides to the corresponding 1-halophospholenes [58].

$$\text{(20.29)}$$

B. Phenylsilane

While hexachlorodisilane is an excellent reagent, it is rather expensive. Some racemization occurs on reduction of cyclic chiral tertiary phosphine oxides with Cl_3SiH and triethylamine. On the other hand, such cyclic chiral tertiary phosphine oxides are reduced by phenylsilane to the corresponding tertiary phosphines with complete retention of configuration [59–62]. In only one case has racemization been reported [63].

$$\text{(20.30)}$$

Phenylsilane permits the selective reduction of 3,4-epoxyphospholane oxides to the corresponding 3,4-epoxyphospholanes [64, 65].

$$\text{(20.31)}$$

Despite the fact that little mechanistic work has appeared concerning reductions of tertiary phosphine oxides with phenylsilane, it is probably the reagent of choice. Phenylsilane may be prepared by treatment of phenyltrichlorosilane with $LiAlH_4$ [66]. After filtration to remove excess $LiAlH_4$, it is critical that

331

the ether or THF solution of phenylsilane be extracted with water prior to distillation. If this is not done, vigorous decomposition during distillation will ensue.

Phenylsilane, diphenylsilane, and polymethylsiloxane reduce a variety of phosphorous oxygen functional groups to P−H bonds. For example, diethyl *n*-butylphosphonate has been reduced by polymethylsiloxane to yield *n*-butyl-phosphine [68].

$$\text{(20.32)}$$

20.6 Reduction of Sulfoxides

Cl_3SiH reduces diaryl sulfoxides to the corresponding sulfides [69].

$$\text{(20.33)}$$

The mechanism of this reaction has been studied [70]. The first order dependence of the reaction rate on the concentration of both the diaryl sulfoxide and Cl_3SiH, the large negative entropy of activations ($\Delta S^+ = 31$ e.u.) as well as the small isotope effects $k_H/k_D = 2.1$–2.4 are all consistent with a four-center transition state [70].

$$Ph_2S\text{-}O \; + \; HSiCl_3 \longrightarrow \begin{bmatrix} Ph_2\overset{+}{S}\text{-}O \\ H\text{-}\underset{=}{Si}Cl_3 \end{bmatrix} \longrightarrow \begin{bmatrix} Ph_2\overset{+}{S} & \overset{-}{O} \\ H & SiCl_3 \end{bmatrix}$$

$$\text{(20.34)}$$

$$Ph_2S \; + \; HOSiCl_3$$

The reduction of dibenzyl sulfoxide with Cl_3SiH results in a mixture of dibenzyl sulfide and the benzyl mercaptal of benzaldehyde [69].

TMS-I has also proved useful for the reduction of sulfoxide to sulfides [71, 72]. Dibenzyl sulfoxide is reduced to dibenzyl sulfide in high yield. TMS-1 may be generated *in-situ* by reaction of trimethylphenylsilane [72] or hexamethyldisilane with iodine [72] or by reaction of TMS-Cl with sodium iodide in acetonitrile solvent [73]. The latter method is faster, possibly due to a combination of a favorable solvent effect and iodide ion catalysis. The following mechanism has been proposed. Nucleophilic attack by the sulfoxide oxygen on the silyl center of TMS-I leads to a dialkyl trimethylsilyloxy sulfonium cation/iodide ion pair. This may collapse to an intermediate which possess a tetra-coordinate sulfur atom (sulfurane). Iodide ion attack on the iodine atom bonded to sulfur leads to the products. Catalysis by iodide and other soft anions such as cyanide, methyl thiolate, and thiocyanate is consistent with this proposal.

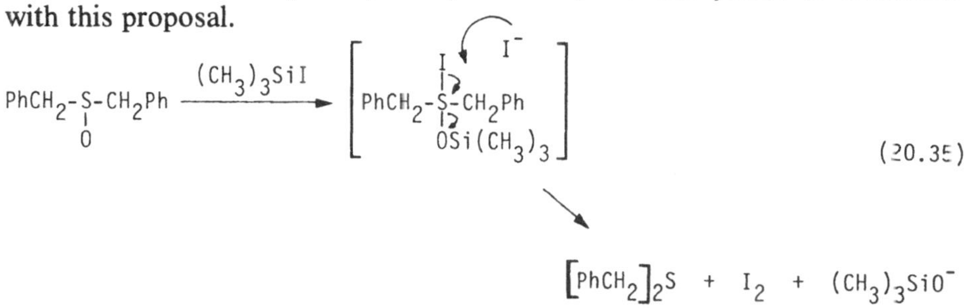

$$PhCH_2-\underset{O}{\overset{|}{S}}-CH_2Ph \xrightarrow{(CH_3)_3SiI} \left[PhCH_2-\underset{OSi(CH_3)_3}{\overset{|}{\underset{I_2}{\overset{I}{S}}}}-CH_2Ph \right] \qquad (20.35)$$

$$\left[PhCH_2\right]_2S \ + \ I_2 \ + \ (CH_3)_3SiO^-$$

TMS-I has been utilized to reduce a sulfoxide to a sulfide in the synthesis of PGI$_2$ a prostacyclic analog [74].

$$\xrightarrow[\underset{N}{}]{\substack{(CH_3)_3SiI \\ \overline{\quad CCl_4 \quad}}}$$

(20.36)

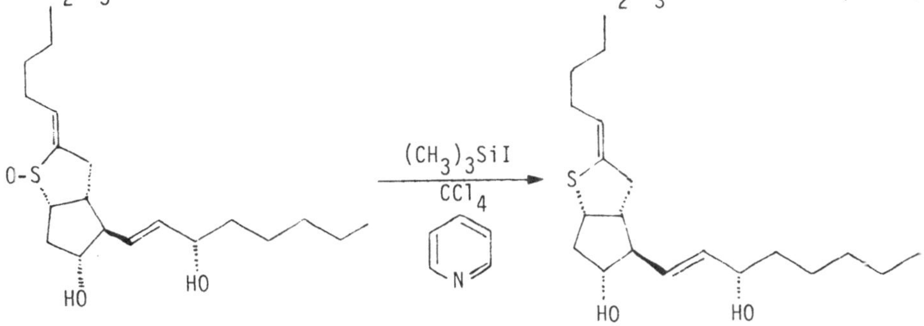

TMS-Br also reduces sulfoxides to sulfides. However, with diphenyl sulfoxide ring brominated diphenyl sulfides are isolated [72]. TMS-Br generated *in-situ* by reaction of TMS-Cl with sodium bromide in acetonitrile also reduces sulfoxides to sulfides. With ethylene present as a halogen scavenger, the problem of aromatic bromination can be eliminated [75]. Diphenyldichloro-silane reacts with DMSO to yield hexaphenylcyclotrisiloxane and dimethyl sulfide. The generality of this reaction has not been explored [76]. Aliphatic and aromatic sulfoxides are readily reduced to the corresponding sulfides by TMS-Cl and zinc in THF [77].

Diaryl, alkyl aryl, and dialkyl sulfoxides are reduced by disilthianes to yield sulfides, siloxanes, and elemental sulfur [78]. This reaction may occur as outlined below.

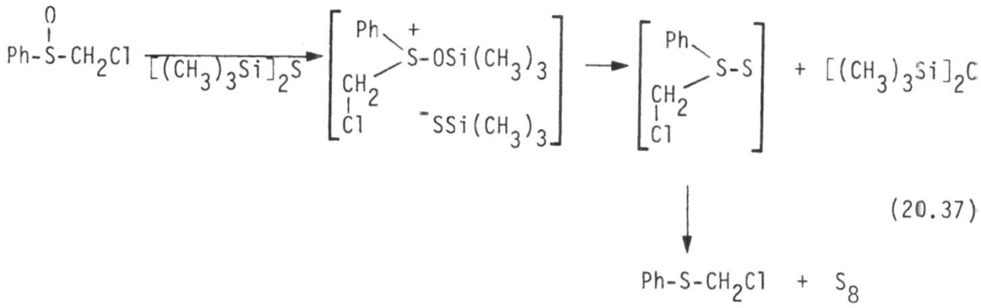

$$Ph-\underset{O}{\overset{\underset{\|}{}}{S}}-CH_2Cl \xrightarrow{[(CH_3)_3Si]_2S} \left[\underset{\underset{Cl}{\overset{|}{CH_2}}}{\overset{Ph}{\diagdown}} \underset{{}^-SSi(CH_3)_3}{\overset{+}{S-OSi(CH_3)_3}} \right] \longrightarrow \left[\underset{\underset{Cl}{\overset{|}{CH_2}}}{\overset{Ph}{\diagdown}} S-S \right] \ + \ [(CH_3)_3Si]_2C$$

(20.37)

$$Ph-S-CH_2Cl \ + \ S_8$$

The combination of TMS-Cl and benzene thiol reduces sulfoxides to sulfides. In the process, benzene thiol is oxidized to diphenyl disulfide [79].

Phenylselenotrimethylsilane is also high effective for the reduction of sulfoxides and selenoxides [80].

$$(20.38)$$

The combination of Cl$_3$SiH and tri-n-propyl amine reduces sulfenyl, sulfinyl, and sulfonyl chlorides as well as sulfenate and sulfinate esters to the corresponding disulfides [81].

$$(20.39)$$

Trimethylsilyl iodide also reduces sulfonyl chlorides and bromides to disulfides [82]. The fact that alkyl sulfinate esters, sulfinyl chlorides and sulfenyl chlorides are reduced by TMS-I to disulfides is consistent with reaction sequence proposed.

$$(20.40)$$

Sulfinic acids are also reduced to disulfides by the combination of thiols and TMS-Cl [83].

$$p\text{-}CH_3Ph\text{-}\overset{\overset{O}{\|}}{S}\text{-}OH \xrightarrow[n\text{-BuSH}]{(CH_3)_3SiCl} p\text{-}CH_3PhSS\text{-}n\text{-}Bu + n\text{-}BuSS\text{-}n\text{-}Bu \qquad (20.41)$$

Thiabenzene-1-oxides are reduced by Cl_3SiH. 1-Methyl-3,5-diphenylthiabenzene-1-oxide gives a mixture of 2H- and 4H-3,5-diphenylthiopyrans [84].

$$\text{(20.42)}$$

20.7 Reduction of Amine Oxides

Both the combination of Cl_3SiH and tertiary aliphatic amines, as well as, hexachlorodisilane reduce a variety of N−O bonds. Tertiary amine oxides are reduced by hexachlorodisilane to the corresponding tertiary amines [47]. The combination of Cl_3SiH and triethylamine has proved effective for reduction of nitrobenzene to aniline [32]. Thermal reaction (250 °C) of 2-nitrobiphenyl with hexamethyldisilane leads to carbazole, 2-amino biphenyl, and hexamethyldisiloxane [85]. The formation of carbazole may implicate a nitrene intermediate [86].

$$\text{(20.43)}$$

A number of aromatic heterocyclic N-oxides have been effectively reduced by treatment with hexachlorodisilane [87].

$$\text{(20.44)}$$

Nitrones are reduced by hexachlorodisilane to the corresponding imines.

$$\text{Ph}\diagdown_{H}\!\!C=N\diagup^{+}\diagdown_{Ph}^{O^-} \xrightarrow{\text{Si}_2\text{Cl}_6} \text{Ph}\diagdown_{H}\!\!C=N\diagdown_{Ph} \qquad (20.45)$$

Pyridine-N-oxides have been reduced by reaction with phenoxypentamethyl disilane [88].

Hexachlorodisilane reduces cyclic *cis*-azoxy compounds to corresponding azo compounds, which often spontaneously lose nitrogen under the reduction conditions [89–91]. Hexachlorodisilane also reduces cyclic *cis*-azo dioxides, C-nitroso dimers, first to the *cis*-azoxy derivatives and then to the azo compounds [90, 92].

$$\xrightarrow{\text{Si}_2\text{Cl}_6} \qquad \xrightarrow{\text{Si}_2\text{Cl}_6} \qquad (20.46)$$

20.8 Reduction of α-Halo Ketones

TMS-I reduces α-halo ketones to ketones [93, 94].

References

1. Kuivila, H.G., Advances in Organometallic Chem., *1*, 47, New York: Academic Press 1964
2. Poller, R.C.: The Chemistry of Organotin Compounds, p. 105–107, New York: Academic Press, 1970
3. Hayashi, K., Iyoda, J., Shiihara, I.: J. Organometal. Chem. *10*, 81 (1967)
4. Bellegarde, B., Pereyre, M., Valade, J.: Bull. Soc. Chem. Fr. 3082 (1967)
5. Pereyre, M., Pijselman, J.: J. Organometal. Chem. *25*, C27 (1970)
6. Pijselman, J., Pereyre, M.: J. Organometal. Chem. *63*, 139 (1973)
7. Lewis, E.S., Grinstein, R.H.: J. Am. Chem. Soc. *84*, 1158 (1962)
8. O'Ferrall, R.A.M.: J. Chem. Soc. B, 785 (1970)
9. Grady, F.L., Kuivila, H.G.: J. Org. Chem. *34*, 2014 (1969)
10. Barnes, M.W., Patterson, J.M.: J. Org. Chem. *41*, 733 (1976)
11. Lipowitz, J., Bowman, S.A.: J. Org. Chem. *38*, 162 (1973)
12. Ueno, Y., Okawara, M.: J. Am. Chem. Soc. *101*, 1893 (1979)
13. For a Review of Silyl Radicals see Davidson, I.M.T., J. Chem. Soc. Quarterly Review, *25*, 111 (1971)
14. Nagai, Y., Yamazaki, K., Shiojima, I., Kobori, N., Hayashi, N.: J. Organometal. Chem. *9*, P21 (1967)
15. Curtice, J., Gilman, H., Hammond, G.S.: J. Am. Chem. Soc. *79*, 4754 (1957)
16. Kerr, J.A., Smith, B.J.A., Trotman-Dickenson, A.F., Young, J.C.: J. Chem. Soc. Chem. Commun. 157 (1966)
17. Kerr, J.A., Smith, B.J.A., Trotman-Dickenson, A.F., Young, J.C.: J. Chem. Soc. A, 510 (1968)
18. Nagai, Y., Yamazaki, K., Shiojima, I.: J. Organometal. Chem. *9*, P25 (1967)
19. Ando, T., Hosaka, H., Funasaka, W., Yamanaka, H.: Bull. Soc. Chem. Japan, *46*, 3513 (1973)

20. Billingham, N.C., Jackson, R.A., Malek, F.: J. Chem. Soc. Chem. Commun 344 (1977)
21. Citron, J.D.: J. Org. Chem. *36*, 2547 (1971)
22. Nakao, R., Fukumoto, T., Tsurugi, J.: J. Org. Chem. *37*, 76 (1972)
23. Nagata, Y., Dohmaru, T., Tsurugi, J.: J. Org. Chem. *38*, 795 (1973)
24. Nakao, R., Fukumoto, T., Tsurugi, J.: J. Org. Chem. *37*, 4349 (1972)
25. Benkeser, R.A.: Accts. Chem. Res. *4*, 94 (1971)
26. Benkeser, R.A., Smith, W.E.: J. Am. Chem. Soc. *90*, 5307 (1968)
27. Matsumoto, H., Ohkawa, K., Nakano, T., Nagai, Y.: Chem. Lett. 721 (1980)
28. Benkeser, R.A., Gaul, J.M., Smith,W.E.: J. Am. Chem. Soc. *91*, 3666 (1969)
29. Burg, A.B.: J. Am. Chem. Soc. *76*, 2674 (1954)
30. Benkeser, R.A., Foley, K.M., Grutzner, J.B., Smith, W.E.: J. Am. Chem. Soc. *92*, 697 (1970)
31. Bernstein, S.C.: J. Am. Chem. Soc. *92*, 699 (1970)
32. Nametkin, N.S., Kuz'min, O.V., Korolev, V.K., Kobrakov, K.I., Patriekeev, A.V.: Izv. Akad. Nauk SSSR, 676 (1978)
33. Nametkin, N.S., Kuz'min, O.V., Korolev, V.K., Kobrakov, K.I.: Dokl. Akad. Nauk. SSSR, *234*, 340 (1977)
34. Benkeser, R.A., Smith, W.E.: J. Am. Chem. Soc. *91*, 1556 (1969)
35. Benkeser, R.A., Li, G.S., Mozdzen, E.C.: J. Organometal. Chem. *178*, 21 (1979)
36. Eaborn, C., "Organosilicon Compounds", pp. 143–146, London: Butterworth, 1960
37. Benkeser, R.A., Gaul, J.M.: J. Am. Chem. Soc. *92*, 720 (1970)
38. Benkeser, R.A., Foley, K.M., Gaul, J.M., Li, G.S.: J. Am. Chem. Soc. *92*, 3232 (1970)
39. Benkeser, R.A., Mozdzen, E.C., Muth, C.L.: J. Org. Chem. *44*, 2185 (1979)
40. Buckle, D.R., Morgan, N.J., Alexander, R.G.: J. Chem. Soc. Perkin *I*, 3004 (1979)
41. Adcock, W., Dewar, M.J.S., Golden, R., Zeb, M.A.: J. Am. Chem. Soc. *97*, 2198 (1975)
42. Adcock, W., Alste, J., Rizui, S.Q.A., Aurangzeb, M.: J. Am. Chem. Soc. *98*, 1701 (1976)
43. Clarke, K., Gregory, D.N., Scrowston, R.M.: J. Chem. Soc. Perkin *I*, 63 (1977)
44. Korpiun, O., Lewis, R.A., Chickos, J., Mislow, K.: J. Am. Chem. Soc. *90*, 4842 (1968)
45. Fritzsche, H., Hasserodt, U., Korte, F.: Chem. Ber. *97*, 1988 (1964)
46. Horner, L., Balzer, W.D.: Tetrahedron Lett. 1157 (1965)
47. Naumann, K., Zon, G., Mislow, K.: J. Am. Chem. Soc. *91*, 7012 (1969)
48. Naumann, K., Zon, G., Mislow, K.: J. Am. Chem. Soc. *91*, 2788 (1969)
49. Knowles, W.S., Sabacky, M.J., Vineyard, B.D., Weinkauff, D.J.: J. Am. Chem. Soc. *97*, 2567 (1975)
50. Tanao, K., Yamamoto, H., Matsumoto, H., Miyake, N., Hayashi, T., Kumada, M.: Tetrahedron Lett. 1389 (1977)
51. Cremer, S.E., Chorvat, R.J.: J. Org. Chem. *32*, 4066 (1967)
52. DeBruin, K.E., Zon, G., Naumann, K., Mislow, K.: J. Am. Chem. Soc. *91*, 7027 (1969)
53. Katz, T.J., Carnahan, Jr., J.C., Clarke, G.M., Acton, N.: J. Am. Chem. Soc. *92*, 734 (1970)
54. Turnblom, E.W., Katz, T.J.: J. Am. Chem. Soc. *93*, 4065 (1971)
55. Turnblom, E.W., Katz, T.J.: J. Am. Chem. Soc. *95*, 4292 (1973)
56. Baccolini, G., Todesco, P.E.: J. Org. Chem. *40*, 2318 (1975)
57. Chan, T.H., Ong, B.S.: J. Org. Chem. *39*, 1748 (1974)

58. Myers, D.K., Quin, L.D.: J. Org. Chem. *36*, 1285 (1971)
59. Marsi, K.L.: J. Am. Chem. Soc. *91*, 4724 (1969)
60. Egan, W., Chauviere, G., Mislow, K., Clark, R.T., Marsi, K.L.: J. Chem. Soc. Chem. Commun. 733 (1970)
61. Marsi, K.L.: J. Org. Chem. *39*, 265 (1974)
62. Marsi, K.L., Tuinstra, H.: J. Org. Chem. *40*, 1843 (1975)
63. Fisher, C., Mosher, H.S.: Tetrahedron Lett. 2487 (1977)
64. Symmes, Jr., C., Quin, L.D.: Tetrahedron Lett. 1853 (1976)
65. Quin, L.D., Symmes, Jr., C., Middlemas, E.D., Lawson, H.F.: J. Org. Chem. *45*, 4688 (1980)
66. Benkeser, R.A., Landesman, H., Foster, D.J.: J. Am. Chem. Soc. *74*, 648 (1952)
67. Zon, G., DeBruin, K.E., Naumann, K., Mislow, K.: J. Am. Chem. Soc. *91*, 7023 (1969)
68. Fritzsche, H., Hasserodt, U., Korte, F.: Chem. Ber. *98*, 1681 (1965)
69. Chan, T.H., Melnyk, A., Harpp, D.N.: Tetrahedron Lett. 201 (1969)
70. Chan, T.H., Melnyk, A.: J. Am. Chem. Soc. *92*, 3718 (1970)
71. Olah, G.A., Narang, S.C., Gupta, B.G.B., Malhotra, R.: Synthesis, 61 (1979)
72. Olah, G.A., Gupta, B.G.B., Narang, S.C.: Synthesis, 583 (1977)
73. Olah, G.A., Narang, S.C., Gupta, B.G.B., Malhotra, R.: Angew. Chem. Int. Ed. *18*, 612 (1979)
74. Nicolaou, K.C., Barnette, W.E., Magolda, R.L.: J. Am. Chem. Soc. *100*, 2567 (1978)
75. Schmidt, A.H., Russ, M.: Chem. Ber. *114*, 1099 (1981)
76. Goossens, J.C., Fr. Pat. 1, 456, 981 (1966), CA. *67*, 54239 (1967)
77. Schmidt, A.H., Russ, M.: Chem. Ber. *114*, 822 (1981)
78. Soysa, H.S.D., Weber, W.P.: Tetrahedron Lett. 235 (1978)
79. Numata, T., Togo, H., Oae, S.: Chem. Lett. 329 (1979)
80. Detty, M.R.: J. Org. Chem. *44*, 4528 (1979)
81. Chan, T.H., Montillier, J.P., Van Horn, W.F., Harpp, D.N.: J. Am. Chem. Soc. *92*, 7224 (1970)
82. Olah, G.A., Narang, S.C., Fields, L.D., Salem, G.F.: J. Org. Chem. *44*, 4792 (1980)
83. Oae, S., Togo, H., Numata, T., Fujimori, K.: Chem. Lett. 1193 (1980)
84. Hortmann, A.G., Harris, R.L.: J. Am. Chem. Soc. *92*, 1803 (1970)
85. Tsui, F.P., Vogel, T.M., Zon, G.: J. Org. Chem. *40*, 761 (1975)
86. Cadogan, J.I.G.: J. Chem. Soc. Quarterly, Review, *22*, 222 (1968)
87. Hortmann, A.G., Koo, J.Y., Yu, C.C.: J. Org. Chem. *43*, 2289 (1978)
88. Sakurai, H., Kira, M., Kumada, M.: Bull. Chem. Soc. Japan, *44*, 1167 (1971)
89. Snyder, J.P., Lee, L., Bandurco, V.T., Yu, C.Y., Boyd, R.J.: J. Am. Chem. Soc. *94*, 3260 (1972)
90. Snyder, J.P., Heyman, M.L., Suciu, E.N.: J. Org. Chem. *40*, 1395 (1975)
91. Olsen, H., Snyder, J.P.: J. Am. Chem. Soc. *99*, 1524 (1977)
92. Greene, F.D., Gilbert, K.E.: J. Org. Chem. *40*, 1409 (1975)
93. Olah, G.A., Arvanaghi, M., Vankar, Y.D.: J. Org. Chem. *45*, 3531 (1980)
94. Ho, T.L.: Syn. Commun. *11*, 101 (1981)
95. Croft, T.S., McBrady, J.J.: J. Org. Chem. *41*, 2256 (1976)

21 Silicon-Sulfur

21.1 Introduction

Silicon-sulfur and selenium compounds have proved to be valuable synthetic reagents [1]. The preparation of both vinyl thio ethers [2, 3] and vinyl sulfinyl ethers [4] by the Peterson reaction has been discussed [2], as well as reductions of sulfoxides by silyl sulfide [5] and silyl selenide [6] reagents (20.6).

Methylthiotrimethylsilane may be thought of as the combination of hard acid, the trimethylsilyl group, with a soft base, the methylthio group. The relative strength of Si−S single bonds (~99 kcal/mol) [7, 8] compared to that of Si−O single bonds (~128 kcal/mol) [8] may account for the facility with which these reagents react with a variety of oxygen functional groups.

21.2 Epoxides and Oxetanes

Methylthiotrimethylsilane reacts with epoxides and oxetanes under Lewis acid catalysis by zinc chloride to yield (2-methylthioethoxy)trimethylsilanes and (3-methylthiopropoxy)trimethylsilanes, respectively [9].

$$\text{(epoxide)} + \text{CH}_3\text{SSi(CH}_3)_3 \xrightarrow{\text{ZnCl}_2} \text{CH}_3\text{S} \diagup\!\diagdown\!\diagup \text{OSi(CH}_3)_3 \qquad (21.1)$$

Propylene oxide reacts under these conditions to yield (1-methylthio-2-propoxy)trimethylsilane. This regiospecificity is expected if the formation of the C−S bond has the characteristic of an S_n2 nucleophilic reaction.

The regiospecific reaction of the S-trimethylsilyl derivative of glutathione with methyl-E-5,6-epoxy-E,E,Z,Z-7,9,11,14-eicosatetraenoate is a key step in the synthesis of A-leukotriene [10].

$$(21.2)$$

The combination of methylthiotrimethylsilane, zinc iodide and tetra-*n*-butylammonium iodide has proved valuable for the cleavage of methyl and benzyl ethers to yield alkoxytrimethylsilanes and dimethylsulfide or benzyl methyl sulfides, respectively [11]. Unlike TMS-I this combination of reagents results in neither competitive formation of alkyl iodides nor in cleavage of acetates or benzoates (Chapter 3).

$$(21.3)$$

Phenylselenotrimethylsilane likewise reacts stereo- and regiospecifically with epoxides to yield *trans*-2-phenylselenoalkoxytrimethylsilanes either under Lewis acid catalysis by zinc iodide [12] or nucleophilic catalysis by potassium fluoride/18-C-6 [13].

$$(21.4)$$

21.3 Aldehydes and Ketones

Phenylthiotrimethylsilane reacts thermally with easily enolizable ketones such as methyl acetoacetate or benzoylacetonitrile to yield trimethylsilyl enol ethers and phenylthiol [16].

$$\underset{\substack{\text{O}\\ \|}}{CH_3-C-CH_2CO_2CH_3} \; + \; PhSSi(CH_3)_3 \; \longrightarrow \; \underset{\substack{OSi(CH_3)_3\\ |}}{CH_3-C=CHCO_2CH_3} \; + \; PhSH \qquad (21.5)$$

These results are related to the reaction of alkylthiotrimethylsilanes with alcohols to yield alkoxyltrimethylsilanes and thiols.

Although aldehydes undergo slow thermal reaction with methylthiotrimethylsilane, most ketones do not react. This reaction can be catalyzed by addition of Lewis acids or by anionic activation. Phenylthiotrimethylsilane or methylthiotrimethylsilane reacts readily with aldehydes in the presence of a catalytic amount of potassium cyanide/18-C-6, or tetra-*n*-butylammonium cyanide to yield O-trimethylsilyl hemithioacetals [17, 18].

$$\underset{\substack{\text{O}\\ \|}}{(CH_3)_2CH-C-H} \; + \; PhSSi(CH_3)_3 \; \xrightarrow[\text{18-C-6}]{\text{KCN}} \; \underset{\substack{OSi(CH_3)_3\\ |\\ SPh}}{(CH_3)_2CH-C-H} \qquad (21.6)$$

In the presence of imidazole or other weak bases and zinc iodide, methylthiotrimethylsilane adds to aldehydes or ketones to yield O-trimethylsilyl hemithioacetals or ketals [18].

$$(21.7)$$

Hexafluoroacetone [14] or chloral [15] react with methylthiotrimethylsilane to yield the corresponding O-trimethylsilyl hemithioketal. No catalyst is required.

Ketones or aldehydes react with methylthiotrimethylsilane in the presence of zinc iodide to yield *bis*(methylthio) ketals or acetals directly [17, 18]. The fact that 1-trimethylsilyloxy-1-methylthiocyclohexane is converted to 1,1-*bis*(methylthio)cyclohexane on treatment with zinc iodide, supports the hypothesis that the O-trimethylsilyl hemithioketal is an intermediate in this reaction.

$$(21.8)$$

A high level of carbonyl differentiation is observed in these reactions. Sterically unhindered ketones are preferentially converted to thioketals [17].

$$\text{(21.9)}$$

Prior preparation of the alkylthiotrimethylsilane is not essential. Thus addition of a thiol to a solution of an aldehyde or ketone, TMS-Cl and pyridine yields the O-trimethylsilyl hemithioketal or acetal directly [19]. The reaction apparently involves *in-situ* formation of the alkylthiotrimethylsilane [18].

$$\text{(21.10)}$$

Similarly, reaction of thiols, benzaldehyde, hexamethyldisilazane and a catalytic amount of imidazole or potassium cyanide/18-C-6 yields the O-trimethylsilyl hemiacetals directly [20]. Aldehydes or ketones react directly with two equivalents of thiols and one equivalent of TMS-Cl to yield thioacetals or thioketals [21]. HCl generated in this reaction is critical for the conversion of the intermediate O-trimethylsilyl hemithioacetals or ketals to thioacetals or ketals. Esters, amides, and C−C double bonds are not affected by these reaction conditions.

$$\text{(21.11)}$$

0-Trimethylsilyl hemithioketals and acetals resist hydrolysis by 5% NaOH or sodium carbonate and are stable in methanol/water, pyridine, HMPT, and other common organic solvents. They are, however, rapidly hydrolyzed to regenerate the ketone or aldehyde by dilute HCl [19]. Solvents effect the reaction of alkyl lithium reagents with 0-trimethylsilyl hemithioketals or acetals. In ether or THF alkyl lithium reagents react at the silyl center (Eq. 21.12). However, in HMPT or THF/TMEDA solvents alkyl lithium reagents react at the central carbon (Eq. 21.13).

$$\underset{\underset{SEt}{\overset{\overset{OSi(CH_3)_3}{|}}{\underset{|}{Ph-C-H}}}}{} \xrightarrow{CH_3Li/THF} \underset{}{\overset{\overset{O}{||}}{Ph-C-H}} + (CH_3)_4Si + Li^{+-}SEt \qquad (21.12)$$

$$\xrightarrow{CH_3Li/HMPA} \underset{\underset{CH_3}{|}}{\overset{\overset{OSi(CH_3)_3}{|}}{Ph-C-H}} + Li^{+-}SEt \qquad (21.13)$$

The sensitivity of 0-trimethylsilyl hemiacetals to Lewis acids has been exploited. Reaction of 0-trimethylsilyl hemiacetals with a mixture of LiAlH₄/AlCl₃ gives sulfides [20].

$$\underset{\underset{SPh}{|}}{\overset{\overset{OSi(CH_3)_3}{|}}{Ph-C-H}} \xrightarrow[AlCl_3]{LiAlH_4} PhCH_2SPh \qquad (21.14)$$

Alkyl or aryl trimethylsilyl sulfides react with α,β-unsaturated ketones or aldehydes in a 1,4-conjugate manner either under nucleophilic activation or electrophilic catalysis by zinc iodide [17, 18].

$$\text{(cyclopentenone)} =O + PhSSi(CH_3)_3 \xrightarrow[18-C-6]{KCN} \text{(ring)} -OSi(CH_3)_3 \qquad (21.15)$$

Neither methylseleno-nor phenylselenotrimethylsilane react with aldehydes at room temperature. However, in the presence of magnesium bromide, zinc chloride or zinc iodide reaction occurs to give 0-trimethylsilyl hemiselenoacetals (Eq. 21.16) [22, 23]. Use of the stronger Lewis acid, AlCl₃ leads to selenoacetals (Eq. 21.17). 0-Trimethylsilyl hemiselenoacetals or ketals can also be prepared directly by reaction of ketones or aldehydes with phenylselenol and TMS-Cl in pyridine [22].

$$\xrightarrow{MgBr_2} \underset{\underset{SeCH_3}{|}}{\overset{\overset{H}{|}}{n\text{-}C_6H_{13}\text{-}C\text{-}OSi(CH_3)_3}} \qquad (21.16)$$

$$n\text{-}C_6H_{13}\overset{\nearrow O}{\underset{\searrow H}{C}} + CH_3SeSi(CH_3)_3$$

$$\xrightarrow{AlCl_3} \underset{\underset{SeCH_3}{|}}{\overset{\overset{SeCH_3}{|}}{n\text{-}C_6H_{13}\text{-}C\text{-}H}} \qquad (21.17)$$

Phenylselenotrimethylsilane adds in a conjugate manner to α,β-unsaturated ketones or aldehydes under the catalytic influence of triphenylphosphine, zinc iodide [23] or potassium fluoride/18-C-6 [13].

$$(21.18)$$

21.4 Esters

Ethyl α-mercapto cinnamates esters have been efficiently prepared by reaction of ethyl S-trimethylsilyl-thioglycolate with aromatic aldehydes and sodium hydride followed by an acidic work-up [74].

$$(21.19)$$

Ethylthiotrimethylsilane reacts with β-propiolactone to yield trimethyl-silyl 3-ethylthiopropionate [24]. Ethylthio or phenylthiotrimethylsilane reacts with alicyclic esters under the influence of AlCl$_3$ to yield thioesters [25].

$$(21.20)$$

On the other hand, Breslow reports that methyl-m-iodobenzoate reacts with ethylthiotrimethylsilane and AlCl$_3$ to yield triethyl-m-iodo-$ortho$-thiobenzoate [26].

Phenylselenotrimethylsilane reacts with alkyl acetates under catalysis by zinc iodide in CCl_4 or toluene to yield alkyl phenyl selenides and acetoxytrimethylsilane. These weakly acidic reaction conditions provide a novel route to such compounds.

$$PhCH_2O-\overset{O}{\overset{\|}{C}}-CH_3 \xrightarrow[\substack{ZnI_2 \\ CCl_4}]{PhSeSi(CH_3)_3} PhCH_2SePh + (CH_3)_3SiO-\overset{O}{\overset{\|}{C}}-CH_3 \qquad (21.21)$$

The fact that both crotyl and 1-methylallyl acetate react with phenylselenotrimethylsilane to yield crotyl phenyl selenide is suggestive of catonic intermediates [27]. δ-Butyrolactone reacts with phenylselenotrimethylsilane under catalysis by potassium fluoride/18-C-6 to yield trimethylsilyl 4-phenylselenobutyrate [13].

$$\overset{O}{\underset{}{\bigcirc}}{=}O + PhSeSi(CH_3)_3 \xrightarrow[18-C-6]{KF} PhSe\diagdown\diagup\diagdown\overset{O}{\overset{\|}{\diagup}}OSi(CH_3)_3 \qquad (21.22)$$

21.5 Cumulenes

Ethylthiotrimethylsilane reacts with phenyl isocyanate to yield N-phenyl-N trimethylsilyl S-ethyl thiourethane [24, 28].

$$(CH_3)_3Si-SEt + Ph-N=C=O \xrightarrow{80°} \underset{(CH_3)_3Si}{\overset{Ph}{\diagdown}}N-\overset{O}{\overset{\|}{C}}-SEt \qquad (21.23)$$

21.6 Allylic Acetals and Benzylic Acetates

Allylic acetals react with phenylthiotrimethylsilane or ethylthiotrimethylsilane and $AlCl_3$ to yield γ-alkoxy allyl sulfides, α,β-unsaturated thioacetals or α,β-unsaturated 0-alkyl hemithioacetals. The particular products formed are dependent on the silyl sulfide, as well as, the allylic acetal utilized [29].

Furfuryl acetates react with phenylselenotrimethylsilane and $TiCl_4$ to yield furfuryl phenyl selenides. It seems likely that these reactions involve carbocation intermediates. Such furfuryl phenyl selenides react with n-butyl lithium to yield furfuryl lithium which undergoes ring opening. Acidic work-up yields α,β,γ,δ-dienones [30, 31] (see 6.2E).

$$(21.24)$$

21.7 Silyl-Pummerer Rearrangements

Trimethylsilylmethyl phenyl sulfoxide was shown by Brook to rearrange thermally at 60 °C to yield trimethylsilyloxymethyl phenyl sulfide. This silyl-Pummerer rearrangement may occur by migration of the trimethylsilyl group from carbon to oxygen to yield an ylid which fragments to a trimethylsilanoate/methylene phenyl sulfonium ion pair which recombine to yield the 0-trimethylsilyl hemithioacetal [32].

$$(21.25)$$

$$(CH_3)_3SiOCH_2SPh$$

The facile acid catalyzed hydrolysis of such 0-trimethylsilyl hemithioacetals to regenerate aldehydes has been previously discussed. The silyl Pummerer rearrangement is the basis for a number of aldehyde syntheses.

Trimethylsilylmethyl phenyl sulfoxide was initially prepared by reaction of trimethylsilylmethyl magnesium chloride with methyl benzene sulfinate [32]. Vedejas found that addition of phenylsulfinyl methyl lithium to TMS-Cl also gave trimethylsilylmethyl phenyl sulfoxide. This order of addition is critical to the success of the reaction [33].

$$(21.26)$$

A. Synthesis of Aldehydes

Metallation of trimethylsilylmethyl phenyl sulfide [34, 35] with *n*-butyl lithium in THF followed by alkylation with primary alkyl bromides or epoxides yields 1-phenylthioalkyltrimethylsilanes. Oxidation of the sulfide to a sulfoxide with MCPBA at −15° followed by a silyl-Pummerer rearrangement and hydrolysis of the 0-trimethylsilyl hemithioacetals gives the desired aldehydes [36, 37]. By comparison, 1,3,dithianes are often difficult to hydrolyze.

$$(21.27)$$

B. Synthesis of Ketones

While it is possible to metallate 1-phenylthioalkyltrimethylsilanes, it has not been possible to get such anions to react with alkyl halides. Hence this methodology is not generally useful for the preparation of ketones. The preparation of alkyl phenyl ketones is an exception. Alkylation of (phenylthio)phenyl-(trimethylsilyl)methyl lithium followed by oxidation with MCPBA and silyl-Pummerer rearrangement yields 1-phenylthio-1-trimethylsilyloxy 1-phenyl-alkane which undergoes facile acid catalyzed hydrolysis to yield the alkyl phenyl ketone [38].

$$(21.28)$$

C. Preparation of 1-Phenylthioalkyltrimethylsilanes

Alkyl lithium reagents will add to either phenyl vinyl sulfide or vinyl tri-methylsilane in ether/TMEDA to yield α-lithioalkyl phenyl sulfides or α-lithio-alkyltrimethylsilanes, respectively. 1-Phenylthioalkyltrimethylsilanes result from reaction of either α-lithioalkyl phenyl sulfides with TMS-Cl (Eq. 21.29) or α-lithioalkyltrimethylsilanes with phenylsulfenyl chloride or diphenyl di-sulfide (Eq. 21.30) [39].

$$\overset{\displaystyle \diagup}{\diagdown}\text{SPh} \xrightarrow[\substack{\text{TMEDA} \\ \text{Et}_2\text{O}}]{\text{RLi}} R \diagdown\diagup \underset{\text{Li}^+}{\overset{\text{SPh}}{\diagdown}} \xrightarrow{(\text{CH}_3)_3\text{SiCl}} R \diagdown\diagup \underset{\text{Si(CH}_3)_3}{\overset{\text{SPh}}{\diagup}} \qquad (21.29)$$

$$\overset{\displaystyle \diagup}{\diagdown}\text{Si(CH}_3)_3 \xrightarrow[\substack{\text{TMEDA} \\ \text{Et}_2\text{O}}]{\text{RLi}} R \diagdown\diagup \underset{\text{Li}^+}{\overset{\text{Si(CH}_3)_3}{\diagdown}} \xrightarrow[\text{PhSSPh}]{\text{PhSCl or}} \qquad (21.30)$$

An alternative approach to 1-phenylthioalkyltrimethylsilanes utilizes phenyl vinyl sulfide [39, 41]. 1-Phenylthio-1-trimethylsilyl ethylene can be oxidized by MCPBA to 1-phenylsulfinyl-1-trimethylsilyl ethylene [40].

$$\text{PhS} \diagdown\hspace{-0.3em}\| \xrightarrow[\substack{\text{THF} \\ \text{HMPT}}]{\text{LDA}} \text{PhS}\diagup\hspace{-0.3em}\underset{\|}{\overset{\text{Li}}{\diagdown}} \xrightarrow{(\text{CH}_3)_3\text{SiCl}} \text{PhS}\diagup\hspace{-0.3em}\underset{\|}{\overset{\text{Si(CH}_3)_3}{\diagdown}} \qquad (21.31)$$

$$\xrightarrow[\text{2) H}_2\text{O}]{\text{1) RLi/TMEDA}} \text{PhS}\diagup\hspace{-0.3em}\underset{\diagdown R}{\overset{\overset{H}{|}\,\text{Si(CH}_3)_3}{|}}$$

D. Synthesis of Aldehydes/Selenium-Silicon Reagents

Trimethylsilylmethyl phenyl selenide has also proved useful for the prepara-tion of aldehydes. Metallation with LDA followed by alkylation with primary alkyl bromides or iodides yields 1-phenylselenoalkyltrimethylsilanes. Oxidation of these with 30% hydrogen peroxide gives the corresponding selenoxide which can undergo a silyl-Pummerer rearrangement to an 0-trimethylsilyl hemiselenoacetal. Hydrolysis of these compounds gives the desired aldehyde. The necessary precursor has been prepared by reaction of sodium phenyl selenide with chloromethyltrimethylsilane [42].

$$\text{PhSeCH}_2\text{Si(CH}_3)_3 \xrightarrow[\text{2) CH}_3(\text{CH}_2)_3\text{CH}_2\text{Br}]{\text{1) LDA/THF}} \underset{\text{(CH}_2)_4\text{CH}_3}{\text{PhSeCHSi(CH}_3)_3} \qquad (21.32)$$

$$\xrightarrow{\text{H}_2\text{O}_2} \underset{\text{(CH}_2)_4\text{CH}_3}{\overset{\overset{\text{O}}{\|}}{\text{PhSeCHSi(CH}_3)_3}} \xrightarrow{\Delta} \underset{\text{(CH}_2)_4\text{CH}_3}{\text{PhSeCHOSi(CH}_3)_3}$$

Attempts to prepare alkyl phenyl ketones by this procedure proved more complicated. Deprotonation of benzyl phenyl selenide with LDA followed by reaction with TMS-Cl gives α-phenylselenobenzyltrimethylsilane. Metallation of this compound followed by reaction with methyl iodide gives α-methyl-α-phenylselenobenzyltrimethylsilane. However, on oxidation with MCPBA the selenoxide undergoes not only the silyl-Pummerer rearrangement but also *syn*-elimination of phenylselenous acid. *Syn*-elimination is much more facile for selenium than for sulfur [43].

$$(21.33)$$

Oxidation of allylic systems such as 1-phenylseleno-1-dimethylphenylsilyl-3-methyl-2-butene leads to 2-methyl-4-dimethylphenylsilyl-3-buten-2-ol. Clearly the silyl-Pummerer is not competitive with the [2,3]-sigmatropic rearrangement of allylic selenoxides [44].

$$(21.34)$$

349

E. Synthesis of α,β-Unsaturated Aldehydes

3-Trimethylsilylallylic alcohols can be converted to α,β-unsaturated aldehydes by reaction with phenylsulfenyl chloride and triethylamine. This results from a [2,3]-sigmatropic rearrangement of the initial adduct to yield an α,β-unsaturated 0-trimethylsilyl hemiacetal [45].

$$(21.35)$$

The required 3-trimethylsilyl allylic alcohols can be prepared by LiAlH$_4$ reduction of 1-(1'-hydroxyalkyl)-2-trimethylsilyl acetylenes.

$$(21.36)$$

Ylides formed by deprotonation of allyl methyl trimethylsilylmethyl sulfonium salts with n-butyl lithium, undergo [2,3] sigmatropic rearrangement to yield homoallylic α-methylthio trimethylsilanes. These can be oxidized with MCPBA to the corresponding sulfoxides which undergo silyl-Pummerer rearrangement to yield β,γ-unsaturated aldehydes after hydrolysis [46].

$$(21.37)$$

21.8 Exchange Reactions

Silyl sulfur reagents undergo exchange reactions with halogen containing substrates: such that one of the products possesses a Si−X bond while the other has a sulfur bonded to the substrate where the halogen was bonded in the starting material. The thermodynamic driving force for these reactions may, in general, be the strength of the Si−X bond which is formed (Si−Cl ~113 kcal/mol) [7].

A. Synthesis of Sulfides

Alkyl halide react with n-butylthiotrimethylsilane to yield alkyl n-butyl sulfide and TMS−X. As expected on the basis of bond energies, primary with the following order of reactivity is observed alkyl halide RI > RBr > RCl [75].

B. Synthesis of Polysulfides

Sulfenyl chlorides react with alkylthiotrimethylsilanes to yield TMS-Cl and unsymmetrical disulfides [47].

$$(21.38)$$

In a similar manner, 1,3-bis(trimethylsilylthio)propane or 2,2-dimethyl-2-sila-1,3-dithiocyclohexane [48] reacts with sulfur dichloride to yield 1,2,3-trithiocyclohexane. 1,4-bis(Trimethylsilylthio)butane reacts with sulfur dichloride to yield 1,2,3-trithiocycloheptane [49]. This procedure is the most direct approach to such cyclic polysulfides.

$$(21.39)$$

C. Synthesis of S-alkyl Thiocarboxylates

Alkylthiotrimethylsilanes react with acid chlorides to yield S-alkyl thiocarboxylates [76].

$$Ph\text{-}\underset{O}{\overset{\parallel}{C}}\text{-}Cl \ + \ (CH_3)_3SiSCH_2CO_2CH_3 \longrightarrow Ph\text{-}\underset{O}{\overset{\parallel}{C}}\text{-}SCH_2CO_2CH_3 \qquad (21.40)$$

2,2-Dimethyl-2-sila-1,3-dithiocyclopentane [50] reacts under high dilution conditions (10^{-2} molar solutions) with α,ω-diacid chlorides to yield macrocyclic tetrathiolactones [50, 51].

$$(CH_3)_2Si \overset{S}{\underset{S}{\big<}} \quad + \quad Cl-\overset{O}{\overset{\|}{C}}-(CH_2)_3-\overset{O}{\overset{\|}{C}}-Cl \longrightarrow \quad \overset{O=C\diagdown^S\diagup\diagdown_S-\overset{C=O}{\underset{|}{}}}{(CH_2)_3 \qquad (CH_2)_3}_{O=C\diagdown_S\diagup\diagup\diagdown_S\diagdown_{C=O}} \quad (21.41)$$

Phenylselenotrimethylsilane reacts in an analogous manner with acid chlorides to yield Se-phenyl selenocarboxylates [52]. Sulfinyl chlorides react with alkoxytrimethylsilane to yield sulfinate esters and TMS-Cl [47].

$$\text{(Ph)}-CH_2\overset{O}{\overset{\|}{S}}\diagdown_{Cl} \quad + \quad EtOSi(CH_3)_3 \longrightarrow \text{(Ph)}-CH_2\overset{O}{\overset{\|}{S}}\diagdown_{OEt} \quad + \quad (CH_3)_3SiCl \quad (21.42)$$

This reaction is analogous to the exchange reaction between carboxylic acid chlorides and alkoxytrimethylsilanes which yield esters and TMS-Cl [54]. Reactions are also observed between methyl benzene sulfenate and TMS-Cl or TMS-CN to yield methoxytrimethylsilane and benzene sulfenyl chloride or phenyl thiocyanate, respectively [47].

D. Sulfur Transfer Reagents

A number of useful sulfur transfer reagents have been prepared by use of organosilicon reagents. For example, 1,1-thiocarbonyl di-imidazole has been prepared by reaction of N-trimethylsilyl imidazole and thiophosgene. Related heterocyclic thiocarbonyl transfer reagents based on benzimidazole, benzotriazole and pyrazole have also been prepared [56].

$$N\overset{\diagup\diagdown}{\diagdown_{\diagup}}N-Si(CH_3)_3 \quad + \quad Cl-\overset{S}{\overset{\|}{C}}-Cl \longrightarrow \quad N\overset{\diagup\diagdown}{\diagdown_{\diagup}}N-\overset{S}{\overset{\|}{C}}-N\overset{\diagup\diagdown}{\diagdown_{\diagup}}N \qquad (21.43)$$

In a similar manner sulfenyl chlorides react with N-trimethylsilyl succinimide to yield N-alkylthio or N-arylthio succinimide [57].

$$\text{(Ph)}-CH_2SCl \quad + \quad (CH_3)_3Si-N\overset{O}{\underset{O}{\big<}} \longrightarrow \text{(Ph)}-CH_2S-N\overset{O}{\underset{O}{\big<}} \qquad (21.44)$$

N-Trimethylsilyl heterocycles react with sulfur dichloride or sulfur monochloride to yield a series of mono or disulfur transfer reagents. These react with thiols to regenerate the heterocycle and yield tri-or tetrasulfides respectively [58].

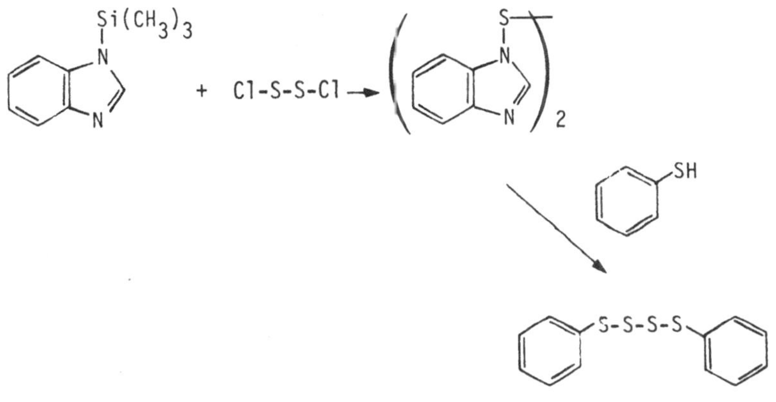

(21.45)

21.9 Miscellaneous

N-(Trimethylsilyl)thioformamide has been prepared by reaction of thioform-
amide with hexamethyldisilazane [59]. Metallation of N-alkyl thioformamides
followed by reaction with TMS-Cl yields N-alkyl-N-trimethylsilyl thioformamides. These exhibit temperature dependent dynamic NMR behavior [60].

N,N-*bis*(Trimethylsilyl)thioformamide has been utilized to prepare N,N-
bis(trimethylsilyl)enamines [61]

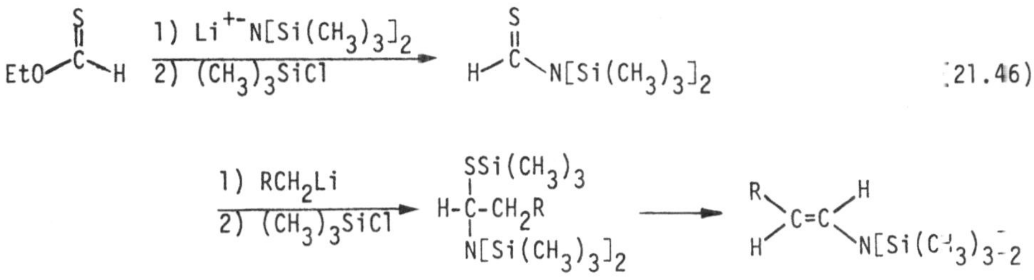

(21.46)

Reductive cleavage of the C−S bond of α-methylthio trimethylsilyl enol
ethers with sodium or sodium/potassium alloy in the presence of TMS-Cl
yields α-trimethylsilyl trimethylsilyl enol ethers [55]. These can be easily
hydrolyzed to acyl trimethylsilanes.

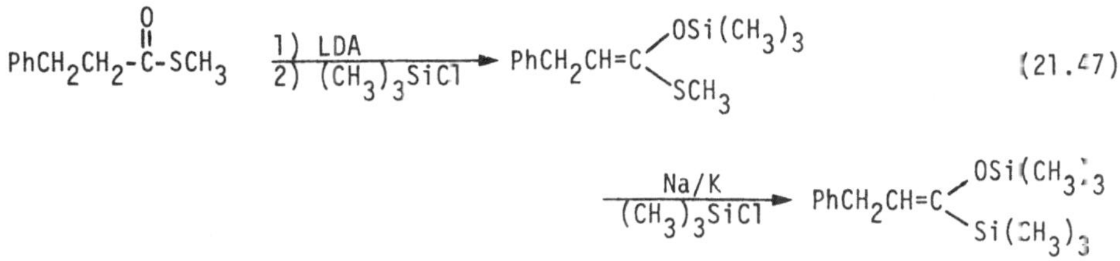

(21.47)

All of the silicon-sulfur reagents we have considered thus far have pos-
sessed organic groups on either silicon or sulfur or both. Silicon sulfide is,

in this regard, unique. It is virtually insoluble in all common organic solvents, except DMSO with which it reacts. Silicon sulfide reacts with ketones possessing electron releasing groups in refluxing chloroform to convert the carbonyl to a thiocarbonyl group [53].

$$(CH_3)_2N-\langle\bigcirc\rangle-\overset{O}{\underset{||}{C}}-\langle\bigcirc\rangle-N(CH_3)_2 \ + \ SiS_2 \qquad (21.48)$$

$$\xrightarrow[\Delta]{CHCl_3} \ (CH_3)_2N-\langle\bigcirc\rangle-\overset{S}{\underset{||}{C}}-\langle\bigcirc\rangle-N(CH_3)_2$$

21.10 Preparation

Alkylthiotrimethylsilanes have been prepared by reaction of TMS-Cl with metal mercaptides [62].

$$CH_3-MgI \ + \ CH_3S-H \longrightarrow CH_3-S-MgI \xrightarrow{(CH_3)_3SiCl} CH_3S-Si(CH_3)_3 \qquad (21.49)$$

Lithium trimethylsilylacetylide reacts with sulfur to yield lithium 2-trimethylsilylethynylthiolate. This ambident anion reacts with TMS-Cl to yield *bis*(trimethylsilyl)thioketene and with TMS-Br to yield 1-trimethylsilylthio-2-trimethylsilyl acetylene. This difference may result from the hard-soft nature of the leaving groups.

$$(CH_3)_3SiC\equiv C^- \xrightarrow{S_8} \left[(CH_3)_3SiC\equiv CS^-\right] \longleftrightarrow \left[(CH_3)_3Si\overset{-}{C}=C=S\right]$$

$$\downarrow (CH_3)_3SiBr \qquad\qquad \downarrow (CH_3)_3SiCl \qquad (21.50)$$

$$(CH_3)_3SiC\equiv CSSi(CH_3)_3 \qquad \underset{(CH_3)_3Si}{\overset{(CH_3)_3Si}{>}}C=C=S$$

bis(Trimethylsilyl)thioketene like di-*t*-butyl thioketene does not dimerize or polymerize [63].

Sodium phenyl selenide, formed by the reduction of diphenyl diselenide with sodium in THF, reacts with TMS-Cl to yield phenylselenotrimethylsilane [64, 65].

$$PhSeSePh \xrightarrow[THF]{Na} PhSe^-Na^+ \xrightarrow{(CH_3)_3SiCl} PhSeSi(CH_3)_3 \qquad (21.51)$$

Magnesium-*p*-tolyl selenide, prepared by reaction of *p*-tolyl magnesium bromide with selenium, reacts with TMS-Cl to yield *p*-tolylselenotrimethylsilane. This approach has also been used to prepare *p*-tolyltellurotrimethylsilane [66].

The reaction of trimethylsilylamines with thiols yields alkylthio- and aryl-thiotrimethylsilanes [67]. Deprotonation of the thiol to yield a thiolate by N-trimethylsilyl imidazole may be an essential step in the reaction [68].

$$(21.52)$$

The reaction of hexamethyldisilazane with thiols can be catalyzed by imidazole [69].

$$[(CH_3)_3Si]_2NH \; + \; H_2S \; \xrightarrow[\text{Imidazole}]{} \; [(CH_3)_3Si]_2S \; + \; NH_3 \qquad (21.53)$$

Likewise phenylselenotrimethylsilane can be prepared by reaction of phenyl-selenol with TMS-Cl in the presence of trimethylamine. The preparation and purification of phenylselenol is, however, difficult [70].

Alkylthio- and arylthiotrialkylsilanes can be prepared by reaction of tri-alkylsilanes with thiols catalyzed by [Ph₃P]₃RhCl [71, 72].

$$PhSH \; + \; Et_3SiH \; \xrightarrow{[Ph_3P]_3RhCl} \; Et_3Si\text{-}SPh \qquad (21.54)$$

Dissolving metal reduction of symmetrical disulfides in the presence of TMS-Cl yields alkylthiotrimethylsilanes [73].

References

1. For a review of silicon-sulfur Chemistry see: Abel, E.W., Armitage, D.A.: Adv. Organometal. Chem. *5*, 2 (1967)
2. Peterson, D.J.: J. Org. Chem. *33*, 780 (1968)
3. Carey, F.A., Court, A.S.: J. Org. Chem. *37*, 939 (1972)
4. Carey, F.A., Hernandez, O.: J. Org. Chem. *38*, 2670 (1973)
5. Soysa, H.S.D., Weber, W.P.: Tetrahedron Lett. 235 (1978)
6. Detty, M.R.: J. Org. Chem. *44*, 4528 (1979)
7. Walsh, R.: Accts. of Chem. Res. *14*, 246 (1981)
8. Schmeisser, M., Muller, H.: On the basis of equilibration studies, Si–S and C–S single bonds appear to be approximately equal strength: Angew. Chem. *69*, 781 (1957)
9. Abel, E.W., Walker, D.J.: J. Chem. Soc. *A*, 2338 (1968)
10. Rokach, J., Girard, Y., Guidon, Y., Atkinson, J.G., Larue, M., Young, R.N., Masson, P., Holme, G.: Tetrahedron Lett. 1485 (1980)

11. Hanessian, S., Guindon, Y.: Tetrahedron Lett. 2305 (1980)
12. Miyoshi, N., Kondo, K., Murai, S., Sonoda, N.: Chem. Lett. 909 (1979)
13. Detty, M.R.: Tetrahedron Lett. 5087 (1978)
14. Abel, E.W., Walker, D.J., Wingfield, N.J.: J. Chem. Soc. *A*, 1814 (1968)
15. Itoh, K., Matsuzaki, K., Ishii, Y.: J. Chem. Soc. *C*, 2709 (1968)
16. Ojima, I., Nagai, Y.: J. Organometal. Chem. *57*, C42 (1973)
17. Evans, D.A., Grimm, K.G., Truesdale, L.K.: J. Am. Chem. Soc. *97*, 3229 (1975)
18. Evans, D.A., Truesdale, L.K., Grimm, K.G., Nesbitt, S.L.: J. Am. Chem. Soc. *99*, 5009 (1977)
19. Chan, T.H., Ong, B.S.: Tetrahedron Lett. 319 (1976)
20. Glass, R.S.: Syn. Comm. *6*, 47 (1976)
21. Ong, B.S., Chan, T.H.: Syn. Commun. *7*, 283 (1977)
22. Dumont, W., Krief, A.: Angew. Chem. Int. Ed. *16*, 540 (1977)
23. Liotta, D., Paty, P.B., Johnston, J., Zima, G.: Tetrahedron Lett. 5091 (1978)
24. Itoh, K., Matsuzaki, K., Ishii, Y.: J. Chem. Soc. *C*, 2709 (1968)
25. Mukaiyama, T., Takeda, T., Atsumi, K.: Chem. Lett. 187 (1974)
26. Breslow, R., Pandey, P.S.: J. Org. Chem. *45*, 740 (1980)
27. Miyoshi, N., Ishii, H., Murai, S., Sonoda, N.: Chem. Lett. 873 (1979)
28. Ricci, A., Danieli, R., Pirazzini, G.: J.C.S. Perkin 1, 1069 (1977)
29. Mukaiyama, T., Takeda, T., Atsumi, K.: Chem. Lett. 1013 (1974)
30. Kuwajima, I., Hoshino, S., Tanaka, T., Shimizu, M.: Tetrahedron Lett. 3209 (1980)
31. Dumont, W., Krief, A.: Angew. Chem. Int. Ed. *15*, 161 (1976)
32. Brook, A.G., Anderson, D.G.: Can. J. Chem. *46*, 2115 (1968)
33. Vedejs, E., Mullins, M.: Tetrahedron Lett. 2017 (1975)
34. Cooper, G.D.: J. Am. Chem. Soc. *76*, 3713 (1954)
35. Corey, E.J., Seebach, D.: J. Org. Chem. *31*, 4097 (1966)
36. Kocienski, P.J.: Tetrahedron Lett. 1559 (1980)
37. Ager, D.J., Cookson, R.C.: Tetrahedron Lett. 1677 (1980)
38. Ager, D.J.: Tetrahedron Lett. 4759 (1980)
39. Ager, D.J.: Tetrahedron Lett. 587 (1981)
40. Harirchian, B., Magnus, P.: J. Chem. Soc. Chem. Commun. 522 (1977)
41. Cookson, R.C., Parsons, P.J.: J. Chem. Soc. Chem. Commun. 990 (1976)
42. Sachdev, K., Sachdev, H.S.: Tetrahedron Lett. 4223 (1976)
43. Reich, H.J., Shan, S.K.: J. Org. Chem. *42*, 1773 (1977)
44. Reich, H.J.: J. Org. Chem. *40*, 2570 (1975)
45. Cutting, I., Parsons, P.J.: Tetrahedron Lett. 2021 (1981)
46. Kocienski, P.J.: J. Chem. Soc. Chem. Commun. 1096 (1980)
47. Harpp, D.N., Friedlander, B.T., Larsen, C., Steliou, K., Stockton, A.: J. Org. Chem. *43*, 3481 (1978)
48. Wieber, M., Schmidt, M.: J. Organometal. Chem. *I*, 336 (1964)
49. Yamazaki, N., Nakahama, S., Yamaguchi, K., Yamaguchi, T.: Chem. Lett. 1355 (1980)
50. Wieber, M., Schmidt, H.: Z. Naturf. *18*, 846 (1963)
51. Shanzer, A., Schwartz, E.: Tetrahedron Lett. 5019 (1979)
52. Derkach, N.Y., Tishchenko, N.P.: Zh. Org. Khim. *13*, 100 (1977)
53. Dean, F.M., Goodchild, J., Hill, A.W.: J. Chem. Soc. *C*, 2192 (1969)
54. For a review see Klebe, J.F.: Adv. Org. Chem. *8*, 97–178 (1972)
55. Kuwajima, I., Mori, A., Kato, M.: Bull. Chem. Soc. Japan, *53*, 2634, (1980)
56. Larsen, C., Steliou, K., Harpp, D.N.: J. Org. Chem. *43*, 337 (1978)
57. Harpp, D.N., Friedlander, B.T., Mullins D., Vines, S.M.: Tetrahedron Lett. 963 (1977)

58. Harpp, D.N., Steliou, K., Chan, T.H.: J. Am. Chem. Soc. *100*, 1222, (1978)
59. Walter, W., Lüke, H.W., Voss, J.: Liebigs. Ann. Chem. 1808 (1975)
60. Walter, W., Lüke, H.W.: Angew. Chem. Int. Ed. *14*, 427 (1975)
61. Walter, W., Lüke, H.W.: Angew. Chem. Int. Ed. *16*, 535 (1977)
62. Hootan, K.A., Allred, A.L.: Inorg. Chem. *4*, 671 (1965)
63. Harris, S.J., Walton, D.R.M.: J. Chem. Soc. Chem. Commun. 1008 (1976)
64. Miyoshi, N., Ishii, H., Kondo, K., Murai, K., Sonoda, N.: Synthesis, 300 (1979)
65. Liotta, D., Markiewicz, W., Santiesteban, H.: Tetrahedron Lett. 4365 (1977)
66. Praefcke, K., Weichsel, C.: Synthesis, 216 (1980)
67. Louis, E., Urry, G.: J. Inorg. Chem. *7*, 1253 (1968)
68. Glass, R.S.: J. Organometal. Chem. *61*, 83 (1973)
69. Harpp, D.N., Steliou, K.: Synthesis, 721 (1976)
70. Derkach, N.Y., Pasmurtseva, N.A., Levchenko, E.S.: Zh. Org. Khim. *7*, 1543 (1971)
71. Ojima, I., Nihonyanagi, M., Nagai, Y.: J. Organometal. Chem. *50*, C26 (1973)
72. Sommer, L.H., Citron, J.D.: J. Org. Chem. *32*, 2470 (1967)
73. Kuwajima, I., Abe, T.: Bull. Chem. Soc. Japan, *51*, 2183 (1978)
74. Hayashi, T., Midorikawa, H.: Tetrahedron Lett. 2461 (1973)
75. Abel, E.W., Armitage, D.A., Bush, R.P.: J. Chem. Soc. 2455 (1964)
76. Rimpler, M.: Chem. Ber. *99*, 1528 (1966)

22 Silicon-Phosphorous

22.1 Introduction

A number of silicon-phosphorous compounds have proved to be useful reagents in organic synthesis. Among these are at least four major types: trimethylsilyl phosphines, $Ph_2PSi(CH_3)_3$; trimethylsilyl phosphites, $(CH_3)_3SiOP(OEt)_2$; trimethylsilyl phosphates, $[(CH_3)_3SiO]_3P=O$, and trimethylsilyl hypophosphites, $[(CH_3)_3SiO]_2P-H$. In general all four react with a single functional group in similar ways and so their chemistry will be examined together.

We have previously considered the preparation of vinyl phosphonates as well as the reaction of trimethylsilyl bromide with dialkylphosphonates (see 6.1 and 3.9).

$$H_2C=CH-\underset{\underset{O}{\|}}{P}-(OEt)_2 \xrightarrow{2(CH_3)_3SiBr} H_2C=CH-\underset{\underset{O}{\|}}{P}-[OSi(CH_3)_3]_2 \xrightarrow{H_2O} H_2C=CH-\underset{\underset{O}{\|}}{P}-(OH)_2$$

$$(22.1)$$

22.2 Alkyl Halides — Arbuzov Reactions

bis(Trimethylsilyl) alkylphosphonates can be prepared by the Arbuzov reaction of primary alkyl halides with *tris*(trimethylsilyl) phosphite [1, 2].

$$\left[(CH_3)_3SiO\right]_3P \ + \ PhCH_2Br \ \longrightarrow \ \left[\begin{array}{c} \overset{+}{PhCH_2-P-[OSi(CH_3)_3]_2} \\ O \\ | \\ (CH_3)_3Si \\ Br^- \end{array} \right] \tag{22.2}$$

$$\downarrow$$

$$PhCH_2-\underset{\underset{O}{\|}}{P}-[OSi(CH_3)_3]_2 \ + \ (CH_3)_3SiBr$$

Arbuzov reaction of *d,l*-3-iodo-1,2-distearoyl propane with *tris*(trimethylsilyl) phosphite gives after hydrolysis *d,l*-2,3-distearoyl propylphosphonic acid which was converted to 2,3-distearoyl propylphosphonyl choline derivatives [3, 73].

Trimethylsilyl phosphinites undergo Arbuzov reaction with alkyl iodides to yield tertiary phosphine oxides [4].

$$(n\text{-Bu})_2\text{POSi}(\text{CH}_3)_3 \xrightarrow{\text{CH}_3\text{I}} (n\text{-Bu})_2\overset{\overset{\text{O}}{\|}}{\text{P}}\text{CH}_3 \ + \ (\text{CH}_3)_3\text{SiI} \qquad (22.3)$$

Arbuzov reaction of *bis*(trimethylsilyl) trimethylsilyloxymethyl phosphinate with 3-chloropropionitrile yields 2-cyanoethyl(hydroxymethyl)phosphinic acid after hydrolysis [5].

$$\text{HOCH}_2-\overset{\overset{\text{O}}{\|}}{\underset{\text{H}}{\text{P}}}-\text{OH} \xrightarrow[\text{CH}_3\text{CN}]{(\text{CH}_3)_3\text{SiNEt}_2} (\text{CH}_3)_3\text{SiOCH}_2\text{P}[\text{OSi}(\text{CH}_3)_3]_2 \qquad (22.4)$$

$$\xrightarrow[\text{2) H}_2\text{O}]{\text{1) ClCH}_2\text{CH}_2\text{CN}} \text{HOCH}_2-\overset{\overset{\text{O}}{\|}}{\underset{\text{OH}}{\text{P}}}-\text{CH}_2\text{CH}_2\text{CN}$$

Trimethylsilyl phosphines react with chloroacetonitrile to yield cyanomethyl phosphines and TMS-Cl [6].

$$\text{Ph}_2\text{PSi}(\text{CH}_3)_3 \ + \ \text{ClCH}_2\text{CN} \longrightarrow \text{Ph}_2\text{PCH}_2\text{CN} \ + \ (\text{CH}_3)_3\text{SiCl} \qquad (22.5)$$

Trimethylsilyl phosphines also react with organogermanium chlorides and organotin chlorides to yield TMS-Cl and organogermanium or organotin phosphines, respectively [7, 8].

$$[(\text{CH}_3)_3\text{Si}]_3\text{P} \ + \ 3(\text{CH}_3)_3\text{SnCl} \longrightarrow [(\text{CH}_3)_3\text{Sn}]_3\text{P} \ + \ 3(\text{CH}_3)_3\text{SiCl} \qquad (22.6)$$

22.3 Acid Chlorides

A. Acyl Phosphonates

Acid chlorides react with silyl phosphites to yield acyl phosphonates. This reaction has been carried out with *tris*(triethylsilyl) phosphite, ethyl *bis*(triethylsilyl) phosphite and diethyl triethylsilyl phosphite [9].

$$\text{EtOP(OSiEt}_3)_2 \ + \ \text{CH}_3-\overset{\overset{\text{O}}{\|}}{\text{C}}-\text{Cl} \xrightarrow{\text{Et}_2\text{O}} \text{EtO}-\overset{\overset{\text{O}}{\|}}{\text{P}} \overset{\text{OSiEt}_3}{\underset{\underset{\overset{\|}{\text{O}}}{\text{CCH}_3}}{}} \ + \ \text{Et}_3\text{SiCl} \qquad (22.7)$$

359

B. Acyl Phosphates

Acyl phosphates are a type of mixed anhydrides. They have been prepared in two ways. Acyl *bis*(tri-*n*-butylstannyl)phosphate reacts with TMS-Cl to yield acyl *bis*(trimethylsilyl)phosphate.

$$[(n\text{-Bu})_3\text{SnO}]_2\underset{\overset{\|}{O}}{P}\text{-O-}\underset{\overset{\|}{O}}{C}\text{-Ph} \xrightarrow{(\text{CH}_3)_3\text{SiCl}} [(\text{CH}_3)_3\text{SiO}]_2\underset{\overset{\|}{O}}{P}\text{-O-}\underset{\overset{\|}{O}}{C}\text{-Ph} \qquad (22.8)$$

Alternatively, tri-*n*-butyltin methoxide reacts with *tris*(trimethylsilyl)phosphate to yield trimethylmethoxysilane and tri-*n*-butylstannyl *bis*(trimethylsilyl)phosphate which reacts with acid chlorides to yield acyl *bis*(trimethylsilyl)phosphates [10]. These easily undergo hydrolysis to yield the desired acyl phosphates.

$$[(\text{CH}_3)_3\text{SiO}]_3\text{P=O} + n\text{-Bu}_3\text{SnOCH}_3 \longrightarrow n\text{-Bu}_3\text{SnO-}\overset{\overset{\text{O}}{\|}}{P}\text{-}[\text{OSi}(\text{CH}_3)_3]_2 + (\text{CH}_3)_3\text{SiOCH}_3$$

$$\swarrow \overset{\text{CH}_3\text{-}\underset{\overset{\|}{O}}{C}\text{-Cl}}{} \qquad (22.9)$$

$$\text{CH}_3\text{-}\underset{\overset{\|}{O}}{C}\text{-O-}\underset{\overset{\|}{O}}{P}\text{-}[\text{OSi}(\text{CH}_3)_3]_2 + n\text{-Bu}_3\text{SnCl}$$

C. Acyl Phosphines

Silyl phosphines also react with acid chlorides to yield acyl phosphines and silyl chlorides [11–13].

$$(22.10)$$

Silyl phosphines react with sulfonyl chlorides in a more complex manner [12].

22.4 Ketones and Aldehydes

Trialkylsilyl phosphites react with ketones or aldehydes to yield 1-trialkylsilyloxyalkyl phosphonates. The reaction of acetaldehyde, TMS-Cl and trimethylphosphite also yields dimethyl (1-trimethylsilyloxyethyl)phosphonate [14].

$$\text{CH}_3\text{-}\underset{\overset{\|}{O}}{C}\text{-H} + (\text{CH}_3)_3\text{SiCl} + (\text{CH}_3\text{O})_3\text{P} \longrightarrow \overset{(\text{CH}_3)_3\text{SiO}}{\underset{}{\text{CH}_3\text{-CH-}\underset{\overset{\|}{O}}{P}(\text{OCH}_3)_2}} + \text{CH}_3\text{Cl} \quad (22.11)$$

In a thorough study, Evans showed that this reaction does not involve prior formation of dimethyl trimethylsilyl phosphite [15]. An alternative possibility involves nucleophilic attack by phosphorous on the carbonyl carbon of acetaldehyde to yield a zwitterionic intermediate. The negatively charged alkoxide anion attacks the silicon of TMS-Cl to give a trimethoxy(1-trimethylsilyloxy-ethyl)phosphonium/chloride ion pair. Chloride attack on a methyl group in an Arbuzov reaction gives methyl chloride and the product.

$$(CH_3O)_3P \;+\; CH_3-C\!\!\begin{array}{c} O \\ \diagdown H \end{array} \longrightarrow \left[\begin{array}{c} H \\ | \\ CH_3-C-P(OCH_3)_3 \\ | \quad + \\ -O \end{array} \right] \tag{22.12}$$

$$\xrightarrow{(CH_3)_3SiCl} \left[\begin{array}{c} H \quad + \\ CH_3-C-P(OCH_3)_2 \\ | \qquad | \\ (CH_3)_3SiO\;\; O \\ \diagdown CH_3 \quad Cl^- \end{array} \right] \longrightarrow \begin{array}{c} H \\ | \\ CH_3-C-P(CCH_3)_2 \\ | \quad || \\ (CH_3)_3SiO\;\; O \end{array}$$

The reaction of dialkyl trimethylsilyl phosphites with ketones or aldehydes also proceeds by nucleophilic attack by phosphorous on the carbonyl carbon to yield a zwitterionic intermediate. 1,4-Intramolecular rearrangement of the trialkylsilyl group from an oxygen bonded to phosphorous to the alkoxide oxygen yields the product. Intramolecular migration of trialkylsilyl groups via front side displacement with retention of configuration at the silyl center is well-known [16].

$$(EtO)_2POSi(CH_3)_3 \;+\; Ph\overset{O}{\overset{||}{C}}H \longrightarrow \left[\begin{array}{c} ^-O\;\; OSi(CH_3)_3 \\ |\quad | \\ Ph-C-P-OEt \\ |\quad |+ \\ H\;\; OEt \end{array} \right] \longrightarrow \begin{array}{c} OSi(CH_3)_3 \\ | \\ Ph-C-P(OEt)_2 \\ |\quad || \\ H\;\; O \end{array} \tag{22.13}$$

As predicted by this mechanism, no crossover products were observed when diethyl trimethylsilyl phosphite, dimethyl t-butyldimethylsilyl phosphite and benzaldehyde were reacted in a 1:1:2 molar ratio [15].

Numerous examples of this reaction have been reported. Much of the original work was done by Russian chemists. Diethyl trimethylsilyl phosphite reacts with aldehydes or ketones to yield diethyl (1-trimethylsilyloxyalkyl)-phosphonates [17, 18]. These are easily hydrolyzed to yield diethyl (1-hydroxyalkyl)phosphonates [17, 18].

$$\begin{array}{c}\bigcirc\!\!=\!O\end{array} \;+\; (EtO)_2POSi(CH_3)_3 \longrightarrow \begin{array}{c} OSi(CH_3)_3 \\ \bigcirc\!\!\overset{|}{\underset{O}{\overset{}{P(OEt)_2}}} \\ || \end{array} \xrightarrow{H_2O} \begin{array}{c} OH \\ \bigcirc\!\!\overset{|}{\underset{O}{\overset{}{P(OEt)_2}}} \\ || \end{array} \tag{22.14}$$

The reaction of diethyl trimethylsilyl phosphite with aromatic aldehydes has been studied [20]. The effect of substituents on reaction rate is consistent with the importance of nucleophilic attack by phosphorous on the carbonyl carbon.

tris(Trimethylsilyl) phosphite reacts with aldehydes or ketones to yield *bis*(trimethylsilyl) 1-trimethylsilyloxyalkyl phosphonates [29, 30]. These can be readily hydrolyzed to yield α-hydroxyalkyl phosphonic acids.

$$
\underset{\substack{\parallel \\ \text{Ph-C-CH}_3}}{\overset{O}{}} \ + \ [(CH_3)_3SiO]_3P \ \longrightarrow \ \underset{\substack{H_3C \ \ O}}{\overset{OSi(CH_3)_3}{Ph-C-P[OSi(CH_3)_3]_2}} \ \overset{H_2O}{\longrightarrow} \ \underset{\substack{H_3C \ \ OH}}{\overset{HO \ \ O}{Ph-C-P-OH}}
$$

$$(22.15)$$

bis(Trimethylsilyl) phenyl phosphinate reacts with aldehydes to yield trimethylsilyl (1-trimethylsilyloxyalkyl) phenyl phosphinate [30].

$$
PhP[OSi(CH_3)_3]_2 \ + \ \underset{\substack{\parallel \\ CH_3-C-H}}{\overset{O}{}} \ \longrightarrow \ \underset{\substack{H \ \ O}}{\overset{(CH_3)_3Si \ \ O \ \ Ph}{CH_3-C-P-OSi(CH_3)_3}}
$$

$$(22.16)$$

Likewise, *bis*(trimethylsilyl)hypophosphite reacts with aromatic aldehydes or ketones [31].

$$(22.17)$$

Trimethylsilyl-N,N,N′,N′-tetraethylphosphorodiamidite reacts with aromatic aldehydes [32] to yield the expected 1 : 1 adducts: N,N,N′N′-tetraethyl-P-[α-trimethylsilyloxybenzyl]phosphonic diamides.

$$
[Et_2N]_2P-O-Si(CH_3)_3 \ + \ \underset{\substack{\parallel \\ H-C-Ph}}{\overset{O}{}} \ \longrightarrow \ \underset{\substack{H}}{\overset{O \ \ OSi(CH_3)_3}{[Et_2N]_2P-C-Ph}}
$$

$$(22.18)$$

Diethyl trimethylsilyl phosphite reacts with ketene to yield diethyl (1-trimethylsilyloxyvinyl)phosphonate which can be hydrolyzed to yield acetyl diethyl phosphonate [17, 19] (see 22.3 A).

$$
(EtO)_2POSi(CH_3)_3 \ + \ CH_2=C=O \ \longrightarrow \ \underset{\substack{OSi(CH_3)_3}}{\overset{O}{(EtO)_2P-C=CH_2}} \ \overset{H_2O}{\longrightarrow} \ \underset{}{\overset{O \ \ O}{(EtO)_2P-C-CH_3}}
$$

$$(22.19)$$

Reaction of diethyl trimethylsilyl phosphite with 2,3-butanedione yields diethyl (1-methyl-1-trimethylsilyloxyacetonyl)phosphonate [21].

$$(EtO)_2POSi(CH_3)_3 \quad + \quad CH_3\text{-}\overset{O}{\underset{\|}{C}}\text{-}\overset{O}{\underset{\|}{C}}\text{-}CH_3 \quad \longrightarrow \quad (EtO)_2\overset{O}{\underset{\|}{P}}\text{-}\underset{\underset{\underset{CH_3}{/}\quad \underset{OSi(CH_3)_3}{\backslash}}{}}{C}\text{-}\overset{O}{\underset{\|}{C}}\text{-}CH_3 \tag{22.20}$$

This is surprising since trialkyl phosphites react with α-diketones to yield cyclic 1:1 adducts [22, 23]. On the other hand, diethyl trimethylsilyl phosphite reacts with benzil to yield diethyl-[1,2-diphenyl-2-trimethylsiloxyvinyl]phosphate [20].

$$(EtO)_2POSi(CH_3)_3 \quad + \quad Ph\text{-}\overset{O}{\underset{\|}{C}}\text{-}\overset{O}{\underset{\|}{C}}\text{-}Ph \quad \longrightarrow \tag{22.21}$$

Similarly, *tris*(trimethylsilyl) phosphite reacts with 2,3-butanedione to yield *bis*(trimethylsilyl) (1,2-dimethyl-2-trimethylsilyloxyvinyl)phosphate [24]. The reason for the difference in behavior of diethyl trimethylsilyl phosphite and *tris*(trimethylsilyl)phosphite toward 2,3-butanedione is not obvious.

Diethyl trimethylsilyl phosphite reacts with both hexafluoroacetone [25, 26] and chloral [27] at low temperature to yield diethyl (1-trifluoromethyl-1-trimethylsilyloxy-2,2,2-trifluoroethyl)phosphonate and diethyl(1-trimethylsilyloxy-2,2,2-trichloroethyl)phosphonate, respectively. These rearrange on heating at 140–160 °C to yield diethyl-(2,2-difluoro-1-trifluoromethylvinyl)-phosphate and diethyl-(2,2-dichlorovinyl)phosphate [26].

$$(EtO)_2POSi(CH_3)_3 \quad + \quad CF_3\text{-}\overset{O}{\underset{\|}{C}}\text{-}CF_3 \quad \xrightarrow{-25°} \quad (EtO)_2\overset{O}{\underset{\|}{P}}\text{-}\underset{\underset{CF_3}{|}}{\overset{\overset{OSi(CH_3)_3}{|}}{C}}\text{-}CF_3 \tag{22.22}$$

The thermal decomposition of dimethyl [α-methyl-α-trimethylsilyloxy-benzyl]phosphonate to yield dimethyl trimethylsilyl phosphite and acetophenone is closely related [28].

22.5 Benzoquinones

Both diethyl trimethylsilyl phosphite [20, 33] and *tris*(trimethylsilyl) phosphite [24] react with *p*-benzoquinones to yield diethyl-4-trimethylsilyloxyphenyl phosphates or *bis*(trimethylsilyl)4-trimethylsiloxyphenyl phosphates, respectively [33].

$$(EtO)_2POSi(CH_3)_3 \ + \ O=\text{(ring)}=O \ \longrightarrow \ (EtO)_2PO-\text{(ring)}-OSi(CH_3)_3 \qquad (22.23)$$

22.6 α-Keto Esters and α-Keto Nitriles

Diethyl trimethylsilyl phosphite reacts with methyl pyruvate and pyruvonitrile to yield 1:1 adducts: diethyl [1-carbomethoxy-1-trimethylsilyloxyethyl) phosphonate and diethyl [1-cyano-1-trimethylsilyloxyethyl] phosphonate, respectively [34].

$$(EtO)_2POSi(CH_3)_3 \ + \ CH_3-\overset{O}{\overset{\|}{C}}-\overset{O}{\overset{\|}{C}}-OCH_3 \ \longrightarrow \ (EtO)_2\overset{O}{\overset{\|}{P}}-\overset{OSi(CH_3)_3}{\underset{CH_3}{\overset{|}{C}}}-CO_2CH_3 \qquad (22.24)$$

tris(Trimethylsilyl) phosphite and *bis*(trimethylsilyl) phenyl phosphinate react with pyruvonitrile in a similar manner to yield *bis*(trimethylsilyl)-[1-cyano-1-trimethylsilyloxyethyl] phosphonate and trimethylsilyl [1-cyano-1-trimethylsilyloxyethyl] phenyl phosphinate [30].

Diethyl trimethylsilyl phosphite reacts with ethyl phenylglyoxylate to yield diethyl [α-carboethoxy-α-trimethylsilylbenzyl] phosphate. Stabilization of the carbanion by adjacent ester and phenyl groups may facilitate the critical rearrangement step which converts a 1,3-phosphonium/alkoxide zwitterionic intermediate into a 1,3-phosphonium/carbanion zwitterionic intermediate [34].

$$(EtO)_2POSi(CH_3)_3 \ + \ PhC-COEt \ \longrightarrow \ \begin{bmatrix} O^- \\ | \\ Ph-C-CO_2Et \\ | \\ (EtO)_2P^+-OSi(CH_3)_3 \end{bmatrix} \qquad (22.25)$$

$$\downarrow$$

$$\begin{bmatrix} Ph-\bar{C}-CO_2Et \\ | \\ O \\ | \\ (EtO)_2P^+-OSi(CH_3)_3 \end{bmatrix} \ \longrightarrow \ \underset{O\diagdown P(OEt)_2}{\overset{Si(CH_3)_3}{\underset{|}{\overset{|}{Ph-C-CO_2Et}}}}$$

bis(Trimethylsilyl) hypophosphite reacts in a similar manner with methyl pyruvate [35].

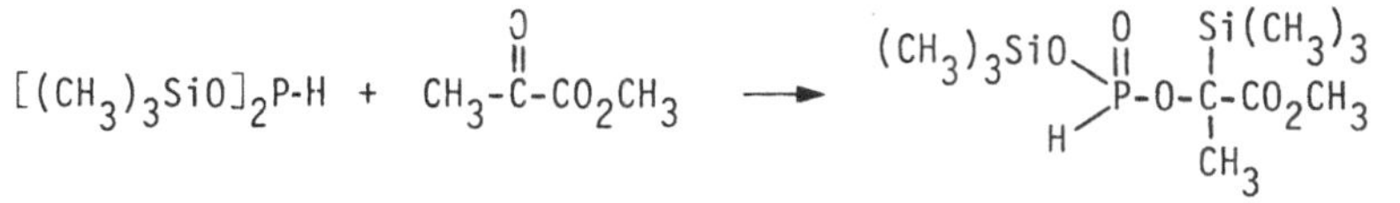

$$[(CH_3)_3SiO]_2P\text{-}H \ + \ CH_3\text{-}\overset{\overset{\displaystyle O}{\|}}{C}\text{-}CO_2CH_3 \quad \longrightarrow \quad (CH_3)_3SiO \underset{H}{\overset{\overset{\displaystyle O}{\|}}{\diagdown}}P\text{-}O\text{-}\underset{CH_3}{\overset{\overset{\displaystyle Si(CH_3)_3}{|}}{C}}\text{-}CO_2CH_3 \qquad (22.26)$$

The reaction of *bis*(trimethylsilyl) hypophosphite with methyl 3,3-dimethyl-2-ketobutyrate is more complicated [36].

22.7 α,β-Unsaturated Carbonyl Compounds

Dimethyl trimethylsilyl phosphite reacts with α,β-unsaturated aldehydes to yield mixtures of 1,2 and 1,4-adducts (Eq. 22.27). Significantly, trimethyl phosphite and TMS-Cl [14] react regiospecifically with α,β-unsaturated aldehydes to yield only 1,2-adducts (Eq. 22.28) [15,37]. α,β-Unsaturated ketones yield only 1,4-adducts with either reagent (Eq. 22.29).

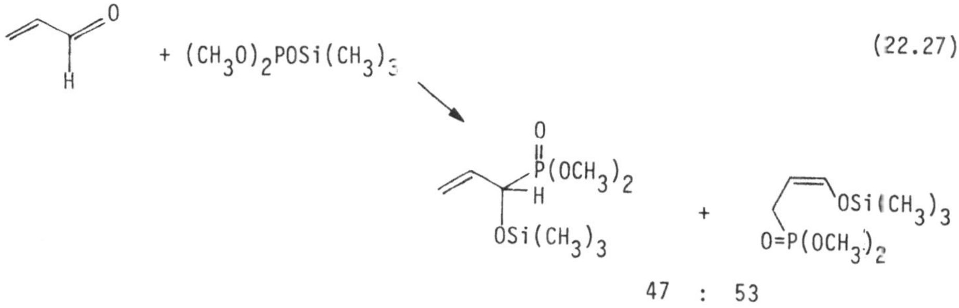

$$(22.27)$$

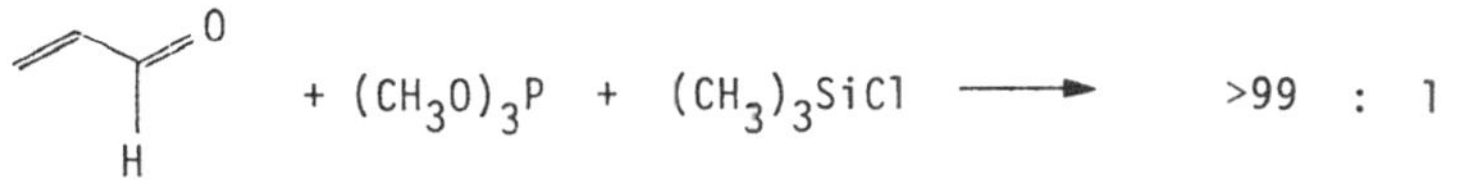

47 : 53

$$(22.28)$$

>99 : 1

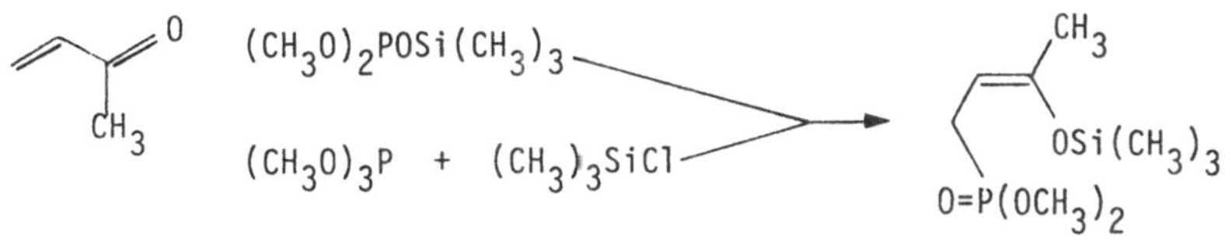

$$(22.29)$$

Based on NMR coupling constants, the stereochemistry of these 1,4-adducts has been determined to be exclusively Z. α,β-Unsaturated ketones which cannot adopt a cisoid geometry, such as 2-cyclohexenone do not react. These facts suggest that the 1,4-adducts may be formed via a cyclic intermediate [15]. Since 1,2 and 1,4 adducts do not interconvert thermally, the ratio of these products must be kinetically controlled.

365

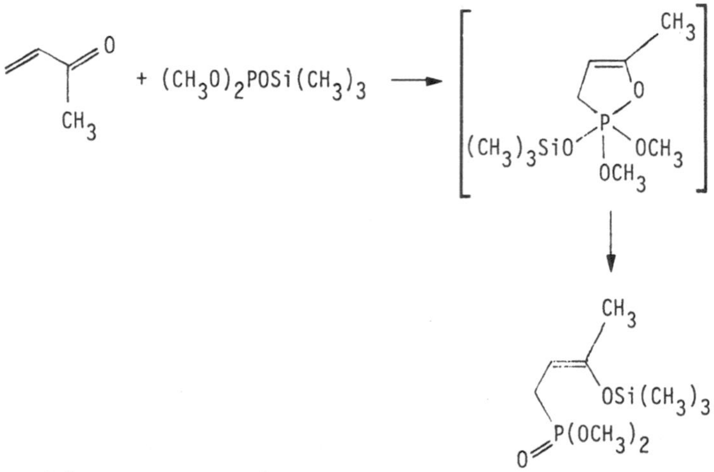

$$\text{(image of reaction scheme)}$$

(22.30)

Diethyl trimethylsilyl phosphite reacts in a 1,4 manner with 5-benzyldiene barbituric acid [38].

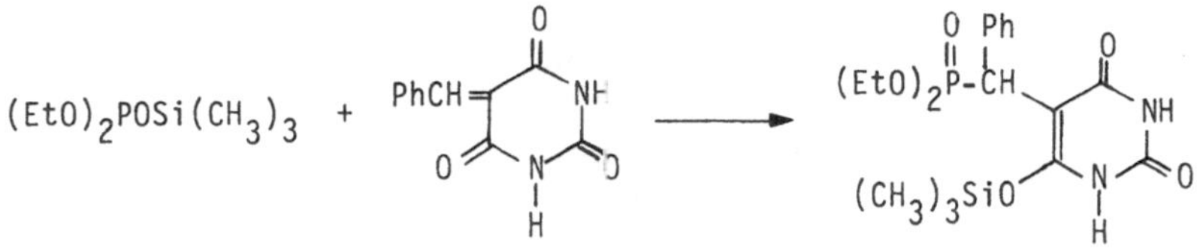

(22.31)

Diethyl trimethylsilyl phosphite reacts with α,β-unsaturated esters such as ethyl acrylate to yield mixtures of adducts [19].

$$(EtO)_2POSi(CH_3)_3 \quad + \quad H_2C=CHCO_2Et$$

(22.32)

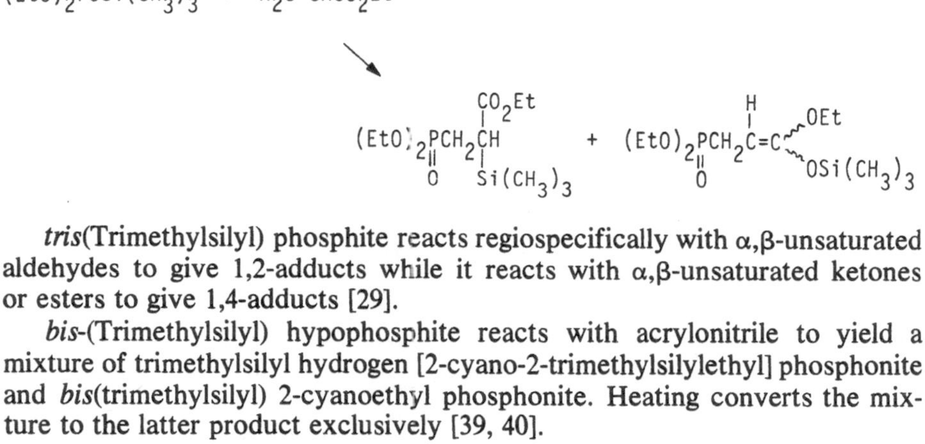

tris(Trimethylsilyl) phosphite reacts regiospecifically with α,β-unsaturated aldehydes to give 1,2-adducts while it reacts with α,β-unsaturated ketones or esters to give 1,4-adducts [29].

bis-(Trimethylsilyl) hypophosphite reacts with acrylonitrile to yield a mixture of trimethylsilyl hydrogen [2-cyano-2-trimethylsilylethyl] phosphonite and bis(trimethylsilyl) 2-cyanoethyl phosphonite. Heating converts the mixture to the latter product exclusively [39, 40].

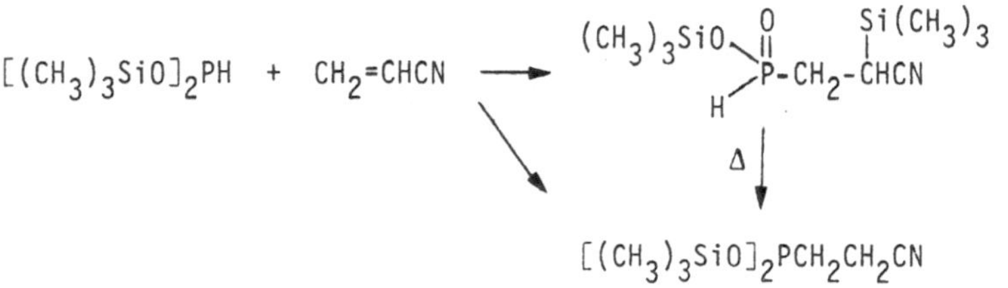

$$[(CH_3)_3SiO]_2PH \quad + \quad CH_2=CHCN$$

(22.33)

$$[(CH_3)_3SiO]_2PCH_2CH_2CN$$

bis(Trimethylsilyl) hypophosphite reacts with styrene to yield *bis*(trimethylsilyl) 2-phenylethyl phosphonite [39].

22.8 α-Haloketones

The reaction of *tris*(trimethylsilyl) phosphite with α-halo ketones occurs by three possible pathways [41]. The first is the Arbuzov reaction which yields *bis*(trimethylsilyl) 2-oxoalkyl phosphonates. Second is the formation of 1:1-adducts: *bis*(trimethylsilyl) (2-halo-1-trimethylsilyloxyalkyl) phosphonates. Third is the Perkow reaction which results in formation of *bis*(trimethylsilyl) vinyl phosphates. These latter two reactions may involve a common initial zwitterionic intermediate.

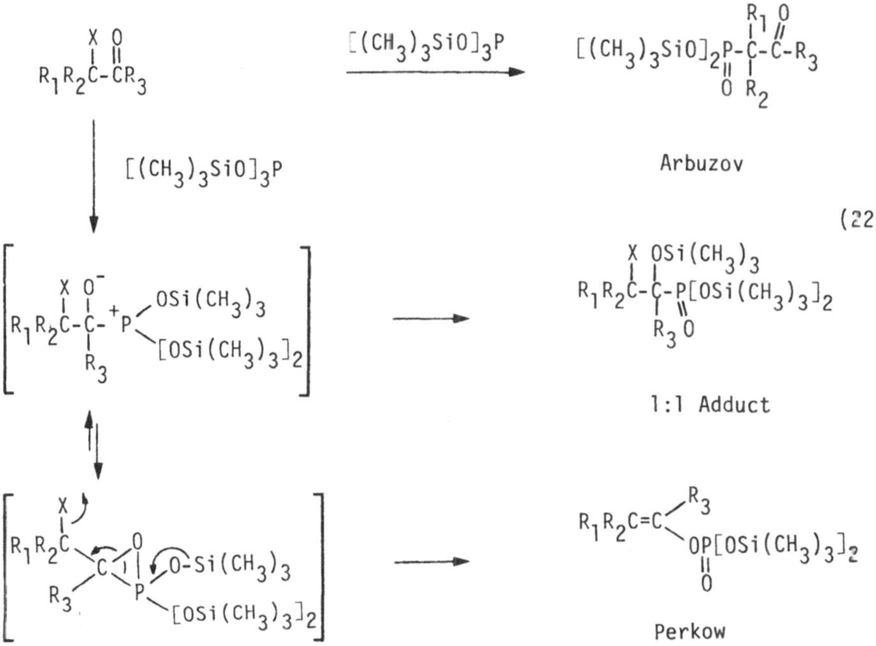

$$[(CH_3)_3SiO]_2P\text{-}\overset{R_1}{\underset{R_2}{\underset{\|}{\underset{O}{C}}}}\text{-}\overset{O}{\overset{\|}{C}}\text{-}R_3$$

Arbuzov

(22.34)

$$R_1R_2\overset{X}{\underset{\|}{C}}\text{-}\overset{OSi(CH_3)_3}{\underset{\underset{O}{R_3}}{C}}\text{-}P[OSi(CH_3)_3]_2$$

1:1 Adduct

$$R_1R_2C=C\overset{R_3}{\underset{OP[OSi(CH_3)_3]_2}{\overset{}{\underset{\|}{O}}}}$$

Perkow

With aliphatic α-haloketones or aldehydes the 1 : 1 adducts predominate. Thus chloroacetone reacts with *tris*(trimethylsilyl) phosphite to give *bis*(trimethylsilyl)-(2-chloro-1-methyl-1-trimethylsilyloxyethyl) phosphonate. This compound can be converted to the corresponding epoxide which is related to the antibiotic phosphonomycin [41, 42].

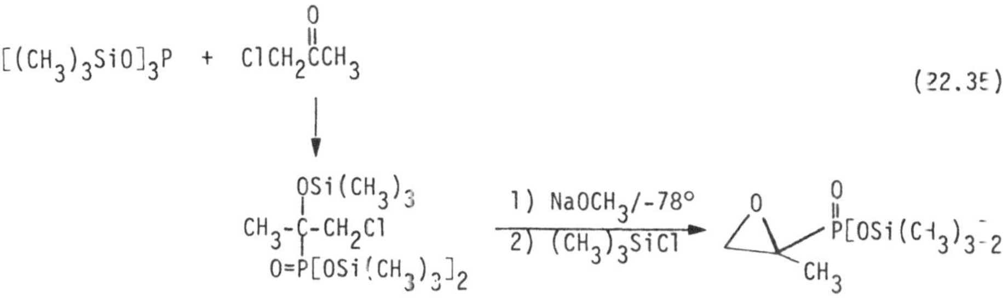

$$[(CH_3)_3SiO]_3P \; + \; ClCH_2\overset{O}{\overset{\|}{C}}CH_3$$

(22.35)

$$CH_3\text{-}\overset{OSi(CH_3)_3}{\underset{O=P[OSi(CH_3)_3]_2}{\underset{|}{C}}}\text{-}CH_2Cl \xrightarrow[\text{2) }(CH_3)_3SiCl]{\text{1) NaOCH}_3/-78°}$$

367

Phenacyl bromide reacts with *tris*(trimethylsilyl) phosphite to yield a mixture of Arbuzov (14%) and Perkow (61%) products (Eq. 22.36) [41, 43]. α-Haloesters yield exclusively Arbuzov products.

$$[(CH_3)_3SiO]_3P \ + \ Ph\text{-}\overset{\overset{\text{O}}{\|}}{C}\text{-}CH_2Br \ \longrightarrow \tag{22.36}$$

$$[(CH_3)_3SiO]_2\overset{\overset{\text{O}}{\|}}{P}CH_2\text{-}\overset{\overset{\text{O}}{\|}}{C}\text{-}Ph \ + \ H_2C=C\overset{\nearrow Ph}{\underset{\searrow O\underset{\underset{\text{O}}{\|}}{P}[OSi(CH_3)_3]_2}{}}$$

Diethyl trimethylsilyl phosphite reacts with bromoacetone to yield a mixture of Arbuzov (24%) and Perkow (65%) products while chloroacetone yields only 1 : 1 type adducts. This difference has been attributed to the increased nucleophilicity of the phosphorous of diethyl trimethylsilyl phosphite compared to *tris*(trimethylsilyl) phosphite and to the relative strength of a C−Br bond compared to a C−Cl bond [41].

$$(EtO)_2\overset{\overset{\text{O}}{\|}}{P}OSi(CH_3)_3 \ + \ BrCH_2\text{-}\overset{\overset{\text{O}}{\|}}{C}\text{-}CH_3 \ \longrightarrow \ (EtO)_2\overset{\overset{\text{O}}{\|}}{P}\text{-}CH_2\text{-}\overset{\overset{\text{O}}{\|}}{C}\text{-}CH_3 \ + \ (EtO)_2\overset{\overset{\text{O}}{\|}}{P}\text{-}O\text{-}\overset{\overset{\text{CH}_3}{|}}{C}=CH_2$$

$$\tag{22.37}$$

$$(EtO)_2\overset{\overset{\text{O}}{\|}}{P}OSi(CH_3)_3 \ + \ ClCH_2\text{-}\overset{\overset{\text{O}}{\|}}{C}\text{-}CH_3 \ \longrightarrow \ (EtO)_2\overset{\overset{\text{O}}{\|}}{P}\text{-}\overset{\overset{\text{OSi(CH}_3)_3}{|}}{\underset{\underset{\text{CH}_3}{|}}{C}}\text{-}CH_2Cl \tag{22.38}$$

bis(Trimethylsilyl) hypophosphite reacts with chloroacetone to yield approximately equal amounts of 1:1 adduct (37,6%) and Perkow reaction product (41,5%) [44].

Phosphoenol pyruvate possesses a high energy phosphate bond, [$\Delta G°$ = −14.8 kcal/mole on hydrolysis]. It can be prepared in an one pot reaction sequence (Eq. 22.39) [45].

$$CH_3\text{-}\overset{\overset{\text{O}}{\|}}{C}\text{-}CO_2H$$

$$(CH_3)_3SiCl \ \Big| \ (CH_3)_2N\!\!-\!\!\langle\text{pyridine}\rangle\!\!-\!\!N \quad Et_3N$$

$$CH_2=\overset{\underset{\underset{\text{OSi(CH}_3)_3}{|}}{|}}{C}\text{-}\overset{\overset{\text{O}}{\|}}{C}\text{-}OSi(CH_3)_3 \ \xrightarrow[-78°]{\underset{\text{CH}_2Cl_2}{Br_2}} \ BrCH_2\text{-}\overset{\overset{\text{O O}}{\|\ \|}}{C}\text{-}C\text{-}OSi(CH_3)_3 \ + \ (CH_3)_3SiBr$$

$$\Big|\ (CH_3O)_2POSi(CH_3)_3$$
Perkow reaction

$$CH_2=\overset{\underset{\underset{\text{O=}\overset{}{P}[OSi(CH_3)_3]_2}{|}}{|}}{C}\text{-}\overset{\overset{\text{O}}{\|}}{C}\text{-}OSi(CH_3)_3 \ \xleftarrow{2(CH_3)_3SiBr} \ CH_2=\overset{\underset{\underset{\text{O=}\overset{}{P}(OCH_3)_2}{|}}{|}}{C}\text{-}\overset{\overset{\text{O}}{\|}}{C}\text{-}OSi(CH_3)_3 \tag{22.39}$$

Enol phosphates have been prepared as outlined [46].

$$
\underset{\text{PhCCH}_2\text{Cl}}{\overset{\overset{\text{O}}{\parallel}}{}}
$$

$$\Big\downarrow\ \text{P(OCH}_3)_3 \tag{22.40}$$

$$
\underset{\underset{\text{O=C(OCH}_3)_2}{\overset{|}{\text{O}}}}{\overset{\text{Ph}}{\diagdown}}\diagup\!\!=
\quad\xrightarrow{\ (\text{CH}_3)_3\text{SiBr}\ }\quad
\underset{\underset{\text{O=P[OSi(CH}_3)_3]_2}{\overset{|}{\text{O}}}}{\overset{\text{Ph}}{\diagdown}}\diagup\!\!=
\quad\xrightarrow[\text{THF}]{\ \text{EtOH, PhNH}_2\ }\quad
\underset{\underset{-\overset{|}{\text{O}}\quad\text{PhNH}_3^+}{\overset{|}{\underset{\text{O=P-OH}}{}}}}{\overset{\text{Ph}}{\diagdown}}\diagup\!\!=
$$

22.9 Carbon-Carbon Bond Formation/Acyl Anion Synthons

Benzaldehyde can be converted to diethyl (α-trimethylsilyloxybenzyl) phosphonates (Eq. 22.13), which can be metallated with LDA. This anion reacts with primary alkyl iodides or bromides to yield diethyl [α-alkyl-$\dot\alpha$-trimethylsilyloxybenzyl] phosphonates. Treatment of these with base gives alkyl aryl ketones [37, 47].

$$
\underset{\underset{\text{O=P(OEt)}_2}{\overset{|}{\underset{|}{\text{Ph-C-H}}}}}{\overset{\text{OSi(CH}_3)_3}{}}
\quad\xrightarrow[\text{2) } n\text{-PrI}]{\text{1) LDA}}\quad
\underset{\underset{\text{(OEt)}_2}{\overset{\text{O=P}}{}}}{\overset{\overset{\text{Si(CH}_3)_3}{\diagup}}{\underset{|}{\overset{|}{\text{Ph-C-CH}_2\text{CH}_2\text{CH}_3}}}}
\tag{22.41}
$$

$$\diagdown\ \text{OH}^-$$

$$
\underset{\text{Ph-C-CH}_2\text{CH}_2\text{CH}_3}{\overset{\overset{\text{O}}{\parallel}}{}}\ +\ (\text{EtO})_2\text{PO}^-\ +\ (\text{CH}_3)_3\text{SiOH}
$$

Diethyl [α-lithio-α-trimethylsilyloxybenzyl] phosphonate also reacts with ketones or aldehydes to yield α-hydroxy ketones [48, 49].

$$
\underset{\underset{\text{Li}}{\overset{|}{\underset{|}{(\text{EtO})_2\text{P-C-OSi(CH}_3)_3}}}}{\overset{\overset{\text{O Ph}}{\parallel\ |}}{}}
\ +\
\text{CH}_3\underset{\text{S}}{\diagup\!\!\diagdown}\underset{\text{C-H}}{\overset{\overset{\text{O}}{\parallel}}{}}
\tag{22.42}
$$

$$
\left[
\underset{\underset{\underset{\text{CH}_3}{\text{S}}}{\overset{|}{\text{H-C-O}^-}}}{\overset{\overset{\text{O Ph}}{\parallel\ |}}{(\text{EtO})_2\text{P-C-O-Si(CH}_3)_3}}
\right]
\quad\longrightarrow\quad
\underset{\underset{\text{H}}{\overset{|}{\text{Ph-C-C}}}}{\overset{\overset{\text{O O}}{\parallel\ \parallel}\ \ \overset{\text{Si(CH}_3)_3}{|}}{}}\underset{\text{S}}{\diagdown\!\!\diagup}\!\!-\!\text{CH}_3
$$

$$(\text{EtO})_2\text{P-O}^-\text{Li}^+$$

Diethyl trimethylsilyl phosphite reacts with α,β-unsaturated aldehydes to yield 1,2-adducts. Metallation of these yields allylic carbanions which react regiospecifically with primary secondary alkyl iodides at the γ-position to yield diethyl (2-alkyl-1-trimethylsilyloxyvinyl) phosphonates. These undergo acidic hydrolysis to yield esters [50].

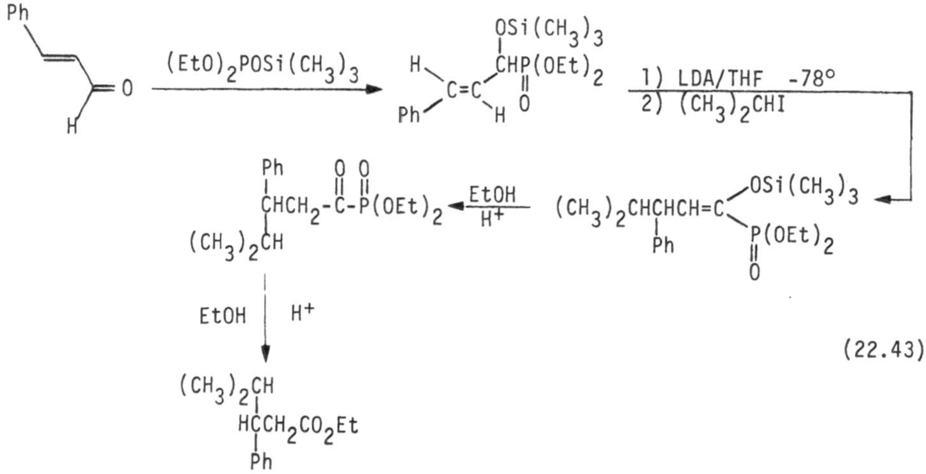

(22.43)

22.10. Oxidation of Trimethylsilyl Phosphites

tris(Trimethylsilyl) phosphite reduces 5′-azido-5′-deoxyribonucleosides to 5′-amino-5′-deoxyribonucleosides as outlined below. The phosphite is oxidized to a phosphoramidate in the process [51].

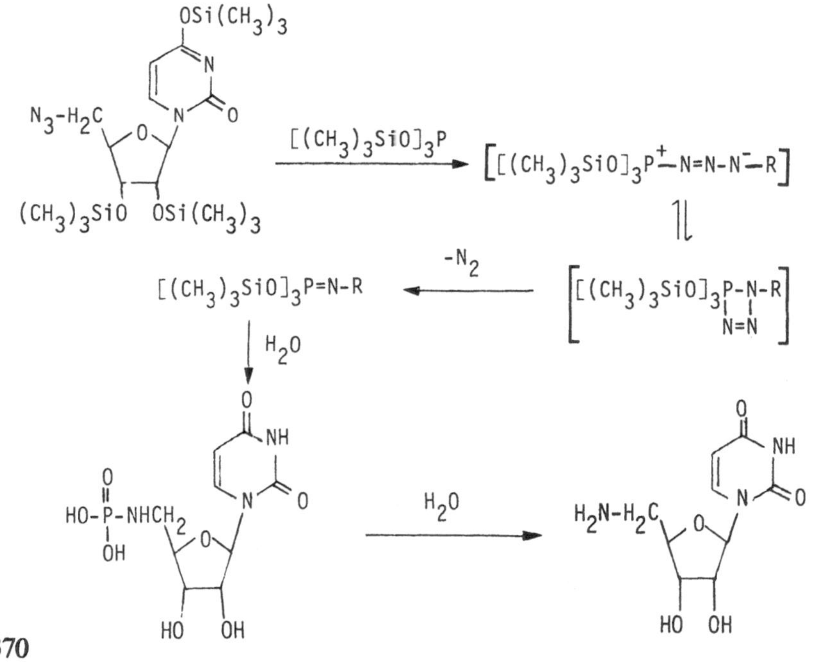

(22.44)

This procedure has been used to prepare 3',5'-dinucleoside phosphoramidates.

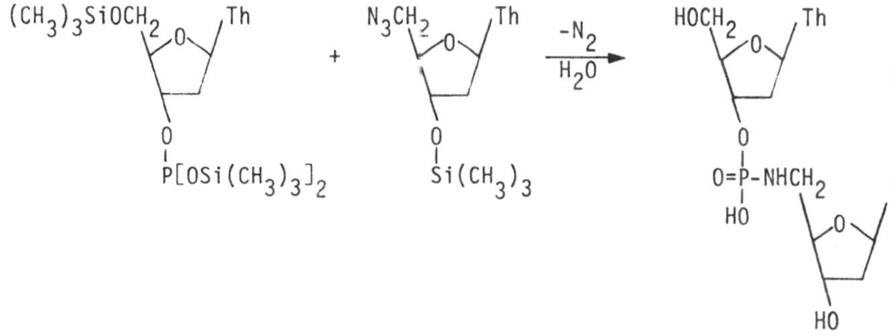

(22.45)

Trimethylsilyl phosphinites react with sulfur to yield trimethylsilylthio-
phosphinates [4]. *bis*(Trimethylsilyl) phenyl phosphonate reacts with sulfur
to yield O,O-*bis*(trimethylsilyl) phenyl phosphonothioate [52, 53].

$$(n\text{-Bu})_2\text{POSi}(CH_3)_3 \ + \ S_8 \ \longrightarrow \ (n\text{-Bu})_2\overset{\overset{\displaystyle S}{\|}}{P}\text{OSi}(CH_3)_3$$

(22.46)

In a similar manner, alkyl *bis*(trimethylsilyl) phosphites react with diaryl
disulfides to yield arylthiotrimethylsilanes and alkyl S-aryl trimethylsilyl thio-
phosphates. This methodology has proved useful for the oxidation of nucleoside phosphites [53, 54, 74].

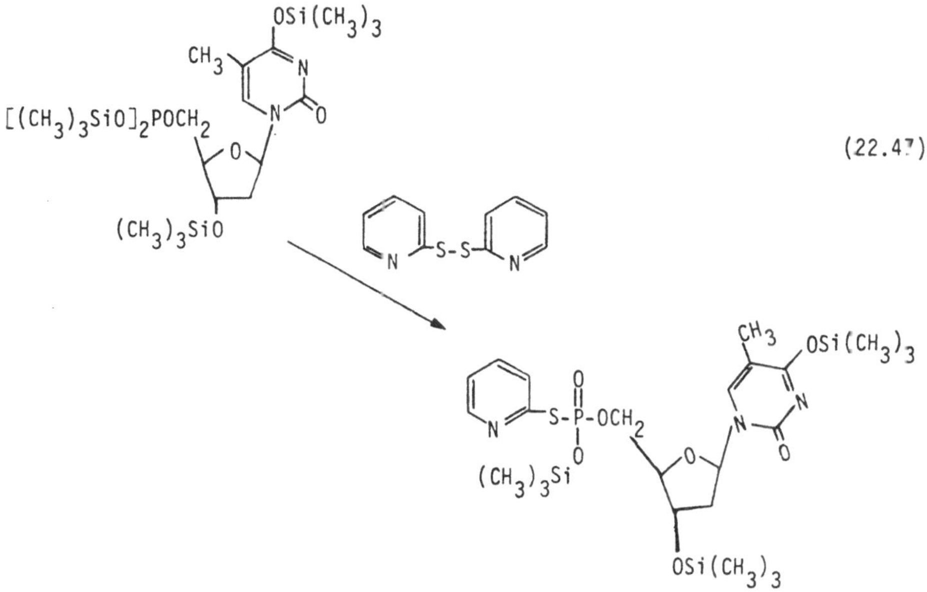

(22.47)

DMSO also oxidizes *bis*-(trimethylsilyl) nucleoside phosphites to *bis*-(trimethylsilyl) nucleoside phosphates [75].

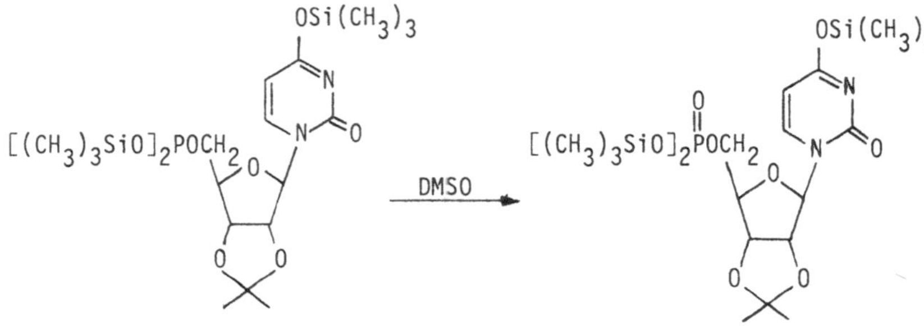

(22.48)

Likewise *tris*(trimethylsilyl phosphite is oxidized by methyl phenyl sulfoxide to *tris*(trimethylsilyl) phosphate [75]. On the other hand, *tris*(trimethylsilyl) phosphite reacts at 130° with 2-nitrobiphenyl to yield carbazole and *tris*-(trimethylsilyl) phosphate.

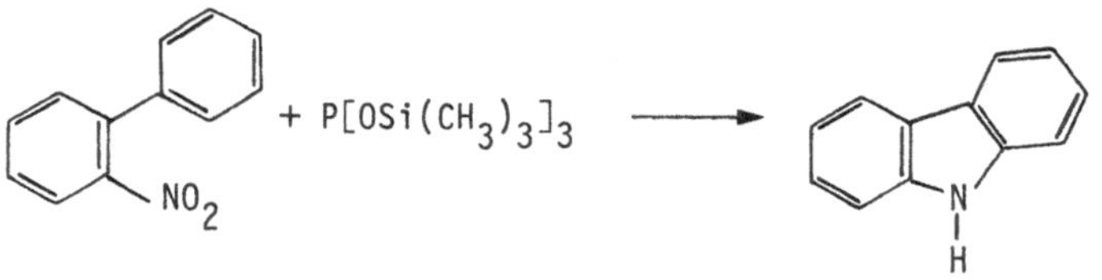

(22.49)

22.11 Miscellaneous Reactions

Under nucleophilic catalysis by potassium phenylthiolate/DC-18-C-6, phenylthiotrimethylsilane reacts with trimethylphosphate to yield first dimethyl trimethylsilyl phosphate and then more slowly methyl *bis*(trimethylsilyl) phosphate and finally *tris*(trimethylsilyl) phosphate. The half-life for the first exchange is significantly shorter than that for the second which in turn is shorter than the third ($t_1 = 7.5$ min, $t_2 = 55$ min, and $t_3 = 455$ min at 30 °C). This difference permits isolation of intermediate products [55]. TMS-Br, while effective for such reactions, is not selective.

$$(CH_3O)_3P{=}O \;+\; PhSSi(CH_3)_3 \xrightarrow[\text{DC-18-C-6}]{PhS^-K^+} (CH_3O)_2P({=}O)OSi(CH_3)_3 \qquad (22.50)$$

$$\xrightarrow[\text{DC-18-C-6}]{PhS^-K^+} CH_3OP(O)[OSi(CH_3)_3]_2$$

Trimethylsilyl polyphosphate may be prepared by addition of P_2O_5 to hexamethyldisiloxane. Unlike polyphosphoric acid, it has good solvent properties and will dissolve a number of organic substrates at room temperature [56]. It has been utilized for the Beckman rearrangement to convert oximes to amides [56, 57].

$$(22.51)$$

2-Trimethylsilylprop-2-enyl esters of phosphoric acid can be used as a protecting group since they are relatively stable to acidic and basic conditions [58]. They are, however, removed by hydrogenolysis over Pd/C or by treatment with tetraethylammonium fluoride.

$$(22.52)$$

They may be prepared by reaction of 2-trimethylsilylprop-2-enol [59] with phosphorodichloridates in pyridine.

22.12 Preparations

Diethyl trimethylsilyl phosphite has been prepared by reaction of diethylphosphite with TMS-Cl and triethylamine [60, 61].

$$(22.53)$$

Dimethyl trimethylsilyl phosphite [62], and dimethyl triethylsilyl phosphite [62] have been prepared by analogous reactions [62]. Dimethyl trimethylsilyl phosphite has been prepared by reaction of dimethyl phosphite with hexamethyldisilazane [63].

Dialkyl phosphites also react with dialkylaminotrialkylsilanes to yield dialkyl trialkylsilyl phosphites [64]. Dimethyl t-butyldimethylsilyl phosphite has been prepared by reaction of dimethylphosphite with sodium hydride and t-butyldimethylchlorosilane [15].

$$(22.54)$$

Detailed instructions for the preparation of *tris*(trimethylsilyl) phosphite by reaction of TMS-Cl with phosphorous acid and triethylamine have been published [41].

$$\text{H-}\overset{\overset{\text{O}}{\|}}{\text{P}}\text{(OH)}_2 \xrightarrow[\text{Et}_3\text{N}]{\text{(CH}_3)_3\text{SiCl}} [\text{(CH}_3)_3\text{SiO}]_3\text{P} \qquad (22.55)$$

bis(Trimethylsilyl) hypophosphite has been prepared by reaction of hypophosphorous acid with TMS-Cl and trimethylamine or with *bis*(trimethylsilyl)acetamide. NOTE: It is inflammable and burns in air [31].

$$\overset{\overset{\text{O}}{\|}}{\text{H}_2\text{POH}} + \text{CH}_3\text{-}\overset{\overset{\text{OSi(CH}_3)_3}{|}}{\text{C}}\text{=NSi(CH}_3)_3 \longrightarrow \text{HP[OSi(CH}_3)_3]_2 \qquad (22.56)$$

bis(Trimethylsilyl) hypophosphite can also be prepared by reaction of hypophosphorous acid with two equivalents of dimethylaminotrimethylsilane [65].

bis(Trimethylsilyl) phenyl phosphinate has been prepared by reaction of phenyl phosphonous acid with hexamethyldisilazane [30].

$$\text{Ph-}\overset{\overset{\text{O}}{\|}}{\text{P}}\overset{\text{OH}}{\underset{\text{H}}{<}} + [\text{(CH}_3)_3\text{Si}]_2\text{NH} \longrightarrow \text{PhP[OSi(CH}_3)_3]_2 \qquad (22.57)$$

Phenyl phosphonous acid also reacts with triethylsilane under catalysis by nickel to yield *bis*(triethylsilyl) phenyl phosphinate [66].

Trimethylsilyl N,N,N′,N′-tetraethylphosphorodiamidite has been prepared by reaction of magnesium bromide N,N,N′,N′-tetraethylphosphorodiamidite with TMS-Cl [67].

$$[\text{Et}_2\text{N}]_2\text{PO}^-\text{MgBr}^+ + \text{(CH}_3)_3\text{SiCl} \longrightarrow [\text{Et}_3\text{N}]_2\text{POSi(CH}_3)_3 \qquad (22.58)$$

Reaction of N,N,N′,N′-tetramethylphosphorodiamido chloride with sodium triethylsilanoate yields triethylsilyl N,N,N′,N′-tetramethylphosphorodiamidite [15].

$$\text{Et}_3\text{SiOH} \xrightarrow{\text{NaH}} \text{Et}_3\text{SiO}^-\text{Na}^+ + [\text{(CH}_3)_2\text{N}]_2\text{PCl} \longrightarrow \text{Et}_3\text{SiOP[N(CH}_3)_2]_2 \qquad (22.59)$$

Secondary phosphine oxides react with alkali metals in aprotic solvents with evolution of hydrogen. The anion thus formed reacts with TMS-Cl to yield trimethylsilyl phosphinites [4].

$$\text{Ph}_2\text{P}\overset{\overset{\text{O}}{\diagup}}{\underset{\text{H}}{\diagdown}} \xrightarrow{\text{K}} \text{Ph}_2\text{PO}^-\text{K}^+ \xrightarrow{\text{(CH}_3)_3\text{SiCl}} \text{Ph}_2\text{POSi(CH}_3)_3 \qquad (22.60)$$

tris(Trimethylsilyl) phosphate can be prepared by reaction of TMS-Cl with phosphoric acid. Triethylbromosilane also reacts with triethylphosphate to yield ethyl bromide and *tris*(triethylsilyl) phosphate [68].

tris(Trimethylsilyl) phosphine undergoes oxidation by nitrogen dioxide to yield *tris*(trimethylsilyl) phosphate [69].

$$[(CH_3)_3Si]_3P \ + \ NO_2 \ \longrightarrow \ [(CH_3)_3SiO]_3P=O \tag{22.61}$$

Silyl phosphines [70] have been prepared by reaction of alkali metal phosphides and chlorosilanes [69–71].

$$PhPK_2 \ + \ 2(CH_3)_3SiCl \ \longrightarrow \ PhP[Si(CH_3)_3]_2 \tag{22.62}$$

Trimethylsilyl diphenyl phosphine has been prepared by Wurtz type reaction of diphenylphosphinous chloride, TMS-Cl and sodium [72] or magnesium [7] in ether solvents.

tris(Trimethylsilyl) phosphine, *t*-butyl *bis*(trimethylsilyl) phosphine and di-*t*-butyl trimethylsilyl phosphine have been prepared by Wurtz type reaction of TMS-Cl and phosphorous trichloride, *t*-butyl dichloro phosphine or di-*t*-butyl phosphinous chloride respectively with magnesium in THF [8].

$$(CH_3)_3CPCl_2 \ + \ 2(CH_3)_3SiCl \ \xrightarrow{\text{Mg/THF}} \ (CH_3)_3CP[Si(CH_3)_3]_2 \tag{22.63}$$

Experimental details of the reaction of aldehydes with TMS-Cl and trialkyl phosphites have been published [15, 49].

$$\underset{\text{Ph-}\overset{\overset{\textstyle O}{\|}}{C}\text{-H}}{} \ + \ (EtO)_3P \ + \ (CH_3)_3SiCl \ \longrightarrow \ \underset{\text{Ph-}\overset{\overset{\textstyle OSi(CH_3)_3}{|}}{\underset{\underset{\textstyle O=P(OEt)_2}{|}}{C}}\text{-H}}{} \tag{22.64}$$

References

1. Voronkov, M.G., Skorik, Y.I.: Zh. Obsh. Khim. *35*, 106 (1965)
2. Hata, T., Sekine, M., Kagawa, N.: Chem. Lett. 635 (1975)
3. Rosenthal, A.F., Vargas, L.A., Isaacson, Y.A., Bittman, R.: Tetrahedron Lett. 977 (1975)
4. Issleib, K., Walther, B.: Angew. Chem. Int. Ed. *6*, 88 (1967)
5. Rosenthal, A.F., Gringauz, A., Vargas, L.A.: J. Chem. Soc. Chem. Commun. 384 (1976)
6. Dahl, O.: Acta. Chem. Scand. *B, 30,* 799 (1976)
7. Schumann, H., duMont, W.W.: Chem. Ber. *108*, 2261 (1975)
8. Schumann, H., Rösch, L.: Chem. Ber. *107*, 854 (1974)
9. Orlov, N.F., Kaufman, B.L.: Zh. Obsh. Khim. *38*, 1842 (1968)
10. Yamaguchi, Y., Kamimura, T., Hata, T.: J. Am. Chem. Soc. *102*, 4534 (1980)
11. Becher, H.J., Fenske, D., Langer, E.: Chem. Ber. *106*, 177 (1973)
12. Kunzek, H., Braun, M., Nesener, E., Rühlmann, K.: J. Organometal. Chem. *49*, 149 (1973)
13. Fenske, D., Langer, E., Heymann, M., Becher, H.J.: Chem. Ber. *109*, 359 (1976)
14. Birum, G.H., Richardson, G.A.: U.S. Patent 3,113,139 (1963)
15. Evans, D.A., Hurst, K.M., Takacs, J.M.: J. Am. Chem. Soc. *100*, 3467 (1978)
16. Brook, A.G.: Accts. Chem. Res. *7*, 77 (1974)

17. Novikova, Z.S., Mashoshina, S.N., Sapozhnikova, T.A., Lutsenko, I.F.: Zh. Obsh. Khim. *41*, 2622 (1971)
18. Nesterov, L.V., Krepysheva, N.E., Sabirova, R.A., Romanova, G.N.: Zh. Obsh. Khim. *41*, 2449 (1971)
19. Novikova, Z.S., Lutsenko, I.F.: Zh. Obsh. Khim. *40*, 2129 (1970)
20. Pudovik, A.N., Kibardin, A.M., Pashinkin, A.P., Sudarev, Y.I., Gazizov, T.K.: Zh. Obsh. Khim. *44*, 522 (1974)
21. Gazizov, T.K., Kibardin, A.M., Pashinkin, A.P., Sudarev, Y.I., Pudovik, A.N.: Zh. Obsh. Khim. *43*, 679 (1973)
22. Ramirez, F.: Pure and Applied Chem. *9*, 337 (1964)
23. Ramirez, F., Desai, N.B.: J. Am. Chem. Soc. *85*, 3252 (1963)
24. Hata, T., Sekine, M., Ishikawa, N.: Chem. Lett. 645 (1975)
25. Pudovik, A.N., Gazizov, T.K., Kibardin, A.M.: Zh. Obsh. Khim. *44*, 1210 (1974)
26. Kibardin, A.M., Gazizov, T.K., Pudovik, A.N.: Zh. Obsh. Khim. *45*, 1982 (1975)
27. Pudovik, A.N., Gazizov, T.K., Sudarev, Y.I.: Zh. Obsh. Khim. *43*, 2086 (1973)
28. Pudovik, A.N., Gazizov, T.K., Sudarev, Y.I.: Zh. Obsh. Khim. *44*, 951
29. Sekine, M., Yamamoto, I., Hashizume, A., Hata, T.: Chem. Lett. 485 (1977)
30. Lebedev, E.P., Pudovik, A.N., Tsyganov, B.N., Nazmutdinov, R.Y., Romanov, G.V.: Zh. Obsh. Khim. *47*, 765 (1977)
31. Hata, T., Mori, H., Sekine, M.: Chem. Lett. 1431 (1977)
32. Pudovik, A.N., Batyeva, E.S., Al'fonsov, V.A.: Zh. Obsh. Khim. *45*, 939 (1975)
33. Pudovik, A.N., Batyeva, E.S., Zamaletdinova, G.U.: Zh. Obsh. Khim. *42*, 2577 (1972)
34. Konovalova, I.V., Burnaeva, L.A., Saifullina, N.S., Pudovik, A.N.: Zh. Obsh. Khim. *46*, 18 (1976)
35. Pudovik, A.N., Romanov, G.V., Nazmutdinov, R.Y., Konovalova, I.V.: Zh. Obsh. Khim. *43*, 678 (1973)
36. Pudovik, A.N., Romanov, G.V., Nazmutdinov, R.Y.: Zh. Obsh. Khim. *45*, 1896 (1975)
37. Evans, D.A., Hurst, K.M., Truesdale, L.K., Takacs, J.M.: Tetrahedron Lett. 2495 (1977)
38. Pudovik, A.N., Batyeva, E.S., Zamaletdinova, G.U.: Zh. Obsh. Khim. *43*, 947 (1973)
39. Pudovik, A.N., Romanov, G.V., Nazmutdinov, R.Y.: Zh. Obsh. Khim. *47*, 555 (1977)
40. Voronkov, M.G., Marmur, L.Z., Dolgov, O.D., Pestunovich, V.A., Pokrovskii, E.I., Popel, Y.I.: Zh. Obsh. Khim. *41*, 1987 (1971)
41. Sekine, M., Okimoto, K., Yamada, K., Hata, T.: J. Org. Chem. *46*, 2097 (1981)
42. Sekine, M., Okimoto, K., Hata, T.: J. Am. Chem. Soc. *100*, 1001 (1978)
43. Hata, T., Sekine, M., Kagawa, N.: Chem. Lett. 635 (1975)
44. Pudovik, A.N., Romanov, G.V., Nazmutdinov, R.Y.: Zh. Obsh. Khim. *44*, 221 (1974)
45. Sekine, M., Futatsugi, T., Yamada, K., Hata, T.: Tetrahedron Lett. 371 (1980)
46. Hata, T., Yamada, K., Futatsugi, T., Sekine, M.: Synthesis, 189 (1979)
47. Hata, T., Hashizume, A., Nakajima, M., Sekine, M.: Tetrahedron Lett. 363 (1978)
48. Koenigkramer, R.E., Zimmer, H.: Tetrahedron Lett. 1017 (1980)
49. Koenigkramer, R.E., Zimmer, H.: J. Org. Chem. *45*, 3994 (1980)
50. Hata, T., Nakajima, M., Sekine, M.: Tetrahedron Lett. 2047 (1979)
51. Hata, T., Yamamoto, I., Sekine, M.: Chem. Lett. 601 (1976)
52. Orlov, N.F., Belokrinitskii, M.A.: Zh. Obsh. Khim. *40*, 504 (1970)
53. Hata, T., Sekine, M.: Tetrahedron Lett. 3943 (1974)

54. Sekine, M., Hata, T.: Tetrahedron Lett. 1711 (1975)
55. Takeuchi, Y., Demachi, Y., Yoshii, E.: Tetrahedron Lett. 1231 (1979)
56. Imamoto, T., Yokoyama, H., Yokoyama, M.: Tetrahedron Lett. 1803 (1981)
57. Cava, M.P., Lakshmikanthan, M.V., Mitchell, M.J.: J. Org. Chem. *34*, 2665 (1969)
58. Chan, T.K., DiStefano, M.: J. Chem. Soc. Chem. Commun. 761 (1978)
59. Chan, T.H., Mychajlowskij, W., Ong, B.S., Harpp, D.N.: J. Org. Chem. *43*, 1526 (1978)
60. Orlov, N.F., Kaufman, B.L., Sukhi, L., Slesar, L.N., Sudakova, E.V.: Khim. Prakt. Primen. Kreminorg. Soedin, Tr. Soveshch. 111 (1966) CA *72*, 217384 (1970)
61. Orlov, N.F., Sudakova, E.V.: Zh. Obsh. Khim. *39*, 222 (1969)
62. Nesterov, L.V., Krepysheva, N.E., Sabirova, R.A., Romanova, G.N.: Zh. Obsh. Khim. *41*, 2449 (1971)
63. Chevnyshev, E.A., Bugerenko, E.F., Akat'eva, A.S., Naumov, A.D.: Zh. Obsh. Khim. *45*, 242 (1975)
64. Pudovik, M.A., Medvedeva, M D., Pudovik, A.N.: Zh. Obsh. Khim. *45*, 700 (1975)
65. Voronkov, M.G., Marmur, L.Z., Dolgov, O.N., Pestunovich, V.A., Pokrovskii, E.I., Popel, Y.I.: Zh. Obsh. Khim. *41*, 1987 (1971)
66. Orlov, N.F., Belokrinitskii, M.A.: Zh. Obsh. Khim. *40*, 504 (1970)
67. Pudovik, A.N., Batyeva, E.S., Al'fonsov, V.A.: Zh. Obsh. Khim. *45*, 248 (1975)
68. Voronkov, M.G., Zgonnik, V.N.: Zh. Obsh. Khim. *27*, 1483 (1957)
69. Parshall, G.W., Lindsey, Jr., R.V.: J. Am. Chem. Soc. *81*, 6273 (1959)
70. For a review of the older literature concerning silyl phosphines see Fritz, G.: Angew. Chem. Int. Ed. *5*, 53 (1966)
71. Baudler, M., Zarkadas, A.: Chem. Ber. *106*, 3970 (1973)
72. Kuchen, W., Buchwald, H.: Chem. Ber. *92*, 227 (1959)
73. Deroo, P.W., Rosenthal, A.F., Isaacson, Y.A., Vargas, L.A., Bittman, R.: Chem. and Phys. of Lipids, *16*, 60 (1976)
74. Hata, T., Sekine, M.: J. Am. Chem. Soc. *96*, 7363 (1974)
75. Sekine, M., Yamagata, H., Hata, T.: Tetrahedron Lett. 375 (1979)

23 Silyl Oxidants

23.1 Introduction

While there are numerous silyl reduction reactions, there are just a few silicon based oxidizing reagents. Oxidation of silyl enol ethers and the modification of lead tetraacetate by TMS-N$_3$ have been previously considered.

23.2 *bis*(Trimethylsilyl) monoperoxysulfate

bis(Trimethylsilyl) monoperoxysulfate is a silyl derivative of Caro's acid. Soluble in aprotic non-polar solvents such as methylene chloride, it has proved useful for Baeyer-Villiger oxidation of ketones to the esters [1].

$$Ph_2C=O \ + \ (CH_3)_3SiO-\overset{\overset{O}{\|}}{\underset{\underset{O}{\|}}{S}}-OOSi(CH_3)_3 \ \longrightarrow \ PhO-\overset{\overset{O}{\|}}{C}-Ph \qquad (23.1)$$

bis(Trimethylsilyl) monoperoxysulfate is prepared by reaction of sulfur trioxide with *bis*(trimethylsilyl) peroxide.

Baeyer-Villiger oxidations of β-trimethylsilyl ketones yield esters of β-hydroxyalkyltrimethylsilanes. Migratory aptitude in Baeyer-Villiger oxidation, may be related to the propensity of the migrating group to bear positive charge. The 2-trimethylsilylethyl group has a migratory aptitude between that of tertiary and secondary alkyl groups [2].

$$(23.2)$$

23.3 *bis*(Trimethylsilyl)peroxide and *t*-Butyl Trimethylsilyl Peroxide

bis(Trimethylsilyl)peroxide might be considered to be analogous to hydrogen peroxide. It oxidizes sulfides to sulfoxides and sulfones, phosphites to phosphates and tertiary phosphines to tertiary phosphine oxides [3, 4].

$$Ph_3P \ + \ (CH_3)_3SiOOSi(CH_3)_3 \ \longrightarrow \ Ph_3P{\rightarrow}O \ + \ (CH_3)_3SiOSi(CH_3)_3 \qquad (23.3)$$

It also reacts with Grignard and organolithium reagents to yield alkoxy- or aryloxytrimethylsilanes and trimethylsilanoate [3, 4].

$$n\text{-BuLi} + (CH_3)_3SiOOSi(CH_3)_3 \ \longrightarrow \ n\text{-BuOSi}(CH_3)_3 + Li^+ \ ^-OSi(CH_3)_3 \qquad (23.4)$$

Si—Si and Si—H bonds have also been oxidized by *bis*(trimethylsilyl)peroxide [5]. *bis*-Trimethylsilyl)peroxide may be prepared by reaction of TMS-Cl with 90% hydrogen peroxide or by reaction of the 1,4-diazo bicyclo [2,2,2] octane/hydrogen peroxide complex with TMS-Cl [6].

t-Butyl trimethylsilyl peroxide also oxidizes tertiary phosphines to tertiary phosphine oxides and phosphites to phosphates [7]. Photolysis of *t*-butyl trimethylsilyl peroxide results in homolytic fission of the O—O bond to yield *t*-butoxy and trimethylsilyloxy radicals [8]. These are able to initiate vinyl polymerizations [9].

23.4 Silyl Hydroperoxides

Trimethylsilyl hydroperoxide/HCl, generated *in-situ*, by reaction of TMS-Cl with aq. hydrogen peroxide, reacts with alkenes to yield chlorohydrins. An intermediate oxirane has been proposed [10].

$$\text{(structure)} + 30\% \ H_2O_2 \ \xrightarrow[\text{THF}]{(CH_3)_3SiCl} \ \text{(structure)} \qquad (23.5)$$

Consistent with this prosposal, triphenylsilyl hydroperoxide [11] was found to epoxidize alkenes [12].

$$\text{(structure)} + Ph_3SiOOH \ \xrightarrow{CH_2Cl_2} \ \text{(structure)} \qquad (23.6)$$

The older literature on silyl peroxides and hydroperoxides has been reviewed [13].

23.5 Silyl Chromate

bis(Triphenylsilyl) chromate oxidizes alkenes to ketones or aldehydes in non-polar solvents such as CCl$_4$ or heptane [14]. It is also a useful catalyst for polymerization of ethylene [14].

$$\text{(structure)} + \text{(structure)} \ \xrightarrow{CCl_4} \ 2Ph\text{-}\underset{\underset{O}{\|}}{C}\text{-H} \qquad (23.7)$$

23.6 *bis*(Silyl) Bromamine

bis(Trimethylsilyl) bromamine reacts with hydrocarbons to yield alkyl bromides and hexamethyldisilazane via a free radical mechanism. The *bis*(trimethylsilyl)aminyl radical is similar in reactivity to an alkoxy or succinimidyl radical [15].

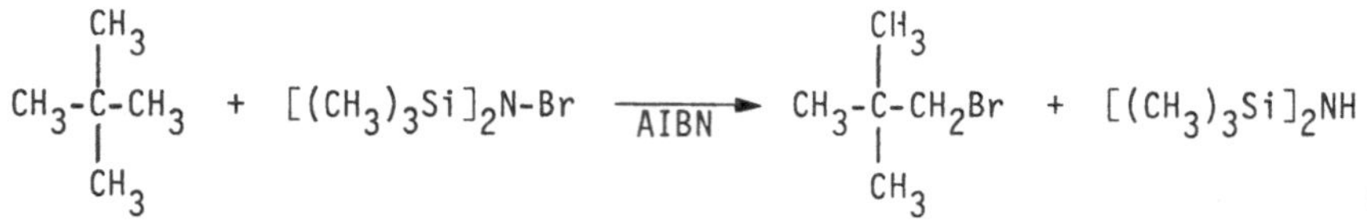
CH3
CH3-C-CH3
CH3
+
[(CH3)3Si]2N-Br
AIBN
CH3
CH3-C-CH2Br
CH3
+
[(CH3)3Si]2NH

(23.8)

bis(Trimethylsilyl)bromamine has been prepared by reaction of hexamethyldisilazane with NBS [16].

23.7 Silica Gel Mediated Oxidations

A number of selective oxidations of substrates absorbed on silica gel by ozone have been reported. Tertiary C–H bonds of hydrocarbons undergo hydroxylation by ozone under these conditions [17].

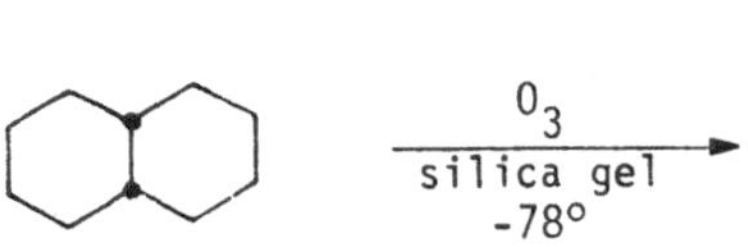
O3
silica gel
-78°
OH

(23.9)

This procedure has been utilized in an efficient synthesis of 1-α,25-dihydroxyvitamin D_3 [18]. Treatment of steroids absorbed on silica gel with ozone results in selective hydroxylation at C-25 [19].

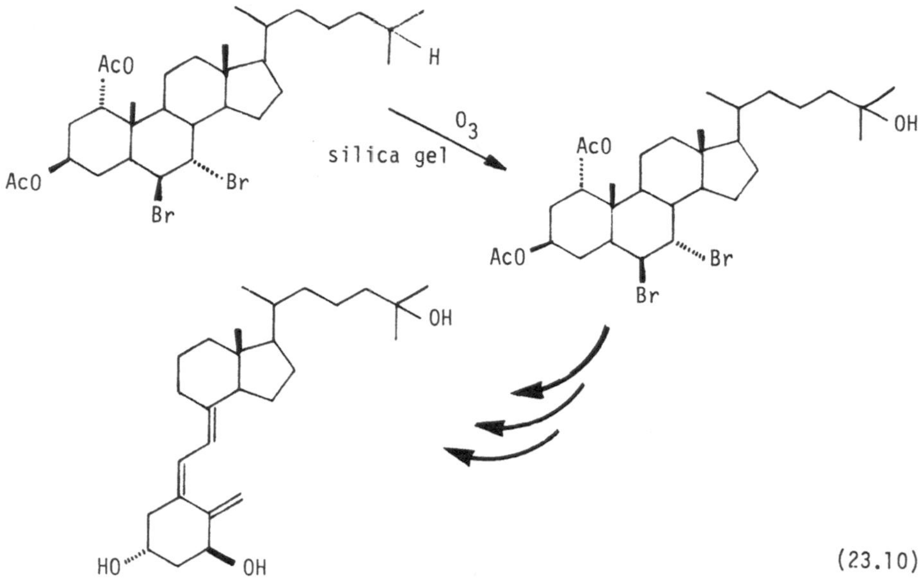
AcO
H
AcO
Br
Br
O3
silica gel
AcO
OH
AcO
Br
Br
OH
HO
OH

(23.10)

Primary amines are oxidized to nitro compounds under these conditions [20]. Reaction of 1,2-alkenes absorbed on silica gel with ozone results in exclusive formation of ozonides. If the silicon gel contains 5% water a 1:1 mixture of aldehyde and carboxylic acid is obtained [21].

$$
\text{H}\overset{O}{\underset{}{\|}}\!\!\sim\!\!\text{CO}_2\text{H} \xleftarrow[\substack{\text{silica gel} \\ 5\% \text{ H}_2\text{O}}]{O_3} \bigcirc\!\!=\!\! \xrightarrow[\substack{\text{silica gel} \\ \text{anhydrous} \\ -78°}]{O_3} \text{(ozonide)}
$$

(23.11)

Chromic acid adsorbed on silica gel has been found to be an effective reagent for the oxidation of primary and secondary hydroxyl groups to aldehydes and ketones, respectively [22, 23]. Pyridinium chromate adsorbed on silica gel permits selective oxidation of primary and secondary alcohols which possess acid labile functional groups, such as a cyclopropane ring or ketal protecting groups [23].

$$
\xrightarrow[\text{SiO}_2]{\text{pyridinium chromate}}
$$

(23.12)

It would appear that much work remains to be done in the area of silyl oxidants.

References

1. Adams, W., Rodriguez, A.: J. Org. Chem. 44, 4969 (1979)
2. Hudrlik, P.F., Hudrlik, A.M., Nagendrappa, G., Yimenu, T., Zellers, E.T., Chin, E.: J. Am. Chem. Soc. 102, 6894 (1980)
3. Brandes, D., Blaschette, A.: J. Organometal. Chem. 49, C6 (1973)
4. Brandes, D., Blaschette, A.: J. Organometal. Chem. 73, 217 (1974)
5. Tamao, K., Kumada, M., Takahashi, T.: J. Organometal. Chem. 94, 367 (1975)
6. Cookson, P.G., Davies, A.G., Fazal, N.: J. Organometal. Chem. 99, C31 (1975)
7. Brandes, D., Blaschette, A.: J. Organometal. Chem. 99, C33 (1975)
8. Edge, D.J., Kochi, J.K.: J. Chem. Soc. Perkin II, 182 (1973)
9. Hahn, W., Metzinger, L.: Makromol. Chem. 21, 113 (1956)
10. Ho, T.L.: Syn. Commun. 9, 37 (1979)
11. Dannley, R., Jalics, G.: J. Org. Chem. 30, 2417 (1965)
12. Rebek, J., McCready, R.: Tetrahedron Lett. 4337 (1979)
13. Brandes, D., Blaschette, A.: J. Organometal. Chem. 78, 1 (1974)
14. Baker, L.M., Carrick, W.L.: J. Org. Chem. 35, 774 (1970)
15. Roberts, B.P., Wilson, C.: J. Chem. Soc. Chem. Commun. 752 (1978)
16. Wiberg, N., Raschig, F.: J. Organometal. Chem. 10, 15 (1967)
17. Cohen, Z., Keinan, E., Mazur, Y., Varkony, T.H.: J. Org. Chem. 40, 2141 (1975)
18. Cohen, Z., Keinan, E., Mazur, Y., Ulman, A.: J. Org. Chem. 41, 2651 (1976)

19. Cohen, Z., Mazur, Y.: J. Org. Chem. *44*, 2318 (1979)
20. Keinan, E., Mazur, Y.: J. Org. Chem. *42*, 844 (1977)
21. Besten, C.E.D., Kinstle, T.H.: J. Am. Chem. Soc. *102*, 5969 (1980)
22. Santaniello, E., Ponti, F., Manzocchi, A.: Synthesis, 534 (1978)
23. Singh, R.P., Subbarao, H.N., Dev, S.: Tetrahedron, *35*, 1789 (1979)

24   Silyl Bases

24.1 Introduction

Trimethylsilyl substituents affect the reactivity, solubility, and selectivity of both alkoxide and amide bases. Since this is one of the last chapters in this monograph certain examples of the use of lithium and sodium *bis*(trimethylsilyl) amide bases have been previously discussed [see: (16.11)]. This chapter is not comprehensive, rather illustrative examples will be presented.

24.2 Lithium 1,1-*bis*(trimethylsilyl) alkoxides

Lithium 1,1-*bis*(trimethylsilyl) alkoxides have proved to be extremely select- ive bases. Their basicity is apparently intermediate between those of tertiary alkoxides and lithium amide bases. This has been attributed to the inductive electron releasing effect of the trimethylsilyl groups. Lithium 1,1-*bis*(trimethyl- silyl) alkoxide bases permit the selective generation of kinetic enolate anions of methyl ketones in the presence of aldehydes. This results in the regio- specific cross-aldol reactions between methyl ketones and aldehydes [1].

$$CH_3(CH_2)_4C\diagdown{}^{O}_{H} \quad + \quad (CH_3)_2CHCH_2C\diagdown{}^{O}_{CH_3} \tag{24.1}$$

$$\xrightarrow[\substack{\displaystyle \overset{\displaystyle Si(CH_3)_3}{\underset{\displaystyle Si(CH_3)_3}{(CH_3)_2CHCH_2CO^-Li^+}}}]{-40°/THF} \quad n-C_5H_{11}-\underset{\underset{H}{|}}{\overset{\overset{OH}{|}}{C}}-CH_2-\overset{O}{\overset{||}{C}}-CH_2CH(CH_3)_2$$

Lithium-1,1-*bis*(trimethylsilyl)-3-methyl-1-butoxide permits the selective generation of ester enolates in the presence of aldehydes [2]. This reaction yields β-hydroxy esters. This provides a viable alternative to the Reformatsky reaction.

$$CH_3CH_2-O-\overset{\overset{\text{O}}{\|}}{C}-CH_3 \quad + \quad PhCH_2CH_2-\overset{\overset{\text{O}}{\|}}{C}-H \tag{24.2}$$

$$\xrightarrow[\underset{\displaystyle\overset{|}{Si(CH_3)_3}}{(CH_3)_2CH-CH_2-\overset{|}{\underset{|}{C}}-O^-Li^+}]{\overset{\displaystyle Si(CH_3)_3}{-30°/THF}} \quad Ph-CH_2CH_2-\overset{\overset{\text{OH}}{|}}{\underset{\overset{|}{H}}{C}}-CH_2-\overset{\overset{\text{O}}{\|}}{C}-O-CH_2CH_3$$

Lactone enolates of γ-butyrolactone and δ-valerolactone can be generated in the presence of aldehydes or ketones by use of lithium 1,1-*bis*(trimethylsilyl) alkoxide bases.

$$\tag{24.3}$$

The enolate anion of succinic anhydride can also be generated in the presence of aldehydes or ketones by reaction with lithio-1,1-*bis*(trimethylsilyl)-3-methyl-1-butoxide. This provide a facile method to prepare β-carbomethoxy-γ-substituted-γ-butyrolactones [3].

$$\tag{24.4}$$

The preparation of the necessary 1,1-*bis*(trimethylsilyl) alcohols has been previously discussed in connection with dissolving metal reductions of esters (see Chapter 19).

24.3 Alkali *bis*(trimethylsilyl) Amides

The first work with sodium and lithium *bis*(trimethylsilyl) amides was reported by Wannagat and Rochow [4–9]. Both are distillable low melting solids. They are prepared as outlined below.

$[(CH_3)_3Si]_2N^-Li^+$ bp   115°/1 mm   mp 70–72

$[(CH_3)_3Si]_2N^-Na^+$ bp   170°/2 mm   mp 165–167°

$$(CH_3)_3SiCl \ + \ NH_3 \longrightarrow [(CH_3)_3Si]_2NH$$

(24.5)

$$[(CH_3)_3Si]_2N^-Na^+ \xleftarrow{\text{NaNH}_2} [(CH_3)_3Si]_2NH \xrightarrow{\text{PhLi}} [(CH_3)_3Si]_2N^-Li^+$$

A. Ketone Enolate Anions

Both lithium and sodium *bis*(trimethylsilyl) amides have proved highly effective bases for the generation of kinetic enolate anions from ketones. Both are soluble in most non-polar solvents. In certain cases different ratios of enolate anions are obtained with lithium *bis*(trimethylsilyl) amide than with sodium *bis*(trimethylsilyl) amide. This results from the more facile isomerization of sodium enolates compared to lithium enolates in the presence of unionized ketone [10, 11].

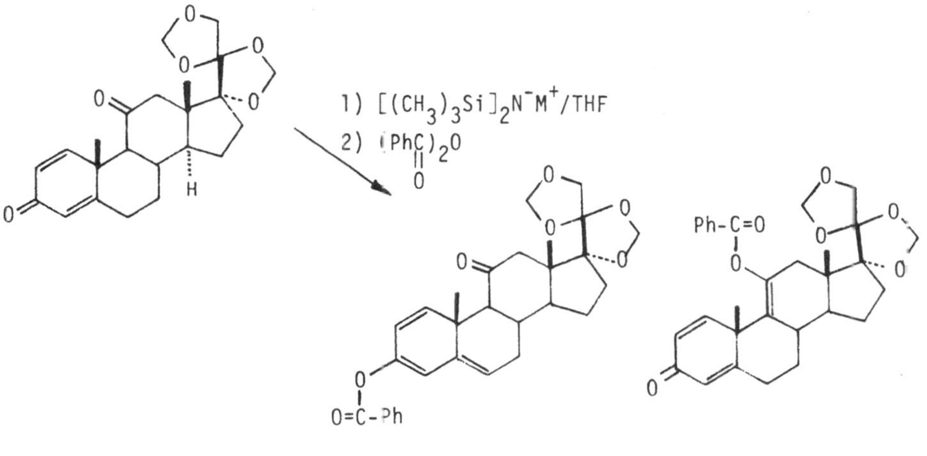

Na^+	1	:	2
Li^+	100	:	0

(24.6)

Alkali metal enolates of ketones generated by reaction with lithium *bis*(trimethylsilyl) amides have been utilized as ketone protecting groups during metal hydride reductions [12].

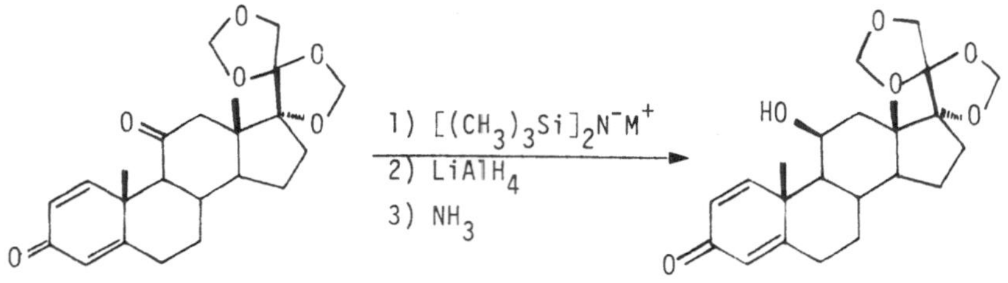

$$
\begin{array}{c}
\text{1) } [(CH_3)_3Si]_2N^-M^+ \\
\hline
\text{2) } LiAlH_4 \\
\text{3) } NH_3
\end{array}
$$

$$(24.7)$$

Δ^4-3-Keto steroids yield kinetic 2,4-dienolate anions on treatment with lithium *bis*(trimethylsilyl) amide. These can be alkylated by additions of methyl iodide or trapped as silyl enol ethers by addition of *t*-butyldimethylchlorosilane [13].

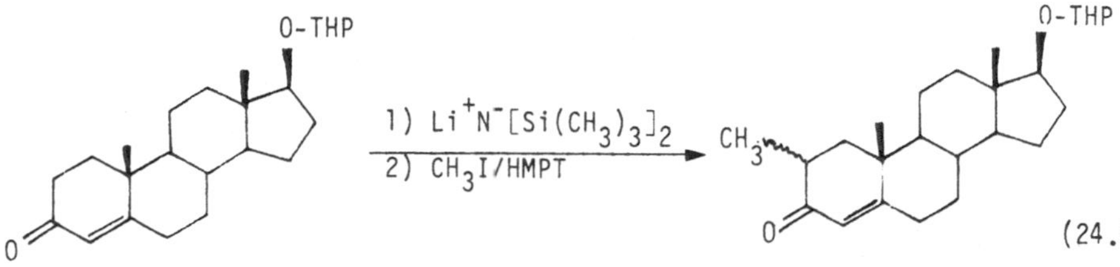

$$
\begin{array}{c}
\text{1) } Li^+N^-[Si(CH_3)_3]_2 \\
\hline
\text{2) } CH_3I/HMPT
\end{array}
$$

$$(24.8)$$

On the other hand, Δ^4-3-keto steroids undergo alkylation with potassium-*t*-butoxide in *t*-butanol and methyl iodide to give 4,4-dimethyl Δ^5-3-keto steroids. This results from alkylation of the thermodynamically more stable 3,5-dienolate anion [14].

Enolate anions of hexamethyl-2,4-cyclohexadienone have been generated by treatment with lithium *bis*(trimethylsilyl) amide [15].

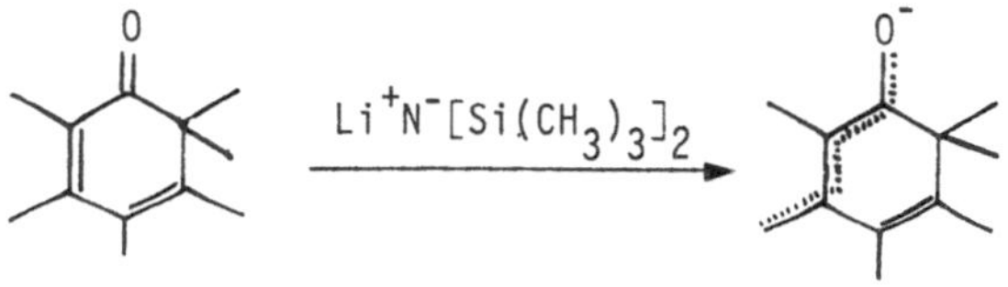

$$Li^+N^-[Si(CH_3)_3]_2$$

$$(24.9)$$

Sodium *bis*(trimethylsilyl) amide has proved a particularly effective base for intramolecular condensation reactions. This methodology has proved useful in the synthesis of sesquiterpenes [16, 17].

The solubility of sodium *bis*(trimethylsilyl) amide in benzene or DME is probably critical to the reaction's success.

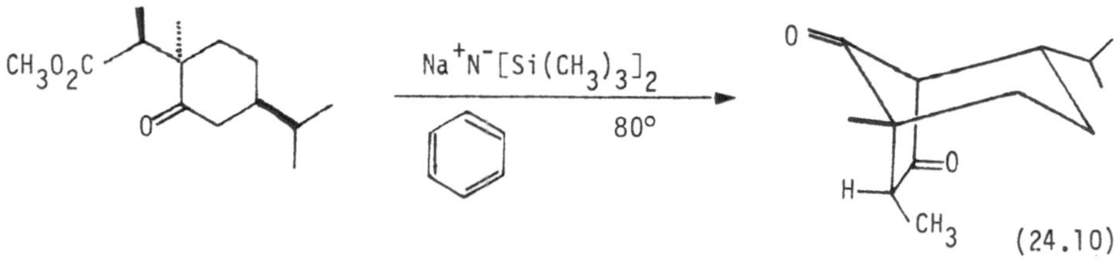

$$
\begin{array}{c}
Na^+N^-[Si(CH_3)_3]_2 \\
\hline
80°
\end{array}
$$

$$(24.10)$$

B. Ester Enolate Anions

Sodium *bis*(trimethylsilyl) amide has proved effective for the preparation of large ring ketones via Dieckman condensation. Such reactions are usually only useful for the preparation of five and six membered ring compounds [18].

$$(24.11)$$

Sodium *bis*(trimethylsilyl) amide quantitatively converts α-bromo esters to the corresponding ester enolates. Addition of aldehydes or ketones to a solution of α-bromo ester enolate gives high yields of glycidic esters [18]. The Darzens condensation usually fails with aldehydes due to competing base catalyzed self-condensation reactions [19].

$$(24.12)$$

C. Cyano-Stabilized Anions

Intramolecular cyclization of protected 3-chloropropionaldehyde cyanohydrins and 4-chlorobutyraldehyde cyanohydrins by treatment with sodium *bis*(trimethylsilyl)amide yields cyanohydrins of cyclopropanones and cyclobutanones, respectively [20].

387

$$(24.13)$$

Epoxynitrile cyclizations leading to cyanocyclobutylcarbinols have been carried out with potassium or lithium *bis*(trimethylsilyl)amide [21].

$$(24.14)$$

Intramolecular cyclization reactions of α-bromo or α-chloro ketals are successful (24.15). These involve S_n2 displacement of halide by a cyano stabilized carbanion. These anions have been generated by deprotonation with potassium or lithium *bis*(trimethylsilyl)amide in benzene [22]. The particular cation can have a dramatic effect on the stereochemistry of cyclization (24.16) [23].

$$(24.15)$$

$$(24.16)$$

D. Ylids

Sodium *bis*(trimethylsilyl)amide is a useful base for the generaticn of lithium, salt free alkylidene triphenylphosphoranes in THF or HMPT. Under these conditions, Wittig reactions with aldehydes lead stereoselective.y to Z-alkenes [24–26].

$$n\text{-}C_4H_9\text{-}CH_2\text{-}\overset{+}{P}Ph_3 \quad \xrightarrow[\text{THF/-78°}]{\begin{array}{l}1)\ \ Na^+N^-[Si(CH_3)_3]_2\\[4pt] 2)\ \ CH_3O_2C\text{-}(CH_2)_8\text{-}\overset{\text{O}}{\underset{\|}{C}}\text{-H}\end{array}}$$

$$CH_3O_2C\diagdown(CH_2)_8\diagup C=C\diagdown\overset{(CH_2)_3CH_3}{\underset{H}{}}$$

Br⁻

Z:E   98:2

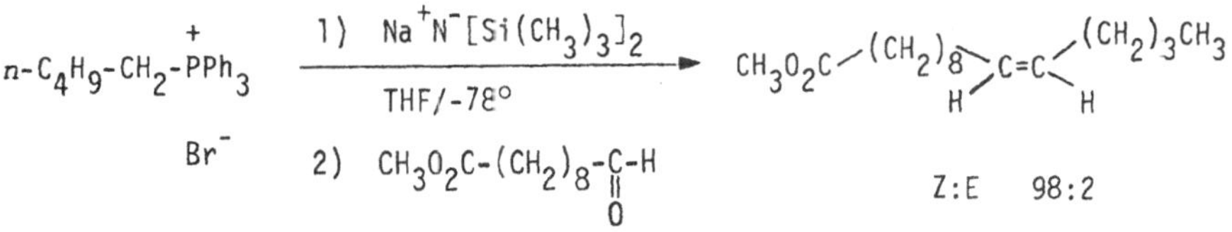

(24.17)

E. Carbenes

Sodium *bis*(trimethylsilyl)amide has proved useful for the *in-situ* generation of monobromo [27, 28] and monochlorocarbene [29] by deprotonation of dibromomethane and methylene chloride, respectively.

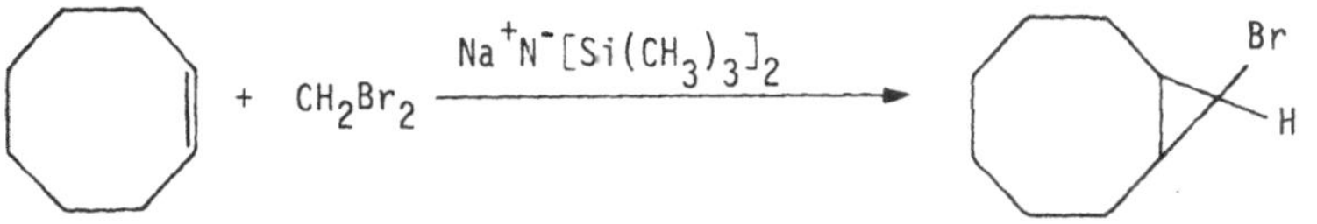

$$+ \ CH_2Br_2 \quad \xrightarrow{Na^+N^-[Si(CH_3)_3]_2}$$

(24.18)

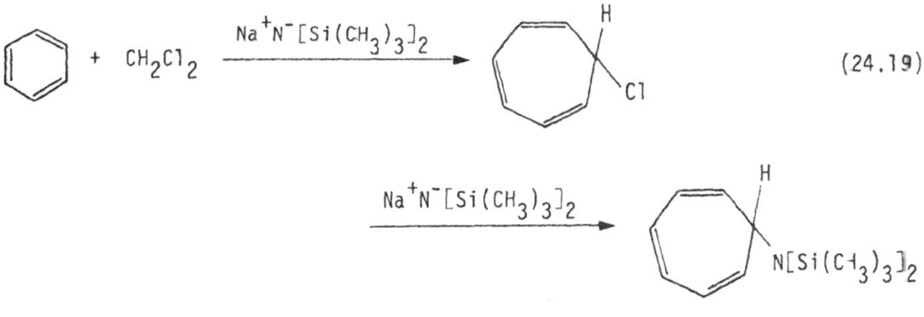

$$+ \ CH_2Cl_2 \quad \xrightarrow{Na^+N^-[Si(CH_3)_3]_2}$$

(24.19)

$$\xrightarrow{Na^+N^-[Si(CH_3)_3]_2}$$

Chloromethylcarbene has been generated by deprotonation of 1,1-dichloroethane with sodium *bis*(trimethylsilyl)amide [30].

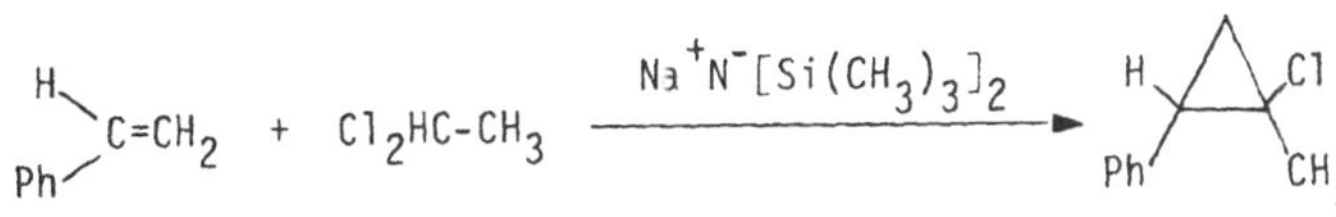

$$\underset{Ph}{\overset{H}{\diagdown}}C=CH_2 \ + \ Cl_2HC\text{-}CH_3 \quad \xrightarrow{Na^+N^-[Si(CH_3)_3]_2}$$

(24.20)

389

References

1. Kuwajima, I., Sato, T., Arai, M., Minami, N.: Tetrahedron Lett. 1817 (1975)
2. Kuwajima, I., Minami, N., Sato, T.: Tetrahedron Lett. 2253 (1976)
3. Minami, N., Kuwajima, I.: Tetrahedron Lett. 1423 (1977)
4. Wannagat, U., Niederprüm, H.: Chem. Ber., *94*, 1540 (1961)
5. Krüger, C.R., Rochow, E.G., Wannagat, U.: Chem. Ber. *96*, 2131 (1963)
6. Krüger, C.R., Rochow, E.G., Wannagat, U.: Chem. Ber. *96*, 2138 (1963)
7. Krüger, C.R., Rochow, E.G.: Angew. Chem. Int. Ed. *2*, 617 (1963)
8. Krüger, C.R., Rochow, E.G.: J. Organometal. Chem. *1*, 476 (1964)
9. Wannagat, U., Niederprüm, H.: Zeit für Anorg. und Allgem. Chem. *308*, 337 (1961)
10. Barton, D.H.R., Hesse, R.H., Tarzia, G., Pechet, M.M.: J. Chem. Soc. Chem. Commun. 1497 (1969)
11. Tanabe, M., Crowe, D.F.: J. Chem. Soc. Chem. Commun. 1498 (1969)
12. Barton, D.H.R., Hesse, R.H., Pechet, M.M., Wiltshire, C.: J. Chem. Soc. Chem. Commun 1017 (1972)
13. Tanabe, M., Crowe, D.F.: J. Chem. Soc. Chem. Commun. 564 (1973)
14. Woodward, R.B., Patchett, A.A., Barton, D.H.R., Ives, D.A.J., Kelly, R.B.: J. Am. Chem. Soc. *76*, 2852 (1951)
15. Hart, H., Love, G.M., Wang, I.C.: Tetrahedron Lett. 1377 (1973)
16. Piers, E., Geraghty, M.B., Kido, F., Soucy, M.: Syn. Commun. *3*, 39 (1973)
17. Piers, E., Britton, R.W., Geraghty, M.B., Keziere, R.J., Smille, R.D.: Can. J. Chem. *53*, 2827 (1975)
18. Hurd, R.M., Shah, D.M.: J. Org. Chem. *38*, 390 (1973)
19. Borch, R.F.: Tetrahedron Lett. 3761 (1972)
20. Stork, G., Depezay, J.C., d'Angelo, J.: Tetrahedron Lett. 389 (1975)
21. Stork, G., Cohen, J.F.: J. Am. Chem. Soc. *96*, 5270 (1974)
22. Stork, G., Gardner, J.O., Boeckman, Jr., R.K., Parker, K.A.: J. Am. Chem. Soc. *95*, 2014 (1973)
23. Stork, G., Boeckman, Jr., R.K.: J. Am. Chem. Soc. *95*, 2016 (1973)
24. Bestmann, H.J., Stransky, W., Vostrowsky, O.: Chem. Ber. *109*, 1694 (1976)
25. Bestmann, H.J., Brosche, T., Koschatzky, K.H., Michaelis, K., Platz, H., Vostrowsky, O.: Tetrahedron Lett. 747 (1980)
26. Schneider, M.P., Goldbach, M.: J. Am. Chem. Soc. *102*, 6114 (1980)
27. Martel, B., Hiriart, J.M.: Angew. Chem. Int. Ed. *11*, 326 (1972)
28. Martel, B., Hiriart, J.M.: Synthesis, 201 (1972)
29. Martel, B., Aly, E.: J. Organometal. Chem. *29*, 61 (1971)
30. Arora, S., Binger, P.: Synthesis, 801 (1974)

25 Silicon-Fluorine

25.1 Introduction

The formation of a Si−F bond (142 kcal/mol) is usually a highly exothermic process. This provides the driving force for a number of useful synthetic reactions. Since this is the last chapter, many of these have been previously considered. Reactions of fluoride ion with organosilicon compounds probably proceed by initial attack of fluoride ion on one of the empty 3d orbitals of silicon to form a pentacoordinate negatively charged species. The fate of this intermediate depends on the other groups bonded to silicon. Alkyltrichlorosilanes react with fluoride ion to form alkyl pentafluorosilicates. This results from sequential loss of chloride ion, a relatively good leaving group, and association of additional fluoride ions (see Chapter 10).

$$\text{R-SiCl}_3 \xrightarrow{\text{F}^-} \left[\text{R-Si} \begin{matrix} \text{Cl} \\ | \\ | \\ \text{F} \end{matrix} \begin{matrix} \text{Cl} \\ \diagdown \\ \text{Cl} \end{matrix} \right]^- \qquad (25.1)$$

$$\text{R-SiCl}_2^= \xrightarrow[\text{-Cl}^-]{\text{F}^-} \xrightarrow[\text{-Cl}^-]{\text{F}^-} \xrightarrow{\text{F}^-} \text{R-SiF}_4^- \xrightarrow{\text{F}^-} \text{R-SiF}_5^=$$

$$\text{Cl}^-$$

25.2 Generation of Carbanions and Enolate Anions

Reactions of many types of organotrimethylsilanes with fluoride ion result in formation of trimethylfluorosilane (TMS-F) and loss of the organic group as an anion. For example, 1-trimethylsilyl alkynes react with fluoride ion to yield TMS-F and relatively stable acetylide anions [1].

$$\text{Ph-C}\equiv\text{C-Si(CH}_3)_3 \xrightarrow[\text{EtOH}]{\text{KF}} \text{Ph-C}\equiv\text{C}^- + (\text{CH}_3)_3\text{SiF} \xrightarrow{\text{EtOH}} \text{Ph-C}\equiv\text{CH} \qquad (25.2)$$

This methodology has been used to remove trimethylsilyl protecting groups from terminal acetylenes. Both potassium fluoride dihydrate in methanol [2] and TBAF in THF [3] have proved effective.

391

The reaction of 1-trimethylsilyl alkynes with ketones or aldehydes under nucleophilic catalysis by TBAF [4] or potassium fluoride/18-C-6 [5] to yield propargyl trimethylsilyl ethers, involves acetylide anions as intermediates (see 9.3 E).

$$Ph-C{\equiv}C-Si(CH_3)_3 \ + \ \overset{O}{\diagdown} \quad \xrightarrow[\text{THF}]{\text{cat. } (n\text{-}Bu)_4N^+F^-} \quad \overset{\displaystyle O-Si(CH_3)_3}{\diagup}{}_{C{\equiv}C-Ph} \qquad (25.3)$$

Allylic trimethylsilanes also react with fluoride ion to generate TMS-F and allylic carbanions. Fluoride ion catalyzes reaction of allylic silanes with aldehydes or ketones to yield homoallylic trimethylsilyl ethers [6–8] (see II. 2 H).

$$\text{(25.4)}$$

+ (CH$_3$)$_3$SiF   (25.4)

The reaction of aliphatic and aromatic aldehydes with propargyl trimethyl-silane to yield rearranged allenic trimethylsilyl ethers is also catalyzed by TBAF [9] (see 9.3 E).

Vinylsilanes do not in general react with fluoride ion to yield fluorosilanes and vinyl carbanions [10]. However, β-hydroxy groups accelerate the rate of cleavage of Si–C sp^2 bonds by fluoride ion. A cyclic transition state has been proposed in which the fluoride ion is both hydrogen bonded to the adjacent hydroxyl group and bonded to the silyl center [10].

$$\text{Ph-CH-CH=CH}_2 \ + \ \text{Ph}_3\text{SiF} \qquad (25.5)$$

Adjacent hydroxy groups also accelerate the cleavage of C–Si bonds of α-silyl epoxides [11]. An oxaranyl anion has been proposed as an intermediate in this reaction. The anchimeric assistance of an adjacent hydroxyl group does not, however permit cleavage of most Si–C sp^3 bonds by fluoride ion.

Fluoride ion induced desilylation of trimethylsilylmethylsulfonium, ammonium, immonium, and phosphonium salts leads to formation of ylids [12].

These reactions are synthetically important in cases where the molecule contains base sensitive functional groups or acidic C−H bonds. These ylids undergo their characteristic reactions. For example, the desilylation of trimethylsilylmethyl iminium salts leads to azomethine ylids which may be trapped via [3 + 2] cycloaddition reactions.

$$PhCH=N-CH_3 \quad + \quad (CH_3)_3SiCH_2O-\overset{O}{\underset{O}{\overset{\parallel}{S}}}-CF_3 \qquad (25.6)$$

The necessary salts have been generated by reaction of trimethylsilylmethyl triflate with amines, imines, sulfides, or phosphines.

Dithianyl anions can be generated by treatment of 2-trimethylsilyl-1,3-dithianes with TBAF in THF [13]. This methodology has been used to prepare spiro alcohols by intramolecular addition of the dithianyl anion to ω-aldehyde functional groups.

$$(25.7)$$

The dithianyl anion also undergoes intramolecular 1,4-conjugate addition to α,β-unsaturated ketones. Neither aldehydes nor α,β-unsaturated ketones are compatible with the usual basic conditions needed to generate dithianyl anions.

Benzoyl trimethylsilanes react with potassium fluoride in moist DMSO or HMPT or with TBAF in moist THF to yield benzaldehyde. If this reaction is carried out in the presence of alkyl halides [49] alkyl aryl ketones are formed. With ketones or aldehydes, the reaction yields α-hydroxy ketones [14]. These reactions may involve direct fluoride attack on the silyl center to form a benzoyl anion.

$$(25.8)$$

An alternative mechanistic possibility involves a Brook rearrangement.

$$(25.9)$$

Fluoride ion catalyzes regiospecific aldol condensations between trimethylsilyl enol ethers and aliphatic or aromatic aldehydes [15].

$$(25.10)$$

Nitro aldol reactions have also been carried out by reaction of silyl nitronates with fluoride ion (see 5.3) [16,17].

In a similar manner, tetraalkylammonium enolates have been generated regiospecifically by reaction of trimethylsilyl enol ethers with benzyltrimethylammonium fluoride in THF. These enolate anions may be alkylated with allylic or benzylic bromides or methyl iodide [18].

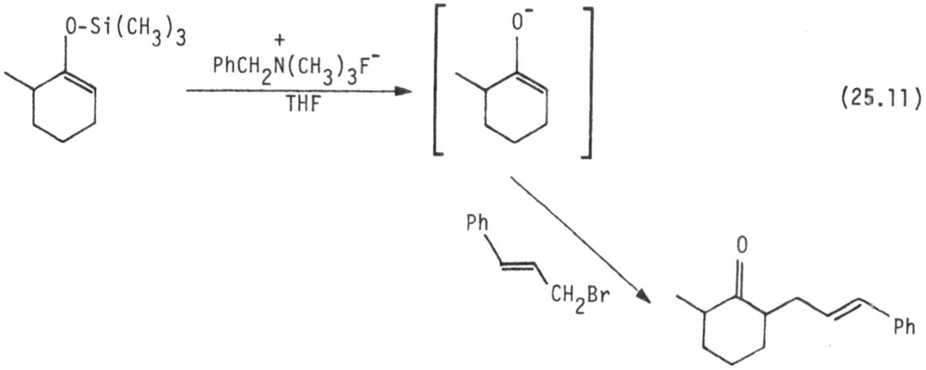

(25.11)

tris(Diethylamino)sulfonium difluorotrimethylsiliconate reacts with trimethylsilyl enol ethers to yield TMS-F and *tris*(diethylamino)sulfonium enolate ions pairs. These enolates can be C-alkylated by primary alkyl iodides, allylic or benzylic bromides or α-bromo esters [19].

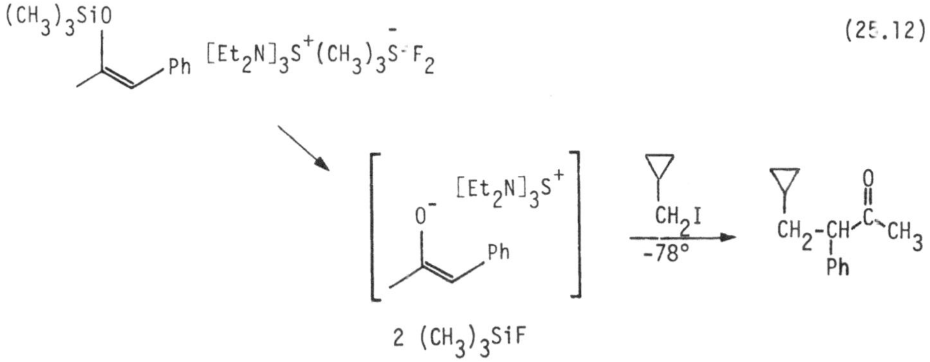

(25.12)

Ketone enolate anions generated by reaction of trimethylsilyl enol ethers with fluoride ion undergo O-acylation by ethyl fluoro formate or carbamoyl fluorides to yield enol carbonates or enol carbamates, respectively [20].

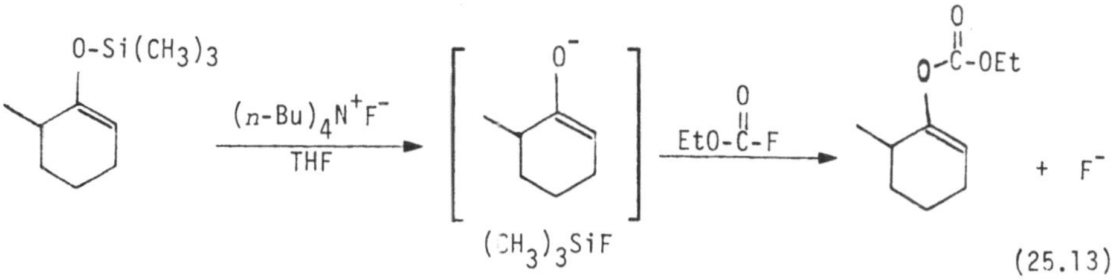

(25.13)

Photocycloaddition reactions of 2-trimethylsilylcyclopentenones with simple alkenes proceed in a highly regiospecific manner to yield head to tail cycloadducts.

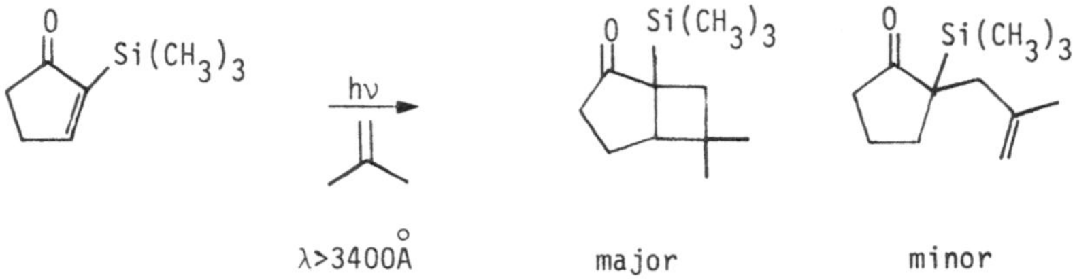
Si(CH3)3
hν
λ>3400Å
major
minor

(25.14)

The trimethylsilyl group can be removed by desilylation with potassium fluoride dihydrate in DMSO. This probably involves formation of the enolate anion of the ketone and TMS-F [21, 22].

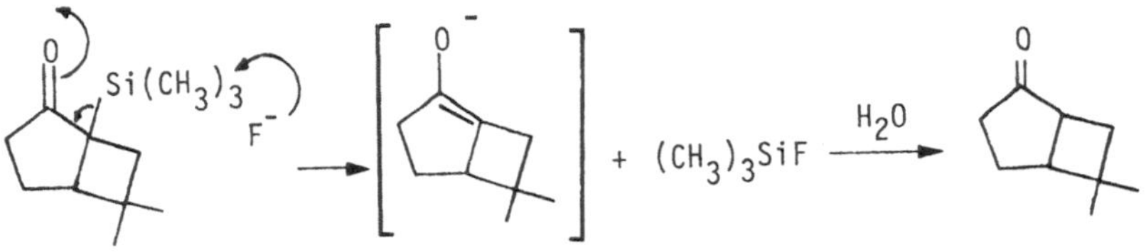
Si(CH3)3
F⁻
(CH3)3SiF
H2O

(25.15)

Similar directing effects were observed in the photocycloaddition reactions of 5-trimethylsilyl uracil with alkenes [22].

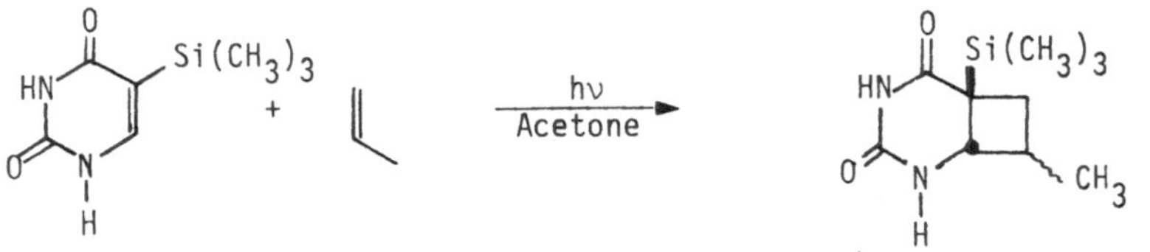
Si(CH3)3
hν
Acetone
CH3

(25.16)

The conversion of ketones to trimethylsilyl enol ethers by reaction with ethyl trimethylsilylacetate and a catalytic amount of TBAF depends on the generation of ester enolates by reaction of fluoride ion with ethyl trimethylsilylacetate.

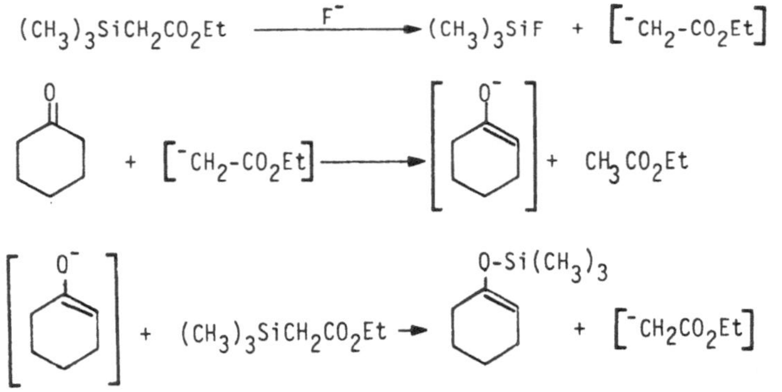
(CH3)3SiCH2CO2Et
F⁻
(CH3)3SiF + [⁻CH2-CO2Et]
[⁻CH2-CO2Et]
CH3CO2Et
(CH3)3SiCH2CO2Et
O-Si(CH3)3
[⁻CH2CO2Et]

(25.17)

On the other hand, reactions of ethyl trimethylsilylacetate with aldehydes yields β-trimethylsilyloxy esters. This difference results from the greater reactivity of aldehydes toward nucleophilic addition. The ester enolate serves as a base towards ketones but reacts as a nucleophile with aldehydes [23].

$$\text{(25.18)}$$

Ethyl trimethylsilylacetate also reacts under fluoride ion catalysis with non-enolizable ketones or aldehydes to yield β-trimethylsilyloxy esters [24].

Intramolecular Williamson ether syntheses have been carried out under fluoride ion activation. Silyl ethers react with fluoride ion to yield reactive alkoxide ions and silyl fluorides. This procedure has proved effective for the synthesis of O-2-isocephams [25].

$$\text{(25.19)}$$

Potassium phenylselenide has been generated by treatment of phenyl trimethylsilyl selenide with potassium fluoride (see eq. 21.22) [26].

25.3. Generation of Carbenes, α-Elimination

Trihalomethyltrimethylsilanes react with potassium fluoride/18-C-6 in diglyme to yield TMS-F and potassium cation trihalomethyl anion pairs. These undergo α-elimination to yield dihalocarbenes [27].

$$\text{(25.20)}$$

1-Halo-1-trimethylsilyl-2-methyl propene undergoes α-elimination on treatment with fluoride ion in diglyme to yield isopropylidene carbene. This reacts *in-situ* with olefins to yield isopropylidene cyclopropanes [28, 29].

$$\text{(25.21)}$$

Similar α-eliminations occur under milder conditions ($-20°$ to $0°$) on treatment of α-trimethylsilylvinyl triflates with potassium fluoride/18-C-6 or anhydrous TBAF or by PTC. Alkylidene carbenes, generated in this way, add to C−C double bonds, to give vinylidene cyclopropanes [30]. They also undergo α-addition to the carbon of isonitriles to yield alkadienylidenamines which undergo hydrolysis to give vinylamides [31].

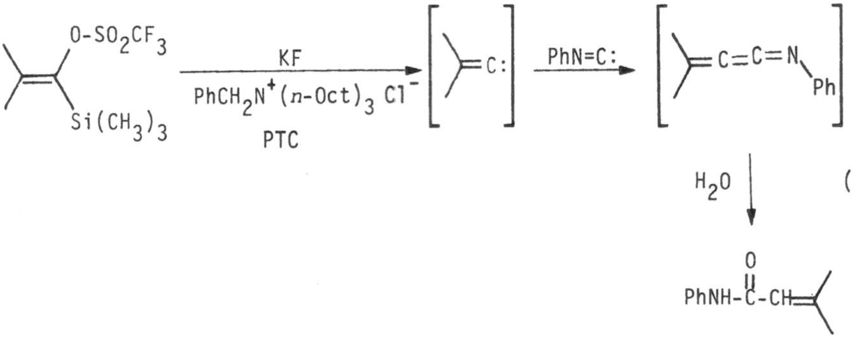

(25.22)

Insertion of alkylidene carbenes into the S−H single bonds of enethiols provides an efficient route to divinyl sulfides [32].

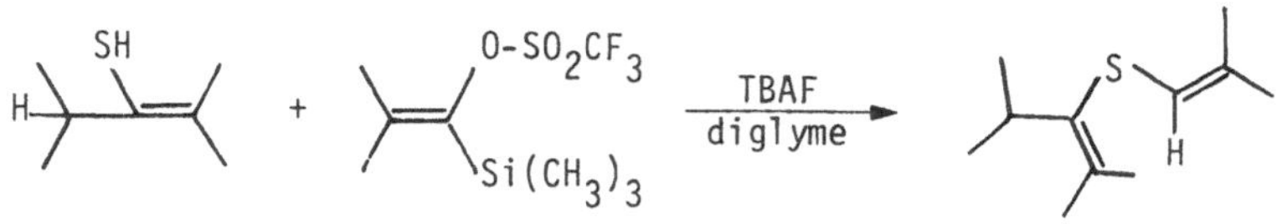

(25.23)

The necessary α-trimethylsilylvinyl triflates can be prepared by reaction of acylsilanes with triflic anhydride and pyridine in methylene chloride [30].

25.4 1,2-, 1,4- and 1,6-Elimination Reactions

Fluoride ion also promotes 1,2-elimination reactions of alkyltrimethylsilanes if the alkyl group is substituted with a leaving group in the β-position. For example, 2-trimethylsilylethyl esters function as carboxyl protecting groups which may be selectively removed by fluoride ion [33, 34].

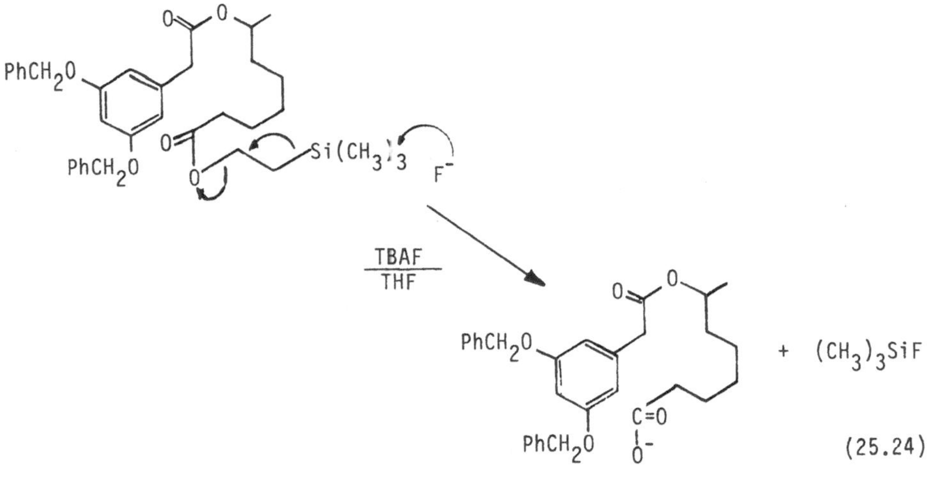

$+$ $(CH_3)_3SiF$

(25.24)

β-Trimethylsilylalkyl phenyl sulfones react with TBAF · 3 H$_2$O in THF to yield TMS-F, phenyl sulfinate ion and an alkene. The facile formation and alkylation of carbanions alpha to a phenylsulfonyl group combined with this fluoride ion mediated elimination reaction provides a new method to prepare terminal olefins [35].

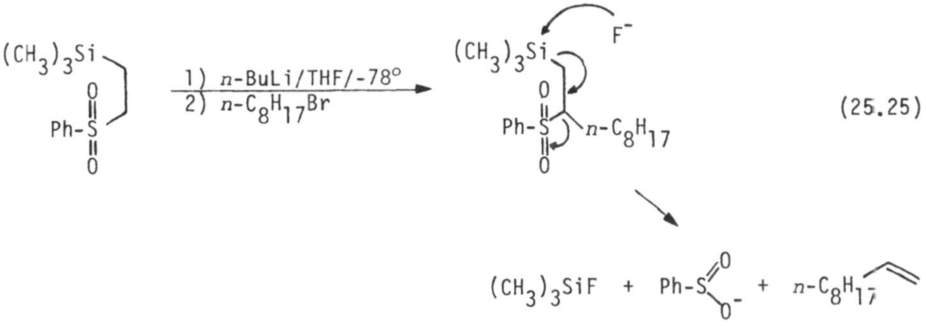

$$
(CH_3)_3Si \quad \xrightarrow[\text{2) } n\text{-}C_8H_{17}Br]{\text{1) } n\text{-}BuLi/THF/-78°} \quad (CH_3)_3Si \quad F^-
$$

$$
Ph\text{-}S \quad\quad Ph\text{-}S\text{-}n\text{-}C_8H_{17}
$$

$$(25.25)$$

$$
(CH_3)_3SiF \;+\; Ph\text{-}S\overset{O}{\underset{O^-}{\diagdown}} \;+\; n\text{-}C_8H_{17}
$$

Such β-trimethylsilylalkyl phenyl sulfones can be prepared by reaction of iodomethyltrimethylsilane with phenylsulfonyl stabilized carbanions.

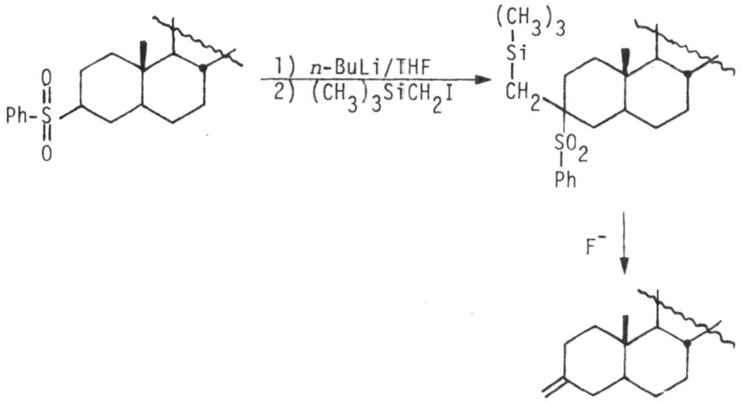

$$
\xrightarrow[\text{2) } (CH_3)_3SiCH_2I]{\text{1) } n\text{-}BuLi/THF}
$$

$$(25.26)$$

2-Triphenylsilyl allylic alcohols do not readily undergo elimination of triphenylsilanol or triphenylsilanoate (see 6.4 E). However, they can be converted to 2-triphenylsilyl allylic chlorides by reaction with thionyl chloride. These undergo elimination on treatment with tetraethylammonium fluoride in DMSO to yield allenes [36, 37].

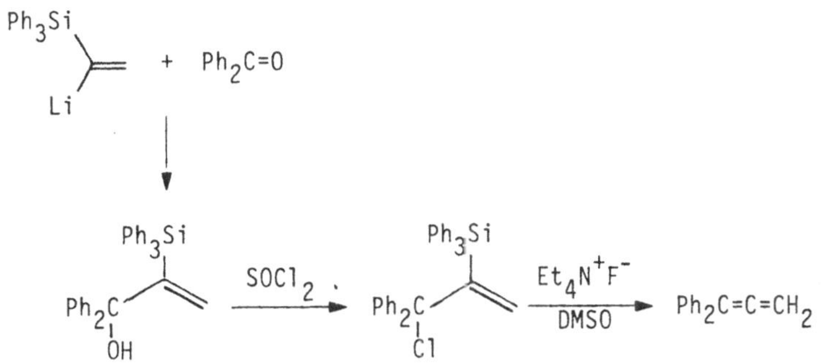

$$
Ph_3Si \quad + \; Ph_2C=O
$$

$$
\downarrow
$$

$$
Ph_3Si \qquad Ph_3Si
$$

$$
Ph_2C \xrightarrow{SOCl_2} Ph_2C \xrightarrow[\text{DMSO}]{Et_4N^+F^-} Ph_2C=C=CH_2
$$

$$
\overset{|}{OH} \qquad\qquad \overset{|}{Cl}
$$

$$(25.27)$$

399

Allene oxides-cyclopropanones have been prepared by fluoride induced elimination from α-chloromethyl-α-silyl epoxides. These reactive intermediates have been trapped *in-situ* by cycloaddition reactions with cyclopentadiene and furan [38, 39].

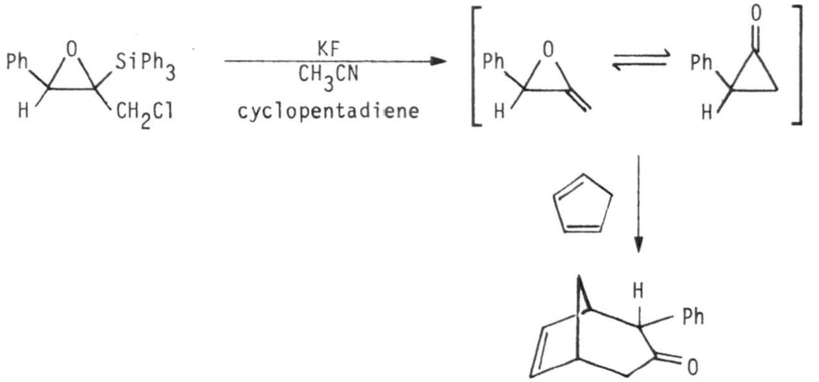

(25.28)

1-Halo-cyclopropenes have been generated by fluoride promoted β-elimination of 1,1-dihalo-2-trimethylsilyl cyclopropanes [40].

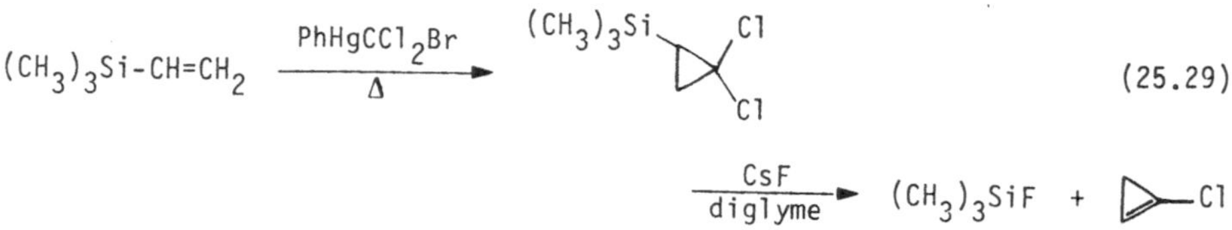

(25.29)

Fluoride ion promotes β-elimination of both *cis* and *trans* β-chlorovinyltrimethylsilanes to yield acetylene and TMS-F. As expected, the *trans* isomer reacts considerably faster than the *cis* [41].

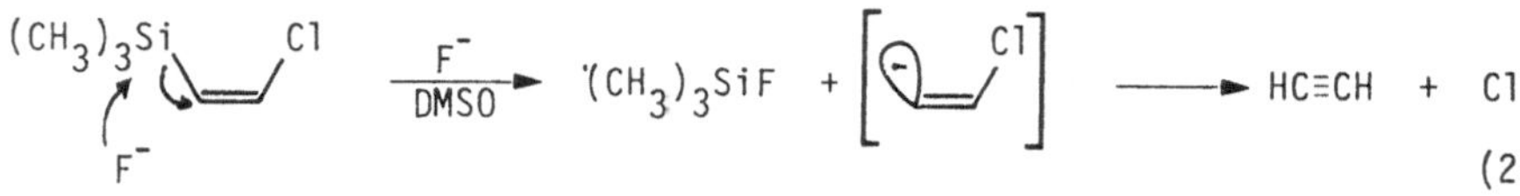

(25.30)

ortho-Halophenyltrimethylsilanes undergo loss of the elements of TMS-X on treatment with trimethylammonium fluoride or potassium-*t*-butoxide in HMPT to yield benzyne as a reactive intermediate. This may be trapped *in-situ* by reaction with furan [42].

$$(25.31)$$

Fluoride ion induced 1,6-elimination of [p-(trimethylsilylmethyl)benzyl]-trimethylammonium iodide provides a convenient route to p-quinodimethane. This reactive intermediate may dimerize to yield [2,2]-paracyclophane or poly-merize to poly-p-xylylene depending on reaction conditions [43].

$$(25.32)$$

o-Xylylene reactive intermediates have been generated by fluoride ion induced 1,4-elimination from *ortho*-(α-trimethylsilylalkyl) benzyltrimethyl-ammonium halides. o-Xylylene undergoes *in-situ* [4 + 2] cycloaddition reactions with alkenes and alkynes substituted with electron withdrawing groups to yield tetrahydronaphthalene and dihydronaphthalene derivatives, respectively [44].

$$(25.33)$$

ortho-[Trimethylsilylmethyl]benzyldimethylamine can be converted to *ortho* [α-trimethylsilylalkyl]benzyldimethylamine by metallation with *n*-butyl lithium followed by reaction with primary alkyl iodides [44]. This methodology has been utilized in an efficient stereoselective synthesis of estrone as outlined [45].

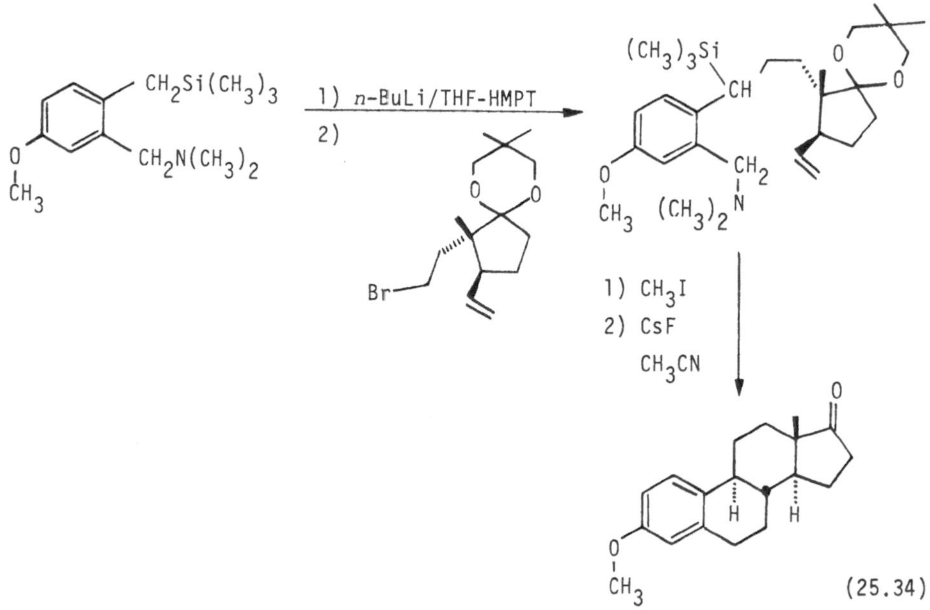

(25.34)

d,1-11-α-Hydroxyesterone methyl ether has been prepared by a closely related intramolecular cycloaddition reaction. The reactive *ortho*-quinodimethane was formed by a fluoride ion induced 1,4-elimination of a 2-trimethylsilylmethyl styrene oxide derivative as outlined below [46].

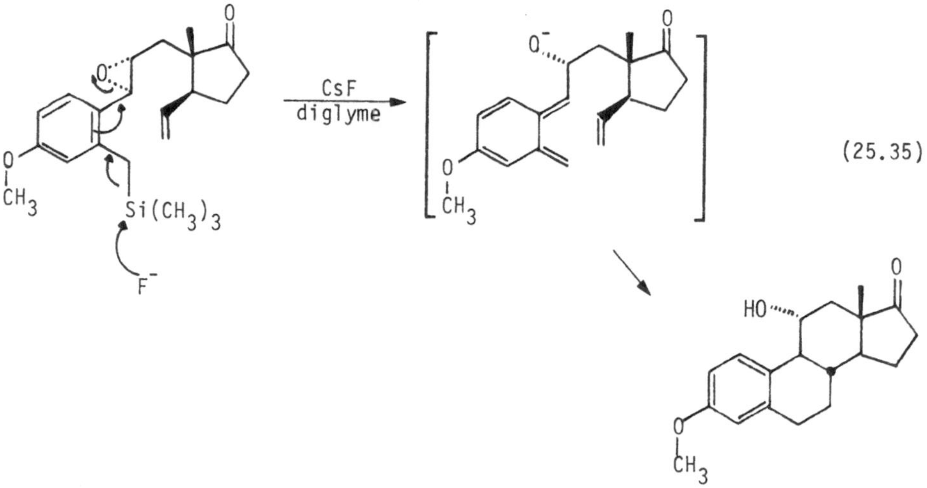

(25.35)

Recently, reactive *o*-quinone methide N-alkylimine intermediates have been generated by fluoride ion induced 1,4-elimination reactions. While intermolecular Diels-Alder reactions with dienophiles fail, they undergo intramolecular Diels-Alder electrocyclic reactions with C−C double bonds to yield nitrogen containing polycyclic molecules [47].

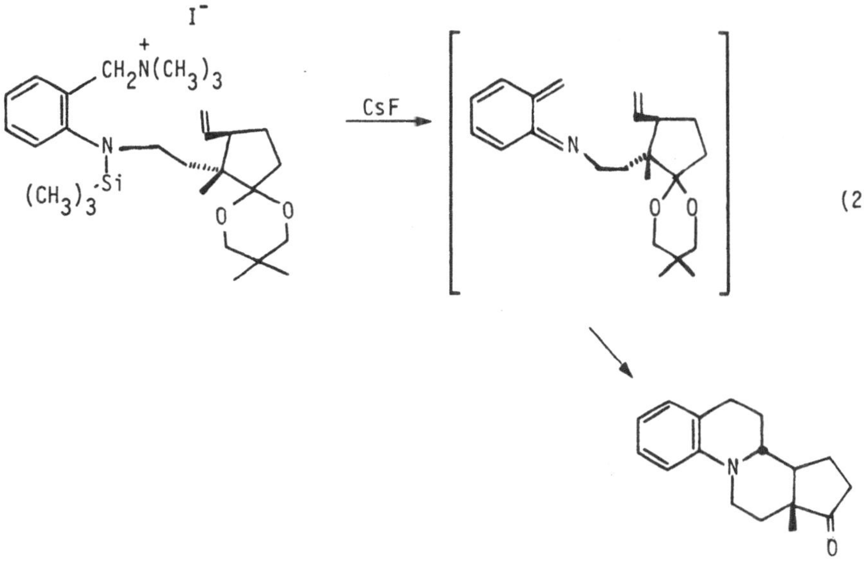

(25.36)

Flash vacuum pyrolysis of *o*-trimethylsilylmethyl benzoyl chlorides at 600° results in elimination of TMS-Cl and formation of benzocyclobutenones [48].

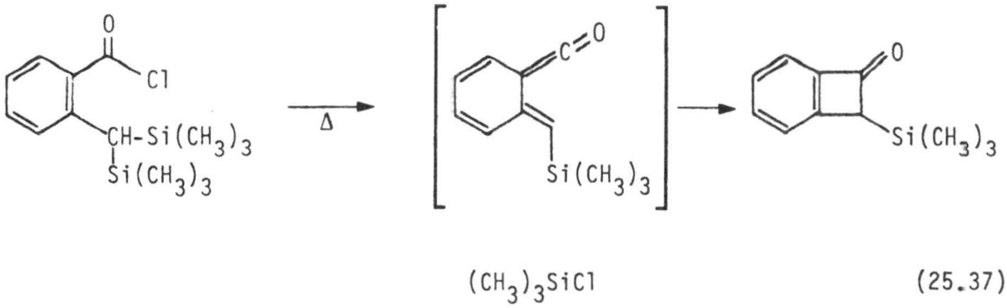

(25.37)

References

1. Kraihanzel, C.S., Poist, J.E.: J. Organometal. Chem. *8*, 239 (1967)
2. Stang, P.J., Ladika, M.: Synthesis, 29 (1981)
3. Holmes, A.B., Raphel, R.A., Welland, N.K.: Tetrahedron Lett. 1539 (1976)
4. Nakamura, E., Kuwajima, I.: Angew. Chem. Int. Ed. *15*, 498 (1976)
5. Holmes, A.B., Jennings-White, C.L.D., Schulthess, A.M., Akinde, B., Walton, D.R.M.: J. Chem. Soc. Chem. Commun. 840 (1979)
6. Sarkar, T.K., Anderson, N.H.: Tetrahedron Lett. 3513 (1978)
7. Hosomi, A., Shirahata, A., Sakurai, H.: Tetrahedron Lett. 3043 (1978)

8. Trost, B.M., Vincent, J.E.: J. Am. Chem. Soc. *102*, 5680 (1980)
9. Pornet, J.: Tetrahedron Lett. 455 (1981)
10. Chan, T.H., Mychajlowskij, W.: Tetrahedron Lett. 3479 (1974)
11. Chan, T.H., Lau, P.W.K., Li, M.P.: Tetrahedron Lett. 2667 (1976)
12. Vedejs, E., Martinez, G.R.: J. Am. Chem. Soc. *101*, 6452 (1979)
13. Grotjahn, D.G., Andersen, N.H.: J. Chem. Soc. Chem. Comm. 306 (1981)
14. Schinzer, D., Heathcock, C.H.: Tetrahedron Lett. 1881 (1981)
15. Noyori, R., Yokoyama, K., Sakata, J., Kuwajima, I., Nakamura, E., Shimizu, M.: J. Am. Chem. Soc. *99*, 1265 (1977)
16. Colvin, E.W., Seebach, D.: J. Chem. Soc. Chem. Comm. 689 (1978)
17. Seebach, D., Beck, A.K., Lehr, F., Weller, T., Colvin, E.: Angew. Chem. Int. Ed. *20*, 397 (1981)
18. Kuwajima, I., Nakamura, E.: J. Am. Chem. Soc. *97*, 3257 (1975)
19. Noyori, R., Nishida, I., Sakata, J.: Tetrahedron Lett. 2085 (1980)
20. Olofson, R.A., Cuomo, J.: Tetrahedron Lett. 819 (1980)
21. Swenton, J.S., Fritzen, Jr., E.L.: Tetrahedron Lett. 1951 (1979)
22. Shih, C., Fritzen Jr., E.L., Swenton, J.S.: J. Org. Chem. *45*, 4462 (1980)
23. Nakamura, E., Murofushi, T., Shimizu, M., Kuwajima, I.: J. Am. Chem. Soc. *98*, 2346 (1976)
24. Nakamura, E., Shimizu, M., Kuwajima, I.: Tetrahedron Lett. 1699 (1976)
25. Just, G., Hakimelahi, G.H., Ugolini, A., Zamboni, R.: Synthesis Comm. *9*, 113 (1979)
26. Detty, M.R.: Tetrahedron Lett. 5087 (1978)
27. Cunico, R.F., Chou, B.B.: J. Organometal. Chem. *154*, C45 (1978)
28. Cunico, R.F., Han, Y.K.: J. Organometal. Chem. *105*, C29 (1976)
29. Cunico, R.F., Han, Y.K.: J. Organometal. Chem. *162*, 1 (1978)
30. Stang, P.J., Fox, D.P.: J. Org. Chem. *42*, 1667 (1977)
31. Stang, P.J., Bjork, J.A.: J. Chem. Soc. Chem. Comm. 1057 (1978)
32. Stang, P.J., Christensen, S.B.: J. Org. Chem. *46*, 823 (1981)
33. Gerlach, H.: Helv. Chim. Acta *60*, 3039 (1977)
34. Sieber, P.: Helv. Chim. Acta, *60*, 2711 (1977)
35. Kocienski, P.J.: Tetrahedron Lett. 2649 (1979)
36. Chan, T.H., Mychajlowskij, W.: Tetrahedron Lett. 171 (1974)
37. Chan, T.H., Mychajlowski, W., Ong, B.S., Harpp, D.N.: J. Org. Chem. *43*, 1526 (1978)
38. Chan, T.H., Li, M.P., Mychajlowskij, W., Harpp, D.N.: Tetrahedron Lett. 3511 (1974).
39. Chan, T.H., Ong, B.S.: J. Org. Chem. *43*, 2994 (1978)
40. Chan, T.H., Massuda, D.: Tetrahedron Lett. 3383 (1975)
41. Cunico, R.F., Dexheimer, E.M.: J. Am. Chem. Soc. *94*, 2868 (1972)
42. Cunico, R.F., Dexheimer, E.M.: J. Organometal. Chem. *59*, 153 (1973)
43. Ito, Y., Miyata, S., Nakatsuka, M., Saegusa, T.: J. Org. Chem. *46*, 1043 (1981)
44. Ito, Y., Nakatsuka, M., Saegusa, T.: J. Am. Chem. Soc. *102*, 863 (1980)
45. Ito, Y., Nakatsuka, M., Saegusa, T.: J. Am. Chem. Soc. *103*, 476 (1981)
46. Djuric, S., Sarkar, T., Magnus, P.: J. Am. Chem. Soc. *102*, 6885 (1980)
47. Ito, Y., Miyata, S., Nakatsuka, M., Saegusa, T.: J. Am. Chem. Soc. *103*, 5250 (1981)
48. Chenard, B.L., Slapak, C., Anderson, D.K., Swenton, J.S.: J. Chem. Soc. Chem. Commun. 179 (1981)
49. Degl'Innocenti, A., Pike, S., Walton, D.R.M., Seconi, G., Ricci, A. Fioreza, M.: J. Chem. Soc. Chem. Commun. 1201 (1980)

Author Index

405

Subject Index

419